THE INTERNATIONAL DIRECTORY OF
CIVIL AIRCRAFT

2001/2002

by Gerard Frawley

Airlife
England

Copyright © 2001 Aerospace Publications Pty Ltd

First published in the UK in 2001
by Airlife Publishing Ltd

British Library Cataloguing-in-Publication Data
 A catalogue record for this book
 is available from the British Library

ISBN 1 84037 282 6

The information in this book is true and complete to the best of our knowledge. All recommendations are made without any guarantee on the part of the Publisher, who also disclaims any liability incurred in connection with the use of this data or specific details.

Printed in Australia

Airlife Publishing Ltd
101 Longden Rd, Shrewsbury SY3 9EB England
E-mail: airlife@airlifebooks.com
Website: www.airlifebooks.com

Contents

Published by Aerospace Publications Pty Ltd (ACN: 001 570 458) PO Box 1777, Fyshwick ACT 2609, Australia. Phone (02) 6280 0111, fax (02) 6280 0007, website address www.ausaviation.com.au – publishers of monthly *Australian Aviation* magazine.

ISBN 1 875671 52 8

Front cover: (top left) Korean Airlines Boeing MD-11F freighter [Paul Merritt]; (top right) Airbus A380 in Emirates colours [Airbus]; (bottom left) The 300th Embraer ERJ 145 in British Airways colours [Embraer]; (bottom right) Agusta Westland A 109 Power [Agusta Westland]. Back cover (clockwise from top left): Cirrus SR20s [Cirrus]; Bombardier Learjet 31A and 60 and Challenger 604 [Bombardier]; Boeing 737-800 with optional winglets [Boeing]; Cessna Stationair floatplane [Gary Gentle]; Airbus A300-600ST [Airbus]; Ilyushin Il-62M [Craig Murray].

Introduction

This is our fourth edition of the *International Directory of Civil Aircraft*. Thank you for purchasing it, I hope you find it of value.

Like its predecessors, this edition aims to present a comprehensive reference on almost every single civil aircraft in use or under development around the world. All told this volume includes 384 aircraft entries, including 10 new types. Ultralights and very light aircraft (VLAs) are not included, but almost everything else is, from popular classic light aircraft such as the venerable Piper Cub to the giant, newly launched Airbus A380 555 seat twin deck airliner.

The new aircraft entries range from the Boeing 747X/747X Stretch to the Ibis Ae270. A small number of entries in the previous edition have been deleted, due to program cancellations or retirements from service. Of those entries carried over, almost everyone has been changed and revised, many quite significantly. In particular aircraft in production evolve over time with improvements made and new subvariants released, and this book details all these changes and is up to date as at late December 2000. Most of the photographs are new.

The aircraft are presented alphabetically by manufacturer and then either by model number, chronologically, or by family types. In some cases aircraft may appear out of strict model number order to allow variants of the same basic family to appear on the same and/or facing pages, allowing easy comparisons of related models.

Aircraft manufacturer mergers and rationalisations in recent years means there is the potential for confusion about under which manufacturer's name and some aircraft entries should appear. The general rule here is if the aircraft is *currently in production* it is listed under the name of its manufacturer (ie Boeing 717 and not McDonnell Douglas MD-95), if the aircraft is out of production, it is listed under the manufacturer's name with which it is most closely related (ie McDonnell Douglas MD-80). If you are unsure where an aircraft appears, try the comprehensive index at the back of the book.

A fully revised and updated *International Directory of Civil Aircraft* is released every two years, with the replacement for this book due to appear in early 2003. In the meantime the next edition of the companion *International Directory of Military Aircraft* is due for release in early 2002. Between them the military and civil aircraft directories provide an unparalleled, affordable reference source on over 700 civil and military aircraft.

Finally, thanks to those that helped with this book, which, with its more than 200,000 words of text and 400 or so photographs, is no small task. Several photographers deserve thanks, including Rob Finlayson, Keith Sadler, Sebastian Zacharias, Viktor Laszlo, Bill Lines, Paul Merritt and Paul Sadler. *Propliner* magazine's Tony Merton Jones allowed me to pick his brains on the status of a number of older airliners/freighters. Numerous aircraft manufacturer PR reps responded to requests for information. Publisher Jim Thorn also leant his hand to proofreading, while Gayla Wilson looked after the book's production. Lastly thanks to Kerrie for her support.

Gerard Frawley
Canberra, January 2001.

Civil Aviation in Review

A new millennium, and a new flagship for the world's airlines.

The year 2000 will go down in aviation history as a particularly significant one, with Airbus' launch of its giant 555 seat A380 airliner. The new jet promises to carry 35% more passengers than Boeing's 747, until now the undisputed 'Queen of the Skies'. But 2000 was also the year that Boeing launched its Longer-Range versions of the 777-200 and 777-300.

The battle lines are now drawn – it will be fascinating to see which of the big two manufacturers is right. Airbus says there is a very significant need for a 500 plus seat airliner as air traffic growth and airport and airways congestion continues, hence the A380. Boeing says international air travellers will continue to demand more frequent, direct services, needing smaller aircraft, thus the emphasis on the 777. Meanwhile both Airbus and Boeing continue to churn out airliners at record or near record rates.

Elsewhere in civil aviation in the two year review period, the regional jet sector has been going from strength to strength, business aircraft sales are booming, and new light aircraft production is the healthiest it has looked in decades. All told at late 2000 it was a very rosy picture for civil aviation as a whole, the only question mark being the health of the global economy, which was showing signs of slowing. When the economy slows, so do aircraft sales.

The launch of the all new A380 is certainly the most exciting and significant event in civil aviation in many years. Perhaps the launch and development of the 747 was more significant – the 747 was about twice as large as the 707s and DC-8s it replaced, whereas the A380 is 'only' a third larger than the 747 – but history nonetheless is unfolding.

The A380 will be a very impressive aircraft. The base A380-800 will seat around 550 passengers, weigh up to 560 tonnes (1,235,000lb) at takeoff, and have a range of 15,100km (8150nm). It will be the second largest aircraft in history, shaded only by the massive, six engined Antonov An-225 (which has a 600 tonne max takeoff weight). A stretched A380 is also planned – the A380-900 will seat 656 passengers and have a 590 tonne (1,301,000lb) max takeoff weight.

Technology wise the A380 will be impressive, although again not quite on the scale that the 747 was to its predecessors (the first 747 was powered by four of the most powerful engines then available – today significantly more powerful engines are available than those for the A380). Nevertheless, the A380 will pioneer new materials, feature new engines and the most advanced flightdeck yet designed for an airliner.

Like all other Airbus airliners except for the A300/A310 twins, the A380 will feature fly-by-wire and sidestick controllers. The new materials include GLARE, a glass fibre/aluminium laminate which will be used for the cargo hold floor and upper fuselage panels. On the flightdeck it will feature large liquid crystal displays, while Flight Management System (FMS) information will be inputted by keyboard with a trackball or touchpad on pull-out platforms in front of the pilots.

But perhaps even more impressive will be the money required – the financial investment needed for the A380 is just as big as the aircraft itself. Airbus estimates A380 development will cost almost $US11 billion, but is confident that the program will make money once it has sold 250 A380s. Another big number is the A380's list price – about $US235 million each. While that seems like a big number for airlines to stomach, because of its size and efficiencies, *per seat* it is cheaper to buy and cheaper to operate than the current 747-400.

Another string in the A380's bow is its deck space – Airbus says the A380 will have 49% more floorspace but only 35% more seats than the 747-400, leaving plenty of room for passenger amenities. Airbus' marketing seems to be getting a bit carried away when it suggests the A380 could be equipped with gymnasiums, bars, casinos and games rooms. But private suites for first class passengers and more room for the other classes throughout the aircraft seems likely, making long distance travel a slightly less arduous ordeal.

The most important number of all though is the number of A380s Airbus can sell and make money on the program, and it is here that Boeing and Airbus widely differ. Through to 2019 Airbus forecasts global demand for 1235 airliners and 315 freighters in the ultra large aircraft category – over

The Airbus A380 was launched in December 2000 and should fly in late 2004. (Airbus)

400 seats – worth around $US343 billion. Over the same period Boeing forecasts a market for 1010 in the 400 plus seat category, of which about half will be in the 500 plus seat (A380) size category. Boeing also believes that demand for these very large aircraft won't be strong until 2010 onwards.

Despite these disparities both Airbus and Boeing forecast 5% annual passenger growth. The difference is Boeing's belief that long range international air travel will continue to fragment, favouring the use of 777 and 767 sized aircraft on nonstop point to point services – hence Boeing's launch in 2000 of the Longer-Range 777-200 and -300 and 767-400 models. Airbus says that there will be more fragmentation (for this it has the A340 and A330 family), but that growing airport and air traffic control congestion means airlines will need very large aircraft to meet air traffic growth.

Boeing's answer to the A380 is the 747X – the 430-422 seat, 16,630km (8975nm) range 747X, and the 504-522 seat, 14,455km (7800nm) range 747X Stretch. These are developments of the 747-400 but with a modified wing and new Rolls-Royce or Engine Alliance powerplants. Boeing says it can develop these aircraft (including the Longer-Range 747-400 which Boeing launched with an order from Qantas in late November 2000) for around $US4 billion – less than half Airbus' A380 development pricetag. Boeing says the 747X and 747X Stretch could enter in service in 2005. But it has been the A380 which has grabbed all the early orders and attention.

Time will tell which manufacturer has got its numbers right. Certainly Airbus either stands to win or lose the most. It will be fascinating to watch.

Super jumbos aside, both Airbus and Boeing have enjoyed bumper sales over the last few years. In 1999 Boeing delivered a record 620 commercial airliners (including 325 737s), in 2000 the Seattle based manufacturer delivered 489 airliners (one fewer than planned despite an engineers' strike which caused production delays). In 2000 Boeing booked firm orders for no fewer than 611 new airliners, wresting sales leadership for the year from Airbus (which sold around 500 airliners). In 1999 the situation was reversed, Airbus sold 476 airliners compared with Boeing's 391.

Significantly, 2000 was Boeing's best year for 777 sales, with 117 signed for (including launch orders for the Longer-Range 777 models). Boeing sees these 777 sales as evidence of the continued move to direct, point to point international services.

Airbus delivered over 310 aircraft in 2000 and will continue to increase production to around 400 in 2002, including no fewer than 30 A320 family aircraft a month. Boeing meanwhile expects to deliver around 530 jets in both 2001 and 2002. Sadly, just a trickle of aircraft have been emerging from Russia's aircraft factories.

Lower down the scale regional jet airliner sales have gone from strength to strength (at the expense of turboprops). In 2000 regional jet manufacturers took 670 orders, while just 70 new turboprop regional airliners were signed for. In 2000 280 regional jets were delivered, compared with 110 turboprops. Illustrating how much sales of turboprop regional airliners have been in decline, in 1992 just 72 regional jets were delivered, compared to 277 turboprops.

The growth in regional jet sales is matched by the proliferation in regional jet types. Fairchild Dornier and Embraer continue work on their 728JET and ERJ 170/190 families, respectively. Bombardier has launched a 90 seat class stretch of the CRJ700, the CRJ900, while suspending the all new BRJ program. Embraer has enlarged its ERJ 145 family to include the ERJ 140 40 seater and the Legacy

Boeing's Longer-Range 777 and 747X models. Boeing says fragmentation of international routes will mean greater demand for its 777s and only a small market for very large aircraft. (Boeing)

business jet (based on the ERJ 135), while Fairchild Dornier has dropped the 428JET. BAE Systems' Avro RJX replacement for the RJ series should fly in early 2001.

Likewise sales of business aircraft have been very strong, in large part fuelled by the recent strength of the US economy. In 2000 the world's corporate aircraft manufacturers delivered a record 740 aircraft.

At the lower end of the general aviation sector, piston powered light aircraft are enjoying a resurgence. In the first nine months of 2000 US manufacturers delivered 1366 piston powered light aircraft. Cessna and Piper production lines are churning out light aircraft in good numbers now, while newcomers Cirrus and Lancair, with the SR20 and Columbia series respectively, are bringing innovation and new products to a market dominated by modern incarnations of ageing designs. Cessna has released new 182 developments and continues to study new aircraft possibilities, as does Piper. Meanwhile Socata continues to work on its jet fuel piston powered range of singles.

In the rotary wing sector too sales have been strong. Consolidation of helicopter manufacturers is continuing – Agusta and Westland and merging to form Agusta Westland, Boeing's light helicopter lines have been taken over by Dutch owned MD Helicopters, Bell and Agusta cooperation under their Bell/Agusta Aerospace Company project has been enlarged to include the all new AB139.

In Europe important structural changes are occurring. Aerospatiale Matra, DaimlerChrysler Aerospace and CASA have merged to form EADS (European Aeronautic, Defence and Space Company), promising new efficiencies, productivity and profitability. EADS will have an 80% shareholding in the new Airbus company which was due to be officially launched in February 2001. The other 20% will be held by BAE Systems.

The Airbus single company structure replaces the cumbersome economic grouping of four partners Airbus has operated under since its creation in 1970. Again the new Airbus company should allow new efficiencies and productivity. As well as its Airbus share, EADS owns Eurocopter and Socata. CASA's light transports now fall under the EADS banners, as does a half share in ATR the other half is owned by Italy's Alenia).

So the last two years have been very good for civil and commercial aviation. Time will tell how the influences of the world economy and strong competition between manufacturers worldwide will impact the next two years.

CIVIL
AIRCRAFT

AASI Jetcruzer 500

Country of Origin: United States of America

Type: Six seat corporate turboprop

Powerplant: One rear mounted 1172kW (1572shp) Pratt & Whitney Canada PT6A-66A turboprop driving a five blade constant speed Hartzell propeller.

Performance: Cruising speed 555km/h (300kt). Initial rate of climb 3200ft/min. Service ceiling 30,000ft. Max range at economical cruising speed with reserves 2592km (1400nm).

Weights: Empty 1725kg (3800lb), max takeoff 2810kg (6200lb).

Dimensions: Wing span 12.85m (42ft 2in), length 9.19m (30ft 2in), height 3.20m (10ft 6in). Wing area 18.0m² (193.2sq ft).

Capacity: Typical accommodation for six including pilot. Can be configured for ambulance, cargo and other utility work.

Production: Deliveries due to begin third quarter 2001. At late 2000 approx 188 orders worth $US226m held.

History: The Jetcruzer 500 is intended as a high speed, low cost single engine corporate turboprop and is the product of Long Beach, California based Advanced Aerodynamics and Structures Inc (AASI).

The Jetcruzer 500 is based on the smaller, unpressurised Jetcruzer 450. Early design work for what would become the Jetcruzer 450 began in 1983. Construction of an Allison 250-C20S powered prototype began in 1988. It flew for the first time on January 11 1989.

In 1990 AASI was formed and took over development of the aircraft, resulting in the first production standard Jetcruzer 450 flying for the first time on September 13 1992. When FAA Part 23 certification was granted on June 14 1994 the Jetcruzer became the first aircraft in the world to be certificated as spin resistant.

AASI elected not to place the 450 into production and instead develop the pressurised Jetcruzer 500. Initial work was on the 500P, which featured a modest 25cm (10in) fuselage stretch, but AASI instead decided to enlarge the design further. The definitive Jetcruzer 500 features a 1.83m (6ft) fuselage stretch over the 450 (increasing cabin length by 90cm (3ft), plus a significantly more powerful PT6A-66 turboprop driving a five (rather than three) blade prop, pressurisation to 30,000ft, an airstair entry door on the right hand side and additional cabin windows.

Other notable Jetcruzer 500 design features include its canard configuration (which allows the main wing to be positioned further aft than normal, so the wing spars do not intrude into the cabin), lack of flaps (reducing pilot workload and manufacturing costs and saving weight), and optional EFIS avionics. Like the 450 the 500 will be certificated as spin resistant. The fuselage is made from composites while the wing and canards are aluminium.

First flight of the Jetcruzer 500 was on August 22 1997, certification is planned for mid 2001. The company opened a new factory for Jetcruzer production at Long Beach Airport in California in November 1998.

The company is also working on the Stratocruzer 1250 13-place twin Williams-Rolls FJ44 powered light corporate jet, but the Jetcruzer 500 remains the priority.

Photo: The canard, rear engine mounted Jetcruzer 500 during early flight testing. (AASI)

Aermacchi SF.260

Country of origin: Italy

Type: Two seat trainer and high performance light aircraft

Powerplant: SF.260A & C – One 195kW (260hp) Lycoming O-540-E4A5 flat six piston engine driving a two blade constant speed propeller.

Performance: SF.260A – Max cruising speed 345km/h (186kt). Initial rate of climb 1770ft/min. Service ceiling 21,370ft. Range with max fuel 2050km (1107nm). SF.260C – Max speed 347km/h (187kt), max cruising speed 330km/h (178kt). Initial rate of climb 1790ft/min. Service ceiling 19,000ft. Max range 1490km (805nm).

Weights: SF.260A – Empty 700kg (1543lb), max takeoff (aerobatic) 1000kg (2205lb), max takeoff (utility) 1102kg (2430lb).

Dimensions: SF.260A – Wing span over tip tanks 8.40m (27ft 7in), length 7.02m (23ft 0in), height 2.60m (8ft 6in). Wing area 10.1m² (108.5sq ft). SF.260C – Wing span 8.35m (27ft 5in), length 7.10m (23ft 4in), height 2.41m (7ft 11in). Wing area 10.1m² (108.7sq ft).

Capacity: Seating for two side by side, plus rear seat capable of seating one adult or two small children.

Production: Over 650 SF.260s have been built of which approximately 170 built for civil customers.

History: The nimble SIAI-Marchetti SF.260 has sold in modest numbers to civil operators worldwide but is also a successful two seat piston military trainer.

The SF.260 was designed by famed Italian aircraft designer Stelio Frati (who was responsible for a number of renowned light aircraft designs) in the early 1960s. It was originally built and flown in 185kW (250hp) Lycoming O-540 powered prototype form by the Aviamilano company as the F.250. However until its takeover by Aermacchi in 1997 SIAI-Marchetti undertook all production (initially under licence, before later assuming full responsibility for the program) of the aircraft as the 195kW (260hp) O-540 powered SF.260. The second SF.260 to fly was the first built by SIAI-Marchetti and the first with the more powerful version of the O-540. This second prototype first flew in 1966.

The initial civil production model was the SF.260A, and a number were sold in the USA as the Waco Meteor. In 1974 production switched to the SF.260B with improvements first developed for the military SF.260M, including a stronger undercarriage, a redesigned wing leading edge and a taller fin. The B was soon followed by the further improved SF.260C, with increased span wing.

While the SF.260 has been further developed into E and F forms these have been sold to military operators only. The 260kW (350shp) Allison 250-B17D turboprop powered SF.260TP meanwhile has been built since the early 1980s, but it too has been sold only to military customers. Nevertheless Italian civil certification was awarded in October 1993, opening the door for possible civil sales.

In 1997 Aermacchi took over SIAI-Marchetti and continues to market the SF.260, with low rate production continuing against military orders.

In civil use the SF.260 is now regarded as something of a classic thoroughbred. Its clean aerodynamic lines, retractable undercarriage and relatively powerful engine guarantee spirited performance.

Photo: An SF.260A. Note the wingtip mounted fuel tanks and rearwards sliding canopy. (Keith Myers)

Aero Boero 95, 115, 150 &180

Country of origin: Argentina

Type: Family of three and four seat light aircraft

Powerplant: AB 95 Standard – One 70kW (95hp) Continental C-90-8F flat four driving a two blade fixed pitch prop. AB 115 Trainer – One 85kW (115hp) Textron Lycoming O-235-C2A. AB 180 RVR – One 135kW (180hp) Textron Lycoming O-360-A1A driving a two blade fixed pitch Sensenich or constant speed Hartzell prop.

Performance: AB 95 – Max speed 204km/h (110kt), cruising speed 170km/h (92kt), long range cruising speed 159km/h (86kt). Range at long range cruising speed 959km (518nm). AB 115 Trainer – Max cruising speed 169km/h (91kt). Initial rate of climb 669ft/min. Range with max fuel 1230km (664nm). AB 180 RVR – Max speed 225km/h (122kt), max cruising speed 201km/h (108kt). Initial rate of climb 1025ft/min. Range with max fuel 1180km (636nm).

Weights: AB 95 – Empty 400kg (882lb), loaded 700kg (1543lb). AB 115 Trainer – Empty 556kg (1226lb), max takeoff 802kg (1768lb). AB 180 RVR – Empty 602kg (1327lb), max takeoff 890kg (1962lb).

Dimensions: AB 95 – Wing span 10.42m (34ft 2in), length 6.91m (22ft 8in), height 2.19m (7ft 2in). AB 115 Trainer & AB 180 RVR – Wing span 10.78m (35ft 5in), length 7.08m (23ft 3in), height 2.05m (6ft 9in). Wing area 17.4m² (187.4sq ft).

Capacity: Accommodation for one pilot and two passengers, or three/four passengers in initial AB 180 model. Ag aircraft fitted with ventral tank pod (for approx 270 litres/60Imp gal/71US gal) and spray bars.

Production: Approx 600 of all variants have been built, including over 300 out of a Brazilian government order for 450.

History: Development from the basic AB 95 (which first flew in 1959) has spawned one of the largest families of GA types yet developed in South America.

Versions of the AB 95 include the AB 95 Standard, the AB 95 De Lujo with a 75kW (100hp) Continental O-200-A engine; the AB 95 A Fumigador ag aircraft with the O-200-A engine and fitted for crop dusting or spraying; the AB 115 BS air ambulance fitted with a stretcher, the more powerful AB 95 B; and the AB 95/115 with a more streamlined engine cowling housing a 85kW (115hp) O-235 engine and main wheel fairings.

From the AB 95/115 Aero Boero developed the AB 115 with increased wing span, greater fin sweepback and longer range, and the AB 115 Trainer. Brazil ordered 450 Trainers in the late 1980s for its aero clubs. Over 300 of these have been delivered to Brazil, with over 400 built in total.

The AB 180 first flew in the late 1960s and was offered in three and four seat versions with differing wingspans and a more powerful engine than those featured on the earlier AB 95 and AB 115. Developments included the AB 180 RV with greater range, reprofiled fuselage and sweptback fin; the glider tug AB 180 RVR; the high altitude AB 180 Condor with optional engine turbocharger; AB 180 Ag agricultural aircraft and the two seat AB 180 PSA preselection aircraft for student pilot flight grading. A biplane AB 180 SP was also developed. The AB 150 RV and AB 150 Ag have less 110kW (150hp) O-320s compared with their corresponding AB 180 models.

Photo: Aero Boero 115 in flight.

Aeronca 7 Champion & 11 Chief

Country of origin: United States of America

Type: Two seat light aircraft

Powerplant: 7AC – One 50kW (65hp) Continental A65-8 flat four piston engine driving a two blade fixed pitch propeller. 11BC – One 63kW (85hp) Continental C85-85F.

Performance: 7AC – Max speed 208km/h (112kt), cruising speed 183km/h (99kt). Service ceiling 12,400ft. Range 740km (400nm). 11 – Max speed 169km/h (91kt), cruising speed 153km/h (83kt). Service ceiling 10,800ft. Range 531km (287nm).

Weights: 7AC – Empty 325kg (740lb), max takeoff 533kg (1220lb). 11 – Empty 329kg (725lb), loaded 567kg (1250lb).

Dimensions: 7AC – Wing span 10.73m (35ft 2in), length 6.65m (21ft 6in), height 2.13m (7ft 0in). Wing area 15.8m² (170sq ft). 11 – Wing span 11.00m (36ft 1in), length 6.35m (20ft 10in), height 2.08m (6ft 10in). Wing area 16.3m² (175.5sq ft).

Capacity: 7 – Pilot and single passenger in tandem. 11 – Accommodation for pilot and passenger side by side.

Production: Approx 10,000 Aeronca Champions (including L-16s and 7200 7ACs) and 1750 Chiefs built between 1946 and 1951.

History: The Aeronca Champion was a highly popular light aircraft in the USA in the intermediate postwar period, with over 10,000 built.

The Champion was based on the prewar Model K Scout, with which it shares an overall similar configuration, but with tandem instead of side by side seating and a reduced span but increased chord flapless wing.

The first production version of the Champion was the 7AC, with succeeding versions similar except for the powerplant fitted. These versions were the 7BC with a 63kW (85hp) Continental C85-12 or O-190-1 (and built in large numbers for the US Army as the L-16 liaison platform); the 7CC with a Continental C90-12F; the 7DC with a Continental C85; and the 7EC with a 67kW (90hp) Continental C90.

Aeronca sold the production rights of the Champion to the Champion Aircraft Corporation in 1951. Champion Aircraft dropped production of its namesake that year and instead developed the 7EC Traveller (which first flew in 1955), 7FC tricycle undercarriage Tri-Traveller and the 110kW (150hp) Lycoming O-320 powered Model 7GCB Challenger, with increased span wing with flaps. The Challenger formed the basis for the Citabria and subsequent Decathlon and Scout, which are described separately under American Champion.

In September 1970 Bellanca acquired the assets of the Champion Aircraft Company and elected to return the Champion to production as the 7ACA Champ. Based on the 7AC, changes included a 45kW (60hp) Franklin 2A-120-B engine in place of the by then out of production Continental, cantilever spring steel main landing gear and modernised interior. Small numbers were built in the early 1970s.

Meanwhile the Aeronca Chief was introduced in 1946. Compared to the Champion it featured a wider cabin for side by side seating. Versions of the Chief (initial production was of the 11AC) were the Scout pilot trainer; 11BC with a dorsal fin and more powerful 63kW (85hp) Continental engine; and 11CC Super Chief with the Continental C85 with improvements to the fuselage giving greater interior space. A further development was the 15AC four seater.

Photo: An Aeronca 11AC Chief. (Lance Higgerson)

Aerospatiale/BAC Concorde

Countries of origin: France and United Kingdom

Type: Medium range supersonic airliner

Powerplants: Four 170.2kN (38,050lb) Rolls-Royce SNECMA Olympus 593 Mk 610 afterburning turbojets.

Performance: Max cruising speed at 51,300ft Mach 2.04, or 2179km/h (1176kt), typical supersonic cruise speed Mach 2.02. Service ceiling 60,000ft. Range with max fuel, reserves and 8845kg (19,500lb) payload 6580km (3550nm).

Weights: Operating empty 78,700kg (173,500lb), max takeoff 185,065kg (408,000lb). Max payload 12,700kg (28,000lb).

Dimensions: Wing span 25.56m (83ft 10in), length 62.17m (203ft 9in), height 11.40m (37ft 5in). Wing area $358.3m^2$ (3856sq ft).

Capacity: Two pilots and flight engineer on the flightdeck. Accommodation for 128 passengers at four abreast with 86cm (34in) pitch in main cabin. Max seating for 144 at 81cm (32in) pitch.

Production: Two prototypes (001 & 002), two preproduction aircraft (01 & 02) and 16 production aircraft. Total 20.

History: Despite first flying over three decades ago, the Concorde is likely to remain the only supersonic airliner to have seen regular, scheduled service for many more years yet.

An engineering masterpiece but commercial failure, the Concorde was the result of a collaborative venture between the aviation industries of Britain and France. It dates back to design work for a supersonic airliner carried out by Sud Aviation and Bristol, whose respective Super Caravelle and Bristol 233 designs were remarkably similar in configuration to each other. The forecast high development costs of any SST program and the similarities in the designs led to a 1962 government agreement between France and Britain which resulted in the British Aircraft Corporation (into which Bristol had been merged) and Sud-Aviation (which became a part of Aerospatiale in 1970) joining to design and develop such an aircraft.

Concorde evolved to be relatively long range aircraft (for the period) capable of flying trans Atlantic sectors. Design of the airframe was refined to feature a highly complex delta wing featuring cambering and ogival leading edges with pairs of afterburning engines mounted in pods under the wing undersurface. Concorde's fuel system was designed to trim the aircraft longitudinally by transferring fuel between tanks to combat the change in the centre of pressure as the aircraft accelerates and decelerates. A distinctive feature is the variable geometry nose which is lowered while taxying, on takeoff and landing to improve the flightcrew's visibility, while Concorde was the first airliner to feature fly-by-wire.

The Concorde first flew on March 2 1969 but did not enter airline service until January 1976. Although a sales failure, Concorde proved very popular in service with its high flying clientele, plying the North Atlantic and often used on charter flights.

Sadly on July 25 2000 an Air France Concorde crashed shortly after takeoff from Paris' Charles de Gualle airport, killing 113. As a result British Airways' seven and Air France's four surviving aircraft were grounded by British and French airworthiness authorities, and they were not expected to resume flying until mid 2001.

Photo: An Air France Concorde on its landing roll. (Craig Murray)

Aerospatiale (Sud) Alouette II & Lama

Country of origin: France

Type: Light utility helicopters

Powerplant: SA 313B Alouette II – One 270kW (360shp) Turbomeca Artouste IIC6 turboshaft driving a three blade main rotor and two blade tail rotor. SA 315B Lama – One 650kW (870shp) Turbomeca Artouste IIIB turboshaft, derated to 410kW (550shp).

Performance: SA 313B – Max speed 185km/h (100kt), max cruising speed 165km/h (90kt). Initial rate of climb 825ft/min. Hovering ceiling in ground effect 5400ft. Range with max fuel 300km (162nm), range with max payload 100km (54nm). SA 315B – Max cruising speed 192km/h (103kt). Max initial rate of climb 1080ft/min. Hovering ceiling in ground effect 16,565ft, out of ground effect 15,090ft. Range with max fuel 515km (278nm).

Weights: SA 313B – Empty 895kg (1973lb), max takeoff 1600kg (3527lb). SA 315B – Empty 1020kg (2250lb), max takeoff 1950kg (4300lb), or 2300kg (5070lb) with external sling load.

Dimensions: SA 313B – Main rotor diameter 10.20m (33ft 5in), fuselage length 9.70m (31ft 10in), height 2.75m (9ft 0in). SA 315B – Main rotor diameter 11.02m (36ft 2in), length overall 12.92m (42ft 5in), fuselage length 10.26m (33ft 8in), height overall 3.09m (10ft 2in). Main rotor disc area $95.4m^2$ (1026.7sq ft).

Capacity: Typical seating for five. Lama can lift a 1135kg (2500lb) external sling load.

Production: 1303 Alouette IIs, including 360 SA 318Cs, were built for military and commercial customers. Sud/Aerospatiale built 407 Lamas, while seven were built in Brazil and more than 240 in India as the HAL Cheetah.

History: Among the first turbine powered helicopters in the world, the Alouette II and Lama remain in service in fairly large numbers worldwide.

For a time the most successful western European helicopter in terms of numbers built, the Alouette II was based on the original Sud-Est Alouette SA 3120 which first flew on March 12 1955. Two prototypes were built and these were powered by Salmson 9 piston engines. Production deliveries of the turbine powered SE 313B Alouette II occurred from 1957, the first machines bound for the French military. Civil certification was awarded on January 14 1958, although most SA/SE 313B production was for military customers.

The Alouette II was soon followed by a more powerful Turbomeca Astazou powered development. This aircraft was designated the SA 318C Alouette II Astazou, and flew for the first time on January 31 1961. Power was supplied by a 395kW (530shp) Astazou IIA derated to 270kW (360shp), which increased the type's maximum speed and max takeoff weight, but otherwise the Alouette II and Alouette II Astazou were similar.

The SA 315B Lama was initially developed for the Indian Army as a utility helicopter with improved hot and high performance. Called Cheetah in Indian service, the Lama mated the Alouette's airframe with the larger Alouette III's dynamic components including Artouste IIIB engine. The Lama's first flight was on March 17 1969. Aerospatiale built 407 through to 1989, while HAL in India continues limited licence production.

Photo: A Helicopters (NZ) SA 315B Lama. (Peter Clark)

Aerospatiale (Sud) Alouette III

Country of origin: France

Type: Light utility helicopter

Powerplant: SA 316C – One 450kW (600shp) derated Turbomeca Artouste IIID turboshaft driving a three blade main rotor and three blade tail rotor. SA 319 – One 450kW (600shp) derated Turbomeca Astazou XIV turboshaft.

Performance: SA 316C – Max speed 220km/h (118kt), max cruising speed 195km/h (105kt). Initial rate of climb 885ft/min. Hovering ceiling in ground effect 7380ft/min. Range with max fuel 540km (290nm). SA 319B – Max cruising speed 197km/h (106kt). Initial rate of climb 885ft/min. Hovering ceiling in ground effect 10,170ft, out of ground effect 5575ft. Range with six passengers 605km (327nm).

Weights: SA 316C – Empty 1134kg (2500lb), max takeoff 2250kg (4960lb). SA 319B – Empty 1140kg (2513lb), max takeoff 2250kg (4960lb).

Dimensions: SA 316/319 – Main rotor diameter 11.02m (36ft 2in), length overall 12.54m (42ft 2in), fuselage length 10.03m (32ft 11in), height 3.00m (9ft 10in). Main rotor disc area 95.4m² (1026.7sq ft)

Capacity: Typical seating for seven, with two passengers and pilot on front bench seat and four on rear bench seat. In aerial ambulance configuration accommodates pilot, two medical attendants and two stretcher patients.

Production: Approximately 1500 Alouette IIIs were built in France, plus production in India (300+), Romania (200) and Switzerland, most for military customers, but some are in civil use.

History: The Alouette III is an enlarged development of the Alouette II series, and was Aerospatiale's most successful helicopter in terms of numbers built until the mid 1980s when surpassed by the Ecureuil.

Like the Alouette II, the Alouette III traces its development back to the Sud-Est SE 3101 Alouette piston powered prototypes, the first of which first flew on July 31 1951. The Alouette III first flew as the SE 3160 on February 28 1959. Compared with the Alouette II, the III is larger and seats seven, but in its initial SA 316A form was powered by the Turbomeca Artouste turboshaft.

The SE 3160 Alouette III remained in production for almost a decade until 1969, when it was replaced by the improved SA 316B with strengthened transmission and a greater max takeoff weight. The SA 316C, with higher rated engine, replaced the SA 316B in production from early 1972.

The SA 319 Alouette III Astazou is, as its name suggest, a development of the SA 316 powered by a derated 450kW (600shp) Turbomeca Astazou XIV turboshaft, which conferred better hot and high performance and improved fuel economy. The SA 319 entered production in 1971 (Sud Aviation had become part of Aerospatiale on January 1 1970).

The SA 319 and SA 316C remained in production side by side through the 1970s and into the early 1980s. HAL of India continues to licence build Alouette IIIs as the Chetak, mainly for that country's military, but also for government and civil customers. ICA of Brasov in Romania licence built SA 316Bs as IAR 316Bs.

Like the Alouette II, the III has been used in a wide range of utility roles, and many armed military variants have been built.

Photo: The Alouette III. (via Tony Arbon)

Aerospatiale SA 330 Puma

Country of origin: France

Type: Twin engine medium lift helicopter

Powerplants: SA 330J – Two 1175kW (1575shp) Turbomeca Turmo IVC turboshafts driving a four blade main rotor and five blade tail rotor. SA 330G/F – Two 1070kW (1435shp) Turbomeca Turmo IIIC4s.

Performance: SA 330J – Max speed 262km/h (141kt), max cruising speed at sea level 257km/h (139kt). Hovering ceiling in ground effect 7315ft. Initial rate of climb 1400ft/min. Max range with standard fuel 550km (297nm).

Weights: Empty 3766kg (8305lb), max takeoff 7500kg (16,535lb) with sling load, standard max takeoff 7400kg (16,315lb).

Dimensions: Rotor diameter 15.08m (49ft 6in), length overall rotors turning 18.15m, fuselage length 14.06m (46ft 2in), height 5.14m (16ft 11in). Main rotor disc area 177.0m² (1905sq ft).

Capacity: Crew of one or two pilots on flightdeck, plus jumpseat. Passenger configurations in main cabin range from 8, 10 or 12 seat executive layouts, or for 17 to 20 passengers in an airline arrangement. A 3200kg (7055lb) external sling load can be carried.

Production: 696 Pumas of different versions, including military, had been sold, when Aerospatiale production ceased in 1987. Limited production has continued in Romania by IAR, largely for that country's military. IAR has built over 160 as the IAR-330L.

History: The Aerospatiale Puma is perhaps the most successful European built medium lift helicopter, and while the majority of Pumas have been sold to military customers (largely for use as troop transports), a significant number are in commercial use.

The Puma was first designed to meet a French army requirement for a medium lift helicopter capable of operating in all weather conditions. The first of two SA 330 prototypes first flew on April 15 1965, with the first production aircraft flying in September 1968. A 1967 decision by Britain's Royal Air Force to order the Puma as its new tactical helicopter transport resulted in substantial Westland participation in the helicopter's design and construction.

Early versions of the Puma were for military customers, including the SA 330B, C, E and H. The initial civil models were the Turmo IIIC powered SA 330F passenger and SA 330G freight versions, which became the first helicopters certificated for single pilot IFR operations in A and B conditions.

The SA 330J is the definitive civil Puma, and compared to the earlier F and G has composite main rotors and an increased maximum takeoff weight. The weather radar equipped J also became the first helicopter certificated for all weather operations including flight in icing conditions, awarded in April 1978.

IPTN of Indonesia assembled a small number of SA 330s before switching to the Super Puma. After Aerospatiale ceased production in 1987, the sole production source for the Puma became IAR of Romania.

The AS 332 Super Puma is a stretched development, and is described separately under Eurocopter.

Photo: A flotation gear equipped SA 330J Puma of Bristow Helicopters used for oil rig support missions. (Bristow)

Aerospatiale SA 341/342 Gazelle

Country of origin: France

Type: Utility helicopter

Powerplant: SA 341G – One 440kW (590shp) max continuous Turbomeca Astazou XIV turboshaft driving a three blade main rotor and Fenestron shrouded tail rotor.

Performance: SA 341G – Max cruising speed at S/L 264km/h (142kt), econ cruising speed at S/L 233km/h (126kt). Initial rate of climb 1770ft/min. Service ceiling 16,400ft. Hovering ceiling out of ground effect 6560ft. Range at S/L with max fuel 670km (361nm), range with a 500kg (1102lb) payload 360km (194nm).

Weights: SA 341G – Empty equipped 917kg (2022lb), max takeoff 1800kg (3970lb).

Dimensions: Main rotor diameter 10.50m (34ft 6in), length overall 11.97m (39ft 4in), fuselage length 9.53m (31ft 3in), height overall 3.15m (10ft 3in). Main rotor disc area 86.5m² (931sq ft).

Capacity: Maximum seating for five including pilot. Rear seat can be folded down to accommodate freight.

Production: More than 1250 Gazelles built in France, although the large majority of these were for military service. Further production took place in the UK with Westland, and the former Yugoslavia.

History: The Gazelle will be long remembered for being the first helicopter to introduce Aerospatiale's (and now Eurocopter's) trademark Fenestron shrouded tail rotor system.

While civil Gazelles are not too common, many are in service as personal or corporate transports. However the Gazelle remains in widespread military service worldwide, and a large number of military variants have been developed.

The Gazelle was designed as a replacement for the popular Alouette II series. Design features included the Alouette II Astazou's powerplant and transmission system, and most noticeably the Fenestron tail rotor, where the tail rotor is housed within the vertical tail.

The prototype SA 340 Gazelle, powered by an Astazou III, first flew on April 7 1967. The Astazou III also powered the subsequent production model, the SA 341, which first flew on August 16 1971.

Like the larger Puma, the Gazelle was the subject of a 1967 agreement that saw it jointly built by Westland in the UK and Aerospatiale in France.

The civil production Gazelle model is the SA 341G, and is powered by the Astazou IIIA. The SA 341G was the first helicopter to be certificated to be flown by one pilot under Cat I weather conditions, achieving this in January 1975 (this was subsequently upgraded to Cat II). The Stretched Gazelle variant of the SA 341G features a slightly modified rear cabin allowing an extra 20cm (8in) of rear legroom.

Further development of the Gazelle resulted in the improved SA 342 with a more powerful Astazou XIV and refined Fenestron design, giving the civil SA 342J a 100kg (220lb) increase in payload. The SA 342 became available from 1977.

When the helicopter subsidiaries of Deutsche Aerospace and Aerospatiale merged to form Eurocopter in 1992, low rate production of the Gazelle for military customers continued.

Photo: An Australian registered SA 341G Gazelle. Note the Fenestron shrouded tail rotor. (Lance Higgerson)

Aerospatiale SA 360 & SA 365 Dauphin

Country of origin: France

Type: Mid size utility helicopters

Powerplant: SA 360 – One 785kW (1050shp) Turbomeca Astazou XVIIIA turboshaft driving a four blade main rotor and Fenestron shrouded tail rotor. SA 365C – Two 505kW (680shp) Turbomeca Arriel turboshafts driving a four blade main rotor and 11 blade Fenestron shrouded tail rotor.

Performance: SA 360 – Cruising speed at S/L 275km/h (148kt), economical cruising speed 245km/h (132kt). Initial rate of climb 1770ft/min. Hovering ceiling in ground effect 7380ft. Range at S/L with max fuel 680km (367nm). SA 365C – Cruising speed 255km/h (137kt). Initial rate of climb 1970ft/min. Hovering ceiling in ground effect 11,710ft, out of ground effect 9315ft. Range at econ cruising speed 465km (251nm).

Weights: SA 360 – Basic operating 1637kg (3609lb), max takeoff 3000kg (6613lb). SA 365C – Empty 1876kg (4136lb), max takeoff 3400kg (7495lb).

Dimensions: SA 360/361 – Main rotor diameter 11.50m (37ft 9in), fuselage length 10.98m (36ft 0in), height 3.50m (11ft 6in). SA 365C – Same except main rotor diameter 11.68m (38ft 4in), length overall 13.32m (43ft 9in).

Capacity: Standard accommodation for 10, including one pilot, in three seat rows, with pilot and one passenger in front row, four passengers in centre row and four passengers in rear row. Max seating for 14. Executive configurations can seat four to six passengers. Air ambulance configuration accommodates up to four stretcher patients and a medical attendant.

Production: Approx 40 SA 360s and 50 SA 365Cs built.

History: The single engine SA 360 Dauphin and twin engine SA 365C Dauphin 2 were developed as replacements for the Alouette III.

The prototype SA 360 first flew on June 2 1972 and was powered by a 730kW (980shp) Turbomeca Astazou XVI turboshaft. After 180 development flights a more powerful 785kW (1050shp) Astazou XVIIIA was substituted, and weights were fitted to the rotor tips to reduce vibration and to eliminate ground resonance. The first prototype flew in this new configuration on May 4 1973, following a second prototype built to the new standard which had flown for the first time that January. The first production aircraft, designated the SA 360C, flew in April 1975.

The SA 361 is a more powerful variant with improved hot and high performance and a greater payload capability. Deliveries of the SA 361 took place from the second half of 1978. A military variant of the SA 361, the SA 361F, was offered fitted with up to eight HOT anti tank missiles, but was not ordered into production.

The twin engine SA 365C Dauphin 2 meanwhile was announced in early 1973. First flight was on January 24 1975. Compared with the SA 360 it features twin Arriel turboshafts and a new engine fairing, a Starflex main rotor hub and a higher max takeoff weight. Production deliveries began in December 1978.

SA 360 and SA 365 production ceased in 1981 in preference for the much improved AS 356N, described under Eurocopter.

Photo: An SA 365C with skid undercarriage. The SA 360 and 365 were offered with wheeled or skid undercarriage. (Jim Thorn)

Aerospatiale N 262, Fregate & Mohawk

Country of origin: France

Type: Short range turboprop commuter airliner

Powerplants: 262 Fregate – Two 843kW (1130shp) Turbomeca Bastan VIIC turboprops driving three blade variable pitch Ratier-Figeac FH.146 propellers. Mohawk 298 – Two 880kW (1180shp) Pratt & Whitney Canada PT6A-45 turboprops driving five blade variable pitch Hamilton Standard props.

Performance: Fregate – Max level speed 418km/h (225kt) at 20,000ft, economical cruising speed 408km/h (220kt). Max range with full fuel and no reserves 2400km (1295nm), range with 26 pax and reserves 1020km (550nm). Mohawk – Max speed 385km/h (208kt), economical cruising speed 375km/h (203kt). Max range with full fuel and no reserves 2132km (1151nm).

Weights: Fregate – Basic empty 6200kg (13,668lb), max takeoff 10,800kg (23,810lb). Mohawk – Empty 7030kg (15,498lb), max takeoff 10,600kg (23,370lb).

Dimensions: Fregate & Mohawk – Wing span 22.60m (74ft 2in), length 19.28m (63ft 3in), height 6.21m (20ft 4in). Wing area 55.0m^2 (592sq ft).

Capacity: Flightcrew of two and max seating for 29 passengers at three abreast. Standard seating layout for 26 passengers.

Production: 110 of all variants of the 262 (including the 298 and miscellaneous military orders) built.

History: The N 262 regional airliner traces back to the Max Holste MH 260 Super Broussard, which first flew on July 29 1960.

The MH 260 was a Turbomeca Bastan turboprop powered development of the one-of MH 250 prototype. The MH 250 was powered by Pratt & Whitney Wasp radial piston engines and first flew on May 20 1959. Nord then built just 10 MH 260s (flown by Air Inter and Norway's Widerøe) before undertaking a significant redesign of the aircraft in 1961. The redesigned Nord N 262, which first flew on December 24 1962, featured a revised fuselage with a circular cross section, pressurisation and more powerful engines.

Four major variants of the 262 were built: the initial production 262A with 805kW (1080shp) Bastan VIC engines; the 262B (just four built for Air Inter), and the 262C and D, later renamed the Fregate, with more powerful Bastan VII engines giving a higher cruising speed and better hot and high performance, and modified wing tips. The Fregate entered production in 1970 as the N 262 following the merger of Nord and Sud which resulted in it becoming an Aerospatiale product.

In the mid to late 1970s US commuter airline Allegheny Airlines – through its subsidiary Mohawk Air Services – extensively upgraded its fleet of 262s, resulting in the Mohawk 298 (the designation being derived from the FAA FAR Part 298 airworthiness regulation). The upgrade involved re-engining the 262s with more powerful Pratt & Whitney Canada PT6A-45 turboprops with five blade props, and fitting new avionics and a new auxiliary power unit.

The first Mohawk 298 flew on January 7 1975, while the last of nine converted was completed in 1978.

Photo: The French air force was the largest Fregate customer. (Armee de l'Air)

Aerospatiale SN 601 Corvette

Country of origin: France

Type: Light corporate jet

Powerplants: Two 11.1kN (2500lb) Pratt & Whitney Canada JT15D-4 turbofans.

Performance: Max cruising speed 760km/h (410kt), economical cruising speed 566km/h (306kt). Max range at max cruising speed with tip tanks and 45 minute reserves 2390km (1290nm), at economical cruising speed 2555km (1380nm). Range with 12 passengers at max cruising speed 1480km (800nm), at economical cruising speed 1555km (840nm).

Weights: Empty 3510kg (7738lb), max takeoff 6600kg (14,550lb).

Dimensions: Wing span 12.87m (42ft 3in), length 13.83m (45ft 5in), height 4.23m (13ft 11in). Wing area 22.0m^2 (236.8sq ft).

Capacity: Flightcrew of one or two pilots. Main cabin seating for between six and 14 passengers, depending on configuration. Galley and toilets were available optionally. Alternative configurations for ambulance, freighter, navigation aid calibration and photography missions offered.

Production: One prototype SN 600 and 39 production SN 601s built, with 32 remaining in service in 2000.

History: Although primarily a small corporate jet transport, Aerospatiale designed the Corvette to fulfil a variety or roles, including commuter airliner, aerial photography, airline pilot training, air ambulance, air taxi, express freight and navigation aid calibration work.

With just 40 built, the Corvette was a commercial failure, and was Aerospatiale's only venture into the executive jet market. The first prototype SN 601 first flew on July 16 1970, but only completed 270 hours of test and development flying before it crashed on March 23 the following year. This aircraft was powered by 9.8kN (2200lb) JT15D-1s.

The subsequent production version, the SN 601, had more powerful JT15D-4 turbofans and a stretched fuselage. The first SN 601, or Corvette 100, first flew on December 20 1972. The second SN 601 Corvette (the first to full production standard) flew on March 7 1973, and a third on January 12 1974.

French civil certification for the Corvette was granted on May 28 1974. Customer deliveries, delayed by strikes at engine manufacturer Pratt & Whitney Canada (then UACL) began the following September.

Production of the Corvette continued until 1977. The initial production schedule called for 20 aircraft to be delivered in 1974 and production of six a month for 1975 and thereafter. However this proved an overly optimistic assessment of potential sales and only 40 were built (including development aircraft). Plans for a 2.08m (6ft 7in) stretched 18 seat Corvette 200 were also dropped.

Many early Corvette customers were French regional airlines (such as Air Alpes and Air Alsace), with others sold to corporate operators in Europe. Outside Europe however the type generated little sales interest in the face of very strong competition. However most of the Corvettes built remain in service today.

Photo: An SN 601 Corvette at Toulouse. This example is used as a corporate jet while others were used as regional airliners, at least early in their careers. (Jim Thorn)

Agusta Westland A 109

Country of origin: Italy

Type: Light twin corporate and utility helicopter

Powerplants: A 109A Mk II – Two Allison 250-C20B turboshafts rated at 300kW (400shp) max continuous operation, or 313kW (420shp) for takeoff, derated to 260kW (346shp) for twin engine operations. A 109E – Two 477kW (640shp) takeoff rated Pratt & Whitney Canada PW206Cs.

Performance: A 109A – Max cruising speed 285km/h (154kt), economical cruising speed 233km/h (126kt). Max initial rate of climb 2110ft/min. Range with standard fuel and no reserves 648km (350nm). A 109E – Max cruising speed 289km/h (156kt). Max initial rate of climb 2080ft/min. Service ceiling 20,000ft. Hover ceiling out of ground effect 13,300ft. Max range 977km (528nm). Max endurance 5hr 10min.

Weights: A 109A Mk II – Empty equipped 1418kg (3126lb), max takeoff 2600kg (5732lb). A 109E – Empty 1570kg (3461lb), max takeoff 2850kg (6283lb).

Dimensions: Main rotor diameter 11.00m (36ft 1in), length with rotors turning 13.05m (42ft 10in), fuselage length 10.71m (35ft 2in), height 3.30m (10ft 10in). Main rotor disc area 95.0m² (1022.9sq ft).

Capacity: Total accommodation for eight people including one pilot. In medevac configuration two stretchers and two medical attendants.

Production: Approximately 500 A 109s of all variants (civil and military) had been built by 2000.

History: The Agusta A 109 is a high performance light twin helicopter, widely used as a corporate transport and for EMS.

The first of four A 109 prototypes flew on August 4 1971. VFR certification was awarded on June 1 1975 although series production had already begun in 1974. First production deliveries took place in late 1976. Single pilot IFR certification was granted in January 1977.

The base A 109A was superseded by the upgraded A 109A Mk II from September 1981. Improvements incorporated in the Mk II included a greater transmission rating, redesigned tailboom and a new tail rotor driveshaft, improved rotor blade life and modern avionics. The Mk II is also available in widebody configuration with increased internal volume courtesy of bulged fuselage side panels and reshaped fuel tanks under the cabin floor. The Mk II Plus has the more powerful 250-C20R-1 engines, as does the A 109C. The 109C also has composite rotor blades.

The A 109K first flew in April 1983 and is powered by two 470kW (640shp) max continuous operation rated Turbomeca Arriel 1K1 turboshafts. The latest A 109 model is the PW206C powered (477kW/640shp takeoff rated) A 109E Power, which first flew on February 8 1995 and was certificated in August 1996. Based on the A 109K2 it also features a strengthened landing gear and improved main rotor. The engines feature FADEC.

The A 109 has been offered in a number of mission specific configurations and is used widely in medevac, police and patrol roles worldwide. For the medevac role a US firm developed the A 109 Max, with extended upward opening side doors and fairings giving greater internal volume.

Agusta and Westland merged in 2000 to form Agusta Westland.

Photo: The P&WC powered A 109 Power. (Agusta Westland)

Agusta Westland A 119 Koala

Country of origin: Italy

Type: Light utility helicopter

Powerplants: One 747kW (1002shp) takeoff rated, 650kW (872shp) max continuous rated Pratt & Whitney Canada PT6B-37 turboshaft driving a four blade main rotor and two blade tail rotor.

Performance: Max cruising speed 260km/h (140kt). Initial rate of climb 1930ft/min. Service ceiling 15,700ft. Hovering ceiling out of ground effect 8200ft, in ground effect 11,810ft. Max range at 5000ft and best range cruising speed 887km (479nm). Endurance at 5000ft and best range cruising speed 5hr 21min.

Weights: Basic empty 1430kg (3150lb), max takeoff with an internal load 2720kg (5997lb), max takeoff with a sling load 2850kg (6283lb).

Dimensions: Main rotor diameter 10.83m (35ft 6in), length overall rotors turning 13.04m (42ft 9in), fuselage length 11.07m (36ft 4in), height overall 3.77m (12ft 4in).

Capacity: One pilot and passenger on flightdeck. Main cabin seats six in standard configuration. In an EMS configuration can accommodate two stretcher patients.

Production: Planned annual production rate of 20 to 25 aircraft per year. Approx 30 sold at time of writing. Second assembly line to be established at Denel in South Africa. First delivery September 2000.

History: The 'widebody' A 119 Koala is a single engine development of the A 109 twin. It is designed for a range of utility transport missions where it makes economic sense to operate a single when the redundancy of a twin is not required.

Agusta began development work on the Koala in 1994, leading to the first prototype's maiden flight in early 1995. A second prototype flew later in that same year. Agusta originally aimed to gain certification for the A 119 in late 1996 but this has been repeatedly delayed and was not achieved until mid 2000. Agusta said causes for the delays included strong sales demand for the A 109 Power, and that it was improving the A 119's performance in response to customer feedback.

One of the Koala's big marketing features is its large 'widebody' fuselage. Agusta says the cabin is 30% larger than those of any other current production single engine helicopter. A measure of the cabin size is that it can accommodate two stretcher patients in an EMS role, along with two medical attendants. Most other single engine helicopters typically are only equipped for a single stretcher because of a lack of space (Agusta Westland sees medical retrieval operators as prime potential Koala customers).

Access to the main cabin is via two large sliding doors, one either side of the fuselage. A baggage compartment in the rear of the fuselage is also accessible in flight.

The first prototype Koala was powered by a Turbomeca Arriel 1 turboshaft but it was subsequently re-engined with a 747kW (1002shp) takeoff rated Pratt & Whitney Canada PT6B-37, which powered the second prototype and features in production aircraft. Another design feature is the Koala's composite four blade main rotor which features a titanium fully articulated maintenance free hub with elastomeric bearings and composite grips.

Photo: The first production A 119 Koala was delivered to Australian transport company Linfox in September 2000. (Paul Sadler)

Agusta Westland EH 101

Countries of origin: Italy and United Kingdom

Type: Commuter, offshore oil rig support & utility helicopter

Powerplants: Three 1230kW (1649shp) max continuous rated General Electric CT7-6-GE-T6A turboshafts driving a five blade main rotor and four blade tail rotor.

Performance: Heliliner – Typical cruising speed 278km/h (150kt), long range cruising speed 260km/h (140kt). Service ceiling 15,000ft. Range offshore IFR equipped, standard fuel and reserves 1130km (610nm), with 30 pax, IFR equipped, fifth fuel tank and reserves 1390km (750nm). Endurance 5hr.

Weights: Heliliner – Operating empty (with IFR, offshore equipped) 9300kg (20,503lb), max takeoff 14,600kg (32,188lb).

Dimensions: Main rotor diameter 18.59m (61ft 0in), length rotors turning 22.80m (74ft 10in), fuselage length 19.53m (64ft 1in), height rotors turning 6.62m (21ft 9in). Main rotor disc area 271.5m² (2922.5sq ft).

Capacity: Flightcrew of two. Main cabin seating for 30 at four abreast and 76cm (30in) pitch. Equipped with galley and toilet.

Production: One sold to the Tokyo police (service entry in March 1999) was first (and at time of writing, only) commercial sale.

History: Agusta Westland (formerly EH Industries) offers commercial developments of its EH 101 aimed at offshore oil rig support, airport/city centre shuttle and utility operations.

EH Industries was a collaborative venture between Westland of the UK and Agusta of Italy – which in 2000 merged to become Agusta Westland – formed to develop an anti submarine warfare helicopter for the Royal Navy and Italian navy. The partnership was formed in 1980 with both companies holding 50% each. From the outset both companies intended to develop civil and commercial models of the EH 101. Westland had design responsibility for the Heliliner, the anti submarine warfare variant was developed jointly, while Agusta headed development of military and utility transport versions with a rear loading ramp.

EH 101 full scale development began in March 1984. The first flight of an EH 101 (the Westland built PP1) was on October 9 1987, while the first civil configured EH 101, PP3, first flew on September 30 1988. The first production EH 101 (a Merlin for the Royal Navy) first flew in December 1995.

While the Royal Navy's EH 101 Merlin ASW helicopters and the Royal Air Force's Merlin HC.3 tactical transports have Rolls-Royce Turbomeca RTM322 engines, Italian and civil EH 101s have General Electric CT7 engines.

The 30 seat Heliliner variant is optimised either for offshore oil rig or airport to city centre transfers, and the rear freight door is offered as an option, while the civil utility version has the rear ramp fitted as standard. Canada's military has ordered 15 similar AW320 Cormorants for search and rescue work.

So far Tokyo's police is the only civil EH 101 customer, its single machine entered service in March 1999. In mid 2000 pre-production EH 101s PP8 and PP9 completed a 6000 hour Intensive Flight Operations Program (IFOP), the second phase of which was based in Aberdeen, UK. The program entailed flying simulated military and civil sorties to demonstrate reliability and maintainability performance.

Photo: Pre-production EH 101 PP8 on a North Sea oil rig in late 1999.

American Champion & Bellanca series

Country or origin: United States of America

Type: Series of two seat utility and aerobatic light aircraft

Powerplant: 7GCBC Explorer – One 120kW (160hp) Textron Lycoming O-320-B2B flat four driving a two blade fixed pitch Sensench propeller. 8GCBC – One 135kW (180hp) Lycoming O-360-C2A driving either a two blade fixed pitch or constant speed prop.

Performance: 7GCBC – Max speed 217km/h (117kt), cruising speed at 75% power 211km/h (114kt), at 65% power 198km/h (107kt). Max initial rate of climb 1345ft/min. Range at 55% power 965km (520nm). 8GCBC – Max speed 217km/h (162kt), cruising speed 209km/h (113kt). Initial rate of climb 1110ft/min. Range 725km (390nm).

Weights: 7GCBC – Empty 544kg (1200lb), max takeoff 816kg (1800lb). 8GCBC – Empty 595kg (1315lb), max takeoff 975kg (2150lb).

Dimensions: 7GCBC – Wing span 10.49m (34ft 5in), length 6.92m (22ft 9in), height 2.36m (7ft 9in). Wing area 16.5m² (165sq ft). 8GCBC – Wing span 11.02m (36ft 2in), length 6.93m (22ft 9in), height 2.64m (8ft 8in). Wing area 16.7m² (180sq ft).

Capacity: Two in tandem. Scout can be fitted for crop spraying.

Production: Over 6000 of all models built. Almost 100 built in 1999.

History: The Citabria, Bellanca and Scout can trace their lineage back to the Aeronca 7 Champion (described separately).

Champion Aircraft Corporation purchased the production rights to the Aeronca 7 in 1951, and from this developed the 7EC Traveller and 7GCB Challenger. The Challenger-based Citabria first flew in May 1964. It had more glass area, a squarer tail and stressing for limited (+5g, -2g) aerobatic flight, while other features were the flapless wing and choice of 75kW (100hp) Continental O-200 or 80kW (108hp) Lycoming O-235 engines. Variants were the 110kW (150hp) O-320 powered 7GCAA and the 7GCBC with a longer span wing fitted with flaps.

Bellanca took over production of the Citabria in September 1970, renaming the 7ECA, which by now was powered by an 85kW (115hp) O-235, as the Citabria; the 7GCAA the Citabria 150 and the 7GCBC the Citabria 150S. Champion initially developed the 7KCAB model, but Bellanca took this over, resulting in the fully aerobatic 8KCAB Decathlon. The ultimate Decathlon design was the 135kW (180hp) AEIO-360 powered Super Decathlon.

The Scout was designed to perform a number of utility roles, and appeared in 1970. The updated 8GCBC followed in 1974 with a 135kW (180hp) O-360.

Bellanca production ended in 1982, while the Champion Aircraft Company produced the range in limited numbers between 1985-86.

American Champion re-introduced all three models into production in 1990-91. American Champion currently builds the baseline 7ECA Citabria Aurora (re-introduced in 1995), the 7GCAA Citabria Adventure, the 7GCBC Citabria Explorer, 8KCAB Super Decathlon and the 8GCBC Scout (and Scout CS with constant speed propeller). These aircraft are basically similar to their earlier namesakes, save for some equipment changes and improvements, including metal spar wings.

The company is also investigating returning the 7ACA Champ into production. A prototype with a 60kW (80hp) Australian Jabiru engine was displayed at Oshkosh 2000.

Photo: An American Champion built 8GCBC Scout. (Bob Grimstead)

Airbus A300B2 & B4

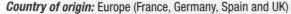

Country of origin: Europe (France, Germany, Spain and UK)

Type: Medium range widebody airliner

Powerplants: A300B2/B4 – Two 227kN (51,000lb) General Electric CF6-50C or 236kN (53,000lb) Pratt & Whitney JT9D-9 turbofans.

Performance: A300B2-200 – Typical high speed cruising speed 917km/h (495kt), typical long range cruising speed 847km/h (457kt). Range with 269 passengers and reserves 3430km (1850nm). A300B4-200 – Same except range with 269 passengers and reserves 5375km (2900nm), range with max fuel 6300km (3400nm).

Weights: A300B2-200 – Operating empty 85,910kg (189,400lb), max takeoff 142,000kg (313,055lb). A300B4-200 – Operating empty 88,500kg (195,109lb), max takeoff 165,000kg (363,760lb).

Dimensions: Wing span 44.84m (147ft 1in), length 53.62m (175ft 11in), height 16.53m (54ft 3in). Wing area 260.0m² (2798.7sq ft).

Capacity: Flightcrew of two pilots and a flight engineer. Seating for between 220 and 336 single class passengers. Typical two class arrangement for 20 business and 230 economy class passengers.

Production: A300B2 and B4 orders stood at 249 when production was completed in 1984. Approx 161 in service at late 2000.

History: The A300 is significant not only for being the world's first widebody twinjet airliner and a commercial success in its own right, but for being the first design and foundation of the success of Airbus, now one of the world's two major jet airliner manufacturers.

Airbus Industrie was formed on December 18 1970 as a consortium with participation from the aerospace industries of France, Germany and the UK (Spain joined later) specifically to develop a twin engined 300 seat widebody 'air bus' to fill an identified market gap.

Original design studies dated back to 1965, with the original 300 seat airliner concept (hence A300) over time evolving into a smaller 250 seater, the A300B. Two prototype A300B1s were built, the first of these flying from Toulouse in southern France on October 28 1972, the second on February 5 the next year. The General Electric CF6 was the powerplant choice for initial A300s. The 2.65m (8ft 8in) longer A300B2 was the first production version. It first flew in June 1973 (the first production B2 flew in April 1974) and entered service with Air France on May 23 1974.

Subsequent versions included the B2-200 with Krueger leading edge flaps and different wheels and brakes; the B2-300 with increased weights for greater payload and multi stop capability; the B4-100, a longer range version of the B2 with Krueger flaps; and the increased max takeoff weight B4-200 which featured reinforced wings and fuselage, improved landing gear and optional rear cargo bay fuel tank. A small number of A300C convertibles were also built, these featured a main deck freight door behind the wing on the left hand side. Late in the A300B4's production life an optional two crew flightdeck was offered as the A300-200FF (customers were Garuda, Tunis Air and VASP).

Production of the A300B4 ceased in May 1984, with manufacture switching to the improved A300-600.

The A300B4 is finding a useful niche as a freighter, with a number of companies (including Airbus) offering and performing conversion programs, involving a forward freight door and strengthened main deck floor.

Photo: A China Airlines A300B4.

Airbus A300-600

Country of origin: Europe (France, Germany, Spain and UK)

Type: Medium range widebody airliner

Powerplants: Two 262.4kN (59,000lb) General Electric CF6-80C2A1s, or two 273.6kN (61,500lb) CF6-80C2A5s, or two 249kN (56,000lb) Pratt & Whitney PW4156s or two 258kN (58,000lb) PW4158 turbofans.

Performance: A300-600R – Max cruising speed 897km/h (484kt), long range cruising speed 875km/h (472kt). Range at typical airline operating weight with 267 passengers with 370km (200nm) reserves and standard fuel 7505km (4050nm) with CF6s, or 7540km (4070nm) with PW4000s. A300-600 – Range at same parameters 6670km (3600nm). A300-600F – Range with max payload, and reserves 4908km (2650nm).

Weights: A300-600 – Operating empty with CF6s 90,115kg (198,665lb), with PW4000s 90,065kg (198,565lb). Max takeoff 165,900kg (365,745lb). A300-600R – Operating empty 91,040kg (200,700lb) with CF6s, or 90,965kg (200,550lb) with PW4000s, max takeoff 170,500kg (375,855lb), or optionally 171,700kg (378,535lb). A300-600F – (CF6 powered) Operating empty 78,335kg (172,700lb), max takeoff 170,500kg (375,900lb).

Dimensions: Wing span 44.84m (147ft 1in), length 54.08m (177ft 5in), height 16.62m (54ft 6.5in). Wing area 260.0m² (2798.7sq ft).

Capacity: Flightcrew of two. Typical two class arrangement for 26 premium class passengers at six abreast and 240 economy class passengers at eight abreast. The A300-600 and -600R can carry 22 LD3 containers in forward and aft belly cargo holds. A300-600F total payload 55,017kg (121,290lb).

Production: 520 A300s of all models ordered by late 2000, of which 271 were for the A300-600. Over 242 A300-600s had been delivered by late 2000, of which 238 were in service.

History: The A300-600 development of the A300B4 incorporated a number of significant improvements and refinements, foremost being a two crew flightdeck and increased range.

Apart from the two crew EFIS flightdeck with digital avionics based on that developed for the A310, changes included the A310's tail empennage which increased freight and passenger payloads, small winglets (an option from 1989, standard from 1991), simplified systems, greater use of composites, Fowler flaps and increased camber on the wings, new brakes and APU, and improved payload/range through an extensive drag reducing airframe clean up and new engines. First flight for the A300-600 was on July 8 1983, the first airline delivery was in March 1984.

The A300-600 was further developed into the longer range A300-600R, its extended range courtesy of a fuel trim tank in the tailplane and higher maximum takeoff weights. First flight was on December 9 1987, first delivery was on April 20 1988 (to American Airlines).

Convertible freight/passenger versions of all variants of the A300 have been offered, as has the all freight A300F4-600. The first new build pure freighter A300, one of 36 ordered by Federal Express, flew in December 1993. UPS is another major A300-600F customer, following its September 1998 order for 30.

Photo: A FedEx A300-600F. (Rob Finlayson)

Airbus A300-600ST Super Transporter

Country of origin: Europe (France, Germany, Spain and UK)

Type: Oversize cargo freighter

Powerplants: Two 262.4kN (59,000lb) General Electric CF6-80C2A8 turbofans.

Performance: Max cruising speed 780km/h (421kt). Max certificated altitude 35,000ft. Range with a 40 tonne (88,105lb) payload 2778km (1500nm), range with a 26 tonne (57,268lb) payload 4630km (2500nm), range with max payload 1666km (900nm).

Weights: Empty 86,500kg (190,700lb), max payload 47,300kg (104,279lb), max takeoff 155,000kg (341,700lb).

Dimensions: Wing span 44.84m (147ft 0in), length 56.16m (184ft 3in), height 17.24m (56ft 7in). Wing area 260m² (2798.7sq ft). Internal useable length 37.70m (123ft 8in), diameter 7.40m (24ft 3in).

Capacity: The A300-600ST's internal main cabin volume is 1400m³ (49,442cu ft), and can carry a range of oversize components, such as a fully equipped A330 or A340 wing shipset, or two A320/321 wing shipsets, or two A310 fuselage sections (front & rear).

Production: Airbus has taken delivery of its four A300-600STs originally on order with a fifth to be delivered in early 2001 to be used exclusively for third party work.

History: The A300-600ST Super Transporter was designed to replace Airbus Industrie's Boeing Stratocruiser based Super Guppy transports, and are used to ferry oversize components such as wings and fuselage sections between Airbus' plants throughout western Europe.

Development of the A300-600ST, nicknamed Beluga and also Super Flipper, began in August 1991. The A300-600ST's tight development program – for what in many ways is effectively a new aircraft – saw the transport rolled out in June 1994, with first flight on September 13 that year. The A300-600ST then entered a 400 flight test program which culminated in mid 1995, with certification awarded that September and with delivery and entry into service with Airbus in January 1996. All of the first four on order had been delivered by mid 1998 (allowing the Super Guppy's retirement in October 1997). A fifth Super Transporter is scheduled to be delivered in early 2001.

The A300-600ST is based on the A300-600 airliner, with which it shares the wing, lower fuselage, main undercarriage and cockpit. The main differences are obvious – a bulged, voluminous main deck, new forward lower fuselage, new enlarged tail with winglets and an upwards hinging main cargo door.

Program management of the A300-600ST is the responsibility of the Special Aircraft Transport Company, or SATIC, an economic interest grouping formed on a 50/50 basis by Aerospatiale and DASA (now both part of EADS) operating on behalf of Airbus Industrie. While much of the work on the aircraft has been performed by the Airbus partners, other European companies are also involved in the program. The aircraft are completed by Sogerma at Toulouse.

The A300-600STs are operated for Airbus by Airbus Transport International (ATI). Apart from its Airbus work ATI increasingly also undertakes commercial third party charter work. The fifth Super Transporter will be used almost exclusively for third party work. The first third party flight was on November 24 1996.

Photo: The fourth A300-600ST. (Paul Merritt)

Airbus A310

Country of origin: Europe (France, Germany, Spain and UK)

Type: Medium to long range widebody airliner

Powerplants: Initial powerplant choice of either two 213.5kN (48,000lb) Pratt & Whitney JT9D-7R4D1s or two 222.4kN (50,000lb) General Electric CF6-80A3 turbofans. Current choices of 238kN (53,500lb) CF6-80C2A2s, 262.4kN (59,000lb) CF6-80C2A8s, 231.2kN (52,000lb) PW4152s, or 249.1kN (56,000lb) PW4156s.

Performance: Max cruising speed 897km/h (484kt), long range cruising speed 850km/h (459kt). Range at typical airliner operating weight with 218 passengers and baggage and reserves 6800km (3670nm) for A310-200, 7982km (4310nm) for CF6 powered A310-300, 9580km (5170nm) for high gross weight A310-300 with CF6s.

Weights: A310-200 with CF6-80C2A2s – Operating empty 80,142kg (176,683lb), max takeoff 142,000kg (313,055lb). A310-300 with CF6-80C2A8s – Operating empty 81,205kg (179,025lb), max takeoff 150,000kg (330,695lb) standard, or higher gross weight options through to 164,000kg (361,560lb).

Dimensions: Wing span 43.89m (144ft 0in), length 46.66m (153ft 1in), height 15.80m (51ft 10in). Wing area 219.0m² (2357.3sq ft).

Capacity: Flightcrew of two. Max passenger capacity at nine abreast 280. Typical two class arrangement for 20 passengers at six abreast and 192 economy class passenger eight abreast. Cargo capacity in fore and aft underfloor compartments can hold 2.44 x 3.17m (88 x 125in) pallets or a total of up to 14 LD3 containers.

Production: Total orders held for the A310 stood at 260 at late 2000, of which more than 255 had been delivered and 214 were in commercial service.

History: The A310 first began life as the A300B10, one of a number of projected developments and derivatives of Airbus' original A300B widebody twinjet airliner.

Compared with the larger A300, the A310 introduced a number of major changes. The fuselage was shortened by 13 frames compared to the A300B, reducing seating to around 200 to 230 passengers and a new higher aspect ratio wing of smaller span and area was developed. New and smaller horizontal tail surfaces, fly-by-wire outboard spoilers and a two crew EFIS flightdeck were incorporated, while the engine pylons were common to suit both engine options (GE and P&W).

The A310 program was formally launched in July 1978 and the prototype first flew on April 3 1982. Service entry was with Lufthansa in April 1983. Early production A310s did not have the small winglets that became a feature of later build A310-200s and the A310-300. The A310-300 is a longer range development of the base A310-200, and has been in production since 1985. This version can carry a further 7000kg (15,430lb) of fuel in the tailplane.

The A310-200F freighter is available new build or as a conversion of existing aircraft and in this role has proven quite popular (over 40 A310-200s have been converted to freighters for freight express giant FedEx). The A310-200C convertible passenger/freighter variant first entered service with Dutch operator Martinair in 1984.

Photo: An Air Plus Comet A310-300 at Madrid. Apart from the shorter fuselage, the A310 can be distinguished from the A300 by the above wing emergency exit. (Rob Finlayson)

Airbus A318

Country of origin: Europe (France, Germany, Spain and UK)

Type: 100 seat regional airliner

Powerplants: Two 97.9kN (22,000lb) Pratt & Whitney PW6122s or 106.8kN (24,000lb) PW6124s or 97.9kN (22,000lb) CFM International CFM56-5B turbofans.

Performance: Range with 109 pasengers and reserves at 59 tonne (129,955lb) takeoff weight 2780km (1500nm), at 61.5 tonne (135,463lb) takeoff weight 3705km (2000nm), at 66 tonne (145,505lb) max takeoff 5180km (2797nm).

Weights: Operating empty 38,950kg (85,870lb), max takeoff 59,000kg (129,955lb) or optionally 61,500kg (135,463lb) or 66,000kg (145,505lb).

Dimensions: Wing span 34.09m (111ft 10in), length 31.45m (103ft 2in), height 12.56m (41ft 3in). Wing area 122.6m2 (1319.7sq ft).

Capacity: Flightcrew of two. Standard seating for 107 passengers (eight premium class at four abreast and 97cm/38in pitch, 99 economy class at six abreast and 81cm/32in pitch). Single class seating for 117 at 81cm (32in) pitch at six abreast.

Production: By late 2000 Airbus held firm orders for 161 A318s. First deliveries planned for late 2002.

History: The A318 will be Airbus' smallest airliner and is the European manufacturer's first foray into the 100 seat market.

Airbus' initial efforts at developing a 100 seat airliner were focused on the all new AE31X program (covering the baseline 95 seat AE316 and 115-125 seat AE317) which Airbus and Alenia, as Airbus Industrie Asia, were developing in conjunction with AVIC of China and Singapore Technologies. The AE31X would have been assembled in China. However in September 1998 Airbus announced termination of the project.

Even before the cancellation of the AE31X program Airbus had been independently studying a minimum change 100 seat derivative of the A319 covered by the A319M5 designation (M5 = minus five fuselage frames). Following the AE31X's cancellation Airbus announced the commercial launch of the A319M5 as the A318 at the 1998 Farnborough Airshow. Industrial launch followed on April 26 1999 with sales commitments for 109. Certification and first deliveries are planned for the last quarter of 2002.

Compared with the A319, the A318 will be 4.5 frames shorter, reducing standard two class seating from 124 to 107. The A318's other significant new feature will be its powerplant, two new Pratt & Whitney PW6000s – either 97.9kN/22,000lb PW6122s or 106.8kN/24,000lb PW6124s (The A318 is the launch aircraft for the PW6000). CFM56s are offered as options. Other changes include a small dorsal fillet added to the tail, modified wing camber, and a reduced size cargo doors (to maintain engine nacelle clearance for loading vehicles).

Otherwise the A318 will retain 95% commonality with the rest of the A320 family, including the advanced flightdeck with side stick controllers and fly-by-wire flight controls allowing a pilot common type rating, and the same six abreast fuselage cross section.

A318 final assembly will take place at Hamburg, Germany, alongside the A319 and A321. The A318 will also be the first airliner application for laser welding, which reduces cost and weight.

Photo: A computer generated image of the A318 in flight. (Airbus)

Airbus A319

Country of origin: Europe (France, Germany, Spain and UK)

Type: Short to medium range narrowbody airliner

Powerplants: Two 98 to 104.5kN (22,000 to 23,500lb) class CFM International CFM56-5A or International Aero Engines IAE V2500-A5 turbofans.

Performance: Speeds similar to A320. Range at 64 tonne (141,095lb) takeoff weight 3391km (1831nm), range at 75,500kg (166,450lb) takeoff weight with 104.5kN (23,500lb) engines 6845km (3697nm).

Weights: Operating empty 40,160kg (88,537lb) or optionally 41,203kg (90,837lb), standard max takeoff 64,000kg (141,094lb) or optionally 75,500kg (166,450lb).

Dimensions: Wing span 34.09m (111ft 10in), length 33.84m (111ft 0in), height 11.76m (38ft 7in). Wing area 122.6m² (1319.7sq ft).

Capacity: Seating for 124 passengers in a typical two class configuration (eight premium class and 116 economy class). High density single class layout can seat 142 passengers.

Production: At late 2000 total orders for the A319 stood at 694 with 305 delivered.

History: The A319 is a shortened, 124 seat class development of Airbus' highly successful single aisle A320, and competes with Boeing's Next Generation 737-700.

The A319 program was launched at the Paris Airshow in June 1993 on the strength of just six orders placed by ILFC late in 1992 and the predicted better prospects of the commercial airliner market, which were certainly realised. The first A319 airline order came from French carrier Air Inter (since merged into Air France), whose order for six was announced in February 1994. Since then Swissair, Air Canada, Lufthansa, Northwest, United, US Airways and British Airways are among the major customers that have ordered more than 600 A319s (all also operate or have on order A320s).

The A319 flew for the first time on August 25 1995 from Hamburg in Germany. European JAA certification and service entry, with Swissair, took place in April 1996.

The A319 is a minimum change, shortened derivative of the highly successful A320. The major difference between the A320 and A319 is that the latter is shorter by seven fuselage frames, while in almost all other respects the A319 and A320 are identical.

Like the A321, A330 and A340, the A319 features Airbus' common two crew glass cockpit with sidestick controllers first introduced on the A320. There are significant crew training cost benefits and operational savings from this arrangement as the A319, A320 and A321 (and soon A318) can all be flown by pilots with the same type rating. Further, the identical cockpit means reduced training times for crews converting to the larger A330 and A340.

A319 (and A321) final assembly takes place in Hamburg. Final assembly of all other Airbus airliners, including the A320, takes place at Toulouse.

The A319 forms the basis for the new baby of the Airbus family, the A318 100 seater (described separately), and the Airbus Corporate Jetliner (also described separately).

Photo: A CFM56 powered US Airways A319. US Airways, like most other A319 customers, has also ordered A320s. (Airbus)

Airbus A320

Country of origin: Europe (France, Germany, Spain and UK)

Type: Short to medium range airliner

Powerplants: Two 111.2kN to 120.1kN (25-27,000lb) CFM International CFM56-5A1 turbofans or 118kN (26,500lb) CFM56-5A3s or 120kN (27,000lb) -5B4s, or two 113.4kN (25,500lb) International Aero Engines IAE V2500-A1 or 117.9kN (26,500lb) V2500-A5s.

Weights: A320-200 – Operating empty with V2500s 42,220kg (93,079lb); with CFM56s 42,175kg (92,980lb). Standard max takeoff for both versions 73,500kg (162,040lb) or optionally 75,500kg (166,445lb) or 77,000kg (169,755lb).

Performance: A320-200 – Max cruising speed 903km/h (487kt) at 28,000ft, econ cruising speed 840km/h (454kt) at 37,000ft. Range with 150 passengers and reserves with CFM56s 4843km (2615nm), or 5639km (3045nm), or 5278km (2850nm); with V2500s 4874km (2632nm) or optionally 5463km (2950nm) or 5676km (3065nm).

Dimensions: Wing span 34.09m (111ft 10in), length 37.57m (123ft 3in), height 11.76m (38ft 7in). Wing area 122.6m² (1319.7sq ft).

Capacity: Flightcrew of two. Main cabin can accommodate a maximum of 179 passengers in a high density layout. Typical two class seating arrangement for 12 passengers at four abreast and 138 at six abreast.

Production: As of late 2000 firm orders for the A320 stood at 1423 with 880 delivered.

History: Perhaps the most important contributor to Airbus Industrie's success as an airliner manufacturer, the four member A320 family is a significant sales success and a technological trailblazer. The 150 seat A320 is the foundation and best selling member of the family.

The A320 is perhaps best known as the first airliner to introduce a fly-by-wire flight control system – where control inputs from the pilot are transmitted to the flying surfaces by electronic signals rather than mechanical means. Apart from a small weight saving, the advantage of Airbus' fly-by-wire system is that as it is computer controlled, an inbuilt flight envelope protection makes it virtually impossible to exceed certain flight parameters such as G limits and the aircraft's maximum and minimum operating speeds and angle of attack limits.

Also integral to the A320 is the advanced electronic flightdeck, with six fully integrated EFIS colour displays and innovative sidestick controllers rather than conventional control columns. The A320 also employs a relatively high percentage of composite materials compared to earlier designs. Two engines are offered, the CFM56 and IAE V2500.

The A320 program was launched in March 1982, first flight occurred on February 22 1987, while certification was awarded on February 26 1988. Launch customer Air France took delivery of its first A320 in March that year.

The initial production version was the A320-100, which was built in only small numbers before being replaced by the definitive A320-200 (certificated in November 1988) with increased max takeoff weight, greater range and winglets. The stretched A321 and shortened A319 and A318 are described separately. All four share a common pilot type rating. A320 family production is due to increase to 30 units a month by the end of 2002, up from the mid 2000 monthly rate of 22.

Photo: An A320 of New York based jetBlue. (Airbus)

Airbus A321

Country of origin: Europe (France, Germany, Spain and UK)

Type: Short to medium range narrowbody airliner

Powerplants: A321-100 – Choice of two 133.4kN (30,000lb) International Aero Engines V2530-A5 or CFM International CFM56-5B1 turbofans. CFM56-5B2s of 139.7kN (31,000lb) available as an option. A321-200 – As above or 142.3kN (32,000lb) CFM56-5B3s or 146.8kN (33,000lb) V2533-A5s.

Performance: A321-100 – Max cruising speed 903km/h (488kt), economical cruising speed 828km/h (447kt). Range with 186 passengers and reserves 4352km (2350nm) with V2530s, 4260km (2300nm) with CFM56s. A321-200 – Range 4907km (2650nm).

Weights: A321-100 – Operating empty 47,776kg (105,330lb) with V2530s, 47,900kg (105,605lb) with CFM56s. Max takeoff (with either engine option) 83,000kg (182,984lb) or 85,000kg (187,390lb). A321-200 – Operating empty 48,024kg (105,875lb) with CFM56-5B3s, 48,139kg (106,130lb) with V2533-A5s, max takeoff 89,000kg (196,210lb).

Dimensions: Wing span 34.09m (111ft 10in), length 44.51m (146ft 0in), height 11.76m (38ft 7in). Wing area 122.6m² (1319.7sq ft).

Capacity: Flightcrew of two. Maximum passenger accommodation in a high density layout of 220 passengers. Passenger accommodation in a typical two class arrangement consists of 16 passengers at four abreast, and 169 passengers at six abreast.

Production: 377 A321s ordered by late 2000 with 172 delivered.

History: The 185 seat A321 is a stretched development of the successful A320.

Airbus launched the A321 program in November 1989 and the first development aircraft first flew on March 11 1993. European certification was awarded in December that year.

Compared with the A320 the A321's major change is the stretched fuselage, with forward and rear fuselage plugs totalling 6.93m (22ft 9in) (front plug immediately forward of wing 4.27m/14ft, rear plug directly behind the wing 2.67m/8ft 9in).

Other changes include strengthening of the undercarriage to cope with the higher weights, more powerful engines, a simplified and refined fuel system and larger tyres for better braking. A slightly modified wing with double slotted flaps and modifications to the flight controls allows the A321's handling characteristics to closely resemble the A320's. The A321 features an identical flightdeck to that on the A318, A319 and A320, and four types share the same type rating.

The basic A321-100 suffers from reduced range compared to the A320 as extra fuel tankage was not added to the initial design to compensate for the extra weight. To overcome this Airbus launched the longer range, heavier A321-200 development in 1995 which has a full pax transcontinental US range. This is achieved through 2900 litres (766US gal/638Imp gal) greater fuel capacity with the installation of an ACT (additional centre tank), higher thrust V2533-A5 or CFM56-5B3 engines and minor structural strengthening.

The A321-200 first flew from the then Daimler Benz Aerospace's Hamburg facilities in December 1996. A321s are assembled at Hamburg, along with the A319.

Photo: Virgin Atlantic operates a single A321-200. (Airbus)

Airbus A330-200 & -500

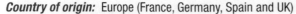

Country of origin: Europe (France, Germany, Spain and UK)

Type: Long range widebody airliners

Powerplants: A330-200 – Choice of two 300.3kN (67,500lb) General Electric CF6-80E1A2s, 286.7kN (64,000lb) Pratt & Whitney PW4164s, or PW4168s or 302.5kN (68,000lb) Rolls-Royce Trent 768 or Trent 772 turbofans.

Performance: A330-200 – Max cruising speed 880km/h (475kt) at 33,000ft, economical cruising speed 860km/h (464kt). Range with max passengers and reserves at 230t MTOW 11,850km (6400nm), at 217t MTOW 8890km (4800nm).

Weights: A330-200 – Operating empty 120,150kg (264,875lb) with CF6 engines, 120,750kg (266,200lb) with PW4168s, or 120,250kg (265,150lb) with Trents. Max takeoff 230,000kg (507,050lb).

Dimensions: A330-200 – Span 60.30m (197ft 10in), length 59.00m (193ft 7in), height 16.83m (55ft 2in). Wing area 363.1m² (3908.4sq ft).

Capacity: A330-200 – Flightcrew of two. Passenger seating arrangements for 256 in three classes or 293 in two classes.

Production: Total A330-200 orders stood at 100 at late 2000, by which stage 67 had been delivered.

History: The A330-200 is a long range, shortened development of the standard A330-300, and could also form the basis for the further shortened, 222 seat long range A330-500, which was under serious design study in late 2000.

Airbus launched development of the A330-200 in November 1995. First flight was on August 13 1997, with certification and first customer deliveries in April 1998.

The A330-200 shares near identical systems, airframe, flightdeck and wings with the A330-300, the only major differences being the fuselage length and bigger tail. Compared with the -300 the A330-200 is 10 fuselage frames shorter, and so has an overall length of 59.00m (193ft 7in), compared with 63.70m (209ft 0in) for the standard length aircraft. This allows the A330-200 to seat 256 passengers in a three class configuration, or alternatively 293 in two classes.

The A330-200 features enlarged horizontal and vertical tail services (to compensate for the loss of moment arm with the shorter fuselage). The addition of a centre fuel tank, which increases the A330-200's fuel capacity, results in the -200's 11,850km (6400nm) range.

The A330-200 would form the basis for the shortened A330-500 which Airbus was seriously studying in 2000. The A330-500 would be shortened by eight frames compared with the -200 (four frames fore and four aft of the wing), allowing it to seat 222 passengers, but otherwise it would be little changed with the same wing and power-plant options. With its comparatively big wing and a 228 tonne (502,200lb) max takeoff weight the -500 would have a range of 12,970km (7000nm). A lighter, 195 tonne (429,515lb) version would fly 8060km (4350nm). The A330-500 would also feature the improved liquid crystal display flightdeck being developed for the A340-500/-600 and enhanced A340-300.

The A330-500's design could be frozen in the third quarter of 2001, allowing a third quarter 2003 first flight and service entry a year later.

Photo: A Rolls-Royce Trent 700 powered SriLankan A330-200. (Paul Merritt)

Airbus A330-300

Country of origin: Europe (France, Germany, Spain and UK)

Type: Large capacity medium to long range airliner

Powerplants: A330-300 – Choice of two 300.3kN (67,500lb) General Electric CF6-80E1A4s, 284.7kN (64,000lb) Pratt & Whitney PW4164s, or 302.5kN (68,000lb) PW4168s or Rolls-Royce Trent 768s, or 320.2kN (72,000lb) Trent 772 turbofans. Long range A330 choice of P&W PW4164s or PW4168s or RR Trent 768s or 772s or 324kN (73,000lb) PW4173s.

Performance: Max cruising speed 880km/h (475kt) at 33,000ft, economical cruising speed 860km/h (464kt). Range with 335 pax and reserves 8340km (4500nm) with CF6s, or 8430km (4550nm) with P&W engines, or 8600km (4640nm) with Trents; A330 longer range version with max passengers range 10,185km (5500nm).

Weights: A330-300 – Operating empty 121,870kg (268,675lb) with CF6 engines, 122,460kg (269,975lb) with PW4000s, and 121,970kg (268,900lb) with Trents. Max takeoff 212,000kg (467,380lb). Long range A330 – Operating empty 122,780kg (270,675lb) with PW4000s or 122,210kg (269,425lb) with CF6s, 122,300kg (269,625lb) with Trents, max takeoff 217,000kg (478,400lb) or 230,000kg (507,060lb).

Dimensions: Wing span 60.30m (197ft 10in), length 63.60m (208ft 8in), height 16.74m (54ft 11in). Wing area 361.6m² (3892.2sq ft).

Capacity: Flightcrew of two. Passenger seating arrangements for 295 in three classes or 335 in two class (30 premium class at 2+3+2 and 305 economy at 2+4+2). Max passengers in high density configuration 440. Front and rear underbelly cargo holds can take 32 LD3 containers or 11 pallets.

Production: Total A330 orders stood at 342 at late 2000, of which over 171 delivered.

History: The A330-300 is the largest Airbus twinjet and is closely related to the four engined long range A340-300/-200 with which it shares near identical systems, airframe, flightdeck and wings.

The A340 and A330 were launched simultaneously in June 1987. Although developed in parallel, the A330-300 made its first flight after the A340, on November 2 1992. It was the first aircraft to achieve simultaneous European Joint Airworthiness Authorities (JAA) and US FAA certification, on October 21 1993. Entry into service (with France's Air Inter) was in January 1994.

Differences from the A340-300/-200 aside from the number of engines are slight changes to the wing and internal systems, including fuel tankage, and the A330-300 and A340-300 share the same fuselage length. The A330 (like the A340) features a number of technologies first pioneered on the A320, including Airbus' common advanced EFIS flightdeck with sidestick controllers and fly-by-wire computerised flight control system.

Airbus has studied various stretched (A330-400) and shortened (A330-100 and -200) A330 variants. One stretched, high capacity concept studied for a time featured lower deck seating in place of the forward freight hold. The shortened, longer range A330-200 was formally launched in 1996, while in 2000 Airbus was developing the further shortened A330-500 as a 222 seat replacement for the A300 and A310. Both are detailed in the next entry.

Photo: A Philippines A330-300. (Sam Chui)

Airbus A340-200 & -300

Country of origin: Europe (France, Germany, Spain and UK)

Type: Long range widebody airliners

Powerplants: A330-200/-300 – Four 145kN (32,550lb) CFM International CFM56-5C3 turbofans (initially 138.8kN/31,200lb CFM56-5Cs) A340-300E – Four 151.2kN (34,000lb) CFM56-5C4s.

Performance: A340-200 – Max cruising speed 914km/h (494kt), econ cruising speed 880km/h (475kt). Range with 263 passengers 13,805km (7450nm). A340-300 – Speeds same. Range with 295 passengers standard -300 13,150km (7100nm), -300E 13,520km (7300nm).

Weights: A340-200 – Operating empty (126,000kg (277,775lb), max takeoff 260,000kg (573,200lb). A340-300 – Operating empty 129,300kg (285,050lb), max takeoff 271,000kg (597,450lb), initially 260,000kg (573,200lb). A340-300E – Operating empty 130,200kg (287,050lb), max takeoff 275,000kg (606,275lb).

Dimensions: A340-200 – Wing span 60.30m (197ft 0in), length 59.39m (194ft 10in), height 16.74m (54ft 11in). Wing area 363.1m² (3908.4sq ft). A340-300 – Same except for length 63.70m (209ft 0in).

Capacity: Flightcrew of two. A340-200 – Typical three class arrangement for 263 passengers, or 303 in two classes. A340-300 – Typical three class accommodation for 303, or 335 in two classes.

Production: A total of 206 A340-200/-300s had been ordered by late 2000, of which 181 had been delivered.

History: The A340-200 and -300 are the initial variants of the successful quad engined A340 family of long haul widebodies.

The A340 and closely related A330 were launched in June 1987. The A340-300 first flew on October 25 1991, certification was in December 1992, and service entry was in March 1993.

The A340 shares the same flightdeck including sidestick controllers and EFIS, plus fly-by-wire, basic airframe, systems, fuselage and wing with the A330 (the flightdeck is also common to the A320 series). Power is from four CFM56s, Airbus says the four engine configuration is more efficient for long range flights (as twins need more power for a given weight for engine out on takeoff performance), and quads are free from ETOPS restrictions.

The A340-300 has the same fuselage length as the A330-300, while the shortened A340-200 traded seating capacity for greater range (first flight April 1 1992). Both feature a third main undercarriage unit, a twin wheel unit, which retracts into the fuselage. The A340-300E features an additional centre fuel tank and greater range.

The 275,000kg (606,275lb) MTOW A340-213X (formerly A340-8000) is based on the -200 but has extra fuel in three additional rear cargo hold tanks and a 15,000km (8100nm) range with 232 three class passengers. One was been built for the Sultan of Brunei.

Airbus is currently working on an improved A340-300 powered by the upgraded CFM56-5C Enhanced, which will offer maintenance cost savings and greater reliability. The improved A340-300 will also include improvements being developed for the A340-500/-600, including liquid crystal displays on the flightdeck, fly-by-wire rudder actuation and additional crew rest facilities. First deliveries would follow certification in the northern spring of 2003.

All versions are offered with underfloor passenger sleepers.

Photo: One of three Egyptair A340-200s. (Airbus)

Airbus A340-500 & -600

Country of origin: Europe (France, Germany, Spain and UK)

Type: Long range widebody airliners

Powerplants: Four 249kN (56,000lb) Rolls-Royce Trent 556 turbofans.

Performance: Typical cruising speed Mach 0.83. A340-500 – Range with 313 passengers 15,742km (8500nm). A340-600 – Range with 380 passengers 13,890km (7500nm).

Weights: A340-500 – Operating empty 170,400kg (375,665lb), max takeoff 365,000kg (804,675lb). A340-600 – Operating empty 177,000kg (390,220lb), max takeoff 365,000kg (804,675lb).

Dimensions: A340-500 – Wing span 63.60m (208ft 8in), length 67.90m (209ft 0in), height 17.80m (58ft 5in). Wing area 437.0m² (4704sq ft). A340-600 – Same except length 73.50m (241ft 2in).

Capacity: A340-500 – Flightcrew of two. Typical three class seating for 316 passengers. A340-600 Typical three class seating for 372.

Production: At late 2000 Airbus held 71 firm orders for the A340-500/-600. First deliveries are planned for June 2002.

History: The 15,740km (8500nm) ultra long range A340-500 and stretched 380 seat A340-600 are new variants of the Airbus A340 quad currently under development.

Compared with the A340-300 the A340-600 will feature a 9.07m (35ft 1in) stretch (5.87m/19ft 3in ahead of the wing and 3.20m/10ft 6in behind), allowing it to seat 372 passengers in a typical three class arrangement. This will give Airbus a true early model 747 replacement and near direct competitor to the 747-400.

The A340-500 meanwhile will be stretched by only 3.19m (10ft 6in) compared with the A340-300, and so will seat 313 in three classes, but it would have a massive range of 15,740km (8500nm), which will make it one of the longest ranging airliners in the world, capable for example of operating Los Angeles/Singapore nonstop.

The two new A340 models share a common wing which is based on the A330/A340's but is 1.6m (5.2ft) longer and has a tapered wingbox insert, increasing wing area and fuel capacity. Both models will feature three fuselage plugs. The other change to the A340 airframe is the use of the A330-200 twin's larger fin and enlarged horizontal area stabilisers. To cope with the increased weights the centre undercarriage main gear is a four wheel bogie, rather than a two wheel unit.

Both new A340s have a high degree of commonality with the A330 and other A340 models. They will feature Airbus' common two crew flightdeck, but with some improvements such as LCD rather than CRT displays and modernised systems.

Power will be from four 249kN (56,000lb) thrust Rolls-Royce Trent 556 turbofans.

The commercial launch for A340-500/-600 was at the 1997 Paris Airshow, the program's industrial launch was in December that year when Virgin Atlantic ordered eight A340-600s and optioned eight. First flight (the -600 will fly first) is planned for May 2001, with first delivery (to Virgin) in June 2002. The A340-500 is due to make its first flight in February 2002.

An 1800 flight hour, three aircraft flight test program is planned for the A340-600, the A340-500 will undergo a further 500 flight hours of testing.

Photo: The A340-600 prototype pictured in December 2000. (Airbus)

Airbus A380

Country of origin: Europe (France, Germany, Spain and UK)

Type: High capacity, long range, twin deck, widebody airliner

Powerplants: A380-800 – Four 302kN (67,890lb) Rolls-Royce Trent 900 or Engine Alliance (GE & P&W) GP7200 turbofans. A380-800HGW – Four 311kN (69,915lb) Trent 900s or GP7200s.

Performance: A380-800 & -800HGW – Max cruising speed Mach 0.88. Long range cruising speed Mach 0.85. Range 15,100km (8150nm).

Weights: A380-800 – Operating weight empty 275,000kg (606,000lb), max takeoff 548,000kg (1,208,000lb). A380-800HGW – Max takeoff 560,000kg (1,235,000lb).

Dimensions: A380-800 – Wing span 79.8m (261ft 10in), length 73m (239ft 6in), height 24.1m (79ft 1in).

Capacity: A380-800 – Flightcrew of two. Standard seating for 555 passengers on two decks in a three class arrangement. Launch customer Qantas plans to fit its aircraft with 523 seats (in three classes). A380 has 49% more floor area but only 35% more seats (in 555 seat configuration) than the 747-400, allowing room for passenger amenities such as bars, gymnasiums and duty free shops.

Production: Program launched Dec 2000 with 50 firm orders.

History: The 555 seat, double deck Airbus A380 is the most ambitious civil aircraft program yet. When it enters service in March 2006, the A380 will be the world's largest airliner, easily eclipsing Boeing's 747.

Airbus first began studies on a very large 500 seat airliner in the early 1990s. The European manufacturer saw developing a competitor and successor to the 747 as a strategic play to end Boeing's dominance of the very large airliner market and round out Airbus' product line-up.

Engineering studies of such an aircraft, designated the A3XX, began in 1994. A 12 abreast single deck design was soon rejected for a twin deck configuration. Design aims included 15% lower direct operating costs per seat compared with the 747-400 and the ability to use existing airport infrastructure with little modifications to the airports.

Airbus formally launched the A380 on December 19 2000 after gaining 50 launch order commitments from five airlines (Emirates, Singapore, Air France, Qantas and Virgin Atlantic) and lessor ILFC. The out of sequence A380 designation was chosen as the '8' represents the twin decks. First flight is planned for the fourth quarter of 2004, service entry, with Singapore Airlines, is scheduled for March 2006.

A380 features include an advanced flightdeck with pull-out keyboards for the pilots, and extensive use of composite materials such as GLARE.

Several A380 models are planned. The basic aircraft is the A380-800 and high gross weight A380-800, with the longer range A380-800R planned. The A380-800F freighter will be able to carry a 150 tonne payload and is due to enter service in 2008. Future models will include the shortened, 480 seat A380-700, and the stretched, 656 seat A380-900. (The -700, -800 & -900 designations were chosen to reflect that the A380 will enter service as a "fully developed aircraft" and that the basic models will not be soon replaced by more improved variants.)

A380 final assembly will take place in Toulouse, France, with interior fitment in Hamburg, Germany. Major A380 assemblies will be transported to Toulouse by ship, barge and road.

Photo: An artist's impression of the A380. (Airbus)

Airbus A319CJ Corporate Jetliner

Country of origin: Europe (France, Germany, Spain and UK)

Type: Long range large corporate jet

Powerplants: Two 120kN (27,000lb) International Aero Engines IAE V2527M-A5 turbofans (CFM International CFM56s optional).

Performance: Max cruising speed Mach 0.82. Max altitude 41,000ft. Range with 12 passengers up to 11,100km (6000nm), range with 40 passengers up to 8300km (4500nm).

Weights: Max takeoff 75,500kg (166,400lb).

Dimensions: Wing span 33.91m (111ft 3in), length 33.80m (110ft 11in), height 11.80m (38ft 8.5in). Wing area 122.4m² (1317.5sq ft).

Capacity: Flightcrew of two. Six standard layouts offered, seating from 10 to 39 passengers.

Production: First customer delivery December 1999, eight completed aircraft due to be delivered by end of 2000, when Airbus held firm orders for 19. Green A319CJ costs $US37m, interior completion can cost $US5-10m. 18 firm orders held at late 2000. Airbus forecasts annual demand for A319CJ class aircraft at 15-20 per year.

History: The Airbus Corporate Jetliner, or A319CJ, is a long range corporate jet development of the A319 airliner which competes directly with the Boeing Business Jet and dedicated long range corporate jets such as the Bombardier Global Express and Gulfstream V.

Airbus launched the A319CJ at the 1997 Paris Airshow and the first A319CJ rolled out in October 1998. The airframe was then due to be fitted with belly auxiliary fuel tanks and flight test instrumentation prior to making a first flight in May 1999. Certification (to FAA Part 121 and JAR OPS) was awarded in July 1999, with the first delivery, to the Al Kharafi Group, that December.

The A319CJ was designed as a minimum change development of the A319. One of its key design features is that the A319CJ can be easily converted to an airliner, thus increasing the aircraft's potential resale value. The A319CJ can be powered by either the IAE V2500 or CFM56, although in October 2000 Airbus signed an agreement with IAE to make the V2500 the 'reference' engine on the aircraft. As a consequence the V2500 powered A319CJ is now offered to potential customers as a package arrangement

The A319's containerised cargo hold means that the CJ's auxiliary fuel tanks can be easily loaded and unloaded, giving operators flexibility to reconfigure the aircraft for varying payload/range requirements. Like the rest of the A320 single aisle family (plus the A330 and A340), the A319CJ shares Airbus' common advanced six screen glass flightdeck with sidestick controllers (but with a new flight management system), plus fly-by-wire flight controls. It also features standard integral airstair and has a higher cruising altitude than the A319 airliner.

Airbus supplies green A319CJ airframes outfitters for interior fitment. Interiors weigh 3.8 tonnes (8500lb) to 4.8 tonnes (10,700lb), and cost from $US8m to $US12m. Outfitting takes from four to eight months.

The first A319CJ order was announced in December 1997. One notable customer is Qatar Air, which has ordered one for use on corporate charters and scheduled airline services. Other customers include the Italian air force and DaimlerChrysler.

Photo: An Italian air force A319CJ. (Airbus)

Air Tractor AT-301, AT-401 & AT-501

Country of origin: United States of America

Type: Piston powered agricultural aircraft

Powerplant: AT-301 – One 447kW (600hp) Pratt & Whitney R-1340 radial piston engine driving a two blade prop. AT-401B – One remanufactured 447kW (600hp) P&W R-1340, two or three blade prop.

Performance: AT-301 – Max speed 266km/h (144kt), economical cruising speed 225km/h (122kt), typical working speed 193-225km/h (104-122kt). Range with max fuel and no reserves 869km (469nm). AT-401B – Max cruising speed 251km/h (135kt), cruising speed 230km/h (124kt), typical working speed 193-225km/h (104-122kt). Range with max fuel and no reserves 1015km (547nm).

Weights: AT-301 – Empty 1656kg (3650lb), loaded 3130kg (6900lb). AT-401B – Empty (spray equipped) 1950kg (4300lb), standard max takeoff 3565kg (7860lb), optional max takeoff 4082kg (9000lb).

Dimensions: AT-301 – Wing span 13.75m (45ft 2in), length 8.23m (27ft 0in), height 2.59m (8ft 6in). Wing area 25.1m² (270sq ft). AT-401B – Same except span 15.57m (51ft 1in). Wing area 28.4m² (306.0sq ft).

Capacity: Pilot only. Chemical spray hopper capacity of 1210 litres in AT-301, 1325 litres in AT-301A/B and 1515 litres in AT-401.

Production: More than 1700 Air Tractors of all models have been built, including more than 665 AT-301s, 250 AT-401s and 11 AT-501s.

History: The AT-301, AT-401 and AT-501 are the radial piston powered members of the series of the successful Air Tractor family.

The Air Tractor was designed by company founder Leland Snow who had earlier designed and built the Snow S-2 ag aircraft (which was later built by Rockwell and Ayres). Leland Snow today remains chairman of the Olney, Texas based company he established. Snow began work on the Air Tractor AT-301 in January 1971 (he formed Air Tractor in 1974). The prototype first flew in September 1973 and the type was awarded FAA certification in November of that year.

The AT-301 was fairly similar in overall configuration to Snow's earlier S-2 series. It was powered by a remanufactured 447kW (600hp) Pratt & Whitney R-1340 (the R-1340 has been out of production since the mid '50s) with an enclosed, single seat cockpit. Spray bars mounted below and behind the wing's leading edge dispensed the hopper's 1210 litre chemical capacity.

Air Tractor introduced the improved AT-301A, with a larger capacity 1325 litre capacity hopper in 1981. The AT-301 and -301A were built side-by-side until 1987 when Air Tractor replaced the AT-301A with the slightly improved, shortlived AT-301B.

Meanwhile in 1986 Air Tractor developed the AT-301 based AT-401, with a 1.22m (4ft 0in) increased span wing, a 1514 litre capacity hopper and increased max takeoff weight. The AT-401 replaced the -301 in 1987 and remains in production as the AT-401B with remanufactured R-1340 and increased span wings with Hoerner wingtips. The AT-401A was a one-off with a PZL-3S radial flown in 1990.

The AT-500 prototype with a 16.15m (53ft 0in) wing span, three blade prop and higher landing gear debuted in 1985. It was the basis for the production 15.24m (50ft) span AT-501 (certificated mid 1987) and 11 were built to 1992 (and they could be converted in the field to turbine AT-502s).

Photo: An AT-401 in standard Air Tractor yellow and blue.

Air Tractor turbine models

Country of origin: United States of America

Type: Turboprop powered agricultural and firebombing aircraft

Powerplant: AT-502 – One 507kW (680shp) Pratt & Whitney Canada PT6A series turboprop, optionally a 560kW (750shp) PT6A, driving a three blade prop. AT-802 – One 966kW (1295shp) PT6-65AG or -67AG, or 1007kW (1350shp) PT6A-67AGR or -67AF driving a five blade prop.

Performance: AT-502 – Max speed 290kmh (155kt), typical operating speeds 195 to 235km/h (105 to 125kt). Initial rate of climb 1080ft/min. Range with max fuel 998km (538nm). AT-802 – Max speed 338km/h (182kt), max cruising speed 314km/h (170kt). Initial rate of climb 800ft/min. Range with max fuel 805km (434nm).

Weights: AT-502 – Empty 1870kg (4123lb), max takeoff 4175kg (9200lb). AT-802 – Empty equipped 2903kg (6400lb), max takeoff 7257kg (16,000lb).

Dimensions: AT-502 – Wing span 15.24m (50ft in), length 9.91m (32ft 6in), height 2.99m (9ft 10in). Wing area 27.9m² (300.0sq ft). AT-802 – Wing span 18.06m (59ft 3in) length 10.87m (35ft 8in), height 3.35m (11ft 0in). Wing area 37.3m² (401.0sq ft).

Capacity: Pilot only, two in tandem in AT-503A and AT-802.

Production: Turbo Air Tractor production includes 18 AT-302s, 86 -400s, 160 -402s, 500 -502s, 70 -602s, and 80 -802s and -802As.

History: The first turbine Air Tractor was the AT-301 based AT-302, which first flew in June 1977.

The AT-302 was powered by a 447kW (600shp) Avco Lycoming LTP 101-600, while the improved AT-301A, introduced in 1979, had a larger, 1514 litre hopper. Just 18 were built through to the mid 1980s.

The first Pratt & Whitney Canada PT6 powered model was the AT-400 Turbo Air Tractor, introduced in 1980. Powered by a 507kW (680shp) PT6A-15AG (or -27 or -28) it featured the AT-302A's 1514 litre hopper. The AT-400A is similar except the buyer supplies its used 410kW (550shp) PT6A-20. The AT-402 first flew in 1988 and features the increased span wings of the piston powered AT-401. The current AT-402A (introduced in 1997) has a 410kW (550shp) PT6A-11AG, joining the standard 507kW (680shp) PT6A powered AT-402B.

The first two seater Air Tractor was the AT-503. First flown in April 1986 it is based on the AT-400 and but features an 820kW (1100shp) PT6A-45R, five blade prop, 1892 litre hopper and tandem seats. It was initially developed for the US State Department for anti drugs work

The single seat AT-502 is based on the AT-503 (first flight April 1987) has a 15.24m (50ft) span wing (as on the piston AT-501) and 507kW (680shp) PT6. The 502 remains in production alongside the AT-502A (first flight Feb 1992) with a far more powerful 820kW (1100shp) PT6A-45R driving a slow turning five blade prop, and the -502A based AT-502B with long span wings with Hoerner wingtips.

The 5.6 tonne MTOW 783kW (1050shp) or 966kW (1295shp) PT6 powered AT-602 (first flight December 1 1995) has a 818 litre hopper.

The heaviest and most powerful Air Tractors are the two seat (and dual controls) AT-802 and single seat AT-802A – the largest purpose designed single engine ag aircraft in production. First flight was in October 1990. The AT 802AF is a single seater optimised for firefighting. Total hopper capacity is 3066 litres.

Photo: An AT-802A. (Robert Wiseman)

Antonov/PZL Mielec An-2 & SAMC Y-5

Countries of origin: Ukraine and Poland

Type: Biplane utility transport

Powerplants: An-2P – One 745kW (1000hp) PZL Kalisz ASz-61IR nine cylinder radial engine driving an AW-2 four blade variable pitch propeller. Y-5B – One 735kW (986hp) PZL Kalisz ASz-61IR-16 or Zhuzhou HS5 nine cylinder radial engine.

Performance: An-2P – Max speed 258km/h (139kt), economical cruising speed 185km/h (100kt). Range with a 500kg (1100lb) payload 900km (485nm). Y-5B – Max speed 220km/h (120kt), typical cruising speed 160km/h (85kt). Range 845km (455nm).

Weights: An-2P – Empty 3450kg (7605lb), max takeoff 5500kg (12,125lb). Y-5B – Max takeoff 5250kg (11,575lb).

Dimensions: Upper wing span 18.18m (59ft 8in), lower 14.14m (46ft 9in), length (tail down) 12.40m (40ft 8in), height (tail down) 4.01m (12ft 2in). Upper wing area 43.5m² (468.7sq ft), lower 28.0m² (301.2sq ft).

Capacity: Flightcrew of one or two pilots. Passenger accommodation for 12 at three abreast. Agricultural versions have large chemical hoppers with spray bars along the lower wing.

Production: More than 5000 An-2s were built in the Ukraine between 1948 and the mid 1960s, before production was transferred to PZL Mielec in Poland, where approximately 12,000 were built through to the early 1990s, with small numbers completed since then. Close to 1000 Y-5s have been built by SAMC in China.

History: The An-2 biplane utility transport was originally designed to meet a USSR Ministry of Agriculture and Forestry requirement, and flew for the first time on August 31 1947.

Entering production and service the following year, Antonov built An-2s were powered by 745kW (1000hp) ASh-62 radials. Soviet production continued through to the mid sixties by which time a number of variants had been developed, including the base model An-2P, An-2S and -2M crop sprayers, An-2VA water bomber, An-2M floatplane and the An-2ZA high altitude meteorological research aircraft.

Production responsibility was transferred to Poland's PZL Mielec in the 1960s, with the first example flying on October 23 1960. Aside from the An-2P, Polish versions include the An-2PK VIP transport, An-2PR for TV relay work, An-2S ambulance, An-2TD paratroop transport, An-2P cargo/passenger version, An-2 Geofiz geophysical survey version, 12 seat passenger An-2T and An-2TP with increased passenger headroom, and agricultural An-2R.

Chinese production as the Y-5 commenced with Nanchang in 1957, before being transferred to the Shijiazhuang Aircraft Manufacturing Company. The main Chinese version was the standard Y-5N which was built until 1986 after 221 had been built. The Y-5B specialist ag aircraft, first flew in June 1989. Versions are the Y5B-100 with wingtip vanes, passenger Y-5B(K), agricultural or passenger Y-5B(D) and Y-5C parachutist version, ordered by the Chinese air force.

The An-3 Antonov built turboprop powered version first flew in the early 1980s powered by a 706kW (946shp) Omsk (Mars) TVD-10, but originally did not enter production. However a 1025kW (1375shp) TVD-20 powered An-3 received Russian certification in August 2000 and is due to enter production.

Photo: A Polish An-2 in Canada. (Gary Gentle)

Antonov An-8, An-10 & An-12 & Xian Y-8

Countries of origin: Ukraine and China (Y-8)

Type: Turboprop freighter

Powerplants: An-12 – Four 2490kW (3495shp) Ivchenko AI-20K turboprops driving AV-68 four blade constant speed propellers. Shaanxi Y-8A – Four 3170kW (4250shp) Zhuzhou WJ6 turboprops driving four blade constant speed propellers.

Performance: An-12 – Max speed 777km/h (420kt), max cruising speed 670km/h (361kt). Range with max payload 3600km (1940nm), range with full fuel load 5700km (3075nm). Y-8A – Max speed 660km/h (357kt), economical cruising speed 530km/h (286kt). Range with max fuel load 5615km (3030nm), range with max payload 1275km (690nm).

Weights: An-12 – Empty 28,000kg (61,730lb), max takeoff 61,000kg (134,480lb). Y-8 – Empty equipped 35,490kg (77,237lb), max takeoff 61,000kg (134,480lb).

Dimensions: An-12 – Wing span 38.00m (124ft 8in), length 33.10m (108ft 7in), height 10.53m (34ft 7in). Wing area 121.7m² (1310sq ft). Y-8 – Same except for length 34.02m (111ft 8in), height 11.16m (36ft 8in). Wing area 121.9m² (1311.7sq ft).

Capacity: Flightcrew of two pilots, flight engineer, radio operator and navigator (the latter in the glazed nose). Can be configured to accommodate 14 passengers plus freight, with military versions carrying up to 90 troops. Max payload 20,000kg (44,090lb).

Production: An-12 production approximately 1200 aircraft. Xian has built over 60 Y-8s for military and civil use. In 2000 approximately 10 An-8s and 150 An-12s in commercial service.

History: The An-12 (NATO reporting name 'Cub') was developed to fulfil a Soviet air force requirement for a turboprop freighter.

The An-12 freighter and civil An-10 were developed in parallel and were based on the twin turboprop An-8. The An-8 first appeared in 1956 and was developed for Aeroflot. It is still in limited commercial service.

The prototype An-12 flew in 1958, powered by Kuznetsov NK-4 turboprops, and was essentially a militarised An-10 with a rear loading cargo ramp. Meanwhile approximately 500 An-10s were built, and they saw service between 1960 and 1972 exclusively with Aeroflot.

Production An-12s are powered by more economical AI-20 turboprops and were built through until 1973. In Soviet military service it was replaced by the Ilyushin Il-76 (described elsewhere). The An-12BP is the basic military transport version of the Cub. Other military versions have been used as Elint and ECM platforms.

The defensive rear gunner's turret is usually faired over on civil operated An-12s. Today large numbers remain in use with charter freight operators.

China's Xian began redesign work of the An-12 in 1969, and has resulted in a number of Chinese versions, built by the Shaanxi Aircraft Company. Civil variants include the Y-8B and pressurised Y-8C, which was developed with cooperation from Lockheed (first flight was in 1990), export Y-8D with some western avionics, the Y-8F livestock carrier, Y-8F100 with improved engines, 2.2m (7ft 10in) stretched Y-8F200, and Y-8H aerial survey model.

Photo: The stretched Xian Y-8F200. (Ian Moy)

Antonov An-22 Antheus

Country of origin: Ukraine

Type: Large capacity turboprop freighter

Powerplants: Four 11,185kW (15,000shp) Kuznetsov (now Kuibyshev) NK-12MA turboprops driving eight blade counter rotating propellers.

Performance: Max speed 740km/h (400kt), cruising speed 580-640km/h (313-345kt). Range with max fuel and 45 tonne (99,200lb) payload 10,950km (5905nm), range with max payload 5000km (2692nm).

Weights: Typical empty equipped 114,000kg (251,325lb), max takeoff 250,000kg (551,160lb).

Dimensions: Wing span 64.41m (211ft 4in), length 57.92m (190ft 0in), height 12.53m (41ft 1in). Wing area 345.0m^2 (3714sq ft).

Capacity: Flightcrew of up to six, comprising two pilots, navigator, flight engineer and a communications specialist. Up to 29 passengers can be accommodated on the upper deck behind the flightdeck. The unpressurised main cabin can house a range of oversize payloads such as main battle tanks and oil drilling equipment. Max payload is 80,000kg (176,350lb).

Production: Approximately 65 built, of which approximately 50 have been operated in Aeroflot colours. Just one example remained in commercial service in 2000, with the Antonov Design Bureau.

History: The massive An-22 is the largest turboprop powered aircraft yet built and was designed in response to a primarily Soviet military requirement for a strategic heavylift freighter.

The An-22 (NATO reporting name 'Cock') made its first flight on February 27 1965 – at that time it was comfortably the largest aircraft in the world. Production of the An-22 for the Soviet air force and Aeroflot continued through the 1960s until 1974. Early production was of the An-22, the definitive An-22A had less nose glazing. A 724 seat passenger carrying variant did not make it off the drawing board.

Notable features of the An-22 include the NK-12 turboprops – which also power the Tupolev Tu-95/Tu-142 'Bear' family of bombers and maritime patrol aircraft and are the most powerful turboprop engines in service – comprehensive navigation and precision drop avionics, and massive undercarriage and tailplane.

The An-22 set 14 payload to height records in 1967, the pinnacle of which was the carriage of 100 tonnes (220,500lb) of metal blocks to an altitude of 25,748ft (7848m). It also established the record for a maximum payload lifted to a height of 2000m (6562ft), carrying a payload of 104,444kg (221,443lb). A number of class speed records were also set in 1972, including a speed of 608.5km/h (328kt) around a 1000km (540nm) circuit with a 50,000kg (110,250lb) payload. Further speed with payload records were established in 1974 and 1975.

As well as operations into the underdeveloped regions of Russia's northeast, Siberia and far east, Aeroflot An-22s were commonly used for military transport, their 'civilian' status allowing much freer access to landing and overflight rights.

Although just one An-22 was in use in 2000, the type's impressive payload capabilities means it remains a useful airlifter. The Antonov Design Bureau's single example is used for freight charters, alongside An-124s.

Photo: The An-22. (Peter Sweetten/Aviation Photography Worldwide)

Antonov An-24 & -26 & Xian Y7 & MA-60

Country of origin: Ukraine (An-24/-26), China (Y7 & MA-60)

Type: Regional airliners and freighters

Powerplants: An-24V – Two 1887kW (2530ehp) Ivchenko (Progress) AI-24A turboprops driving four blade constant speed propellers. Y7-100 – Two 2080kW (2790shp) Wongan WJ5A I turboprops.

Performance: An-24V – Max cruising speed 500km/h (270kt), long range cruising speed 450km/h (243kt). Range with max payload 550km (296nm), range with max fuel 2400km (1295nm). Y7-100 – Max cruising speed 476km/h (257kt). Range with 52 pax 910km (491nm).

Weights: An-24V – Empty equipped 13,300kg (29,320lb), max takeoff 21,000kg (46,300lb). Y7-100 – Operating empty 14,900kg (32,850lb), max takeoff 21,800kg (48,060lb).

Dimensions: An-24V – Wing span 29.20m (95ft 10in), length 23.53m (77ft 3in), height 8.32m (27ft 4in). Wing area 75.0m^2 (807sq ft). Y7-100 – Wing span 29.64m (97ft 3in), length 23.71m (77ft 10in), height 8.55m (28ft 1in). Wing area 75.0m^2 (807sq ft).

Capacity: Flightcrew of two pilots and flight engineer, plus optional radio operator. Seating for up to 50 at four abreast.

Production: Over 1200 An-24s built, most in the Ukraine. Approx 880 An-24s in commercial service in 2000. Y7 production continues. Approx 470 An-24s, 265 An-26s, 60 An-30s and 70 An-32s are in civil use.

History: The An-24 is the original aircraft in a prolific and highly successful family of twin turboprop civil and military transports.

The An-24 first flew in April 1960 and entered service with Aeroflot in September 1963. Aeroflot was the largest An-24 operator, with others going to Soviet client nations.

Versions of the An-24 include the An-24V and the An-24T freighter. A small turbojet in the right engine nacelle to boost takeoff performance resulted in the An-24RT and An-24RV. The An-24P firebomber was also developed before Ukrainian production ceased in 1978.

The An-24 was developed into the An-26 'Curl' military tactical transport with more powerful engines and redesigned tail, which itself evolved into the An-32 with enhancements for better hot and high performance. Over 550 An-26s are in civil service, with 1410 built.

The An-30 development was built in limited numbers and is used largely for aerial survey and cartography work. This version is identifiable by its extensive nose glazing.

The An-32 first flew in 1976 and features much more powerful 3760kW (5042ehp) Progress engines for improved hot and high performance. The An-32 features above wing mounted engines to give the larger diameter props adequate ground clearance.

China's Xian Aircraft Company is now the sole production source for the An-24 as the Y7. The improved Y7-100, developed with the technical assistance of HAECO in Hong Kong during the 1980s, incorporates a revised passenger interior and flightdeck, and wingtip winglets.

The Y7-200A features 2050kW (2750shp) Pratt & Whitney Canada PW127C turboprops and Collins EFIS avionics. If first flew in December 1993 and was certificated in 1998. The Y7-200B has Collins avionics but Chinese engines. The Y7H and Y7H-500 are versions of the An-26. The ultimate development is the stretched, P&WC PW127 powered MA-60, which was publicly unveiled at the 2000 Zhuhai Airshow.

Photo: The Xian MA-60. (Ian Moy)

Antonov/PZL Mielec An-28 & An-38

Countries of origin: Ukraine and Poland

Type: Regional airliner and utility transports

Powerplants: An-28 – Two 715kW (960shp) PZL Rzeszów built RKBM/Rybinsk (Glushenkov) TVD-10B turboprops driving three blade propellers. M-28 – Two 820kW (1100shp) Pratt & Whitney Canada PT6A-65Bs driving five blade props. An-38-100 – Two 1118kW (1500shp) Honeywell TPE331-14GR-801E turboprops.

Performance: An-28 – Max cruising speed 350km/h (189kt), economical cruising speed 335km/h (181kt). Range with 20 passengers 510km (274nm), range with a full fuel load and 1000kg (455lb) payload 1365km (736nm). M-28 – Economical cruising speed 270km/h (146kt). Initial rate of climb 2657ft/min. Range with max fuel and 1000kg (2205lb) payload 1365km (735nm). An-38-100 – Max speed 405km/h (219kt), cruising speed 380km/h (205kt). Range with 27 passengers and reserves 600km (324nm).

Weights: An-28 – Empty equipped 3900kg (8598lb), max takeoff 6500kg (14,330lb). M-28 – Empty equipped 3917kg (8635lb), max takeoff 7000kg (15,432lb). An-38-100 – Empty 5300kg (11,684lb), max takeoff 8800kg (19,400lb).

Dimensions: An-28/M-28 – Span 22.06m (72ft 5in), length 13.10m (42ft 12in), height 4.90m (16ft 1in). Wing area 39.7m² (427.5sq ft). An-38 – Same except length 15.67m (51ft 5in), height 4.30m (14ft 1in).

Capacity: An-28/M-28 – Flightcrew of two. Typical passenger seating for 17 at three abreast and 72cm (28in) pitch. High density seating for 20. An-38 – Standard seating for 26 three abreast, optionally 27.

Production: Approx 200 An-28s built, with 80 in commercial service. Over a dozen M-28s have been ordered. Six An-38s in service.

History: The An-28 was the winner of a competition against the Beriev Be-30 for a new light passenger and utility transport for Aeroflot's short haul routes. The An-38 is a stretched development

The An-28 is based on the earlier An-14. It combines the An-14's high wing layout, twin fins and rudders with a new and far larger fuselage and turboprop engines.

The An-28 made its first flight as the An-14M in September 1969 in the Ukraine, while a preproduction aircraft first flew in April 1975. Production of the An-28 was transferred to Poland's PZL Mielec in 1978, although it was not until July 22 1984 that the first Polish built production aircraft flew. The An-28's Soviet type certificate was awarded in April 1986.

PZL Mielec has been the sole source for production An-28s, and has developed the westernised M-28 Skytruck version powered by 820kW (1100shp) Pratt & Whitney Canada PT6A-65B turboprops with five blade Hartzell propellers, plus some western (Bendix-King) avionics. Originally designated the An-28PT, first flight was in July 1993 and it is in limited production. The M-28 received Polish certification equivalent to US FAR Part 23 in March 1996.

The An-28 also forms the basis for the Antonov developed stretched 26 seat An-38 which first flew on June 23 1994. Variants are the AlliedSignal (now Honeywell) TPE331 powered An-38-100 (the first two prototypes were to this standard) and An-38K convertible, and Omsk TVD-20 powered An-38-200. Russian certification was granted in April 1997.

Photo: The TPE331 powered An-38. (Paul Merritt)

Antonov An-72 & An-74

Countries of origin: Ukraine and Russia

Type: STOL capable freighter

Powerplants: Two 63.7kN (14,330lb) ZMKB Progress D-36 turbofans.

Performance: An-72 – Max speed 705km/h (380kt), cruising speed range 550 to 600km/h (295 to 325kt). Service ceiling 35,000ft. Range with max fuel and reserves 4800km (2590nm), with a 7500kg (16,535lb) payload 2000km (1080nm). An-74 – Speeds similar. Range with reserves and a 10,000kg (22,025lb) payload 1150km (620nm), or with a 1500kg (3310lb) payload 5300km (2860nm).

Weights: An-72 – Empty 19,050kg, max takeoff (from a 1800m/5900ft runway) 34,500kg (76,060lb). Max takeoff from a 600-800m (1970-2630ft) runway 27,500kg (60,625lb).

Dimensions: Wing span 31.89m (104ft 8in), length 28.07m (92ft 1in), height 8.65m (28ft 5in). Wing area 98.6m² (1062sq ft).

Capacity: Flightcrew of three (two pilots and a flight engineer) for the An-72. An-74 also has provision for a radio operator. Main cabin designed primarily for freight, in which role it can carry a payload of 10 tonnes (22,045lb) including four UAK-2.5 containers, or four 2.5 tonne (5510lb) PAV-2.5 pallets. An-72 can seat 68 on removable seats, while the An-74 when configured for combi passenger/freight tasks can carry eight support crew.

Production: Production totals more than 160, mostly for military customers. Most built in Ukraine but production transferred to Omsk in Russia in 1993. Approx eight An-72s and 39 An-74s in commercial use.

History: The An-72 was designed as a replacement for the An-26 tactical transport for the Soviet air force, but variants including the An-74 are in use as commercial freighters.

The first of five flying An-72 prototypes first flew on August 31 1977, although it was not until December 1985 that the first of eight extensively revised preproduction An-72s with lengthened fuselage and longer span wings flew. Included in this pre-series batch were two An-74s, differing from the An-72s in their ability to operate in harsh weather conditions in polar regions. Other changes include greater fuel capacity and an increased max takeoff weight.

The most significant design feature of the An-72 and An-74 is the use of the Coanda effect to improve STOL performance, which utilises engine exhaust gases blown over the wing's upper surface to boost lift. Other features include multi slotted flaps, rear loading ramp and multi unit landing gear capable of operations from unprepared strips.

Versions of the An-72/74 family (NATO codename 'Coaler') include the An-72 base model with extended wings and fuselage compared to the prototypes, the An-72S VIP transport and An-72P maritime patrol aircraft.

Versions of the An-74 include the base An-74, the increased MTOW and payload An-74-200 freighter and further improved An-74T-200A, the An-74TK-100 and -74TK-200 convertible passenger/freighter models (with seating for up to 52 passengers), and the An-74TK-200D Salon VIP transport. Antonov has also worked on two stretched developments, An-74-400 and An-174. Antonov has also been working on the An-74TK-300 with new Progress D-426T1 turbofans mounted in pods under the wings.

Photo: The An-74TK is built in -100 and -200 forms. (Paul Merritt)

Antonov An-124

Country of origin: Ukraine

Type: Heavylift freighter

Powerplants: An-124 – Four 229.5kN (51,590lb) ZMKB Progress (Lotarev) D-18T turbofans.

Performance: An-124 – Max cruising speed 865km/h (468kt), typical cruising speeds 800 to 850km/h (430 to 460kt). Range with max payload 4500km (2430nm), range with max fuel 16,500km (8900nm).

Weights: An-124 – Operating empty 175,000kg (385,800lb), max takeoff 405,000kg (892,875lb).

Dimensions: Wing span 73.30m (240ft 6in), length 69.10m (226ft 9in), height 20.78m (68ft 2in). Wing area 628.0m² (6760sq ft).

Capacity: Flightcrew of six – two pilots, two flight engineers, navigator and communications operator. Upper deck behind the flightdeck area features galley, rest room and two relief crew cabins. Upper deck behind the wing can accommodate up to 88 passengers. Main deck cargo compartment can carry a range of bulky and oversized cargos. The An-124's total payload in weight is 150 tonnes (330,695lb).

Production: About 60 An-124s have been built, of which 25 were in commercial use in 2000.

History: For a time the massive An-124 held the mantle of the world's largest aircraft before the arrival of the An-225, a stretched six engine derivative. It is commonly used for oversize freight charters.

Developed primarily as a strategic military freighter (in which role it can carry missile units and main battle tanks), the first prototype An-124 flew on December 26 1982. A second prototype, named Ruslan (after a Russian folk hero), made the type's first western public appearance at the Paris Airshow in June 1985, preceding the type's first commercial operations in January 1986. Since that time the An-124 has set a wide range of payload records.

Notable features include nose and tail cargo doors, 24 wheel undercarriage allowing operations from semi prepared strips, the ability to 'kneel' to allow easier front loading, and fly-by-wire control system.

The two major An-124 variants are the basic An-124 and similar Russian civil certificated An-124-100. Various upgrades have been proposed, including the western avionics equipped An-124-100M built in prototype form but not flown, the three crew EFIS flightdeck equipped An-124-102 and the An-124FFF firebomber. Numerous re-engine studies have also been conducted, including using Rolls-Royce RB211-524Gs, General Electric CF6-80s (as the An-124-130) and even Aviadvigatel NK-93 propfans.

Antonov has developed a multistage life extension program for the An-124 for existing and new build An-124-100s. After a break of five years deliveries of new build An-124s resumed in August 2000.

The An-225 Myria was based on the An-124 but features six (instead of four) D-18T turbofans, a stretched fuselage and a 600 tonne (1,322,750lb) max takeoff weight. Two were built (only one flew) intended to transport the Russian Buran space shuttle. A third is partly assembled and may yet be completed. First flight was in 1988. After they had been dormant for many years in 2000 Antonov was planning to refurbish an An-225 to use it for commercial freight charters. It could lift payloads of up to 250 tonnes.

Photo: An An-124-100. (Paul Merritt)

Antonov An-140

Country of origin: Ukraine

Type: Turboprop regional airliner

Powerplants: An-140 – Two 1839kW (2466shp) Motor-Sich Al-30 Series 1 turboprops (licence built Klimov TV3-117s) driving six blade propellers, or two 1864kW (2500shp) Pratt & Whitney Canada PW127A turboprops.

Performance: An-140 with Al-30s – Max cruising speed 575km/h (310kt), economical cruising speed 520km/h (280kt). Range with 52 passengers 2100km (1133nm), range with a 6000kg (13,227lb) payload at 520km/h (280kt) 900km (486nm). An-140 with PW127s – Range with 52 passengers 2500km (1349nm).

Weights: An-140 – Max takeoff 19,150kg (42,218lb).

Dimensions: An-140 – Wing span 24.51m (80ft 5in), length 22.61m (74ft 2in), height 8.23m (26ft 11in).

Capacity: An-140 – Flightcrew of two. Typical passenger seating for 52 at four abreast and 75cm (30in) pitch or 48 at 81cm (32in) pitch. Forward starboard freight door allows 1900 to 3650kg (4188 to 8046lb) of palletised freight and 36 or 20 passengers to be carried in a combi configuration.

Production: Air Ukraine has firm orders for four, first delivered mid 2000, out of a total requirement for up to 40. Aeroflot signed an MoI covering 50 An-140As in 1999.

History: Antonov's An-140 is a promising all new 50 seat regional twin turboprop regional airliner, developed as a replacement for the ageing An-24.

Antonov announced development of the An-140 in 1993. The first An-140 prototype rolled out from the Kiev factory on June 6 1997 and flew for the first time on September 17 that year. The second flying prototype was completed in late 1998, while the first production standard An-140 flew on October 11 1990. Service entry was with Air Ukraine in mid 2000.

The An-140 is of conventional design and construction, with US and European certification planned in addition to Russian/CIS certification. The basic version is powered by Motor-Sich Al-20s which are licence built Klimov TV3-117VMA-SBM1s, while Pratt & Whitney Canada PW127As will be optional. The flightdeck features conventional instruments, the main cabin seats 52 in a four abreast configuration. The rear main passenger door features integral stairs, while a forward starboard side freight door allows cargo to be carried. The rear of the cabin also features a galley, coat stowage and a toilet.

Versions apart from the basic An-140 will include the An-140A for Aeroflot which will be powered by PW127As, the An-140T and An-140TK freighters which would have a large freight door on the rear port side, the 3.80m (12ft 6in) stretched 68 seat An-140-100, and the An-142 with a rear loading freight. Military versions are also planned.

Series production of the An-140 is being undertaken at Kharkov by KhGAPP in the Ukraine and at Samara, Russia, by Aviacor. In 1996 Antonov signed an agreement with HESA of Iran for licence assembly of an An-140 model called the Iran 140 at a new plant at Esfahan. Initial Iran 140s will be assembled from supplied kits, with gradually increasing Iranian local content.

Photo: The second prototype An-140. (Ian Moy)

ATR 42

ATR 72

Countries of origin: France and Italy

Type: 42 seat turboprop regional airliner

Powerplants: ATR 42-300 – Two flat rated 1340kW (1800shp) Pratt & Whitney Canada PW120 turboprops driving four blade c/s Hamilton Standard propellers. ATR 42-500 – Two PW127Es derated to 1610kW (2160shp) driving six blade Ratier-Fagiec/Hamilton Standard props.

Performance: ATR 42-300 – Max cruising speed 490km/h (265kt) econ cruising speed 450km/h (243kt). Range at max cruising speed 4480km (2420nm), or 5040km (2720nm) at econ cruising speed. ATR 42-500 – Cruising speed 563km/h (304kt). Max range 1850km (1000nm).

Weights: ATR 42-300 – Operating empty 10,285kg (22,674lb), max takeoff 16,700kg (36,817lb). ATR 42-500 – Operating empty 11,250kg (24,802lb), max takeoff 18,600kg (41,005lb).

Dimensions: Wing span 24.57m (80ft 8in), length 22.67m (74ft 5in), height 7.59m (24ft 11in). Wing area 54.5m² (586.6sq ft).

Capacity: Flightcrew of two. Maximum passenger accommodation for 50, 48 or 46 at 76cm (30in) pitch and four abreast. Typical seating arrangement for 42 at 81cm (32in) pitch.

Production: As at late 2000 total orders for all versions of the ATR 42 stood at 363 with 360 delivered.

History: Aerospatiale and Aeritalia (now Alenia) established Avions de Transport Regional or ATR in 1980 to develop a family of regional airliners. The program has proved very successful for its two partners, the 600th ATR was delivered in early 2000, and is one of the west's most successful turboprop airliner programs.

The ATR 42 was the consortium's first aircraft and was launched in October 1981. The first of two ATR 42 prototypes first flew on August 16 1984 and Italian and French authorities granted certification in September 1985. The ATR 42 entered service on December 9 1985.

The ATR 42-300 was the standard production version of the ATR 42 family until 1996 and features greater payload range and a higher takeoff weight than the prototypes. The similar ATR 42-320 (also withdrawn in 1996) differed in having more powerful PW121 engines for better hot and high performance, while the ATR 42 Cargo is a quick change freight/passenger version of the 42-300.

The significantly improved ATR 42-500 features a revised interior, more powerful PW127Es for a substantially increased cruising speed (565km/h/305kt) driving six blade propellers, a 1850km (1000nm) maximum range, the EFIS flightdeck, elevators and rudders of the stretched ATR 72 (described separately), plus new brakes and landing gear and strengthened wing and fuselage for higher weights. The first ATR 42-500 delivery was in October 1995.

For a short time ATR was part of the Aero International (Regional) regional airliner consortium established in January 1996 to incorporate ATR, Avro and Jetstream. AI(R) was disbanded in mid 1998.

In mid 2000 ATR launched a freighter conversion program for both the 42 and 72, involving installing a forward freight door and modifying the cabin for freight. The ATR 42 Freighter can carry a 5.8 tonne payload. DHL Aviation Africa was the launch customer with the two converted ATR 42-300s redelivered in September and December 2000.

Photo: An Air Botswana ATR 42 at Johannesburg. (Rob Finlayson)

Countries of origin: France and Italy

Type: 70 seat turboprop regional airliner

Powerplants: ATR 72-200 – Two 1610kW (2160shp) Pratt & Whitney Canada PW124B turboprops driving four blade Hamilton Standard propellers. ATR 72-210 – Two 1850kW (2480shp) P&WC PW127s.

Performance: ATR 72-200 – Max cruising speed at 15,000ft 526km/h (284kt), economical cruising speed 460km/h (248kt). Range with reserves at max optional weight 1195km (645nm), range with 66 pax 2665km (1200nm).

Weights: Operating empty 12,500kg (27,558lb), max takeoff 21,500kg (47,400lb).

Dimensions: Wing span 27.05m (88ft 9in), length 21.17m (89ft 2in), height 7.65m (25ft 1in). Wing area 61.0m² (656.6sq ft).

Capacity: Flightcrew of two. Max seating for 74 passengers at four abreast and 76cm (30in) pitch. Typical seating for between 64 and 70 passengers, with seat pitch starting from 81cm (32in). With larger forward freight door fitted it can accommodate a payload of 7200kg (15,875lb) in 13 containers. ATR 52C – 7500kg (16,535lb) payload comprising pallets or five LD3 containers.

Production: As at late 2000 260 ATR 72s had been ordered, out of total ATR orders for 623, with 254 delivered.

History: The ATR 72 is a stretched development of the popular ATR 42 and was launched in January 1986.

The first of three ATR 72 development aircraft first flew on October 27 1988, followed by the awarding of French and then US certification in late 1989. Entry into service was on October 27 1989.

Significant differences between the ATR 72 and the smaller and older ATR 42 include a 4.50m (14ft 9in) fuselage stretch and reworked wings. The ATR 72's wings are new outboard of the engine nacelles and with 30% of it made up of composite materials, comprising composite spars and skin panels and a carbon fibre wing box.

Aside from the baseline ATR 72-200, three developments have been offered, the ATR 72-210, ATR 72-500 and the ATR 52C. The ATR 72-210 is the current production model and is optimised for operations in hot and high conditions. It has more powerful PW127 engines for better takeoff performance.

The ATR 72-500 (for a time the ATR 72-210A) further improved hot and high model and was certificated in early 1997. It features PW127Fs driving six blade composite Hamilton Standard propellers.

The ATR 52C is an unlaunched freight derivative with a redesigned tail to incorporate a rear loading ramp, intended for military and commercial operators. As with the ATR 42, a military maritime patrol version, known as the Petrel 72, has also been offered.

ATR has studied a number of developments which have not seen the light of day. The ATR 82, a 78 seat stretched development, would have been powered by two Allison AE 2100 turboprops (ATR studied turbofans for a time) and would have had a cruising speed as high as 610km/h (330kt). The ATR 82 was suspended in early 1996.

In 1998 the ATR 42/72 was also considered as the basis for the ATR AirJet regional jet family which would have featured the ATR's fuselage, a new wing and turbofan engines.

Photo: An Air New Zealand/Mount Cook ATR 72-500. (Peter Clark)

Auster J series

Aviat Husky A-1

Country of origin: United Kingdom

Type: Two, three and four seat light aircraft

Powerplants: J/1 – One 75kW (100hp) Blackburn Cirrus. J/5B & J/5F – One 97kW (130hp) de Havilland Gipsy Major. J/5G – One 116kW (155hp) Blackburn Cirrus Major 3. All were inline four cylinder piston engines driving two blade fixed pitch propellers.

Performance: J/1 – Max speed 193km/h (104kt), cruising speed 160km/h (86kt). Initial rate of climb 568ft/min. Range with no reserves 515km (278nm). J/5G – Max speed 204km/h (110kt), cruising speed 177km/h (96kt). Initial rate of climb 710ft/min. Range with no reserves 780km (421nm). J/5F – Max speed 212km/h (114kt), cruising speed 180km/h (97kt). Initial rate of climb 705ft/min. Range with no reserves 435km (235nm).

Weights: J/1 – Empty 477kg (1052lb), max takeoff 840kg (1850lb). J/5B – Empty 605kg (1334lb), max takeoff 1090kg (2400lb). J/5G – Empty 620kg (1367lb), max takeoff 1110kg (2450lb). J/5F – Empty 600kg (1323lb), max takeoff 885kg (1950lb).

Dimensions: J/1 – Wing span 10.97m (36ft 0in), length 7.14m (23ft 5in), height 1.98m (6ft 6in). Wing area 17.2m² (185sq ft). J/5B – Same except for length 7.11m (23ft 4in), height 2.30m (7ft 6in). J/5G – Same except for length 7.06m (23ft 2in), height 2.30m (7ft 6in). J/5F – Same except for length 7.16m (23ft 6in), height 1.98m (6ft 6in). Wing area 15.2m² (164sq ft).

Capacity: Two pilots side by side, plus room for one or two passengers, depending on model type. Most J/5s seat four.

Production: Approximate production totals for the series are: J/1 – 420; J/1B – 87; J/1N – 43; J/2 – 44; J/4 – 26; J/5 – 58; J/5B – 92; J/5G – 92; J/5P – 24; J/5F – 56; J/5K, L, R & Q – 40 plus.

History: The Auster marque traces its lineage back to the Taylorcraft Aeroplanes (England) company, which produced Taylorcrafts (described separately) under licence, and built over 1600 spotter (Air Observation Post) aircraft for Britain's Royal Air Force and Army (many of which were resold to private operators).

The first civil Auster (as Taylorcraft become known as in 1946) was the Mk 5 J/1 Autocrat, which was essentially similar to the military Mk V, but had a Cirrus Minor 2 engine in place of the Mk 5's Lycoming, upholstered seats and a small number of other refinements.

The J/1 Autocrat served as the basis for a family of civil aircraft. The next to appear was the two seat side by side J/2 Arrow family, with a 56kW (75hp) Continental, and was further developed into the J/4 Archer, which replaced the Continental with a Cirrus Minor engine. The J/1N Alpha was an attempt to increase sales and overcome the problems associated with fitting the Cirrus Minor engine to the J/1 with less equipment and minor improvements.

Most Auster J/5 models were four seaters except for the initial J/5 which was an Autocrat with a more powerful engine, while the J/5B incorporated the enlarged four seat cabin. The J/5F Aiglet trainer was a fully aerobatic two seat trainer. The J/5D, introduced in 1959, was the last of the line and featured metal wing spars and ribs and Lycoming power (more than 160 were built, including 150 in Portugal by OGMA under licence). Auster was taken over by Beagle in 1960.

Photo: An Auster J/1N Alpha. (Gerard Frawley)

Country of origin: United States of America

Type: Two seat utility light aircraft

Powerplant: A-1A – One 135kW (180hp) Textron Lycoming O-360-A1P flat four piston engine driving a two blade constant speed Hartzell propeller.

Performance: A-1/A-1A – Cruising speed at 75% power 225km/h (122kt), cruising speed at 55% power 212km/h (115kt). Stalling speed with flaps extended 67km/h (37kt). Initial rate of climb 1500ft/min. Service ceiling 20,000ft. Range with max fuel and reserves at 75% power cruising speed 1020km (550nm).

Weights: A-1A – Empty 540kg (1190lb), max takeoff (landplane) 857kg (1890lb), floatplane 984kg (2170lb).

Dimensions: A-1A – Wing span 10.82m (35ft 6in), length 6.88m (22ft 7in), height 2.01m (6ft 7in). Wing area 17.0m² (183.0sq ft).

Capacity: Seating for two in tandem.

Production: 400 A-1s built, approx 120 A-1As built.

History: The Aviat Husky utility is a very successful two seat light aircraft in the spirit of the popular Piper Super Cub. It also has the distinction of being the only all new light aircraft designed and placed into series production in the United States in the mid to late 1980s.

The Husky was originally designed by Christen Industries, the company also responsible for the kit built Christen Eagle aerobatic biplane and previous owner of the Pitts Special aerobatic biplane series (described separately, Aviat now owns Pitts and Christen). Initial design work began in late 1985, with aid of Computer Aided Design. The prototype Husky first flew in 1986 and the US FAA certification was awarded the following year. Production deliveries followed shortly afterwards.

Husky design features include a braced high wing, seating for two in tandem and dual controls. This high wing arrangement was selected for good all round visibility, essential for the many observation and patrol roles the Husky is suited for. Power is supplied by a relatively powerful, for the Husky's weight, 135kW (180hp) Textron Lycoming O-360 flat four turning a constant speed two blade prop. The good power reserves and wing also give good field performance. Unlike most current light aircraft the Husky's structure features steel tube frames and Dacron covering over all but the rear of the fuselage, plus metal leading edges on the wings. Options include floats, skis and banner and glider hooks.

The basic Husky A-1 was replaced in production by the increased span wing A-1A in 1998. The A-1B is similar to the A-1A but is designed for mission specific government agencies work and has an increased 907kg (2000lb) max takeoff weight.

With more than 500 built since production began, the Husky has also quietly gone about becoming one of the largest selling light aircraft GA designs of recent times. Many are used for observation duties, fisheries patrol, pipeline inspection, border patrol, glider towing and a range of other utility missions. Notable users include the US Departments of the Interior and Agriculture and the Kenya Wildlife Service which bought seven for aerial patrols of elephant herds as part of the fight against illegal ivory poaching.

Photo: A Canadian registered Husky A-1. (Gary Gentle)

Aviat Pitts Special

Country of origin: United States of America

Type: Single and two seat competition aerobatic biplanes

Powerplants: S-1S – One 135kW (180hp) Lycoming IO-360 fuel injected flat four piston engine driving a two blade fixed pitch propeller. S-2B – One 195kW (260hp) Textron Lycoming AEIO-540-D4A5 flat six driving a two blade constant speed Hartzell propeller.

Performance: S-1S – Max speed 283km/h (153kt), max cruising speed 227km/h (123kt). Initial rate of climb 2600ft/min. Service ceiling 22,300ft. Max range with no reserves 507km (275nm). S-2B – Max cruising speed 282km/h (152kt). Initial rate of climb 2700ft/min. Service ceiling 21,000ft. Range with max fuel at economical cruising speed 513km (277nm).

Weights: S-1S – Empty 326kg (720lb), max takeoff 520kg (1150lb). S-2B – Empty 520kg (1150lb), max takeoff 737kg (1625lb).

Dimensions: S-1S – Wing span 5.28m (17ft 4in), length 4.71m (15ft 6in), height 1.91m (6ft 3in). Wing area 9.2m² (98.5sq ft). S-2B – Wing span upper 6.10m (20ft 0in), lower 5.79m (19ft 0in), length 5.71m (18ft 9in), height 2.02m (6ft 8in). Wing area 11.6m² (125.0sq ft).

Capacity: S-1 series seats pilot only. S-2 series seats two, except for S-2S which seats pilot only.

Production: Current Aviat production is of the S-1T, S-2B and S-2S. Factory production includes 360 S-2Bs and 36 S-2S.

History: The designer of the original Pitts Special aerobatic biplane, Curtiss Pitts, could hardly have appreciated that his design would continue in production for over five decades, and that it would come to be considered by the general public as the definitive aerobatic and display flying aircraft.

The original prototype of the S-1 Special first flew in September 1944. The aircraft was of steel tube construction with fabric covering over wooden spars, while the two wings were braced with wire. Power in early aircraft was supplied by 65 to 95kW (90 to 125hp) four cylinder Continentals or Lycomings. Later models were higher powered and of conventional metal construction.

Factory production of the basic single seat S-1 Special included the S-1S with a 135kW (180kW) Lycoming IO-360, driving a fixed pitch prop, and the current S-1T. The S-1T was introduced to production in 1981, and features a 150kW (200hp) Lycoming (now Textron Lycoming) AEIO-360 driving a constant speed prop and with symmetrical wings. Homebuilt versions of the S-1 include the S-1D and S-1E (for which plans or kits have also been offered), while the S-1S and S-1T are also available in kit form.

The two seat S-2 Special is of the same configuration as the single seat S-1 but is larger overall, and generally regarded as a more capable aerobatic aircraft due to its larger size and heavier weight, more power and aerodynamic changes. The S-2 is offered in single seat 195kW (260hp) AEIO-540 powered S-2S form, while two seat models are the 150kW (200hp) IO-360 powered S-2A, and current production 195kW (260hp) powered and fully aerobatic with two occupants S-2B. The S-2C has aerodynamic changes.

The Pitts Special is marketed and built by Aviat in Wyoming.

Photo: The Pitts Special remains popular for recreational and competition aerobatics and airshow displays. This is an S-2B. (Gary Gentle)

Aviation Traders ATL-98 Carvair

Country of origin: United Kingdom

Type: Freighter/utility transport

Powerplants: Four 1080kW (1450hp) Pratt & Whitney R-2000-7M2 Twin Wasp 14 cylinder twin row radial engines driving three blade Hamilton Standard Hydromatic variable pitch propellers.

Performance: Max speed 402km/h (217kt), max cruising speed 342km/h (185kt), economical cruising speed at 10,000ft 334km/h (180kt). Service ceiling at 33,110kg (73,000lb) 18,700ft. Range with max fuel and 4500kg (10,000lb) payload 5560km (3000nm). Range with 8035kg (17,700lb) payload 2745km (1480nm).

Weights: Empty equipped 18,762kg (41,365lb), max takeoff 33,475kg (73,800lb).

Dimensions: Wing span 35.82m (117ft 6in), length 31.27m (102ft 7in), height 9.09m (29ft 10in). Wing area 135.8m² (1462sq ft).

Capacity: Flightcrew of three. Maximum seating in a passenger configuration for 85 at five abreast at 86cm (34in) pitch. When used as a car ferry it was typically outfitted to carry five cars plus 22 passengers in the rear cabin.

Production: Total Carvair conversions number 21, the last of which was completed in 1968. Two remained in commercial service in 2000 one with Hawkair Aviation in Canada and one in Georgia in the USA. A third flyable example was in storage in South Africa.

History: Aviation Traders developed the Carvair in response to Channel Air Bridge's requirement for an air ferry capable of transporting passengers and their cars between the United Kingdom and continental Europe.

Although its external appearance is quite different, the Carvair is a conversion of the Douglas DC-4 airliner (or C-54 Skymaster in military guise), large numbers of which were available after World War 2. The airframe from the wings rearward is that of a standard DC-4, except for a lengthened vertical tail for enhanced controllability. The major modifications performed on the forward fuselage centred on a new lengthened nose section with a hydraulically operated cargo door and an elevated flightdeck (somewhat similar in appearance to that which would appear on the Boeing 747 several years later) which allowed nose loading for cars.

The Carvair first flew on June 21 1961 and the type subsequently entered service in March 1962 with British United Air Ferries (into which Channel Air Bridge had been merged, it later became British Air Ferries and is now known as British World Airways). Deliveries to other operators included three for Aer Lingus of Ireland and two for Aviaco of Spain, with other aircraft operated by French, Australian (Ansett) and Luxembourg carriers.

Aviation Traders also proposed a Carvair type conversion of the larger Douglas DC-6, DC-6B and DC-7, with the option of re-engining with Rolls-Royce Dart turboprops, although these plans never came to fruition.

In 2000 one Carvair was operated by Hawkair Aviation in British Colombia, Canada, registered C-GAAH. Another operates from Bear Creek/Tara Field in Georgia in the USA, while a third is in Zaire. All are ex Ansett machines.

Photo: This flyable Carvair is now in Zaire. (Keith Gaskell)

Ayres Turbo-Thrush

Country of origin: United States of America

Type: Agricultural aircraft

Powerplant: S2R-T34 – One 560kW (750shp) Pratt & Whitney Canada PT6A-34AG turboprop driving a three blade prop. 660 – Options of 917kW (1230shp) PT6A-65AG or 783kW (1050shp) PT6A-60 or 701kW (940shp) Honeywell TPE331-10 driving a five blade prop.

Performance: S2R-T34 – Max speed with spray equipment 256km/h (138kt), cruising speed at 50% power 240km/h (130kt), working speed range at 30 to 50% power 143 to 240km/h (82 to 130kt). Initial rate of climb 1740ft/min. Service ceiling 25,000ft. Ferry range at 40% power 1230km (665nm). 660 – Cruising speed 281km/h (152kt), working speeds 161-282km/h (87-152kt). Initial rate of climb 1250ft/min. Ferry range 966km (521nm).

Weights: S2R-T34 – Empty 1633kg (3600lb), max takeoff (ag category) 2720kg (6000lb). 660 – Empty 2381kg (5250lb), typical operating weights 5600kg (12,500lb).

Dimensions: S2R-T34 – Wing span 13.54m (44ft 5in), length 10.06m (33ft 0in), height 2.79m (9ft 2in). Wing area 30.3m² (326.6sq ft). 660 – Wing span 15.25m (50ft), length 10.22m (33ft 6in), height 2.80m (9ft 9in). Wing area 34.8m² (375sq ft).

Capacity: Pilot only, but optional second seat. Hopper capacities of 2498 litres (660US gal), 1930 litres (510US gal) and 1515 litres (400US gal).

Production: Approx 400 Turbo Thrushes built.

History: The Turbo Thrush family of turboprop agricultural aircraft is offered in three hopper capacity variants.

Ayres' first experience with the Thrush was when it contracted Serv-Aero Engineering to develop a turbine conversion of the Thrush Commander. The Thrush Commander/PT6 conversion first flew on September 9 1975 and Ayres marketed production conversions. Then in 1977 Ayres acquired from Rockwell the Thrush Commander-600 and -800 design rights and production facilities (in Albany, Georgia).

The initial production turbine S2R had a standard 560kW (750shp) PT6A-34 (with other PT6A models offered optionally) and a 1514 litre (400US gal) hopper. It remains in production today offered with 373-507kW (500-680shp) PT6A or TPE331 turbines and has a 4222kg (9300lb) typical operating weight.

The 1930 litre (510US gal) capacity hopper first appeared on the piston R-1820 powered Bull Thrush. Today turbine 1930 litre (510US gal) hopper equipped Thrushes are offered with 507-917kW (680-1230shp) PT6As or 560-701kW (750-940shp) TPE331s. Typical operating weight is 4400kg (9700lb).

The latest development is the 660 Turbo Thrush with its 2498 litre (660US gal) hopper. Again it is offered powered by either the PT6A or TPE331 turbines. The 660 Turbo Thrush was certificated in March 2000.

Two special missions developments are the S2R-T65 NEDS Narcotics Eradication Delivery System for the US State Department (who ordered 19 during the 1980s), and the TPE331 powered Vigilante surveillance and close air support version (ff 1989, some are used in Africa for game hunting surveillance). The Sea Thrush firebomber was a version fitted with floats to scoop up water.

Photo: A TPE331 powered Ayres Turbo Thrush.

Ayres LM 200 Loadmaster

Country of origin: United States of America

Type: Twin turboprop utility transport

Powerplants: One 2013kW (2700shp) LHTEC CTP800-4T turboprop – two linked CTP800s turboprops – driving a four blade constant speed propeller through a combining gearbox.

Performance: Estimated – Max cruising speed approx 370km/h (200kt), econ cruising speed 278km/h (150kt). Range with max payload 518km (280nm), with a 1815kg (4000lb) payload 2945km (1590nm). Ferry range 3020km (1630nm).

Weights: Empty equipped 4080kg (9000lb), max takeoff 8620kg (19,000lb).

Dimensions: Wing span 19.51m (64ft 0in), length 19.61m (64ft 4in), height 7.00m (23ft 0in). Wing area 42.5m² (458.0sq ft).

Capacity: Will be certificated for single pilot operations. Various configurations offered. Can carry 3945kg (9000lb) of freight in four standard size LD3 containers, or up to 34 passengers in a high density seating arrangement, or 19 in a standard configuration. Different military versions could seat troops or be configured for surveillance with workstations for operators.

Production: Firm orders for 104 from Federal Express and a number of smaller operators. First deliveries planned for 2001. Ayres has forecast a market for up to 600 Loadmasters by 2010. Unit cost approx $US3.5m to $US4m.

History: The Loadmaster will be a unique twin engine utility transport, similar in size to some smaller regional airliners, designed for a multitude of roles ranging from the carriage of containerised freight through to passenger transport and firebombing.

Largely at the request of Federal Express Ayres has been developing the Loadmaster to fulfil freight and utility tasks. Unlike any other aircraft close to its size, the Loadmaster is being designed with a pallet freight handling system which will allow the aircraft to interface easily into large package freight operators' networks.

Another important market Ayres sees for the Loadmaster is for use as both a regional airliner and a freighter in developing countries where inadequate surface transportation systems and continued population and economic growth means good air transport links are important. Ayres is also pitching the Loadmaster at potential government users and military operators.

In November 1996 Federal Express signed a letter of intent for 50 with options on a further 200. FedEx will uses its Loadmasters to complement its smaller Cessna Caravans and larger Fokker F27s.

Design features of the Loadmaster include its twin LHTEC (Light Helicopter Turbine Engine Company – AlliedSignal/Allison) CTP800 turboprops (a commercial turboprop variant of the military T800) driving a single propeller through a combining gearbox, its raised flightdeck, fixed undercarriage, high mounted wing and square sided fuselage.

Various developments of the basic aircraft have been studied including a floatplane and the military LM250 with a more powerful engine.

The first of three prototypes had still not flown by late 2000. Production aircraft will be built at a new factory at Dotham, Alabama.

Photo: A model of the Loadmaster as it will appear in Federal Express colours. (Ayres)

BAE Systems Avro RJ70 & BAe 146-100

Country of origin: United Kingdom

Type: Regional jet airliners

Powerplants: BAe 146-100 – Four 30.0kN (6700lb) Textron Lycoming ALF 502R-3s or four 31.0kN (6970lb) ALF 502R-5 turbofans. RJ70 – Four 27.3kN (6130lb) or 31.1kN (7000lb) AlliedSignal LF 507 turbofans.

Performance: BAe 146-100 – Cruising speed 767km/h (414kt), long range cruising speed 670km/h (361kt). Range with standard fuel 3000km (1620nm), range with max payload 1630km (880nm). RJ70 – Cruising speed 763km/h (412kt), long range cruising speed 720km/h (389kt). Range with max fuel 3074km (1660nm), range with max payload 2047km (1104nm).

Weights: 146-100 – Operating empty 23,288kg (51,342lb), max takeoff 38,100kg (84,000lb). RJ70 – Operating empty 23,900kg (52,690lb), max takeoff 43,091kg (95,000lb).

Dimensions: Wing span 26.21m (86ft 0in), length 26.20m (86ft 0in), height 8.61m (28ft 3in). Wing area 77.3m² (832.0sq ft).

Capacity: Flightcrew of two. Single class seating for alternatively 70 passengers at 84cm (33in) pitch five abreast, or 82 passengers six abreast in a 84cm (33in) pitch configuration, or up to 94 six abreast at 74cm (29in) pitch. Quiet Trader freighter version of the 146-100 capable of carrying standard size pallets or LD3 containers.

Production: 37 146-100s (including three VIP examples operated by the Royal Air Force) built before production ceased in 1992. 12 RJ70s were ordered and built.

History: The BAe 146-100 and Avro RJ70 are the smallest of this three fuselage length family of quiet, regional jet airliners whose origins lie in the early 1970s.

In August 1973 the then Hawker Siddeley Aviation announced it was designing the HS.146, a short range quiet airliner powered by four small turbofans, financed in part with British government aid. Large scale development lasted just a few months before a worsening economic recession made the risk of the project seem unjustifiable. Development then continued on a limited scale, but it was not until July 1978 that the project was officially relaunched, by which time Hawker Siddeley had been absorbed into the newly created British Aerospace.

The resulting BAe 146-100 made its first flight on September 3 1981. Certification was granted in early 1983 with first deliveries following shortly afterwards in May 1983.

In 1990 BAe first offered the improved RJ70 and RJ80, both of which are based on the 146-100. Seating 70 and 80 passengers respectively, these designs were optimised matured into the Avro RJ70 with improved FADEC equipped LF 507 engines and digital avionics. First RJ70 deliveries occurred in late 1993 but the type is now out of production due to low customer interest.

The RJ series was originally marketed and manufactured by Avro Aerospace, a separate BAe company. Subsequent plans for a partnership with Taiwan Aerospace, which would have seen the RJ series built in Taiwan fell through and Avro subsequently became part of the AI(R) consortium. AI(R) disbanded in mid 1998 and the Avro RJ range again became a British Aerospace (now BAE Systems) product.

Photo: One of two Druk Air/Royal Bhutan Airlines BAe 146-100s. (Rob Finlayson)

BAE Systems Avro RJ85 & BAe 146-200

Country of origin: United Kingdom

Type: Regional jet airliners

Powerplants: BAe 146-200 – Four 31.0kN (6900lb) Textron Lycoming ALF 502R-5 turbofans. RJ85 – Four 31.0kN (6970lb) Honeywell LF 507 turbofans.

Performance: 146-200 – Cruising speed 767km/h (414kt), long range cruising speed 669km/h (377kt). Range with standard fuel 2910km (1620nm), range with max payload 2095km (1130nm). 146-200QC in freighter configuration – Same except range with standard fuel 1935km (1045nm). RJ85 – Cruising speed 763km/h (412kt), long range cruising speed 720km/h (389kt). Range with standard fuel 2963km (1600nm), range with max payload 2129km (1150nm).

Weights: 146-200 – Operating empty 23,882kg (52,651lb), max takeoff 42,185kg (93,000lb). RJ85 – Operating empty 24,600kg (54,239lb), max takeoff 43,998kg (97,000lb).

Dimensions: Wing span 26.21m (86ft), length 28.60m (93ft 10in), height 8.59m (28ft 2in). Wing area 77.3m² (832sq ft).

Capacity: Flightcrew of two. Max seating in passenger cabin for 112 at six abreast and 74cm (29in) pitch. More typical seating configuration for 85 (hence RJ85 designation) at five abreast and 84cm (33in) pitch. 146-200 & RJ85 QT freighters can accommodate six standard 2.74 x 2.24m (108 x 88in) pallets, or a max of nine standard LD3 containers. Max payload of the BAe 146-200QT freighter is 11,827kg (26,075lb), max payload of the BAe 146-200QC is 10,039kg (22,132lb).

Production: Production of the 146-200 ceased in early 1993, after 113 examples had been built. By late 2000 79 RJ85s had been ordered and delivered out of total RJ family sales of 160.

History: The BAe 146-200 is a stretch of the 146-100, while the Avro RJ85 in turn is a modernised upgrade of the 146-200.

The 146-200 is essentially similar to its smaller stablemate, but has a 2.39m (7ft 8in) longer fuselage, is slightly higher, features 35% greater underfloor cargo volume, has slightly different performance figures and heavier weights. The stretch consists of five extra fuselage frame pitches. The first BAe 146-200 made the type's maiden flight on August 1 1982, while the UK CAA awarded the 146-200's type certificate on February 4 the following year.

Versions of the 146-200 include the 'Quiet Trader' freighter, which has been fairly successful because of its low external noise footprint, and the 'Quick Change' passenger or freight convertible.

The improved Avro RJ85 first flew on March 23 1992, and like the smaller RJ70 and larger RJ100, is a modernised development of the basic 146, with improvements including more reliable and efficient FADEC equipped AlliedSignal (now Honeywell) LF 507 engines, enhanced 'Spaceliner' cabin and a digital flightdeck.

British Aerospace (and for a time the AI(R) consortium and now BAE Systems) was quite successful in marketing the RJ85 in particular to 'blue chip' airline customers and the 146/RJ line is now profitable.

Further improvements to the basic design (particularly new engines) are now being developed for the Avro RJX, described separately.

Photo: A BAe 146-200 operated by Manx at London's Heathrow Airport. The 146/RJ family members are renowned for their low external noise levels. (Trent Jones)

BAE Systems Avro RJ100 & BAe 146-300

BAE Systems Avro RJX

Country of origin: United Kingdom

Type: Regional airliners

Powerplants: BAe 146-300 – Four 31.0kN (6900lb) Textron Lycoming ALF 502R-5 turbofans. RJ100 – Four 31.1kN (7000lb) Honeywell LF 507 turbofans.

Performance: 146-300 – Max operating speed Mach 0.73, cruising speed 790km/h (426kt), long range cruising speed 700km/h (377kt). Range with standard fuel 2817km (1520nm), range with max payload 1927km (1040nm). RJ100 – Max operating speed Mach 0.73, cruising speed 763km/h (412kt), long range cruising speed 720km/h (389kt). Range with max fuel 2760km (1490nm), range with max payload 2129km (1150nm).

Weights: 146-300 – Operating empty 24,878kg (54,848lb), max take-off 44,225kg (97,500lb). 146-300QT – Operating empty 23,126kg (50,985lb), max takeoff same. RJ100 – Operating empty 25,600kg (56,438lb), max takeoff initially 44,225kg (97,500lb), later 46,039kg (101,500lb). RJ100QT – Operating empty 23,706kg (52,263lb), max takeoff same as 100. RJ115 – Operating empty 26,156kg (57,665lb), max takeoff as 100.

Dimensions: Wing span 26.21m (86ft 0in), length 30.99m (101ft 8in), height 8.61m (28ft 3in). Wing area 77.3m^2 (832sq ft).

Capacity: Flightcrew of two plus a maximum of 128 passengers at six abreast and 74cm (29in) pitch. Seating arrangements also for 100 at 84cm (33in) pitch and five abreast, and 116 at six abreast. 146-300QT and RJ100QT can accommodate standard 2.74 x 2.24m (108 x 88in) pallets, or LD3 containers. Max payload of 12,490kg (26,075lb). RJ115 would seat 116 to 128.

Production: Production of the 146-300 ceased in early 1993, after 71 examples had been built. By late 2000 69 RJ100s had been ordered of which 63 had been delivered. No RJ115s had been sold.

History: The 146-300 and RJ100 and RJ115 are the longest and largest members of the four engined BAe 146 and Avro/Aero International (Regional) regional jet families.

The 146-300 is a further stretched derivative of the original short fuselage BAe 146-100, but unlike the midsize 200 series, was not developed until later in the 1980s. The first 146-300, an aerodynamic prototype based on the original prototype 146-100, flew for the first time on May 1 1987, with certification granted that September.

The RJ100 is an improved derivative of the 146-300, sharing the latter's fuselage length but with new LF 507 engines, 'Spaceliner' interior and digital flightdeck, plus other minor improvements. First flight was on May 13 1992

The RJ100 has also been marketed as the RJ115 which would feature mid cabin emergency exits allowing it to seat 116 to 128 in a high density six abreast seating configuration. The RJ115 would also feature the higher design weights later made standard on the RJ100 and the latter's optional greater fuel capacity, but none have been built or sold.

Like the 146-200 and RJ85, freighter versions of the 146-300 and RJ100 are known as Quiet Traders, or QTs.

The improved RJX is described separately.

Photo: An Aer Lingus Avro RJ100. (Rob Finlayson)

Country of origin: United Kingdom

Type: Regional jet airliners

Powerplants: Four 31.1kN (7000lb) Honeywell AS977-1A turbofans.

Performance: Max speed Mach 0.70. RJX-70 – Range 3500km (1890nm). RJX-85 – Range 3296km (1780nm). RJX-100 – Range 3019km (1630nm).

Weights: RJX-70 – (Estimated) Operating empty 23,650kg (52,140lb). RJX-85 – Operating empty 24,500kg (54,013lb). RJX-100 – Operating empty 25,450kg (56,108lb).

Dimensions: RJX-70 – Wing span 26.34m (86ft 5in), length 26.20m (86ft 0in), height 8.61m (28ft 3in). Wing area 77.3m^2 (832.0sq ft). RJX-85 – Wing span 26.34m (86ft 5in), length 28.60m (93ft 10in), height 8.59m (28ft 2in). Wing area 77.3m^2 (832sq ft). RJX-100 – Wing span 26.34 m (86ft 5in), length 30.99m (101ft 8in), height 8.61m (28ft 3in). Wing area 77.3m^2 (832sq ft).

Capacity: Flightcrew of two. RJX-70 – Typical seating for 70 at five abreast or 82 at six abreast. RJX-85 – Typical seating for 85 at five abreast or 100 at six abreast. RJX-100 – Typical seating for 100 at five abreast or 112 at six abreast.

Production: First deliveries planned for late 2001. Launch order from Druk Air for 2 RJX-85, options for six RJX-100s placed by CityFlyer.

History: The Avro RJX range is a modernised development of the Avro RJ family, with the key change being new Honeywell AS900 powerplants which promise greater range, improved fuel burn and lower maintenance costs.

BAe Regional Aircraft (now BAE Systems Regional Aircraft) announced it was conditionally offering the improved RJX range on February 16 1999 at the Avalon Airshow (near Melbourne, Australia). At the same time BAe announced the selection of the Honeywell AS977 turbofan. At that stage certification was planned for December 2000 and service entry in May 2001.

The RJX was formally launched on March 21 2000 (somewhat later than envisaged when the program was announced). Assembly of the first RJX, an RJX-85, began before formal launch in March 2000, and it was expected to make its first flight in February 2001. The first RJX-100 will fly in April 2001. At late 2000 BAE Systems anticipated certification being awarded in December 2001.

The RJX's AS977 powerplant is a two spool design with dual FADEC, and compared with the LF507 it replaces, should produce 5% more thrust in the climb, and have 15% lower fuel burn, 20% lower direct engine operating costs, lower emissions, and even quieter noise levels. The RJXs will have an up to 17% range increase and a 227kg (500lb) empty weight reduction over the RJs.

Like the earlier Avro RJ and BAe 146, the RJX family is offered in three sizes – the 70 seat RJX-70, 85 70 RJX-85 and 100 seat RJX-100. The airframes are unchanged from the corresponding RJ models apart from the engine nacelles and pylons (supplied by GKN Westland). BAE Systems calls the engine, nacelle, pylon and associated accessories package the IPPS (Integrated Power Plant System).

Like the RJ series, Avro offers the RJX as the Avro Business Jet.

Photo: The first two RJXs at Woodford. In the foreground is the first RJX-100, behind it the first RJX-85. (BAE Systems)

BAC One-Eleven

Country of origin: United Kingdom

Type: Short haul airliner

Powerplants: Srs 200 – Two 45.9kN (10,330lb) Rolls-Royce Spey Mk 506 turbofans. Srs 400 – Two 50.7kN (11,400lb) Spey Mk 511s. Srs 500 – Two 55.6kN (12,500lb) Spey Mk 512-14DWs.

Performance: Max cruising speed 870km/h (470kt), econ cruising speed 742km/h (400kt). Series 200 – Range with typical payload 1410km (760nm). Srs 400 – Range with typical payload 2300km (1240nm). Srs 500 – Range with typical payload 2745km (1480nm).

Weights: Srs 200 – Empty 21,049kg (79,000lb), max takeoff 35,833kg (79,000lb). Srs 400 – Empty 22,493kg (49,857lb), max takeoff 40,153kg (88,500lb). Srs 500 – Operating empty 24,758kg (54,582lb), max takeoff 47,400kg (104,500lb).

Dimensions: Srs 200, 300, 400 – Wing span 26.97m (88ft 6in), length 28.50m (93ft 6in), height 7.47m (24ft 6in). Wing area 93.2m² (1003sq ft). Srs 500 – Wing span 28.50m (93ft 6in), length 32.61m (107ft 0in). Wing area 95.8m² (1031sq ft).

Capacity: Flightcrew of two. Srs 200, 300, 400 & 475 – Single class seating for up to 89 passengers. Srs 500 – typical seating for 97-109 passengers, max seating for 119.

Production: UK total 235, comprising 58 Srs 200s, nine Srs 300s, 70 Srs 400s, 86 Srs 500s and 12 production 475s. Nine 561s built in Romania. Approximately 90 One-Elevens were in service in late 2000.

History: The One-Eleven can trace its origins back to the proposed Hunting H.107 jet airliner project of 1956.

Protracted development followed, but by 1961, when Hunting had been absorbed into the British Aircraft Corporation (BAC), a larger Rolls-Royce Spey turbofan powered design was finalised.

British United Airways placed a launch order for 10 of the new jets, then known as the BAC.111, in May 1961. The new aircraft took to the skies for the first time on August 20 1963, while the first production Series 200 first flew on December 19 1963. Certification was eventually awarded on April 6 1965, following a troubled flight test program, during which one prototype crashed with the loss of its crew, the cause attributed to deep stall from the rear engine and the T-tail configuration. With the deep stall issue resolved, the BAC.111 entered service on April 6 1965.

Development of the basic Series 200 led to the higher weight Series 300, followed by the Series 400 designed for American requirements with a higher US equipment content.

The 4.11m (13ft 6in) stretched Series 500 could seat up to 119 and was the most popular One-Eleven model (with 86 built). It first flew (converted from a -400) on June 30 1967. The Series 475 was optimised for hot and high operations and combined the Series 500's more powerful engines with the earlier shorter length fuselage.

The last UK built One-Eleven (by this time a British Aerospace product) flew in 1982, when production was progressively being transferred to Romaero in Romania where nine were built.

In the mid 1990s Romaero was working on a Rolls-Royce Tay 650 powered development called the Airstar 2500. The Airstar was planned to fly in late 1996 but the program has been suspended.

Photo: A Nationwide 111-200 at Johannesburg. (Rob Finlayson)

Beagle B.121 Pup

Country of origin: United Kingdom

Type: Two, three and four place light aircraft

Powerplant: 100 – One 75kW (100hp) Rolls-Royce Continental O-200-A flat four piston engine driving a two blade fixed pitch propeller. 150 – One 110kW (150hp) Lycoming O-320-A2B flat four. 160 – One 120kW (160hp) Lycoming IO-320.

Performance: 100 – Max speed 204km/h (110kt), max cruising speed 190km/h (103kt), economical cruising speed 153km/h (83kt). Initial rate of climb 575tft/min. Range with no reserves 916km (495nm). 150 – Max speed 222km/h (120kt), max cruising speed 211km/h (114kt), economical cruising speed 175km/h (95kt). Initial rate of climb 800ft/min. Range with no reserves 708km (382nm), range with optional additional fuel and no reserves 1019km (550nm).

Weights: 100 – Empty 482kg (1063lb), max takeoff 725kg (1600lb). 150 – Empty 522kg (1151lb), max takeoff 873kg (1925lb).

Dimensions: 100 – Wing span 9.45m (31ft 0in), length 6.99m (22ft 11in), height 2.29m (7ft 6in). Wing area 11.2m² (120sq ft). 150 – Same except length 7.06m (23ft 2in).

Capacity: 100 – Two side by side, plus two children behind. 150 – Three adults and one child.

Production: 173 Pups built, consisting of 66 Pup 100s, 98 Pup 150s, and 9 Pup 160s.

History: The Pup was one of two new designs to be produced by the British Executive and General Aviation Ltd or Beagle company, which was formed in October 1960 following the merger of Auster and Miles.

The Pup evolved from the Miles M.117 project, which was to have made extensive use of plastics. A range of (conventional construction) Pups was planned, from a 75kW (100hp) two seat trainer through to retractable undercarriage four seaters, a light twin and a fully aerobatic 155kW (210hp) military trainer, the Bull Pup. All would have featured metal construction.

The Pup made its first flight on April 8 1967 and deliveries of the initial Pup 100 began a year later in April 1968.

In the meantime Beagle had flown the first of the more powerful Pup 150s in October 1967. The 150 featured a 110kW (150hp) engine, as its designation reflects, and seating for an extra adult.

Another more powerful variant originally designed in response to an Iranian Civil Air Training Organisation requirement was the Pup 160. The Pup 160 featured a 120kW (160hp) IO-320 Lycoming, but only nine were built.

Continuing financial difficulties finally forced Beagle to close its doors in January 1970 after building 152 Pups, despite holding orders for an additional 276. As a consequence plans for the extended Pup based family came to nought. A further 21 near complete aircraft were subsequently assembled.

The Bulldog military basic trainer development first flew in May 1969. Scottish Aviation (which took over the design following Beagle's collapse) built 328 150kW (200hp) Lycoming IO-360 powered Bulldogs for a number of air forces, including Britain's Royal Air Force.

Scottish Aviation became part of British Aerospace in the late 1970s.

Photo: The Pup is one of the few light aircraft to feature control sticks and not control columns. This is a Pup 150. (Paul Sadler)

Beagle B.206

Country of origin: United Kingdom

Type: Six/eight place cabin twin

Powerplants: B.206C – Two 230kW (310hp) Continental GIO-470-A geared, fuel injected flat six piston engines driving three blade constant speed propellers. B.206-S – Two 255kW (340hp) Continental GTSIO-520-C geared, turbocharged and fuel injected engines.

Performance: B.206C – Max speed 354km/h (191kt), max cruising speed 333km/h (180kt), economical cruising speed 298km/h (160kt). Initial rate of climb 1170ft/min. Range with no reserves 2905km (1570nm). B.206-S – Max speed 415km/h (224kt), max cruising speed 380km/h (205kt), economical cruising speed 301km/h (163kt). Initial rate of climb 1340ft/min. Range with no reserves 2462km (1330nm).

Weights: B.206C – Empty equipped 2381kg (5250lb), max takeoff 3401kg (7499lb). B.206-S – Empty equipped 2450kg (5400lb), max takeoff 3401kg (7499lb).

Dimensions: Wing span 13.96m (45ft 10in), length 10.26m (33ft 8in), height 3.43m (11ft 4in). Wing area 19.9m² (214sq ft).

Capacity: Standard seating for eight.

Production: Total production run of 79 aircraft included one 206X; one 206Y; two 206Z; 20 206R Bassets for the Royal Air Force; 11 B.206C; 43 206-S; and one Series 3.

History: The cabin class Beagle B.206's origins lie in a late 1950s Bristol project for a four seat twin.

Although the Bristol 220 was not built, when Bristol's managing director moved to the newly established Beagle in 1960 he took the design with him. Beagle then developed the 220 into the 206 and the prototype B.206X first flew on August 15 1961. The five/six seat, 195kW (260hp) Continental IO-470 powered prototype was considered too small and the design evolved into the B.206Y with 230kW (310hp) GIO-470 engines, greater wing span, a larger cabin with increased seating capacity, greater fuel capacity and increased weights.

This allowed the B.206 to meet a Royal Air Force requirement for a communications aircraft to transport V-bomber support crews. Twenty were ordered (not the originally planned buy of 80) in preference to the de Havilland Dove. In RAF service the B.206 was designated the CC.1 Basset, and deliveries began in May 1965.

Following the B.206Y were two evaluation B.206Z aircraft, then the initial civil production version, the Series 1 B.206C. Poor hot and high performance was in part responsible for slow sales and so Beagle designed the Series 2 B.206-S with more powerful turbocharged GTSIO-520 engines. The B.206-S also introduced a slightly revised cabin to seat eight with the entry door repositioned from above the wing to the rear port side fuselage. The B.206-S proved far more capable but was too late to compete in a marketplace already dominated by Cessna's 400 series and Piper's PA-31 Navajo.

A commuter airliner development was also built in prototype form, the 10 seat Series 3 with a further enlarged cabin. The Series 3 design died when Beagle entered liquidation in early 1970.

In the 1980s in the US, South Florida Aviation refurbished several 206s with 280kW (375hp) GTSIO-520-Ms, a new instrument panel and numerous other improvements

Photo: A Beagle 206-S. (Stewart Wilson)

Beechcraft Model 18

Country of origin: United States of America

Type: Light utility transport

Powerplants: Super H18 – Two 335kW (450hp) Pratt & Whitney R-985AN-14B Wasp Junior nine cylinder radial piston engines driving two blade constant speed propeller. Turboliner – Two 525kW (705ehp) AiResearch (Garrett) TPE331-1-101B turboprops driving three blade constant speed Hartzell propellers.

Performance: Super H18 – Max cruising speed 354km/h (191kt), economical cruising speed 298km/h (160kt). Initial rate of climb 1400ft/min. Service ceiling 21,400ft. Range with max fuel 2460km (1330nm). Turboliner – Max speed 450km/h (243kt), economical cruising speed 412km/h (222kt). Initial rate of climb 1520ft/min. Service ceiling 24,000ft. Range with max fuel and reserves 3340km (1800nm), range with max payload and reserves 555km (300nm).

Weights: Super H18 – Empty equipped 2650kg (5845lb), max takeoff 4490kg (9900lb). Turboliner – Empty (airliner) 2993kg (6600lb), max takeoff 5215kg (11,500lb).

Dimensions: Super H18 – Wing span 15.14m (49ft 8in), length 10.70m (35ft 3in), height 2.84m (9ft 4in). Wing area 33.5m² (360.7sq ft). Turboliner – Wing span 14.02m (46ft 0in), length 13.47m (44ft 3in), height 2.92m (9ft 7in). Wing area 34.8m² (374sq ft).

Capacity: Most Beech 18s seat two crew and seven to nine passengers in main cabin. Volpar Turboliner conversion seats up to 15.

Production: Over 9000 Beech 18s of all models built between 1937 and 1969, of which 2000 were built postwar. Wartime military production accounts for majority of Beech 18s built (approx 5000).

History: Beech's most successful twin aircraft, more than 9000 Beech 18s were built over an uninterrupted three decade long production run, and while many of those were built against wartime military contracts, vast numbers went on to see civil service.

The prototype Beech 18 first flew on January 15 1937. The design followed conventional design wisdom at the time, including twin radial engines, metal construction and taildragger undercarriage, while less common were the twin tail fins. Early production aircraft were either powered by two 225kW (300hp) Jacobs L-6s or 260kW (350hp) Wright R-760Es. The Pratt & Whitney Wasp Junior became the definitive engine from the prewar C18S onwards.

The demands of World War 2 significantly boosted the already successful Beech 18's fortunes, with 5000 built as C-45s for the US Army Air Force for use as transports and multi engine pilot trainers.

Postwar, large numbers of C-45s entered civil service, while Beech resumed production of the C18S. Progressive development resulted in the D18S of 1946, the Continental powered D18C of 1947, the E18S of 1954, the G18S from 1959 and the H18 with optional tricycle undercarriage from 1962. Beech production ceased in 1969.

The Beech 18 has also been the subject of numerous conversions. Volpar has offered tricycle undercarriage conversions, conversions with TPE331 turboprops and stretched fuselage and TPE331 powered conversions (described in the specifications above). Hamilton meanwhile converted Beech 18s as Westwinds with Pratt & Whitney Canada PT6 turboprops and also offered stretches.

Photo: A H18S. (Tony Arbon)

Beech Musketeer, Sierra & Sundowner

Beechcraft 35 Bonanza

Country of origin: United States of America

Type: Four seat light aircraft

Powerplant: B19 – One 112kW (150hp) Lycoming O-320-E2D flat four piston engine driving a two blade fixed pitch propeller. C23 – One 135kW (180hp) Lycoming O-360-A4K. C23R – One 150kW (200hp) fuel injected Lycoming IO-360-A1B6 driving a variable pitch propeller.

Performance: B19 – Max speed 225km/h (169kt), long range cruising speed 182km/h (98kt). Initial rate of climb 700ft/min. Range with reserves 1420km (1064nm). C23 – Max speed 228km/h (123kt), long range cruising speed 182km/h (98kt). Initial rate of climb 700ft/min. Range with reserves 1168km (631nm). C23R – Max speed 262km/h (141kt), long range cruising speed 213km/h (115kt). Initial rate of climb 927ft/min. Range with reserves 1271km (686nm).

Weights: B19 – Empty 630kg (1390lb), max takeoff 1020kg (2250lb). C23 – Empty 681kg (1502lb), max takeoff 1111kg (2450lb). C24R – Empty 777kg (1713lb), max takeoff 1250kg (2750lb).

Dimensions: B19, C23 & C23R – Wing span 10.00m (32ft 9in), length 7.84m (25ft 9in), height 2.51m (8ft 3in). Wing area 13.6m^2 (146sq ft).

Capacity: Standard seating for four except two in Sport III.

Production: 4455 built, including 2390 Musketeers, I/II/III/Custom & Sundowners; 904 Sports; 793 Super R/Sierras; and 369 Supers.

History: Beechcraft's Musketeer family of four seaters competed with the more successful Cessna 172 and Piper Cherokee.

The bonded honeycomb construction wing, O-320 powered Musketeer first flew in October 1961 with deliveries beginning in late 1962 (for the 1963 model year). Some 553 were built in the first year, but none were built for the 1964 model year while Beech developed the improved A23 Musketeer II with a fuel injected 125kW (165hp) Continental IO-346 engine.

In the 1965 model year Beech offered a three model range (which it dubbed the Three Musketeers) – the A23A Musketeer Custom III with greater max takeoff weight, the reduced MTOW A23-19 Musketeer Sport III two seat trainer with a 110kW (150hp) Lycoming O-320, and the 150kW (200hp) IO-346 powered and increased MTOW A23-24 Musketeer Super III. For 1968 the Super III's Continental IO-346 was replaced by a 135kW (180hp) Lycoming O-360 to become the B23, while the Sport III became the Model 19A, both it and the Custom were certificated for aerobatics.

From the 1970 model year the three introduced a more rounded fuselage, more steeply raked windscreen and pointed propeller spinner. They were renamed the Musketeer B19 Sport, C23 Custom and A24 Super respectively, and were joined by the retractable undercarriage A24R Super R.

The Musketeer name was dropped in 1971, with the Custom renamed the Sundowner, the Super R the Sierra, and the Musketeer Sport becoming simply the Sport, while the Super was dropped.

The Sierra underwent significant changes for the 1974 model year becoming the B24R with a new cowling, quieter engine and more efficient prop. Further aerodynamic clean ups were introduced in 1977, the Sport was dropped in late 1978, while Sundowners and Sierras were built until 1983.

Photo: A C23 Sundowner. (Bill Lines)

Country of origin: United States of America

Type: Four & six seat high performance light aircraft

Powerplant: D35 – One 153kW (205hp) Continental E-185-11 flat six piston engine driving a two blade constant speed propeller. P35 – One 195kW (260hp) fuel injected Continental IO-470-N. V35TC – One 210kW (285hp) turbocharged and fuel injected Continental TSIO-520-D.

Performance: D35 – Max speed 306km/h (165kt), cruising speed 281km/h (152kt). Initial rate of climb 1100ft/min. Range with no reserves 1247km (673nm). P35 – Max speed 330km/h (178kt), cruising speed 306km/h (165kt). Initial rate of climb 1150ft/min. Range with optional fuel and no reserves 1955km (1056nm). V35TC – Max speed 386km/h (208kt), max cruising speed 360km/h (194kt), long range cruising speed 262km/h (141kt). Initial rate of climb 1225ft/min. Range with reserves & std fuel 917km (495nm), with opt fuel 1770km (955nm).

Weights: D35 – Empty 760kg (1675lb), max takeoff 1236kg (2725lb). P35 – Empty 841kg (1855lb), max takeoff 1418kg (3125lb). V35TC – Empty 907kg (2000lb), max takeoff 1542kg (3400lb).

Dimensions: D35 – Wing span 10.00m (32ft 10in), length 7.67m (25ft 2in). Wing area 16.5m^2 (177.6sq ft). P35 – Wing span 10.20m (33ft 6in), length 7.65m (25ft 1in). Wing area 16.8m^2 (181sq ft). V35TC – Wing span 10.20m (33ft 6in), length 8.04m (26ft 5in), height 2.31m (7ft 7in). Wing area 16.8m^2 (181sq ft).

Capacity: Models 35 through to J35 seat four people, K35 optional fifth passenger, later models from S35 onwards six people.

Production: Approximately 10,400 Model 35 Bonanzas of all variants were built between 1945 and 1982.

History: The distinctive Model 35 Bonanza is one of general aviation's most famous and prolific types, and enjoyed a production life spanning four decades.

The Bonanza first flew on December 22 1945. Featuring metal construction, retractable undercarriage and high performance, it heralded a new class of high performance GA aircraft. The design also featured the distinctive V-tail, incorporated for aerodynamic efficiency and reduced weight. Deliveries of production aircraft began in 1947.

Subsequent development led to a significant family of subtypes. Briefly these are the A35 of 1949 with a greater max takeoff weight; the B35 with a 146kW (196hp) E-185-8 engine; the 153kW (205hp) E-185-11 powered C, D and E models through to 1954; the F and G35 with third cabin window and 170kW (225hp) E-225-8 of the mid fifties; the 180kW (240hp) Continental O-470-G powered H35 of 1957; the fuel injected 187kW (250hp) powered J35; 1960's M35 with larger rear windows; and the N35 and P35 with a 195kW (260hp) IO-470-N and greater max takeoff weight.

Then followed the redeveloped S35 of 1964 with six seats and redesigned rear cabin, optional three blade prop, 215kW (285hp) IO-520-B engine and yet greater weights; the heavier V35; and turbocharged V35TC of 1966; V35A and V35A-TC of 1968 with increased rake windscreen; and the V35B and V35B-TC (just seven built) from 1970. The V35B remained in production until 1982 and underwent a number of detail changes in that time.

Photo: A C35 Bonanza. (Bill Lines)

Beechcraft 77 Skipper

Country of origin: United States of America

Type: Two seat light aircraft

Powerplant: One 85kW (115hp) Lycoming O-235-L2C flat four piston engine driving a two blade fixed pitch propeller.

Performance: Max speed 196km/h (106kt), max cruising speed 195km/h (105kt), long range cruising speed 158km/h (85kt). Initial rate of climb 720ft/min. Range with reserves 764km (413nm).

Weights: Empty 500kg (1103lb), max takeoff 760kg (1675lb).

Dimensions: Wing span 9.14m (30ft 0in), length 7.32m (24ft 0in), height 2.41m (7ft 11in). Wing area 12.1m² (129.8sq ft).

Capacity: Two seated side by side.

Production: Production of the Skipper ceased in 1981 after 312 had been built.

History: Beech developed the Skipper as a low expense two seat trainer in response to the growing costs (mainly fuel) of pilot training in the mid 1970s.

Starting life as the Beech PD (for Preliminary Design) 285, the new Skipper was intended to be a simple and cost effective new generation pilot training aircraft, combining low purchasing and operating costs with lightweight but sturdy construction. A PD285 prototype first flew on February 6 1975, but this differed from production aircraft in that it was powered by a 75kW (100hp) Continental O-200 engine and featured a conventional low set tailplane.

Protracted development meant that the first of the definitive Model 77 Skippers did not fly until September 1978, by which time the 85kW (115hp) Lycoming O-235 engine and T-tail had been settled upon. In the Beech product line-up the Skipper was to replace the two seat Model 19 Sport variant of the Musketeer family, production of which ended in 1978.

US FAA certification for the Skipper was awarded in April 1979, and the first production aircraft were delivered in May 1979 to Beechcraft's own Beech Aero Center pilot training centres.

Production lasted just three years until mid 1981 (at the time Beech said the halt in production was a "suspension" pending an improvement in market conditions). During that time little more than 300 Skippers had been built (at a rate of about 10 per month). Unsold Skipper stocks kept the type available for a further year.

The Skipper was in direct competition with Piper's very successful PA-40 Tomahawk and Cessna's 152. The Tomahawk was developed in a very similar time scale to the Skipper (entering service in early 1978) and both aircraft share a T-tail, low wing and canopy style cabin configuration (with 360° all round vision and a door on each side), and the Lycoming O-235 powerplant. Of the three the Skipper was the least successful, being comfortably outsold by the Cessna and Piper products.

Other features of the Skipper design are a NASA developed GA(W)-1 high lift wing (the result of joint NASA and Beech research into high lift, supercritical aerofoils) bonded metal construction, tubular spars, and flap and aileron actuation by torque tubes rather than the more conventional cable and pulley system. New construction techniques were intended to reduce manufacturing costs.

Photo: 312 Beech Skippers were built. (Bill Lines)

Beechcraft 76 Duchess

Country of origin: United States of America

Type: Four place light twin

Powerplants: Two 135kW (180hp) Lycoming O-360-A1G6D flat four piston engines driving two blade constant speed propellers.

Performance: Max speed 317km/h (171kt), max cruising speed 307km/h (165kt), recommended cruising speed at 10,000ft 293km/h (158kt), long range cruising speed 280km/h (151kt). Initial rate of climb 1248ft/min. Max range with reserves 1445km (780nm).

Weights: Empty 1110kg (2446lb), max takeoff 1780kg (3900lb).

Dimensions: Wing span 11.58m (38ft 0in), length 8.85m (29ft 1in), height 2.89m (9ft 6in). Wing area 16.8m² (181.1sq ft).

Capacity: Seats for four.

Production: 437 Duchesses were built between 1978 and 1982.

History: The Model 76 Duchess was one of a new class of light four place twins developed in the mid 1970s.

The prototype of the Duchess, designated the PD289, made its first flight in September 1974, although a further 30 months of development work passed before the first production Model 76 first flew on May 24 1977. Certification was granted in early 1978, with first deliveries commencing in that May.

The Duchess was positioned between the Bonanza and the Baron in the Beechcraft model range. Beech developed it for its Beech Aero Centers, and pitched it at the personal use light twin, light charter and multi engine training markets. Design aims included good low speed and single engine handling.

Aside from the prototype PD289, no variations of the Duchess 76 were built before production ended in 1982. All Duchesses therefore feature two Lycoming O-360 engines (with counter rotating propellers), a T-tail (incorporated to reduce control forces and improve elevator response), entry doors on either side of the cabin and electric trim and flap controls (the prototype PD289 featured manually operated flaps). The fuselage was based loosely on the single engine Sierra's, and like the Sierra and its Musketeer predecessors featured a bonded honeycomb construction wing. The Sierra and Duchess also share common structural components.

Beech offered three factory option packages on the Duchess – the Weekender, Holiday and Professional – and 11 factory installed avionics packages.

Beech developed the Duchess for low cost, high volume production, but the falling popularity of light twins, an economic recession and crippling product liability laws in the USA all contributed to a relatively short production run which wound up in 1982. Sales had peaked in 1979 when 213 were built.

Like its contemporaries the Grumman/Gulfstream American Cougar and Piper Seminole, the Duchess' success was hampered through unfortunate timing. Ever increasing advances in engine efficiency, safety and reliability led to a rise in popularity for big high performance singles such as Beech's own Bonanza series, which lacked the maintenance overheads of two engines, but had comparable performance. However the Duchess did enjoy a degree of success as a twin engine trainer, to a greater extent than the Seminole and Cougar.

Photo: A Duchess used by BAE Systems Flight Training. (Robert Wiseman)

Beechcraft 60 Duke

Country of origin: United States of America

Type: Four or six place light business twin

Powerplants: 60 – Two 285kW (380hp) Lycoming TIO-541-E1A4 turbocharged fuel injected flat six piston engines driving three blade constant speed Hartzell propellers. B60 – Two 285kW (380hp) Avco Lycoming TIO-541-E1C4s.

Performance: 60 – Max speed 460km/h (248kt), cruising speed 395km/h (214kt). Range with optional fuel and 45 minute reserves 1890km (1020nm). B60 – Max level speed 455km/h (246kt) at 23,000ft, max cruising speed 443km/h (239kt) at 25,000ft, cruising speed 431km/h (233kt) at 25,000ft. Initial rate of climb 1601ft/min. Service ceiling 30,000ft. Max range at 20,000ft with reserves 2078km (1122nm).

Weights: 60 – Empty equipped 1860kg (4100lb), max takeoff 3050kg (6725lb). B60 – Empty equipped 1987kg (4380lb), max takeoff 3073kg (6775lb).

Dimensions: Wing span 11.96m (39ft 3in), length 10.31m (33ft 10in), height 3.76m (12ft 4in). Wing area 19.8m² (212.9sq ft).

Capacity: Standard seating for four with optional fifth and sixth seats and toilet.

Production: Beechcraft built 584 Dukes between 1968 and 1982, including 113 60s, 121 A60s and 350 B60s.

History: Between the Beech Baron and Queen Air in size, performance and general capabilities, the Duke was a pioneer in the pressurised high performance light business twin class.

Beechcraft began design work on its new Model 60 in early 1965, with the first flight of the prototype occurring the following year on December 29. US FAA Certification was awarded on February 1 1968.

Design features of the Duke include turbocharged Lycoming TIO-541 engines driving three blade propellers and a 0.32 bars (4.6psi) cabin pressure differential. The airframe was based loosely on the Baron's wing and undercarriage, plus a new fuselage employing bonded honeycomb construction. Optional fuel tanks in the wings were offered, increasing range.

Deliveries of the initial 60 model began in July 1968. Further development led to the improved A60. Appearing in 1970 it introduced an enhanced pressurisation system and longer life yet lighter turbochargers which increased the maximum altitude at which the engine could deliver maximum power, thus improving performance.

The definitive model of the Duke family is the B60. New interior arrangements and more improvements to the turbochargers were the main changes to this model, which first appeared in 1974. Production ceased in 1982. The Duke B60 accounted for about two thirds of all Duke production, although the B60's production total of 350 is relatively small for a US GA type of its era.

Since its appearance the Duke has been regarded as something of a hot ship, with its high performance in a relatively small package the main attraction. However, this image did not translate into anything other than modest sales because of the Duke's relatively complex systems (turbochargers and pressurisation among them) and high operating costs.

Photo: A brightly painted Duke A60. (Keith Myers)

Beechcraft Queen Air

Country of origin: United States of America

Type: Utility, light executive transport and commuter airliner

Powerplants: 65 – Two 255kW (340hp) IGSO-480-A1E6 Lycoming fuel injected supercharged flat six piston engines driving three blade constant speed propellers. B80 – Two 285kW (380hp) Lycoming IGSO-540-A1D piston engines.

Performance: 65 – Max speed 385km/h (208kt), max cruising speed 344km/h (186kt), long range cruising speed 267km/h (144kt). Range with reserves and standard fuel 1682km (908nm), with optional fuel 2670km (1442nm). B80 – Max speed 400km/h (215kt), max cruising speed 362km/h (195kt), typical cruising speed 335km/h (181kt). Range with reserves 1950km (1053nm).

Weights: 65 – Empty 2324kg (5123lb), max takeoff 3719kg (8200lb). B80 – Empty 2394kg (5277lb), max takeoff 3992kg (8800lb).

Dimensions: Wing span 15.32m (50ft 3in), length 10.82m (35ft 6in), height 4.33m (14ft 3in). Wing area 27.3m² (294sq ft).

Capacity: One or two pilots and up to nine passengers in commuter configuration, or six passengers in executive transport role.

Production: 1001 Queen Airs of all models built (404 Model 65s & A65s, 42 Model 70s, 510 Model 80s and 45 Model 88s), including 71 A65s as the U-8F Seminole for the US Army.

History: The versatile Queen Air is Beech's largest and heaviest piston twin apart from the WW2 era radial powered Beech 18. It remained in production for two decades, and provided the basis for the very popular turboprop King Air (described under Raytheon).

The prototype Model 65 Queen Air made its first flight on August 28 1958, with deliveries of production aircraft beginning in late 1960. This first model combined the wings, undercarriage, Lycoming engines and tail surfaces of the Model E50 Twin Bonanza with a new and substantially larger fuselage. A Queen Air 65 established a new class altitude record of 34,882ft in 1960.

Many variants subsequently followed, including the 3630kg (8000lb) max takeoff weight Model 80 with more powerful 285kW (380hp) engines and swept fin and rudder. This model evolved into the A80, the first to be offered as a commuter airliner. Introduced in 1964, the A80 had a redesigned nose and interior, increased wing span and a 227kg (500lb) greater takeoff weight.

The pressurised 88 first appeared in 1965. It combined the pressurised, circular window fuselage of the King Air 90 turboprop, the longer wingspan of the A80 and a 3992kg (8800lb) MTOW.

The Model B80 was the last major production model and appeared in 1966. It featured the longer span wing and the 88's MTOW. In 11 seat commuter form it was marketed as the Queen Airliner. The model A65 was essentially a Model 65 with the swept fin and rudder of the Model 80, and entered production in 1967. The Model 70 entered production in 1969, it featured the longer span wings, 3720kg (8200lb) MTOW and 255kW (340hp) engines.

Production of the Queen Air ceased in 1977.

At the peak of its popularity the Queen Air was used in a variety or roles ranging from commuter airliner to air ambulance, corporate transport, freighter, and photo survey.

Photo: The short lived model A65 Queen Air. (Lance Higgerson)

Beechcraft 99 Airliner

Country of origin: United States of America

Type: Commuter airliner

Powerplants: B99 – Two 505kW (680shp) Pratt & Whitney Canada PT6A-28s turboprops driving three blade constant speed Hartzell propellers. C99 – Two 535kW (715shp) PT6A-36s.

Performance: B99 – Max cruising speed 460km/h (247kt). Initial rate of climb 2090ft/min. Range at max cruising speed 1665km (900nm), range at cruising speed 1887km (1019nm). C99 – Max speed 496km/h (268kt) at 8000ft, cruising speed at 8000ft 461km/h (249kt). Range with max fuel and reserves 1686km (910nm).

Weights: B99 – Empty equipped 2620kg (5777lb), max takeoff 4944kg (10,900lb). C99 – Operating empty 3040kg (6700lb), max takeoff 5125kg (11,300lb).

Dimensions: B99 – Wing span 14.00m (45ft 11in), length 13.58m (44ft 7in), height 4.38m (14ft 4in). C99 – Same except for wing span 13.98m (45ft 11in). Wing area 26.0m² (279.7sq ft).

Capacity: Flightcrew of one or two. Typical passenger accommodation for 15 at two abreast. Baggage stowed in nose compartment and underbelly cargo pod. Some used as corporate aircraft.

Production: Total Model 99 production of 239, comprising 164 99s, A99s, A99-As and B99s between 1967 and 1975 and production of 75 C99s between 1980 and 1986, when production ceased.

History: The Beech 99 commuter airliner is an evolution of the successful Queen Air/King Air series, and shares the King Air's basic powerplant and layout, but with a stretched fuselage.

Design of the 99 began in the late 1960s, in part to find a replacement for the venerable Beech 18. In December 1965 Beech flew a stretched fuselage Queen Air development aircraft, while re-engined with Pratt & Whitney Canada PT6A-20 turboprops it served as the 99 prototype, first flying in this configuration in July 1966. Apart from the PT6 turboprops and stretched Queen Air fuselage the unpressurised 99 featured an airstair incorporated in the main cabin door and was offered with an optional cargo door allowing it to carry a mix of passengers and freight, separated by a moveable bulkhead.

The first customer 99 Airliner was delivered in May 1968. At the time the 99 was Beech's largest aircraft yet and Beech was optimistically forecasting a production rate of 100 per year. Subsequent models were the flat rated 507kW (680shp) PT6A-27 powered A99, and the B99 with an increased gross weight. The 99 was available in two variants, the 99 Airliner and the 99 Executive, a corporate transport version with seating for between eight and 17 passengers.

Production of early models was halted in 1975. Then in 1979 Beech launched the improved Commuter C99 (plus the larger 1900, described separately) as part of Beech's return to the commuter airliner market. A converted B99 fitted with P&WC PT6A-34 engines served as the C99 prototype, and flew in this form for the first time on June 20 1980.

Production aircraft featured PT6A-36 engines, and deliveries recommenced following certification, both in July 1981. Shortly afterwards it became known as the C99 Airliner.

C99 production ceased in 1986.

Photo: A Beech 99 with optional 1.0m³ (35.3cu ft) underbelly cargo pod. (Steve Allsopp)

Beechcraft Starship 2000

Country of origin: United States of America

Type: Corporate transport

Powerplants: Two 895kW (1200shp) Pratt & Whitney Canada PT6A-67As turboprops driving five blade constant speed propellers.

Performance: 2000 – Max cruising speed 622km/h (335kt), economical cruising speed 546km/h (295kt). Initial rate of climb 3225ft/min. Max range 2630km (1634nm). 2000A – Max cruising speed 621km/h (335kt), economical cruising speed 570kt (307kt). Initial rate of climb 2748ft/min. Range with reserves 2920km (1576nm).

Weights: 2000 – Empty equipped 4484kg (9887lb), max takeoff 6531kg (14,400lb). 2000A – Empty equipped 4574kg (10,085lb), max takeoff 6758kg (14,900lb).

Dimensions: Wing span 16.60m (54ft 5in), length 14.05m (46ft 1in), height 3.94m (12ft 11in). Wing area 26.1m² (280.9sq ft).

Capacity: Flightcrew of one or two pilots. Standard passenger layout for eight in 2000 or six in 2000A.

Production: Production ceased in early 1995 after three prototypes, 18 Starship 2000s and 32 Starship 2000As had been built

History: Despite its extensive use of modern technologies and innovative design the Starship was a commercial failure.

Conceived as a new generation light corporate transport in the King Air class, the Starship traces back to the 85% scale proof of concept demonstrator built by Scaled Composites, which first flew in August 1983. The prototype Starship 2000 proper made its first flight on February 26 1986, provisionally powered by PT6A-65 turboprops. A second prototype equipped with Collins avionics entered the flight test program in June 1986, while a third development aircraft took flight in January 1987. Initial US FAA certification was awarded on June 14 1988, while the first production example flew on April 25 1989.

The Starship incorporates many innovations. Foremost of these is its rear mounted laminar flow wing and variable geometry canards or foreplanes. The foreplanes sweep forward with flap extension for pitch trim compensation, designed to make it impossible for the Starship to stall on takeoff or landing.

The wing itself is constructed almost entirely of composites (something which attracted much criticism because of the associated difficulties of inspecting it thoroughly), and has tip mounted tails. The rear mounted engines are in a pusher arrangement, being behind the cabin noise is reduced, while their relatively close proximity to each other also improves single engine handling. The EFIS flightdeck has Collins avionics with colour and monochrome CRTs.

The improved Starship 2000A was certificated in April 1992. It introduced changes including seating for six instead of eight, a slightly higher max takeoff weight and increased range.

A lack of customer interest forced Beech to terminate Starship production in early 1995 after just 53 had been built (including three prototypes), a somewhat inglorious end to a technologically innovative and seemingly promising design.

Photo: The composite construction Starship 2000 was perhaps ahead of its time. It is interesting to note that subsequent designs to feature extensive use of composite materials (such as the Raytheon Premier) have composite fuselages but metal wings. (Howard Geary)

Bell 47

Country of origin: United States of America

Type: Two or three seat light utility helicopter

Powerplant: 47G – Various Lycoming flat six piston engines ranging in output from 150kW (200hp) to 210kW (280hp), including the 47G-3B-2A's 210kW (280hp) Lycoming TVO-435-F1A, driving two blade main and tail rotors. 47J Ranger – One 230kW (305hp) Lycoming VO-540-B1B flat six.

Performance: 47G-3B-2A – Max speed 169km/h (91kt), cruising speed 135km/h (73kt) at 5000ft. Initial rate of climb 880ft/min. Range 397km (214nm) at 6000ft. 47J Ranger – Max speed 169km/h (91kt), cruising speed 130km/h (70kt). Initial rate of climb 800ft/min. Range with max fuel and no reserves 413km (223nm).

Weights: 47G-3B-2A – Empty 858kg (1893lb), max takeoff 1340kg (2950lb). 47J Ranger – 785kg (1730lb), max takeoff 1340kg (2950lb).

Dimensions: 47G-3B-2A – Rotor diameter 11.32m (37ft 2in), fuselage length 9.63m (31ft 7in), height 2.83m (9ft 4in). Main rotor disc area 100.8m² (1085sq ft). 47J Ranger – Same except for fuselage length 9.90m (32ft 5in).

Capacity: 47G – Pilot and two passengers on a single bench seat. 47J Ranger – One pilot and three passengers.

Production: Bell built more than 4000 47s between the late 1940s and 1974. Agusta-Bell of Italy licence built over 1200; Kawasaki of Japan 239; and Westland of the UK 239.

History: The familiar and distinctive Bell 47 is an especially significant aircraft as it was one of the world's first practical helicopters.

The ubiquitous Bell 47 dates back to Bell's Model 30 of 1943, an experimental helicopter evaluated by the US Army (which ordered 10). The first subsequent prototype Bell Model 47 (with a car type cabin and two seats) first flew on December 8 1945. In May 1946, this early model Bell 47 became the first helicopter in the world to gain civil certification.

The first civil variants to see production were the similar Model 47B, and the 47B-3 with an open cockpit. The 47D followed and was the first model to feature the famous 'goldfish bowl' canopy and the distinctive uncovered tail boom. The Model 47E was similar but powered by a 150kW (200hp) Franklin engine.

The definitive Model 47G followed the 47E into production in 1953, and it was this variant, in a number of successively more powerful versions, that remained in production until 1974, testament to the utility and success of Bell's basic design. The 47G had optional metal rotor blades and was powered by a range of Lycoming engines outputting 150 to 210kW (200 to 280hp).

The Model 47H is based on the 47G, but with a fully enclosed fuselage and conventional cabin, and formed the basis for the 47J Ranger. The Ranger had a further enlarged cabin with seating for four, and entered production in 1956. The 47J-2 Ranger introduced powered controls and metal blades as standard, and was powered by a 195kW (260hp) VO-540.

Kawasaki in Japan licence built a development of the 47G, the KH-4 with more traditional style enclosed cabin.

Large numbers of Bell 47s have also seen military service.

Photo: A Kawasaki Bell KH-4. (Robert Wiseman)

Bell 206 JetRanger

Countries of origin: USA and Canada

Type: Light utility helicopter

Powerplant: 206B JetRanger II – One 300kW (400shp) Allison 250-C20 turboshaft driving a two blade main rotor and two blade tail rotor. 206B-3 JetRanger III – One 315kW (420shp) Rolls-Royce (Allison) 250-C20J.

Performance: 206B – Max cruising speed 219km/h (118kt). Initial rate of climb 1540ft/min. Range 702km (379nm). 206B-3 – Max speed 225km/h (122kt), max cruising speed 214km/h (115kt). Initial rate of climb 1280ft/min. Range with max fuel and no reserves 732km (385nm).

Weights: 206B – Empty 660kg (1455lb), max takeoff 1360kg (3000lb). 206B-3 – Empty 737kg (1635lb), max takeoff with external load 1521kg (3350lb), with internal load 1451kg (1500lb).

Dimensions: Main rotor diameter 10.16m (33ft 4in), fuselage length 9.50m (31ft 2in), height 2.91m (9ft 7in). Main rotor disc area 81.1m² (872.7sq ft).

Capacity: Total accommodation for five, including one pilot and one passenger in the front, and three behind them on the rear bench seat. Max internal payload (Model 206B) 635kg (1400lb), max external sling load 680kg (1500lb).

Production: Over 7700 military and civil versions of the JetRanger have been built by Bell in the USA and Canada, Agusta-Bell in Italy and other licensees. More than 4400 built for civilian customers.

History: The JetRanger series has become the definitive turbine powered light utility and corporate helicopter of the past three decades.

The JetRanger can trace its lineage back to an unsuccessful contender for a US Army competition for a light observation helicopter, which was won by the Hughes 500. This first Model 206 made its first flight on December 8 1962, while the following civil 206A, powered by a 235kW (317shp) Allison 250-C18A, followed, flying on January 10 1966. Deliveries of the first production JetRangers began late in that same year.

In the early 1970s production switched to the Model 206B JetRanger II with a 300kW (400shp) 250-C20 turboshaft, while conversion kits to upgrade earlier As to the new standard were made available. The third major variant of the JetRanger is the 315kW (420shp) 250-C20B powered JetRanger III, with first deliveries commencing in late 1977. Once again Bell offered a conversion kit to update earlier JetRangers to the new standard. Other features introduced on the JetRanger III were a larger and improved tail rotor and minor modifications.

JetRanger production was transferred from Texas to Mirabel in Canada in 1986, where the current production model remains the 206B-3 JetRanger III.

The JetRanger was also accepted by the US Army as an observation helicopter as the OH-58 Kiowa, and variants of the Kiowa remain in production in the USA. Military 206Bs were also built in Australia for the Australian Army, where plans were also held to build civilian 206Bs for the Australian market under licence by CAC, but these fell through.

Photo: The Bell 206 JetRanger remains without doubt the most popular light turbine helicopter in the world. Pictured is a JetRanger II used for crop spraying. (Gwydir Air)

Bell 206L LongRanger

Countries of origin: USA and Canada

Type: Light utility helicopter

Powerplant: 206L LongRanger I – One 315kW (420shp) Allison 250-C20B turboshaft driving a two blade main rotor and two blade tail rotor. 206L-1 LongRanger II – One 375kW (500shp) Allison 250-C28B. 206L-3 LongRanger III & 206L-4 LongRanger IV – One 485kW (650shp) Allison (now Rolls-Royce) 250-C30P.

Performance: 206L – Max speed 232km/h (125kt), cruising speed 229km/h (124kt). Hovering ceiling in ground effect 8200ft. Range 628km (339nm). 206L-1 – Same except for range 692km (374nm). 206L-3 – Max speed 241km/h (130kt), max cruising speed 203km/h (110kt). Range with no reserves 666km (360nm) at 5000ft. 206L-4 – Same except for range 661km (357nm) at 5000ft.

Weights: 206L – Empty 844kg (1861kg), max takeoff 1814kg (4000lb). 206L-1 – Empty 980kg (2160lb), max takeoff 1882kg (4150lb). 206L-3 – Empty 998kg (2200lb), max takeoff 1882kg (4150lb), or 1927kg (4250lb) with external sling load. 206L-4 – Empty 1031kg (2274lb), max takeoff 2018kg (4450lb), or 2064kg (4550lb) with external sling load.

Dimensions: Main rotor diameter 11.28m (37ft 0in), fuselage length 206L & 206L-1 10.13m (33ft 3in), 206L-3 10.44m (34ft 3in), 206L-4 – 9.81m (32ft 2in); height 3.14m (10ft 4in). Main rotor disc area 99.9m² (1075.2sq ft).

Capacity: Total seating for seven, including five passengers in main rear cabin, or four in an optional executive layout. Can accommodate two stretchers and two medical attendants for aerial ambulance.

Production: More than 1600 LongRangers have been delivered.

History: Bell developed the LongRanger to offer a light helicopter with greater capacity and utility over the JetRanger.

Bell announced it was developing a stretched JetRanger in September 1973, the subsequent Model 206L first flew on September 11 1974, and production began in early 1975. The LongRanger seats a further two passengers compared to the JetRanger, and introduced a more powerful engine and Noda-Matic transmission suspension system for less vibration and greater passenger comfort.

Subsequent versions have been the 206L-1 LongRanger II, introduced in 1978, the 206L-3 LongRanger III, and the current 206L-4 LongRanger IV, introduced in 1992. Each subsequent version features increasingly more powerful engines and other minor improvements. LongRanger production, along with the JetRanger, was transferred to Mirabel in Canada in 1986 (although dynamic components continued to be built at Bell's Fort Worth, Texas plant, as is the case for all Canadian built Bells).

The LongRanger has found favour not only as a corporate transport, but with police and medical services worldwide, its extra cabin size providing a very useful increase in utility.

During the mid 1990s Bell offered a twin engined LongRanger, the TwinRanger, while US company Tridair offers the twin engine Gemini ST conversion of the LongRanger (both are described separately). The LongRanger also forms the basis of the 407.

Photo: Note this LongRanger's optional raised undercarriage for improved ground clearance and emergency inflatable floats on the skids.

Bell TwinRanger & Tridair Gemini ST

Countries of origin: United States of America & Canada

Type: Twin engine light utility helicopters

Powerplant: Two 335kW (450shp) takeoff rated Allison 250-C20R turboshafts driving a two blade main rotor and two blade tail rotor.

Performance: 206LT – Max cruising speed 217km/h (117kt), economical cruising speed 200km/h (108kt). Service ceiling 10,000ft. Hovering ceiling in ground effect 10,000ft, out of ground effect 6900ft. Range with max fuel and no reserves at long range cruising speed 463km (250nm). 206L-3ST – Max cruising speed 217km/h (117kt). Initial rate of climb 1550ft/min. Service ceiling 20,000ft. Hovering ceiling in ground effect 15,800ft. Range with max payload and max internal fuel 643km (347nm).

Weights: 206LT – Standard empty 1246kg (2748lb), max takeoff 2018kg (4450lb), or 2064kg (4550lb) with an external sling load. 206L-3ST – Empty 1175kg (2590lb), max takeoff 1928kg (4250lb).

Dimensions: Main rotor diameter 11.28m (37ft 0in), length overall 13.02m (42ft 9in), fuselage length 9.81m (32ft 3in), height 3.14m (10ft 4in). Main rotor disc area 99.9m² (1075.2sq ft).

Capacity: Typical seating for seven, plus pilot, in three rows (3+2+3). Executive configuration has club seating for four in main cabin.

Production: Conversions to Gemini ST configuration commenced in early 1994. Deliveries of new build 206LTs began in early 1994. Only 13 were built.

History: Bell's 206LT TwinRanger, was, as its name suggests, a new build twin engined development of the 206L LongRanger, while Tridair helicopters in the USA offers its twin engine Gemini ST conversion for existing LongRangers.

The name TwinRanger predates the 206LT to the mid 1980s when Bell first looked at developing a twin engine version of the LongRanger. The Model 400 TwinRanger did fly (maiden flight was on April 4 1984) and it featured two Allison 250 turboshafts, the four blade main rotor developed for the military Bell 406/OH-58D Kiowa and a reprofiled fuselage, but development was later suspended.

The 206LT TwinRanger is based on Tridair Helicopters' Gemini ST conversion program. Tridair announced it was working on a twin engine conversion of the LongRanger in 1989, and the prototype flew for the first time on January 16 1991. Full FAA certification was awarded in November and covers the conversion of LongRanger 206L-1s, L-3s and L-4s to Gemini ST configuration.

In mid 1994 the Gemini ST made history when it was certificated as the first Single/Twin aircraft, allowing it to operate either as a single or twin engine aircraft throughout all phases of flight. This unique certification allows it to operate with a single engine for maximum economy (for ferrying etc), with the extra redundancy and performance of a twin available when required.

Bell's 206LT TwinRanger was a new build production model equivalent to Tridair's Gemini ST and based on the LongRanger IV. The first example was delivered in January 1994. The TwinRanger has been replaced by the 427, described separately.

Photo: The reprofiled engine/transmission coaming is the most notable difference between the TwinRanger/Gemini ST and the single engine LongRanger. (Bell)

Bell 204, 205 & 214B

Country of origin: United States of America

Type: Medium twin utility helicopter

Powerplant: 204B – One 820kW (1100shp) Lycoming T5311A turboshaft driving a two blade main rotor and a two blade tail rotor. 205A-1 – One 932kW (1250shp) T5313B Lycoming turboshaft derated from 1050kW (1400shp).

Performance: 204B – Max speed 222km/h (120kt), max cruising speed 217km/h (117kt). Initial rate of climb 1600ft/min. Range with reserves 370km (200nm). 205A-1 – Max speed 204km/h (110kt), cruising speed 180km/h (97kt). Initial rate of climb 1680ft/min. Range 553km (300nm) at 8000ft.

Weights: 204B – Empty 2085kg (4600lb), max takeoff 4310kg (9500lb). 205A-1 – Empty 2414kg (5323lb), max takeoff 4765kg (10,500lb) with external load.

Dimensions: 204B – Main rotor diameter 14.63m (48ft 0in), fuselage length 12.69m (41ft 8in), height 4.45m (14ft 7in). Main rotor disc area 168.0m² (1808sq ft). 205A-1 – Same except for fuselage length 12.65m (41ft 6in).

Capacity: 204B – Total accommodation for 10 people, including one or two pilots, or 1360kg (3000lb) of freight. 205A-1 – Total accommodation for 15 including one or two pilots or 1815kg (4000lb) of cargo internally, or 2270kg (5000lb) externally on a sling load. Air ambulance configuration for six stretchers and one or two medical attendants.

Production: Over 60 civil Model 204Bs had been delivered by 1967, while further examples were built by Agusta-Bell up until 1973. 12,000 Model 205s (including civil 205A-1s) were built by Bell and Agusta-Bell up to the early 1980s. Numerous ex military 204s and 205s converted for commercial use.

History: The Bell Model 204B and 205A-1 are the civil counterparts to the highly successful UH-1B and UH-1H Iroquois military helicopters.

Bell designed the Model 204 in response to a 1955 US Army requirement for a utility helicopter. The 204 was something of a quantum leap forward in helicopter design as it was one of the first to be powered by a turboshaft. The turboshaft engine radically improved the practicality of the helicopter due to its lower maintenance and operating costs, lower fuel consumption, light weight and high power to weight ratio. The use of a turboshaft in the 204 allowed it to carry a useful payload over respectable ranges and at reasonable speeds, which resulted in the 204 and subsequent 205 becoming the most successful western helicopter series in terms of numbers built.

The UH-1B, from which the 204B was derived, was first delivered in March 1961. The subsequent Model 205A-1 is based on the UH-1H, which, when compared to the B model, is greater in length and capacity, has better performance and a more powerful engine.

In civil guise the 204 and 205 have been operated in a number of utility roles including as aerial cranes and firebombing.

The 214B Biglifter is based on the 205 but is powered by a very powerful 2185kW (2930shp) Lycoming LTC4B turboshaft (with more than twice the output of the 205's T53). Its main use is as an aerial crane. Iran's Army took delivery of 287 during the 1970s while smaller numbers were built for civil customers through to 1981.

Photo: An ex military UH-1B (204) used for crop spraying. (Gordon Reid)

Bell 212 Twin Two-Twelve

Countries of origin: USA and Canada

Type: Medium twin utility helicopter

Powerplant: One 1340kW (1800shp) (derated to 960kW/1290shp) Pratt & Whitney Canada PT6T-3 or PT6T-3B Turbo Twin-Pac, comprising two coupled PT6 turboshafts sharing a common gearbox with a single output shaft, driving a two blade main rotor and two blade tail rotor.

Performance: Max speed 206km/h (111kt), long range cruising speed 193km/h (104kt). Initial rate of climb 1320ft/min. Range with standard fuel at long range cruising speed 450km (243nm).

Weights: Empty VFR configuration 2765kg (6097lb), IFR configuration 2847kg (6277lb); max takeoff (with or without an external load) 5080kg (11,200lb).

Dimensions: Main rotor diameter 14.69m (48ft 2in), length overall 17.46m (57ft 3in), fuselage length 12.92m (42ft 5in), height 4.53m (14ft 10in). Main rotor disc area 168.1m² (1809.6 sq ft).

Capacity: Total seating for 15, including one or two pilots. Max weight on an external sling load 2270kg (5000lb).

Production: Approximately 950 212s, including military aircraft, had been delivered by 2000, when it remained available to order. Production totals augmented by Agusta-Bell examples, although these are mainly military versions. Bell production transferred to Canada in 1988.

History: The Model 212 is a twin engined development of Bell's earlier and highly successful Model 204 and 205 series.

Bell announced its decision to develop the Model 212 in early May 1968 in large part in response to a Canadian Armed Forces requirement for a twin engined development of the CUH-1H (Model 205) then entering military service in that country, and following successful negotiations with Pratt & Whitney Canada and the Canadian government. Development of the Model 212 was a joint venture between Bell, Pratt & Whitney Canada and the Canadian government, the latter providing financial support. The resulting helicopter (designated CUH-1N in Canadian and UH-1N in US military service) first flew in 1969 and was awarded commercial certification in October 1970. The first Canadian CUH-1Ns were handed over in May 1971.

The most significant feature of the Twin Two-Twelve is the PT6T Twin-Pac engine installation. This consists of two PT6 turboshafts mounted side by side and driving a single output shaft via a combining gearbox. The most obvious benefit of the new arrangement is better performance due to the unit's increased power output. However, the Twin-Pac engine system has a major advantage in that should one engine fail, sensors in the gearbox instruct the remaining operating engine to develop full power, thus providing a true engine out capability, even at max takeoff weight.

Aside from the twin engines, the 212 features only minor detail changes over the earlier Model 205 and UH-1H, including a slightly reprofiled nose. The 212 is also offered with a choice of IFR or VFR avionics suites. Production was transferred to Bell's Canadian factory in August 1988. Today it remains available to order (a single example was delivered in 1988, none were delivered in 1999).

Photo: The reprofiled nose and engine fairings help distinguish the 212 from the 205. (Robert Wiseman)

Bell 412

Countries of origin: USA and Canada

Type: Medium twin utility helicopter

Powerplants: 412 – One 1350kW (1800shp) (derated to 980kW/1308shp for takeoff) Pratt & Whitney Canada PT6T-3B Turbo Twin-Pac, consisting of two PT6 turboshafts linked through a combining gearbox, driving a four blade main rotor and two blade tail rotor. 412SP – One 1044kW (1400shp) takeoff rated PT6T-3B-1 Turbo Twin-Pac. 412EP – One 1342kW (1800shp) takeoff rated PT6T-3D Turbo Twin-Pac.

Performance: 412 – Max speed 240km/h (130kt) at sea level, cruising speed 235km/h (127kt). Max range 455km (245nm), or 835km (450nm) with auxiliary tanks. 412SP – Max speed 260km/h (140kt), max cruising speed 230km/h (124kt). Initial rate of climb 1350ft/min. Range with max payload and reserves 695km (374nm), max range with standard fuel 656km (354nm). 412EP – Max cruising speed 226km/h (122kt). Range at 5000ft 745km (402nm).

Weights: 412 – Empty equipped 2753kg (6070lb), max takeoff 5216kg (11,500lb). 412SP – Empty equipped (IFR) 3001kg (6616lb), max takeoff 5397kg (11,900lb). 412EP – Empty equipped (standard) 3079kg (6789lb), max takeoff 5397kg (11,900lb).

Dimensions: Main rotor diameter 14.02m (46ft 0in), length overall rotors turning 17.12m (56ft 2in), fuselage length 12.70m (41ft 9in), height 4.57m (15ft 0in). Main rotor disc area 154.4m² (1662sq ft).

Capacity: Total seating for 15, including one or two pilots. Maximum external sling load 2040kg (4500lb).

Production: Approx 580 Bell 412s of all models, civil and military, have been built. Production of the 412 switched to Bell's Canadian plant in February 1989 after 213 had been built in the US.

History: The Bell 412 family is four blade main rotor development of the 212.

Bell announced development of the 412 on September 8 1978, and two 212s were converted to the new standard to act as development aircraft for the program. The first of these flew in August 1979, and the 412 was awarded VFR certification in January 1981, with the first delivery the same month.

Subsequent development led to the 412SP, or Special Performance, with increased fuel capacity, higher takeoff weight and more optional seating arrangements. The 412HP, or High Performance, superseded the 412SP in production in 1991. Features include improved transmission for better hovering performance.

The current standard production model is the 412EP, or Enhanced Performance. The 412EP features a PT6T-3D engine and a dual digital automatic flight control system fitted as standard, with optional EFIS displays. Fixed tricycle landing gear is optional. The 412 Plus design study announced in 1999 would feature a 5647kg (12,450lb) max takeoff weight.

Meanwhile in Indonesia, IPTN has a licence to build the 412SP, which it calls the NBell-412. The licence covers up to 100 NBell-412s.

Like the 212, the 412 is in widespread use for a number of utility roles, including EMS and oil rig support. It too is in military service, Canada once again being a major customer (including 100 412EP based CH-146 Griffons).

Photo: Note the emergency floats on this 412. (Wayne Grant)

Bell 214ST

Country of origin: United States of America

Type: Medium twin utility helicopter

Powerplants: Two 1215kW (1625shp) General Electric CT7-2A turboshafts linked through a combining gearbox driving a two blade main rotor and two blade tail rotor.

Performance: Max cruising speed 260km/h (140kt) at 4000ft, or 264km/h (143kt) at sea level. Max initial rate of climb 1780ft/min. Service ceiling with one engine out 4800ft. Hovering ceiling in ground effect 6400ft. Ferry range with auxiliary fuel 1020km (550nm), range with standard fuel and no reserves 805km (435nm).

Weights: Empty 4300kg (9481lb), max takeoff 7938kg (17,500lb).

Dimensions: Main rotor diameter 15.85m (52ft 0in), length overall rotors turning 18.95m (62ft 2in), fuselage length 15.03m (49ft 4in), height overall 4.84m (15ft 11in). Main rotor disc area 197.3m² (2124sq ft).

Capacity: Pilot and copilot and up to 16 or 17 passengers. Freight volume of 8.95m³ (316cu ft). Can carry an external sling freight load of 3630kg (8000lb).

Production: The 214ST was in production from 1980 to 1990, during which time 100 were built.

History: Despite sharing a common model number with the 214 Huey Plus and Big Lifter (described separately), the Bell 214ST is a larger, much modified helicopter.

Bell's biggest helicopter yet was developed to meet an Iranian requirement for a larger transport helicopter with better performance in its hot and high environment than its 214 Isfahans. Bell based its proposal on the 214 but made substantial design changes, resulting in what is essentially an all new helicopter with little commonality with the smaller 214 series.

The 214ST features two General Electric CT7 turboshafts (the commercial equivalent of the military T700), a stretched fuselage seating up to 17 in the main cabin, glassfibre main rotor blades, and lubrication free elastomeric bearings in the main rotor hub. The ST suffix originally stood for Stretched Twin, reflecting the changes over the 214, but this was later changed to stand for Super Transporter.

The 214ST was to have been built under licence in Iran as part of that country's plans to establish a large army air wing (other aircraft ordered in large numbers under this plan were the 214A Isfahan and AH-1J SeaCobra), but the Islamic revolution and fall of the Shah in 1979 put paid to these plans.

Undeterred, Bell continued development of the 214ST – which first flew in February 1977 – for civil and military customers. Three preproduction 214STs were built from 1978 and 100 production aircraft were built through to 1990.

Most 214ST sales were to military customers. Ironically Iraq was the 214ST's largest customer, taking delivery of 45 during 1987 and 1988, some most likely seeing service in the Gulf War.

Civil applications for the 214ST are numerous, including oil rig support, where its twin engine configuration and 17 passenger main cabin are useful assets.

Photo: The 214ST is Bell's largest helicopter, and differs considerably from the similarly designated 214A and 214B. (Robert Wiseman)

Bell 222 & 230

Countries of origin: Canada and USA

Type: Light twin corporate and utility helicopters

Powerplants: 222B – Two 505kW (680shp) Avco (Textron) Lycoming LTS 101-750C turboshafts driving a two blade main rotor and two blade tail rotor. 230 – Two 520kW (700shp) takeoff rated Allison 250-C30G2 turboshafts.

Performance: 222B – Max cruising speed 240km/h (130kt). Initial rate of climb 1730ft/min. Hovering ceiling in ground effect 10,300ft. Range with no reserves 724km (390nm). 230 – Max cruising speed (with wheels) 261km/h (141kt), economical cruising speed (with wheels) 256km/h (138kt). Service ceiling 15,500ft. Hovering ceiling in ground effect 12,400ft. Range at economical cruising speed, with standard fuel, wheels and no reserves 558km (301nm), or 713km (385nm) with skids; range with wheels and auxiliary fuel, no reserves 702km (380nm).

Weights: 222B – Empty equipped 2076kg (4577lb), max takeoff 3472kg (8250lb). 230 – Empty with wheels 2312kg (5097lb), max takeoff 3810kg (8400lb).

Dimensions: 222B – Main rotor diameter 12.80m (42ft 0in), fuselage length 12.85m (42ft 2in), height 3.51m (11ft 6in). Main rotor disc area 128.7m² (1385.4sq ft). 230 – Main rotor diameter 12.80m (42ft 0in), length overall 15.23m (50ft 0in), fuselage length with wheels 12.87m (42ft 3in), with skids 12.81m (42ft 0in), height overall with skids 3.20m (12ft 2in). Main rotor disc area 128.7m² (1385.4sq ft).

Capacity: Standard seating for eight, including pilot, in four rows. Alternatively four in main cabin in club configuration.

Production: 184 Bell 222s built. Bell built 38 230s between 1992 and August 1995.

History: Bell announced the all new 222 twin, the first commercial light twin helicopter to be developed in the US, in April 1974.

The 222 first flew on August 13 1976. The new helicopter incorporated a number of advanced features including the Noda Matic vibration reduction system developed for the 214ST, stub wings housing the retractable undercarriage, and dual hydraulic and electrical systems.

The 222 was certificated in December 1979 and deliveries commenced in early 1980. Three initial versions were offered, the basic 222, the single/dual pilot IFR certificated corporate 222 Executive, and dual pilot IFR over water certificated 222 Offshore.

Subsequent development led to the more powerful 222B with a larger diameter main rotor, introduced in 1982. Versions were the basic 222B, 222B Executive certificated for dual pilot IFR operations and with a corporate interior, and the 222B based 222UT Utility Twin, with skid landing gear.

The Bell 230 is a development of the 222 with two Allison 250 turboshafts instead of the 222's LTS 101s plus other refinements. First flight of a 230, a converted 222, took place on August 12 1991, and Transport Canada certification was awarded in March 1992. The first delivery of a production 230 occurred that November and customers had a choice of skid or wheel undercarriage. Production ceased in 1995 after 38 had been built. The 230 has been replaced by the stretched, more powerful 430, described separately.

Photo: A Bell 222UT. (Martin Grimm)

Bell 430

Countries of origin: Canada and USA

Type: Light twin corporate utility helicopter

Powerplants: Two 584kW (783shp) takeoff rated, 521kW (699shp) max continuous rated Rolls-Royce 250-C40B turboshafts driving a four blade main rotor and two blade tail rotor.

Performance: Max cruising speed at sea level (with retractable gear or skids) 260km/h (140kt), economical cruising speed 256km/h (138kt) with retractable undercarriage, 237km/h (128kt) with skids. Service ceiling 18,340ft. Hovering ceiling in ground effect 11,350ft, out of ground effect 8750ft. Max range with reserves, standard fuel and retractable undercarriage 503km (272nm), with skids 644km (348nm).

Weights: Empty equipped 2406kg (5305lb) with retractable undercarriage, 2388kg (5265lb) with skids, max takeoff with internal load 4082kg (9000lb), max takeoff with sling load and optional MTOW with skids 4220kg (9300lb).

Dimensions: Main rotor disc diameter 12.80m (42ft 0in), length overall rotors turning 15.30m (50ft 3in), fuselage length inc tailskid 13.44m (44ft 1in), height to top of rotor head with wheels 3.72m (12ft 3in), with standard skids 4.03m (13ft 3in), optional skids 4.24m (13ft 11in). Main rotor disc area 128.7m² (1385.4sq ft).

Capacity: Typical seating configuration for 10 comprising pilot and passenger, with eight passengers in main cabin behind them in three rows of seats. Six and eight place executive layouts offered. In EMS role can carry one or two stretcher patients with four or three medical attendants respectively. Max hook capacity 1585kg (3500lb).

Production: Approximately 75 built.

History: Bell's 430 twin helicopter is a stretched and more powerful development of the 230.

Bell began preliminary design work on the 430 in 1991, even though the 230 itself had only flown for the first time in August that year. The 430 program was formally launched in February 1992. Two prototypes were modified from Bell 230s, and the first of these flew in its new configuration on October 25 1994. The second prototype featured the full 430 avionics suite, its first flight was on December 19 1994.

The first 430 production aircraft was completed in 1995, while Canadian certification was awarded on February 23 1996, allowing first deliveries from the middle of that year. Meanwhile 230 production had wound up in August 1995, making way for the 430.

Compared with the 230, the 430 features several significant improvements. Perhaps the most important of these is the new four blade, bearingless, hingeless, composite main rotor. Other changes include the 46cm (1ft 6in) stretched fuselage, allowing seating for an extra two passengers, 10% more powerful Rolls-Royce (Allison) 250 turboshafts (with FADEC) and an optional EFIS flightdeck. As well as the optional EFIS displays the 430 features as standard a Rogerson-Kratos Integrated Instrument Display System (IIDS), comprising two LCD displays to present engine information. The 430 is offered with either skids or retractable wheeled undercarriage.

Between August 17 and September 3 1996 Americans Ron Bower and John Williams broke the round the world helicopter record with a Bell 430, flying westwards from England.

Photo: Bell 430 with retractable undercarriage. (Bell)

Bell 407

Countries of origin: Canada and USA

Type: Light utility helicopter

Powerplants: One 605kW (814shp) takeoff rated, 520kW (700shp) max continuous rated Rolls-Royce (Allison) 250-C47 turboshaft driving a four blade main rotor and two blade tail rotor.

Performance: Max cruising speed at sea level 237km/h (128kt), max cruising speed at 4000ft 243km/h (131kt), economical cruising speed at 4000ft 213km/h (115kt). Service ceiling 18,690ft. Hovering ceiling in ground effect 12,200ft, out of ground effect 10,400ft. Max range 577km (312nm). Endurance 3hr 42min.

Weights: Empty equipped 1178kg (2598lb), max takeoff with internal load 2268kg (5000lb), max takeoff with sling load 2495kg (5500lb).

Dimensions: Main rotor disc diameter 10.67m (35ft 0in), length overall rotors turning 12.70m (41ft 8in), fuselage length 9.77m (32ft 1in), height overall 3.56m (11ft 8in). Main rotor disc area 89.4m^2 (962.1sq ft).

Capacity: Typical seating configuration for seven comprising pilot and passengers, with five passengers in main cabin. Max hook capacity 1200kg (2645lb).

Production: Over 450 407s delivered by late 2000.

History: Bell's popular 407 is a development of its JetRanger and LongRanger light singles.

Development work on Bell's New Light Aircraft replacement for the LongRanger and JetRanger dates back to 1993. The end result was the 407, an evolutionary development of the LongRanger.

A modified 206L-3 LongRanger served as the concept demonstrator 407 and first flew in this form on April 21 1994, while the 407 was first publicly announced at the Las Vegas Heli-Expo in January 1995.

The 407 concept demonstrator mated the LongRanger's fuselage with the tail boom and dynamic system of the military OH-58D Kiowa (which has a four blade main rotor). Fake fairings were used to simulate the wider fuselage being developed for the production standard 407. The first preproduction 407 flew in June 1995, the first production 407 flew in November 1995. Customer deliveries commenced the following February.

Compared with the LongRanger, the 407 features the four blade main rotor developed for the OH-58, which uses composite construction, and the blades and hub have no life limits. Benefits of the four blade main rotor include improved performance and better ride comfort. Another big change over the LongRanger is the 18cm (8in) wider cabin, increasing internal cabin width and space, plus 35% larger main cabin windows. Power is from a more powerful Rolls-Royce (Allison) 250-C47 turboshaft fitted with FADEC, allowing an increase in max takeoff weight and improving performance at hotter temperatures and/or higher altitudes. The tail boom is made from carbonfibre composites, while in 1995 Bell studied fitting the 407 with a shrouded tail rotor. The instrument panel features Litton liquid crystal displays.

Bell looked at the 407T twin 407 for a time, but opted instead to develop the essentially all new twin PW206D powered 427.

Photo: The 407 became an overnight sales success, with over 450 delivered by the end of 2000. (Paul Sadler)

Bell 427

Countries of origin: Canada, USA and South Korea

Type: Light twin utility helicopter

Powerplants: Two 456kW (611shp) takeoff rated, 405kW (543shp) max continuous rated Pratt & Whitney Canada PW206D turboshafts driving a four blade main rotor and two blade tail rotor.

Performance: Max speed 255km/h (138kt), cruising speed 246km/h (133kt). Hovering ceiling in ground effect 16,000ft, out of ground effect 7500ft. Range 704km (380nm). Max endurance 4hr.

Weights: Empty 1743kg (3842lb), max takeoff 2880kg (6350lb).

Dimensions: Main rotor diameter 11.28m (37ft 0in), fuselage length 10.94m (35ft 11in). Main rotor disc area 99.9m^2 (1075.2sq ft).

Capacity: Pilot and up to seven passengers (in a 2+3+3 arrangement), or pilot and passenger side by side with seating for four in a club configuration in main cabin. In medevac configuration two stretcher patients and two medical attendants.

Production: First deliveries January 2000. Over 80 ordered by end 2000.

History: Bell's latest helicopter, the 427 is a replacement for the 206LT TwinRanger and the cancelled 407T, which was to be a twin engine 407 (described separately).

When Bell first looked at a twin engine version of its new 407 light single, the company originally anticipated developing the 407T which would have been a relatively straightforward twin engine development (with two Allison-250C22Bs). However, Bell concluded that the 407T would not offer sufficient payload/range performance, and so began studies of a new light twin.

The result was the all new 427, which Bell announced at the Heli Expo in Dallas in February 1996. Prior to this announcement Bell had signed a collaborative partnership agreement with South Korea's Samsung Aerospace Industries covering the 427. Samsung builds the 427's fuselage and tailboom, and may later assemble any 427s sold in South Korea and China at its Sachon plant (Samsung also builds the left and right fuselage halves and the tailboom for the Bell 212 and 412). Bell builds the 427's flight dynamics systems at Fort Worth in Texas, with final assembly at Bell's Mirabel, Quebec plant.

The 427 was the first Bell designed entirely on computer (including using CATIA 3D modelling). Compared to the 407 the 427's cabin is 33cm (13in) longer, is largely of composite construction and lacks the roof beam which obstructs the cabin on the 206/206L/407.

Power is from two FADEC equipped Pratt & Whitney Canada PW206 turboshafts, driving the composite four blade main rotor and two blade tail rotor (based on those on the OH-58D Kiowa and Bell 407) through a new combining gearbox. The main rotor's soft-in-plane hub features a composite flexbeam yoke and elastomeric joints, eliminating the need for lubrication and any form of maintenance. The 427's glass cockpit features an integrated instrument display system (IIDS). A hinged main cabin door is standard but a sliding door is optional.

First flight was on December 11 1997 and Canadian certification was awarded on November 19 1999. First customer deliveries followed US certification in January 2000. US FAA dual pilot IFR certification was awarded in May 2000.

Photo: A Chinese registered Bell 427. (Ian Moy)

Bell/Agusta BA609

Country of origin: United States of America

Type: Six to nine seat corporate/utility tiltrotor

Powerplants: Two 1447kW (1940shp) Pratt & Whitney Canada PT6C-67A turboshafts driving three blade proprotors.

Performance: Provisional – Max cruising speed 510km/h (275kt), normal cruising speed 465km/h (260kt). Service ceiling 25,000ft. Max range, no reserves 1390km (750nm), max endurance with no reserves 3.0hr.

Weights: Provisional – Max useful load 2500kg (5500lb), max takeoff 7258kg (16,800lb).

Dimensions: Proprotor diameter 7.9m (26ft), span between proprotor centres 10m (33ft), fuselage length 13.4m (44ft), width overall rotors turning 18.3m (60ft), height 4.6m (15ft).

Capacity: To be certificated for single pilot IFR operation. Main cabin seats six to nine passengers depending on configuration. Could also be configured for search and rescue/medevac.

Production: First deliveries planned for 2003. In 2000 Bell Agusta held 80 advance orders for the BA609.

History: The Bell Agusta BA609 is on track to become the first civil application of the revolutionary tiltrotor technology, taking advantage of Bell's vast experience with the military V-22 Osprey.

Bell pioneered the tiltrotor concept with the experimental XV-3 which first flew as early as 1957 and then with NASA developed the XV-15 experimental demonstrator which first flew in 1977. In conjunction with Boeing it is building the military V-22 Osprey – deliveries of which to the US Marine Corps are now underway.

In November 1996 Bell and Boeing announced that they intended to use their expertise and experience with the V-22 to develop a nine seat civil tiltrotor. The Bell Boeing 609 was formally unveiled on November 18 1996, however in March 1998 Boeing announced its withdrawal from the program as a risk sharing partner to remain as a major subcontractor.

Then in September 1998 (at the Farnborough Airshow) Bell announced that Agusta would become a risk sharing development partner in the redesignated BA609. The two companies formed the Bell Agusta Aerospace Company joint venture based in Fort Worth, Texas, which is also developing the AB139 twin (described separately). Bell has a majority holding in Bell Agusta and has program lead on the BA609, while Agusta is leading development of the AB139. Production BA609s will be built at Bell's Amarillo, Texas Tiltrotor Assembly Center and at Agusta's facility near Milan in Italy.

First flight for the BA609 is planned for August 2001 with certification and first deliveries scheduled for late 2003 (somewhat delayed from the original announced schedule of first flight in mid 1999 and deliveries in 2001).

The BA609 will incorporate advanced technologies such as a three LCD screen glass cockpit, fly-by-wire flight controls and a composite construction fuselage. Power will be from two PT6C-67A turboshafts. Unlike the V-22 it features a T-tail (with conventional elevators but no rudder). In May 2000 Bell Agusta announced that Japan's Fuji Heavy Industries had been selected to build the BA609's composite fuselage.

Photo: The BA609 mockup. (Bell Agusta)

Bell/Agusta AB139

Countries of origin: Italy & USA

Type: Medium lift helicopter

Powerplants: Two 1252kW (1679shp) takeoff rated Pratt & Whitney Canada PT6C-67C turboshafts driving a five blade main rotor and four blade tail rotor.

Performance: Max cruising speed 157kt (290km/h). Initial rate of climb 2000ft/min. Hovering ceiling out of ground effect 12,000ft. Max range with no reserves 750km (400nm). Endurance with no reserves 3.9hr.

Weights: Max takeoff 6000kg (13,227lb). Useful load (external) 2700kg (6000lb).

Dimensions: Main rotor diameter 13.80m (45ft 3in), length overall rotors turning 16.65m (54ft 8in), height overall rotors turning 4.95m (16ft 3in). Main rotor disc area 149.6m² (1610.0sq ft).

Capacity: Flightcrew of one or two. Main cabin seating for up to 15 passengers on three rows of five seats (the first row rearward facing, the second and third rows forward facing). In EMS configuration can carry six stretcher patients and four medical attendants.

Production: First deliveries planned for 2002. Launch orders from Bristow Helicopters placed in late 1999. Anticipated market for 900 over the next two decades.

History: The all new AB139 medium lift helicopter is the second product of the Bell/Agusta Aerospace Company (BAAC) joint venture, after the BA609 tiltrotor.

The new six tonne class AB139 is aimed at offshore oil rig support, corporate transport, and utility work, and will complement the Bell 212/412, as it is slightly larger with significantly improved performance. Military variants will also be offered. BAAC says the AB139 grew out of a comprehensive market survey which measured the requirements of operators in its size class.

The joint venture company publicly announced details of the AB139 on September 8 1999 at the Farnborough Airshow, while a mockup was displayed at the following year's Paris Airshow. Three development AB139s are being built, with first flight expected in late 2000, with certification and first deliveries in 2002.

Features of the new helicopter include a 291km/h (157kt) cruising speed, delivered courtesy of the twin PT6C engines and the five blade fully articulated main rotor and four bladed canted tail rotor, plus a Honeywell Primus Epic integrated glass cockpit, and a large, unobstructed main cabin with seating for 15.

Unlike the BA609 tiltrotor, AgustaWestland is the lead partner on the AB139, responsible for the new helicopter's design and development and production, while the manufacturing workshare is split 75:25 to the Italian manufacturer's benefit. Engine manufacturer Pratt & Whitney Canada and avionics provider Honeywell are risk sharing partners in the program, along with Kawasaki, for the transmission input module, Poland's PZL Swidnik, which is supplying airframe components, and landing gear and air-conditioning system supplier Liebherr of Germany. Final assembly will be undertaken at AgustaWestland's Vergiate plant, while Bell will establish a second line to build AB139s for North American customers.

Photo: A mockup of the Bell/Agusta AB139. (Gerard Frawley)

Beriev Be-32

Country of origin: Russia

Type: Regional airliner and utility transport

Powerplants: Be-32K – Two 820kW (1100shp) P&W-Rus PK6A-65B turboprops driving three blade constant speed propellers.

Performance: Be-32K – Max cruising speed 480km/h (259kt), economical cruising speed 363km/h (196kt). Range with 16 passengers at max cruising speed 600km (324nm), at economical cruising speed 885km (477nm). Corporate transport range with seven passengers at max cruising speed 1450km (780nm), at economical cruising speed 2050km (1105nm).

Weights: Be-32K – Max takeoff 7300kg (16,090lb).

Dimensions: Wing span 17.00m (55ft 9in), length 15.70m (51ft 6in), height 5.52m (18ft 2in). Wing area 32.0m² (344.45sq ft).

Capacity: Flightcrew of two. Standard passenger seating for 16. Corporate shuttle configuration seats seven. Ambulance configuration accommodates nine stretcher patients, six seated patients and one medical attendant.

Production: Eight Be-30s were built in the late 1960s before program terminated. One of the original Be-30s converted to operate as the Be-32, then Be-32K demonstrator. Moscow Airways announced an order for 50 Be-32s in 1993.

History: The Beriev Be-32 is a modern development of the Be-30 commuter that was originally developed for Aeroflot in the late 1960s.

The Beriev Be-30 was designed against an Aeroflot requirement for a twin turboprop airliner and utility transport in the late 1960s. The prototype first flew on March 3 1967. Eight development aircraft were built in the late 1960s, but the project was cancelled when Aeroflot chose the Czech L 410 (described separately) in preference to Beriev's design. Since then the Be-30 lay dormant until Beriev resurrected it as the Be-32, firstly to claim time to height records in the mid 1970s, and then in the early 1990s in a bid to attract new business and gain scarce hard currency.

Beriev first exhibited the improved Be-32 at the 1993 Paris Airshow, the design bureau claiming that the Be-32 incorporated a number of improvements, including more powerful engines. This demonstrator was one of the original Be-30s modified to the new configuration.

Features of the basic Be-32 included Mars (formerly Omsk) TVD-10B turboprops, use of Glass Fibre Reinforced Plastics in the wingtips, tail surfaces and wing/fuselage fillets, and honeycomb panelling covering sections of the wing and tail.

The Pratt & Whitney-Rus PK6A powered Be-32K first flew on August 15 1995. The 820kW (1100shp) PK6A-65B is a Russian built version of Pratt & Whitney Canada's successful PT6A. (The Be-32K prototype is powered by Canadian built PT6A-65Bs.)

Moscow Airways placed an order for 50 Be-32s in 1993, but this sale appears to have lapsed. Be-32 production machines would be built at the Irkutsk Aviation Production Plant (where the Be-200 amphibian, refer next entry, is also scheduled to be built) although little apparent progress has been made in recent years.

Photo: The resurrected Russian TVD-10B powered Be-32 demonstrator. This aircraft was re-engined with Pratt & Whitney PT6As.

Beriev Be-200

Country of origin: Russia

Type: Firefighting and multirole amphibian

Powerplants: Two 73.6kN (16,550lb) ZMKB Progress D-436TP turbofans.

Performance: Max speed 720km/h (388kt), max cruising speed 700km/h (377kt). Initial rate of climb 2755ft/min. Service ceiling 36,090ft. Range with 66 passengers 900km (486nm), with 12 passengers in a corporate configuration 3200km (1727nm), with 3000kg (6614lb) freight payload 2500km (1350nm). Range with max fuel 3850km (2078nm).

Weights: Max takeoff 37,200kg (79,365lb).

Dimensions: Wing span (over winglets) 32.78m (107ft 7in), length 32.05m (105ft 2in), height 8.90m (29ft 3in). Wing area 117.4m² (1264.2sq ft).

Capacity: Flightcrew of two. In firefighting configuration can uplift 12 tonnes (26,460lb) of water. Alternative seating for 68 economy class, or 10 to 32 first class passengers, with a seating pitch up to 102cm (40in). Ambulance configuration seats seven medical attendants and 30 stretcher patients. Can carry 8 tonnes (17,635lb) of freight in cargo configuration.

Production: Deliveries due from late 2001.

History: The Beriev Be-200 jet powered multirole amphibian is based on the larger military A-40 Albatross.

Beriev has extensive experience in building large amphibious aircraft, including the turboprop ASW Be-12 Tchaika and the Be-42 Albatross jet (NATO reporting name 'Mermaid').

The Be-200 is based on the Be-42 (which first flew in 1986) but is smaller overall and designed for civil roles, in particular firefighting. The all metal hull design is based on the Be-42's, and the Be-200 has a mildly swept wing with winglets, above fuselage mounted turbofan engines and a swept T-tail.

The airframe is strengthened to cope with the demands of water operations and firebombing and there is some use of advanced aluminium lithium alloys. The two crew flightdeck features an ARIA-2000 EFIS avionics suite (ARIA is a collaboration between the Russian avionics research institute and Honeywell). The ARIA-2000 suite includes specialist firefighting functions including an automatic glidescope and water source/drop zone memorisation.

Design work on the Be-200 began in 1989. It is being marketed by Betair, a collaboration between Beriev and Irkutsk in central Russia where the aircraft will be built.

After a number of delays the first flight took place on September 24 1998 from Irkutsk Aviation Production Organisation's airfield in Irktusk, Siberia, however, the Be-200 continues to be hamstrung by funding shortfalls and delays. By late 2000 additional funding was still required to complete certification (to Russia's new AP-25 standard, equivalent to the US's FAR and Europe's JAR 25 standard). This would allow deliveries to Russia's ministry of emergency services (which has ordered seven) from late 2001. Beriev is also looking at gaining western certification.

Firebombing versions would be designated Be-200ChS, the Be-210 is a proposed 72 seat airliner version.

Photo: The Be-200 prototype at the 1999 Paris Airshow. (Paul Merritt)

Beriev Be-103

Country of origin: Russia

Type: Six seat amphibious light aircraft

Powerplants: Two 157kW (210hp) Teledyne Continental IO-360-ES4 flat six piston engine driving three blade propellers.

Performance: Max cruising speed 260km/h (140kt). Service ceiling 9840ft. Takeoff run on land 310m (1020ft), takeoff run from water 440m (1445ft). Range with max payload 500km (270nm), range with max fuel 1350km (729nm).

Weights: Empty equipped 1540kg (3395lb), max takeoff 2270kg (5004lb).

Dimensions: Wing span 12.72m (41ft 9in), length 10.65m (34ft 11in), height 3.75m (12ft 4in). Wing area 25.1m² (270.2sq ft).

Capacity: Seating for six in pairs. Ambulance configuration accommodates pilot, stretcher patient and three seated passengers/medical attendants.

Production: Beriev estimates sales for up to 600, including over 200 for export. First customer is Russia's Border Guards.

History: The Beriev Be-103 six seat amphibian is the only aircraft of its type currently available, and consequently could establish itself some useful market niches.

The Beriev Aviation Company, based at Taganrog on Russia's Sea of Azoz, has specialised in amphibious aircraft design and development since 1948, and probably has more experience in this area than any other company today. Since the end of the Cold War Beriev has focused its efforts on civil aircraft which have export potential, including the Be-32, Be-200 and the uniquely configured Be-103.

Beriev began design work on the Be-103 in 1992. The first prototype was publicly displayed for the first time at the Gelendzhik Hydroaviation Show on the Black Sea in September 1996, before making its first flight on July 15 1997. Unfortunately this aircraft was short-lived, it crashed while practising for the Moscow Airshow on August 18 1997.

However by that stage a second prototype was well advanced and it first flew on November 17 1997. This aircraft made the Be-103's first flight from water on April 24 1998, but unfortunately it too crashed, on April 26 1999. Flight testing resumed when the first of three preproduction Be-103s first flew on February 19 1999, by which stage eight production aircraft were under construction.

The Be-103's unique configuration features a low mounted, large area wing, with its two engines rear mounted on pylons on either side for the fuselage. The first prototype Be-103 was powered by VOKBM/Bakanov M-17F piston engines, while production aircraft will be powered by Teledyne Continental IO-360s. A Russian domestic market version has been under consideration powered by the ubiquitous VOKBM M-14 nine cylinder radial, which would be mounted above the fuselage.

The Be-103 is designed to be certificated against Russian AP-23 and US FAR Part 23 requirements. Options will include autopilot, GPS and weather radar.

Beriev says the Be-103 is suitable for a number of roles including tourist flights, medical transport and freight work.

Photo: The short-lived first prototype Beriev Be-103. (Sebastian Zacharias)

Boeing Stearman

Country of origin: United States of America

Type: Two seat sport, utility and agricultural biplane

Powerplant: One 170kW (225hp) Lycoming R-680 seven cylinder radial piston engine driving a two blade fixed pitch propeller, or alternatively a 165kW (220hp) Continental W-670-6 or 170kW (225hp) Jacobs R-755-7 piston radial. Many later converted with a 335kW (450hp) Pratt & Whitney R-985-A6-1 radial piston engine.

Performance: Max cruising speed 200km/h (108kt), typical cruising speed range 148 to 170km/h (80 to 92kt). Initial rate of climb 1000ft/min. Service ceiling 11,200ft. Range with max fuel at 148km/h (80kt) cruising speed 605km (325nm).

Weights: Basic operating 940kg (2075lb), max takeoff 1275kg (2810lb), or max takeoff in ag configuration 2040kg (4500lb).

Dimensions: Wing span 9.80m (32ft 2in), length 7.62m (25ft 0in), height 2.79m (9ft 2in). Wing area 27.6m² (297.4sq ft).

Capacity: Typical seating for two in tandem, or single pilot only when used for agricultural work.

Production: Total production 8584. Postwar more than 2100 were converted for agricultural spraying work. Several hundred continue to fly with private owners.

History: The Boeing Stearman is perhaps the most widely known and recognised biplane in the USA, as it was that country's primary basic trainer throughout World War 2.

This famous biplane began life as a design of the Wichita, Kansas based Stearman division of United Aircraft (at that time United Aircraft also owned Boeing and United Air Lines), which Boeing acquired as a wholly owned subsidiary in 1934. At the time of the takeover development on the X70 training biplane was well advanced, and Stearman continued work on the type under Boeing ownership. The prototype of the Stearman Model 75, as the X70 became, flew for the first time in 1936. That year Stearman delivered the first production Model 35s, as the PT-13, to the US Army Air Corps. That service immediately found the Lycoming R-680 powered PT-13 to be an ideal basic trainer, the airframe was rugged and forgiving, and the slow turning radial engine reliable and reasonably economical.

America's entry into World War 2 brought with it massive requirements for pilot training and the US Army and Navy went on to buy thousands of PT-13s and Continental engined PT-17s and N2Ss. During the war almost all American pilots undertook basic training on the PT-13 or PT-17, and the type was exported to Canada (as the Kaydet), Britain and other nations. Apart from in Canada the Kaydet name was unofficially widely adopted for the type.

Postwar, the Stearman's rugged construction and good low speed handling saw large numbers converted for agricultural spraying work. Many conversions involved replacing the Stearman's fabric covering with metal (to avoid problems with chemical contamination), while many were fitted with more powerful 335kW (450hp) P&W R-985-A6-1 radials.

Today several hundred Stearmans are still flown in private hands, although its crop spraying days are mostly over.

Photo: Stearmans are easily recognised by their large radial engine and biplane configuration. (Alan Scoot)

Boeing C-97 Stratofreighter

Country of origin: United States of America

Type: Freighter

Powerplants: KC-97G – Four 2610kW (3500hp) Pratt & Whitney R-4360-59B Wasp Major 28 cylinder radial piston engines driving four blade constant speed propellers.

Performance: KC-97G – Max speed 603km/h (325kt), cruising speed 482km/h (260kt). Service ceiling 35,000ft. Range with max fuel 6920km (3735nm).

Weights: KC-97G – Empty 37,450kg (82,500lb), max takeoff 79,450kg (175,000lb).

Dimensions: KC-97G – Wing span 43.05m (141ft 3in), length 35.81m (117ft 5in), height 11.67m (38ft 3in). Wing area 164.5m² (1769sq ft).

Capacity: Flightcrew of two pilots, flight engineer, and, in military service, a navigator and radio operator. When configured for passengers can seat more than 100 (Stratocruisers in airline service typically seated 55). All surviving Stratofreighters used as freighters.

Production: Total military Model 367 production of 27 C-97s and 808 KC-97s, in addition to which 55 civil Model 377 Stratocruiser airliners were built. A handful of Stratofreighters remained in commercial use in 2000.

History: Boeing's Stratofreighter formed the backbone of the US Air Force's Military Air Transport Service (MATS) during the early 1950s, and more than 800 were built for use as freighters and air-to-air refuellers.

The Model 367 Stratofreighter is based on the Boeing B-29 Superfortress, the Allies' most technologically advanced bomber to see service in World War 2, and an aircraft famous (or infamous) for dropping the only atomic bombs used operationally in warfare on Japan in the closing stages of that conflict. The B-29 flew for the first time in September 1942 by which time Boeing had already studied a transport version, utilising the B-29's wing, engines, tail and lower fuselage, combined with a new upper fuselage section. The new double lobe fuselage shape was very distinctive, and also formed the basis for future Boeing jet airliner fuselage cross sections.

The US Army Air Force was impressed with Boeing's proposals and ordered three prototypes be built, the first of which flew on November 15 1944. Ten development YC-97s were subsequently ordered, the last of which represented production aircraft, featuring the more powerful R-4360 engines and taller tail developed for the B-50, an improved B-29. The first production C-97A was delivered in October 1949.

Development of the C-97 led to the C-97C, which was used for casualty evacuation, and the KC-97E, KC-97F and KC-97G aerial tankers. More than 590 KC-97Gs were built. The KC-97 was the US Air Force's primary tanker until replaced by the jet powered KC-135, the predecessor to the Boeing 707. Small numbers of 377 Stratocruiser airliners were also built, but the last of these have long been retired.

Many Stratofreighters survived their military service to be acquired by civilian operators for use as freighters and fire bombers. A small number still operate in Alaska.

Photo: Small numbers of C-97s are still flying in commercial service. The C-97/377 was notorious for its engine problems.

Boeing 707

Country of origin: United States of America

Type: Medium to long range airliner and freighter

Powerplants: 707-120B – Four 75.6kN (17,000lb) Pratt & Whitney JT3D-1 turbofans. 707-320B – Four 80kN (18,000lb) JT3D-3s or four 84.4kN (19,000lb) JT3D-7s.

Performance: 707-120B – Max speed 1010km/h (545kt), max cruising speed 1000km/h (540kt), economical cruising speed 897km/h (484kt). Range with max payload 6820km (3680nm), range with max fuel 8485km (4580nm). 707-320B – Max speed 1009km/h (545kt), max cruising speed 974km/h (525kt), long range cruising speed 885km/h (478kt). Range with max passengers 6920km (3735nm), range with max fuel and 147 passengers 9265km (5000nm).

Weights: 707-120B – Operating empty 55,589kg (122,533lb), max takeoff 116,575kg (257,000lb). 707-320B – Empty 66,406kg (146,400lb), max takeoff 151,315kg (333,600lb).

Dimensions: 707-120B – Wing span 39.90m (130ft 10in), length 44.07m (144ft 6in), height 12.94m (42ft 5in). Wing area 226.3m² (2433sq ft). 707-320B – Wing span 44.42m (145ft 9in), length 46.61m (152ft 11in), height 12.93m (42ft 5in). Wing area 283m² (3050sq ft).

Capacity: Flightcrew of three or four. 707-120 max seating for 179, or 110 in two classes (44 first and 66 economy). 707-320B – Max seating for 219, or 189 single class at 81cm (32in) pitch, or 147 in two classes. Convertible or freighter versions – 13 A type containers.

Production: 707 production ended in 1978 with 878. Military 707 airframes built to 1990. Approx 100 remain in commercial service.

History: The 707's jet speed, long range, high seating capacity and operating economics revolutionised airliner travel when it was introduced into service in 1958. The 707 also laid the foundations for Boeing's subsequent dominance of the jet airliner market.

Recognising the jet engine's potential for commercial aviation, Boeing (at great financial risk) decided to develop a jet powered transport that could fulfil military tanker transport roles but also be easily adapted to become an airliner. The resulting prototype, known as the Dash 80, flew for the first time on July 16 1954. Impressed, the US Air Force ordered it into production as the KC-135 tanker/transport (more than 700 were built). The success of the KC-135 paved the way for the commercial 707, which was a similar swept wing four jet design, but had a longer and slightly widened fuselage.

The first production 707 (a 707-120 for PanAm) flew on December 20 1957, and entered service later the following year. Developments of the 707-120 include the similar 707-220, the shorter -138 for Qantas, and the stretched 707-320, which flew in July 1959. The 707-320 and -120 were later re-engined with JT3D turbofans (in place of the original JT3 turbojets) to become the 707-320B, and the 707-120B respectively. The 707-320C was a convertible model, the 707-420 was powered by Rolls-Royce Conways, while the proposed CFM56 powered 707-700 upgrade was flight tested in the late 1970s but never entered production.

Most 707s in service today have been converted to freighters, while others are used as corporate transports.

Photo: A Saudi Arabian government 707-320C VIP aircraft (operated by Saudi Arabian Airlines. (John Adlard)

Boeing 720

Country of origin: United States of America

Type: Medium range narrowbody airliner

Powerplants: 720B – Four 75.6kN (17,000lb) Pratt & Whitney JT3D-1 turbofans or four 80kN (18,000lb) JT3D-3s.

Performance: 720B – Max speed 1009km/h (545kt), max cruising speed 983km/h (530kt), economical cruising speed 896km/h (484kt). Range with maximum payload and no reserves 6687km (3610nm), range with max fuel 8428km (4550nm).

Weights: 720B – Operating empty 51,203kg (112,883lb), max takeoff 106,140kg (234,000lb).

Dimensions: Wing span 39.88m (130ft 10in), length 41.68m (136ft 9in), height 12.66m (41ft 7in). Wing area 234.2m² (2521sq ft).

Capacity: Flightcrew of three comprising two pilots and a flight engineer. Typical seating for 112 in two classes, max seating for 149.

Production: Between 1959 and 1969 Boeing built 65 720s and 89 720Bs (many 720s were converted to 720Bs). Small numbers used as corporate transports.

History: The 720 is a smaller capacity, lighter, medium range variant of the 707, given its own model number to indicate significant engineering changes.

Introduced in 1959, the 720 (originally designated 707-020) retained the same basic structure as the 707-120, but was 2.54m (8ft 4in) shorter, which reduced seating to 112 in a typical two class arrangement. Other changes were made to the wing which introduced full span leading edge flaps, while a glove between the inner engines and the fuselage increased wing sweep and wing area and decreased the wing's thickness/chord ratio. The changes to the wing made it more aerodynamically efficient, permitting higher cruising speeds and lowered minimum speeds (which aided field performance).

Like the early 707s the first 720s had JT3C turbojets, although less powerful models lacking water injection because of the 720's lighter weight. Compared with the 707-120 the 720 also had reduced fuel capacity and a lower max takeoff weight. But many components were interchangeable between the 720 and 707, while inside the cabin the 720 and 707 shared the same passenger interior and flightdeck.

The initial 720 (bound for launch customer United) first flew on November 23 1959. Certification was awarded on June 30 1960, and entry into service with United Airlines was on July 5 that year.

The availability of the far more fuel efficient Pratt & Whitney JT3D turbofan resulted in the 720B, which was powered by either JT3D-1s or -3s. First flight of the 720B was on October 6 1960, with certification awarded on March 3 1961. The 720B also featured a higher maximum zero fuel weight (significantly boosting payload/range) and an increased max takeoff weight due to the heavier turbofan engines.

Major 720 operators included American Airlines (a number of its 720s were converted to 720Bs with turbofan engines), United, Eastern, Northwest Orient and Western, while operators outside the US included Lufthansa and Avianca.

Today a handful are used as corporate transports, although none are understood to be in commercial service.

Photo: Pratt & Whitney uses this 720B as an engine testbed. Here it is shown testing the new PW6000 turbofan bound for the Airbus A318.

Boeing 717

Country of origin: United States of America

Type: 100 seat regional airliner

Powerplants: 717-200BGW – Two 82.3kN (18,500lb) Rolls-Royce BR715 A1-30 turbofans. 717-200HGW – Same or optionally 89.9kN (20,000lb) or 93.4kN (21,000lb) BR715s.

Performance: 717-200BGW – Cruising speed 811km/h (438kt). Range with 106 passengers 2645km (1430nm). 717-200HGW – Cruising speed same. Range with 106 passengers 3815km (2060nm).

Weights: 717-200BGW – Operating empty 31,674kg (69,830lb), max takeoff 49,940kg (110,100lb) or 51,710kg (114,000lb). 717-200HGW – Operating empty 32,110kg (70,790lb), max takeoff 54,885kg (121,000lb).

Dimensions: Wing span 28.44m (93ft 3in), length 37.82m (124ft 0in), height 8.87m (29ft 1in). Wing area 93.0m² (1000.7sq ft).

Capacity: Flightcrew of two. Typical two class seating for 106 passengers at five abreast in main cabin. Single class seating for 117.

Production: At late 2000 149 717s had been ordered, of which 38 had been delivered.

History: The 100 seat 717 is the latest development of the DC-9/MD-80/MD-90 family and the only Douglas airliner which Boeing retained in its product line-up follow the 1997 merger with McDonnell Douglas. It is designed for high cycle, short range operations.

McDonnell Douglas first announced the MD-95 at the June 1991 Paris Airshow. At the time MDC anticipated a formal program launch by late 1991 and a first flight in July 1994. As it happened program launch was not until October 1995 when US airline ValuJet (now AirTran Airlines) ordered 50 and optioned 50.

In January 1998 Boeing (following the August 1997 Boeing/McDonnell Douglas merger) relaunched the MD-95 as the 717-200. First flight took place on September 2 1998, certification was awarded on September 1 1999 while the first delivery, to AirTran, was on September 23 that year.

Initially MDC studied powering the MD-95 with Pratt & Whitney JT8D-218s or Rolls-Royce Tays. In February 1994 however MDC announced it had chosen the new BMW Rolls-Royce (now just Rolls-Royce) BR715 over the JT8D-200 and an engine from the proposed 'Project Blue' teaming of General Electric, SNECMA, MTU and P&W.

Other 717-200 features include a fuselage 1.45m (4ft 9in) longer than the DC-9-30's, a wing based on the DC-9-34's, an advanced six LCD screen Honeywell EFIS flightdeck, and a cabin interior similar to that developed for the MD-90. It is offered in standard 717-200BGW (Basic Gross Weight) and extended range 717-200HGW (High Gross Weight) forms. In addition, 80 seat shortened 717-100 (formerly MD-95-20) and 130 seat stretched 717-300 (formerly MD-95-50) models have been studied, as has a business jet variant.

Companies participating in 717 production include Alenia (fuselage), Korean Air (nose), AIDC of Taiwan (empennage), ShinMaywa of Japan (engine pylons and horizontal stabilizers), Israel Aircraft Industries (undercarriage), and Fischer of Austria (interior). Final assembly is at Boeing's Long Beach plant, in the same building that the DC-9 and MD-80 were built in.

Photo: A 717 operated by Australia's Impulse Airlines. (Boeing)

Boeing 727-100

Country of origin: United States of America

Type: Short to medium range narrowbody airliner

Powerplants: 727-100 – Three 62.3kN (14,000lb) Pratt & Whitney JT8D-7 turbofans.

Performance: Max speed 1017km/h (549kt), max cruising speed 977km/h (527kt), economical cruising speed 917km/h (495kt). Range with max payload 3260km (1760nm).

Weights: 727-100 – Empty equipped 36,560kg (80,602lb), max takeoff 72,570kg (160,000lb).

Dimensions: 727-100 – Wing span 32.92m (108ft 0in), length 40.59m (133ft 2in), height 10.36m (34ft 0in). Wing area 157.9m² (1700sq ft).

Capacity: Flightcrew of three (two pilots and flight engineer). Typical two class seating for 94, max seating for 131.

Production: Of the 582 727-100s built, approx 275 remained in commercial service in late 2000, with 40 more used as corporate jets.

History: The 727 short to medium range trijet is the world's second most successful jet airliner built and an important part of the Boeing success story.

Initial design studies began in 1956, although for a time it appeared that a new short/medium range airliner would not be built at all due to Boeing's financial position before sales of the 707 had taken off. Boeing persisted however and began serious development of the 727 in June 1959. The program was launched on the strength of orders for 80 from Eastern and United in 1960.

The 727 pioneered the rear trijet configuration, with power from three specially designed Pratt & Whitney JT8D turbofans (although Rolls-Royce Speys were originally considered). The trijet design was settled upon as it gave the redundancy of three engines, better climb performance than a twin and improved operating economics over a four engine jet. The 727 also introduced an advanced wing with outer leading edge Krueger flaps, inner leading edge slats and trailing edge triple slotted Fowler flaps. The 727 retained the 707's fuselage cross section, but with a redesigned smaller lower fuselage due to the need to carry less baggage on shorter range flights, and it has limited parts commonality with the 707 and 720. The 727 was also the first Boeing airliner to feature an APU (auxiliary power unit).

The prototype 727 first flew on February 9 1963, with certification granted in December that year. The first 727 entered service with Eastern Airlines on February 9 the following year.

Development of the initial 727-100 resulted in a small family of sub variants, including higher gross weight options for the basic passenger carrying 727, the 727-100C Convertible and 727-100QC Quick Change, both with a large freight door on the forward left hand side of the fuselage. Many were subsequently converted to pure freighters. The stretched 727-200 is described separately.

Production of the 727-100 ceased in 1973.

During the 1990s Dee Howard in the USA upgraded 45 727-100 freighters for express freight operator UPS with Rolls-Royce Tay turbofans, improving performance, reducing fuel consumption and allowing the aircraft to meet Stage 3 noise requirements.

Photo: A 727-100 of South Africa's Nationwide. (Rob Finlayson)

Boeing 727-200

Country of origin: United States of America

Type: Short to medium range narrowbody airliner

Powerplants: Three 64.5kN (14,500lb) Pratt & Whitney JT8D-9 turbofans, or 67.2kN (15,000lb) JT8D-11s, or 68.9kN (15,500lb) JT8D-15s or 71.1kN (16,000lb) JT8D-17s (Advanced only), or 77.3kN (17,400lb) JT8D-17Rs (Advanced only).

Performance: Advanced 727-200 – Max speed 1017km/h (549kt), max cruising speed 953km/h (515kt), economical cruising speed 865km/h (467kt). Range with max payload 3965km (2140nm), range with max fuel 4450km (2400nm).

Weights: Advanced 727-200 – Operating empty 45,360kg (100,000lb), max takeoff 95,030kg (209,500lb).

Dimensions: Wing span 32.92m (108ft 0in), length 46.69m (153ft 2in), height 10.36m (34ft 0in). Wing area 157.9m² (1700sq ft).

Capacity: 727-200 – Max seating for 189 at six abreast and 76cm (30in) pitch, typical two class seating for 14 premium class and 131 economy class passengers. 727-200F – Typical max payload comprises 11 2.23m x 3.17m (7ft 4in x 10ft 5in) pallets.

Production: 1831 727s of all models built when production ceased in 1984, including 1249 -200s. Approx 900 in service at late 2000.

History: The 727-100 had been in service barely a year when Boeing began serious consideration of a stretched development.

This resulted in the 727-200, which Boeing announced it was developing in August 1965. The 727-200 was essentially a minimum change development of the -100, the only major change being the 6.10m (20ft) fuselage stretch, which increased maximum seating to 189 passengers. The 727-200's stretch consisted of two 3.05m (10ft) plugs, one forward and one rear of the wing. Otherwise the 727-100 and -200 shared common engines, fuel tank capacity and the same maximum takeoff weight.

The 727-200 first flew on July 27 1967, with certification granted in late November that year. The -200 was placed into service by launch customer Northeast Airlines (this airline was later acquired by Delta) the following month, by which time total 727 orders for both models exceeded 500.

The 727-200 helped broaden the sales appeal of the 727 considerably and snared significant sales. However the -200 was restricted by its relatively short range, due to it having the same fuel capacity as the 727-100, so Boeing developed the increased range Advanced 727-200. First flown in March 1972 changes introduced on the Advanced model included increased fuel capacity, and thus range, the option of more powerful engines, quieter engine nacelles and strengthened structure. The Advanced remained the primary 727-200 production model until production ceased in 1984.

The 727-200 remains popular with passengers and pilots but it does not meet Stage 3 noise requirements. To overcome this a number of hushkit programs are on offer while Valsan converted 23 727s to its Stage 3 compliant Quiet 727 standard (before the company collapsed). This retrofit included installing JT8D-217s on the outer pylons and acoustic treatment of the centre engine.

Photo: A 727-200 of British Airways' franchise operator of South Africa lands at Johannesburg. (Rob Finlayson)

Boeing 737-100 & 737-200

Country of origin: United States of America

Type: Short range narrowbody airliner

Powerplants: 737-100 – Two 62.3kN (14,000lb) Pratt & Whitney JT8D-7 turbofans. 737-200 – Two 64.5kN (14,500lb) JT8D-9As, or two 68.9kN (15,500lb) JT8D-15s, or two 71.2kN (16,000lb) JT8D-17s, or two 77.4kN (17,400lb) JT8D-17Rs with automatic reverse thrust.

Performance: 737-100 – Max speed 943km/h (509kt), economical cruising speed 852km/h (460kt). Range with max fuel 2855km (1540nm). 737-200 – Max speed 943km/h (509kt), max cruising speed 927km/h (500kt), economical cruising speed 796km/h (430kt). Range with 115 passengers and reserves between 3520km (1900nm) and 4260km (2300nm) depending on weight options and engines.

Weights: 737-100 – Empty 25,878kg (57,000lb), max takeoff 49,940kg (110,000lb). 737-200 – Operating empty 27,448kg (60,600lb), max takeoff 52,390kg (115,500lb), or optionally 58,740kg (129,500lb).

Dimensions: 737-100 – Wing span 28.35m (93ft 0in), length 28.67m (94ft 0in), height 11.29m (37ft 0in). Wing area 91.1m^2 (980sq ft). 737-200 – Same except for length 30.53m (100ft 2in).

Capacity: Flightcrew of two. 737-100 – Typical single class seating for 100. 737-200 – Typical single class seating for 115, max seating for 130 at 74cm (29in) pitch. 737-200C & QC payload 15,545kg (34,270lb), consisting of pallets or containers.

Production: 1144 737-100s and 200s built, comprising 30 -100s and 1114 -200s, including 19 737-200 T-43A navigation trainers for the USAF and 104 737-200Cs. Approximately 3 -100s and 820 737-200s remained in service in late 2000.

History: The 737-100 and -200 are the first generation models of the world's most successful jet airliner family, Boeing's 737 twinjet.

Boeing conceived the 737 as a short range small capacity airliner to round out its jet airliner family beneath the 727, 720 and 707. Announced in February 1965, the 737 was originally envisioned as a 60 to 85 seater, although following consultation with launch customer Lufthansa, a 100 seat design was settled upon. Design features included two underwing mounted turbofans and 60% structural and systems commonality with the 727, including the same six abreast seating fuselage cross section.

The 737-100 first flew on April 9 1967 and entered service with Lufthansa in February 1968, while the last of 30 built was delivered to Malaysia-Singapore Airlines in October 1969.

By this time the larger capacity 1.93m (6ft 4in) stretched 737-200 was in service. The first 737-200 had flown for the first time on August 8 1967, with first delivery, to United, that December.

Developments of the -200 include the -200C convertible and quick change -200QC, while an unprepared airfield kit was also offered. The definitive Advanced 737-200 appeared in 1971, featuring minor aerodynamic refinements and other improvements.

Sales of the 737-200 far exceeded that of the shorter -100 and the 737-200 remained in production until 1988, by which time it had been superseded by the improved 737-300, after 1114 had been built. Many of those still in service have been fitted with Stage 3 engine hushkits.

Photo: A 737-200 of Argentina's LAPA. (Rob Finlayson)

Boeing 737-300

Country of origin: United States of America

Type: Short to medium range narrowbody airliner

Powerplants: Two 89.0kN (20,000lb) CFM International CFM56-3B-1 turbofans, or optionally two 97.9kN (22,000lb) CFM56-3B-2s.

Performance: Max cruising speed 908km/h (491kt), long range cruising speed 794km/h (429kt). Range with 128 passengers and standard fuel 3362km (1815nm), range with 128 pax and max fuel 4973km (2685nm). High gross weight version max range 6300km (3400nm) with 140 passengers.

Weights: Operating empty 32,881kg (72,490lb), standard max takeoff 56,740kg (124,500lb), high gross weight option 62,823kg (138,500lb).

Dimensions: Wing span 28.88m (94ft 9in), length 33.40m (109ft 7in), height 11.13m (36ft 6in). Wing area 105.4m^2 (1135sq ft).

Capacity: Flightcrew of two. Typical two class seating for 128 (eight premium class four abreast and 120 economy class six abreast), standard one class seating for 141 at six abreast and 81cm (31in) pitch, max seating for 149 at 76cm (30in) pitch.

Production: Grand total 737 orders stand at over 4600, of which 1113 were for the -300. Approximately 1084 737-300s were in airline service at late 2000.

History: The 737-300 was the first and most popular of the three member second generation CFM56 powered 737 family, which also comprises the stretched 737-400 and shortened 737-500. Now dubbed the 737 Classic family, in all 3132 737s of the three models were built between 1984 and 1999, significantly contributing to make the 737 series the world's best selling airliner family.

Boeing announced it was developing the 737-300 in March 1981. This new variant started off as a simple stretch over the 737-200 but Boeing decided to adopt the CFM International CFM56 high bypass turbofan (jointly developed by General Electric and SNECMA) to reduce fuel consumption and comply with the then proposed International Civil Aviation Organisation Stage 3 noise limits.

Despite the all new engines and the 2.64m (104in) fuselage stretch, the 737-300 retains 80% airframe spares commonality and shares the same ground handling equipment with the 737-200. A number of aerodynamic improvements were incorporated to further improve efficiency including modified leading edge slats and a new dorsal fin extending from the tail. Another feature was the flattened, oval shaped engine nacelles for the larger fan diameter CFM56s, while the nosewheel leg was extended to increase ground clearance for the new engines.

Other internal changes included materials and systems improvements first developed for the 757 and 767 programs, including an early generation EFIS flightdeck with four colour CRT screens.

The 737-300 first flew on February 24 1984, with first deliveries in November that year. Through to 1999 1113 737-300s were built, and it forms the backbone of many airlines' short haul fleets across the globe. The final 737-300 was delivered to Air New Zealand on December 17 1999.

The 737-300's 1113 production run was just one short of the 737-200's 1114, making the latter the most popular 737 model.

Photo: A 737-300 of Chinese airline Zhongyuan Airlines. (Sam Chui)

Boeing 737-400

Country of origin: United States of America

Type: Short to medium range airliner

Powerplants: Two 97.9kN (22,000lb) CFM International CFM56-3B-2 turbofans, or optionally 104.5kN (23,500lb) CFM56-3C-1s.

Performance: Max cruising speed 912km/h (492kt), long range cruising speed 813km/h (439kt). Standard version range with max payload 4005km (2160nm), typical range with 146 passengers 3630km (1960km). High gross weight option range with 146 passengers 3850km (2080nm).

Weights: Standard version operating empty 34,564kg (76,200lb), max takeoff 62,820kg (138,500lb). High gross weight operating empty 34,827kg (76,780lb), max takeoff 68,040kg (150,000lb).

Dimensions: Wing span 28.88m (94ft 9in), length 36.45m (119ft 7in), height 11.13m (36ft 6in). Wing area 105.4m² (1135sq ft).

Capacity: Flightcrew of two. Typical two class seating for 146 (eight premium, 138 economy), typical all economy for 159 at 81cm (32in) pitch, or max seating for 168.

Production: Total 737-400 production of 486, with the last delivered in January 2000. Of those approximately 477 were in airline service at late 2000.

History: Boeing announced it was developing a new higher capacity version of the fast selling 737-300 in June 1986.

The new aeroplane, the 737-400, was developed as a 150 seat class 727 replacement. Although Boeing had initially developed the 180 to 200 seat 757 to replace the successful 727, there still existed a considerable market for a near direct size replacement for the popular trijet. By developing the 737-400 as a minimum change stretch of the 737-300, Boeing was also able to offer considerable commonality, and thus cost, benefits to operators already with the 737-300, and to a lesser extent, the 737-200 in their fleets.

The major change to the 737-400 over the smaller -300 is a 3.05m (10ft 0in) fuselage stretch, consisting of a 1.83m (6ft 0in) stretch forward and a 1.22m (4ft 0in) plug rear of the wing. The stretch increases maximum passenger seating to 188. To cope with the increased weights, more powerful CFM56s are fitted. Other changes were minor, such as a tail bumper fitted to protect against over rotation at takeoff, something that could have become a problem due to the increased fuselage length.

A higher gross weight longer range version was also offered. It introduced increased fuel capacity plus strengthened undercarriage and structures, but was otherwise identical to the standard 737-400.

The 737-400 first flew on February 19 1988 and it entered airline service in October that year with Piedmont. Of the 737-300/-400/-500 Classic family the -400 proved the second most popular, its larger capacity and transcontinental US range meaning it found a very useful market for Boeing as a 727 replacement. The last 737-400 (and last 737 Classic) was delivered to CSA Czech Airlines on February 25 2000 (after rollout on December 9 1999). The -400 was replaced in the Boeing line-up by the Next Generation 737-800.

Photo: A 737-400 of new Australian domestic airline Virgin Blue. The 737-400 can be distinguished from the -300 by its two above wing emergency exits, rather than one. (Paul Merritt)

Boeing 737-500

Country of origin: United States of America

Type: Short to medium range airliner

Powerplants: Two 82.3kN (18,500lb) CFM International CFM56-3B-1 turbofans, or 89.0kN (20,000lb) CFM56-3C-1s.

Performance: Max cruising speed 912km/h (492kt), economical cruising speed 795km/h (430kt). Standard range with max passengers 2815km (1520nm), higher gross weight option range with max passengers 4444km (2400nm).

Weights: Operating empty (standard and high gross weight models) 31,983kg (70,510lb), standard max takeoff 52,390kg (115,500lb), high gross weight max takeoff 60,555kg (133,500lb).

Dimensions: Wing span 28.88m (94ft 9in), length 31.01m (101ft 9in), height 11.13m (36ft 6in). Wing area 105.4m² (1135sq ft).

Capacity: Flightcrew of two. Typical two class seating for 108 (eight first and 100 economy), or max single class seating for 132 at 76cm (30in) pitch.

Production: Total 737-500 production of 389, with the last delivered in 1999. Of those 384 were in airline service at late 2000.

History: The 737-500 was the shortest and smallest member of the second generation 737-300/-400/-500 Classic family, and the last to be developed.

When the new stretched 737-300 first appeared it was intended to supplement, rather than replace, the 737-200. However the evolution of the 737-300 into a family of models led to the development of a new model comparable in size to the 737-200, but offering better fuel economy and extensive commonality with the 737-300 and -400 models. This was the 737-500, known before its May 1987 formal launch as the 737-1000.

Like the preceding 737-300 and 737-400, the 737-500 is powered by CFM International CFM56s turbofans, in this case either 82.3kN (18,500lb) CFM56-3B-1s or 89.0kN (20,000lb) CFM56-3C-1s. All three second generation 737 models share extensive systems and structure commonality, and a common aircrew type rating. These benefits offer real cost savings to an airline with two or more variants of the family in its fleet.

The 737-500 is 31.01m (101ft 9in) in length, comparable to the 737-200's 30.53m (100ft 2in). Like the -300 and -400, a higher gross weight longer range version was offered, featuring auxiliary fuel tanks and uprated engines.

The 737-500's first flight occurred on June 30 1989, FAA certification was awarded on February 12 1990, with service entry later that same month. The last of 389 was delivered to All Nippon on July 21 1999.

The 737-500' appeals most to airlines with large 737-400 and 737-300 fleets. Because the -500 is a shortened development of the -300, it still carries much of the structural weight needed for the higher weight models, which makes it less efficient than if it was designed specifically for its size category. However for 737-300/-400 operators, the extensive commonality benefits (including crewing) more than compensate for this.

Photo: A 737-5L9 of British Airways franchise airline Maersk Air. (Keith Gaskell)

Boeing 737-600 & -700

Country of origin: United States of America

Type: Short to medium range narrowbody airliners

Powerplants: 737-600 – Two 86.7kN (19,500lb) CFM56-7B18 turbofans, or 101kN (20,600lb) CFM56-7B22s on high gross weight version. 737-700 – Two 91.6kN (20,600lb) CFM56-7B20s or 101kN (22,700lb) CFM56-7B24s on HGW version.

Performance: Typical cruising speed Mach 0.785. Max certificated altitude 41,000ft. 737-600 – Range with 110 pax 2480km (1340nm) or 5648km (3050nm) for HGW version. 737-700 – Range with 126 pax 2852km (1540nm) or 6037km (3260nm) for HGW version.

Weights: 737-600 – Operating empty 37,104kg (81,800lb), max take-off 56,245kg (124,000lb), HGW max takeoff 65,090kg (143,500lb). 737-700 – Operating empty 38,147kg (84,100lb), max takeoff 60,330kg (133,000lb), HGW max takeoff 70,080kg (154,500lb).

Dimensions: 737-600 – Wing span 34.31m (112ft 7in), length 31.24m (102ft 6in), height 12.57m (41ft 3in). Wing area 125.0m² (1344sq ft). 737-700 – Same except length 33.63m (110ft 4in), height 12.55m (41ft 2in).

Capacity: Two flightcrew. 737-600 – 110 two class passengers or 132 single class. 737-700 – 126 in two classes or 149 in a single class.

Production: 86 737-600s ordered and 38 delivered at late 2000; 781 737-700s ordered with 254 delivered at late 2000.

History: The 737-600 and -700 are the smaller members of Boeing's successful Next Generation 737-600/-700/-800/-900 family.

The improved Next Generation Boeing 737 family (originally covered by the 737-X designation) was launched in November 1993. The 737-700 was the first member of the new family to be developed, and is based on the 737-300, while the 737-600 is based on the 737-500.

The 737-700 rolled out on December 7 1996, was certificated in November 1997 and entered service (with Southwest) the following month. The 737-600 was launched on March 15 1995, first flew on January 22 1998, and entered service (with SAS) that September.

Among the many changes, the Next Generation 737s feature more efficient CFM56-7B turbofans. The CFM56-7 combines the core of the CFM56-5 with the CFM56-3's low pressure compressor and a 1.55m (61in) fan. The 737's new wing has greater chord, span and wing area, while the tail surfaces are also larger. The 2.4m (8ft) high winglets first developed for the Boeing Business Jet development are now offered as an option on the 737-700 (and -800).

The Next Generation 737s cruise at Mach 0.78 to Mach 0.80, while the larger wing allows greater fuel tankage and transcontinental USA range. Other features include a 777 style EFIS flightdeck with six flat panel LCDs which can be programmed to present information as on the 777 or as on the 737-300/-400/-500 series, the latter allowing a common pilot type rating for the two 737 families.

The Boeing Business Jet or BBJ (described separately) is based on the fuselage of the 737-700 with the larger 737-800's wing. The BBJ's airframe also forms the basis for the convertible passenger/freighter variant of the -700, the 737-700QC, which has been ordered by the US Navy as the C-40A (to replace the DC-9 based C-9 Skytrain II). The C-40 first flew on April 17 2000.

Photo: A Midway 737-700. (Rob Finlayson)

Boeing 737-800 & -900

Country of origin: United States of America

Type: Short to medium range narrowbody airliners

Powerplants: 737-800 – Two 107.6kN (24,200lb) CFM56-7B24s, or two 121.4kN (27,300lb) CFM56-7B27s on high gross weight versions. 737-900 – Two 117kN (26,300lb) CFM56-7B26s, or 121.4kN (27,300lb) CFM56-7B27s in high gross weight versions.

Performance: Typical cruising speed Mach 0.785. Max certificated altitude 41,000ft. 737-800 – Standard range with 162 passengers 3685km (1990nm) or 5445km (2940nm) for high gross weight version. 737-900 – Standard range with 177 passengers 3815km (2060nm), high gross weight version 5083km (2458nm).

Weights: 737-800 – Operating empty 41,145kg (90,710lb), max take-off 70,535kg (155,500lb), high gross weight max takeoff 79,015kg (174,200lb). 737-900 – Operating empty 42,493kg (93,680lb), max takeoff 74,840kg (164,000lb), HGW max takeoff 79,015kg (174,200lb).

Dimensions: 737-800 – Wing span 34.31m (112ft 7in), length 39.47m (129ft 6in), height 12.55m (41ft 2in). Wing area 125.0m² (1344sq ft). 737-900 – Same except length 42.11m (138ft 2in).

Capacity: Flightcrew of two. 737-800 – Typical two class seating for 162 with 12 first class passengers at four abreast and 91cm (36in) pitch and 150 economy class at six abreast and 81cm (32in) pitch. Max single class seating for 189 at 76cm (30in) pitch. 737-900 – Typical two class seating for 177, with 12 first class at four abreast and 91cm (36in) pitch, max seating for 189 in a single class at 81cm (32in) pitch.

Production: 766 737-800s ordered by late 2000 with 370 delivered, while 46 737-900s were on order, first deliveries planned for 2001.

History: Boeing's Next Generation 737-800 and 737-900 are the largest members of the strong selling 737 family. Unlike the other Next Generation 737s, the -800 and -900 introduce new fuselage lengths, extending 737 single class seating range out to 189, compared with 100 in the original 737-100.

Like the -600 and -700, the -800 and -900 feature the Next Generation improvements including more efficient CFM56-7B turbofans, the new wing with greater chord, span and wing area, larger tail surfaces and the 777 style EFIS flightdeck with six flat panel LCDs which can present information as on the 777 or as on the 737-300/-400/-500 series, the latter allowing a common pilot type rating for the two 737 families. BBJ style winglets are now offered as options on the -800.

Until its launch on September 5 1994 the 737-800 was known as the 737-400X Stretch. Compared with the -400 the -800 is 3.02m (9ft 9in) longer, taking typical two class seating from 146 to 162, while range is significantly increased. The -800 has sold strongly since its launch, and at late 2000 was just a handful of units behind the 737-700, then the highest selling Next Generation model. First flight was on July 31 1997, first delivery (to Hapag Lloyd) was in April 1998.

The 737-900 is the largest and latest member of the 737 family, and was launched on September 10 1997 with an order for 10 from Alaska Airlines. A 1.57m (5ft 2in) plug forward of the wing and a 1.07m (3ft 6in) plug rear compared with the -800 increases seating to 177 in two classes (maximum seating is the same as the 737-800's due to emergency exit requirements). First flight was on August 3 2000.

Photo: The 737-900 first flew on August 3 2000.

Boeing 747-100 & -200

Country of origin: United States of America

Type: Long range high capacity widebody airliners

Powerplants: 747-200B – Four 243.5kN (54,750lb) Pratt & Whitney JT9D-7R4G2s, or four 233.5kN (52,500lb) General Electric CF6-50E2s, or 236.2kN (53,110lb) Rolls-Royce RB211-524D4s.

Performance: 747-200B – Max speed 981km/h (530kt) (with RR engines), economical cruising speed 907km/h (490kt). Range with 366 pax and reserves 12,778km (6900nm). 747-200F – Range with 90,270kg (200,000lb) payload 9075km (4900nm) with CF6-80C2s.

Weights: 747-200 – Operating empty with JT9Ds 169,960kg (374,400lb), with CF6-80C2s 172,730kg (380,800lb), with RB211s 174,000kg (383,600lb). Max takeoff 377,840kg (833,000lb). 747-200F – Operating empty with JT9Ds 155,220kg (342,200lb), max takeoff 377,840kg (833,000lb).

Dimensions: Wing span 59.64m (195ft 8in), length 70.66m (231ft 10in), height 19.33m (63ft 5in). Wing area 511m² (5500sq ft).

Capacity: Flightcrew of three (two pilots and flight engineer). Seating arrangements include 397 in three classes, 452 in two classes (32 first & 420 economy), all economy seating for 447 nine abreast or up to 500 ten abreast. 747-200F – Max payload of 112,400kg (247,800lb).

Production: 747-100/-200 in production to 1991. 167 -100s, 9 -100Bs, 29 -100SR, 224 -200Bs, 13 -200Cs, 69 -200Fs and 77 -200Ms built, plus 12 military aircraft. Approx 80 -100s and 335 -200s in service in late 2000.

History: The hugely significant 747 revolutionised airline transport. Far bigger than any airliner before it, the 747 slashed operating costs per seat and thus cut the cost of long haul international airline travel.

Boeing conceived the 747 in the mid 1960s following its missing out on a US Air Force contract for an ultra large strategic transport (which resulted in the Lockheed C-5 Galaxy), when it identified a market for a high capacity 'jumbo jet'. Boeing was able to draw upon design experience with the USAF transport and launched the new airliner on July 25 1966. First flight occurred on February 9 1969, certification was awarded on December 30 that year.

The basic 747-100 entered service with launch customer Pan American in January 1970. Progressive development of the 747 led to the 747-200B with higher weights, more powerful engines and longer range. The -200B first flew in October 1970, while nine higher weight 747-100Bs were built. Developments included the 747-200F freighter, the -100SR (short range) optimised for high cycle short sector operations and the -200C (Combi).

The 747, with its distinctive upper deck (initially used as a first class bar/lounge area before giving way to passenger seats) four double bogey main undercarriage units, and 360 plus seat passenger seating capacity was a huge leap in size over the 707s and DC-8s it would replace. It was the first aircraft to use high bypass ratio turbofans, and the first widebody, or twin aisle, airliner, with nine or 10 abreast seating in economy class.

The 747 holds a place in the public eye unlike any other aircraft. Nicknamed the 'Jumbo Jet' and 'Queen of the Skies', it successfully opened up international air travel to millions.

Photo: A Northwest Airlines 747-200 converted freighter. (Rob Finlayson)

Boeing 747SP

Country of origin: United States of America

Type: Long range high capacity widebody airliner

Powerplants: Four 218.4kN (48,750lb) Pratt & Whitney JT9D-7AW turbofans, or 222.8kN (50,100lb) Rolls-Royce RB211-524Bs or 229.5kN (51,600lb) RB211-524Cs, or 206.8kN (46,500lb) General Electric CF6-45A2s or CF6-50E2-Fs.

Performance: Max speed 1000km/h (540kt). Range with 331 passengers and baggage 10,840km (5855nm), range with 276 passengers 12,325km (6650nm), ferry range with max fuel and 13,610kg (30,000lb) payload 15,400km (8315nm).

Weights: Operating empty 147,420kg (325,000lb), max takeoff 317,515kg (700,000lb).

Dimensions: Wing span 59.64m (195ft 8in), length 56.31m (184ft 9in), height 19.94m (65ft 5in). Wing area 511m² (5500sq ft).

Capacity: Flightcrew of three comprising two pilots and one flight engineer. Max high density single class seating for 440, typical two class seating for 28 first class and 288 economy class passengers

Production: Just 43 747SPs were built, of which 17 were in commercial service in 2000.

History: Boeing developed the 747SP ('Special Performance') in the mid 1970s as a longer range, shortened 747, trading passenger seating for range.

The 747SP first flew on July 4 1975, certification was awarded on February 4 1976 and first delivery (to Pan American) was in March 1976.

The 747SP's fuselage is shortened by 14.35m (47ft 1in) compared to other 747 models, while its vertical tail was increased in height to compensate for the shorter fuselage. Structurally the 747SP was lightened in some areas because of the significant reduction in gross weights. Overall though the 747SP retained 90% commonality of components with the 747-100 and -200. While shortening the 747's fuselage increased the fuel fraction and thus range, it also meant that seating capacity was reduced, typically to 316 in two classes.

The 747SP's range was well illustrated by the delivery flight of a South African Airways SP, which over March 23/24 1976 flew nonstop with 50 passengers from Paine Field in Washington State to Cape Town, South Africa, a distance of 16,560km (8940nm). This world nonstop record for a commercial aircraft stood until 1989 when a Qantas 747-400 flew 17,945km (9688nm) nonstop from London to Sydney.

Sales of the 747SP were modest despite the increased range, as the SP had poorer operating economics per seat compared to the 747-200. However the 747SP did pioneer a number of long range nonstop services that are now commonly flown by the 747-400.

Notable SP customers included South African Airways (who found the SP's extended range a great asset in bypassing African nations that denied it landing rights while South Africa's apartheid policies were in place), Qantas and PanAm, the latter pioneering nonstop trans Pacific Los Angeles/Sydney services.

In 2000 two ex PanAm 747SPs flew on with United Airlines, while other operators included Qantas, Syrianair and Iran Air.

Photo: South African Airways operates two 747SPs. (Rob Finlayson)

Boeing 747-300

Country of origin: United States of America

Type: Long range high capacity widebody airliner

Powerplants: Four 243.5kN (54,750lb) Pratt & Whitney JT9D-7R4G2 turbofans, or 236.3kN (53,110lb) Rolls-Royce RB211-524D4s, or 233.5kN (52,500kN) General Electric CF6-50E2s, or 252.2kN (56,700lb) CF6-80C2B1s.

Performance: Max speed (with CF6-80s) 996km/h (538kt), max cruising speed 939km/h (507kt), economical cruising speed 907km/h (490kt), long range cruising speed 898km/h (485kt). Range with 400 passengers and reserves with JT9Ds 11,675km (6300nm), with CF6-50s 11,297km (6100nm), with CF6-80s 12,408km (6700nm), with RB211s 11,575km (6250nm).

Weights: Operating empty 174,134kg (383,900lb) with JT9Ds, 175,721kg (387,400lb) with CF6-50s, 176,901kg (390,000lb) with CF6-80s or 178,171kg (392,800lb) with RB211s. Max takeoff 351,535kg (775,000lb), or 356,070kg (785,000lb), or 362,875kg (800,000lb), or 371,945kg (820,000lb), or 377,840kg (833,000lb).

Dimensions: Wing span 59.64m (195ft 8in), length 70.66m (231ft 10in), height 19.33m (63ft 5in). Wing area 511m² (5500sq ft).

Capacity: 747-300 – Flightcrew of three, with two pilots and one flight engineer. Typical two class seating arrangement for 470 (50 business class including 28 on the upper deck and 370 economy class).

Production: 81 delivered 1983-90 with 75 in service in late 2000.

History: Boeing's 747-300 was the first 747 model with increased passenger capacity, introducing the distinctive stretched upper deck which can seat up to 69 economy class passengers.

The 747-300 was the end result of a number of Boeing studies which looked at increasing the 747's seating capacity. Concepts studied included fuselage plugs fore and aft of the wing increasing seating to around 600, or running the upper deck down the entire length of the fuselage. In the end Boeing launched the more modest 747SUD (Stretched Upper Deck) development on June 12 1980.

The 747SUD designation was soon changed to 747EUD (for Extended Upper Deck), and then 747-300. The new model first flew on October 5 1982 and was first delivered to Swissair on March 28 1983.

Compared to the -200, the -300's upper deck is stretched aft by 7.11m (23ft 4in), increasing economy class seating from 32 to a maximum of 69. The lengthened upper deck features two new emergency exit doors and allows an optional flightcrew rest area immediately aft of the flightdeck to be fitted. Access is via a conventional rather than spiral staircase as on the earlier models.

Otherwise the 747-300 is essentially little changed from the 747-200 and features the same takeoff weight and engine options. 747-300 variants include the 747-300M Combi and the short range 747-300SR built for Japan Air Lines for Japanese domestic services.

The extended upper deck was also offered as a retrofit to existing 747-100/-200s, although the only airline to take up this option was KLM. KLM later converted two to freighters, resulting in the first 747 freighters with the stretched upper deck. Boeing's own 747-300 freighter conversions, the 747-300 Special Freighter, was first delivered to Atlas Air in October 2000.

Photo: A Japanese Airlines 747-300SR. (Craig Murray)

Boeing 747-400 & Longer-Range 747-400

Country of origin: United States of America

Type: Long range high capacity widebody airliner

Powerplants: Four 252.4kN (56,750lb) Pratt & Whitney PW4056 turbofans or 266.9kN (60,000lb) PW4060s, or 275.8kN (62,000lb) PW4062s, 252.4kN (56,750lb) General Electric CF6-80C2B1Fs or 273.6kN (61,500lb) CF6-80C2B1F1s or -80C2B7Fs, or 258.0kN (58,000lb) Rolls-Royce RB211-524G or -524Hs, or 262.4 to 266.9kN (59 to 60,000lb) RB211-524G/H-Ts.

Performance: Max cruising speed 939km/h (507kt), long range cruising speed 907km/h (490kt). Design range with 420 three class pax at 396,895kg (875,000lb) MTOW 13,491km (7284nm) with PW4000s, 13,444km (7259nm) with GEs, 13,214km (7135nm) with RB211s.

Weights: Standard operating empty with PW4056s 180,985kg (399,000lb), with CF6-80C2B1Fs 180,755kg (398,500lb), with RB211s 181,755kg (400,700lb); operating weights at optional MTOW with PW4056s 181,485kg (400,100lb), with CF6-80C2B1Fs 181,255kg (399,600lb), with RB211s 182,255kg (401,800lb). Max takeoff 362,875kg (800,000lb), or optionally 377,845kg (833,000lb), or 385,555kg (850,000lb), or 396,895kg (875,000lb).

Dimensions: Wing span 64.44m (211ft 5in), length 70.67m (231ft 10in), height 19.41m (63ft 8in). Wing area 541.2m² (5825sq ft).

Capacity: 747-400 – Flightcrew of two. Typical three class seating for 416 (23 first, 78 business and 315 economy class pax). 747-400 747-400F – 30 pallets on the main deck and 32 LD1 containers in the lower hold. Max revenue payload 113 tonnes.

Production: Orders for the 747-400 as of late 2000 stood at 608 (incl 88 freighters) with 535 delivered. Total 747 sales stood at 1332.

History: The long range 747-400 is the best selling model of Boeing's 747 family.

Boeing launched the 747-400 in October 1985 and the first development aircraft first flew on April 29 1988. US certification (with PW4000s) was awarded in January 1989.

The 747-400 externally resembles the -300, but it is a significantly improved aircraft. Changes include a new, two crew digital flightdeck with six large CRT displays, an increased span wing with winglets (the -400 was the first airliner to introduce winglets), new engines, recontoured wing/fuselage fairing, a new interior, lower basic but increased max takeoff weights, and greater range.

Variants include the basic passenger 747-400, the winglet-less 747-400 Domestic optimised for Japanese short haul domestic sectors (seating up to 568), the 747-400M Combi passenger/freight model, and the 747-400F Freighter (which combines the 747-200F's fuselage with the -400's wing).

On November 28 2000 Boeing launched the Longer-Range 747-400, following a launch order for six from Australian airline Qantas. The Longer-Range 747-400 (previously the 747-400X) will have the 747-400F's stronger wing, increased fuel capacity, a 413,140kg (910,825lb) max takeoff weight, 265 to 282kN (59,500 to 63,300lb) thrust class engines, a 14,240km (7690nm) range, an upgraded LCD glass flightdeck based on that in the 777, and a revised interior, again based on the 777's. Service entry will be in 2002.

Photo: A Qantas 747-400 in F1 Grand Prix markings. (Sam Chui)

Boeing 747X & 747X Stretch

Country of origin: United States of America

Type: Long range high capacity widebody airliners

Powerplants: 747X & 747X Stretch – 302.5kN (68,000lb) class Engine Alliance GP7168 or Rolls-Royce Trent turbofans.

Performance: 747X – Cruising speed Mach 0.86. Range with 430 passengers 16,650km (8985nm). 747X Stretch – Cruising speed Mach 0.86. Range with 504 passengers 14,445km (7800nm). 747X Stretch Freighter – Range with 150t payload 8100km (3400nm).

Weights: 747X – Max zero fuel weight 290,300kg (640,000lb), max takeoff 473,100kg (1,043,000lb). 747X Stretch – Max zero fuel weight 308,440kg (680,000lb), max takeoff 473,100kg (1,043,000lb).

Dimensions: 747X – Wing span 69.8m (228ft 11in), length 73.5m (241ft 0in), height 21.5m (70ft 5in). 747X – Wing span 69.8m (228ft 11in), length 79.8m (262ft 0in), height 19.9m (65ft 2in).

Capacity: 747X – Flightcrew of two. Typical three class seating for 430 or 442 with optional overhead crew berths and galley stowage. 747X Stretch. Typical three class seating for 504 or 522 with optional overhead crew berths and galley stowage. High density version could seat up to 660 in a single class. 747X Stretch Freighter – Payload 150 tonnes (330,400lb), total cargo volume 892m² (9601sq ft).

Production: Boeing forecasts a market for 1010 747 size and larger aircraft to 2020, of which 330 will be for 500+ seaters.

History: The 747X and 747X Stretch and longer range and higher capacity developments of the 747-400.

Boeing has studied various growth 747 models over the last few years. In 1996 Boeing was close to launching the 747-500X and -600X models, but dropped the program in January 1997. The 747-500X would have featured a 5.6m (16.4ft) stretch, seating for 462 and a range of 16,100km (8700nm). The larger 747-600X was to be further stretched to 85m (279ft), seat 548 and have a 14,350km (7750nm) range. Both would have had a new 777 style flightdeck, fly-by-wire controls, a new wing and new engines.

Against a backdrop of increased interest in Airbus' 550 seat A3XX, in June 2000 Boeing revealed details of its proposed new 747X family (as well as the 747-400X, described in the 747-400 entry). Three 747X models were announced, the slightly stretched, 430 seat ultra long range (16,650km/8985nm) 747X, and the stretched, 504 seat 747X Stretch, plus the 150 tonne payload 747X Stretch Freighter.

Other changes would include a new glass cockpit based on that in the 777 (while still allowing a common type rating with the 747-400), a modified wing with slightly increased span (giving 17% more area and 27 more fuel capacity of the 747-400 wing), all new main landing gear, 777 style overhead 'pivot' bins, and a Mach 0.86 cruise speed.

Boeing is offering the 747X/747X Stretch with the option of crew berths and galley cart stowage relocated above the rear main cabin in the crown of the fuselage, freeing main deck space for extra seats. Alternatively the crown space could be used for passenger sleeping berths.

If the 747X/74X Stretch is launched in the first half of 2001 it could enter service in late 2005. Boeing says the development cost for the program is in the region of $US4-6bn.

Photo: The 747X Stretch. (Boeing)

Boeing 757-200

Country of origin: United States of America

Type: Medium range narrowbody airliner

Powerplants: Two 178.8kN (40,200lb) Rolls-Royce RB211-535E4 turbofans, or 193.5kN (43,500lb) RB211-535E4-B2, or 162.8kN (36,600lb) Pratt & Whitney PW2037s, or 178.4kN (40,100lb) PW2040s, or 189.5kN (42,600lb) PW2043s.

Performance: Max cruising speed 914km/h (493kt), economical cruising speed 850km/h (460kt). Range with 201 passengers and PW2037s 4760km (2570nm), with PW2040s 7280km (3920nm), with RB211-535E4s 4400km (2375nm), with RB211-535E4-Bs 6845km (3695nm). 757-200PF – Speeds same. Range with 22,680kg payload and P&W engines 7195km (3885nm), with RR engines 6857km (3700nm).

Weights: Operating empty with PW2037s 58,325kg (128,580lb), with PW2040s 58,390kg (128,730lb), with RB211-535E4s 58,550kg (129,080lb), with RB211-535E4-Bs 58,620kg (129,230lb). Max takeoff with PW2037s or RB211-535E4s 99,790kg (220,000lb), with PW2040s or RB211-535E4-Bs 115,665kg (255,000lb) or 115,895kg (255,550lb).

Dimensions: Wing span 38.05m (124ft 10in), length 47.32m (155ft 3in), height 13.56m (44ft 6in). Wing area 185.3m² (1994sq ft).

Capacity: Flightcrew of two. 757-200 – Typical passenger arrangements vary from 178 two class (16 first & 162 economy), or 201 (12 first & 189 economy) or 208 (12 first and 196 economy) or 214 to 239 in all economy class. 757-200PF – Maximum of 15 standard 2.24 x 2.74m (88 x 108in) freight pallets on main deck.

Production: 997 757-200s had been ordered by late 2000, of which over 930 had been delivered. Total 757 sales stand at 1026.

History: After a slow sales start, the medium range single aisle 757 has become yet another sales success story for Boeing.

Boeing considered a number of proposals for a successor to the 727 trijet during the 1970s, with many of these designs featuring the nose and T-tail of the earlier jet. It was not until later in that decade however that Boeing settled on a more conventional design featuring the same cross section as the 727 (not to mention the 737, 707 and 720) but with the fuselage considerably longer in length, an all new wing, nose and flightdeck and fuel efficient high bypass turbofan engines.

Boeing launched development of the 757 in March 1979 following orders from British Airways and Eastern. Developed in tandem with the larger widebody 767 the two types share a number of systems and technologies, including a common early generation EFIS flightdeck.

First flight was on February 19 1982 and the 757 entered service in January the following year. Subsequent versions to appear are the 757-200PF Package Freighter, a pure freighter, and the 757-200M Combi (only one has been built). The stretched 757-300 is described separately.

The 757-200SF (Special Freighter) is a freighter conversion of passenger 757-200s offered by Boeing Airplane Services. DHL will be the launch operator, with converted ex British Airways aircraft.

Boeing has also studied the longer range 757-200X which would feature the strengthened wing of the 757-300, auxiliary fuel and a 9260km (5000nm) range, and the 757 based BBJ 3.

Photo: An America West 757-200 (with RB211s). (Rob Finlayson)

Boeing 757-300

Country of origin: United States of America

Type: Medium range narrowbody airliner

Powerplants: Two 193.5kN (43,500lb) Rolls-Royce RB211-535E4-B turbofans, or 178.8kN (40,200lb) RB211-535E4s, or 189.5kN (42,600lb) Pratt & Whitney PW2043s, or 178.4kN (40,100lb) PW2040s.

Performance: Cruising speed Mach 0.80. Range with PW2040s 4137km (2234nm), with PW2043s 6417km (3465nm), with RB211-535E4s 3805km (2055nm), or with RB211-535E4-Bs 6000km (3240nm).

Weights: Operating empty with RB211s 63,855kg (140,780lb), with PW2000s 63,655kg (140,330lb), max takeoff with PW2040s/535-E4s 108,860kg (240,000lb), with PW2043/535E4-Bs 122,470kg (270,000lb).

Dimensions: Wing span 38.05m (124ft 10in), length 54.43m (178ft 7in), height 13.56m (44ft 6in). Wing area 185.3m² (1994sq ft).

Capacity: Flightcrew of two. Typical two class arrangement seats 243 passengers (12 first and 231 economy class). Max seating for 279 passengers in a high density configuration 71-74cm (28-29in) pitch.

Production: Total 757-300 orders stood at 44 at late 2000, of which 15 had been delivered.

History: The stretched, 240 seat Boeing 757-300 is the first significant variant of the basic 757-200 and was developed in part with the European vacation charter market in mind.

Although design work on the original 757 began in the late 1970s and its entry into service was in 1983, it wasn't until over a decade later in the mid 1990s that Boeing began to study a stretched development of its popular narrowbody twin. This new 757 stretch was covered by the 757-300X designation until its launch at the Farnborough Airshow in England in September 1996.

The most obvious change over the 757-200 is the -300's 54.43m (178ft 7in) long fuselage, which is 7.11m (23ft 4in) longer than the standard aircraft (and only fractionally shorter than the 767-300). This fuselage stretch allows a 20% increase in seating to 225 to 279 passengers, depending on the interior configuration. Lower hold freight capacity is also increased by 40% over the 757-200 by virtue of the longer fuselage.

Another feature of the 757-300 is its new interior which is based on that developed for the Next Generation 737 models. Features include a new sculptured ceiling, larger overhead bins, indirect overhead lighting and vacuum toilets.

The 757-300 shares the -200's cockpit, wing, tail and powerplant options, although the -300 features strengthened structure and landing gear to cope with the increased weights, new wheels, tyres and brakes, and a tailskid.

The 757-300 first flew on August 3 1998, with certification awarded on January 27 1999. Entry into service with launch customer Condor (the charter arm of German carrier Lufthansa) was in March that year.

The -300's 29 month development program from final configuration to planned first delivery is the fastest for any Boeing airliner (the 777-300 took 31 months for example). Other customers at late 2000 were Icelandair, Arkia Israeli Airlines, American Trans Air, JMC Airlines and Continental.

Photo: Boeing claims the 757-300 has the lowest operating costs per seat of any narrowbody airliner. (Viktor László)

Boeing 767-200

Country of origin: United States of America

Type: Medium to long range widebody airliner

Powerplants: 767-200 – Two 213.5kN (48,000lb) Pratt & Whitney JT9D-7R4D turbofans, or 222.4kN (50,000lb) PW4050s, or 233.5kN (52,500lb) General Electric CF6-80C2B2s. 767-200ER – Two PW4050s (as above), or 231kN (52,000lb) PW4052s, or 252.4kN (56,750lb) PW4056s, or 257.7kN (57,900lb) CF6-80C2B4Fs.

Performance: 767-200 – Max cruising speed 914km/h (493kt), economical cruising speed 854km/h (461kt). Range of basic aircraft with JT9Ds 5855km (3160nm), medium range version with CF6s 7135km (3850nm). 767-200ER – Speeds same. Range with PW4056s 12,269km (6625nm), with CF6s 12,352km (6670nm).

Weights: 767-200 – Empty with JT9Ds 74,752kg (164,800lb), with CF6s 74,344kg (163,900lb). Operating empty with JT9Ds 80,920kg (178,400lb), with CF6s 80,510kg (177,500lb). Max takeoff 136,078kg (300,000lb), medium range max takeoff 142,881kg (315,000lb). 767-200ER – Empty with PW4056s 76,566kg (168,800lb), with CF6-80C2B4s 76,476kg (168,600lb), operating empty with PW4056s 84,415kg (186,100lb), with CF6-80C2B4Fs 84,370kg (186,000lb). Max takeoff with PW4056s or CF6-80C2B4Fs 175,540kg (387,000lb).

Dimensions: Wing span 47.57m (156ft 1in), length 48.51m (159ft 2in), height 15.85m (52ft 0in). Wing area 283.3m² (3050sq ft).

Capacity: Flightcrew of two, or optionally three. Typical two class seating for 18 premium and 198 economy class pax. Max seating for 290 at eight abreast and 76cm (30in) pitch. Underfloor cargo holds can accommodate up to 22 LD2 containers.

Production: Total 767 sales of 902 at late 2000. Total 767-200/200ER orders stood at 239, of which 231 had been delivered.

History: The narrowest widebody in service, the 767 started life as an advanced technology mid to large size airliner in the late 1970s.

Launched in July 1978, the 767 was developed in tandem with the narrowbody 757 with which it shares a common two crew EFIS flightdeck (with six colour CRT displays) and many systems. The 767 also features a unique width fuselage typically seating seven abreast in economy, and a new wing design with greater sweepback (compared to the 757) which was designed with high altitude cruise in mind.

The 767 program also features a high degree of international participation, with Japanese companies in particular having a large share of construction.

Initially Boeing intended to offer two versions, the longer 767-200 and short fuselage 767-100 (which was not launched as it was too close in capacity to the 757). The 767 first flew on September 26 1981, and entered service (with United) on September 26 1982 (certification with P&W engines was awarded on July 30 1982).

The longer range 767-200ER (Extended Range) version features higher weights and an additional wing centre section fuel tank. It first flew on March 6 1984, and service entry, with Ethiopian Airlines, was two months later. The -200ER accounts for 111 of the total 239 767-200s ordered.

The last airliner 767-200/-200ER was delivered in 1994 until a November 1998 order from Continental saw it return to production.

Photo: A Malev Hungarian Airlines 767-200. (John Adlard)

Boeing 767-300

Country of origin: United States of America

Type: Medium to long range widebody airliner

Powerplants: Two 213.5kN (48,000lb) Pratt & Whitney JT9D-7R4 turbofans or 222.4kN (50,000lb) JT9D-7R4Es, or 222.4kN (50,000lb) PW4050s, or 233.5kN (52,000lb) PW4052s, or 213.5kN (48,000lb) General Electric CF6-80As or 213.5kN (48,000lb) CF6-80A2s, or 231.3kN (52,500lb) CF6-80C2B2s, or 257.5kN (57,900lb) CF6-80C2B4Fs, or 269.9kN (60,000lb) Rolls-Royce RB211-524Gs. 767-300ER – Same options or 252.4kN (56,750lb) PW4056s or 266.9kN (60,000lb) CF6-80C2B6s.

Performance: 767-300 – Max cruising speed 900km/h (486kt), economical cruising speed 850km/h (460kt). HGW version range with design payload and PW4050s 7835km (4230nm), with CF6-80C2B2s 7890km (4260nm). 767-300ER – Range with design payload with PW4060s 10,880km (5875nm), with CF6-80C2B4Fs 10,195km (5505nm).

Weights: 767-300 – Empty with PW4050s 79,560kg (175,400lb), with CF6-80C2B2s 79,379kg (175,000lb). Operating empty with PW4050s 87,135kg (192,100lb), with CF6-80C2B2s 86,955kg (191,700lb). Higher gross weight version max takeoff with PW4050s or CF6-80C2B2s 159,210kg (351,000lb). 767-300ER – Empty with PW4060s 81,374kg (179,400lb), with CF6-80C2B4s 80,603kg (177,700lb). Operating empty with PW4060s 90,535kg (199,600lb), with CF6-80C2B4s 90,175kg (198,800lb). Max takeoff with PW4060s 181,890kg (401,000lb), with CF6-80C2B4Fs 175,540kg (387,000lb).

Dimensions: Wing span 47.57m (156ft 1in), length 54.94m (180ft 3in), height 15.85m (52ft 0in). Wing area 283.3m² (3050sq ft).

Capacity: Flightcrew of two. Typical three class layout for 210, two class 269 (24 premium & 245 economy seven abreast) max seating for 350 at eight abreast. Underfloor capacity for 20 LD2s.

Production: 615 767-300s (comprising 104 -300s, 475 -300ERs & 36 -300Fs) ordered by late 2000, of which 569 had been delivered.

History: Boeing announced that it was developing a stretched development of the 767-200 in February 1982.

The resulting 767-300 features a 6.42m (21ft 1in) stretch consisting of fuselage plugs forward (3.07m/10ft 1in) and behind (3.35m/11ft) the wing centre section. The flightdeck and systems were carried directly over from the 767-200, the only other changes were minor, and related to the increased weights of the new version. Initially the max takeoff weight was the same as the later 767-200ER.

The 767-300 first flew on January 30 1986, and was awarded certification and entered service in September that year. The higher weight Extended Range ER version first flew on December 19 1986, while Rolls-Royce RB211-524G engines became available from 1989.

In 1993 Boeing launched the 767-300F General Market Freighter. Changes include strengthened undercarriage and wing structure, a cargo handling system, no cabin windows and a main deck freight door. Capacity is 24 containers.

In 2000 Boeing was studying the 14,170km (7650nm) range 767-300ERX with increased fuel, more powerful engines, and the 777 style flightdeck from the stretched 767-400ER (described separately).

Photo: A Lan Chile 767-300. (Rob Finlayson)

Boeing 767-400ER

Country of origin: United States of America

Type: Long range widebody airliner

Powerplants: 767-400ER – Two 281.6kN (63,300lb) Pratt & Whitney PW4062 turbofans, or two 282.5kN (63,500lb) General Electric CF6-80C2B8Fs. Longer Range 767-400ER – Two 320kN (72,000lb) class Rolls-Royce Trent 600 or Engine Alliance GP7172 turbofans.

Performance: 767-400ER – Typical cruising speed 854km/h (461kt). Design range at max takeoff weight with max passengers 10,343km (5580nm) with PW4062s, 10,418km (5625nm) with CF6-80C2B8Fs. LR 767-400ER – Max range 11,390km (6150nm).

Weights: 767-400ER – Operating empty with PW4062s 103,145kg (227,400lb), 103,100kg (227,300lb) with CF6-80C2B8Fs, max takeoff 204,120kg (450,000lb). LR 767-400ER – Max takeoff 210,920kg (465,000lb).

Dimensions: Wing span 51.92m (170ft 4in), length 61.36m (201ft 4in), height 16.86m (55ft 4in). Wing area 290.7m² (3129.0sq ft).

Capacity: Flightcrew of two. Typical three class arrangement for 245 passengers, comprising 20 first class at 152cm (60in) pitch, 50 business at 97cm (38in) and 175 economy at 81cm (32in). Typical two class seating for 305, single class seating for up to 375.

Production: Orders for the 767-400ER as of late 2000 stood at 48 with 12 delivered.

History: Boeing's 767-400 is a stretched, upgraded development of the popular 767-300ER, and is offered in standard 767-400ER and Longer-Range 767-400ER forms.

Design work on the then 767-400ERX began in late 1996 when Boeing enlisted engineering support from the then independent McDonnell Douglas (Boeing and McDonnell Douglas merged in August 1997). The basic 767-400ER was formally launched in January 1997 when Delta Airlines ordered 21, while first flight was on October 9 1999. First delivery was to Delta on August 29 2000.

The most significant change with the 767-400 is the 6.4m (21ft) fuselage stretch. The 767-400's wing, compared to the 767-300's, features 2.34m (7ft 8in) long raked wingtips which improve aerodynamic efficiency. Winglets were originally considered but the wingtip extensions proved more efficient. The wing is also made from increased gauge aluminium with thicker spars. Other features include a new APU, new tailskid, increased weights, and all new, 46cm (18in) taller landing gear. The wheels, tyres and brakes are common with the larger 777.

Inside, the 767-400ER features a 777 style advanced flightdeck with six multifunction LCDs, which can present information in the same format as earlier 767s, allowing a common pilot type certificate, or as for the 777 and Next Generation 737s. The all new cabin interior is similar to that in the 777.

On September 13 2000 Boeing launched the Longer-Range 767-400ER, which will be delivered from mid 2004. The Longer-Range 767-400ER will feature new 320kN (72,000lb) Rolls-Royce Trent 600 or Engine Alliance GP7172 turbofans (being developed for advanced 747 models), additional fuel carried in the horizontal tail and an increased max takeoff, allowing it to fly 11,390km (6150nm).

Photo: A Delta 767-400ER. (Rob Finlayson)

Boeing 777-200

Boeing 777-300

Country of origin: United States of America

Type: Long and ultra long range widebody airliners

Powerplants: 777-200ER – Two 374kN (84,000lb) PW4084s, or 378kN (85,000lb) General Electric GE90-85Bs, or 373kN (84,000lb) Rolls-Royce Trent 884s; or 400kN (90,000lb) class Pratt & Whitney PW4090s, GE90-90B1s, or Trent 890s; or 409kN (92,000lb) GE90-92Bs. 777-200LR – Two 489kN (110,000lb) GE90-110B1s.

Performance: Typical cruising speed 905km/h (490kt). 777-200ER – 263 tonne MTOW range 11,037km (5960nm), 286 tonne MTOW range 13,240km (7150nm). 777-200LR – Max range 16,405km (8860nm).

Weights: 777-200ER – Empty 142,430kg (314,000lb) with 374kN/84,000lb engines, 143,015kg (315,300lb) with 400kN/90,000lb engines, max takeoff optionally 263,085kg (580,000lb) or 286,897kg (632,500lb). 777-200LR – Max takeoff 341,105kg (752,000lb).

Dimensions: 777-200 – Wing span 60.93m (199ft 11in), length 63.73m (209ft 1in), height 18.51m (60ft 9in). Wing area 427.8m² (4605sq ft).

Capacity: Flightcrew of two. Passenger seating for 305 in three classes or up to 440. Underfloor capacity for up to 32 LD3 containers.

Production: 468 777-200s ordered at late 2000 (inc 376 ERs & 3 LRs) with 273 delivered.

History: Boeing's advanced widebody 777 twin has been progressively developed into increasingly longer range developments.

The 777 was originally conceived as a stretched 767, but Boeing instead adopted an all new design with a unique fuselage cross section, fly-by-wire (a Boeing first), an advanced glass flightdeck with five liquid crystal displays, composites (10% by weight), and advanced and extremely powerful engines. The 777 was also offered with optional folding wings where the outer 6m/21ft of each would fold upwards.

The basic 777-200 as launched in October 1990 was offered in two versions, the basic 777-200 (initially A-Market) and the increased weight longer range 777-200IGW (Increased Gross Weight, initially B-Market). The IGW has since been redesignated 777-200ER.

The 777-200 first flew on June 12 1994, with FAA and JAA certification awarded on April 19 1995. The FAA awarded full 180 minutes ETOPS clearance for PW4074 -200s on May 30 that year. First customer delivery was to United Airlines in May 1995. The first 777-200IGW/ER was delivered to British Airways in February 1997.

The 777-100X was a proposed shortened ultra long range (16,000km/8635nm) model, dropped in favour of the 777-200X. The 777-200X evolved into the Longer-Range 777-200 which was formally launched along with the equivalent LR 777-300 on February 29 2000. First flight is planned for early 2003.

Boeing claims the Longer-Range 777-200 will be the world's longest ranging airliner, capable of flying 16,405km (8860nm) – 18 hours flying time. It will achieve this with awesomely powerful 489kN (110,000lb) thrust GE90-110B1 turbofans, a significantly increased max takeoff weight and optional auxiliary fuel tanks in the rear cargo hold. Other changes include 2m (6.5ft) raked wingtips, new main landing gear, structural strengthening and optional overheard crew and flight attendant rest stations above the cabin.

The stretched 777-300 is described separately.

Photo: A Japan Air System 777-200s. (Rob Finlayson)

Country of origin: United States of America

Type: Long and ultra long range high capacity widebody airliners

Powerplants: 777-300 – Either two 400kN (90,000lb) Pratt & Whitney PW4090 turbofans, or 436kN (98,000lb) PW4098s, or 409kN (92,000lb) Rolls-Royce Trent 892s, or 409kN (92,000lb) General Electric GE90-92Bs. 777-300ER – Two 511kN (115,000lb) GE90-115Bs.

Performance: Typical cruising speed 893km/h (482kt). 777-300 – Range with 368 three class passengers 10,595km (5720nm). 777-300ER – Max range 13,330km (7200nm).

Weights: 777-300 – Operating empty 160,120kg (353,600lb), basic max takeoff 263,080kg (580,000lb), high gross weight MTOW 299,380kg (660,000lb). 777-300ER – Max takeoff 341,105kg (752,000lb).

Dimensions: 777-300 – Wing span 60.93m (199ft 11in), or folded 47.32m (155ft 3in), length 73.86m (242ft 4in), height 18.51m (60ft 9in). Wing area 427.8m² (4605sq ft).

Capacity: Flightcrew of two. Typical passenger accommodation for 368 (30 first, 84 business and 254 economy) to 394 in three class arrangements, 400 to 479 in two class arrangements or up to 550 in an all economy high density configuration. Underfloor capacity for 20 standard LD3 containers or eight 2.55 x 3.17m (96 x 125in) pallets.

Production: 93 777-300s ordered as of late 2000 with 34 delivered.

History: Boeing's 777-300 is the world's largest twin engined aircraft, powered by the world's most powerful turbofan engines, and is the world's longest airliner and fastest widebody twin.

The stretched 777-300 was designed as a replacement for early generation 747s (747-100s and -200s). Compared to the older 747s the basic 777-300 has comparable passenger capacity and range, but burns one third less fuel and with 40% lower maintenance costs.

Compared with the 777-200 the -300 features a 10.13m (33ft 3in) stretch, comprising plugs fore and aft of the wings. The longer fuselage allows seating for up to 550 passengers in a single class high density configuration. The -300 also features a strengthened undercarriage, airframe and inboard wing. Other changes include a tailskid and ground manoeuvring cameras mounted on the horizontal tail and underneath the forward fuselage.

Boeing announced it was developing the 777-300 at the Paris Airshow in mid June 1995. The 777-300 first flew on October 16 1997 and made history on May 4 1998 when it was awarded type certification including an immediate 180min ETOPS approval. Service entry with Cathay Pacific was later in that month.

The Longer-Range 777-300 is being developed alongside the LR 777-200 – both were launched on February 29 2000. Both will feature a 341 tonne max takeoff weight, which, with auxiliary fuel, will give the LR 777-300 a range of 13,330km (7200nm), comparable to the slightly larger 747-400. Common changes include 2m (6.5ft) raked wingtips, new main landing gear, structural strengthening and optional overheard crew and flight attendant rest stations above the cabin. The LR 777-300 will be powered by the 511kN (115,000lb) GE90-115Bs – the world's most powerful jet engine.

First flight is due in early 2003.

Photo: A Trent powered Cathay Pacific 777-300. (Rob Finlayson)

Boeing Business Jets

Country of origin: United States of America

Type: Long range large capacity corporate jets

Powerplants: Two 117.4kN (26,400lb) CFM56-7 turbofans.

Performance: BBJ – Max cruising speed Mach 0.82, normal cruising speed Mach 0.80, long range cruising speed Mach 0.79. Initial cruise altitude 38,000ft, max certificated altitude 41,000ft. Range with eight passengers 11,480km (6200nm), with 25 passengers 11,075km (5980nm), with 50 passengers 10,205km (5510nm). BBJ 2 – Range with eight passengers 10,620km (5735nm), with 25 passengers 10,120km (5465nm), with 50 passengers 9140km (4935nm).

Weights: BBJ – Typical operating empty 42,895kg (94,570lb), max takeoff 77,560kg (171,000lb). BBJ 2 – Typical operating empty 45,730kg (100,815lb), max takeoff 79,015kg (174,200lb).

Dimensions: BBJ – Wing span incl winglets 35.79m (117ft 5in), length 33.63m (110ft 4in), height 12.05m (41ft 2in). Wing area 125.0m² (1345.5sq ft). BBJ 2 – Same except length 39.47m (129ft 6in).

Capacity: Flightcrew of two. BBJ – Main cabin interiors to customer preference. Typical configuration includes a crew rest area, forward lounge, private suite with double bed and private bathroom facilities including shower, 12 first class sleeper seats at four abreast and 152cm (60in) pitch, and rear galley and bathroom facilities. Alternatively rear cabin can seat 24 passengers at two abreast and feature a conference area or exercise gym, or up to 63 passengers at six abreast.

Production: By late 2000 total BBJ orders stood at 52 with 39 delivered and 15 in service. Completed aircraft cost approx $US42 to 47m.

History: Boeing Business Jets offers two 737 based corporate jets, the 737-700 based BBJ and the 737-800 based BBJ 2.

Boeing Business Jets is a joint venture formed by Boeing and General Electric in July 1996 to develop and market a corporate version of the popular 737 airliner, initially focusing on the 737-700 based BBJ (or 737-700BBJ). The first BBJ rolled out from Boeing's Renton plant on August 11 1998 and flew for the first time on September 4 that year. On October 30 the US FAA awarded certification to the developed 737-700 airframe on which the BBJ is based. The first completed BBJ was delivered on September 4 1999.

The BBJ combines the Next Generation 737-700's airframe combined with the strengthened wing, fuselage centre section and landing gear of the larger and heavier 737-800, with three to 10 belly auxiliary fuel tanks. It features the Next Generation 737 flightdeck six LCD screens, equipped with embedded dual GPS, TCAS, enhanced GPWS and Flight Dynamics head-up guidance system. Following their certification in September 2000, winglets became a standard option.

The BBJ 2 was launched in October 1999 and is based on the stretched 737-800 airframe, offering 25% greater cabin space (and 100% more baggage space) but has slightly reduced range. It is fitted with between three and seven auxiliary belly fuel tanks. The first BBJ 2 airframe is due to be delivered for interior outfitting in February 2001.

Boeing supplies unfurnished or 'green' BBJ airframes to DeCrane of Georgetown, Delaware, for long range fuel tank installation. From DeCrane the BBJ is flown to a customer specified completion centre for interior fitout and exterior painting.

Photo: A winglet equipped BBJ. (Paul Merritt)

Boeing (MDC) MD-11

Country of origin: United States of America

Type: Long range widebody airliner

Powerplants: Three 266.9kN (60,000lb) Pratt & Whitney PW4460s, 276kN (62,000lb) PW4462s, or 273.6kN (61,500lb) General Electric CF6-80C2D1F turbofans.

Performance: MD-11 – Max cruising speed 945km/h (510kt), economical cruising speed 876km/h (473kt). Range with 298 passengers and reserves 12,633km (6821nm). MD-11F – Range 7242km (3910nm). MD-11 Combi – Range with 183 passengers, six freight pallets and reserves 12,392km (6691nm). MD-11ER – Range with 298 passengers 13,408km (7240nm).

Weights: MD-11 – Operating empty 130,165kg (286,965lb) with CF6s, standard max takeoff 273,314kg (602,555lb), optional 285,990kg (630,500lb). MD-11F – Operating empty 113,920kg (251,150lb), max takeoff same. MD-11 Combi – Operating empty 131,035kg (288,885lb) passenger, max takeoff same. MD-11CF – Operating empty passenger configuration 131,525kg (289,965lb), freighter configuration 115,380kg (254,372lb), max takeoff same. MD-11ER – Max takeoff 285,989kg (630,500lb).

Dimensions: Wing span 51.66m (169ft 6in), length 61.21m (200ft 10in) with PW4460s, 61.62m (202ft 2in) with CF6s, height 17.60m (57ft 9in). Wing area 338.9m² (3648.0sq ft).

Capacity: Flightcrew of two. MD-11 – Max single class seating for 410, can seat 298 in three classes, 323 in two.

Production: 200 MD-11 ordered (comprising 136 MD-11, 5 MD-11C and 59 MD-11F). 198 delivered by late 2000.

History: The McDonnell Douglas/Boeing MD-11 is a modernised, slightly stretched and re-engined development of the DC-10 trijet.

Launched on December 30 1986 (following a launch order from British Caledonian for three placed earlier that month), the MD-11 was the result of a two year study to find a replacement for the DC-10. First flight occurred on January 10 1990, certification was granted in November that year, with service entry that December.

Compared to the DC-10, the MD-11 introduced a 5.71m (18ft 9in) fuselage stretch, winglets, modified tail with less sweepback, an advanced two crew six screen EFIS flightdeck, restyled main cabin interior and new engine options. Variants offered were the longer range MD-11ER available from early 1996, MD-11F freighter, and MD-11C Combi and MD-11CF convertible passenger/freighter models.

McDonnell Douglas at various times proposed MD-11 developments aimed at increasing seating through stretches and underfloor panorama deck seating. In 1996 MDC looked closely at the MD-XX, MD-11 variants with a new wing. Two versions were proposed, one with the standard MD-11 fuselage and a 15,565km (8400nm) range, the other a stretched 375 seater. These were not launched.

In November 1997 following the Boeing/McDonnell Douglas merger Boeing announced that the MD-11 would be kept in production, primarily as a freighter. However in June 1998 Boeing reversed that decision, saying that due to a lack of market demand MD-11 production would be wound up. The last MD-11 built, a MD-11F for Lufthansa Cargo, was due to be delivered in early 2001.

Photo: A FedEx MD-11F. (Rob Finlayson)

Boeing Vertol (Kawasaki) KV 107

Country of origin: United States of America

Type: Medium to heavylift utility helicopter

Powerplants: Two 930kW (1250shp) General Electric CT58-110-1 or Ishikawajima-Harima built CT58-IHI-110-1 turboshafts driving two three-blade rotors.

Performance: KV 107/II-2 – Max speed 270km/h (146kt), economical cruising speed 232km/h (125kt). Initial rate of climb 1440ft/min. Hovering ceiling out of ground effect 8800ft. Range with a three tonne (6600lb) payload and reserves 175km (95kt).

Weights: KV 107/II-2 – Empty equipped 4868kg (10,723lb), max takeoff 8618kg (19,000lb).

Dimensions: Diameter of each rotor 15.24m (50ft 0in), fuselage length 13.59m (44ft 7in), height 5.09m (16ft 9in). Rotor disc area (total) 364.6m² (3925sq ft).

Capacity: Flightcrew of two. Typical seating for 23 to 25 passengers in airliner configuration, or 12 passengers and freight in combi configuration. Executive configuration seats six to 11 passengers in main cabin.

Production: Total BV/KV 107 production approximately 650, with almost all for military customers. Small numbers remain in commercial service.

History: Boeing Vertol's Model 107 is best known as the military CH-46 Sea Knight, but small numbers were built as airliners and utility transports for commercial customers.

The then independent Vertol company (previously Piasecki) designed the 107 in the late 1950s as a medium lift helicopter for US Army evaluation. Three prototype Lycoming turboshaft powered Vertol 107s were built (the Army ordered 10) designated YHC-1As, and first flight occurred on August 27 1958. By that time though the Army's interest had switched to what would become the Chinook and it did not order the 107. However in February 1961 Vertol (Boeing acquired Vertol in 1960) won a US Marine Corps competition with a developed General Electric T58-GE-8 powered version of the BV 107, and the type was ordered into production as the CH-46A Sea Knight.

The commercial 107 is based on the CH-46A powered by the CT-58-110 (equivalent to the military T58-GE-8). The first commercial 107 to fly was one of the three original development aircraft built for the US Army converted to the new standard, its first flight in the new configuration was on October 25 1960. Offered in two forms, the KV 107/II-1 utility transport and KV 107/II-2 airliner, only the latter was built. KV 107/II-2 customers included New York Airlines, who ordered three configured to seat 25, Columbia Helicopters in the US (Columbia still operates KV 107s) and Japan's Air Lift.

A more powerful 1045kW (1400shp) CT58-140-1 powered longer range KV 107/II-A-17 was offered and one was built for the Tokyo Police.

Japan's Kawasaki built all commercial 107s, and has held manufacturing rights to the 107 since 1965. Kawasaki has also built KV 107s for the Japanese military and Saudi Arabia.

Photo: This Japanese KV 107 is pictured in Australia where it was used in support of a testing program of a space re-entry vehicle. (Richard Koehne)

Boeing Commercial Chinook

Country of origin: United States of America

Type: Heavylift utility and airliner helicopter

Powerplants: Two 3040kW (4075shp) takeoff rated Lycoming AL 5512 turboshafts driving two three-blade rotors.

Performance: LR, MLR & ER – Max speed 278km/h (150kt), max cruising speed 270km/h (145kt), long range cruising speed 250km/h (135kt). Max initial rate of climb at MTOW 1180ft/min. Range – LR & MLR with max fuel 1150km (620nm), ER with max fuel 1918km (1035nm). UT – Max speed 260km/h (140kt), max cruising speed 260km/h (140kt), long range cruising speed 250km/h (135kt). Max initial rate of climb at MTOW 1500ft/min. Range with max internal load 425km (230nm).

Weights: LR – Empty 11,748kg (25,900lb), max takeoff 22,000kg (48,500lb), or 23,133kg (51,000lb) with an external load. ER – Empty 12,020kg (26,500lb), max takeoff same. MLR – Empty 11,113kg (24,500lb), max takeoff same. UT – Empty 9797kg (21,600lb), max takeoff 19,051kg (42,000lb), or 23,133kg (51,000lb) with an external sling load.

Dimensions: Rotor diameter (both) 18.29m (60ft 0in), length overall 30.18m (99ft 0in), fuselage length 15.87m (52ft 1in), height 5.68m (18ft 8in). Rotor disc area (total) 525.4m² (5655sq ft).

Capacity: Two pilots on flightdeck. Seating for 44 at four abreast in main cabin. Combi versions seat between eight and 32 with rear cabin loaded with freight, or between 22 and 32 with freight on one side of main cabin. Max internal load of LR and MLR models 9070kg (20,000lb), ER and UT models 8730kg (19,250lb). Max external sling load 12,700kg (28,000lb).

Production: Approximately a dozen Commercial Chinooks were built in the early to mid 1980s. Most remain in service.

History: The Boeing Helicopters Model 234 Commercial Chinook is a variant of the successful CH-47 Chinook military airlifter.

The Chinook was developed for the US Army and first flew in September 1961, and since then has been developed into a number of progressively improved variants and remains in production (over 1160 have been built). The Commercial Chinook was not launched until 1978, following a British Airways Helicopters order for three for North Sea oil rig support missions. The Commercial Chinook's first flight occurred on August 19 1980, certification was granted in June 1981, and service entry was the following month.

Largely identical in configuration to the CH-47, the Commercial Chinook retains the former's rear cargo ramp, but has a slightly reprofiled nose, commercial avionics and large passenger windows along both sides of the main cabin.

The initial orders were for the 234 LR Long Range, which compared with the CH-47 has roughly twice the fuel load, plus a 44 seat passenger interior based on that used in Boeing jetliners. A number of other versions were offered – the 234 ER Extended Range with additional tankage, the 234 UT Utility, and 234 MLR Multi purpose Long Range which can be used for either passenger or freight operations, or a combination of both.

Photo: Oregon based Columbia Helicopters is a large Boeing 234 Commercial Chinook operator. (Steve Bottom)

Bombardier CRJ100 & CRJ200

Country of origin: Canada

Type: Regional jet airliner

Powerplants: 100 – Two 41.0kN (9220lb) General Electric CF34-3A1 turbofans. 200 – Two 41.0kN (9220lb) CF34-3B1s.

Performance: 100 – High speed cruise 851km/h (459kt), typical cruising speed 786km/h (424kt). Range with max payload at long range cruising speed with reserves 1815km (980nm). 200LR – Speeds same. Range with max payload at long range cruising speed and reserves over 3713km (2005nm).

Weights: 100 – Empty 13,236kg (29,180lb), operating empty 13,653kg (30,100lb), max takeoff 21,523kg (47,450lb). 200LR – Empty 13,243kg (29,195lb), operating empty 13,740kg (30,292lb), max takeoff 24,040kg (53,000lb).

Dimensions: Wing span 21.21m (69ft 7in), length 26.77m (87ft 10in), height 6.22m (20ft 5in). Wing area 54.5m² (587.1sq ft).

Capacity: Flightcrew of two. Typical one class seating for 50 at four abreast and 79cm (31in) pitch. Max seating for 52. Corporate Jetliner corporate shuttle configurations seat from 18 to 30.

Production: Total CRJ100/200 airliner orders at late 2000 of 754 (236 100s and 520 200s), of which over 446 had been delivered.

History: Bombardier's Canadair Regional Jet pioneered the 50 seat jet class, and has since become a runaway sales success.

The Canadair Regional Jet – or CRJ – was based on the Challenger corporate jet and was designed to offer the high speed advantages of much larger jets, with similar standards of service while at the same time offering operating economics, particularly over longer stage lengths, close to that of comparable size turboprops.

Canadair originally studied a 24 seat stretched regional airliner development of the CL-600 Challenger business jet up to 1981. Design studies for a stretched airliner based on the much improved CL-601 Challenger were first undertaken in 1987, leading Canadair to launch the Regional Jet program on March 31 1989. The first of three development aircraft first flew on May 10 1991. Transport Canada certification was awarded on July 31 1992, allowing the first customer delivery to Lufthansa that October.

Major changes over the Challenger apart from the stretched fuselage include a new wing optimised for airline operations, higher design weights, EFIS flightdeck with Collins Pro-Line 4 avionics suite, new undercarriage, additional fuel capacity and slightly more powerful CF34 engines.

The original CRJ100 series – the 100, 100ER and 100LR – was augmented by the 200 series (with more efficient engines) in 1995. The Series 200 is available in standard 200, long range 200ER with optional greater fuel capacity, and the extended range Series 200LR (all three are offered in B form with CF34-3B1s for improved hot and high performance). The corporate shuttle configured Corporate Jetliner and the SE (Special Edition) business jet are also offered. In all 13 corporate configured CRJs had been delivered by late 2000.

The stretched CRJ700 and CRJ900 are described separately. Over 900 CRJs (including the CRJ700 and CRJ900) have been sold

Photo: A CRJ200 of Australia's Kendell Airlines (a subsidiary of Ansett Australia). (Bombardier)

Bombardier CRJ700 & CRJ900

Country of origin: Canada

Type: Regional jet airliners

Powerplants: CRJ700 – Two 56.4kN (12,670lb) or 61.3kN (13,790lb) with automatic power reserve General Electric CF34-8C1 turbofans. CRJ900 – Two 63.4kN (14,255lb) with APR CF34-8C5s.

Performance: CRJ700 – High speed cruise 860km/h (464kt), normal cruising speed 818km/h (442kt). Max certificated altitude 41,000ft. Range with 70 passengers and reserves 3124km (1687nm). ER variant range with 70 passengers and reserves 3674km (1984nm). CRJ900 – Speeds same. Range with 86 passengers 2774km (1498km), ER version range with 86 passengers 3208km (1732nm).

Weights: CRJ700 – Operating empty 19,731kg (43,500lb), standard max takeoff 32,999kg (72,750lb), ER max takeoff 34,020kg (75,000lb). CRJ900 – Operating empty 21,546kg (47,500lb). Max takeoff 36,514kg (80,500lb). CRJ900ER – Max takeoff 37,241kg (82,500lb).

Dimensions: CRJ700 – Wing span 23.01m (75ft 6in), length 32.41m (106ft 4in), height 7.29m (23ft 11in). CRJ900 – Same except length 36.19m (118ft 9in).

Capacity: CRJ700 – Flightcrew of two. Typical main cabin seating for 70 passengers at 79cm (31in) pitch and four abreast. Optionally can seat 72 or 78 passengers. CRJ900 – Standard seating for 86 or 90 passengers.

Production: 184 CRJ700s and 14 CRJ900s ordered at late 2000.

History: Bombardier's 70 seat CRJ700 and 90 seat CRJ900 are stretched developments of the fast selling 50 seat CRJ series.

Bombardier began development work on the CRJ700 in 1995 leading to a formal launch in January 1997 and first flight on May 27 1999. CRJ700 certification is scheduled for late 2000 with customer deliveries in the first quarter of 2001.

Compared with the 50 seat CRJ100/200, the CRJ700 is stretched by 4.72m (15ft 6in) with plugs forward and aft of the wing, while the cabin is 6.02m (19ft 9in) longer, aided by moving the rear pressure bulkhead 1.29m (4ft 3in) aft. The cabin windows are raised by 12cm (5in), the cabin floor is lowered slightly and the ceiling raised to provide 1.90m (6ft 3in) headroom, and an underfloor baggage compartment beneath the forward fuselage is added. Other changes include relocating the APU to the rear fuselage and redesigned overhead stowage bins.

Wing span is increased with a 1.83m (6ft 0in) wing root plug, while the leading edge is extended and high lift devices added. The main undercarriage units are lengthened and fitted with new wheels, tyres and brakes. The flightdeck features six liquid crystal displays presenting information from the Collins Pro Line 4 EFIS avionics suite.

Bombardier launched the further stretched, 90 seat class CRJ900 at the Farnborough Airshow in July 2000. First flight is scheduled for the first quarter of 2001 (by a prototype converted from a CRJ700 development aircraft), type certification is planned for the third quarter of 2002 and customer deliveries are planned for the first quarter of 2003.

Changes over the CRJ700 include the stretched fuselage (by 3.68m/12ft 1in), 5% more powerful engines, strengthened main landing gear, upgraded wheels and brakes, a strengthened wing, an additional underfloor baggage door and two additional overwing exits.

Photo: A computer generated image of the CRJ900. (Bombardier)

Bombardier de Havilland Dash 8-100 & Q200

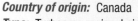

Country of origin: Canada

Type: Turboprop regional airliners

Powerplants: 100 – Two 1490kW (2000shp) Pratt & Whitney Canada PW120A turboprops driving four blade constant speed Hamilton Standard propellers. 100B – Two 1605kW (2150shp) PW121As. Q200 – Two 1605kW (2150shp) PW123C or PW123Ds.

Performance: 100A – Max cruising speed 490km/h (265kt), long range cruising speed 440km/h (237kt). Initial rate of climb 1560ft/min. Range with full passenger load, fuel and reserves 1520km (820nm), range with a 2720kg (6000lb) payload 2040km (1100nm). 100B – Same except max cruising speed of 500km/h (270kt). Q200 – Max cruising speed 546km/h (295kt). Initial rate of climb 1475ft/min. Range with 37 passengers 1795km (970nm).

Weights: 100A – Operating empty 10,250kg (22,600lb), max takeoff 15,650kg (34,500lb). 100B – Operating empty 10,273kg (22,648lb), max takeoff 16,465kg (36,300lb). Q200 – Operating empty 10,486kg (23,117lb), max takeoff 16,465kg (36,300lb).

Dimensions: Wing span 25.91m (85ft 0in), length 22.25m (73ft 0in), height 7.49m (24ft 7in). Wing area 54.4m² (585.0sq ft).

Capacity: Flightcrew of two. Typical passenger seating for 37 at four abreast and 79cm (31in) pitch, max seating for 40.

Production: At late 2000 299 Dash 8-100/Q100s ordered and 94 Dash 8-200/Q200s ordered with 1 Q100 and 4 Q200s to be delivered.

History: Bombardier's de Havilland Dash 8 is the west's second most successful regional turboprop airliner family (after the Fokker F27).

De Havilland Canada began development of the Dash 8 in the late 1970s in response to what it saw as considerable market demand for a new generation 30 to 40 seat commuter airliner. The first of two preproduction aircraft first flew on June 20 1983, while Canadian certification was awarded on September 28 1984. The first customer delivery was to norOntair of Canada on October 23 1984.

Like the Dash 7 (described under de Havilland), the Dash 8 features a high mounted wing and T-tail, and has an advanced flight control system and large full length trailing edge flaps. The Dash 8 is powered by two Pratt & Whitney Canada PW120 series (originally designated PT7A) turboprops.

The initial Dash 8 Series 100 was followed by the Series 100A in 1990. The 100A introduced a revised interior with extra headroom and PW120A turboprops. The Series 100B was offered from 1992 with more powerful PW121s for better climb and airfield performance.

The improved performance Dash 8-200 was announced in 1992 and delivered from April 1995. It features more powerful PW123C engines which give a 56km/h (30kt) increase in cruising speed, as well as greater commonality with the stretched Dash 8-300. The 200B derivative has PW123Ds for better hot and high performance.

From the second quarter of 1996 all Dash 8s delivered have been fitted with a computer controlled noise and vibration suppression system (or NVS). To reflect this the designation was changed to Dash 8Q (Q for 'quiet'). In 1998 that was changed again to Dash 8 Q100 and Dash 8 Q200 when a new interior was introduced.

The stretched Q300 and Q400 are described separately.

Photo: An Air Ontario Dash 8-100. (Gary Gentle)

Bombardier de Havilland Dash 8 Q300

Country of origin: Canada

Type: Turboprop regional airliner

Powerplants: 300A – Two 1775kW (2380shp) Pratt & Whitney Canada PW123 turboprops driving four blade propellers or optional 1865kW (2500shp) PW123Bs. Q300 HGW – Two 1865kW (2500shp) PW123Bs.

Performance: Q300 – Max cruising speed 532km/h (287kt). Initial rate of climb 1800ft/min. Service ceiling 25,000ft. Range with full passenger load and reserves 1538km (830nm), with 2720kg (6000lb) payload 1612km (870nm). Q300 HGW – Max cruising speed 528km/h (285kt). Range with 50 passengers 1625km (878nm), with 50 passengers and auxiliary fuel 2179km (1177nm).

Weights: 300 – Operating empty 11,657kg (25,700lb), standard max takeoff 18,642kg (41,100lb). Q300 HGW – Operating empty 11,743kg (25,888lb), max takeoff 19,505kg (43,000lb).

Dimensions: Wing span 27.43m (90ft 0in), length 25.68m (84ft 3in), height 7.49m (24ft 7in). Wing area 56.2m² (605sq ft).

Capacity: Flightcrew of two. Standard single class seating for 50 passengers at four abreast and 81cm (32in) pitch.

Production: Total orders for Dash 8-300s stood at over 199 by late 2000, of which 166 had been delivered.

History: With the success of the Dash 8-100 series, a stretched version with greater capacity was a logical development.

De Havilland Canada (now part of Bombardier) launched full scale development of a 50 seat stretched version of its Dash 8 regional airliner during 1986, approximately two years after the standard fuselage length aircraft had entered service. The first series 300 aircraft was modified from the prototype Dash 8, and flew for the first time in its new configuration on May 15 1987. Canadian certification was granted in February 1989, with the first delivery, to Time Air, following late that same month. US certification was awarded in June 1989.

The stretch comprises fuselage plugs forward and aft of the wing, increasing length by 3.43m (11ft 3in). In addition, the wings are greater in span. The fuselage stretch increases typical seating capacity to 50 (at 81cm/32in pitch), or for up to 56 (at 74cm/29in pitch). Other changes compared with the Dash 8-100 were minor, but included a larger, repositioned galley, larger toilet, additional wardrobe, dual air conditioning packs, a new galley service door and optional APU.

The standard Dash 8-300 was followed in 1990 by the 300A which introduced optional higher gross weights, interior improvements (as on the Dash 8-100A), and standard PW123A engines (with PW123Bs optional). The 300B was introduced in 1992 and had 1865kW (2500shp) PW123Bs and the 300A's optional high gross weight as standard. The 300E had 1775kW (2380shp) PW123Es rated to 40 degrees, thus improving hot and high performance.

Like the Dash 8Q-200, all Dash 8-300s built since the second quarter of 1996 have been fitted with a computer controlled noise and vibration suppression system (or NVS) and so from then all models were designated Dash 8Q-300s. In 1998 the aircraft was again renamed, this time to Dash 8 Q300 when a new interior was also introduced. The Q300 is offered in basic (PW123/PW123B powered) and optional high gross weight (PW123B powered) forms.

Photo: A Qantas New Zealand Dash 8-300. (Ronn Hann)

Bombardier de Havilland Dash 8 Q400

Country of origin: Canada

Type: 70 seat regional turboprop airliner

Powerplants: Two 3410kW (4573shp) takeoff rated Pratt & Whitney Canada PW150A turboprops driving six blade Dowty propellers.

Performance: Max cruising speed 648km/h (350kt). Max certificated ceiling 25,000ft, or optionally 27,000ft. Max range with 70 passengers and reserves 2400km (1296nm).

Weights: Operating empty 16,580kg (36,520lb), max takeoff 27,330kg (60,198lb) or high gross weight 28,690kg (63,250lb).

Dimensions: Wing span 28.42m (93ft 3in), length 32.84m (107ft 9in), height 8.36m (27ft 5in). Wing area 63.1m² (679.0sq ft).

Capacity: Flightcrew of two. Can seat 70 passengers at 79cm (31in) pitch or 78 at 76cm (30in) pitch in a single class arrangement.

Production: Total Q400 firm sales at late 2000 stood at 68 of which 17 had been delivered.

History: Bombardier's 70 seat de Havilland Dash 8 Q400 (or Q400 for short) is the latest and longest member of the successful Dash 8 family, but with its new engines, avionics and systems, a modified wing and stretched fuselage is basically an all new aeroplane.

De Havilland was already working on a further stretch of the Dash 8 when Bombardier acquired the company from Boeing in 1992, although the program was not formally launched until June 1995. Rolled out on November 21 1997, the Q400 made its first flight on January 31 1998. Five Q400s were used in the 1900 flying hour flight test program, culminating in Canadian certification being awarded on June 14 1999 and US certification on February 8 2000. The first delivery, to launch customer SAS Commuter was on January 20 2000, about 10 months later than originally planned.

The Q400 is pitched at the short haul regional airliner market for stage lengths of 550km (300nm) or less. Bombardier says the Q400's breakeven load factor for a 360km (195nm) stage length is just 29 passengers.

The Q400 features a new fuselage stretched 6.83m (22ft 5in) compared with the Q300 mated with the familiar Dash 8 nose section and vertical tail, while the horizontal tail is new. The fuselage's cross section and structure is based on the earlier Dash 8's but with two entry doors at the forward and aft ends of the fuselage on the left side, with emergency exit doors opposite them on the right side.

The Q400's inner wing section and wing fuselage wing join are new, while the outer wing has been strengthened. Power is from two FADEC equipped 3410kW (4573shp) Pratt & Whitney Canada PW150As driving six blade, slow turning Dowty propellers.

The Q400 is fitted with Bombardier's NVS active noise and vibration system which reduces cabin noise to levels comparable to the CRJ jet airliner. This is achieved through the use of computer controlled active tuned vibration absorbers (ATVAs) mounted on the airframe.

The flightdeck features five large Sextant LCD colour displays which present information to the pilots in a similar format to earlier Dash 8s, allowing a common type rating.

Other new features include the main landing gear, wheels, tyres and brakes, a third hydraulic system and a bullet fairing at the tip of the fin.

Photo: An SAS Commuter Q400. (Bombardier)

Bombardier Canadair CL-215 & CL-415

Country of origin: Canada

Type: Firebomber and utility amphibians

Powerplants: CL-215 – Two 1565kW (2100hp) Pratt & Whitney R-2800-CA3 18 cylinder radial piston engines driving three blade constant speed propellers. CL-415 – Two 1775kW (2380shp) Pratt & Whitney Canada PW123AF turboprops driving four blade constant speed Hamilton Standard props.

Performance: CL-215 – Max cruising speed 290km/h (157kt). Initial rate of climb 1000ft/min. Range at max cruising speed 1715km (925nm), at long range cruising speed 2095km (1130nm). CL-415 – Max cruising speed 376km/h (203kt), long range cruising speed 270km/h (145kt), patrol speed 240km/h (130kt). Initial rate of climb 1375ft/min. Ferry range with 500kg (1100lb) payload 2426km (1310nm).

Weights: CL-215 firebomber – Empty 12,220kg (26,941lb), max takeoff from water 17,100kg (37,700lb), from land 19,730kg (43,500lb). CL-415 firebomber – Operating empty 12,882kg (28,400lb), max takeoff from land 19,890kg (43,850lb), from water 17,168kg (37,850lb).

Dimensions: CL-215 – Wing span 28.60m (93ft 10in), length 19.82m (65ft 1in), height 8.98m (29ft 6in). Wing area 100.3m² (1080sq ft). CL-415 – Same except wing span over wingtips 28.63m (93ft 11in).

Capacity: Flightcrew of two, plus accommodation in special missions variants for a third flightdeck member, a mission specialist and two observers. Fire retardant capacity 6123kg (13,500lb). Passenger configuration for 30 at 79cm (31in) pitch, or in a combi configuration for 11, with firebombing tanks retained and freight in forward fuselage.

Production: Total CL-215 production of 125. As of late 2000 55 CL-415s had been ordered.

History: The piston CL-215 and turboprop CL-415 SuperScooper are purpose designed amphibious firebomber aircraft.

The CL-215 is powered by two Pratt & Whitney R-2800 radials, and is capable of scooping up 5455 litres (1200Imp gal/1440US gal) of water in 12 seconds from a water source such as a lake. The CL-215 first flew on October 23 1967, and first delivery was to the French civil protection agency in June 1969. Production of batches of CL-215s continued through to 1990.

Originally the subsequent CL-215T was to be a straightforward turboprop powered development of the CL-215, and Canadair converted two aircraft in 1989 to act as development aircraft. The first of these flew on June 8 that year. Retrofit kits for CL-215s to the new standard were offered, but Canadair elected not to build new CL-215Ts, and instead developed the CL-415.

The primary improvement introduced on the CL-415 over the CL-215T is an EFIS avionics suite, while other improvements, some of which first appeared on the CL-215T, include winglets and finlets, higher weights and an increased capacity firebombing system. Like the CL-215 its principle mission is that of a firebomber, but various special mission (including SAR and maritime patrol) and transport configurations are available.

The first CL-415 flew in December 1993 and was delivered from April 1994. The new CL-415GR ordered by Greece has higher operating weights.

Photo: A French Securite Civile CL-415. (Bombardier)

Bombardier Learjet 35, 36 & 31

Country of origin: United States of America

Type: Light corporate jets

Powerplants: Two 15.6kN (3500lb) Garrett TFE731-2-2B turbofans. 31A – Honeywell TFE731-2-3Bs.

Performance: 35A & 36A – Max speed 872km/h (470kt), max cruising speed 852km/h (460kt), economical cruising speed 774km/h (418kt). Service ceiling 41,000ft. Range with four passengers, max fuel and reserves 4070km (2195nm) for 35A, 4673km (2522nm) for 36A. 31A – Max cruising speed 891km/h (481kt), typical cruising speed at 45,000ft 832km/h (450kt). Max certificated altitude 51,000ft. Range with two crew, four passengers and IFR reserves 2344km (1266nm), or 2752km (1486nm) for 31A/ER.

Weights: 35A and 36A – Empty equipped 4590kg (10,120lb), max takeoff 8300kg (18,300lb). 31A – Empty 4651kg (10,253lb), operating empty 5035kg (11,100lb), max takeoff 7030kg (15,500lb), or optionally 7711kg (17,000lb). 31A/ER – Max takeoff 7711kg (17,000lb).

Dimensions: Wing span (over tip tanks) 12.04m (39ft 6in), length 14.83m (48ft 8in), height 3.73m (12ft 3in). Wing area 23.5m^2 (253.3sq ft). 31A – Same except for wing span 13.35m (43ft 10in). Wing area 24.6m^2 (264.4sq ft).

Capacity: Flightcrew of two. Seating for up to eight in main cabin in 35 and 31, or up to six in 36A. Some aircraft configured as package freighters.

Production: 676 Learjet 35s and 36s delivered. US Air Force and Air National Guard ordered 84 35As as C-21s. More than 200 31s built. At late 2000 634 Learjet 35s, 55 36s and 159 31s were in service.

History: The Learjet 35 and 36 are stretched, turbofan powered developments of the initial Learjet models, the 23, 24 and 25.

The availability of the Garrett AiResearch TFE731 turbofan in the late 1960s led to a development of the Learjet 25 that was initially known as the 25B-GF (Garrett Fan). A testbed Lear 25 with a TFE731 on its left side flew in May 1971, while the definitive Learjet 35 prototype first flew on August 22 1973.

Aside from turbofans, the 35 and longer range 36 differ from the earlier Learjet 25 in having a 0.33m (1ft 1in) fuselage stretch. The Learjet 35 has seating for up to eight, but has less fuel than the longer range 36, which can only seat up to six, as both types share the same maximum takeoff weight. The 35 and 36 were certificated in July 1974.

Improvements to the two models led to the 35A and 36A from 1976, with higher standard max takeoff weights. Both models remained in production until 1994.

Development of the 35 and 36 range was taken one step further with the Learjet 31, which combines the 35/36's fuselage and powerplants with the more modern wing of the 55 (now also on the 60) and delta fins under the tail. A 31 development aircraft first flew in May 1987 and certification was awarded in August 1988.

The improved 31A and 31A/ER are the current production models, the 31A/ER being an extended range variant with a higher maximum takeoff weight and more fuel. A new interior with increased headroom was introduced in 1995.

Bombardier acquired Learjet in 1990.

Photo: A Learjet 31A in flight. (Bombardier)

Bombardier Learjet 45

Country of origin: United States of America

Type: Small to mid size corporate jet

Powerplants: Two 15.7kN (3500lb) Honeywell TFE731-20 turbofans.

Performance: High speed cruise 867km/h (468kt), normal cruising speed 846km/h (457kt), long range cruising speed 787km/h (425kt). Max certificated altitude 51,000ft. Max range with four passengers and IFR reserves 3926km (2120nm).

Weights: Empty 5693kg (12,550lb), basic operating empty 6146kg (13,550lb), max takeoff 9298kg (20,500lb).

Dimensions: Wing span 14.58m (47ft 10in), length 17.81m (58ft 5in), height 4.37m (14ft 4in). Wing area 29.0m^2 (311.6sq ft).

Capacity: Flightcrew of two. Main cabin seating for eight or nine passengers (typically eight).

Production: 100th Learjet 45 delivered October 2000.

History: Bombardier's Learjet 45 is proving a popular addition to the upper end of the small sized (or 'super-light') corporate jet market.

Bombardier division Learjet announced it was developing the Model 45 at the US National Business Aviation Association's annual convention in Dallas in September 1992. First flight was on October 7 1995 (the 32nd anniversary of the first flight of the original Lear 23), and, after some delays, US FAA certification was granted on September 22 1997. The first customer aircraft was delivered in January 1998, the 100th was delivered in October 2000.

The 45 is of classic Learjet design and layout but is effectively an all new aircraft, designed with the aid of 3D computer modelling. Design changes made early into the 45's design life included a larger fin and rudder, extended engine pylons, smaller delta fins, full span elevators, and single piece flaps.

Larger than the Learjet 31 and smaller than the 60, the 45 features a 1.50m (4.9ft) high and 1.55m (5.1ft) wide cabin which is designed to accommodate double club seating, a galley and a full width aft rest room. The wing spar is recessed beneath the cabin floor. Eight windows line each side of the cabin.

The flightdeck features a four screen (two primary flight displays and two multifunction displays) Honeywell Primus 1000 integrated avionics suite, while an APU is standard.

The -20 FADEC equipped version of the proven Honeywell (formerly AlliedSignal) TFE731 engine was developed in cooperation with Learjet for the 45 and incorporates 60 design changes.

Bombardier announced performance improvements for the 45 at the 1999 Paris Airshow. These include restyled seats, reduced cabin noise and improvements to the cabin air system.

While Learjet holds overall 45 program leadership, with responsibility for the aircraft's design, other Bombardier subsidiaries also participate in Learjet 45 production. De Havilland Inc in Canada is responsible for wing construction, while Shorts of Northern Ireland in the UK builds the fuselage and empennage.

Significant Learjet 45 customers include Bombardier's own Flexjets fractional ownership scheme which has ordered 40, and Singapore Airlines which uses four for pilot training.

Photo: A Learjet 45 was the 2000th Learjet delivered, in August 1999. (Bombardier)

Bombardier Learjet 55 & 60

Country of origin: United States of America

Type: Mid size corporate jets

Powerplants: 55 – Two 16.5kN (3700lb) Garrett TFE731-3A-2B turbofans. 60 – Two 20.5kN (4600lb) Pratt & Whitney Canada PW305A turbofans.

Performance: 55C – Max speed 884km/h (477kt), max cruising speed 843km/h (455kt), economical cruising speed 778km/h (420kt). Service ceiling 51,000ft. Range with two crew, four passengers and reserves 4442km (2397nm) for 55C/LR. 60 – High cruising speed 859km/h (464kt), normal cruising speed 839km/h (453kt), long range cruising speed 782km/h (422kt). Max certificated altitude 51,000ft. Range with two crew, four passengers and IFR reserves 4628km (2499nm).

Weights: 55C – Empty 5832kg (12,858lb), operating empty 6013kg (13,258lb), max takeoff 9525kg (21,000lb). 60 – Empty 6282kg (13,850lb), basic operating empty 6641kg (14,640lb), max takeoff 10,659kg (23,500lb).

Dimensions: 55 – Wing span 13.34m (43ft 9in), length 16.79m (55ft 1in), height 4.47m (14ft 8in). Wing area 24.6m² (264.5sq ft). 60 – Same except length 17.88m (58ft 8in),

Capacity: 55 – Flightcrew of two. Six different main cabin arrangements offered with seating ranging from four to eight. 60 – Flightcrew of two. Optional seating arrangements for six to nine passengers.

Production: Production of the Model 55 ceased in 1990 after 147 had been built. 141 55s in service at late 1998. Deliveries of Model 60 began in January 1993, with more than 190 delivered by late 2000.

History: The Learjet 55 and its follow-on successor, the Learjet 60, are the largest members of the Learjet family, and date back to development work undertaken in the late 1970s.

In designing the 55, Learjet (or Gates Learjet as the company was then known as) took the wing of the earlier Longhorn 28/29 series and married it to an all new, larger 10 seat fuselage. The original Model 55 Longhorn prototype first flew on November 15 1979. The first production aircraft meanwhile flew on August 11 1980, with the first delivered in late April 1981 (after FAA certification was granted in March that year).

Development of the 55 led to a number of sub variants, including the 55B which introduced a digital flightdeck, modified wings, improved interior, and most importantly, the previous optional higher takeoff weights becoming standard. The 55C introduced 'Delta Fins' which gave a number of performance and handling advantages, the 55C/ER is an extended range version with additional fuel in the tail cone (the additional tank can be retrofitted to earlier aircraft), while the 55C/LR introduced more fuel capacity.

The improved Learjet 60 first flew in its basic definitive form in June 1991 (the modified Learjet 55 prototype earlier served as a proof of concept aircraft for the 60 with Garrett engines). It differs from the 55 in having a 1.09m (43in) fuselage stretch and new Pratt & Whitney Canada PW305 turbofans. Certification of the 60 was awarded in January 1993, with first deliveries following shortly afterwards.

A revised interior was introduced in 1998.

Photo: The 60 is the largest member of Bombardier's Learjet family.

Bombardier Continental Jet

Countries of origin: Canada & USA

Type: Medium size corporate jet

Powerplant: Two 28.9kN (6500lb) with automatic power reserve Honeywell AS907 turbofans.

Performance: High speed cruising speed 870km/h (470kt) or Mach 0.82, normal cruising speed 850km/h (460kt) or Mach 0.80. Balanced field length 1510m (4950ft), landing distance 810m (2650ft). Max operating altitude 45,000ft, initial cruise altitude 41,000ft. Max range with eight passengers and NBAA IFR reserves at Mach 0.80 5740km (3100nm).

Weights: Basic operating 10,138kg (22,350lb), max takeoff 17,010kg (37,500lb).

Dimensions: Wing span 19.46m (63ft 10in), length 20.91m (68ft 7in), height 6.19m (20ft 4in). Wing area 48.5m² (522sq ft).

Capacity: Flightcrew of two. Typical cabin arrangement for eight, with a two seat lounge opposite two facing seats, with club seating for four behind them, or double club seating.

Production: First delivery of a 'green' Continental Jet planned for first quarter 2002. Over 100 on order.

History: Bombardier's all new Continental Jet is a transcontinental range eight seat corporate jet which will sit in the company's model line-up between the Learjet 60 and Challenger 604.

Bombardier revealed it was developing the Continental Jet at the National Business Aviation Association's annual convention in Las Vegas in October 1998 and formally launched the aircraft at the Paris Airshow the following June. First metal for the prototype was cut in October 1999 with rollout and first flight planned for mid 2001. Certification is planned for the third quarter of 2002 with the first delivery of a 'green' aircraft to Bombardier's Tuscon, Arizona completion centre for interior fitment scheduled for the fourth quarter of 2002.

The Continental Jet (its engineering designation is BD-100) will be powered by two Honeywell (formerly AlliedSignal) AS907 turbofans. The flightdeck will feature a Rockwell Collins Pro Line 21 avionics system displaying information on four large screen liquid crystal displays. The main cabin will seat eight passengers in a standard double club arrangement and will feature a flat floor and stand-up headroom.

The Continental Jet will be largely built from conventional materials with limited use of composites for some non structural fairings. Flight controls are manual apart from fly-by-wire spoilers on the wings. The wings themselves feature a 27° sweepback and winglets.

Final assembly of Continental Jets will be at Bombardier's Learjet facilities in Wichita, Kansas. Fellow Bombardier subsidiaries Canadair and Shorts are also involved in the program – Canadair will build the cockpit, forward fuselage and primary flight controls, Shorts will build the centre fuselage.

Other non Bombardier suppliers include Japan's Mitsubishi heavy Industries which designed and is building the wing, and Taiwan's AIDC which builds the rear fuselage and tail. Boeing Australia builds the composite tailcone, Messier Dowty supplies the undercarriage, Huriel-Dubois the thrust reversers and GKN Westland the engine nacelles.

Photo: Mating of the prototype Continental Jet's wing and fuselage on November 19 2000 at Wichita. (Bombardier)

Bombardier Canadair 601 & 604 Challenger

Country of origin: Canada

Type: Long range corporate jets

Powerplants: 601 – Two 40.7kN (9140lb) General Electric CF34-3A turbofans. 604 – Two CF34-3Bs flat rated to 38.8kN (8729lb) without automatic power reserve, or 41.0kN (9220lb) with.

Performance: 601-1A – Max cruising speed 851km/h (460kt), typical cruising speed 819km/h (442kt), long range cruising speed 786km/h (424kt). Max operating altitude 45,000ft. Range with max fuel and reserves 6208km (3352nm). 601-3A – Normal cruising speed 851km/h (460kt). Service ceiling 41,000ft. Range with max fuel, five pax and reserves 6236km (3365nm). 604 – Max cruising speed 882km/h (476kt), normal cruising speed 851km/h (459kt), long range cruising speed 787km/h (425kt). Certificated ceiling 41,000ft. Range with max fuel, five pax and reserves 7550km (4077nm) at long range cruising speed, 6980km (3769nm) at normal cruising speed.

Weights: 601-3A – Empty 9049kg (19,950lb), operating empty 11,605kg (25,585lb), max takeoff 19,550kg (43,100lb). 601-3A – Empty 9292kg (20,485lb), operating empty 11,566kg (25,500lb), max takeoff 19,550kg (43,100lb) or optionally 20,457kg (45,100lb). 604 – Empty 9806kg (21,620lb), operating empty 12,079kg (26,630lb), max takeoff 21,591kg (47,600lb), or optionally 21,863kg (48,200lb).

Dimensions: Wing span 19.61m (64ft 4in), length 20.85m (68ft 5in), height 6.30m (20ft 8in). Wing area 48.3m² (520.0sq ft).

Capacity: Flightcrew of two. Various seating options available depending on customer preference, maximum permissible seating for 19.

Production: Challenger 601 production completed, with 66 601-1As, 134 601-3As and 59 601-3Rs delivered. Over 165 604s delivered. 500th Challenger (of all models) delivered in October 2000.

History: The Challenger 601 addressed the original CL-600 Challenger's weight problems and replaced the troubled ALF 502 turbofans, creating a highly successful full size corporate jet.

Troubles with the Avco Lycoming powered CL-600 Challenger (described under Canadair) led Canadair (now a division of Bombardier) to develop a vastly improved variant in the form of the General Electric CF34 powered Challenger 601. Another important change was the addition of winglets, which have also been offered as a retrofit to earlier aircraft. The 601 first flew on April 10 1982 and for a time was offered alongside the CL-600. The CL-600 was dropped from the model line in 1983.

The improved 601-3A first flew in 1987, this variant introduced an EFIS glass flightdeck and upgraded engines. Available from 1989, the 601-3R was an extended range model with higher weights (the range increase modifications can also be retrofitted to 601-3As).

Further enhancements led to the Challenger 604. Improvements include an advanced Collins Pro-Line IV EFIS avionics system with colour displays, higher weights, CF34-3B turbofans and increased fuel tankage. Many other minor changes were incorporated based on Bombardier's experience with the Canadair Regional Jet. First flight with CF34-3A engines was in September 1994, first flight with the CF34-3B engines was on March 17 1995. Transport Canada certification was granted that September. First delivery was in January 1996.

Photo: Boeing operates this Challenger 604. (Tim Dath)

Bombardier Global Express

Country of origin: Canada

Type: Ultra long range, high speed, high capacity corporate jet

Powerplants: Two 65.6kN (14,750lb) Rolls-Royce BR710A2-20 turbofans.

Performance: High speed cruise 935km/h (505kt) or Mach 0.88, normal cruising speed 904km/h (488kt) or Mach 0.85, long range cruising speed 850km/h (459kt) or Mach 0.80. Range with eight passengers, four crew and reserves at long range cruising speed 12,038km (6500nm), at normal cruising speed 11,297km (6100nm). Range with max payload at normal cruising speed 9241km (4990nm), at long range cruise speed 9852km (5320km).

Weights: Operating empty 22,135kg (48,800lb), max takeoff 42,410kg (93,500lb), optional max takeoff 43,091kg (95,000lb) or 43,545kg (96,000lb).

Dimensions: Span over winglets 28.65m (94ft 0in), length 30.30m (99ft 5in), height 7.57m (24ft 10in). Wing area 94.95m² (1022sq ft).

Capacity: Flightcrew of two plus one or two flight attendants. Typical arrangements seat from eight to 18 passengers. Can be fitted with a galley, crew rest station, work stations, a conference/lounge/dining area, a stateroom with a fold out bed, toilet, shower and wardrobe. High density 30 seat corporate shuttle configuration offered.

Production: At late 2000 18 Global Expresses were in service with a further 39 at Bombardier's completion centres.

History: The Global Express is one of a new class of ultra long range corporate jets, and competes against the Gulfstream V, Boeing 737 BBJ and Airbus A319CJ (all described separately).

Bombardier's Canadair division announced development of the Global Express (engineering designation BD-700) in October 1991 at the annual NBAA conference in the USA. Officially launched on December 20 1993, it first flew on October 13 1996, with Canadian certification awarded on July 31 1998 with US certification that November. First customer delivery of a completed aircraft was in July 1999.

The fly-by-wire Global Express shares the CRJ's fuselage cross section, but is otherwise an all new design. It features an advanced all new supercritical wing with a 35° sweep and winglets, plus a new T-tail. The engines are Rolls-Royce BR710s with FADEC. The advanced flightdeck features a six screen Honeywell Primus 2000 XP EFIS suite and is offered with optional heads-up displays.

Three Bombardier divisions are involved with the Global Express – Canadair is the Global Express' design leader and manufactures the nose; Shorts is responsible for the design and manufacture of the engine nacelles, horizontal stabiliser and forward fuselage; and de Havilland at Downsview is responsible for final assembly and builds the rear fuselage and vertical tail. In addition, Japan's Mitsubishi Heavy Industries builds the wing and centre fuselage sections in Nagoya.

Bombardier's performance enhancement program for the Global Express will yield aerodynamic, weight and hence performance improvements. The improvements will be fitted to new build aircraft and offered as a retrofit on existing Global Expresses.

Five are being fitted with ground imaging radar for Britain's Royal Air Force under the ASTOR program.

Photo: A Global Express owned by Samsung. (John Adlard)

Brantly B-2 & 305

Country of origin: United States of America

Type: Light piston powered utility helicopters

Powerplant: B-2B – One 135kW (180hp) Textron Lycoming IVO-360-A1A fuel injected flat four piston engine driving a three blade main rotor and two blade tail rotor. 305 – One 225kW (305hp) Textron Lycoming IVO-540-B1A fuel injected flat six.

Performance: B-2B – Max level speed 161km/h (87kt), max cruising speed (at 75% power) 145km/h (78kt). Initial rate of climb 1900ft. Service ceiling 10,800ft. Hovering ceiling in ground effect 6700ft. Range with max fuel and reserves 400km (217nm). 305 – Max speed 193km/h (104kt), max cruising speed 177km/h (96kt). Initial rate of climb 975ft/min. Service ceiling 12,000ft. Hovering ceiling in ground effect 4080ft. Range with max fuel and reserves 354km (191nm).

Weights: B-2B – Empty 463kg (1020lb) or 481kg (1060lb) with floats, max takeoff 757kg (1670lb). 305 – Empty 815kg (1800lb), max takeoff 1315kg (2900lb).

Dimensions: B-2B – Main rotor diameter 7.24m (23ft 9in), length overall 8.53m (28ft 0in), fuselage length 6.62m (21ft 9in), height 2.06m (6ft 9in). Main rotor disc area 41.2m² (443.0sq ft). 305 – Main rotor diameter 8.74m (28ft 8in), length overall 10.03m (32ft 11in), fuselage length 7.44m (24ft 5in), height 2.44m (8ft 1in). Main rotor disc area 60.0m² (654.4sq ft).

Capacity: B-2 series has seating for two side by side. 305 has seating for five with two forward individual seats and rear bench seat for three.

Production: Exact production unclear, but includes more than 400 B-2 series. Production has resumed with Chinese financial backing.

History: The Brantly B-2 series of light helicopters first flew in the early 1950s and returned to production in the early 1990s, while the larger five seat 305 dates to the early 1970s.

The original B-2 two seat light helicopter was designed and built by N Brantly, and flew for the first time on February 21 1953. Certification was awarded in April 1959 allowing production deliveries to get underway soon after. The initial production B-2 model featured a 135kW (180hp) VO-360-A1A flat four, the same basic powerplant that powered the B-2 series through to the 1990s. The initial B-2 was followed by the improved B-2A with a redesigned cabin and the B-2B, which became the definitive production model.

Brantly also developed a larger five seat Model 305 based on the B-2, with a larger cabin and more powerful VO-540 engine. The 305 first flew in January 1964 and was certificated in July the following year.

Brantly production ceased in the early 1970s after more than 400 B-2s had been built. However production resumed in 1976 when the Hynes company acquired the design and production rights to what became the Brantly-Hynes B-2 and 305.

Brantly-Hynes continued low rate manufacture of both models through to the mid 1980s when it too ceased production. Then in 1989 James Kimura formed Brantly Helicopter Industries to build both models, and low rate production resumed for a time.

Brantly International Inc took over the B-2B's FAA production certificate in July 1996 and resumed low rate B-2B production at Vernon, Texas. A number of equipment improvements have been incorporated.

Photo: A new production Brantly International B-2B. (Paul Sadler)

Bristol 170 Freighter

Country of Origin: United Kingdom

Type: Short range freighter/utility transport

Powerplant: Mk 31 – Two 1475kW (1980hp) Bristol Hercules 734 14-cylinder sleeve valve radial piston engines driving four blade propellers.

Performance: Mk 31 – Max cruising speed 311km/h (168kt) at 10,000ft, economical cruising speed 262km/h (141kt). Range with maximum payload 1320km (715nm), range with maximum fuel 2785km (1505nm).

Weights: Mk 31 – Empty 12,247kg (27,000lb), max takeoff 19,958kg (44,000lb).

Dimensions: Mk 31 – Wing span 32.92m (108ft 0in), length 20.83m (68ft 4in), height 6.56m (21ft 6in). Wing area 138.0m² (1487sq ft).

Capacity: Mk 31 payload of 5670kg (12,500lb), or alternatively seating for 15 to 23 passengers, depending on configuration. Mk 32 could seat up to 60 passengers.

Production: Total Bristol 170 production 214 aircraft. In late 2000 one example was in commercial service in Canada with Hawkair Aviation Services in British Colombia who was rebuilding a second machine.

History: Design of the Bristol Freighter began in 1944 in anticipation of demand for a rugged airliner and freighter once WW2 was over, plus potential military requirements.

Bristol's Type 170 started out as a private venture design and was developed under the leadership of technical director L G Frise (who also designed the Frise aileron). Design features of the 170 include its slab sided fuselage, fixed taildragger undercarriage, clamshell style nose doors, raised flightdeck, and a relatively large wing of two spar construction with swept back leading edge and straight trailing edge. As originally proposed the 170 was to be powered by improved sleeve valve Bristol Perseus radials.

The 170 soon caught the British Air Staff's attention which considered the design well suited for use in the India-Burma theatre carrying supplies and vehicles to jungle strips. Two prototypes were ordered with a slightly enlarged fuselage and more powerful Hercules 630 radials.

The 170 made its first flight from Filton on December 2 1945 and while it was too late to be ordered into production for military service in WW2 the type's potential had been demonstrated. The second prototype, configured in 32 seat Wayfarer airliner form (without the nose freight doors) flew the following April. Civil certification was granted in June 1946.

Early production was of the Mk I Freighter and Mk II Wayfarer. The Mark XI (later the Mk 21) was unveiled at the 1947 SBAC airshow and introduced rounded wingtips and more powerful Hercules 672 engines, allowing an increase in gross weight of 1360kg (3000lb). The Mk 31 introduced more powerful engines and remained in production until 1950.

The final 170 model is the Mk 32, developed at the request of Silver City Airways. The Mk 32 featured a lengthened nose which allowed it to carry three cars, rather than two, in a car ferry configuration.

Photo: Hawkair Aviation's Bristol Freighter. Hawkair is the last Bristol 170 operator in the world. (Hawkair Aviation)

British Aerospace/Hawker Siddeley 748

Country of origin: United Kingdom

Type: Regional airliner

Powerplants: Srs 2A – Two 1700kW (2280ehp) Rolls-Royce Dart RDa.7 Mk 534-2 or Mk 535-2 turboprops driving four blade propellers. Super 748 – Two 1700kW (2280ehp) Dart Mk 552-2s.

Performance: Srs 2A – Cruising speed 452km/h (244kt). Range with max payload and reserves 1360km (735nm), range with max fuel and reserves 3130km (1690nm). Super 748 – Cruising speed 452km/h (244kt). Initial rate of climb 1420ft/min. Range with max payload and reserves 1715km (926nm), range with max fuel, 3360kg (7800lb) payload and reserves 2892km (1560nm).

Weights: Srs 2A – Operating empty 12,159kg (26,806lb), max takeoff 21,092kg (46,500lb). Super 748 – Empty 6676kg (14,720lb), max takeoff 12,430kg (27,400lb).

Dimensions: Srs 2A – Wing span 30.02m (98ft 6in), length 20.42m (67ft 0in), height 7.57m (24ft 10in). Wing area 75.4m² (810.8sq ft). Super 748 – Same except for wing span 31.23m (102ft 6in). Wing area 77.0m² (828.9sq ft).

Capacity: Flightcrew of two. Typical seating for between 48 and 51 passengers, at four abreast and 76cm (30in) pitch. Max seating for 58.

Production: Production ended in 1988 by which time 381 had been built, including 89 assembled in India, comprising 20 Srs 1, 85 Srs 2, 123 Srs 2A, 33 Srs 2B/Super 748 and 31 Andovers. Approx 115 in commercial use in 2000.

History: The HS.748 proved to be a quite successful turboprop airliner and today remains popular both as an airliner and freighter.

Avro designed the HS.748 in a bid to re-enter the civil market in anticipation of a decline in its military aircraft business (following Britain's famous 1957 Defence White Paper). Surfacing in 1958 as the Avro 748, the design became part of the Hawker Siddeley group when it formed in 1959 with the merger of several British aviation companies including Hawker and Avro. The new aircraft first flew on June 24 1960, with four prototype aircraft (two for static testing) built. The first production Series 1 flew on August 30 1961.

Series 1 production aircraft were powered by two 1400kW (1880ehp) Dart RDa.6 Mk 514 turboprops, and the first entered service in December 1961 with Skyways Airways.

The Series 2, in its 2, 2A and 2C (with large freight door) variants, was the most successful of the line, the first flying on November 6 1961. The Series 2 introduced higher weights and more powerful engines. The Series 2B appeared in 1977, offering a range of aerodynamic and other improvements, including an increased wing span.

The most advanced 748 variant, the Super 748, first flew in July 1984. Based on the 2B, it also featured a modernised flightdeck, improved efficiency and hushkitted Dart engines, and new galley and internal fittings. Production ended in 1988 with the last flying in December 1988 and being delivered the following month.

India's HAL licence built 89 748s between 1961 and 1984.

The Andover was a military variant with a rear loading freight door and 'kneeling' undercarriage. Small numbers of ex British and New Zealand air force Andovers are presently in commercial service.

Photo: A Bali Air HS.748 Series 2A. (Rob Finlayson)

British Aerospace ATP

Country of origin: United Kingdom

Type: Turboprop powered regional airliner

Powerplants: ATP – Two 1978kW (2653shp) Pratt & Whitney Canada PW126A turboprops driving six blade constant speed BAe/Hamilton Standard propellers. J61 – Two 2050kW (2750shp) PW127Ds.

Performance: ATP – Max cruising speed 493km/h (266kt), economical cruising speed 437km/h (236kt). Range with max payload and reserves 630km (340nm), with 69 passengers and reserves 1480km (800nm). J61 – Max cruising speed 500km/h (270kt). Range with 70 passengers and reserves 1180km (637nm).

Weights: ATP – Operating empty 14,193kg (31,290lb), max takeoff 22,930kg (50,550lb). J61 – Max takeoff 23,678kg (52,200lb).

Dimensions: Wing span 30.63m (100ft 6in), length 26.01m (85ft 4in), height 7.59m (24ft 11in). Wing area 78.3m² (842.84sq ft).

Capacity: Flightcrew of two. Typical one class seating for 64 to 68 in ATP or 70 in Jetstream 61 at four abreast and 79cm (31in) pitch. Combi versions can take passengers and freight.

Production: Total ATP and Jetstream 61 production of 65 (including 2 J61s) built between 1986 and 1993, of which approx 57 are in service.

History: British Aerospace's ATP was a stretched and modernised development of the HS.748, but did not achieve the sales success of its smaller brethren and was effectively in production for barely five years.

British Aerospace announced it was developing an advanced derivative of the 748 in March 1984. The BAe ATP, or Advanced TurboProp, first flew on August 6 1986, while the first production aircraft flew in February 1988. Certification was granted in March 1988 and the ATP entered airline service that May.

Compared to the 748 the ATP features a stretched fuselage (with square rather than round windows) taking maximum seating up to 72 passengers, while Pratt & Whitney Canada PW126 turboprops drive slow turning six blade propellers. Much of the systems and equipment was new or significantly improved. The flightdeck has EFIS instrumentation, while the cabin interior was modernised. The nose was reprofiled and some sweep back was added to the vertical and horizontal tails.

The further improved Jetstream 61 (or J61) was marketed by the newly created Jetstream Aircraft division of British Aerospace in the mid 1990s. Apart from the name change it introduced a number of minor technical changes including an interior based on the Jetstream 41 (including the innovative arm rests incorporated into the cabin walls for window seats), more powerful PW127D engines and increased operating weights giving higher speeds and longer range. The Jetstream 61 was certificated in June 1995, but marketing efforts ceased when AI(R) was formed because it was a direct competitor to the now disbanded consortium's far more successful ATR 72. Just two J61s were completed and they and 11 ATP airframes were scrapped.

Meanwhile the last three whitetail ATPs were not sold until late 1998 (two went to British World, one to Sun-Air of Scandinavia) after production had effectively ceased in 1993. ATP customers included British Airways, British Midland, United Feeder Services, Indonesia's Merpati and Bangladesh Biman.

Photo: A British World ATP. (Keith Gaskell)

British Aerospace Jetstream 31 & 32

British Aerospace Jetstream 41

Country of origin: United Kingdom

Type: 18 seat regional airliner

Powerplants: J31 – Two 700kW (940shp) Garret TPE331-10 turboprops driving four blade props. Super 31 – Two 760kW (1020shp) TPE331-12UARs.

Performance: J31 – Max cruising speed 482km/h (260kt), long range cruising speed 426km/h (230kt). Initial rate of climb 2200ft/min. Range with 19 pax and reserves 1185km (640nm), 1760km (950nm) with 12 pax or 2130km (1150nm) with nine pax. Super 31 – Max cruising speed 490km/h (264kt), long range cruising speed 452km/h (244kt). Initial rate of climb 2240ft/min. Range with 19 pax and reserves 1192km (643nm).

Weights: J31 – Operating empty 4360kg (9613lb), max takeoff 6950kg (15,322lb). Super 31 – Operating empty 4578kg (10,992lb), max takeoff 7350kg (16,204lb).

Dimensions: Wing span 15.85m (52ft 0in), length 14.37m (47ft 2in), height 5.37m (17ft 6in). Wing area 25.1m² (270sq ft).

Capacity: Flightcrew of two. Main cabin seating for up to 19 at three abreast and 79cm (31in) pitch, or 12 passengers in a corporate shuttle configuration, or nine in an executive layout.

Production: Total J31 deliveries of 381, including 161 Super J31s. 221 in service in late 2000.

History: The successful Jetstream 31 traces its ancestry to the Turbomeca Astazou powered Handley Page HP.137 Jetstream 1.

The HP.137 was designed as early ago as 1965, and flew for the first time on August 18 1967. Initial Handley Page production aircraft were powered by 635kW (850hp) Astazou XIVs and named Jetstream 1 (36 built), but deliveries were delayed by excess weight and drag problems. To overcome these problems Handley Page developed the Jetstream 2 with more powerful 800kW (1073shp) Astazou XIVCs. However Handley Page ran into serious financial difficulties in the late 1960s (causing the US Air Force to cancel an order for 10 Garrett TPE331 powered Jetstream C-10As [3Ms]) and it folded in 1969, bringing to an end development of the more powerful Jetstream 2 and plans to market a civil version of the 3M in the USA.

Development of the Jetstream 2 however resumed in 1970 as the Jetstream 200 under the control of the newly formed Jetstream Aircraft in collaboration with Scottish Aviation. Scottish Aviation later assumed overall responsibility for the Jetstream and built a number for Britain's military. Development continued after Scottish Aviation was merged into British Aerospace in 1977, and work on the Jetstream 31 (or J31) began in 1978. The first flight of the Garrett TPE331 powered Jetstream 31 (a converted HP.137) occurred on March 28 1980. UK certification was granted in June 1982.

Subsequent development led to the Super 31, certificated in October 1988. The Super 31 or J32 features uprated engines, higher weights and better performance. The last J31/J32 was built in 1993.

Since 1997 British Aerospace (now BAE Systems) Asset Management has been offering for sale or lease the upgraded J32EP (Enhanced Performance). Its minor aerodynamic and drag improvements enhance payload range and hot and high performance.

Photo: A Jetstream 31. Note underbelly pod. (Gerard Williamson)

Country of origin: United Kingdom

Type: 29 seat regional turboprop airliner

Powerplants: Two 1120kW (1500shp) AlliedSignal TPE331-14GR/HR turboprops driving five blade propellers on initial production aircraft, later two 1230kW (1650shp) TPE331-14s.

Performance: Max speed 547km/h (295kt), economical cruising speed 482km/h (260kt). Service ceiling 26,000ft. Range (initial production) with 29 passengers and reserves 1263km (681nm), definitive production standard 1433km (774nm).

Weights: Empty 6350kg (14,000lb), max takeoff initial production 10,433kg (23,100lb), definitive max takeoff 10,895kg (24,000lb).

Dimensions: Wing span 18.29m (60ft 0in), length 19.25m (63ft 2in), height 5.74m (18ft 10in). Wing area 32.6m² (350.8sq ft).

Capacity: Flightcrew of two. Main cabin seating for up to 29 at three abreast, seating for 27 with galley. Corporate shuttle configured J41s seat 16 at two abreast.

Production: Orders for the Jetstream 41 stood at 100 in May 1997 when BAe announced it was terminating production. 93 are in service.

History: The Jetstream 41 is a stretched and modernised development of the 19 seat Jetstream 31, and was designed to compete in the 29 seat commuter airliner class alongside such types as the Brasilia, Dornier 328 and Saab 340.

The Jetstream 41 (or J41) is based on the J31, but features a 4.88m (16ft) fuselage stretch, consisting of a 2.51m (8ft 3in) plug forward of the wing and a 2.36m (7ft 9in) stretch rear. The increased span wing (with reworked ailerons and flaps) is mounted lower on the fuselage so that it does not carry through the fuselage and interrupt the interior cabin aisle, unlike on the Jetstream 31. Other airframe modifications included a new reprofiled six piece windscreen and extended wing root fairing with greater baggage capacity. More powerful AlliedSignal TPE331 turboprops, mounted in new nacelles with increased ground clearance, drive advanced five blade McCauley propellers. The flightdeck has modern EFIS glass displays.

Development work on the J41 was announced in mid 1989, resulting in the type's first flight on September 25 1991. Three further aircraft were also used in the flight test program, with European JAA certification being awarded on November 23 1992. The first delivery occurred two days later on November 25.

From mid 1994, all aircraft delivered benefited from various payload and range performance improvements, resulting from uprated engines and a higher maximum takeoff weight.

BAe established a separate Jetstream Aircraft division in mid 1993 to market the Jetstream 41. In January 1996 the J41 became part of the Aero International (Regional) stable, but in May 1997 BAe announced that it was terminating J41 production (the AI(R) consortium was disbanded in 1998). Just over 100 had been built when production was terminated, in part victim to a market segment that has lost its popularity with the world's airlines.

Field Aircraft of the UK and Pilatus of Switzerland were risk sharing partners, while Gulfstream was tasked with building wingsets.

Photo: A South African Airlink J41 photographed at Johannesburg. (Rob Finlayson)

Britten-Norman Islander

Countries of origin: United Kingdom & Romania

Type: Commuter airliner and light utility transport

Powerplants: BN-2A – Two 195kW (260hp) Lycoming O-540-E4C flat sixes. BN2B-20 – Two 225kW (300hp) Textron Lycoming IO-540K1B5s.

Performance: BN-2A – Max speed 273km/h (147kt), max cruising speed 257km/h (140kt), econ cruising speed 246km/h (133kt). Initial rate of climb 970ft/min. Service ceiling 13,200ft. Range at econ cruise 1400km (755nm). BN2B-20 – Max speed 280km/h (150kt), max cruising speed 264km/h (142kt), econ cruising speed 245km/h (132kt). Initial rate of climb 1130ft/min. Service ceiling 17,200ft. Range at econ cruise and std fuel 1136km (613nm), with opt fuel 1965km (1060nm).

Weights: BN-2A – Empty equipped 1627kg (3588lb), max takeoff 2993kg (6600lb). BN2B-20 – Empty equipped 1925kg (4244lb), max takeoff 2993kg (6600lb).

Dimensions: Wing span 14.94m (49ft 0in), length 10.86m (35ft 8in), height 4.18m (13ft 9in). Wing area 30.2m² (325.0sq ft).

Capacity: Flightcrew of two pilots or pilot and passenger on flightdeck, with seating for eight in main cabin.

Production: Over 1220 delivered since 1969, including production in the UK and Romania and military Defenders. Approx 70 BN2Ts built.

History: The BN-2 (now BN2) Islander was Britten-Norman's second original design, work on which began during 1963.

Developed as a Dragon Rapide replacement, the emphasis in designing the Islander was on producing a rugged and durable aircraft that had good field performance, low operating costs and was easy to maintain. One unusual feature is that there is no centre aisle between the seats in the main cabin, instead there are three doors along each side of the fuselage for passenger boarding. The prototype was powered by two 155kW (210hp) IO-360s and flew on June 13 1965.

The first production Islanders were powered by 195kW (260hp) IO-540s. Simply designated BN-2, the first flew in 1967. Twenty-three were built before production switched to the BN-2A which introduced fairings to the main undercarriage legs, wing leading edge and flap droop, and an increased max takeoff weight. From 1970 the base A model was the BN-2A-6, the BN-2A-7 had extended wingtips, while the BN-2A-2 and BN-2A-3 were powered by the 225kW (300hp) IO-540, the latter with the extended wingtips.

Appearing in 1972 were the 195kW (260hp) powered BN-2A-26 and extended wingtips BN-2A-27, and the 225kW (300hp) BN-2A-20 and extended wingtips BN-2A-21, all four models having higher weights.

Further improvements came with the BN2B range with higher weights, improved interior and instrument panel and shorter diameter props. The -26, -27, -20 and -21 variants were available as before. The -27 and -21 were later dropped while the -20BN2B-20 and BN2B-26 remain in production. Approx 160 have been built.

The turboprop (Allison/Rolls-Royce 250) powered BN2T Turbine Islander has been built since 1981. Most of the 70 or so built have been for military customers. The Turbine 4000 is a further development.

Britten Norman was bought by Omani interests in May 2000. BN aircraft are built by subsidiary Romaero in Romania before being ferried to the UK for completion.

Photo: A BN-2A-26 Islander. (Gerard Williamson)

Britten-Norman Trislander

Country of origin: United Kingdom

Type: Commuter airliner

Powerplants: Three 195kW (260hp) Lycoming O-540-E4C5 flat six piston engines driving two blade constant speed Hartzell propellers. An optional 1.56kN (350lb) auxiliary rocket engine for use on takeoff was also offered.

Performance: Max speed 290km/h (156kt), cruising speed at 75% power 267km/h (144kt), cruising speed at 50% power 241km/h (130kt). Initial rate of climb 980ft/min. Service ceiling 13,150ft. Max range 1610km (868nm).

Weights: Empty equipped 2650kg (5843lb), max takeoff 4536kg (10,000lb).

Dimensions: Wing span 16.15m (53ft 0in), length 15.01m (49ft 3in), height 4.32m (14ft 2in). Wing area 31.3m² (337.0sq ft).

Capacity: Usually one pilot and passenger on flightdeck. Seating for 16 passengers two abreast at 79cm (31in) pitch in main cabin.

Production: UK production total 74. Three new Trislanders being built in late 2000.

History: Britten Norman adopted a unique three engined configuration for the Trislander (at least for a piston powered aircraft) when it developed this stretched version of the Islander.

Britten-Norman research revealed a market for a stretched development of the Islander, and the company concluded that such an aircraft would need a 50% increase in internal capacity. The company's novel approach to the need for more power for the enlarged Islander was to add a third engine, rather than two engines of increased power output. A nose mounted engine was considered, but due to the Islander's nose configuration, Britten-Norman settled on mounting the engine on the vertical tail, resulting in the BN-2A Mk III Trislander.

The tail mounted engine involved significant modification to the tail and strengthening of the rear fuselage. Other changes over the Islander include a 2.29m (7ft 6in) fuselage stretch forward of the wing, new main landing gear and larger diameter wheels and tyres.

The first Trislander was converted from the second Islander prototype, and it first flew in its new form on September 11 1970. Early production Trislanders were also conversions of Islanders, while subsequent Trislanders were built on the same production line as the Islander. The first production Trislander flew on March 6 1971, certification was granted on May 14, and the first delivery to a customer occurred on June 29 that year.

Britten-Norman Trislander production originally ceased in 1982 after 73 were ordered (by which stage the company had been acquired by Pilatus). Plans to produce the Trislander in the USA as the Tri-Commutair by the International Aviation Corporation, and in Australia never came to fruition. However one of 12 kits built for the Tri-Commutair project was assembled in Guernsey in the UK and flew in March 1996.

In May 1999 Britten-Norman announced it had an order for three new Trislanders for China Northern Airlines to be built from late 2000. They will feature new avionics (including GPS and weather radar) and a modern interior.

Photo: The uniquely configured Trislander. (Richard Koehne)

Canadair CL-44 & Yukon

Country of origin: Canada

Type: Medium range airliner and freighter

Powerplants: CL-44D-4 – Four 4270kW (5730shp) Rolls-Royce Tyne 515/50 turboprops driving four blade propellers.

Performance: CL-44D-4 – Max cruising speed 647km/h (349kt), cruising speed 621km/h (335kt). Service ceiling 30,000ft. Range with max payload 4625km (2500nm), range with max fuel 8990km (4855nm).

Weights: CL-44D-4 – Operating empty 40,345kg (88,952lb), max takeoff 95,250kg (210,000lb).

Dimensions: CL-44D-4 – Wing span 43.37m (142ft 4in), length 41.73m (136ft 11in), height 11.18m (36ft 8in). Wing area 192.7m² (2075sq ft).

Capacity: Flightcrew of two pilots and one flight engineer. CL-44D-4 – Max single class seating for 178 passengers (or 214 in the CL-44J). Max payload 29,959kg (66,048kg).

Production: A total of 27 civil CL-44s built (including one CL-400 conversion), and 12 military CC-106 Yukons, many of which later entered civil service. Up to five remained in service in 2000 as freighters.

History: Based on the Bristol Britannia, the Canadair CL-44 resulted from a mid 1950s Royal Canadian Air Force requirement for a maritime patrol aircraft.

What resulted was the CP-107 Argus. The Argus differed from the Britannia in a number of significant respects – it was powered by Wright Turbo Compound radial engines (selected in place of turboprops to give better endurance at low level), and had a redesigned unpressurised fuselage incorporating a weapons bay. With Canadair already producing the Argus, it was a relatively simple matter to offer a Britannia based design to meet an RCAF requirement for a freighter.

The freighter became the CC-106 Yukon (or to Canadair the CL-44D). Twelve were built, featuring Rolls-Royce Tyne turboprops, lengthened fuselage and wings and a conventional side loading large freight door. The first Yukon flew on November 15 1959.

Canadair then began to offer the Yukon to commercial customers and developed the CL-44D-4, which featured the hinged tail which considerably simplified loading. The first CL-44D-4 flew on November 16 1960, and at that time the model was the largest commercial freighter on offer in the world.

Most CL-44s in civil service have been used as freighters, but Icelandic airline Loftleidir operated three CL-44D-4s plus a single CL-44J as airliners. The J, or the CL-400, differed from the D-4s in that it featured a 4.62m (15ft 2in) fuselage stretch. Only one was built, while two Loftleidir CL-44D-4s were converted to CL-44Js.

One CL-44 was converted by Conroy Aircraft in the US as a large volume freighter with a new enlarged fuselage (similar to the Boeing 337 Super Guppy conversions), and it flew after conversion for the first time on November 26 1969.

Several ex military Yukons found their way into civil service after retirement in 1973. In 2000 at least two and as many as five were operational with with South Africa based Africargo (the only CL-44s left flying in the world).

Photo: HeavyLift operated this Conroy converted CL-44. (Bill Lines)

Canadair CL-600 Challenger

Country of origin: Canada

Type: Medium to long range corporate jet

Powerplants: Two 33.6kN (7500lb) Avco Lycoming ALF 502L turbofans.

Performance: Max speed 904km/h (488kt), max cruising speed 890km/h (480kt), long range cruising speed 800km/h (432kt). Max operating altitude 45,000ft. Range with reserves (later build aircraft) 6300km (3402nm), or 5925km (3200nm) (earlier build aircraft).

Weights: Early build aircraft – Operating empty 10,353kg (22,825lb), max takeoff 18,325kg (40,400lb). Later build aircraft – Empty 8369kg (18,450lb), operating empty 10,285kg (22,675lb), max takeoff 18,201kg (40,125lb).

Dimensions: Wing span 18.85m (61ft 10in), length 20.85m (68ft 5in), height 6.30m (20ft 8in). Wing area 41.8m² (450sq ft).

Capacity: Flightcrew of two. Various customer seating options including 14, 15, 17 or 18 passenger configurations.

Production: 83 Challenger CL-600s built between 1978 and 1983. Production of the Challenger 604 continues, described separately under Bombardier. (500th Challenger was delivered in October 2000.)

History: The Canadair CL-600 Challenger had a troubled early history but formed the basis for what became a very successful business jet.

In 1976 Canadair purchased the exclusive production, development and marketing rights to an all new business jet developed by Learjet designer Bill Lear. Known as the LearStar 600, this design was first conceived in 1974. Notable for its large size cabin, the LearStar promised long range and good operating economics and was also one of the first aircraft to be designed with a supercritical wing. Lear initially planned that the LearStar would be a trijet, but the design had evolved to become a twin by the time Canadair purchased the rights.

Canadair launched development of the LearStar design as the CL-600 Challenger on October 29 1976 with 53 firm orders. Canadair made a small number of changes to the design including repositioning the horizontal tailplane to the top of the fin.

Three development Challengers were built, the first flying on November 8 1978, the others flying in March and July the following year. However the first aircraft crashed in a deep stall accident and while certification was granted in August 1980, temporary restrictions limited maximum takeoff weight to 14,970kg (33,000lb) and maximum speed to 587km/h (317kt), with flight into known icing conditions and the use of thrust reversers prohibited.

A major weight and drag reduction program pared back the Challenger's weight, improving range. The General Electric CF34 powered Challenger CL-601 (described under Bombardier) further addressed performance shortfalls and overcame problems with the CL-600's ALF 502 turbofan.

One version that failed to see the light of day was the CL-610 Challenger E, which would have featured a fuselage stretch allowing seating for 24 passengers, but Canadair suspended development in 1981.

Production of the CL-600 ceased in 1983, having switched to the much improved CL-601. The 600 can be distinguished from the 601 (and current 604) by its different nacelles and its lack of winglets, although some have had winglets retrofitted.

Photo: A CL-600 Challenger gets airborne.

CAP Aviation (Mudry) CAP Series

Country of origin: France

Type: Single and two seat aerobatic light aircraft

Powerplant: 10 B – One 135kW (180hp) Textron Lycoming AEIO-360-B2F fuel injected flat four piston engine driving a two blade fixed pitch Hoffmann propeller. 21 – One 150kW (200hp) AEIO-360-A1B driving a two blade variable pitch Hartzell prop. 232 – One 224kW (300hp) AEIO-540-L1B5 flat six driving a three or four blade constant speed Mühlbauer propeller.

Performance: 10 B – Max speed 270km/h (146kt), max cruising speed at 75% power 250km/h (135kt). Initial rate of climb 1575ft/min. Service ceiling 16,400ft. Range with max fuel 1000km (540nm). 21 – Max cruising speed at 75% power 265km/h (143kt). Initial rate of climb 2755ft/min. Endurance with max fuel two hours. 232 – Max speed 339km/h (183kt). Initial rate of climb 3000ft/min. Service ceiling 15,000ft. Range with max fuel 1200km (647nm).

Weights: 10 B – Empty equipped 550kg (1213lb), max takeoff in aerobatic category 760kg (1675lb), or 830kg (1829lb) in utility category. 21 – Empty 500kg (1103lb), max takeoff 620kg (1367lb). 232 – Empty 590kg (1300lb), max takeoff 816kg (1800lb).

Dimensions: 10 B – Wing span 8.06m (26ft 5in), length 7.16m (23ft 6in), height 2.55m (8ft 5in). Wing area 10.9m² (116.8sq ft). 21 – Wing span 8.08m (26ft 6in), length 6.46m (21ft 3in), height 1.52m (5ft 0in). Wing area 9.2m² (99.0sq ft). 231 – Wing span 8.08m (26ft 6in), length 6.75m (22ft 2in), height 1.90m (6ft 3in). Wing area 9.9m² (106.1sq ft).

Capacity: Two side by side in CAP 10, all others pilot only.

Production: More than 290 CAP 10s and 10Bs, 40 CAP 21s, approximately 30 231s and 231 EXs and 20 232s built.

History: The successful CAP series of aerobatic aircraft dates back to the Piel C.P.30 Emeraude of the early 1960s.

Claude Piel designed the two seat Emeraude in France in the early 1960s for kit builders, but more than 200 were built in four different factories across Europe. The Emeraude first flew in 1962 and was built in basic 50kW (65hp) Continental A65 power C.P.30 form and 65kW (90hp) Continental C90 C.P.301 Super Emeraude form.

One of the companies to build the Emeraude was CAARP, a company owned by Auguste Mudry. CAARP used the basic Emeraude design as the basis for the CAP 10, which was a similar aircraft other than its 135kW (180hp) Lycoming IO-360 engine and stressing for aerobatic flight. The prototype CAP 10 first flew in August 1968. CAARP built 30 CAP 10s for the French air force before Mudry started production for civil orders in 1972 at his other aviation company, Avions Mudry.

The CAP 10 remains in production today in 10 B form with an enlarged tail. The CAP 20 meanwhile was a single seat development with a 150kW (200hp) AEIO-360 engine.

The updated CAP 21 replaced the CAP 20 in 1981. The CAP 21 combined the fuselage of the CAP 20 with an all new wing and new undercarriage, and forms the basis for the similar CAP 231, CAP 231 EX (with a carbon fibre wing) and the current production CAP 232.

Akrotech Europe (owned by Aeronautique Service) took over the CAP series in early 1997 following Mudry's bankruptcy. Akrotech renamed itself CAP Aviation in January 1999.

Photo: An Australian registered CAP 232. (Michael Johnson)

Cessna 150 & 152

Country of origin: United States of America

Type: Two seat primary and aerobatic capable trainer

Powerplants: 150 & 150M – One 75kW (100hp) Continental O-200-A flat four piston engine driving a two blade fixed pitch prop. A152 Aerobat – One 80kW (108hp) Lycoming O-235-N2C.

Performance: 150 – Max speed 200km/h (108kt), optimum cruising speed 196km/h (106kt). Initial rate of climb 640ft/min. Service ceiling 15,300ft. Range 563km (304nm). 150M – Max speed 201km/h (109kt), max cruising speed 196km/h (106kt), economical cruising speed 159km/h (86kt). Initial rate of climb 670ft/min. Service ceiling 12,250ft. Max range with no reserves 909km (490nm), or 1424km (769nm) with optional fuel. A152 – Max speed 200km/h (108kt), cruising speed 195km/h (105kt). Initial rate of climb 715ft/min. Range 575km (310nm).

Weights: 150 – Empty 447kg (985lb), max takeoff 681kg (1500lb). 150M – Empty 458kg (1010lb), max takeoff 726kg (1600lb). A152 – Empty 513kg (1131lb), max takeoff 760kg (1675lb).

Dimensions: 150 – Wing span 10.17m (33ft 4in), length 6.56m (21ft 6in), height 2.11m (6ft 11in). Wing area 14.8m² (159.5sq ft). 150M – Wing span 10.21m (33ft 6in), length 6.58m (21ft 7in), height 2.39m (7ft 10in). Wing area 14.6m² (157sq ft). A152 – Wing span 10.17m (33ft 4in), length 7.25m (24ft 1in), height 2.59m (8ft 6in). Wing area 14.9m² (160sq ft).

Capacity: Seating for two side by side.

Production: Total 150 and 152 production of 31,289 over 27 years, comprising 6860 US built 152s, 589 French built 152s, 22,082 US built 150s and 1758 French built 150s.

History: The introduction of the Cessna 150 marked Cessna's return to the two seat trainer market after a six year absence and resulted in the most prolific and successful two seat trainer line in history.

Development of the original 150 began in the mid 1950s, resulting in a first flight in September 1957. This modern, all new aircraft followed the Cessna conventions then gaining favour of a strut braced high wing, all metal construction and tricycle undercarriage. Production began in September 1958.

A continuous process of model improvement followed, although throughout the 150 model life the Continental O-200-A powerplant remained unchanged. One of the most significant model changes was the 150D of 1964 which introduced the wraparound rear window. The 150G introduced the swept back fin and rudder.

Most versions were built in Standard, Commuter and Trainer forms with differing equipment levels, while licence production in France was undertaken by Reims. Aerobat versions were stressed for limited aerobatic work.

The 152 was a response to availability problems with 80/87 octane fuel, and used the 150's fuselage coupled with a Lycoming O-235 running on 100 Octane (initially a 82kW/110hp O-235-L, later a 81kW/108hp O-235-N). The 152 replaced the 150 from 1977 and remained in production until late 1985. It too was progressively updated, offered in A152 Aerobat form and also built in France.

Photo: A Cessna A150K Aerobat. The 150 is a popular basic trainer. (Paul Sadler)

Cessna 170

Country of origin: United States of America

Type: Four seat light aircraft

Powerplant: 170 – One 108kW (145hp) Continental C145-2 flat six piston engine driving a two blade fixed pitch McCauley propeller. 170B – One 108kW (145hp) Continental O-300-A.

Performance: 170 – Max speed 225km/h (122kt), max cruising speed 195km/h (106kt). Initial rate of climb 690ft/min. Service ceiling 15,000ft. Range 952km (514nm). 170B – Max speed 230km/h (124kt), max cruising speed 195km/h (106kt). Initial rate of climb 690ft/min. Service ceiling 15,500ft. Range 950km (513nm).

Weights: 170 – Empty 554kg (1220lb), max takeoff 998kg (2200lb). 170B – Empty 547kg (1205lb), max takeoff 998kg (2200lb).

Dimensions: Wing span 10.97m (36ft 0in), length 7.61m (24ft 11.5in), height 2.01m (6ft 7in). Wing area 16.2m² (174sq ft).

Capacity: Typical seating for four.

Production: 5173 Cessna 170s were built between 1948 and 1957, including 730 170s and 1537 170As.

History: A larger four seat development of the earlier Cessna Model 140, the four seat 170 was in production for almost a decade, and was the predecessor to the successful and long running 172 series.

Cessna developed the four place 170 as a low cost four seater to round out its product line. The prototype Cessna 170 (NX41691) flew for the first time in September 1947, while the first production 170 flew on February 27 1948. Notable features included the six cylinder 110kW (145hp) Continental C145 engine (later redesignated O-300A), extensive metal construction and the characteristic Cessna braced high wing.

The first production Cessna 170s were delivered from March 1948, but this model was soon replaced by the improved 170A. The primary improvement with the 170A was metal instead of fabric covered wings with larger flaps, but it also featured a single strut under each wing (instead of two) and an increased tail area (identical to that used on the larger Cessna 195).

The third and final major variant appeared in 1953. The Cessna 170B featured the most significant revisions to the line, including the large semi Fowler wing flaps (first developed for the military L-19 Bird Dog and dubbed 'Para-lift' by Cessna marketing) that were to become characteristic of later single engine Cessna models, revised tail wheel steering, larger rear windows and revised and lengthened engine cowling.

The 170 remained in production until 1957, by which stage its popularity had waned and sales of the new 172 had taken off. The early 172 was a direct development of the 170, but introduced tricycle undercarriage and squared up vertical tail surfaces. The 170's most popular year was 1952 when 1186 were built.

It is interesting to note that the 170 laid the foundation for Cessna's two most successful single engine light aircraft lines, the 172 and 182, plus the 180 and 185. As well as the 172 tricycle undercarriage development, the 170 also formed the basis for the 180, which started as a more powerful, higher performance version of the 170, while the subsequent 182 was originally a tricycle undercarriage 180.

Photo: A Cessna 170 (note wing struts). (Bill Lines)

Cessna 180 & 185

Country of origin: United States of America

Type: Four to six seat utility light aircraft

Powerplant: 180 – One 168kW (225hp) Continental O-470-A flat six piston engine driving a two blade constant speed McCauley prop. 180G – One 172kW (230hp) O-470-R. A185F – One 225kW (300hp) fuel injected IO-520-D driving a three blade constant speed prop.

Performance: 180 – Max speed 267km/h (144kt), cruising speed 260km/h (140kt). Initial rate of climb 1150ft/min. Service ceiling 20,000ft. Range 1247km (673nm). 180G – Max speed 273km/h (147kt), max cruising speed 260km/h (141kt), long range cruising speed 195km/h (105kt). Initial rate of climb 1090ft/min. Service ceiling 19,600ft. Range with no reserves 1490km (804nm). A185F – Max speed 283km/h (153kt), max cruising speed 272km/h (147kt), long range cruising speed 207km/h (111kt). Initial rate of climb 1075ft/min. Service ceiling 17,900ft. Range with reserves 1575km (850nm).

Weights: 180 – Empty 690kg (1520lb), max takeoff 1158kg (2550lb). 180G – Empty 692kg (1525lb), max takeoff 1270kg (2800lb). A185F – Empty 783kg (1727lb), max takeoff 1520kg (3350lb).

Dimensions: 180 – Wing span 10.98m (36ft 0in), length 7.98m (26ft 2in), height 2.29m (7ft 6in). Wing area 16.2m² (174sq ft). 180G – Wing span 11.02m (36ft 2in), length 7.77m (25ft 6in), height 2.29m (7ft 6in). Wing area 16.2m² (174sq ft). A185F – Wing span 10.92m (35ft 10in), length 7.81m (25ft 8in). Wing area 16.2m².

Capacity: 180 has standard seating for four, 180 Skywagon and 185 have seating for six. 180H has optional 1360kg (3000lb) cargo pod. Often used with rear seats removed for cargo work. 185 Ag Carryall is fitted with a 571 litre (126Imp gal/151US gal) chemical hopper.

Production: Total 180 production of 6210. Total 185 production 4339 aircraft including 265 U-17A and 215 U-17B military variants and 109 Ag Carryalls.

History: The 180 started life as a more powerful development of the 170 four seater 'tourer', but evolved into a family of useful utility aircraft that was in production for over three decades.

The first 180s were essentially Model 170s with a more powerful 170kW (225hp) O-470-A engine. The first of the type flew in 1952 and deliveries began in February the following year. The 180's career as a high performance single was short lived due to the arrival of the tricycle 180 based 182 in 1956, but by then the type had established itself a useful niche as a utility aircraft.

Progressive updating of the line led to a range of updated models including the 170kW (230hp) 180A, and 1964's 180G with a third cabin window which from 1966 was offered as a six seater, by then having the same fuselage as the more powerful 185 Skywagon. The Skywagon name was applied to the 180 in 1969. The 180 remained in production until 1981.

The first 185 Skywagon flew in July 1960. It differed from the 180 in having a more powerful engine (195kW/260hp) and larger cabin, allowing six seats. Updated models include the 225kW (300hp) A185E from 1967 and the versatile Ag Carryall (introduced in late 1971) with removable chemical spraying equipment. From 1980 the previously optional three bladed prop became standard equipment.

Photo: A float equipped A185F. (Steve Allsopp)

Cessna 172 Skyhawk (O-300 models)

Country of origin: United States of America

Type: Four seat light aircraft

Powerplants: 172 – One 108kW (145hp) Continental O-300-A flat six piston engine driving a two blade fixed pitch McCauley propeller. 175A – One 130kW (175hp) Continental GO-300-C geared flat six. 172F – One 108kW (145hp) Continental O-300-C.

Performance: 172 – Max speed 217km/h (117kt), cruising speed 200km/h (108kt). Initial rate of climb 660ft/min. Service ceiling 15,100ft. Range with no reserves 1000km (539nm). 175A – Max speed 236km/h (128kt), max cruising speed 225km/h (121kt), long range cruising speed 170km/h (91kt). Initial rate of climb 850ft/min. Service ceiling 15,900ft. Range with no reserves 957km (517nm). 172F – Max speed 222km/h (120kt), max cruising speed 211km/h (114kt), long range cruising speed 164km/h (88kt). Initial rate of climb 645ft/min. Service ceiling 13,100ft. Max range with no reserves 1158km (625nm).

Weights: 172 – Empty 572kg (1260lb), max takeoff 998kg (2200lb). 175A – Empty 607kg (1339lb), max takeoff 1066kg (2350lb). 172F – Empty 599kg (1320lb), max takeoff 1043kg (2300lb).

Dimensions: 172 – Wing span 10.92m (35ft 10in), length 8.20m (26ft 11in), height 2.59m (8ft 6in). Wing area 16.2m² (175sq ft). 175A – Wing span 10.97m (36ft 0in), length 8.08m (26ft 6in), height 2.72m (8ft 11in). 172F – Wing span 11.02m (36ft 2in), length 8.07m (26ft 6in), height 2.72m (8ft 11in).

Capacity: Typical seating for four in all models.

Production: Total Cessna 172 family production over 43,500, of which the civil Continental powered models account for about 15,800. Production ran from 1955 to 1967. Approximately 2190 175 Skylarks built.

History: The Cessna 172 is without doubt the most successful mass produced light aircraft in history. From 1955 through to 1967 the Skyhawk was powered by the six cylinder Continental O-300, before this engine was replaced by the four cylinder Lycoming O-320.

The Cessna 172 started life as a relatively simple tricycle undercarriage development of the taildragger 170, with a fairly basic level of standard equipment. First flight was in November 1955. The 172 became an overnight sales success and over 1400 were built in 1956, its first full year of production.

The basic 172 remained in production until replaced by the 172A of early 1960. The 172A introduced a swept back tail and rudder, while the 172B of late 1960 introduced a shorter undercarriage, equipment changes and for the first time the Skyhawk name.

The 172D of 1963 introduced the cut down rear fuselage with wraparound rear window. The 172F introduced electric flaps and was built in France by Reims Cessna as the F172 through to 1971. It also formed the basis for the US Air Force's T-41A Mescalero primary trainer. The 172G of 1966 introduced a more pointed spinner, while the 172H (built until late 1967) was Cessna's last Continental powered 172.

The 175 Skylark meanwhile was powered by a 130kW (175hp) geared GO-300, while the GO-300 powered P172D Powermatic of 1963 had a constant speed prop. The 1966 R172E had a Continental IO-360 and a constant speed prop. It was built in France as the FR172.

The O-320 powered 172 models are described separately.

Photo: A Cessna 172E Skyhawk. (Bill Lines)

Cessna 172 Skyhawk (O-320 models)

Country of origin: United States of America

Type: Four seat light aircraft

Powerplants: 172N – One 120kW (160hp) Lycoming O-320-H2AD flat four piston engine driving a two blade fixed pitch propeller. R172 Hawk XP – One 145kW (195hp) Continental IO-360-KB fuel injected flat six driving a two blade constant speed propeller.

Performance: 172N – Max speed 232km/h (125kt), max cruising speed 226m/h (122kt). Initial rate of climb 770ft/min. Service ceiling 14,200ft. Max range with 45min reserves and standard fuel 1065km (575nm), with optional fuel 1390km (750nm). R172 – Max speed 246km/h (133kt), max cruising speed 241km/h (130kt), long range cruising speed 177km/h (95kt). Initial rate of climb 870ft/min. Service ceiling 17,000ft. Max range with 45min reserves and standard fuel 1065km (575nm), with optional fuel 1510km (815nm).

Weights: 172N – Empty 649kg (1430lb), max takeoff 1043kg (2300lb). R172 – Empty 710kg (1565lb), max takeoff 1157kg (2550lb).

Dimensions: 172N – Wing span 10.92m (35ft 10in), length 8.21m (26ft 11in), height 2.68 (8ft 10in). Wing area 16.3m² (175sq ft). R172 – Span 10.92m (35ft 10in), length 8.28m (27ft 2in), height 2.68m (8ft 10in).

Capacity: Typical seating for four in all models.

Production: Total Cessna 172 family production over 42,500, of which about 22,000 were basic Lycoming powered 172s built 1968-1985.

History: In the late 1960s Cessna re-engined its already highly successful 172 four seater with the four cylinder Lycoming O-320. These O-320 powered models were the most successful to bear the Skyhawk name, as they were in production during GA's golden years, the 1970s.

Cessna re-engined the 172 with the Lycoming O-320-E as compared with the O-300 it had two less cylinders (and thus lower overhaul costs), a 200 hour greater TBO, improved fuel efficiency and more power. Even so, Cessna thought 172 production would be shortlived as the similarly powered but more modern 177 Cardinal was released at the same time. In spite of the Cardinal the Lycoming powered 172 was a great success and easily outsold and outlived its intended replacement.

The first O-320 Skyhawk was the 172I introduced in 1968. The 1969 172K introduced a redesigned fin, reshaped rear windows and optional increased fuel capacity, while 1970's 172K sported conical camber wingtips and a wider track undercarriage. The 172L in production in the 1971/72 model years was the first to feature the enlarged dorsal fin fillet.

The 172M of 1973/76 gained a drooped wing leading edge for improved low speed handling. The 172M was also the first to introduce the optional 'II' package of higher standard equipment. Also in 1976 Cessna stopped marketing the aircraft as the 172.

The 172N was powered by a 120kW (160hp) O-320-H designed to run on 100 octane fuel, but the engine proved troublesome and was replaced by the similarly rated O-320-D in the 172P of 1981. The P was the last basic 172 model, remaining in production until 1985.

Higher performance 172s include the R172 Hawk XP, powered by a 145kW (195hp) Continental IO-360 and the 135kW (180hp) Lycoming O-360 powered, retractable undercarriage 172RG Cutlass.

Photo: A Canadian Cessna 172L Skyhawk. (Gary Gentle)

Cessna 172R Skyhawk & 172S Skyhawk SP

Country of origin: United States of America

Type: Four seat light aircraft

Powerplants: 172R – One 120kW (160hp) Textron Lycoming IO-360-L2A fuel injected flat four piston engine driving a two blade fixed pitch McCauley propeller. 172S – One 135kW (180hp) IO-360-L2A.

Performance: 172R – Max cruising speed at sea level 228km/h (123kt), cruising speed at 75% power at 8000ft 226km/h (122kt). Initial rate of climb from sea level 720ft/min. Service ceiling 13,500ft. Range 1272km (687nm). 172S – Max cruising speed at sea level 233km/h (126kt), cruising speed at 75% power at 8500ft 229km/h (124kt). Initial rate of climb 730ft/min. Range 880km (475nm).

Weights: 172R – Empty 726kg (1600lb), max takeoff 1111kg (2450lb). 172SP – Operating empty 730kg (1610lb), max takeoff 1160kg (2555lb)

Dimensions: Wing span 11.00m (36ft 1in), length 8.20m (26ft 11in), height 2.72m (8ft 11in). Wing area 16.3m² (175.5sq ft).

Capacity: Typical seating for four.

Production: 1000th 172R/172S delivered October 1999.

History: The hot selling Cessna 172R Skyhawk is one of three models Cessna returned to production in the mid 1990s after a decade long break from piston light aircraft manufacture.

Recession and crippling product liability laws in the USA forced Cessna to stop production of light aircraft in 1985. Following the passing in August 1994 of the General Aviation Revitalisation Act (in the USA) Cessna announced it would resume light aircraft production.

The new 172R Skyhawk features a fuel injected Textron Lycoming IO-360-L2A engine which Cessna says is significantly quieter than the O-320 it replaced as it produces its max power at only 2400rpm. Other changes include a new interior with contoured front seats which adjust vertically and recline, an all new multi level ventilation system, standard four point intercom, interior soundproofing, and energy absorbing 26g seats with inertia reel harnesses.

The 172R features epoxy corrosion proofing, stainless steel control cables, a dual vacuum pump system, tinted windows, long range fuel tanks, backlit instruments with non glare glass and an annunciator panel. 172R options include two avionics packages (one with GPS, the other with IFR GPS and a single axis autopilot) and wheel fairings.

An engineering prototype 172R (a converted 1978 172N) powered by an IO-360 first flew in April 1995, while the first new build pilot production 172R first flew on April 16 1996. This aircraft was built at Wichita, while production 172Rs are built at an all new factory in Independence, Kansas.

The higher performance 172S Skyhawk SP delivered from July 1998 features an IO-360-L2A (as on the 172R) but rated at 135kW (180hp) by increasing rpm. It also features a 45kg (100lb) increase in useful payload, a new prop and standard leather interior.

In 2000 a limited number of Millennium Edition Skyhawk SPs were introduced, featuring a new interior, optional IFR GPS, new paint and other detail improvements. Further improvements for all Cessna piston aircraft were announced in October 2000, including an optional 13cm (5in) multifunction liquid crystal display, and a revised interior.

Photo: A New Zealand registered Cessna 172R. (Peter Clark)

Cessna 177 Cardinal

Country of origin: United States of America

Type: Four seat light aircraft

Powerplant: 177 – One 112kW (150hp) Lycoming O-320-E2D flat four piston engine driving a two blade fixed pitch McCauley propeller. 177B – One 135kW (180hp) Lycoming O-360-A1F6D driving a two blade constant speed McCauley prop. 177RG – One 150kW (200hp) Lycoming IO-360-A1B6 fuel injected flat four.

Performance: 177 – Max speed 227km/h (123kt), cruising speed 210km/h (113kt). Initial rate of climb 670ft/min. Service ceiling 12,700ft. Range 1215km (655nm). 177B – Max speed 250km/h (136kt), cruising speed 230km/h (124kt). Initial rate of climb 840ft/min. Service ceiling 14,600ft. Range 1120km (604nm). 177RG – Max speed 290km/h (156kt), long range cruising speed 223km/h (120kt). Initial rate of climb 925ft/min. Service ceiling 17,100ft. Max range with reserves 1657km (895nm).

Weights: 177 – Empty 608kg (1340lb), max takeoff 1067kg (2350lb). 177B – Empty 680kg (1495lb), max takeoff 1135kg (2500lb). 177RG – Empty 800kg (1671lb), max takeoff 1270kg (2800lb).

Dimensions: 177 – Wing span 10.85m (35ft 8in), length 8.22m (27ft 0in), height 2.77m (9ft 1in). Wing area 16.2m² (174sq ft). 177B – Wing span 10.82m (35ft 6in), length 8.44m (27ft 8in), height 2.62m (8ft 7in). Wing area 16.2m² (174sq ft). 177RG – Same except for length 8.31m (27ft 3in).

Capacity: Typical seating for four.

Production: 4240 177s built between 1968 and 1978, including 1490 RGs (including 176 RGs by Reims in France).

History: The Cessna 177 Cardinal was developed in the mid 1960s as an all new replacement for the 172 family.

Announced in late 1967, this new aircraft featured a wide and fairly spacious cabin, a rear set flush riveted high wing which offered good visibility in turns, a single piece all moving tailplane, a high level of standard equipment and the 110kW (150hp) O-320-E recently installed on the 172 driving a fixed pitch prop. Offered in two versions, the standard 177 and up-spec Cardinal, it entered the marketplace priced around 10% more than the then current 172 model.

While not a failure, the 177 failed to attract anywhere near the sales volume of the 172 (in its first full year – 1968 – 601 were built, about half the number of 172s built that year). A perceived shortcoming of the initial model was a lack of power, this was addressed with the 135kW (180hp) O-360-A powered 177A introduced in late 1968. The increase in engine power and hence performance lifted the 177B into a more upmarket four seater market niche between the 172 and 182.

The 1970 model 177B introduced a revised aerofoil, conical camber wingtips, cowl flaps and a constant speed propeller. An up market version known as the Cardinal Classic appeared in 1978 with full IFR instrumentation and luxury interior fittings.

The 177RG was announced in December 1970, and, as its designation suggests, featured hydraulically actuated retractable undercarriage, plus a 150kW (200hp) fuel injected IO-360-A engine and a constant speed prop.

Both the 177B and 177RG remained in production until 1978.

Photo: An American registered 177RG Cardinal. (Gary Gentle)

Cessna 182 Skylane

Country of origin: United States of America

Type: Four seat light aircraft

Powerplants: 182 – One 170kW (230hp) Continental O-470-R flat six piston engine driving a two blade constant speed propeller. TR182 – One 175kW (235hp) Lycoming O-540-L3C5D turbocharged flat six. 182R – One 170kW (230hp) Continental O-470-U.

Performance: 182 – Max speed 257km/h (140kt), cruising speed 253km/h (136kt). Initial rate of climb 1200ft/min. Service ceiling 20,000ft. Range 1078km (582nm). TR182 – Max speed 346km/h (187kt), economical cruising speed 232km/h (125kt). Initial rate of climb 1040ft/min. Service ceiling 20,000ft. Range 1870km (1010nm). 182R – Max speed 275km/h (149kt), cruising speed 246km/h (133kt). Initial rate of climb 865ft/min. Service ceiling 14,900ft. Range with max fuel and reserves 1898km (1025nm).

Weights: 182 – Empty 735kg (1621lb), max takeoff 1160kg (2550lb). TR182 – Empty 837kg (1845lb), max takeoff 1406kg (3100lb). 182R – Empty 786kg (1733lb), max takeoff 1406kg (3100lb).

Dimensions: 182 – Wing span 10.98m (36ft 0in), length 25.17m (25ft 2in), height 2.80m (9ft 2in). Wing area 16.2m² (174sq ft). TR182 & 182R – Wing span 10.92m (35ft 10in), length 8.53m (28ft 0in), height 2.82m (9ft 3in). Wing area 16.2m² (174sq ft).

Capacity: Typical seating for four.

Production: 21,864 182s (including 169 R182s by Reims) built through to 1985.

History: The popular, relatively high performance Cessna 182 began life as a tricycle development of the 180.

The first Model 182 appeared in 1956 while the Skylane name was first introduced with the 1958 182A development to denote an optional higher level of equipment. Major changes were introduced with 1960's 182C, including a third window on each side of the cabin, a swept vertical tail and a 45kg (100lb) increase in gross weight. The 182D of 1961 had shorter undercarriage and a redesigned engine cowl.

The 182E of 1962 introduced the cut down rear fuselage with wrap around rear window, improved O-470-R engine, more fuel and optional autopilot. The 182F had more fuel and could seat six with an optional rear cabin seat for two children. The 182G to 182L models introduced detail changes (some 182Js, as A182s, were built in Argentina). The 182M (1970) has an increased takeoff weight, 1972 182N introduced the 'Camber Lift' wing with bonded leading edge and tubular spring steel main undercarriage legs. The 182P (1977) introduced the O-470-U which ran on 100 octane fuel. The 182Q and 182R had a bonded wing with integral fuel tanks.

The retractable undercarriage Skylane RG arrived in 1977, giving a significant speed increase. A further performance boost came with the introduction of the turbocharged 175kW (235hp) Lycoming O-540-L engine on the T182RG, which became available from 1979. The AiResearch turbocharger meant that maximum power could be delivered right up to the 182's service ceiling of 20,000ft. A turbocharged fixed gear model was also offered, but only small numbers were built.

Cessna 182 production initially ceased in 1985, the new build 182S, 182T and T182 are described separately.

Photo: A 182C Skylane. (Bill Lines)

Cessna 182S/T Skylane & T182 Turbo Skylane

Country of origin: United States of America

Type: Four seat light aircraft

Powerplants: 182S – One 170kW (230hp) Textron Lycoming IO-540-AB1A5 flat six piston engine driving a three blade constant speed propeller. T182 – One 175kW (235hp) TIO-540-AK1A turbocharged flat six.

Performance: 182S – Max speed at sea level 268km/h (145kt), cruising speed at 80% power 260km/h (140kt). Initial rate of climb 924ft/min. Service ceiling 18,100ft. Range with reserves at 75% power at 6000ft 1519km (820nm), at 55% power at 10,000ft 1793km (968nm). T182 – Max cruising speed at 20,000ft 315km/h (170kt), cruising speed at 88% power at 12,000ft 296km/h (160kt). Initial rate of climb 1060ft/min.

Weights: 182S – Standard empty 875kg (1928lb), max takeoff 1406kg (3100lb).

Dimensions: 182S – Wing span 11.00m (36ft 1in), length 8.53m (28ft 0in), height 2.82m (9ft 3in).

Capacity: Typical seating for four.

Production: 182S deliveries began April 1997. 900 built by late 2000. T182 deliveries due January 2001.

History: The 182S, 182T and T182 Skylane are new production models of Cessna's popular 182.

The popularity of Cessna's higher performance 182 (at least compared with the 172) is well illustrated by its 20,000+ production run through to 1985 (second only to the 172). So it's not surprising that the 182 was one of three models Cessna nominated to return to production following the signing of the General Aviation Revitalisation Bill in the USA in 1994.

The new production 182S was based on the 182R but significantly features a new powerplant, a Textron Lycoming IO-540 driving a three blade propeller, in place of the earlier Continental IO-470 (Textron owns both Cessna and Lycoming). Numerous detail changes and improvements were also incorporated, including a metal instrument panel, Honeywell avionics, and interior improvements.

Cessna built three preproduction 182S Skylanes at its Wichita, Kansas facility, the first of which first flew on July 16 1996. US FAA certification was awarded on October 3 1996 and the first production 182S was delivered from Cessna's new Independence, Kansas plant (built specifically for new production of Cessna singles) in April 1997.

In April 2000 the limited edition Millennium Edition Skylane was introduced, featuring a new interior with leather seats, optional IFR GPS, new paint and other detail improvements.

In October 2000 Cessna announced the improved 182T and the reintroduction of a turbocharged Skylane with the T182. Both feature aerodynamic improvements, while the T182, like the original turbocharged Skylane, features a TIO-540, improving rate of climb, takeoff performance and high altitude performance.

T182 Turbo Skylane and 182T deliveries are due to begin in January 2001. They will incorporate improvements for all Cessna piston singles announced in October 2000, including an optional 13cm (5in) multifunction liquid crystal display, and a revised interior.

Photo: The 182S Skylane. (Cessna)

Cessna 188 Ag Wagon series

Country of origin: United States of America

Type: Agricultural aircraft

Powerplant: Ag Truck – One 225kW (300hp) Continental IO-520-D fuel injected flat six piston engine driving a two blade fixed pitch or three blade constant speed McCauley propeller. Ag Husky – One 230kW (310hp) Continental TSIO-520-T turbocharged and fuel injected flat six driving a three blade constant speed McCauley prop.

Performance: Ag Truck – Max speed 196km/h (106kt), max cruising speed 187km/h (101kt). Initial rate of climb 465ft/min. Service ceiling 7800ft/min. Range with max fuel and reserves at 75% power 465km (252nm). Ag Husky – Max speed 209km/h (113kt), max cruising speed (75% power) 196km/h (106kt). Initial rate of climb 510ft/min. Certificated service ceiling 14,000ft. Range with max fuel and reserves at max cruising speed 402km (217nm).

Weights: Ag Truck – Empty 1015kg (2235lb), max takeoff 1495kg (3300lb), max takeoff restricted ag category 1905kg (4200lb). Ag Husky – Empty 1045kg (2305lb), max takeoff restricted ag category 1995kg (4400lb).

Dimensions: Ag Truck – Wing span 12.70m (41ft 8in), length 7.90m (25ft 11in), height 2.49m (8ft 2in). Wing area 19.1m² (205sq ft). Ag Husky – Same except for length 8.08m (26ft 6in).

Capacity: Pilot only in all models. Standard hopper capacity of 757 litres (166Imp gal/200US gal) for Ag Wagon & Ag Pickup; Ag Truck & Ag Husky have a 1059 litre (233Imp gal/280US gal) capacity.

Production: Approximate total of 3975 including 53 Ag Pickups, 1589 Ag Wagons, 1949 Ag Trucks and 385 Ag Huskies.

History: The successful Ag Wagon 188 series was Cessna's only purpose designed agricultural aircraft.

Cessna's Model 188 resulted from research and consultation with agricultural aircraft operators conducted in the early 1960s. The design Cessna settled upon was of the conventional agricultural aircraft arrangement with a braced low wing (unique among Cessna singles) with seating for the pilot only. Like other ag aircraft the chemical hopper is of fibreglass and the rear fuselage is of semi monocoque construction and sealed to reduce the potential for damage from chemical contamination.

The prototype Cessna 188 Ag Wagon first flew on February 19 1965, while type approval was awarded the following February. The 188 was initially offered in two forms, the 170kW (230hp) Continental O-470-R powered 188 (which was named the Ag Pickup from 1972) and the 250kW (300hp) Continental IO-520-D powered 188A Ag Wagon.

The 1972 model year also saw the introduction of the most successful 188 model, the Ag Truck. The Ag Truck has the same powerplant as the Ag Wagon, but a larger hopper and a higher max takeoff weight. The ultimate 188 model is the Ag Husky, which was introduced in 1979. It features a turbocharged TSIO-520-T and a further increased max takeoff weight.

Production of the Ag Pickup was suspended in 1976, the Ag Wagon in 1981, and the Ag Truck and Ag Husky in 1985, when all Cessna light aircraft manufacturing was suspended.

Photo: An A188 Ag Wagon. Note removed lower engine cowling. (Les Bushell)

Cessna 205, 206 & 207

Country of origin: United States of America

Type: Six-eight seat utility light aircraft

Powerplant: 207A – One 225kW (300hp) Continental IO-520-F fuel injected flat six driving a three blade c/s McCauley prop. 206H – One 224kW (300hp) Textron Lycoming IO-540-AC1A driving a three blade c/s prop. T206H – One 231kW (310hp) turbocharged TIO-540-AJ1A.

Performance: 207A – Max speed 278km/h (150kt), max cruise 266km/h (144kt), long range cruise 220km/h (118kt). Initial rate of climb 810ft/min. Service ceiling 13,300ft. Range with std fuel 870km (470nm), with opt fuel 1280km (690nm). 206H – Max speed 278km/h (150kt), cruise speed at 75% power at 6500ft 143kt (265km/h). Initial rate of climb 920ft/min. Service ceiling 16,000ft. Range at 75% power 1120km (605nm), at 55% power 1352km (730nm). T206H – Max speed 315km/h (170kt), cruise speed at 75% at 20,000ft 306km/h (165kt). Initial rate of climb 1010ft/min. Service ceiling 27,000ft. Range at 75% power 1052km (568nm), at 55% power 1320km (713nm).

Weights: 207A – Empty 951kg (2095lb), max takeoff 1639kg (3612lb). 206H – Empty 974kg (2146lb), max ramp 1640kg (3614lb). T206H – Empty 1011kg (2227lb), max ramp 1641kg (3616lb).

Dimensions: 206H & T206H – Wing span 10.97m (36ft 0in), length 8.62m (28ft 3in), height 2.83m (9ft 4in). Wing area 16.2m² (174sq ft). 207A – Wing span 10.92m (35ft 10in), length 9.68m (32ft 9in).

Capacity: 205 & 206 seat six, 207 seats seven or eight.

Production: 574 205s, 7556 206s and 790 207s were built through to 1984. Approx 400 206H & T206H delivered to late 2000.

History: The popular 205/206/207 line began life as a six seat utility flying station wagon.

In its initial form the 205 was essentially a fixed undercarriage derivative of the 210B Centurion, optimised for utility roles. Introduced to the Cessna lineup in 1962, the 205 was powered by the same IO-470 engine as the 210B and featured an additional small cargo door on the left side of the fuselage.

The 205 was built until 1964 when it was replaced by the more powerful 206, which featured larger double cargo doors on the right fuselage side and was known as the Super Skywagon. Continuous improvement followed, including introduction of turbocharged and fuel injected models. The 'Super' prefix was dropped in 1969 and the Stationair name was adopted in 1971. Production originally ceased in 1985.

The 207 Skywagon featured a 1.07m (3ft 6in) fuselage stretch (allowing seating for seven) and became available from 1969. Known as the Stationair 7 from 1978, it was replaced by the 207A Stationair 8 from 1979 with seating for eight. Production ended in 1984.

The 206 was the third Cessna single to be returned to production at the company's new Independence plant in Kansas. Two versions are offered, the normally aspirated 206H and turbo T206H. The T206H first flew on August 6 1996, powered by a TIO-580, while the normally aspirated 206H, powered by an IO-580, followed on November 6. A decision to switch to the TIO-540 and IO-540 because of reliability concerns delayed production. The 206H was certificated on September 9 1998, the T206H on October 1. Deliveries began that December. Millennium Edition models were offered during 2000.

Photo: The new 206H. (Cessna)

Cessna 210 Centurion

Country of origin: United States of America

Type: High performance four to six seat light aircraft

Powerplant: 210L – One 225kW (300hp) Continental IO-520-L fuel injected flat six piston engine driving a three blade constant speed McCauley prop. T210M – One 230kW (310hp) fuel injected and turbocharged TSIO-520R, driving a constant speed three blade prop. P210R – One 240kW (325hp) turbocharged and fuel injected TSIO-520-CE.

Performance: 210L – Max speed 324km/h (175kt), max cruising speed 317km/h (171kt), long range cruising speed 249km/h (134kt). Initial rate of climb 950ft/min. Service ceiling 17,300ft. Max range with reserves 1972km (1065nm). T210M – Max speed 380km/h (205kt), max cruising speed 367km/h (198kt), long range cruising speed 260km/h (140kt). Initial rate of climb 1030ft/min. Service ceiling 28,500ft. Range at long range cruising speed 1455km (785nm). P210R – Max speed 417km/h (225kt) at 20,000ft, max cruising speed 394km/h (213kt) at 23,000ft. Initial rate of climb 1150ft/min. Service ceiling 25,000ft. Range with reserves and optional fuel 2205km (1190nm).

Weights: 210L – Empty 1015kg (2238lb), max takeoff 1725kg (3800lb). T210M – Empty 1022kg (2250lb), max takeoff 1725kg (3800lb). P210R – Empty 1120kg (2470lb), MTOW 1860kg (4100lb).

Dimensions: 210 – Wing span 11.15m (36ft 9in), length 8.59m (28ft 2in). Wing area 16.3m² (175.5sq ft). T210M – Wing span 11.21m (36ft 9in), length 8.59m (28ft 2in), height 2.87m (9ft 5in). Wing area same. P210R – Wing span 11.84m (38ft 10in), length 8.59m (28ft 2in), height 2.95m (9ft 8in). Wing area 17.2m (185.5sq ft).

Capacity: Typical seating for four with optional seating for extra two children in some models, or seating for six adults in later versions.

Production: Total 210, T210 and P210 production 9240 (including 843 P210s).

History: During its production life the Cessna 210 was at the top of the Cessna single piston engine model lineup, positioned between the 182 and the 310 twin.

The 210 first flew in January 1957 and it was the first single engine Cessna aircraft to feature retractable undercarriage and swept back vertical tail surfaces. The 210 entered production in late 1959, and from that time the line was constantly updated.

Notable early upgrades include the 210B which introduced the wraparound rear windows, the 210D with a more powerful (213kW/285hp) engine and introduced the Centurion name, and the turbocharged T210F. The 210G dispensed with the traditional strutted wing in favour of a cantilever wing, increased fuel capacity, restyled rear windows and enlarged tail surfaces. The 210K had a 224kW (300hp) IO-520-L. Continual development of the 210 and T210 range continued through until production ceased in 1985.

A significant development of the T210 was the high performance, pressurised P210 which first appeared in 1978. The pressurisation system (based on that in the 337 Skymaster) meant that the cabin's internal altitude was equivalent to 8000ft when flying at 17,350ft. P210s can be identified by their four small cabin windows.

Photo: The P210 was the first pressurised single to reach quantity production. (Keith Myers)

Cessna 310 & 320

Country of origin: United States of America

Type: Four to six seat light piston twins

Powerplants: 310B – Two 180kW (240hp) Continental O-470-M flat six piston engines driving two blade constant speed McCauley propellers. T310P – Two 213kW (285hp) turbocharged and fuel injected TSIO-520-Bs. 310R – Two 213kW (285hp) Continental IO-520-MB fuel injected piston engines.

Performance: 310B – Max speed 383km/h (207kt), cruising speed 291km/h (157kt). Initial rate of climb 1800ft/min. Service ceiling 19,800ft. Range with no reserves 1617km (873nm). T310P – Max speed 442km/h (237kt), max cruising speed 418km/h (226kt) at 20,000ft, long range cruising speed 288km/h (156kt) at 10,000ft. Initial rate of climb 1862ft/min. Service ceiling 28,600ft. Range at max cruise with no reserves and standard fuel 1226km (662nm) at 10,000ft, 3146km (1699nm) at 20,000ft. 310R – Max speed 383km/h (207kt), max cruising speed 360km/h (195kt), long range cruising speed 267km/h (144kt). Initial rate of climb 1662ft/min. Service ceiling 19,750ft. Max range with reserves 1170km (632nm), with reserves and optional fuel 2840km (1535nm).

Weights: 310B – Empty equipped 1436kg (3166lb), max takeoff 2190kg (4830lb). T310P – Empty 1493kg (3292lb), max takeoff 2268kg (5400lb). 310R – Empty equipped 1480kg (3260lb), max takeoff 2495kg (5500lb).

Dimensions: 310B – Wing span 10.88m (35ft 9in), length 8.23m (27ft 0in), height 3.20m (10ft 6in). Wing area 16.3m² (175sq ft). T310P – Wing span 11.25m (36ft 11in), length 8.92m (29ft 3in), height 3.02m (9ft 11in). Wing area 16.6m² (179sq ft). 310R – Wing span 11.25m (36ft 11in), length 9.74m (32ft 0in), height 3.25m (10ft 8in). Wing area 16.6m² (179sq ft).

Capacity: Typical seating for four or five, with an optional sixth seat.

Production: Total 310 and 320 production was 6013 aircraft, of which 575 were 320s and 196 were for the US military.

History: The sleek Cessna 310 was the first twin engine design from Cessna to enter production after WW2.

The 310 first flew on January 3 1953. The modern lines of the new twin were backed up by innovative features such as engine exhaust thrust augmentor tubes and the storage of all fuel in tip tanks. Deliveries commenced in late 1954.

The first significant upgrade to the 310 line came with the 310C of 1959, which introduced more powerful 195kW (260hp) IO-470-D engines. The 310D of 1960 featured swept back vertical tail surfaces. An extra cabin window was added with the 310F. A development of the 310F was the turbocharged 320 Skyknight, with TSIO-470-B engines and a fourth cabin side window. The Skyknight was in production between 1961 and 1969 (the 320E was named the Executive Skyknight), when it was replaced by the similar Turbo 310.

The 310G introduced the 'stabila-tip' tip tanks, while the 310K replaced the rear two windows on each side with a single unit. Subsequent significant developments include the 310Q and turbocharged T310Q with redesigned rear cabin with a skylight window, and the final 310R and T310R, identifiable for their lengthened noses. Production ended in 1980.

Photo: A Cessna 320 Skyknight. (Gary Gentle)

Cessna 336 & 337 Skymaster

Country of origin: United States of America

Type: Six seat light piston twins

Powerplants: 337D – Two 157kW (210hp) Continental IO-360-C fuel injected flat six piston engines driving two blade constant speed props. T337G – Two 170kW (225hp) turbocharged and fuel injected TSIO-360-Cs.

Performance: 337D – Max speed 320km/h (173kt), max cruising speed at 75% power 306km/h (567kt), econ cruising speed 232km/h (125kt). Initial rate of climb 1200ft/min. Service ceiling 19,500ft. Range at max cruise with no reserves and std fuel 1223km (660nm), with opt fuel 1706km (921nm). T337G – Max speed 402km/h (217kt), max cruising speed 380km/h (205kt), long range cruising speed 273km/h (147kt). Initial rate of climb 1250ft/min. Operational ceiling 20,000ft. Range with no reserves 2422km (1308nm) at 16,000ft.

Weights: 337D – Empty 1204kg (2655lb), max takeoff 1995kg (4400lb). T337G – Empty 1444kg (3184lb), MTOW 2132kg (4700lb).

Dimensions: 337D – Wing span 11.58m (38ft 0in), length 9.07m (29ft 9in), height 2.84m (9ft 4in). Wing area 18.7m² (201sq ft). T337G – Wing span 11.63m (38ft 2in), length 9.07m (29ft 9in), height 2.84m (9ft 4in). Wing area 18.7m² (201sq ft).

Capacity: Typical seating for six. Optional underbelly cargo pod.

Production: 336 total production of 195 between 1962 and 1964. 337 production comprised 1859 337s, 332 pressurised 337s and 513 military versions. Reims built 67 standard and 27 pressurised 337s.

History: Cessna's 336 and 337 Skymaster twins were designed to overcome conventional twins' problems of engine out asymmetric flight handling characteristics through their distinctive push-pull engines and twin boom configuration.

Cessna called the layout concept Centre Line Thrust, as the nose mounted tractor and rear fuselage mounted pusher engines eliminated asymmetric handling problems normally experienced when one of a twin's engines fails. The concept was recognised by the US FAA which created a new centre thrust rating for pilots to be rated on the type.

The fixed undercarriage Model 336 first flew on February 18 1961, but significant improvements to the design were made before production aircraft were delivered. Changes included more powerful engines, a larger fuselage with seating for six, and revised wing, tail and rear engine cowling. The 336 was delivered from mid 1963 and production lasted until late 1964 when it was replaced by the 337 Super Skymaster ('Super' was later dropped) which was released in February 1965.

The improved 337 Super Skymaster ('Super' was dropped in 1972) introduced retractable undercarriage, more powerful 160kW (210hp) engines, a dorsal air intake for the rear engine, variable cowl flaps, repositioned forward engine and cowl for improved visibility, and higher weights.

The turbocharged T337 was first released in the 1967 model year, dropped in 1972 and relaunched in 1978, while the ultimate 337 was the T337G Pressurised Skymaster, introduced from August 1972.

Development of the 337 continued in France by Reims after Cessna production ended in 1980, resulting in the FTB337 STOL and the military FTMA Milirole. Cessna also built more than 500 337s as O-2s for the US Air Force, used largely in the Forward Air Control role.

Photo: A 337G Super Skymaster. (Robert Wiseman)

Cessna 340 & 335

Country of origin: United States of America

Type: Six seat business twins

Powerplants: 340A – Two 230kW (310hp) Continental TSIO-520-NB turbocharged and fuel injected flat six piston engines driving three blade constant speed McCauley propellers. 335 – Two 225kW (300hp) TSIO-520-EBs.

Performance: 340A – Max speed 452km/h (244kt), max cruising speed 425km/h (230kt), economical cruising speed 315km/h (170kt) at 25,000ft. Initial rate of climb 1650ft/min. Service ceiling 29,800ft. Range with reserves at economical cruising speed 2603km (1405nm), at max cruising speed 774km (418nm). 335 – Max speed 425km/h (230kt), max cruising speed 390km/h (211kt), economical cruising speed 313km/h (169kt). Initial rate of climb 1400ft/min. Service ceiling 26,800ft. Range at max cruising speed 2016km (1088nm), range at economical cruising speed 2542km (1372nm).

Weights: 340A – Empty 1780kg (3921lb), max takeoff 2719kg (5990lb). 335 – Empty equipped 1800kg (3963lb), max takeoff 2719kg (5990lb).

Dimensions: Wing span 11.62m (28ft 1in), length 10.46m (34ft 4in), height 3.84m (12ft 7in). Wing area 17.1m² (184sq ft).

Capacity: Typical seating for six, including one pilot.

Production: 1287 340s and 64 335s were built. The 340 was in production between 1971 and 1984, the 335 between 1979 and 1981.

History: The Cessna 340 at its release joined the Beechcraft Duke as the only other six seat pressurised piston twin from a major manufacturer, positioned in Cessna's product line between the 310 and the eight seat 414 and 421.

Development of the 340 began in 1969, but the loss of the prototype early in 1970 set back the development program so that production deliveries did not begin until early 1971. The resulting aircraft borrowed heavily from other Cessna twins of the time including the wings from the 414 and the 310's undercarriage and a similar tail unit. Design features of the new aircraft included a pressurisation system with a differential of 0.29bars (4.2psi) that kept the cabin's internal altitude at 8000ft while the aircraft was at 20,000ft, an all new fail safe fuselage and an integral airstair door.

Initial production 340s were powered by two 210kW (285hp) turbocharged Continental TSIO-520-K engines, but these were replaced on the improved 340A, which was first introduced in 1976. Power for the 340A was supplied by two 230kW (310hp) TSIO-520-NBs, while other improvements included reduced diameter props and a slight increase in weights. The 340A was offered in optional 340A II and 340A III forms with various levels of IFR avionics fitted.

The Cessna 335 is an unpressurised, lighter weight and thus lower cost development of the 340. Available from 1979, aside from being unpressurised it differed from the 340 in having 225kW (300hp) TSIO-520-EB engines, but externally the two were identical. Although Cessna marketing claimed the 335 was the lowest priced cabin class business twin on the market, just 64 335s were built before production was terminated in 1980.

Production of the 340 continued until 1984.

Photo: A Cessna 340A III. (Theo Van Loon)

Cessna 411, 401 & 402

Country of origin: United States of America

Type: Freighter, 10 seat commuter, or six to eight seat business twins

Powerplants: 411A – Two 255kW (340hp) Continental GTSIO-520-C turbocharged, geared and fuel injected flat six piston engines driving three blade constant speed propellers. 402C – Two 240kW (325hp) turbocharged and fuel injected TSIO-520-VBs.

Performance: 411A – Max speed 431km/h (233kt), max cruising speed 396km/h (214kt), long range cruising speed 283km/h (153kt). Initial rate of climb 1900ft/min. Service ceiling 26,000ft. Range with std fuel (no res) 2003km (1081nm), with opt fuel 2310km (1247nm). 402C – Max speed 428km/h (230kt), max cruising speed 394km/h (213kt), long range cruising speed 304km/h (164kt). Initial rate of climb 1450ft/min. Ceiling 26,900ft. Range at econ cruising speed 2360km (1273nm).

Weights: 411A – Empty 1973kg (4350lb), max takeoff 2948kg (6500lb). 402C – Empty (Businessliner) 1845kg (4069lb), max takeoff 3107kg (6850lb).

Dimensions: 411 – Wing span 12.15m (39ft 10in), length 10.20m (33ft 6in), height 3.52m (11ft 7in). Wing area 18.6m² (200sq ft). 402C – Wing span 13.45m (44ft 2in), length 11.09m (36ft 5in), height 3.49m (11ft 6in). Wing area 21.0m² (225.8sq ft).

Capacity: 411 & 401 – Standard seating for six with a centre aisle between the four main cabin seats. 402 – Six to eight seats in corporate configured Businessliner, 10 seats or freight in Utililiner.

Production: 301 Cessna 411s, 404 Cessna 401s and 1535 Cessna 402s were built.

History: The 411 was Cessna's entry into the eight seat cabin class twin market that had previously been dominated by the Beech Queen Air.

Much more modern than the Queen Air, the 411 was lighter, smaller and faster. The prototype first flew in July 1962 and differed from the following production aircraft in having two blade props and direct drive engines, as opposed to the geared GTSIO-520-C engines driving three blade props of production aircraft.

Deliveries commenced in October 1964. Optional features for corporate configured aircraft included folding tables, a toilet and refreshment centre. The 411 was followed up by the 411A from 1967 with lighter and more efficient props and optional extra fuel capacity.

Production of the 411 ceased in 1968, replaced by the 401 and 402, which had first been introduced in late 1966. These developments of the 411 were lighter, less powerful and had direct drive engines, and thus were less costly to operate. While the 401 and 402 were essentially the same aircraft, the 401 was optimised for corporate transport and was fitted with fewer seats than the 402, which was configured for commuter and freighter work. A number of versions of both models were developed with minor refinements, including the 402A, which had a lengthened nose, square windows and an optional 10th seat.

The 402B replaced the 401 and 402A from mid 1972, and was offered in Businessliner corporate and Utililiner convertible passenger/freighter configurations and introduced rectangular cabin windows. The 402C appeared in late 1978 and featured the longer span wings from the 414A and 421C (without tip tanks) and more powerful engines. It remained in production until 1985.

Photo: A Cessna 402B. (Mike McHugh)

Cessna 421 & 414

Country of origin: United States of America

Type: Pressurised six to eight seat cabin twins

Powerplants: 421C – Two 280kW (374hp) Continental GTSIO-520-L geared, turbocharged and fuel injected flat six piston engines driving three blade constant speed McCauley propellers. 414A – Two 230kW (310hp) TSIO-520-NBs.

Performance: 421C – Max speed 478km/h (258kt), max cruising speed 447km/h (241kt) at 25,000ft, long range cruising speed 356km/h (192kt) at 25,000ft. Initial rate of climb 1940ft/min. Service ceiling 30,200ft. Max range at 25,000ft with reserves and standard fuel 2016km (1089nm) or 2748km (1484nm) with optional fuel. 414A – Max speed 436km/h (235kt), cruising speed 420km/h (227kt), economical cruising speed 340km/h (183kt). Initial rate of climb 1520ft/min. Service ceiling 30,800ft. Range with reserves at economical cruising speed 2460km (1327nm), at max cruising speed 2036km (1100nm).

Weights: 421C – Empty equipped 2298kg (5067lb), max takeoff 3379kg (7450lb). 414A – Empty 1976kg (4356lb), max takeoff 3062kg (6750lb).

Dimensions: 421C – Wing span 12.53m (41ft 2in), length 11.09m (36ft 5in), height 3.49m (11ft 6in). Wing area 20.0m² (215sq ft). 414A – Wing span 13.45m (44ft 2in), length 11.09m (36ft 5in), height 3.49m (11ft 6in). Wing area 21.0m² (225.8sq ft).

Capacity: Standard seating for six, optional seating for eight in 421 and 414A, seven in 414.

Production: 1901 Model 421s and 1055 Model 414s built, production of both ceased in 1985.

History: The lineage of the 421 and 414 traces back to the 411, the 421 beginning life as a pressurised development of the 411.

The prototype 421 first flew in October 1965 (three years after the 411). In comparison to the 411 on which it was based, the 421 introduced a cabin pressurisation system (with a differential of 0.3 bar/4.2psi), more powerful geared and turbocharged GTSIO-520-D engines (the turbochargers also drove the pressurisation system) and a higher max takeoff weight. Deliveries of production 421s began in May 1967, Cessna at the time claiming it as the cheapest pressurised twin on the market.

Minor improvements were introduced with the 421A in 1969, while the 421B Golden Eagle of 1970 featured a number of significant improvements including lengthened nose (by 71cm/2ft 4in) and wing span, and GTSIO-520-H engines which retained their power rating to a higher altitude than before. The 421C Golden Eagle was available from late 1975, introducing a bonded wet wing with no tip tanks, higher vertical tail, more efficient props and new trailing link undercarriage.

The 414 was developed as a less powerful, lighter, simpler and lower cost 421. First flown in 1968, it entered production in 1969. It features the fuselage of the 401 and 402 (themselves lighter developments of the 411) with the 421's pressurised fuselage, plus direct drive, rather than geared engines. The improved 414A Chancellor appeared in 1978, introducing the bonded wet wing without tip tanks and the Golden Eagle's longer nose. It remained in production until 1985.

Photo: A 414. (Paul Sadler).

Cessna 404 Titan

Country of origin: United States of America

Type: Ten seat corporate and utility piston twin

Powerplants: Two 280kW (375hp) Continental GTSIO-520-M geared, turbocharged and fuel injected flat six piston engines driving three blade constant speed McCauley propellers.

Performance: Max speed 430km/h (238kt), max cruising speed 402km/h (217kt) at 20,000ft, 369km/h (199kt) at 10,000ft, economical cruising speed 302km/h (163kt) at 20,000ft, 259km/h (140kt) at 10,000ft. Initial rate of climb 1940ft/min. Service ceiling 26,000ft. Range with 936kg (2064lb) useable fuel and reserves at 75% power at 20,000ft 2717km (1466nm), at 10,000ft 2501km (1350nm), at economical cruising speed at 20,000ft 3410km (1840nm), at 10,000ft 3404km (1837nm).

Weights: Empty 2192kg (4834lb) for Ambassador, 2205kg (4861lb) for Courier, 2133kg (4702lb) for Freighter, max takeoff (all variants) 3810kg (8400lb).

Dimensions: Wing span 14.12m (46ft 4in) or 14.23m (46ft 8in) in late production aircraft, length 12.04m (39ft 6in), height 4.04m (13ft 3in). Wing area 22.5m² (242sq ft).

Capacity: Pilot and copilot on flightdeck, seating for eight or nine in main cabin.

Production: 378 Titans built between 1976 and 1982.

History: In July 1975 Cessna announced it was developing a new piston twin suitable for airline, freight and corporate work, capable of taking off with a 1560kg (3500lb) payload from a 770m (2530ft) strip, similar in concept to the successful 402, but larger overall.

The resulting aircraft was the Model 404 Titan, Cessna's largest piston engined twin. It shares the same basic fuselage as the turbine powered 441 Conquest which was developed concurrently, but differs in having geared 280kW (375hp) piston engines and it is unpressurised. Other features include a bonded wet wing (then appearing on a number of 400 series Cessna twins) and the trailing link main undercarriage design shared with the Conquest.

The prototype Titan first flew on February 26 1975, production deliveries got underway in October the following year. Throughout the Titan's model life (Cessna dropped references to the 404 model number in its marketing in the late 1970s) it was offered in three major versions, each differing in internal equipment fit.

The base aircraft was the Titan Ambassador, configured for passenger operations, while the Titan Courier was convertible from passenger to freight configurations, and the Titan Freighter was a pure cargo aircraft. The Titan Freighter was specially equipped for freight operations with a strengthened floor, cargo doors and walls and a ceiling made from impact resistant polycarbonate material. All were offered with II and III avionics equipment levels (as with other Cessna twins). The fully IFR III pack avionics suite included a weather radar.

The Titan underwent minor modifications from 1980 when the wing span was increased and the wingtips redesigned, but production was to last for only another two years until 1982, by which time 378 had been built.

Photo: Titans are popular workhorses among commuter, charter and special mission operators worldwide. (Richard Hall)

Cessna Corsair, Conquest I & II & Caravan II

Countries of origin: USA and France (Caravan II)

Type: Turboprop powered executive transports

Powerplants: 441 – Two 474kW (636shp) Garrett TPE331-8-410S/402S turboprops driving either Hartzell or McCauley props. F406 – Two 373kW (500shp) Pratt & Whitney Canada PT6A-112 turboprops driving three blade McCauley propellers.

Performance: 441 – Max speed 547km/h (295kt), max cruising speed 543km/h (293kt). Initial rate of climb 2435ft/min. Service ceiling 37,000ft. Max range with reserves at long range cruising speed 3048km (1646nm), range with max payload and reserves 2724km (1471nm). F406 – Max cruising speed 455km/h (246kt). Initial rate of climb 1850ft/min. Service ceiling 30,000ft. Range with max fuel at max cruising speed 2135km (1153nm).

Weights: 441 – Empty 2588kg (5706lb), max takeoff 4468kg (9850lb). F406 – Standard empty 2283kg (5033lb), max takeoff 4468kg (9850lb).

Dimensions: 441 – Wing span 15.04m (49ft 4in), length 11.89m (39ft 0in), height 4.01m (13ft 1in). Wing area 23.6m² (253.6sq ft). F406 – Wing span 15.08m (49ft 6in), length 11.89m (39ft 0in), height 4.01m (12ft 7in). Wing area 23.5m² (252.8sq ft).

Capacity: 425 – Typical accommodation one or two pilots and four passengers in corporate configured main cabin, optional passenger seating for six. 441 – One or two pilots and up to nine passengers.

Production: Over 230 Corsair/Conquest Is delivered by the end of 1987 by which time production had been suspended. 370 Model 441s were built. Over 90 F406-5s built thus far.

History: The Corsair and Conquest I, and the 441 Conquest II are the turboprop powered equivalents of the 421 Golden Eagle and 404 Titan respectively. The Reims Caravan II is an unpressurised development.

The Model 441 Conquest was the first to be developed, it was designed concurrently with the piston engined 404 Titan in the mid 1970s. Development was announced in November 1974, and the first flight occurred in August 1976. First customer deliveries were from September 1977. The 441 shares a common fuselage with the Titan, but has a longer span (bonded and wet) wing, a pressurised fuselage, and most significantly, Garrett TPE331 turboprop engines. A PT6A powered 441, the 435, flew during 1986, but it did not enter production.

The 425 Corsair meanwhile was introduced to the Cessna model lineup from 1980. Based on the Model 421 Golden Eagle, it differs from its donor aircraft in having turboprop engines (in this case PT6As). Design work on the Corsair began in 1977, first flight was on September 12 1978 and first deliveries took place in November 1980.

From 1983 Cessna renamed the Corsair the Conquest I, while the Conquest became the Conquest II. Production of both ceased in 1986.

The French built Reims Aviation F406 Caravan II meanwhile is essentially an unpressurised Conquest II but powered by 373kW (500shp) PT6A-112s. The F406 first flew on September 22 1983 with deliveries from late 1984. The Caravan II is the only Cessna 400 series twin currently in production, Reims offers it in a variety of configurations including 12 passenger airliner, freighter and Vigilant maritime patrol and special missions versions.

Photo: A Reims Caravan II with cargo pod. (Richard Koehne)

Cessna T303 Crusader

Country of origin: United States of America

Type: Six seat corporate and utility transport

Powerplants: Two 185kW (250hp) Continental TSIO-520-AE turbo-charged and fuel injected flat six piston engines driving three blade constant speed counter rotating McCauley propellers.

Performance: Max speed 400km/h (216kt) at 18,000ft, max cruising speed 363km/h (196kt), economical cruising speed 333km/h (180kt). Initial rate of climb 1480ft/min. Service ceiling 25,000ft. Range with max fuel and reserves at 71% power at 20,000ft 1658km (895nm), at economical cruising speed and 10,000ft 1890km (1020nm).

Weights: Empty 1526kg (3364lb), max takeoff 2336kg (5150lb).

Dimensions: Wing span 11.90m (39ft 0.5in), length 9.27m (30ft 5in), height 4.06m (13ft 4in). Wing area 17.6m² (189.2sq ft).

Capacity: Normal seating for pilot and five passengers with central aisle between seats. Can be configured with a club seating arrangement for four in the main cabin, or for aerial ambulance or freighter work.

Production: In production between 1981 and 1985, 297 Crusaders were sold.

History: Cessna's Model 303 started life as a four seat twin, intended for the light transport and training role.

A prototype four seat Cessna 303 first flew on February 14 1978. Powered by two 120kW (160hp) Lycoming O-320 engines and featuring extensive use of bonded structures and a supercritical wing section, it would have competed against the Beech Duchess, Grumman GA-7 (Cougar) and Piper Seminole. However, a reappraisal of market demand for the aircraft led to Cessna rethinking the 303 design, and the outcome was a larger six seater aircraft aimed at charter and corporate uses which could replace the Cessna 310 in the company's product line-up (Cessna 310 production wound up in 1980).

The new model, designated the T303 for its turbocharged (and fuel injected) Continental TSIO-520 engines, flew for the first time on October 17 1979. Certification was granted in August 1981, and first production deliveries commenced in October 1981. For a time the T303 was named the Clipper, but this was changed to Crusader as PanAm held the rights to the Clipper name.

The T303 incorporated a number of advanced features, being the first entirely new piston twin from Cessna in over a decade. Features included bonded structures around the integral fuel tank, and counter rotating propellers, while standard equipment included integral airstairs and a full IFR avionics suite (Cessna claimed the latter as a first for its class).

Only minor changes were introduced during production, including the addition of anti ice equipment as an option in 1982, and in 1983 the rear cabin bulkhead was moved aft slightly which increased baggage space and allowed the addition of a cargo door.

Production of the Crusader wound up in 1985 as part of the general decline in light aircraft sales during that period, terminating prematurely what looked to be a promising program. The cancellation also put paid to rumours that Cessna planned to develop more powerful, pressurised, and turboprop powered versions of the aircraft.

Photo: Crusader sales were limited by a declining GA market (which was in part caused by harsh US product liability laws). (John Wiebusch)

Cessna Caravan & Grand Caravan

Country or origin: United States of America

Type: Single turboprop utility transport

Powerplant: 208A – One 450kW (600shp) Pratt & Whitney Canada PT6A-114 turboprop driving a three blade variable pitch Hartzell propeller. 208-675, 208B Super Cargomaster & Grand Caravan – One 505kW (675shp) PT6A-114A.

Performance: 208A – Max cruising speed 340km/h (184kt). Initial rate of climb 1215ft/min. Range with max fuel and reserves 1797km (970nm), range with max fuel and reserves 2066km (1115nm). 208B Super Cargomaster – Max cruising speed 317km/h (171kt). Max initial rate of climb 770ft/min. Range with max fuel and reserves 2000km (1080nm). Grand Caravan – Max cruising speed 337km/h (182kt). Max initial rate of climb 975ft/min. Range with max fuel and reserves 1667km (900nm).

Weights: 208A – Empty 1725kg (3800lb), max takeoff 3310kg (7300lb). 208B Super Cargomaster – Empty 2073kg (4570lb), max takeoff 3970kg (8750lb). Grand Caravan – Empty equipped 2250kg (4965lb), max takeoff 3970kg (8750lb).

Dimensions: 208A – Wing span 15.88m (52ft 1in), length 11.46m (37ft 7in), height 4.32m (14ft 2in). Wing area 26.0m² (279.4sq ft). 208B – Same except for length 12.67m (41ft 7in).

Capacity: 208A – Pilot and typically nine passengers, or up to 14 with an FAA FAR Part 23 waiver. Cargo capacity 1360kg (3000lb). 208B – Passenger accommodation same. Cargo capacity for 1587kg (3500lb). Grand Caravan – One pilot and up to 14 passengers.

Production: Over 1200 delivered by late 2000.

History: With sales exceeding the 1200 mark the useful Caravan is a popular utility workhorse.

Design work for the Caravan dates back to the early eighties. First flight of a prototype occurred on December 9 1982 and certification was granted in October 1984. When production began the following year it became the first all new single engine turboprop powered aircraft to enter production.

The Caravan has had a close association with US package freight specialist Federal Express (FedEx), on whose request Cessna especially developed two pure freight versions. The first of these was the 208A based Cargomaster (40 delivered), the second was the stretched 208B Super Cargomaster (260 delivered). The first Super Cargomaster flew on March 3 1986 and features a 1.22m (4ft) stretch and greater payload capacity, including an under fuselage cargo pannier. FedEx's aircraft lack cabin windows.

The Super Cargomaster formed the basis for 208B Grand Caravan, which first flew in 1990 and is powered by a 505kW (675shp) PT6A-114 (which also powers Super Cargomasters built from 1991). It can seat up to 14 passengers.

Announced at the 1997 NBAA convention, the 208-675 or Caravan 675 has replaced the basic 208A. It combines the standard length airframe with the more powerful PT6A-114 of the 208B.

Underbelly cargo pods and floats are offered as options on the Caravan family, and the type is easily converted from freight to passenger configurations. A military/special missions version of the 208A, dubbed the U-27, has also been offered.

Photo: A Grand Caravan over New Zealand. (Peter Clark)

Cessna Citation & Citation I

Country of origin: United States of America

Type: Light corporate jets

Powerplants: Citation – Two 9.79kN (2200lb) Pratt & Whitney JT15D-1 turbofans. Citation I – Two 9.79kN (2200lb) JT15D-1A1Bs.

Performance: Citation – Max speed 647km/h (350kt), max cruising speed 644km/h (348kt). Initial rate of climb 3350ft/min. Service ceiling 38,400ft. Range with eight people on board and reserves at high speed cruise 2250km (1215nm). Citation I – Cruising speed 662km/h (357kt). Initial rate of climb 2720ft/min. Range with max fuel, 710kg (1560lb) payload and reserves 2460km (1328nm).

Weights: Citation – Empty 2455kg (5408lb), max takeoff 4920kg (10,850lb). Citation I – Empty equipped 3008kg (6631lb), max takeoff 5380kg (11,850lb).

Dimensions: Citation – Wing span 13.32m (43ft 9in), length 13.26m (43ft 6in), height 4.36m (14ft 3in). Wing area 24.2m² (260sq ft). Citation I – Same except for wing span 14.35m (47ft 1in). Wing area 25.9m² (278.5sq ft).

Capacity: Two pilots for Citation and Citation I, single pilot for Citation I/SP. Optional main cabin layouts for five, six or seven passengers.

Production: Over 690 Citations, Citation Is and I/SPs were built between 1971 and 1985.

History: The highly popular Citation and Citation I pioneered the entry level light business jet market, and their success formed the basis for the world's largest family of corporate jets.

Cessna became the first of the big three American manufacturers (Piper, Beech and Cessna) to develop a jet powered transport. In October 1968 Cessna announced its plans to build a new eight place jet powered business aircraft that would be capable of operating into airfields already served by light and medium twins. Dubbed the Fanjet 500, the prototype first flew on September 15 1969. Soon after Cessna named the new jet the Citation.

A relatively long development program followed, during which time a number of key changes were made to the design including a longer forward fuselage, repositioned engine nacelles, greater tail area and added horizontal tail dihedral. In this definitive form the Citation was granted FAA certification on September 9 1971.

Improvements including higher gross weights and thrust reversers were added to the line in early 1976, followed shortly after by the introduction of the enhanced Citation I later that same year. Citation I improvements included higher weights, JT15D-1A engines and an increased span wing. A further model to appear was the Citation I/SP, which is certificated for single pilot operation. The I/SP was delivered in early 1977.

Production of the Citation I ceased in 1985, its place in the Citation line left vacant until the arrival of the CitationJet (described separately) some years later.

Direct developments of the Citation were the Citation II (now Citation Bravo) and Citation V (now Citation Ultra Encore).

Photo: The original Citation and Citation I pioneered a new era in corporate transportation. This shot shows to good effect the type's low ground clearance and tailplane dihedral. This is a Citation I. (Rob Finlayson)

Cessna CitationJet, CJ1 & CJ2

Country of origin: United States of America

Type: Light corporate jets

Powerplants: CitationJet & CJ1 – Two 8.45kN (1900lb) Williams Rolls-Royce FJ44-1A turbofans. CJ2 – Two 10.7kN (2400lb) FJ44-2Cs.

Performance: CitationJet – Max cruising speed at 3990kg (8800lb) AUW 704km/h (380kt). Initial rate of climb 3311ft/min. Certificated ceiling 41,000ft. Range with max fuel and reserves 2750km (1485nm). CJ1 – Range with pilot, three passengers and IFR reserves 2315km (1250nm). CJ2 – Max cruising speed at 33,000ft 741km/h (400kt). Service ceiling 45,000ft. Range with max fuel 3195km (1724nm).

Weights: CitationJet – Empty 2794kg (6160lb), max takeoff 4717kg (10,400lb). CJ1 – Empty 2927kg (6453lb), max takeoff 4808kg (10,600lb). CJ2 – Max takeoff 5618kg (12,375lb).

Dimensions: CitationJet & CJ1 – Wing span 14.26m (46ft 10in), length 12.98m (42ft 7in), height 4.18m (13ft 8in). Wing area 22.3m² (240.0sq ft). CJ2 – Wing span 15.09m (49ft 6in), length 14.29m (46ft 11in), height 4.24m (13ft 11in). Wing area 24.53m² (264.0sq ft).

Capacity: CitationJet & CJ1 – Two flightdeck positions, one for pilot, other for a copilot or passenger. Main cabin seats five in standard layout. CJ2 – Main cabin seats six in standard club arrangement.

Production: 359 production CitationJets built to early 2000 when replaced by CJ1. First CJ2 due delivery late 2000, over 100 on order.

History: The CitationJet is a highly successful light business jet and has spawned the CJ1 and CJ2 improved and stretched developments, respectively.

Cessna launched the new Model 525 CitationJet at the annual US National Business Aviation Association convention in 1989. First flight occurred on April 29 1991, FAA certification was awarded on October 16 1992 and the first delivery was on March 30 1993.

The CitationJet is effectively an all new aircraft. The same basic Citation forward fuselage is mounted to a new T-tail configured tailplane and a new supercritical laminar flow wing, and it features Williams Rolls FJ44 turbofans (with paddle thrust reversers) and trailing link main undercarriage. The CitationJet's fuselage is 27cm (11in) shorter than the Citation/Citation I's, while cabin height is increased courtesy of a lowered centre aisle. It features EFIS avionics and is certificated for single pilot operation.

At the 1998 NBAA convention Cessna revealed the improved CJ1 and stretched CJ2. The CJ1 has replaced the CitationJet and introduced a Collins Pro Line 21 EFIS avionics suite and a moderate increase in maximum takeoff weight. The first production CJ1 was delivered on March 31 2000.

The CJ2 meanwhile is a stretched, faster and more powerful development. A CitationJet was converted to act as the CJ2 prototype and first flew as such on April 27 1999. Certification was awarded on June 21 2000 with first customer deliveries expected late that year.

The CJ2 features an 89cm (35in) cabin and 43cm (17in) tailcone stretch allowing standard seating for six in the main cabin. Like the CJ1 it features Collins Pro Line 21 EFIS avionics, plus uprated FJ44-2C engines, increased span wings, larger area tail, six cabin windows per side and greater range.

Photo: The CJ2. (Cessna)

Cessna Citation II & Bravo

Country of origin: United States of America

Type: Light corporate jets

Powerplants: S/II – Two 11.1kN (2500lb) Pratt & Whitney Canada JT15D-4Bs turbofans. Bravo – Two 12.8kN (2887lb) Pratt & Whitney Canada PW530As.

Performance: S/II – Cruising speed 746km/h (403kt). Initial rate of climb 3040ft/min. Range with two crew, four passengers and reserves 3223km (1739nm). Range with max fuel 3700km (1998nm). Bravo – Max cruising speed 745km/h (402kt). Max initial rate of climb 3195ft/min. Max certificated altitude 45,000ft. Range with four passengers and reserves 3704m (2000nm).

Weights: S/II – Empty equipped 3655kg (8060lb), max takeoff 6850kg (15,100lb). Bravo – Empty 3992kg (8750lb), max takeoff 6713kg (14,800lb).

Dimensions: S/II – Wing span 15.91m (52ft 3in), length 14.39m (47ft 3in), height 4.57m (15ft 0in). Wing area 31.8m² (342.6sq ft). Bravo – Wing span 15.90m (52ft 2in), length 14.39m (47ft 3in), height 4.57m (15ft 0in). Wing area 30.0m² (322.9sq ft).

Capacity: S/II – Flightcrew of two. Main cabin can be optionally configured to seat 10, but standard interior layout for six. Can be configured as an air ambulance with one or two stretchers and up to four medical attendants. Bravo – Standard seating for seven with max seating for 10 in main cabin.

Production: 733 Citation IIs built through to late 1994. Bravo deliveries began Feb 1997, approx 130 delivered by late 2000.

History: The early success of the original Citation led Cessna to develop a larger capacity Citation model in the mid 1970s.

Cessna announced the stretched Citation in September 1976. The fuselage was extended by 1.14m (3ft 9in) to increase maximum seating capacity to 10, while more powerful Pratt & Whitney Canada JT15D-4 engines and greater fuel tankage meant higher cruise speeds and longer range. Increased baggage capacity and increased span wings were also added.

The new Model 550 Citation II first flew on January 31 1977 and FAA certification for two pilot operation was awarded in March 1978. The II/SP is certificated for single pilot operation.

Major improvements were made to the design with the arrival of the Model S550 Citation S/II. Announced in October 1983, this improved version first flew on February 14 1984. Certification, including an exemption for single pilot operation, was granted that July. Improvements were mainly aerodynamic, including a new wing designed using supercritical technology plus JT15D-4B turbofans. The S/II initially replaced the II in production from 1984, but the II returned to the line-up from late 1985, and both variants remained in production until the introduction of the Bravo.

The Bravo features new P&WC PW530A turbofans, modern Honeywell Primus EFIS avionics suite, a revised interior based on that introduced in the Citation Ultra and other improvements such as trailing link main undercarriage. The Bravo first flew on April 25 1995 and was granted certification in August 1996. First delivery was in February 1997.

Photo: A Citation Bravo. (Cessna)

Cessna Citation V, Ultra & Ultra Encore

Country of origin: United States of America

Type: Small to mid size corporate jets

Powerplants: V – Two 12.9kN (2900lb) Pratt & Whitney Canada JT15D-5A turbofans. Ultra – Two 13.6kN (3045lb) JT15D-5Ds. Ultra Encore – Two 14.9kN (3360lb) P&WC PW535As.

Performance: V – Cruising speed 790km/h (427kt). Initial rate of climb 3650ft/min. Range with six passengers, two crew and reserves 3558km (1920nm). Ultra – Max cruising speed 796km/h (430kt). Initial rate of climb 4100ft/min. Certificated ceiling 45,000ft. Range with five passengers 3630km (1960nm). Ultra Encore – Max cruising speed at mid cruise weight 798km/h (431kt). Certificated ceiling 45,000ft. Max range with IFR reserves 3150km (1700nm).

Weights: V – Empty equipped 4004kg (8828lb), max takeoff 7212kg (15,900lb). Ultra – Empty 4196kg (9250lb), operating empty 4377kg (9650lb), max takeoff 7393kg (16,300lb). Ultra Encore – Empty approx 4526kg (9977lb), max takeoff 7544kg (16,630lb).

Dimensions: V & Ultra – Wing span 15.91m (52ft 3in), length 14.90m (48ft 11in), height 4.57m (15ft 0in). Wing area 31.8m² (342.6sq ft). Ultra Encore – Same except height 4.63m (15ft 1in).

Capacity: V – Typical seating for eight passengers. Ultra/Ultra Encore – Standard seating arrangements for seven or eight passengers.

Production: 262 Citation Vs built through to mid 1994. Approx 340 Ultras built. Ultra Encore deliveries due to begin second quarter 2000.

History: The Citation V, Citation Ultra and Ultra Encore are the largest straight wing members of Cessna's highly successful Citation family.

Cessna publicly announced it was developing a stretched development of the Citation II at the annual NBAA convention in New Orleans in 1987. Earlier in August that year the first engineering prototype Model 560 Citation V had successfully completed the type's maiden flight. A preproduction prototype flew in early 1986, while US certification was granted on December 9 1988. Deliveries began the following April.

The Citation V was based on the Citation II/SP, but differences over the smaller jet include more powerful Pratt & Whitney Canada JT15D-5A turbofans and a slight fuselage stretch, allowing seating in a standard configuration for eight passengers. The Citation V proved quite popular, with 262 built through to mid 1994 before production switched to the modernised Ultra.

Cessna announced development of the upgraded Citation V Ultra in September 1993. FAA certification was granted in June 1994, allowing for deliveries of production aircraft to commence soon after. Compared with the Citation V, the Ultra features more powerful 13.6kN (3045lb) Pratt & Whitney Canada JT15D-5D engines and Honeywell Primus 1000 EFIS avionics with three CRT displays (two primary flight displays and one multifunction display).

The Citation Ultra Encore is a new development announced at the 1998 NBAA convention. Compared with the Ultra the Encore introduces new Pratt & Whitney Canada PW535 engines, plus trailing link main undercarriage, more fuel payload, updated interior and improved systems. The Ultra's Honeywell Primus 1000 EFIS avionics suite is retained.

The Ultra Encore first flew on July 9 1998, certification was awarded on May 26 2000 with service entry on September 29 2000.

Photo: The Ultra Encore is the latest development of the Citation V. (Cessna)

Cessna Citation Excel

Country of origin: United States of America

Type: Small to mid size corporate jet

Powerplants: Two 16.9kN (3804lb) Pratt & Whitney Canada PW545A turbofans.

Performance: Max cruising speed at 35,000ft 795km/h (429kt). Initial rate of climb 3790ft/min. Max certificated altitude 45,000ft. Range at economical cruising speed with two crew, four passengers and reserves 3852km (2080nm).

Weights: Standard empty 5402kg (11,910lb), max takeoff 9071kg (20,000lb).

Dimensions: Wing span 16.98m (55ft 10in), length 15.79m (51ft 10in), height 5.24m (17ft 3in). Wing area 34.5m² (369.7sq ft).

Capacity: Flightcrew of two. Choice of four interior configurations with seating for up to 10 passengers in main cabin.

Production: First delivery July 1998, 100th delivered in August 2000.

History: One of the latest members of Cessna's extensive line of Citation business jets, the popular Citation Excel combines the cabin width and standup headroom cabin dimensions of the Citation X in a new small/medium size package.

The new Excel followed from customer consultation over advances in engine and airframe technology. The basis of the Excel is a shortened Citation X fuselage (the same fuselage cross section as was used in the Citation III, VI and VII), combined with a modified unswept supercritical wing based on the Citation V Ultra's, the V's cruciform tail configuration and new Pratt & Whitney Canada PW545A series turbofans.

Other design features include trailing link main undercarriage units and a standard Honeywell Primus 1000 three 20 x 18cm (8 x 7in) screen EFIS avionics package (two Primary Flight Displays, one for each pilot, and a multifunction display).

Cessna claims the Citation Excel's cabin is the largest of any light business jet. It features standup headroom and a dropped aisle that runs the length of the main cabin. Seated head and elbow room is greater than that in the Citation II and V, while the cabin length is similar to the Citation I, II, VI and VII.

The Excel was one of the first applications for the new generation PW500 series engines. The Excel's 16.9kN (3804lb) PW545As (derated from 19.9kN/4450lb, with a TBO of 5000 hours) are fitted with Nordam thrust reversers as standard and the engines allow it to cruise at 801km/h (432kt).

Cessna announced it was developing the Excel at the NBAA convention in October 1994. Prototype construction began in February 1995 and it flew for the first time on February 29 1996. The first production Excel rolled out in November 1997 and the type was certificated in April 1998, with deliveries beginning mid that year at which stage over 200 were on order.

Cessna delivered the 100th Excel in August 2000, at which time the company was building one every three days. Cessna says this is the fastest ramp-up of production of any Citation jet yet.

Photo: According to Cessna, the Excel (pictured here landing) combines the cabin size of a mid size jet with the operational flexibility of a light jet. (Cessna)

Cessna Citation III, VI & VII

Country of origin: United States of America

Type: Medium size corporate jets

Powerplants: III & VI – Two 16.2kN (3650lb) Garrett TFE731-3B-100S turbofans. VII – Two 18.2kN (4080lb) AlliedSignal TFE731-4R-2Ss.

Performance: III & VI – Max cruising speed 874km/h (472kt). Initial rate of climb 805ft/min. Range with two crew and four passengers and reserves 4348km (2346nm). VII – Max cruising speed 881km/h (476kt). Initial rate of climb 4442ft/min. Range with six passengers and reserves 4110km (2220nm).

Weights: III & VI – Empty 5357kg (11,811lb), operating empty 5534kg (12,200lb), max takeoff 9980kg (22,000lb). VII – Empty 5316kg (11,720lb), max takeoff 10,183kg (22,450lb).

Dimensions: Wing span 16.31m (53ft 6in), length 16.90m (55ft 6in), height 5.12m (16ft 10in). Wing area 29.0m² (312.0sq ft).

Capacity: Flightcrew of two. Typical main passenger cabin seating for six, or optionally up to nine.

Production: Total of 202 Citation IIIs delivered when production ceased in 1992. A total of 39 Citation VIs had been built when production ceased in 1995, while 119 VIIs were built to September 2000.

History: The all new Cessna Model 650 Citation III was designed as a high performance, mid size long range corporate jet to supplement the much smaller Citation I and II.

Development of this very different Citation began in 1978. As it evolved, the III had little in common with the previous Citation models other than the name. The new design featured a swept supercritical wing optimised for high speed long range flight, new Garrett TFE731 turbofans, a T-tail, and a new fuselage.

The new jet made its first flight on May 30 1979 with a second prototype flying on May 2 1980. Certification was granted on April 30 1982, first customer deliveries occurring the following year. The Citation III set two time to height records for its class in 1983 and a class speed record by flying from Gander to Le Bourget in 5hr 13min.

Production improvements to the Citation III were first proposed in the cancelled Citation IV. This model was announced in 1989 and was to feature longer range through greater fuel tankage, and better short field performance. In its place instead Cessna developed the Citation VI and VII. The Citation VI was offered as a low cost development of the III with a different avionics package and a standard interior layout, with customised interiors unavailable. First flight of the Citation VI took place in 1991 but only 39 were built when production was wound up in May 1995.

The Citation VII meanwhile features a number of improvements including more powerful engines for improved hot and high performance. The first Citation VII prototype flew in February 1991 and the type was certificated in January 1992. The 119th and last Citation VII (and Cessna Model 650) was rolled out from Cessna's Wichita's facilities on September 15 2000. This last aircraft was delivered to United Foods, which also took delivery of the first Citation III. The VII will be replaced in Cessna's model line-up by the forthcoming Citation Sovereign.

One of the last majors customers for the VII was Executive Jet Aviation which ordered 20 for its NetJets fractional ownership scheme.

Photo: A Canadian registered Citation III. (Gary Gentle)

Cessna Citation Sovereign

Country of origin: United States of America

Type: Mid size corporate jet

Powerplants: Two 25.3kN (5690lb) Pratt & Whitney Canada PW306C turbofans.

Performance: Max cruising speed 821km/h (444kt), econ cruising speed 796km/h (430kt). Certificated ceiling 47,000ft. Time to 43,000ft 26min. Takeoff distance at max takeoff weight 1220m (4000ft). Range with eight passengers 4630km (2500nm).

Weights: Not published at late 2000 except design max payload weight 1134kg (2500lb), full fuel payload 726kg (1600lb).

Dimensions: Wing span 19.24m (63ft 1in), length 18.87m (61ft 11in), height 5.85m (19ft 2in). Wing area 47.9m² (516.0sq ft).

Capacity: Flightcrew of two. Typical seating for eight passengers in a double club arrangement, max seating for 12.

Production: First customer deliveries scheduled for early 2004. Over 80 advance orders placed.

History: Cessna is developing the new Citation Sovereign mid size corporate jet to meet what it sees as a large replacement market for ageing business aircraft such as the Falcon 10, Westwind and Sabreliner.

Cessna revealed the Citation Excel based Model 680 Citation Sovereign at the October 1998 NBAA exhibition in Las Vegas. At that time certification was planned for the second quarter of 2002 with deliveries in the third quarter of that year, but delays will now see assembly of the Sovereign prototype begin in the second quarter of 2001, first flight in the first quarter of 2002, FAA certification in late 2003 and first customer deliveries in early 2004.

The Sovereign is based on the Excel's fuselage and shares some common systems but features an all new wing and numerous other differences. Cessna looked at an all new fuselage cross section for the Sovereign but opted instead to stretch the Excel fuselage (by 1.5m/ 4.9ft) to keep down costs and reduce development time. Even so Cessna claims the Sovereign's eight seat cabin will have 40% more volume than the Bombardier Learjet 60 and 18% more than the Raytheon Hawker 800XP.

Power for the Sovereign will be from two FADEC equipped 25.3kN (5690lb) Pratt & Whitney Canada PW306Cs. The PW306 was selected in part as it also powers the 328JET regional airliner which should give maintenance and reliability benefits because of the airline industry's more rigorous operating demands.

The mildly swept wing is an all new, supercritical design, based on Cessna's experience with the Citation III/VII, V and X. The horizontal stabiliser is also slightly swept. The Sovereign will enjoy good field performance, being able to operate from 1220m (4000ft) runways at max takeoff weight. Another feature is trailing link main undercarriage.

The Sovereign will be equipped with a Honeywell Epic CDS avionics suite, with four 20 x 25cm (8 x 10in) colour flat panel liquid crystal displays, a digital dual channel autopilot and flight director, dual long range navigation systems and dual attitude/heading reference systems. Other standard equipment will include TCAS and an EGPWS (enhanced ground proximity warning system).

Photo: A computer generated image of the Citation Sovereign in flight.

Cessna Citation X

Country or origin: United States of America

Type: Long range, high speed, mid size corporate jet

Powerplants: Two 28.7kN (6442lb) Rolls-Royce AE 3007C turbofans, from 2001 30.1kN (6764lb) AE 3007C-1s.

Performance: Max cruising speed at mid cruise weight Mach 0.91 (934km/h/504kt) at 37,000ft. Initial rate of climb 4000ft/min. Max certificated altitude 51,000ft. Range with reserves 6020km (3250nm).

Weights: Typical empty equipped 9705kg (21,400lb), max takeoff 16,195kg (35,700lb). MTOW from 2001 16,389kg (36,100lb).

Dimensions: Wing span 19.48m (63ft 11in), length 22.00m (72ft 2in), height 5.77m (18ft 11in). Wing area 49.0m² (527.0sq ft).

Capacity: Flightcrew of two. Main cabin seating for up to 12 passengers seated on individual seats and couches in a high density configuration. Other interiors to customer preference, including eight passenger seats in a double club arrangement.

Production: First production Citation X delivered in June 1996. 125 Citation Xs had entered service by late 2000.

History: The Citation X is Cessna's largest, fastest and longest range Citation yet, and is the fastest corporate jet in service.

The Citation X (as in the Roman numeral, not the letter, and Cessna's Model 750) is also the largest member of business aviation's biggest corporate jet family, the Citation series.

The design objectives behind the Citation X included transcontinental USA and trans Atlantic range in a mid size package that cruises faster than any other business jet available. This high speed cruise capability means the X can save up to one hour's flight time on transcontinental US flights, flying from Los Angeles to New York with normal wind conditions in 4 hours 10 minutes. Because of its ability to cruise at high speed at high altitudes, Cessna also says the Citation X consumes less fuel than current jets on such a transcontinental flight.

The X's FADEC equipped Rolls-Royce (formerly Allison) AE 3007A turbofans are very powerful for an aircraft of the X's size, while the highly swept (37°) wings are also long in span. Other design features include the fuselage cross section of the Citation III/ VI/VII but with more efficient use of internal space that allows greater head and shoulder room, an area ruled, waisted rear fuselage, trailing link main undercarriage units and a Honeywell Primus 2000 EFIS avionics suite with five colour CRT displays.

Cessna announced that it was developing the Citation X in October 1990 at that year's NBAA conference. The prototype flew for the first time on December 21 1993, certification was granted on June 3 1996, with the first customer delivery (to golfer Arnold Palmer) that month.

A Citation X was the 2500th Citation to be delivered, handed over on September 10 1997. The USA's National Aeronautics Association awarded its prestigious Collier Trophy to the Citation X design team in February 1997.

From January 2001 Xs will feature slightly more powerful engines, giving better field performance, and a 182kg (400lb) increase in maximum takeoff weight. Previously optional equipment, such as TCAS (Traffic Collision Avoidance System) and EGPWS (Enhanced Ground Proximity Warning System), also becomes standard.

Photo: The Citation X. (Rolls-Royce)

Chichester-Miles Leopard

Cirrus Design Corp Cirrus SR20 & SR22

Country of origin: United Kingdom

Type: High performance jet powered four seat light aircraft

Powerplants: Prototype – Two 1.33kN (300lb) Noel Penny NPT 301 turbofans. 2nd aircraft – Two 3.11kN (700lb) Williams International FJX turbofans. Production aircraft – Two Williams International FJX-2s.

Performance: Prototype aircraft – Max cruising speed 655km/h (354kt). Initial rate of climb 2350ft/min. Range with no reserves 1300km (700nm). Production aircraft (estimated) – Max speed 869km/h (469kt), max and econ cruising speed at 45,000ft 804km/h (434kt). Initial rate of climb 6430ft/min. Service ceiling 55,000ft. Range with max payload 2780km (1500nm), range with max fuel 3545km (1915nm).

Weights: Prototype – Basic empty 795kg (1750lb), max takeoff 1155kg (2550lb). Production aircraft (estimated) – Empty equipped 998kg (2200lb), max takeoff 1815kg (4000lb). Production aircraft – Wing span 7.62m (25ft 0in), length 7.85m (25ft 9in). Wing area 5.97m² (64.3sq ft).

Dimensions: Prototype – Wing span 7.16m (23ft 6in), length 7.54m (24ft 9in), height 2.06m (6ft 9in). Wing area 5.9m² (62.9sq ft).

Capacity: Standard seating for four.

Production: Prototype and preproduction aircraft only built at the time of writing, with design of production aircraft continuing.

History: The Leopard is arguably the most advanced high performance light aircraft yet designed and flown.

The sleek Leopard dates back to the early 1980s when Ian Chichester-Miles, a former Chief Research Engineer at BAe Hatfield, established Chichester-Miles Consultants. CMC completed construction of a Leopard mockup in early 1982 and then contracted Designability Ltd to perform detail design work and build a prototype.

CMC originally hoped that the prototype Leopard would fly in early 1987, however various delays meant that it did not fly until December 12 1988. Since then development has progressed slowly.

The program suffered a setback when the Leopard's engine supplier Noel Penny ceased trading, and all flying stopped while a preproduction aircraft powered by Williams International FJX turbofans was designed and built. This aircraft was displayed at the 1996 Farnborough Airshow and flew for the first time on April 9 1997.

Production Leopards will incorporate a number of advanced design features including all composite construction; supercritical, laminar flow, swept wings; liquid deicing and decontamination system along the wings and tailplane; and EFIS avionics (the prototype features simpler avionics and pressurisation systems and liquid deicing on the tailplane only). The preproduction Leopard incorporates most of these features bar the FJX-2 engines. The Leopard also does not feature spoilers or ailerons, instead roll, pitch and yaw control is provided by the all moving fin and differentially actuated tailplanes.

The first production standard Leopard was due to fly in 2000, with certification and production planned for 2002-03. Proposed production versions include the basic Leopard Jet 3, full performance Leopard Jet 4, Leopard Jet 6 with oval side windows and side entry door and military trainer Leopard T-Jet.

Photo: The second development Leopard. (Paul Merritt)

Country of origin: United States of America

Type: Four seat high performance light aircraft

Powerplant: SR20 – One 150kW (200hp) Teledyne Continental IO-360-ES fuel injected flat six piston engine driving a two or three blade Hartzell propeller. SR22 – One 230kW (310hp) IO-550-N.

Performance: SR20 – Cruising speed at 75% power 295km/h (160kt). Initial rate of climb 920ft/min. Service ceiling 17,500ft. Range with reserves 1480km (800nm). SR22 – Cruising speed at 75% power 333km/h (180kt). Initial rate of climb 1300ft/min. Range at long range cruising speed over 1850km (1000nm).

Weights: SR20 – Empty 885kg (1950lb), max takeoff 1315kg (2900lb).

Dimensions: SR20 – Wing span 10.85m (35ft 7in), length 8.00m (26ft 3in), height 2.82m (9ft 3in). Wing area 12.6m² (135.0sq ft).

Capacity: Typical seating for four.

Production: At late 2000 459 SR20s and 178 SR22s on order. Over 90 SR20s delivered by late 2000.

History: Cirrus Design's SR20 and SR22 are all new, modern high performance four seat light aircraft, and are among the most promising all new light aircraft to emerge in a generation.

Cirrus Design Corporation began life as a designer and manufacturer of kit aircraft. The company's piston or turbine powered kit built VK30 four seater in fact forms the basis of the SR20 design, even though the VK30 features a pusher engine. The VK30 first flew in February 1988 but kit production ceased in 1993 to allow Cirrus to relocate its manufacturing facilities to Duluth, Minnesota, and to concentrate on designing and manufacturing a family of fully certificated and factory built GA aircraft.

Details of the SR20 were publicly revealed at the Oshkosh EAA Convention in July 1994. What was revealed is one of the most advanced four seaters in production or under serious development. The SR20 features composite construction, advanced avionics including a 26cm (10in) multifunction display, side mounted control yokes, a 150kW (200hp) Teledyne Continental IO-360 flat six piston engine with a single lever operating both mixture and throttle, and a car-like interior.

The SR20 is also fitted standard with a Ballistic Recovery System (BRS) parachute (a first for a certificated production aircraft), while various energy absorbing features have been designed into the airframe to reduce deceleration loads and increase its ability to absorb energy in the event of an impact.

Apart from its high levels of technology, Cirrus claims that the SR20 offers significant improvements over current four seaters in the areas of performance, price, interior cabin space and internal noise levels.

The SR20 prototype first flew on March 31 1995. FAA FAR Part 23 certification was awarded on October 23 1998 (delayed because Cirrus decided to redesign the wing to lower the stall speed and improve lateral control). First customer delivery was on July 20 1999.

The SR22 is a higher performance development which was publicly revealed on October 20 2000. It is based on the SR20 but features a much more powerful 230kW (310hp) Teledyne Continental IO-550-N. Certification and first deliveries are planned for late 2000, with around 20% of SR20 buyers switching their orders to the new development.

Photo: An SR20 in flight. (Cirrus)

Commander 114B & 115

Country of origin: United States of America

Type: Four seat high performance light aircraft

Powerplant: 115 – One 195kW (260hp) Textron Lycoming IO-540-T4B5 fuel injected flat six piston engine driving a three blade constant speed McCauley propeller. 114TC – One 200kW (270hp) turbocharged and fuel injected TIO-540-AG1A.

Performance: 115 – Max speed 304km/h (164kt), cruising speed at 75% power 296km/h (160kt), economical cruising speed at 65% power 287km/h (155kt). Initial rate of climb 1070ft/min. Range at 75% power 1585km (855nm), range at 65% power 1742km (940nm), at 55% power 1862km (1005nm). 114TC – Max speed 364km/h (197kt), cruising speed at 75% power 328km/h (177kt). Initial rate of climb 1050ft/min. Service ceiling 25,000ft. Range at 75% power 1240km (670nm), at 65% power 1445km (780nm).

Weights: 115 – Empty 954kg (2102lb), max ramp 1480kg (3260lb). 114TC – Empty 1018kg (2245lb), max takeoff 1500kg (3305lb)

Dimensions: Wing span 9.98m (32ft 9in), length 7.59m (24ft 11in), height 2.57m (8ft 5in). Wing area 14.1m² (152sq ft).

Capacity: Typical seating for four.

Production: Approx 160 Commander 114B/TC/ATs built. Deliveries of 115s began in mid 2000.

History: The Commander 114B and recently released 115 are modernised developments of the Rockwell Commander 114.

The Rockwell Commander 114 was itself a more powerful development of the Commander 112 of 1970, one of only two new GA designs from Rockwell. Unfortunately for Rockwell, the 150kW (200hp) powered 112 was widely regarded as underpowered. To address concerns with the 112, Rockwell developed the 114 which incorporated a number of improvements plus most importantly a 195kW (260hp) six cylinder engine.

The 112 and 114 remained in production with Rockwell until 1979. In 1981 Rockwell's General Aviation Division was sold to Gulfstream Aerospace. Gulfstream held the manufacturing rights for the Commander family but never built the 112 or 114, instead selling the rights to the newly formed Commander Aircraft Company in 1988.

Under Commander Aircraft Company's stewardship, the basic 114 design was improved and updated considerably. The main changes to the Commander 114B over the original 114 included a restyled engine cowling to reduce drag and other aerodynamic improvements, a quieter and more efficient three blade McCauley Black Mac propeller, and a new luxury leather and wool interior.

The revised Commander 114B was issued a new Type Certificate on May 4 1992 and production aircraft were delivered from later that year.

Commander also offered the 114AT optimised for pilot training and the turbocharged 200kW (270hp) TIO-540 powered 114TC, which entered service in 1995.

On March 29 2000 Commander announced the introduction of the improved Commander 115 series, which is available in 115, 115TC and 115AT forms. Engine, airframe and systems improvements and an upgraded avionics package are incorporated while range is significantly increased.

Photo: The turbocharged Commander 114TC. (Commander)

Convair CV-240, 340 & 440

Country of origin: United States of America

Type: Short haul commercial transports

Powerplants: CV-240 – Two 1490kW (2000hp) Pratt & Whitney R-2800-CA18 Double Wasp piston radial engines driving three blade constant speed propellers. CV-340 – Two 1790kW (2400hp) R-2800-CB16 Double Wasps. CV-440 – Two 1865kW (2500hp) R-2800-CB16 or -CB17 Double Wasps.

Performance: CV-240 – Cruising speed 435km/h (235kt). Range with max fuel 2900km (1565nm). CV-340 – Cruising speed 457km/h (247kt). Typical range with max payload 935km (505nm). CV-440 – Max cruising speed 483km/h (261kt), economical cruising speed 465km/h (250kt). Service ceiling 24,900ft. Range with max payload 756km (408nm), range with max fuel 3106km (1677nm).

Weights: CV-240 – Empty 12,520kg (27,600lb), max takeoff 18,956kg (41,790lb). CV-340 – Empty 13,375kg (29,486lb), max takeoff 21,320kg (47,000lb). CV-440 – Empty 15,110kg (33,314lb), max takeoff 22,544kg (49,700lb).

Dimensions: CV-240 – Wing span 27.97m (91ft 9in), length 22.76m (74ft 8in), height 8.20m (26ft 11in). Wing area 75.9m² (817sq ft). CV-340 – Wing span 32.12m (105ft 4in), length 24.13m (79ft 2in), height 8.58m (28ft 2in). Wing area 85.5m² (920sq ft). CV-440 – Same as CV-340 except for length 24.84m (81ft 6in).

Capacity: CV-240 – Flightcrew of two or three. Passenger seating for up to 40, or a 4240kg (9350lb) payload. CV-340 – Flightcrew of two or three. Passenger seating for up to 52, or a 6075kg (13,391lb) payload. CV-440 – Flightcrew of two or three. Passenger seating for up to 52, or a 5820kg (12,836lb) payload.

Production: 176 CV-240s, 133 civil and 99 military (C-131 Samaritan) CV-340s and 153 CV-440s were built.

History: The Convair CV-240, 340 and 440 was one of the closest designs to come near to being a Douglas DC-3 replacement as despite a glut of cheap DC-3s in the postwar years this family of airliners achieved considerable sales success.

Design of the original CV-110 was initiated in response to an American Airlines request for a DC-3 replacement. American found the CV-110 (which first flew on July 8 1946) to be too small and asked that the CV-110 be scaled up in size, and this resulted in the CV-240 ConvairLiner. The CV-240 was arguably the most advanced short haul airliner of its day, and first flew on March 16 1947 and entered service on June 1 1948.

The success of the CV-240 led to the 1.37m (4ft 6in) stretched CV-340, which first flew on October 5 1951, and the CV-440 (often called the Metropolitan) which incorporated some aerodynamic improvements and first flew on October 6 1955.

The CV-240, CV-340 and CV-440 sold in large numbers, mainly to airlines in North America, and formed the backbone of many airlines' short to medium haul fleets. Today the small number that remain in service are mainly used as freighters.

Many of the surviving aircraft have been converted with turboprops, and these conversions are discussed in the following entry.

Photo: A Portuguese registered Convair 440 operated by the UK's Atlantic Airways, part of Coventry based Air Atlantique. (Dave Fraser)

Convair CV-540, 580, 600, 640 & CV5800

Country of origin: United States of America

Type: Short haul turboprop converted commercial transports

Powerplants: CV-580 – Two 2800kW (3750shp) Allison 501-D13H turboprops driving four blade propellers. CV-640 – Two 2255kW (3025hp) Rolls-Royce R.Da.10/1 Darts. CV5800 – Two 3430kW (4600shp) Allison 501-D22Gs.

Performance: CV-580 – Max cruising speed 550km/h (297kt) at 20,000ft. Range with 2270kg (5000lb) payload 3650km (1970nm), range with max fuel 4773km (2577nm). CV-640 – Cruising speed 483km/h (260kt). Range with max payload 1979km (1069nm), range with max fuel 3138km (1695nm).

Weights: CV-580 – Operating empty 13,732kg (30,275lb), max take-off 26,371kg (58,140lb). CV-640 – Operating empty 13,733kg (30,275lb), max takeoff 25,855kg (57,000lb). CV5800 – Operating empty 15,043kg (33,166lb), max takeoff 28,576kg (63,000lb).

Dimensions: CV-580 – Wing span 32.12m (105ft 4in), length 24.84m (81ft 6in), height 8.89m (29ft 2in). Wing area 85.5m² (920sq ft). CV5800 – Same except for length 29.18m (95ft 9in).

Capacity: Flightcrew of two or three. Passenger seating for up to 56 at four abreast and 76cm (30in) pitch. CV5800 – Seating for 76.

Production: 170 CV-340s and CV-440s converted to CV-580s, 38 CV-240s converted to CV-600s, 27 CV-340s and CV-440s converted to CV-640s. 87 CV-580s, 5 CV-600s and 13 CV-640s were in commercial service in late 2000. Two CV5800 conversions in service.

History: The original piston Convairs have been the subject of a number of turboprop modification programs, the types's inherent strength and reliability making it a popular choice for conversions.

As early as 1950 the potential of turboprop powered CV-240s was recognised, leading to first flight of the Allison 501 powered CV-240 Turboliner that December, while an Allison 501D powered YC-131C conversion of the CV-340 for the US Air Force first flew on June 19 1954. One other early conversion occurred in 1954 when D Napier and Sons in Britain converted CV-340s with that company's 2280kW (3060hp) Eland N.El.1 turboprops as the CV-540. Six -540s were converted for Allegheny Airlines in the USA, although these aircraft were later converted back to piston power. Canadair meanwhile built 10 new aircraft with Eland engines for the Royal Canadian Air Force from 1960.

The most popular Convair conversions were those done by PacAero in California for Allison, and this involved converting CV-340s and CV-440s to CV-580s with Allison 501D turboprops, plus modified tail control surfaces and a larger tail area. The first such conversion flew on January 19 1960, although it was not until June 1964 that a converted aircraft entered service (with Frontier Airlines).

Convair's own conversion program involved Rolls-Royce Darts, and the first of these flew on May 2 1965. Thus converted CV-240s became CV-600s, while CV-340s and CV-440s became CV-640s.

Kelowna Flightcraft in Canada has offered the most ambitious Convair conversion program, the CV5800, which stretches a CV-580 by 4.34m (14ft 3in) and reverts to the CV-440's original tail unit. Production conversions also have the options of a new freight door and new avionics. Two are in service with Contract Air Cargo in the US.

Photo: A Convair CV-580 airliner. (John Wiebusch)

Curtiss C-46 Commando

Country of origin: United States of America

Type: Freighter

Powerplants: C-46 – Two 1495kW (2000hp) Pratt & Whitney R-2800-34 Double Wasp 18 cylinder radial piston engines driving three blade constant speed propellers. C-46R – Two 1565kW (2100hp) Pratt & Whitney R-2800 C or CA series radial pistons.

Performance: C-46 – Typical cruising speed 300km/h (162kt). Range with 2585kg (5700lb) payload 1880km (1017nm). C-46R – Max speed 435km/h (235kt), max cruising speed 378km/h (204kt). Service ceiling 22,000ft. Range with max fuel 2897km (1564nm).

Weights: C-46 – Operating empty 14,970kg (33,000lb), max payload 5265kg (11,630lb), max takeoff 21,772kg (48,000lb). C-46R – Empty 13,290kg (29,300lb), max takeoff 22,680kg (50,000lb).

Dimensions: Wing span 32.92m (108ft 0in), length 23.27m (76ft 4in), height 6.60m (21ft 8in). Wing area 126.2m² (1358sq ft).

Capacity: Flightcrew of two pilots and optional flight engineer. Typical accommodation for freight, but in an airliner configuration can seat 36, or in military configuration 50 troops.

Production: 3182 Commandos built for US armed forces (as the C-46 for the USAAF and R5C for the USN). Many hundreds subsequently converted for civil service. Approx 16 in service as of late 2000.

History: The Curtiss Commando came into widespread civilian service as both an airliner and a freighter after a large number were built as transports for the US military during World War 2, although the original Curtiss design was intended as an airliner.

Originally intended as a competitor to the highly successful Douglas DC-3, which was the preeminent airliner of the time, the Curtiss CW-20 was designed to operate on routes of up to 1000km (540nm), which at the time accounted for 90% of the US domestic airline system. The CW-20 featured two 1270kW (1700hp) Wright R-2600 Twin Cyclone radial engines, twin vertical tails and a pressurised double lobe, or 'double bubble' fuselage. Accommodation would have been for 36 passengers plus four crew.

Later in timing than the DC-3, the CW-20 first flew on March 26 1940. In July that year an impressed US Army Air Force ordered 20 unpressurised CW-20s, which it named the C-46 Commando. The first production aircraft was completed in May 1942, by which time the powerplant choice had been switched to P&W R-2800s, and the first deliveries to the US Army occurred that July.

Initially the C-46 was troubled with reliability problems in military service, but these were soon overcome and the Commando proved to be a useful transport with its relatively cavernous freight hold.

A proposed postwar commercial version was the CW-20E, but it failed to attract customer interest and thus all Commandos to enter civilian service were ex military aircraft. Many were purchased by American operators for freight work while several hundred operated in Latin America. One postwar version though was the Riddles Airlines C-46R which had more powerful engines and better performance. Thirty or so were converted.

In 2000 five Commandos were believed to be operational in Alaska, four in Canada, and as many as seven in Bolivia.

Photo: A C-46 freighter in Alaska. (Rob Finlayson)

Dassault Mystère/Falcon 10 & 100

Country of origin: France

Type: Light corporate jet

Powerplants: 10 & 100 – Two 14.4kN (3230lb) Garrett TFE731-2 turbofans.

Performance: 10 – Max cruising speed 912km/h (492kt). Range with four passengers and reserves 3560km (1920nm). 100 – Max cruising speed same. Range with four passengers and reserves 3480km (1880nm).

Weights: 10 – Empty equipped 4880kg (10,760lb), max takeoff 8500kg (18,740lb). 100 – Empty equipped 5055kg (11,145lb), max takeoff 8755kg (19,300lb).

Dimensions: Wing span 13.08m (42ft 11in), length 13.86m (45ft 6in), height 4.61m (15ft 2in). Wing area 24.1m² (259sq ft).

Capacity: Flightcrew of two on flightdeck. Main cabin is typically configured to seat four in an executive club seating arrangement. Main cabin can seat up to seven in Falcon 10 or eight in Falcon 100 in a high density layout. Can be configured for air ambulance, aerial photography and navaid calibration missions.

Production: In addition to three prototypes, 226 Falcon 10s and Falcon 100s (including seven military MERs & 31 Falcon 100s), were built between 1973 and 1990, of which 172 10s and 35 100s were in civil service in late 2000.

History: The smallest of Dassault's corporate jet family, the Falcon 10 and Falcon 100 series (Mystère 10 and Mystère 100 in France) sold in good numbers during a production run that lasted almost two decades.

In concept a scaled down Falcon/Mystère 20, the Falcon 10/100 was an all new design except for similar high lift wing devices. It was conceived in the late 1960s, the second member of the Dassault Falcon family to be developed. Dassault originally intended the Falcon 10 be powered by two General Electric CJ610 turbojets, and a CJ610 powered prototype first flew on December 1 1970.

Flight testing was delayed until May 1971 while changes were made to the wing design, including increasing the wing sweepback angle. The second prototype was the first to be powered by Garrett TFE731 turbofans, and it completed its first flight on October 15 1971. Flight testing was completed with the aid of a third prototype, and French and US certification was awarded in September 1973. Deliveries of production aircraft began that November.

While almost all Falcon 10 production was for civil customers, the French navy ordered seven, designated the Mystère 10 MER, as multi purpose pilot trainers. Missions include simulation of targets for Super Etendard pilots and instrument training.

The improved Falcon 100 replaced the Falcon 10 in production in the mid 1980s. Certificated in December 1986, changes included an optional early EFIS glass cockpit, a higher maximum takeoff weight, a fourth cabin window on the right side and a larger unpressurised rear baggage compartment.

Production of the Falcon 100 ceased in 1990 with the last delivered that September.

Photo: A New Zealand registered Falcon 100. Like the larger Falcon 50 and 900, the Falcon 10 and 100 are powered by the popular Garrett (later AlliedSignal, now Honeywell) TFE731. (Bill Lines)

Dassault Mystère/Falcon 20 & 200

Country of origin: France

Type: Mid size corporate jet and multirole utility transport

Powerplants: 20 – Two 20.0kN (4500lb) General Electric CF700-2D-2 turbofans. 200 – Two 23.1kN (5200lb) Garrett ATF 3-6A-4Cs.

Performance: 20 – Max cruising speed 863km/h (466kt), economical cruising speed 750km/h (405kt). Service ceiling 42,000ft. Range with max fuel and reserves 3300km (1780nm). 200 – Max cruising speed 870km/h (470kt), economical cruising speed 780km/h (420kt). Service ceiling 45,000ft. Range with max fuel, eight passengers and reserves 4650km (2510nm).

Weights: 20 – Empty equipped 7530kg (16,600lb), max takeoff 13,000kg (28,660lb). 200 – Empty equipped 8250kg (18,290lb), max takeoff 14,515kg (32,000lb).

Dimensions: Wing span 16.32m (53ft 7in), length 17.15m (56ft 3in), height 5.32m (17ft 6in). Wing area 41.0m² (441.33sq ft).

Capacity: Flightcrew of two. Typical main cabin seating for between eight and 10 passengers, up to 14 in a high density configuration.

Production: Production ended in 1988 when the last Falcon 200 was delivered, by which time 38 200s and 476 20s (including HU-2Js) had been delivered. The last 20 was completed in late 1983. In 2000 430 Falcon 20s and 32 Falcon 200s remained in corporate use.

History: The Mystère or Falcon 20 and 200 family remains Dassault's most successful business jet program thus far, with more than 500 built and most still in service.

Development of the original Mystère 20 traces back to a joint collaboration between Sud Aviation (which later merged into Aerospatiale) and Dassault in the late 1950s. Prototype construction began in January 1962, leading to a first flight on May 4 1963. This first prototype shared the production aircraft's overall configuration, but differed in the powerplant. The prototype was initially powered by 14.7kN (3300lb) Pratt & Whitney JT12A-8 turbojets, whereas production Mystère 20s (or Falcon 20s outside France) were powered with General Electric CF700s. The first GE powered 20 flew on New Year's Day 1965. Throughout the type's production life Aerospatiale built the tail and rear fuselage. The 20 remained in production until 1983.

The Falcon 200 is a re-engined development of the 20 which Dassault first publicly announced at the 1979 Paris Airshow. A converted Falcon 20 served as the prototype, and first flew with the new Garrett ATF 3-6A-4C engines on April 30 1980. French DGAC certification was awarded in June 1981.

Apart from the Garrett engines, the Falcon 200 (initially the 20H) introduced greater fuel capacity and much longer range, redesigned wing root fairings and some systems and equipment changes. The 200 remained in production until 1988.

The Guardian is a maritime surveillance variant of the Falcon 200 sold the French navy (as the Gardian) and the US Coast Guard (HU-2J).

AlliedSignal (now Honeywell) offers a Falcon 20 re-engine program with its TFE731 turbofan. More than 100 Falcon 20s have now been re-engined with 21.1kN (4750lb) TFE731-5ARs or -5BRs.

In 1973 Dassault flew the prototype Falcon 30, a 30 seat regional airliner stretched development of the 20, but it did not enter production.

Photo: A US registered Falcon 20. (Gary Gentle)

Dassault Falcon 50

Country of origin: France

Type: Long range mid size corporate jet

Powerplants: 50 – Three 16.5kN (3700lb) AlliedSignal TFE731-3 turbofans. 50EX – Three 16.5kN (3700lb) Honeywell TFE731-40s.

Performance: 50 – Max cruising speed 880km/h (475kt), long range cruising speed 797km/h (430kt). Max operating altitude 45,000ft. Range with eight passengers and reserves 5715km (3084nm). 50EX – Range with eight passengers at Mach 0.80 5602km (3025nm), at Mach 0.75 6083km (3285nm).

Weights: 50 – Empty equipped 9150kg (20,170lb), standard max takeoff 17,600kg (38,800lb), or optionally 18,500kg (40,780lb). 50EX – Empty equipped 9603kg (21,270lb), standard max takeoff 18,007kg (39,700lb), optional max takeoff 18,497kg (40,780lb).

Dimensions: Wing span 18.86m (61ft 11in), length 18.52m (61ft 11in), height 6.98m (22ft 11in). Wing area 46.8m^2 (504.1sq ft).

Capacity: Flightcrew of two pilots. A number of cabin seating arrangements offered. Seating for eight or nine with aft toilet, or for up to 12 with forward toilet. Max accommodation for 19. Can accommodate three stretchers and two medical attendants in a medevac role.

Production: More than 300 have been delivered since 1979 including almost 50 50EXs.

History: The trijet Falcon 50 is a very substantial long range upgrade based on the earlier twinjet Mystère/Falcon 20 and 200 family.

The Dassault Falcon 50 was developed for long range trans Atlantic and transcontinental flight sectors, using the Falcon 20 as the design basis. However, to meet the 6440km (3475nm) range requirement significant changes mean that the Falcon 50 is for all intents and purposes an all new aircraft.

Key new features include three 16.6kN (3700lb) Garrett TFE731 turbofans, in place of the Falcon 20's two General Electric CF700s, mounted on a new area ruled tail section, plus a new supercritical wing of greater area than that on the 20 and 200. Falcon 20 components carried over include the nose and fuselage cross section.

The first flight of the prototype Falcon 50 occurred in November 1976, although it wasn't until March 7 1979 that FAA certification was granted. In the meantime the design had been changed to incorporate the supercritical wing, although the original wing's basic planform was retained. A second prototype first flew on February 18 1978, the first preproduction aircraft following on June 13 1978. First customer deliveries began in July 1979.

In April 1995 Dassault announced the long range Falcon 50EX with more fuel efficient TFE731-40 turbofans, 740km (400nm) greater range (at Mach 0.80) than the base Falcon 50 and a new EFIS flightdeck based on the Falcon 2000's with Collins Pro Line 4 avionics. The 50EX also features as standard equipment items offered as options only on the standard Falcon 50.

The Falcon 50EX's maiden flight was on April 10 1996, with French and US certification in November and December 1996 respectively. First delivery (to Volkswagen) was in the following January.

The Surmar is a maritime patrol version of the 50 ordered by the French navy (fitted with a FLIR and search radar).

Photo: A Falcon 50. (Trent Jones)

Dassault Falcon 900

Country of origin: France

Type: Large intercontinental range corporate jet

Powerplants: 900B – Three 21.1kN (4750lb) AlliedSignal TFE731-5BRs. 900EX – Three 22.3kN (5000lb) Honeywell TFE731-60s.

Performance: 900B – Max cruising speed 927km/h (500kt), economical cruising speed Mach 0.75. Max certificated altitude 51,000ft. Range with 15 passenger and reserves 7116km (3840nm), with eight passengers and reserves at Mach 0.80 7150km (3860nm). 900EX – Range with eight passengers at Mach 0.80 8020km (4330nm), at long range cruising speed 8335km (4500nm).

Weights: 900B – Empty equipped 10,255kg (22,611kg), max takeoff 20,640kg (45,500lb). 900EX – Empty equipped 10,830kg (23,875lb), max takeoff 21,909kg (48,300lb).

Dimensions: Wing span 19.33m (63ft 5in), length 20.21m (66ft 4in), height 7.55m (24ft 9in). Wing area 49.0m^2 (527.43sq ft).

Capacity: Flightcrew of two. Main passenger cabin seating for eight and 15 passengers, or up to 18 in a high density configuration.

Production: Over 255 Falcon 900s (inc 7 900Cs & 70 900EXs) in service in 2000.

History: The Falcon 900 intercontinental range trijet is a substantially revised development of the Falcon 50.

Dassault announced it was developing a new intercontinental range large size business jet based on the Falcon 50 on May 27 1983 at the Paris Airshow. The prototype, *Spirit of Lafayette*, flew for the first time on September 21 1984. A second prototype flew on August 30 1985. French certification was awarded on March 14 1986, FAA certification followed on March 21, and first customer deliveries occurred in December that year.

While of similar overall configuration to the Falcon 50, the Falcon 900 introduced an all new wider and longer fuselage which can seat three passengers abreast. The main commonality with the Falcon 50 is the wing, which despite being designed for a considerably lighter aircraft, was adapted almost directly unchanged. In designing the Falcon 900 Dassault made use of computer aided modelling, while the aircraft's structure incorporates a degree of composite materials.

From 1991 the standard production model was the Falcon 900B, which differs from the earlier 900 in having more powerful engines and increased range. Earlier production 900s can be retrofitted to 900B standard.

The Falcon 900EX is a longer range development launched in October 1994. It features TFE731-60s, a Honeywell Primus 4000 EFIS avionics suite, optional Flight Dynamics head-up displays, increased fuel capacity and greater range. Its first flight was on June 1 1995 and first delivery was in May 1996.

The latest Falcon 900 model is the 900C. Revealed in 1998, the C is a development of the B but incorporates the advanced Honeywell Primus avionics of the 900EX. The 900C replaced the 900B in the Falcon product line with first deliveries in early 2000.

From 2003 the 900EX will introduce Dassault's EASy avionics operating system with four colour displays, cursor control devices and multifunction keyboards.

Photo: A Falcon 900. (John Adlard)

Dassault Falcon 2000

Country of origin: France

Type: Transcontinental range mid to large size corporate jet

Powerplants: 2000 – Two 26.3kN (5918lb) CFE (General Electric & Honeywell) CFE738-1-1B turbofans. 2000EX – Two 31.1kN (7000lb) Pratt & Whitney Canada PW308Cs.

Performance: 2000 – Max cruising speed Mach 0.84 or 891km/h/481kt, normal cruising speed Mach 0.80 or 850km/h/459kt, long range cruising speed Mach 0.80 or 850km/h (459kt). Max certificated altitude 47,000ft. Range at 0.80 Mach with six passengers 5633km (3040nm). 2000EX – Normal cruising speed Mach 0.80 or 850km/h/459kt. Range at 0.80 Mach with six passengers 7041km (3800nm).

Weights: 2000 – Empty equipped 9405kg (20,735lb), standard max takeoff 16,238kg (35,800lb), optional max takeoff 16,556kg (36,500lb). 2000EX – Max takeoff 18,478kg (40,700lb).

Dimensions: Wing span 19.33m (63ft 5in), length 20.22m (66ft 4in), height 7.06m (23ft 2in). Wing area 49.0m^2 (527.6sq ft).

Capacity: Flightcrew of two. Main cabin seating typically for eight passengers, or up to 12 in a high density layout.

Production: Over 124 delivered by late 2000 with total sales of 200.

History: The Falcon 2000 is a twin engine, slightly smaller development of the Falcon 900 trijet.

The Falcon 2000 shares the 900's wing and forward fuselage, but there are a number of design changes. From the start the Falcon 2000 was designed with a range of 5560km (3000nm) in mind, which is less than the intercontinental 900's range. This design range removed the need for the redundancy of three engines for long range overwater flights, allowing the two new CFE738 engines to be fitted, with considerable maintenance and operating economics benefits over a trijet configuration. The CFE738 engine was developed specifically for the Falcon 2000 by CFE, a partnership of General Electric and AlliedSignal (now Honeywell). Meanwhile, the 2000's fuselage is 1.98m (6ft 6in) shorter than the 900. Another noticeable design change between the 900 and 2000 is the area ruled rear fuselage.

The wing, compared to the 900's, features a modified leading edge and the inboard slats have been removed, while the cockpit features a Collins four screen EFIS avionics system with optional Flight Dynamics head-up displays.

Dassault announced it was developing the Falcon 2000, then known as the Falcon X, in June 1989. First flight occurred on March 4 1993 and certification was awarded in November 1994. The first customer delivery occurred in March 1995.

In October 2000 at that year's NBAA convention Dassault announced the extended range Falcon 2000EX. The 2000EX will be powered by Pratt & Whitney Canada PW308C engines with a 1732kg (3815lb) increase in fuel capacity, giving it a 7040km (3800nm) range, 25% better than the standard 2000, allowing westbound nonstop flights from Europe to the east coast of the USA.

First flight is planned for the fourth quarter of 2001 with customer deliveries in early 2003. The standard 2000 will remain in production alongside the 2000EX. The 2000EX will be offered with Dassault's EASy avionics operating system from 2004.

Photo: The Falcon 2000 is currently Dassault's fastest selling product.

De Havilland Canada DHC-1 Chipmunk

Country of origin: Canada

Type: Two seat light aircraft

Powerplant: One 108kW (145hp) de Havilland Gipsy Major 8 four cylinder inverted inline piston engine driving a two blade fixed pitch wooden propeller.

Performance: Max speed at sea level 223km/h (120kt), cruising speed 200km/h (108kt). Initial rate of climb 900ft/min. Service ceiling 17,200ft. Max range 450km (243nm). Endurance 2.3 hours.

Weights: Empty 526kg (1158lb), max takeoff 914kg (2014lb).

Dimensions: Wing span 10.46m (34ft 4in), length 7.75m (25ft 5in), height 2.13m (7ft 0in). Wing area 15.9m^2 (172sq ft).

Capacity: Seating for two in tandem. Small numbers were modified for crop spraying and fitted with a chemical hopper in place of the front cockpit.

Production: 1291 Chipmunks built, including 217 in Canada, 60 under licence in Portugal and 1014 in Britain. Most built originally for military customers, but hundreds now fly with private operators.

History: Affectionately known as the Chippie, de Havilland Canada's Chipmunk was designed in response to a growing need to replace the Royal Air Force's ageing Tiger Moth two seat basic trainer biplane (described separately).

With a full design workload (courtesy of the revolutionary Comet jet airliner project among others) de Havilland decided to hand design responsibility for the new trainer to its Canadian subsidiary, de Havilland Canada. Design leadership for DHC's first aircraft was the responsibility of W J Jakimuk who had emigrated to Canada from Poland in 1940 and was previously responsible for the design of the PZL 24 and PZL 50 Jastrab fighters and the DH.95 Flamingo airliner.

His new aircraft was designated the DHC-1 Chipmunk and flew for the first time on May 22 1946. Features of the design included a de Havilland Gipsy Major engine and all metal construction (but with fabric covered control surfaces). First deliveries took place from 1947.

Canadian built DHC-1B-1s and DHC-1B-2s (60 were built for the RCAF) were known as the T.30 in British service, and many featured clear view blown canopies. However the bulk of Chipmunk production was undertaken by de Havilland in Britain. British production models included the initial T.10 and T.20 for the RAF, and civilian T.21.

Civilianised versions of RAF aircraft became available in large numbers from the late 1950s, with civilianised T.10s becoming Mk.22s, while Mk.22As were modified ex RAF T.10s with greater fuel capacity.

Farm Aviation Services in the UK heavily modified five Chipmunks with a hopper tank in place of the forward cockpit for spraying duties, these aircraft were designated Mk.23s. Three similar conversions were performed in Australia by Sasin/Aerostructures as the SA29 Spraymaster.

Today the Chipmunk remains a very popular sport and private aircraft, while a small number are still used for pilot training and tailwheel endorsements. Some have also been extensively modified with the installation of Lycoming or Continental engines, blown canopies and wheel spats.

Photo: A Chipmunk finished in the original British Airways colour scheme. (Keith Gaskell)

De Havilland Canada DHC-2 Beaver

Country of origin: Canada

Type: STOL utility transport

Powerplant: Mk I – One 335kW (450hp) Pratt & Whitney R-985 Wasp Junior nine cylinder radial piston engine driving a two blade variable pitch prop. Mk III – One 578eshp Pratt & Whitney Canada PT6A-6 or PT6A-20 turboprop driving a three blade constant speed prop.

Performance: Mk I – Max speed 225km/h (121kt), max cruising speed 217km/h (117kt), normal cruising speed 201km/h (109kt). Initial rate of climb 1020ft/min. Service ceiling 18,000ft. Max range with reserves 1252km (676nm). Mk III – Max speed 274km/h (148kt), max cruising speed 253km/h (137kt), long range cruising speed 225km/h (122kt). Initial rate of climb 1185ft/min. Service ceiling 20,000ft. Max range with reserves 1090km (588nm).

Weights: Mk I – Empty 1293kg (2850lb), max takeoff 2313kg (5100lb). Mk I seaplane – Operating empty 1506kg (3316lb), max takeoff 2309kg (5090lb). Mk III – Empty 1175kg (2590lb), max takeoff 2436kg (5370lb).

Dimensions: Mk I – Wing span 14.63m (48ft 0in), length 9.25m (30ft 4in), height 2.75m (9ft 0in). Wing area 23.1m² (250sq ft). Mk I – seaplane – Same except for length 9.98m (32ft 9in), height 3.18m (10ft 5in). Mk III – Same as Mk I except for length 10.74m (35ft 3in).

Capacity: Standard seating for eight including the pilot, seating for 11 in Turbo Beaver. The 'Ag-Beaver' is fitted with a 0.99m³ (35cu ft) chemical hopper.

Production: 1692 Beavers built between 1948 and 1968, including approximately 60 Turbo Beavers. 974 were delivered to the US military and many others delivered to foreign military air arms. Several hundred remain in service with civilian operators.

History: De Havilland Canada's first purpose designed utility aircraft, the Beaver was that company's most successful program sales wise (both military or civil), with almost 1700 built in a production run lasting two decades.

Beaver development work began in 1946 and the Ontario Department of Lands and Forests had considerable input into the final design and configuration. A prototype flew on August 16 1947, with seating for five or six, the production Beaver grew slightly to seat an extra two passengers by the time civil certification was awarded in March 1948.

The only major development of the Beaver (aside from a single prototype powered by a 410kW/550hp Alvis Leonides 502/4 radial engine) was the Turbo Beaver. First flown in December 1963 it featured a Pratt & Whitney (then United Aircraft Canada) PT6A-6 turboprop, which offered lower empty and higher takeoff weights, and even better STOL performance. The Turbo Beaver's cabin was also longer due to a forward fuselage extension, allowing maximum accommodation for 11, including the pilot. Externally, the Turbo Beaver had a much longer and reprofiled nose, and a larger swept vertical tail.

About 60 new build Turbo Beavers were built (the first was delivered to the Ontario Department of Lands in December 1964) while DHC also offered conversion kits enabling piston powered Beavers to be upgraded to Turbo standard. Many after-market conversions have also been performed. Others have been fitted with Garrett TPE331s.

Photo: A Beaver floatplane. (Lenn Bayliss)

De Havilland Canada DHC-3 Otter

Country of origin: Canada

Type: STOL utility transport

Powerplant: One 447kW (600hp) Pratt & Whitney R-1340-S1H1-G or R-1340-S3H1-G nine cylinder radial piston engine driving a three blade Hamilton Standard constant speed propeller.

Performance: Max speed 257km/h (140kt), economical cruising speed at sea level 195km/h (105kt). Initial rate of climb 850ft/min. Service ceiling 18,800ft. Max range with reserves 1520km (820nm), range with a 950kg (2100lb) payload and reserves 1410km (760nm).

Weights: Landplane – Basic operating 2010kg (4431lb), max takeoff 3629kg (8000lb). Floatplane – Basic operating 2219kg (4892lb), max takeoff 3614kg (7967lb).

Dimensions: Wing span 17.69m (58ft 0in), length 12.80m (41ft 10in), height 3.83m (12ft 7in), floatplane height 4.57m (15ft 0in). Wing area 34.8m² (375sq ft).

Capacity: Flightcrew of one or two. Normal main cabin seating for nine passengers, max seating for 10. As an aerial ambulance can carry six stretchers and four passengers or three stretchers and seven passengers.

Production: A total of 460 Otters built including for military air arms in 11 nations.

History: The second in de Havilland Canada's successful line of rugged and useful STOL utility transports, the Otter was conceived to be capable of performing the same roles as the earlier and highly successful Beaver, but was bigger.

Although the same overall configuration of the Beaver, the Otter is much larger overall. The Otter began life as the King Beaver, but compared to the Beaver is longer, has greater span wings and is much heavier. Seating in the main cabin is for 10 or 11, whereas the Beaver could seat six. Power is supplied by a nine cylinder, 450kW (600hp) Pratt & Whitney R-1340 Wasp radial. Like the Beaver the Otter can be fitted with skis and floats. The amphibious floatplane Otter features a unique four unit retractable undercarriage, with the wheels retracting into the floats.

De Havilland Canada began design work on the DHC-3 Otter in January 1951, the company's design efforts resulting in the type's first flight on December 12 1951. Canadian certification was awarded in November 1952.

De Havilland Canada demonstrated the Otter to the US Army, and subsequently that service went on to become the largest DHC-3 operator (designated U-1). Other military users included Australia, Canada, India and Norway.

Small numbers of Otters were converted to turbine power by Cox Air Services of Alberta, Canada. Changes included a Pratt & Whitney Canada PT6A turboprop, a lower empty weight of 1692kg (3703lb) and a higher maximum speed of 267km/h (144kt). It was called the Cox Turbo Single Otter. A number of other after-market PT6 conversions have also been offered.

The Otter found a significant niche as a bush aircraft and today it remains highly sought after.

Photo: The Otter is substantially larger than the Beaver despite its similar overall configuration. (Gerard Williamson)

De Havilland Canada DHC-4 Caribou

Country of origin: Canada

Type: STOL utility transport

Powerplants: DHC-4A – Two 1080kW (1450shp) Pratt & Whitney R-2000-7M2 14 cylinder twin row radial piston engines driving three blade propellers.

Performance: DHC-4A – Max speed 347km/h (187kt), normal cruising speed 293km/h (158kt). Initial rate of climb 1355ft/min. Service ceiling 24,800ft. Range with max payload 390km (210nm), range with max fuel 2105km (1135nm).

Weights: DHC-4A – Basic operating 8293kg (18,260lb), standard max takeoff 12,930kg (28,500lb), military overload max takeoff 14,195kg (31,300lb).

Dimensions: Wing span 29.15m (95ft 8in), length 22.13m (72ft 7in), height 9.68m (31ft 9in). Wing area 84.7m² (912sq ft).

Capacity: Flightcrew of two. Can carry almost four tonnes (8000lb) of cargo in freighter configuration, or seat approximately 30 passengers.

Production: Caribou production ended in 1983 after 307 had been built, most for military customers. A small number survive in commercial service in 2000 in Spain and North America (incl Alaska).

History: De Havilland Canada's fourth design was a big step up in size compared with its earlier products, and was the first powered by two engines, but the Caribou was similar in that it is a rugged STOL utility. The Caribou was primarily a military tactical transport that in commercial service found itself a small niche.

De Havilland Canada designed the DHC-4 in response to a US Army requirement for a tactical airlifter to supply the battlefront with troops and supplies and evacuate casualties on the return journey. With assistance from Canada's Department of Defence Production DHC built a prototype demonstrator that first flew on July 30 1958.

Impressed with the DHC-4's STOL capabilities and potential, the US Army ordered five for evaluation as YAC-1s and went on to become the largest Caribou operator, taking delivery of 159. The AC-1 designation was later changed to CV-2, and then C-7 when the US Army's CV-2s were transferred to the US Air Force in 1966. US and Australian Caribou saw extensive service during the Vietnam conflict. In addition some US Caribou were captured by North Vietnamese forces and remained in service with that country through to the late 1970s. Other notable military operators included Canada, Malaysia, India and Spain.

The majority of Caribou production was for military operators, but the type's ruggedness and excellent STOL capabilities also appealed to a select group of commercial users. US certification was awarded on December 23 1960. Ansett-MAL, which operated a single example in the New Guinea highlands, and AMOCO Ecuador were early customers, as was Air America (a CIA front in South East Asia during the Vietnam War era for covert operations). Other Caribou entered commercial service after being retired from their military users.

Today only a handful are in civil use as the Caribou's thirsty twin row radial engines make commercial operations uneconomic where its STOL performance is not important. A turboprop development of the Caribou, the DHC-5 Buffalo, was quite successful as a military airlifter but did not see commercial service

Photo: The civil Caribou fleet is dwindling. (Paul Howard)

De Havilland Canada DHC-6 Twin Otter

Country of origin: Canada

Type: STOL turboprop regional airliner and utility transport

Powerplants: 100 – Two 431kW (578shp) Pratt & Whitney Canada (formerly United Aircraft of Canada) PT6A-20 turboprops driving three blade propellers. 300 – Two 460kW (620shp) P&WC PT6A-27s.

Performance: 100 – Max cruising speed 297km/h (160kt). Range with max fuel 1427km (771nm), range with 975kg (2150lb) payload 1344km (727nm). 300 – Max cruising speed 338km/h (182kt). Initial rate of climb 1600ft/min. Range with 1135kg (2500lb) payload 1297km (700nm), range with a 860kg (1900lb) payload and wing tanks 1705km (920nm).

Weights: 100 – Basic operating empty 2653kg (5850lb), max takeoff 4763kg (10,500lb). 300 – Operating empty 3363kg (7415lb), max takeoff 5670kg (12,500lb).

Dimensions: 100 – Wing span 19.81m (65ft 0in), length 15.09m (49ft 6in), height 5.94m (19ft 6in). Wing area 39.0m² (420sq ft). 300 – Same except for length 15.77m (51ft 9in), or 15.09m (49ft 6in) for floatplane variants.

Capacity: Flightcrew of two. Standard regional airliner interior seats 20 at three abreast and 76cm (30in) pitch.

Production: 115 Series 100s, 115 Series 200s and 614 Series 300s built.

History: The Twin Otter remains popular for its rugged construction and useful STOL performance, and after the Bombardier CRJ is Canada's most successful commercial aircraft program.

Development of the Twin Otter began in January 1964 when de Havilland Canada started design work on a new STOL twin turboprop commuter airliner (seating between 13 and 18) and utility transport based on the piston single DHC-3 Otter. The new aircraft was designated the DHC-6 and prototype construction began in November that year, resulting in the type's first flight on May 20 1965. After receiving certification in mid 1966, the first Twin Otter entered service with long time de Havilland Canada supporter the Ontario Department of Lands.

Design features included a stretched Otter fuselage, a longer span Otter based wing with double slotted trailing edge flaps and ailerons that can act in unison to boost STOL performance, and twin PT6A turboprops. The first production aircraft were Series 100s. Compared with the later Series 200s and 300s, the 100s are distinguishable by their shorter, blunter noses.

The main addition to the Series 200, which was introduced in April 1968, was the extended nose, which, together with a reconfigured storage compartment in the rear cabin, greatly increased baggage stowage area.

The definitive Series 300 was introduced from the 231st production aircraft in 1969. It too featured the lengthened nose, but also introduced more powerful engines, thus allowing a 450kg (1000lb) increase in takeoff weight and a 20 seat interior. Production ceased in late 1988. In addition, six 300S enhanced STOL performance DHC-6-300s were built in the mid 1970s.

Examples of all models have been fitted with skis and floats.

Photo: This Twin Otter has been modified with enlarged windows for sightseeing. (Keith Gaskell)

De Havilland Canada Dash 7

Country of origin: Canada

Type: STOL turboprop regional airliner

Powerplants: Four 835kW (1220shp) Pratt & Whitney Canada PT6A-50 turboprops driving four blade propellers.

Performance: Max cruising speed 428km/h (230kt), long range cruising speed 400km/h (215kt). Service ceiling 21,000ft. STOL takeoff distance at 18,600kg (41,000lb) TO weight 670m (2260ft). Range with 50 passengers and reserves 1270km (690nm), range with standard fuel and three tonne payload 2168km (1170nm). 150 – Range with 50 passengers at max cruising speed 2110km (1140nm), with max fuel 4670km (2525nm).

Weights: 100 – Operating empty 12,560kg (27,690lb), max takeoff 19,958kg (44,000lb). 150 – Operating empty 12,465kg (27,480lb), max takeoff 21,320kg (47,000lb).

Dimensions: Wing span 28.35m (93ft 0in), length 24.58m (80ft 8in), height 7.98m (26ft 2in). Wing area 79.9m² (860.0sq ft).

Capacity: Flightcrew of two. Max seating for 54 at four abreast and 74cm (29in) pitch, 50 passengers at 81cm (32in) pitch. In freighter configuration can carry five standard pallets.

Production: 111 Dash 7s were built between 1977 and 1988. 65 were in commercial service as of late 2000.

History: The four engine de Havilland Canada Dash 7 remains unrivalled because of its impressive STOL performance and low noise.

The Dash 7 (or DHC-7) was designed as a STOL (short takeoff and landing) 50 seat regional airliner capable of operating from strips as short as 915m (3000ft) in length. (At the time it was envisaged that many cities would develop inner city 'STOL parts'.) Design features include an advanced wing and four Pratt & Whitney PT6A turboprops. Double slotted trailing edge flaps run the entire span of the high mounted wing, dramatically increasing the lifting surface available for takeoff. Extra lift is also generated by the airflow over the wing from the relatively slow turning propellers. The wings also feature two pairs of spoilers each – the inboard pair also operate as lift dumpers, the outboard pair can act differentially in conjunction with the ailerons to boost roll control.

Financial backing from the Canadian Government allowed the launch of the DHC-7 program in the early 1970s, resulting in the maiden flight of the first of two development aircraft on March 27 1975. The first production Dash 7 flew on March 3 1977, the type was certificated on May 2 1977 and it entered service with Rocky Mountain Airways on February 3 1978.

The standard passenger carrying Dash 7 is the Series 100, while the type was also offered in pure freighter form as the Series 101. The only major development of the Dash 7 was the Series 150, which featured a higher max takeoff weight and greater fuel capacity, boosting range. The Series 151 was the equivalent freighter. However just one Series 150 was built, for Canada's Department of the Environment for ice reconnaissance.

Production of the Dash 7 ended in 1988, following Boeing's takeover of de Havilland Canada. The last was delivered to Austria's Tyrolean Airways in December 1988.

Photo: A Dash 7 of Canadian operator Trans Capital. (Gary Gentle)

De Havilland DH.82 Tiger Moth

Country of origin: United Kingdom

Type: Two seat biplane light aircraft

Powerplant: DH.82A – One 97kW (130hp) de Havilland Gipsy Major 1 inline and inverted four cylinder piston engine driving a fixed pitch two blade wooden propeller.

Performance: DH.82A – Max speed 175km/h (95kt), max cruising speed 160km/h (87kt), economical cruising speed 145km/h (78kt). Initial rate of climb 673ft/min. Service ceiling 13,600ft. Range with max fuel 459km (248nm).

Weights: DH.82A – Empty 506kg (1115lb), max takeoff 828kg (1825lb).

Dimensions: Wing span 8.94m (29ft 4in), length 7.29m (23ft 11in), height 2.70m (8ft 10in). Wing area 22.2m² (239sq ft).

Capacity: Seating for two in tandem open cockpits. Flown solo from rear cockpit due to weight and balance considerations.

Production: 8492 Tiger Moths built, including 5161 in the UK (including 1153 prewar), 1747 in Canada, 1085 in Australia, 345 in New Zealand, 91 in Portugal, 37 in Norway and 23 in Sweden.

History: One of the most famous biplanes in the world, the much loved Tiger Moth was produced in large numbers for WW2 service as a basic pilot trainer, and today is a highly sought after private aircraft.

The DH.82 Tiger Moth is a development of de Havilland's successful and famous Moth line of biplanes. Based on the DH.60T Moth Trainer, the Tiger Moth first flew on October 26 1931. Like the earlier Moth and Gipsy Moth the new aircraft was a two place biplane and featured a Gipsy Major engine and wooden and metal construction. Difficulty bailing out in an emergency was a problem with the earlier aircraft, and this was addressed through repositioning the struts forward of the front cockpit. To counter centre of gravity problems that would have resulted, the wings were given a modest sweepback angle.

The DH.82 attracted the interest of Britain's Royal Air Force, and the first of what would ultimately be several thousand Tiger Moths entered service with the RAF in 1932. Initial production DH.82s were powered by 90kW (120hp) engines, while the DH.82A introduced in 1937 featured a 97kW (130hp) engine, and was the most produced version. Most prewar production was against military orders, although some civil machines were built.

As Britain's standard basic pilot training aircraft, production of the Tiger Moth increased greatly during WW2, and some 4000 were built in the UK. During the war large numbers were also built in Canada (as the DH.82C with a Gipsy Major IC or 120kW/160hp Pirate D.4 engine), Australia and New Zealand.

Postwar, surplus military Tiger Moths proved extremely popular with private owners. Many examples were converted for agricultural work, particularly in Australia and New Zealand, while small numbers of the four seat Jackaroo conversion were built from 1957.

Today the Tiger Moth remains very popular for recreational flying while some earn their keep operating joyflights. In some countries Tiger Moth populations are in fact growing as retired machines are restored and returned to the air.

Photo: The Tiger Moth is popular for its relaxed paced, open cockpit flying. (Paul Sadler)

De Havilland DH.104 Dove

Country or origin: United Kingdom

Type: Eight seat commuter airliner and executive transport

Powerplants: Dove 1 – Two 245kW (330hp) de Havilland Gipsy Queen 70-3 supercharged inverted six cylinder inline engines driving three blade constant speed propellers. Dove 8 – Two 300kW (400hp) Gipsy Queen 70 Mk.3s.

Performance: Dove 1 – Max speed 338km/h (182kt), max cruising speed 322km/h (174kt), long range cruising speed 266km/h (144kt). Initial rate of climb 750ft/min. Service ceiling 20,000ft. Max range 1610km (890nm). Dove 8 – Max speed 370km/h (200kt), max cruising speed 338km/h (183kt), long range cruising speed 300km/h (163kt). Initial rate of climb 1135ft/min. Service ceiling 21,700ft. Max range 1416km (765nm).

Weights: Dove 1 – Empty 2563kg (5650lb), max takeoff 3856kg (8500lb). Dove 8 – Empty 2869kg (6325lb), MOTW 4060kg (8950lb).

Dimensions: Wing span 17.37m (57ft 0in), length 11.96m (39ft 3in), height 4.06m (13ft 4in). Wing area 31.1m² (335sq ft).

Capacity: Flightcrew of two pilots. Main cabin seating for eight passengers, max cabin seating for 11 in a modified cabin arrangement.

Production: 544 Doves built, including 200 for military operators. 17 Riley 400 conversions performed. Small numbers remain in service.

History: The Dove was Britain's first successful postwar civil aircraft, and one of the few successful Brabazon Committee projects.

The Brabazon Committee was established during WW2 to define requirements for British postwar civil aircraft. While the government established committee was responsible for a number of failures such as the Bristol Brabazon, it also resulted in the highly successful Vickers Viscount (described elsewhere) and the de Havilland Dove.

The Dove was developed in response to a requirement for a small feederliner for UK and Commonwealth domestic services. The resulting aircraft featured new versions of the Gipsy Queen engine, a raised flightdeck and separate passenger cabin and all metal construction. The first DH.104 Dove flew for the first time on September 25 1945.

Steady sales success as a regional airliner and corporate transport (particularly in the US) was boosted by significant military orders (RAF versions were known as the Devon, Royal Navy aircraft the Sea Devon).

The Dove remained in production until the mid 1960s (by which time it was a Hawker Siddeley product), and a number of variants were built. These were the initial Series 1, the executive interior Series 2, the military Series 4, the Series 5 with greater range and more powerful engines, the Series 6 (and 6A for the US) executive version of the Series 5, Series 6BA with more powerful engines, Series 7 (Series 7A for the US) with more powerful engines and raised Heron style flightdeck, and Series 8 (8A or Custom 800 in the US) with five seat interior.

In the USA Riley Aeronautics offered conversions of the Dove with two 300kW (400hp) Lycoming IO-720 flat eight piston engines fitted with turbochargers. The conversion is known as the Riley 400 (later Riley Turbo Exec 400), and aside from the engines, customers could fit a swept back tail, a new instrument panel and a steel spar capped wing. The first Riley 400 flew in 1963. Max cruising speed was 474km/h (255kt), range with max fuel was 2075km (1120nm).

Photo: A Riley 400 converted Dove. (David Daw)

De Havilland DH.114 Heron

Country of origin: United Kingdom

Type: 14 seat commuter airliner

Powerplants: Series 2 – Four 185kW (250hp) de Havilland (later Bristol Siddeley) Gipsy Queen 30 Mk 2 six cylinder inline piston engines driving two blade de Havilland constant speed propellers. Series 2E/A1 – Four 215kW (290hp) Lycoming IO-540-B1A5 flat six piston engines driving three blade constant speed props.

Performance: Series 2 – Cruising speed 307km/h (166kt), economical cruising speed 295km/h (160kt). Initial rate of climb 1075ft/min. Service ceiling 17,200ft. Range with max fuel and reserves 2873km (1550nm).

Weights: Empty 3848kg (8484lb), max takeoff 6124kg (13,500lb).

Dimensions: Wing span 21.80m (71ft 6in), length 14.80m (48ft 6in), height 4.75m (15ft 7in). Wing area 46.4m² (499sq ft).

Capacity: Flightcrew of two. Typical main cabin seating for 14 at two abreast with a central aisle. Alternative seating for 15 or 17. Executive versions with seating for eight.

Production: 149 Herons built comprising 51 Series 1s and 98 Series 2. Conversions include 28 Riley Herons, six by Tawron, 29 by Prinair and 13 Saunders ST-27s. A handful remain in commercial service.

History: The DH.114 Heron is a stretched, four engined development of de Havilland's successful DH.104 Dove.

Only a few years later in development than the Dove on which it was based, design work on the Heron began in the late 1940s, resulting in the prototype's first flight on May 10 1950 (the Dove first flew in 1945).

In designing the Heron, de Havilland made as much use of Dove componentry as possible, and so both types feature the distinctive slightly raised cockpit and separate main cabin and metal construction. Initial Heron production aircraft also featured fixed undercarriage (unlike the retractable gear Dove). Major differences include the four 185kW (250hp) Gipsy Queen engines (as opposed to two 255 to 300kW/340 to 400hp Gipsy Queen 70s), greater span wings, a longer and taller fuselage and greater seating capacity. The first Series 1 production Herons were delivered to New Zealand National Airways in 1952.

Also in 1952 the first Series 2 Heron first flew on December 14. The 2's main improvement over the 1 was retractable undercarriage, which for a weight penalty of 75kg (165lb) increased cruising speed by 32km/h (17kt), while other standard and optional improvements were minor in nature. The Heron 2A was certificated for use in the USA, and an equivalent 2B executive version was also offered. The 2C and equivalent executive 2D have greater weights.

The Heron has been the subject of numerous conversion programs. In the USA Riley converted 20 to be powered by Lycoming IO-540s (eight more were converted in Australia), while Prinair converted a further 29 to Lycoming power.

The most ambitious Heron conversions were performed by Saunders, whose ST-27 conversions (six were ordered) feature two 560kW (750shp) Pratt & Whitney Canada PT6A-34 turboprops and a stretched fuselage seating 23 passengers. In addition, Tawron converted six Series 1 Herons with Continental engines.

Photo: A Lycoming powered Heron.

Dornier Do 27

Country of origin: Germany

Type: Four to six seat STOL utility light aircraft

Powerplant: Do 27H-2 – One 255kW (340hp) Lycoming GSO-480-B1B6 flat six piston engine driving a three blade Hartzell propeller. Do 27Q-5 – One 200kW (270hp) GSO-480-B1A6 driving a two blade prop.

Performance: Do 27H-2 – Max speed 245km/h (132kt), high speed cruise 212km/h (115kt), economical cruising speed 180km/h (97kt). Initial rate of climb 965ft/min. Service ceiling 22,000ft. Range with max fuel and no reserves 1360km (735nm). Do 27Q-5 – Max speed 232km/h (125kt), 75% power cruising speed 211km/h (114kt), 60% power cruising speed 190km/h (103kt), economical cruising speed 175km/h (95kt). Initial rate of climb 650ft/min. Service ceiling 10,800ft. Range with max fuel and no reserves 1102km (595nm).

Weights: Do 27H-2 – Empty equipped 1170kg (2580lb), max takeoff 1848kg (4070lb). Do 27Q-5 – Empty equipped 1130kg (2490lb), max takeoff 1848kg (4070lb).

Dimensions: Do 27H-2 & Q-5 – Wing span 12.00m (39ft 5in), length 9.60m (31ft 6in), height 2.80m (9ft 2in). Wing area 19.4m² (208.8sq ft).

Capacity: Pilot and passenger side by side with between four and six passengers behind them on two facing bench seats. Can carry freight with rear seats removed.

Production: Total Do 27 production of over 620.

History: The Dornier Do 27 was the first military aircraft to be manufactured in quantity in what was West Germany since World War 2, and it was also built in limited numbers for civil customers.

The Do 27 traces back to the Do 25, which Professor Claude Dornier (Dornier was responsible for the Do 17 medium bomber in WW2) designed in Spain for a Spanish military requirement for a light general purpose utility aircraft. Two prototype Do 25s were built, the first was powered by a 110kW (150hp) ENMA Tigre G-IVB engine and flew for the first time on June 25 1954. Subsequently CASA built 50 production aircraft as Do 27As for the Spanish air force (Spain designated the type C.127).

Following this success the German military ordered the Do 27 in large numbers. Some 428 were delivered to Germany's armed forces from the mid 1950s to 1960. Small numbers were built for other military customers, and others for commercial use.

Features of the Do 27 design include a flat six Lycoming engine, a wide and relatively roomy cabin, all metal construction apart from fabric covered double slotted flaps and ailerons on the wings (the ailerons are split, the inner portions of which can also act as flaps), wide track undercarriage and excellent STOL performance. The STOL performance in particular suited the Do 27 for use in developing countries, and several have seen service in Africa and Papua New Guinea.

Do 27 models include the initial Do 27A and dual control Do 27B for Germany; the Do 27H series that was based on the A-4 but with a more powerful engine and three blade prop; and the Do 27Q series, equivalent to the Do 27A. The Do 27 T-1 was built in prototype form only, it featured a Turbomeca Astazou turboprop. Do 27 production ceased in 1966. In addition over 60 twin engine Do 28s were built in the early 1960s (powered by two 216kW/290hp Lycoming IO-540s).

Photo: A Do 27A-4. (Jim Thorn)

Dornier Do 28 & 128

Country of origin: Germany

Type: STOL utility transports

Powerplants: Do 28D-2 – Two 285kW (380hp) Lycoming IGSO-540-A1E flat six piston engines driving three blade constant speed Hartzell propellers. 128-6 – Two 300kW (400shp) Pratt & Whitney Canada PT6A-110 turboprops driving three blade Hartzell propellers.

Performance: Do 28D-2 – Max speed 325km/h (175kt), max cruising speed 306km/h (165kt), economical cruising speed 241km/h (130kt). Initial rate of climb 1160ft/min. Service ceiling 25,200ft. Range with max payload 1050km (566nm). 128-6 – Max speed 340km/h (183kt), max cruising speed 330km/h (178kt), econ cruising speed 256km/h (138kt). Initial rate of climb 1260ft/min. Service ceiling 32,600ft. Range with max fuel at econ cruising speed 1825nm (985nm), with a 805kg (1774lb) payload 1460km (788nm).

Weights: Do 28D-2 – Empty 2328kg (5132lb), max takeoff 3842kg (8470lb). 128-6 – Empty 2540kg (5600lb), max takeoff 4350kg (9590lb).

Dimensions: Do 28D-2 – Wing span 15.55m (51ft 0in), length 11.41m (37ft 5in), height 3.90m (12ft 10in). Wing area 29.0m² (312sq ft). 128-6 – Same except for wing span 15.85m (52ft 0in).

Capacity: One or two pilots on flightdeck and seating in main cabin for 10 or 12 seats two abreast with a centre aisle.

Production: Total Do 28 and 128-2 production was over 200 units including military orders, total 128-6 production approximately 25.

History: The Dornier Do 28 Skyservant was the second aircraft to bear the Do 28 designation, but is similar only in overall configuration to the first Do 28.

Dornier's original Do 28 first flew in 1959 and was a twin engined development of the high wing single engine Do 27 utility (powered by two 216kW/290hp Lycoming IO-540s). The Do 28 Skyservant first flew on February 23 1966, and while it retained the earlier Do 28's high wing and unique fuselage side mounted engine configuration, was a completely new aircraft. Other design features of this unusual looking aircraft were the fixed tailwheel undercarriage, with the faired mainwheels mounted under the engines. FAA certification was granted on April 19 1968.

The Do 28 was developed into a number of progressively improved variants, from the original D, through the D-1 and D-2, to the 128-2, introduced in 1980. Each variant introduced a number of detail changes. Most Do 28 production was for military customers, notably Germany, although a small number were delivered to commercial operators.

An initial turboprop version of the Do 28, designated the Do 28D-5X, first flew in April 1978, fitted with two Avco Lycoming LTP 101-600-1As derated to 300kW (400shp).

However production turboprop Dornier 128-6s feature Pratt & Whitney Canada PT6As, with the first such configured aircraft flying in March 1980. Only a about two dozen were built between then and 1986, when production ceased, and again most aircraft were for military customers.

Photo: A Hungarian registered Do 128-6. Note the extended flaps. (Sebastian Zacharias)

Douglas DC-3

Country of origin: United States of America

Type: Short range airliner and utility transport

Powerplants: Two 895kW (1200hp) Pratt & Whitney R-1830-S1C3G Twin Wasp 14 cylinder twin row radial piston engines driving three blade variable pitch propellers, or two 895kW (1200hp) Wright SGR-1820 Cyclone nine cylinder radials.

Performance: Max speed 346km/h (187kt), economical cruising speed 266km/h (143kt). Initial rate of climb 1130ft/min. Range with max fuel 2420km (1307nm), range with max payload 563km (305nm).

Weights: Typical operating empty 8030kg (17,720lb), max takeoff 12,700kg (28,000lb).

Dimensions: Wing span 28.96m (95ft 0in), length 19.66m (64ft 6in), height 5.15m (16ft 11in). Wing area 91.7m^2 (987sq ft).

Capacity: Flightcrew of two. Seating for between 28 and 32 passengers at four abreast or 21 three abreast.

Production: 10,655 built in the USA, including 430 for commercial operators prior to US entry to WW2. 2500 or so built in Russia under licence. Approximately 400 remained in service in 2000.

History: No greater accolade for the DC-3 exists than the fact that over six decades after its first flight several hundred remain in commercial service worldwide. Durability, longevity and profitability are but three of this historically significant aircraft's virtues.

Development of the DC-3 traces back to the earlier one-off Douglas Commercial 1 (DC-1) and subsequent DC-2 (198 built) which made their first flights in 1933 and 1934 respectively. In 1934 American Airlines requested that Douglas develop a larger more capable version of the DC-2 for transcontinental US sleeper flights. The resulting DC-3 (or DST – Douglas Sleeper Transport as it then was) flew for the first time on December 17 1935.

An almost instant sales success, the DC-3 became the mainstay of the US domestic airline network in the years prior to World War 2. Aside from passenger comfort and appeal, the DC-3 offered profitability, with the result that over 400 had been sold to airlines prior to late 1941.

The entry of the United States into WW2 in December 1941 had a profound effect on the fortunes of the already successful DC-3. The US Army Air Force's requirements for transport aircraft were admirably met by the in-production DC-3, with the result that as the C-47 Skytrain it became the standard USAAF transport during the war. More than 10,000 were built for service with US and allied air arms.

After the war many of these aircraft became surplus to requirements and were sold off at bargain prices. The result was that demilitarised C-47s became the standard postwar aircraft of almost all the world's airlines and the backbone of the world airline industry well into the 1950s. Its availability and reliability meant it proved extremely popular. Even by the early 1960s 1500 or so remained in airline service.

A postwar update of the DC-3, the Super DC-3, involving a stretched airframe and more powerful engines, was commercially unsuccessful in the face of cheap second hand DC-3s and the more advanced Convair 340 and Martin 2-0-2/-4-0-4. The Super DC-3 first flew in June 1949 and a small number were built for the US Navy as the R4D-8 and for a US domestic airline, and a few remain in service.

Photo: A Canadian registered Super DC-3. (Gary Gentle)

Douglas DC-4

Country of origin: United States of America

Type: Piston engined airliner and freighter

Powerplants: Four 1080kW (1450shp) Pratt & Whitney R-2000-2SD-BG Twin Wasp 14 cylinder twin row radial piston engines driving three blade constant speed propellers.

Performance: Max speed 451km/h (244kt), cruising speed 365km/h (197kt). Service ceiling 22,300ft. Range with a 5200kg (11,440lb) payload 4023km (2172nm).

Weights: Empty 19,660kg (43,300lb), MTOW 33,112kg (73,000lb).

Dimensions: Wing span 35.81m (117ft 6in), length 28.60m (93ft 10in), height 8.38m (27ft 6in). Wing area 135.6m^2 (1460sq ft).

Capacity: Flightcrew of three, standard passenger seating for 44, max seating for 86. Most surviving aircraft configured as freighters.

Production: Total DC-4 production comprised one DC-4E, 78 commercial DC-4s, 1162 military C-54 Skymasters and 42 Canadair developed Merlin powered derivatives. Almost 80 remain in commercial service, most as freighters.

History: The original DC-4 dates back to a 1936 United Air Lines requirement for a four engined long range airliner.

United looked to Douglas to fulfil the requirement, who designed the highly ambitious DC-4E (E for experimental). This four engined behemoth was flight tested in 1939. It was over twice the size of the DC-3 (its wingspan was 42.17m/138ft 3in, and length 29.76m/97ft 7in), had triple tail surfaces, tricycle undercarriage, was pressurised and potentially could fly nonstop from Chicago to San Francisco.

However all the ground breaking new technology on the DC-4E meant that it was costly, complex and had higher than anticipated operating costs, so instead Douglas developed an all new the design, the smaller and simpler definitive DC-4.

The new DC-4 was developed under the darkening clouds of WW2, and upon the USA's entry into war all DC-4s then on the production line (US airlines had ordered 61 off the drawing board) were requisitioned for the US military. The result was that the first DC-4 flew for the first time on February 14 1942 in military markings as the C-54 Skymaster. The DC-4 was found to admirably suit the USAAF's requirement for a long range cargo transport, and 1162 were built through the war years (some were built for the US Navy as the R5D).

As was the case with the DC-3, the end of war meant that much of that number were surplus and over 500 were leased or sold to the world's airlines in 1945/46. In addition Douglas built a further 78 DC-4s (designated DC-4-1009) to new orders, the first of which was delivered to Western Air Lines in January 1946. Over the years the survivors have been passed down to charter and freight airlines, and today about 80 survive in service as freighters.

Notable developments of the DC-4 include Aviation Trader's much modified Carvair freighter while Canadair built a number with Rolls-Royce Merlin engines and pressurised fuselages. The DC-4 also formed the basis for the larger DC-6 and DC-7 which are described separately (the DC-4 was the first airliner to introduce a circular section, constant diameter fuselage which made stretching the basic aircraft relatively simple).

Photo: The South African Historic Flight's DC-4. (Paul Merritt)

Douglas DC-6

Country of origin: United States of America

Type: Piston engined airliner and freighter

Powerplants: DC-6 – Four 1340kW (1800hp) Pratt & Whitney R-2800-CA15 Double Wasp 18 cylinder twin row radial piston engines (with a maximum output rating of 1790kW/2400hp with water injection) driving three blade constant speed Hamilton Standard propellers. DC-6B – Four 1685kW (2500hp) R-2800-CB17s.

Performance: DC-6 – Cruising speed 501km/h (270kt). Initial rate of climb 1070ft/min. Max range 7376km (3983nm). DC-6B – Cruising speed 507km/h (274kt). Service ceiling 25,000ft. Range with max payload 4835km (2610nm), range with max fuel 7595km (4100nm).

Weights: DC-6 – Empty 23,840kg (52,567lb), max takeoff 44,129kg (97,200lb). DC-6B – Empty 25,110kg (55,357lb), max takeoff 48,534kg (107,000lb).

Dimensions: DC-6 – Wing span 35.81m (117ft 6in), length 30.66m (100ft 7in), height 8.66m (28ft 5in). Wing area 135.9m² (1463sq ft). DC-6B – Same except length 32.18m (105ft 7in).

Capacity: DC-6 – Flightcrew of three or four. Passenger seating typically for 48 to 56, but most aircraft now operated as freighters equipped to carry freight. DC-6B – Typical passenger seating for 54, with max seating for 102, but now usually configured for freight.

Production: Total DC-6 production of 665, comprising 174 DC-6s, 73 DC-6As, 288 DC-6Bs, 105 C-118s and 25 R6Ds. Approximately 100 remain in service.

History: The DC-6 was developed in response to a military airlift requirement and went on to become Douglas' most successful four engined piston airliner.

During the latter stages WW2 Douglas began work on an developed DC-4 for postwar commercial use. However the improved DC-4 (which would feature a 2.11m/6ft 11in fuselage stretch and P&W R-2800 Double Wasp engines) soon attracted the attention of the US Army Air Force, which devised a requirement which the new transport was developed against. A prototype was built, designated XC-112, but it did not fly until February 15 1946, by which time the war was over and the military requirement no longer stood.

However US airlines had already shown strong interest in the new transport, with launch orders for the DC-6 placed in September 1944. The first production DC-6 first flew in June 1946 and service entry, with United Air Lines, occurred on April 27 1947. However entry into service was not smooth with the fleet grounded for four months from November that year after two internal fuselage fires.

The availability of the more powerful R-2800 engines with water/methanol injection prompted Douglas to develop the further stretched DC-6A Liftmaster freighter (first flight September 29 1949) and the equivalent passenger DC-6B (first flight February 2 1951). The DC-6C, the last DC-6 model to be developed, was a convertible passenger/freight version of the DC-6A.

Meanwhile renewed military interest in the DC-6 was sparked by the Korean War, with the result that large numbers of USAF C-118s and USN R6D-1s were built. Many of these were later sold to civilian operators.

Photo: A DC-6 freighter climbs from Anchorage, Alaska. (Paul Merritt)

Douglas DC-7

Country of origin: United States of America

Type: Piston engine airliner and freighter

Powerplants: DC-7F & DC-7C – Two 2535kW (3400hp) Wright R-3350-EA1 or -EA4 Turbo Compound 18 cylinder radial piston engines driving four blade constant speed propellers.

Performance: DC-7F – Typical cruising speed 555km/h (300kt). Range with max fuel and no reserves 7130km (3850nm). DC-7C – Typical cruising speed 555km/h (330kt). Range with max payload 5810km (3135nm), range with max fuel and no reserves 9077km (4900nm).

Weights: DC-7F – Basic operating 30,030kg (66,200lb), max takeoff 57,153kg (126,000lb). DC-7C – Basic operating 36,287kg (80,000lb), max takeoff 64,865kg (143,000lb).

Dimensions: DC-7F – Wing span 35.81m (117ft 6in), length 33.24m (108ft 11in), height 8.71m (28ft 7in). Wing area 136.0m² (1463sq ft). DC-7C – Wing span 38.86m (127ft 6in), length 34.21m (112ft 3in), height 9.70m (31ft 10in). Wing area 152.0m² (1637sq ft).

Capacity: Flightcrew of three. DC-7/DC-7B could seat up to 99 in a high density configuration, the DC-7C up to 105. Capacity of DC-7F conversion of the DC-7B is 15,700kg (34,600lb).

Production: DC-7 production was 338, comprising 105 DC-7s, 112 DC-7Bs and 121 DC-7Cs. Approximately 40 remain in service.

History: Douglas' largest and last piston engined airliner, the DC-7 was one of the first airliners capable of nonstop trans Atlantic crossings between New York and London.

Originally the DC-7 designation had applied to a commercial development of the C-74 Globemaster I that Pan Am had ordered. As it emerged however the DC-7 arose from an American Airlines requirement for a stretched longer range development of the DC-6 to compete with TWA's Lockheed Super Constellations on nonstop transcontinental US services. The resulting aircraft had the same wing as the DC-6, with a stretched DC-6 fuselage (by 1.02m/3ft 4in), more powerful Wright Turbo Compound engines (with exhaust driven turbochargers) and extra fuel allowing nonstop transcontinental US range in both directions.

The prototype DC-7 first flew on May 18 1953, and the type entered service with American between New York and Los Angeles that November. Production of the initial DC-7 was solely for US domestic operators. The extended range DC-7B had extra fuel capacity in extended nacelle tanks and higher weights, allowing Pan American to inaugurate nonstop New York/London services from June 1955.

While the DC-7B could fly New York/London nonstop, wind conditions usually forced reverse services to make a refuelling stop at Gander. Consequently Douglas developed the ultimate DC-7 model, the DC-7C 'Seven Seas'. The DC-7C featured extra fuel capacity, a further 1.02m (3ft 4in) fuselage stretch, extended span wings (by 3.05m/10ft) with new centre section, more powerful engines, taller vertical tail surfaces, and a higher max takeoff weight. As a result it could cross the North Atlantic nonstop in either direction. It entered service in April 1956, although sales were restricted by the coming availability of jets.

Today a small number DC-7s survive, mainly as freighters. Douglas offered DC-7F conversions from 1959 (the DC-7F described above is based on the DC-7B). Others are used for firebombing.

Photo: A DC-7C converted as a firebomber. (Gordon Reid)

Douglas DC-8 Series 10 to 50

Country of origin: United States of America

Type: Medium to long range airliner and freighter

Powerplants: Series 50 – Four 80.1kN (18,000lb) Pratt & Whitney JT3D-3 turbofans.

Performance: Series 50 – Max cruising speed 933km/h (504kt). Range with max payload 9205km (4970nm), max range 11,260km (6078nm).

Weights: Series 50 – Operating empty 60,020kg (132,325lb), max takeoff 147,415kg (325,000lb).

Dimensions: Wing span 43.41m (142ft 5in), length 45.87m (150ft 6in), height 12.91m (42ft 4in). Wing area 257.6m² (2773sq ft) on early aircraft, 266.5m² (2868sq ft) on later aircraft.

Capacity: Flightcrew of three. Mixed class seating for 132, typical all economy seating for 144, or up to 179 in high density single class layout. A number of aircraft are converted for VIP/executive use. Freighter versions can carry approximately 15 tonnes (34,000lb) of cargo consisting of pallets or containers.

Production: 295 Series 10, 20, 30, 40 and 50 DC-8s built between the late 1950s and 1968. Approximately 40 DC-8-50s remain in commercial service.

History: The popular DC-8 was Douglas' first jet powered airliner, and the USA's second successful jet powered transport behind the Boeing 707.

Despite its stronghold on the world airliner market in the early 1950s, and the appearance of the jet powered de Havilland Comet in 1949, Douglas moved cautiously into the field of jet powered transports, a decision which was to cost it in potential sales over the following decades.

Douglas announced it was developing the jet powered DC-8 airliner in June 1955, a year after the first flight of the Boeing Model 367-80 prototype, the 707 predecessor. The first DC-8 flew on May 30 1958, five months before the 707 entered service with Pan Am. A concerted flight test program involving nine aircraft led to certification being awarded on August 31 1959. Entry into commercial service with launch customers United and Delta was on September 18 that year.

Unfortunately for Douglas, the earlier availability of the 707 meant that initial sales of the DC-8 were relatively slow. However the emergence of Douglas' design had already forced Boeing to widen the fuselage width of the 707, and unlike the Boeing the DC-8 was offered in domestic and intercontinental versions from the start.

Versions of the initial short fuselage DC-8 were: the Series 10, the initial domestic version with 60.1kN (13,500lb) P&W JT3C-6 turbojets – 28 were built for Delta and United; the similar Series 20 but with more powerful 74.7kN (16,800lb) JT4A-9 turbojets; the intercontinental Series 30 and Series 40, powered by JT4A-11s or Rolls-Royce Conways respectively; and the Series 50, perhaps the definitive short fuselage model and a direct competitor to the 707-320B/C, with 80.1kN (18,000lb) JT3D-3 turbofans. Convertible 50CF and pure freight 50AF Jet Trader versions were also offered, while others were subsequently converted to freighters.

The short fuselage DC-8s were replaced in production by the substantially larger stretched DC-8 Super Sixty series.

Photo: A DC-8-50AF freighter. (Robert Wiseman)

Douglas DC-8 Super 60 & 70 Series

Country of Origin: United States of America

Type: Long range medium capacity airliner and freighter

Powerplants: DC-8-61 & 62 – Four 80.1kN (18,000lb) Pratt & Whitney JT3D-3B turbofans. DC-8-63 – Four 84.5kN (19,000lb) JT3D-7s. DC-8-70 series – Four 97.9kN (22,000lb) CFM International CFM56-2C5s.

Performance: DC-8-60 – Max cruising speed 965km/h (521kt). Range with max payload DC-8-61 6035km (3256nm); DC-8-62 9620km (5210nm); DC-8-63 7240km (3907nm). DC-8-70 – Max cruising speed 887km/h (479kt), economical cruising speed 850km/h (459kt). Range with max payload (Super 73) 8950km (4830nm).

Weights: DC-8-61 – Operating empty 67,538kg (148,897lb), max takeoff 147,415kg (325,000lb). DC-8-62 – Operating empty 64,366kg (141,903lb), max takeoff 151,950kg (335,000lb). DC-8-63 – Operating empty 69,739kg (153,749lb), max takeoff 158,760kg (350,000lb). DC-8-73 – Operating empty 75,500kg (166,500lb), max takeoff 162,025kg (355,000lb).

Dimensions: DC-8-61 & 71 – Wing span 43.41m (142ft 5in), length 57.12m (187ft 5in), height 12.92m (42ft 5in). Wing area 267.9m² (2884sq ft). DC-8-62 & 72 – Span 45.23m (148ft 5in), length 47.98m (157ft 5in), height 12.92m (42ft 5in). Wing area 271.9m² (2927sq ft). DC-8-63 & 73 – Wing span 45.23m (148ft 5in), length 57.12m (187ft 5in), height 12.92m (45ft 5in). Wing area 271.9m² (2927sq ft).

Capacity: Flightcrew of three. Max seating capacity 259 or standard seating for between 180 and 220 in Series 61, 63, 71 & 73. Super 62 & 72 standard seating for 189. Super 60 and 70 freighters payload between 40,405kg (89,000lb) and 49,585kg (109,217lb).

Production: 262 Super 60 series built with 110 70 series conversions. Approx 90 Super 60s and 100 Super 70s in service in late 2000.

History: The successful DC-8 Super 60 airliners are stretched developments of the DC-8 Series 50. The Super 70s are Super 60s re-engined with CFM56 high bypass turbofans.

Douglas announced the DC-8 Super Sixty series in April 1965. The first, a DC-8-61, first flew on March 14 1966, followed by the first flights of the DC-8-62 on August 29 1966 and the DC-8-63 on April 10 1967. The DC-8-61 differed from the earlier DC-8-50 in having two fuselage plugs which increased length by 11.18m (36ft 8in), increasing max seating capacity to 259 (the largest of any single aisle airliner prior to the 757-300) and underfloor freight capacity by 80%. Intended for domestic operations, its max takeoff weight was identical to the DC-8-50.

The Super 62 was intended for long range operations and featured only a modest 2.04m (6ft 8in) stretch compared to the Series 50, greater wing span, revised engine nacelles and pylons and significantly increased fuel capacity. The Super 63 meanwhile combined the DC-8-61's fuselage with the DC-8-62's wings. It was the final DC-8 variant in production, the last was delivered in May 1972.

McDonnell Douglas initiated a re-engining program of Super 60 series aircraft with CFM International CFM56 engines in the early 1980s, known as the Super 70 Series. The first converted airframe flew in August 1981. The Super 70 aircraft are considerably quieter than their predecessors, with better fuel economy and greater range.

Photo: A DC-8-62F freighter. (Trent Jones)

EADS CASA C-212 Aviocar

Country of origin: Spain

Type: STOL turboprop regional airliner and utility transport

Powerplants: C-212C – Two 580kW (775shp) Garrett AiResearch TPE331-5-251C turboprop engines driving four blade propellers. Series 300 – Two 670kW (900shp) Honeywell TPE331-10R-513Cs.

Performance: C-212C – Max speed 370km/h (199kt), max cruising speed 359km/h (194kt), economical cruising speed 315km/h (170kt). Range with max fuel and 1045kg (2303lb) payload 1760km (950nm), range with max payload 480km (258nm). Series 300 – Max operating speed 370km/h (200kt), max cruising speed 354km/h (191kt), economical cruising speed 300km/h (162kt). Range with 25 passengers and reserves at max cruising speed 440km (237nm), with 1700kg (3770lb) payload 1435km (775nm).

Weights: C-212C – Empty 3700kg (8157lb), max takeoff 6300kg (13,890lb). Series 300 – Empty 3780kg (8333lb), operating empty 4560kg (10,053lb), max takeoff 7700kg (16,975lb).

Dimensions: C-212C & Series 200 – Wing span 19.00m (62ft 4in), length 15.20m (49ft 11in), height 6.30m (20ft 8in). Wing area 40.0m^2 (430.6sq ft). Series 300 – Wing span 20.28m (66ft 7in), length 16.15m (53ft 0in), height 6.60m (21ft 8in). Wing area 41.0m^2 (441.3sq ft).

Capacity: Flightcrew of two. Max passenger seating for 26, typical layout for 22 passengers at three abreast. Freighter version can accommodate three LD3 containers or two LD2s or two LD727/DC-8s. Max payload 2700kg (5950lb).

Production: Over 370 Aviocars of all models built, including 170 for commercial operators and 265 for military customers. IPTN in Indonesia has built over 90 NC-212s under licence.

History: Initially conceived as a light STOL transport for the Spanish air force, the C-212 has found a handy market niche and is highly regarded for its utility in underdeveloped regions.

Designed to replace the Spanish air force's mixed transport fleet of Douglas C-47 Dakotas and Junkers Ju 52s still in service in the 1960s, the C-212 was also developed with the intention of offering a civil variant. Design work began in the late 1960s, the first prototype made the type's first flight on March 26 1971. Preproduction examples followed, before the type entered air force service in 1974. The first commercial version was delivered in July 1975.

The basic civil version was designated the C-212C, the military version the C-212-5. Production of these models ceased in 1978, CASA switching to the Series 200 with more powerful engines and higher operating weights. The first Series 200, a converted C-212C prototype, flew for the first time in its new configuration on April 30 1978. A third development of the Aviocar is the Series 300 which first flew in 1984 and was certificated in late 1987. Improvements to this model are newer engines and winglets.

The latest development is the C-212-400, which first flew on April 4 1997. It features TPE331-12JR engines which maintain their power output to a higher altitude for improved hot and high performance and an EFIS flightdeck. The Patrullero is offered in a number of mission specific configurations.

Photo: A C-212-400 Patrullero of Spain's Ministry of Agriculture, Fisheries and Foord. (EADS)

EADS CASA/IAe CN-235

Countries of Origin: Spain and Indonesia

Type: Utility transport and 45 seat regional airliner

Powerplants: Two 1395kW (1870shp) General Electric CT7-9C turboprops driving four blade constant propellers.

Performance: CN-235-100 – Max speed 509km/h (275kt), max cruising speed 454km/h (245kt). Initial rate of climb at sea level 1780ft/min. Range with max payload and reserves at 18,000ft 796km (430nm).

Weights: CN-235-100 – Operating empty 9800kg (21,605lb), max takeoff 15,100kg (33,290lb).

Dimensions: Wing span 25.81m (84ft 8in), length 21.40m (70ft 3in), height 8.18m (26ft 10in). Wing area 59.1m^2 (636.17sq ft).

Capacity: Flightcrew of two. Passenger accommodation in airliner version for 45 four abreast. Quick change convertibles can carry mixtures of passengers and LD2 or LD3 containers. Cargo version can carry four LD3s or five LD2s or palletised freight.

Production: Out of total orders for 260 CN-235s, 47 have been to civil customers. Over 26 are currently in airline service.

History: The CN-235 regional airliner and military transport was designed and developed under the Airtech banner as a 50:50 joint venture between CASA of Spain (now part of EADS) and Indonesian Aerospace (formerly IPTN).

One prototype was built in both countries and these rolled out simultaneously on September 10 1983. The Spanish prototype flew first, on November 11 1983, with the Indonesian built aircraft following on December 30 that year. Certification by both Spanish and Indonesian authorities and first deliveries (from the Indonesian line) occurred in December 1986. Entry into commercial service was in March 1988.

Final assembly lines for the CN-235 are in Spain and Indonesia, but all other manufacture is not duplicated. EADS (CASA) builds the centre and forward fuselage, wing centre section and inboard flaps, and engine nacelles, while Indonesian Aerospace (IAe) builds outer wings and flaps, ailerons, the rear fuselage and the tail unit.

The initial production CN-235-10 was soon replaced by the CASA built CN-235-100 and IPTN's CN-235-110, incorporating CT7-9C engines in place of CT7-7As, and new composite engine nacelles. Further improvements led to the CASA CN-235-200 and similar IAe CN-235-220 with increased operating weights, better field performance and greater range, with structural improvements and improved leading edge flaps and rudder. The CN-235-220 was certificated in March 1992. CASA and IAe now develop their own CN-235 variants independently.

Other variants on the CN-235 theme are the CN-235 QC quick change variant capable of carrying passengers or freight or both; IAe's CN-235 MPA maritime patrol aircraft and CASA's CN-235MP Persuader (which while primarily aimed at military customers, have customs and boarder patrol applications); and the widely ordered CN-235 M multirole military freighter. IAe has marketed military CN-235s as the Phoenix. CASA has developed the stretched C-295 primarily for military use.

The CN-235 has succeeded in achieving only a small number of commercial orders, mostly from Indonesian and Spanish operators. In contrast it has won a significant number of military orders from around the world.

Photo: A Merpati CN-235 airliner. (John Sise)

EADS Socata Tampico, Tobago & Trinidad

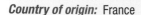

Country of origin: France

Type: Four/five seat light aircraft

Powerplant: TB 9 Tampico Club – One 120kW (160hp) Textron Lycoming O-320-D2A flat four piston engine driving a two blade fixed pitch Sensenich propeller. TB 20 Trinidad – One 185kW (250hp) Textron Lycoming IO-540-C4D5D fuel injected flat six piston engine driving a two blade constant speed Hartzell prop.

Performance: TB 9 – Max speed 226km/h (122kt), max cruising speed 198km/h (107kt), economical cruising speed 194km/h (105kt). Initial rate of climb 750ft/min. Max certificated altitude 11,000ft. Max range 1030km (555nm). TB 20 – Max speed 310km/h (167kt), max cruising speed 301km/h (163kt), economical cruising speed 291km/h (157kt). Initial rate of climb 1260ft/min. Service ceiling 20,000ft. Range with max fuel and reserves at 75% power 1640km (885nm), at 65% power 1785km (964nm), max range 2052km (1108nm).

Weights: TB 9 – Empty 647kg (1426lb), max takeoff 1060kg (2335lb). TB 20 – Empty 800kg (1763lb), max takeoff 1400kg (3086lb).

Dimensions: TB 9 & TB 20 – Wing span 9.76m (32ft 0in), length 7.70m (25ft 3in), height 3.02m (9ft 11in). Wing area 11.9m² (128.1sq ft).

Capacity: Typical seating for four or five, with pilot and passenger on front bucket seats and two or three passengers on rear bench seat.

Production: Over 1900 built including over 470 Tampicos/Tampico Clubs, over 725 Tobagos and 680 Trinidads and Trinidad TCs.

History: Socata's popular 'Caribbean' TB series of light singles spans from the basic fixed gear Tampico Club to the turbocharged 315km/h (170kt) cruise Trinidad TC.

Design work on the TB singles began in the mid 1970s, in part as a replacement for Socata's successful Rallye family. The first prototype, a TB 10 but powered by a 120kW (160hp) Lycoming O-320, flew for the first time on February 23 1977. Production began in 1979.

Three distinct versions of the TB series have been built. The TB 9 Tampico is marketed as a trainer and is powered by a four cylinder 120kW (160hp) Lycoming O-320. Until the late 1980s it was available with a fixed pitch propeller as the Tampico FP, or with a constant speed prop as the Tampico CS. Both the Tampico FP and CS had a more up market interior than the later TB 9 Tampico Club, which has a two blade fixed pitch Sensenich propeller. The Tampico Sprint meanwhile was launched in 1997 and introduced faired, trailing link undercarriage and a new prop, increasing cruising speed by 18km/h (10kt).

The TB 10 Tobago and TB 200 Tobago XL feature faired undercarriage, higher weights, a higher level of interior equipment, more powerful engines and constant speed props. The Tobago is powered by a 135kW (180hp) O-360, the TB 200 Tobago XL a 150kW (200hp) fuel injected IO-360.

The top of the range models are the retractable undercarriage TB 20 Trinidad and TB 21 Trinidad TC. The Trinidad is powered by a 185kW (250hp) IO-540, the Trinidad TC a similarly rated turbocharged TIO-540. The TB 20C has a port side freight door.

In early 2000 Socata switched production to the improved GT (Generation Two) series of all four models. The GTs feature the slightly enlarged cabin developed for the MR series.

Photo: A Tampico Sprint. (EADS Socata)

EADS Socata MS 180 & MS 250 Morane

Country of origin: France

Type: Four/five seat light aircraft

Powerplant: MS 180 – One 135kW (180hp) Morane Renault MR 180 turbocharged and intercooled direct injection flat four piston running on jet fuel driving a three blade constant speed Hartzell propeller. MS 250 – One 185kW (250hp) MR 250.

Performance: MS 180 – Max cruising speed at 10,000ft 248km/h (134kt). Time to 8500ft 14min 50sec, time to 12,000ft 23min 30sec. Service ceiling 17,000ft. Max range 1845km (996nm). MS 250 – Max cruising speed at 15,000ft 350km/h (189kt). Time to 8000ft 7min 10sec, to 12,000ft 10min 50sec. Service ceiling 23,000ft. Max range 2655km (1433nm).

Weights: Weights not published at late 2000.

Dimensions: MS 180/MS 250 – Wing span 9.76m (32ft 0in), length 7.70m (25ft 3in), height 3.02m (9ft 11in). Wing area 11.9m² (128.1sq ft).

Capacity: Typical seating for four or five.

Production: Deliveries due to begin in 2001.

History: Socata's MS 180 and MS 250 Morane light singles are the first applications for new technology Morane Renault direct injection diesel piston engines which run on jet fuel/Avtur.

Morane Renault is the marketing name for the Societe de Motorisations Aeronautiques (SMA), jointly established in 1997 by Socata parent Aerospatiale and Renault Sport, the motorsport arm of the French car manufacturer, to develop new technology piston engines for use by Socata and other aircraft builders.

Morane Renault is currently developing three new diesel direct injection turbocharged engines, the direct drive 135kW (180hp) MR 180, and the geared 185kW (250hp) MR 250 and 225kW (300hp) MR 300. The major benefit of these engines is that they will run on jet fuel, which is cheaper and more readily available than Avgas. The engines will be computer controlled, allowing the use of a single power lever on aircraft they power.

The MR engines will cost about the same as conventional piston engines, but operating costs are predicted to be as much as 30 to 40% lower due to a 3000 hour TBO (time between overhaul), lower maintenance costs, better fuel efficiency and the affordability of jet fuel.

A Morane Renault engine got airborne for the first time aboard a modified Socata Trinidad on March 3 1998. This was an MR 250 derated to 150kW (200hp) due to a gearbox limitation. Morane Renault expects the engines to be certificated in late 2000.

Socata's new Morane singles will be the first applications for the new technology engines. The MS 180 will be based on the fixed undercarriage TB 10 Tobago but powered by an MR 180, while the MR 250 powered MS 250 is based on the retractable undercarriage Trinidad. First deliveries are planned for 2001.

In addition, Socata plans to offer an MR 300 powered development of its Epsilon two seat trainer as the MS 300 and has looked at a development of the TB 360 Tangara with Morane power.

Like the GT series of the TB family, the MR 180 and MR 250 will also feature an enlarged cabin and redesigned interior.

Photo: The Trinidad with the MR 250 engine. (Morane Renault)

EADS Socata TBM 700

Country of origin: France

Type: Single engine corporate turboprop

Powerplant: One 522kW (700shp) flat rated Pratt & Whitney Canada PT6A-64 turboprop driving a four blade constant speed Hartzell propeller.

Performance: Max cruising speed 555km/h (300kt), economical cruising speed 450km/h (243kt). Initial rate of climb 2380ft/min. Max certificated altitude 30,000ft. Range with max payload and reserves at max cruising speed 1666km (900nm), at economical cruising speed 2000km (1079nm). Range with max fuel at max cruising speed 2500km (1350nm), at economical cruising speed 2870km (1550nm).

Weights: Empty equipped 1860kg (4101lb), max takeoff 2984kg (6578lb).

Dimensions: Wing span 12.68m (41ft 7in), length 10.64m (34ft 11in), height 4.35m (14ft 3in). Wing area 18.0m² (193.8sq ft).

Capacity: Pilot and one passenger (or copilot) on flightdeck. Main cabin seating for up to five, or typical accommodation for four in a club arrangement. The TBM 700 is also offered as a freighter.

Production: More than 185 built by late 2000. Total of 25 ordered for the French air force and army.

History: Socata's TBM 700 is a high performance single engine turboprop powered light business and corporate transport.

The TBM 700 is mainly optimised as a business transport and competes with Beech's C90 King Air series. Unlike the similarly sized C90 King Air though, the TBM 700's single engine layout is a major conceptual difference. With its single PT6 turboprop, rather than two on the King Air, the TBM 700 offers significantly lower operating costs yet comparable performance.

The TBM 700 was originally developed in partnership between Socata (then Aerospatiale's General Aviation division, now part of EADS) in France and Mooney in the USA, hence the TBM designation. The two companies formed TBM SA to build and market the TBM 700, with development responsibility for the project divided on a 70/30 basis between Socata and Mooney respectively.

The first of three TBM 700 prototypes first flew on July 14 1988. French certification was granted in January 1990. Shortly after the delivery of the first production aircraft in December 1990, Mooney withdrew from the program, leaving Socata with full responsibility for the aircraft.

The pressurised TBM 700 is of conventional design and construction, with a small amount of composite materials used in some areas. Flight controls, flaps and most of the empennage and fin are made from Nomex honeycomb and metal sheets. Leading edges and undercarriage doors meanwhile are made from a carbon and fibreglass composite. Entry to the cabin is through a split upward/downward opening door in the rear port fuselage.

Apart from the base aircraft the TBM 700 is offered as the TBM 700C freighter with a freight door and separate port side cockpit door. A French customer placed the TBM 700 freighter into service in November 1999. Development of the stretched TBM 700S ceased in 1995.

Photo: A US registered TBM 700 corporate transport. The TBM 700 is smaller than the Caravan and PC-12. (EADS Socata)

Embraer EMB-121 Xingu

Country of origin: Brazil

Type: Twin turboprop corporate transport

Powerplants: Xingu I – Two 505kW (680shp) Pratt & Whitney Canada PT6A-28 turboprops driving three blade constant speed Hartzell propellers. Xingu II – Two 559kW (750shp) PT6A-135s driving four blade props.

Performance: Xingu I – Max cruising speed 450km/h (243kt), econ cruising speed 365km/h (197kt). Initial rate of climb 1400ft/min. Service ceiling 26,000ft. Range with max fuel 2352km (1270nm). Xingu II – Max cruising speed 474km/h (256kt), economical cruising speed 380km/h (205kt). Initial rate of climb 1800ft/min. Service ceiling 28,000ft. Range with max fuel 2278km (1230nm), with max payload 1630km (880nm).

Weights: Xingu I – Empty equipped 3620kg (7984lb), max takeoff 5670kg (12,500lb). Xingu II – Empty equipped 3710kg (8179lb), max takeoff 5670kg (12,500lb).

Dimensions: Wing span 14.45m (47ft 5in), length 12.25m (40ft 2in), height 4.74m (15ft 7in). Wing area 27.5m² (296.0sq ft).

Capacity: Flightcrew of one or two, plus typical main cabin seating for five or six passengers, max seating in main cabin for nine. The cabin features a standard toilet and galley.

Production: Total Xingu I & II production 105 aircraft, including military orders, comprising 89 Xingu Is and 16 Xingu IIs. Over 60 currently in use as corporate transports, largely in Europe and South America, including French military aircraft.

History: The sleek looking Xingu corporate transport coupled the Bandeirante's wing with an all new fuselage, but was only built in modest numbers.

The Xingu flew for the first time on October 10 1976, with a production aircraft following on May 20 1977. The first customer delivery occurred later that same year (to the Copersucar-Fittipaldi Formula One racing team). Design features included a wing based on that on the EMB-110P2 but with reduced span and modified tips, and Pratt & Whitney Canada PT6A turboprops.

The major customer for the Xingu I was the French military, with a total order for 41 (for aircrew training and liaison duties for the air force and navy), which accounted for almost half of all EMB-121 production.

Several derivatives of the Xingu design were proposed, including the original EMB-120, the Araguia, a commuter airliner which would have seated 25, and the EMB-123 Tapajós. The Tapajós would have had more powerful 835kW (1120shp) PT6A-45 engines (which also would have powered the Araguia), increased wing span and a lengthened fuselage.

A more modest development did enter production, the EMB-121B Xingu II. This introduced more powerful PT6A-135 engines, four blade props, increased fuel tankage and small strakes added to each side of the tail cone. Similar in size, powerplant and performance to the Raytheon Beech King Air B200, the Xingu II made its first flight on September 4 1981. Embraer introduced an improved interior for the Xingu II in 1984.

Production ceased in August 1987 after 105 Xingus had been built.

Photo: A Xingu II. (Embraer)

Embraer EMB-110 Bandeirante

Country of origin: Brazil

Type: 15-18 seat turboprop regional airliner

Powerplants: Two 560kW (750shp) Pratt & Whitney Canada PT6A-34 turboprops driving three blade constant speed Hartzell propellers.

Performance: EMB-110P – Max speed 460km/h (248kt), max cruising speed 417km/h (225kt), economical cruising speed 326km/h (176kt). Initial rate of climb 1788ft/min. Service ceiling 22,500ft. Range at long range cruising speed with reserves 2000km (1080nm). EMB-110P2A/41 – Max cruising speed 413km/h (222kt), economical cruising speed 341km/h (184kt). Range with max fuel 1964km (1060nm).

Weights: EMB-110P – Empty equipped 3515kg (7751lb), max takeoff 5700kg (12,566lb). EMB-110P2A/41 – Operating empty 3590kg (7915lb), max takeoff 5900kg (13,010lb).

Dimensions: Wing span 15.33m (50ft 3in), length 15.10m (50ft 4in), height 4.92m (16ft 2in). Wing area 29.1m² (313sq ft).

Capacity: Flightcrew of two. Typical passenger seating for 18 at three abreast, max seating for 21 at 74cm (29in) pitch.

Production: 500 Bandeirantes built, the last of which were delivered to the Brazilian military in 1990. Over 200 remain in airline service.

History: The Embraer EMB-110 Bandeirante (often dubbed 'Bandit'), was Embraer's first successful commercial aircraft program.

The EMB-110 was developed at the Brazilian Institute of Research and Development in response to a Brazilian Ministry of Aeronautics specification for a general purpose light transport suitable for military and civilian duties. The new design was developed with the assistance of well known French designer Max Holste, and the first of three YC-95 prototypes first flew on October 26 1968.

Embraer (or Empresa Brasilera de Aeronáutica SA) was established the following year, and development and production of the C-95 became one of the company's first responsibilities. The first production standard EMB-110 Bandeirante (Portuguese for Pioneer) flew on August 9 1972, and the first entered airline service in April 1973.

Initial Bandeirante models were the 12 seat transport EMB-110, the aerial photography EMB-110B and maritime patrol EMB-111 for the Brazilian air force; the initial airline version, the 15 seat EMB-110C; and the seven seat EMB-110E executive transport.

The 18 seat enlarged EMB-110P gave rise to the main production models, the convertible passenger/freight EMB-110P1 with larger rear door and the passenger EMB-110P2 with airstair, which both appeared in 1977. The P1/41 and P2/41 introduced a higher maximum takeoff weight.

From 1983 Embraer built the EMB-110P1A, P1A/41, P2A and P2A/41, which featured dihedral on the tailplane among other minor improvements. The EMB-110P1A/41 and P2A/41 versions of the P1A were certificated to US FAA SFAR-41 standards.

Bandeirante production ceased in May 1990, the final aircraft being delivered to the Brazilian air force although a further two were completed in 1992 for the Colombian air force. Today the Bandeirante's virtues of reliability and good operating economics means that it remains popular with its operators.

Photo: 200 Bandeirantes remains in service. (Gerard Williamson)

Embraer EMB-120 Brasilia

Country of origin: Brazil

Type: 30 seat turboprop regional airliner

Powerplants: Two 1340kW (1800shp) Pratt & Whitney Canada PW118 or PW118A turboprops driving four blade Hamilton Standard propellers.

Performance: EMB-120 – Max cruising speed 555km/h (300kt) with PW118s, or 574km/h (310kt) with PW118As, long range cruising speed 482km/h (260kt). Initial rate of climb 2120ft/min. Service ceiling 30,000ft with PW118s, or 32,000ft with PW118As. Range with max passengers and reserves 1020km (550nm) with PW118s, or 926km (500nm) with PW118As. EMB-120ER – Max cruising speed 555km/h (300kt) with PW118s, or 580km/h (313kt) with PW118As, long range cruising speed 500km/h (270kt). Initial rate of climb 2500ft/min. Service ceiling 29,000ft with PW118s, or 32,000ft with PW118As. Range with max pax and reserves 1556km (840nm) with PW118s, or 1500km (810nm) with PW118As.

Weights: EMB-120 – Empty equipped 7100kg (15,655lb), max takeoff 11,500kg (25,353lb). EMB-120ER – Empty equipped 7140kg (15,741lb), max takeoff 11,990kg (26,433lb).

Dimensions: EMB-120 – Wing span 19.78m (64ft 11in), length 20.00m (65ft 8in), height 6.35m (20ft 10in). Wing area 39.4m² (424.42sq ft). EMB-120ER – Same except for length 20.07m (65ft 10in).

Capacity: Flightcrew of two. Standard main cabin seating for 30 at three abreast and 79cm (31in) pitch. Optional passenger seating for 24 or 26 with greater baggage/cargo space. Alternative interior arrangements for executive and cargo roles.

Production: Approx 360 Brasilias built by late 2000, with over 290 in service in 2000.

History: The 30 seat Brasilia has proved to be a popular regional turboprop airliner, enjoying strong sales in the face of fierce competition from the slightly larger Saab 340 and Dash 8.

Embraer first began design work on a new regional turboprop airliner in the late 1970s when the company studied stretching its EMB-121 Xingu corporate turboprop to a 25 seat regional airliner. While this was the first aircraft to bear the EMB-120 designation (it was named the Araguia), the production EMB-120 is an all new aircraft.

Design studies of the definitive EMB-120 began in September 1979, first flight of a PW115 powered prototype took place on July 27 1983, and entry into service was in October 1985 with Atlantic Southcoast Airlines.

Versions of the EMB-120 include: the initial production EMB-120; the Reduced Takeoff weight EMB-120RT; the Extended Range EMB-120ER; the EMB-120 Cargo freighter; mixed passenger/freight EMB-120 Combi; and EMB-120 Convertible. Hot and high versions of these models (offered from 1986) have PW118A engines, which retain their power ratings to a higher altitude.

Since 1994 the standard Brasilia production model has been the EMB-120ER Advanced (first delivered to Skywest Airlines in May 1993). The ER Advanced incorporates a range of external and interior improvements and an increased maximum takeoff weight.

The fuselage of the EMB-120 also forms the basis for the very successful ERJ regional jet family.

Photo: An EMB-120ER Brasilia. (Rob Finlayson)

Embraer ERJ 135, ERJ 140 & Legacy

Country of origin: Brazil

Type: 37 and 44 seat regional jet airliners & corporate jet (Legacy)

Powerplants: ERJ 135LR – Two 33.0kN (7426lb) Rolls-Royce AE 3007A1/3 turbofans. ERJ 140LR – Same.

Performance: ERJ 135LR – Max cruising speed 834km/h (450kt). Service ceiling 37,000ft. Range with 37 passengers 3138km (1700nm). ERJ 140LR – Same except range with 44 passengers 3019km (1630nm).

Weights: ERJ 135LR – Operating empty 11,420kg (25,176lb), max takeoff 20,000kg (44,092lb). ERJ 140LR – Operating empty 11,740kg (25,882lb), max takeoff 21,100kg (46,517lb).

Dimensions: ERJ 135 & Legacy – Wing span 20.04m (65ft 9in), length 26.34m (86ft 5in), height 6.75m (22ft 2in). Wing area 51.2m² (550.9sq ft). ERJ 140 – Same except length 28.45m (93ft 5in).

Capacity: Flightcrew of two. ERJ 135 – Flightcrew of two. Standard seating for 37 passengers at three abreast. ERJ 140 – Standard seating for 44 passengers at three abreast.

Production: By late 2000 firm ERJ 135 orders stood at 279 with approximately 50 delivered. 25 firm Legacy orders at late 2000.

History: The ERJ 135 and more recent ERJ 140 are shortened developments of the 50 seat ERJ 145, while the Legacy is a corporate jet development of the ERJ 135.

Embraer launched the ERJ 135 on September 16 1997 with the prototype flying just nine and a half months later on July 4 1998. A second prototype first flew in October 1998, US FAA certification was awarded on July 16 1999 and first delivery was to Continental Express on July 23 1999.

The ERJ 135 is a fairly straightforward development of the 145. Both 135 prototypes were converted from ERJ 145 prototypes, requiring little modification other than the removal of two fuselage plugs totalling 3.50m (11ft 6in) in length. The only other notable change is the derated Rolls-Royce (Allison) AE 3007 turbofans. Like the ERJ 145 therefore, the 135 also features a Honeywell Primus 1000 avionics suite with five large multifunction displays in the cockpit and three abreast passenger seating.

Also in common with the ERJ 145, the 135 is offered in standard ERJ 145ER and extended range ERJ 145LR forms. The LR features an additional fuel tank and slightly uprated engines.

In September 1999 Embraer launched the third member of its regional jet family, the 44 seat ERJ 140. The ERJ 140 is also a minimum change development, and differs from the 135 and 145 only in its fuselage length and seating capacity. First flight was on June 27 2000 and deliveries are scheduled for the first quarter of 2001.

The 140 is largely aimed at US airlines who have to contend with pilot labour agreement restrictions on the numbers of 50 seater jets they can operate. American Eagle is launch customer.

Meanwhile at Farnborough 2000 Embraer launched development of the ERJ 135 based Legacy corporate jet. Due to fly in February 2001 with certification later that year, the Legacy will feature additional fuel giving a range with eight passengers of 5930km (3200nm).

Photo: The prototype ERJ 140. The 140 has 98% structure, parts and systems commonality with its stablemates the 135 and 140. (Paul Merritt)

Embraer ERJ 145

Country of origin: Brazil

Type: 50 seat regional jet airliner

Powerplants: ERJ 145ER – Two 31.3kN (7040lb) Rolls-Royce AE 3007A turbofans. ERJ 145LR – Two 33.0kN (7426lb) AE 3007A1s.

Performance: High speed cruising speed 833km/h (450kt). Service ceiling 37,000ft. ERJ 145ER – Range with 50 passengers at long range cruising speed 2445km (1320nm). ERJ 145LR – Range with 50 passengers 2870km (1550nm).

Weights: ERJ 145ER – Operating empty 11,667kg (25,722lb), max takeoff 20,600kg (45,415lb). ERJ 145LR – Operating empty 12,007kg (26,470lb), max takeoff 22,000kg (48,500lb).

Dimensions: Wing span 20.04m (65ft 9in), length 29.87m (98ft 0in), height 6.75m (22ft 2in). Wing area 51.2m² (550.9sq ft).

Capacity: Flightcrew of two. Standard passenger accommodation for 50 at three abreast and 79cm (31in) pitch. Alternative seating for 48 or 49 with wardrobe fitted.

Production: First deliveries late December 1996. At late 2000 orders stood at 536, of which approx 250 had been delivered.

History: Following a chequered early development history, the 50 seat ERJ 145 regional jet has become a runaway sales success.

Embraer began working on 50 seat regional jet concepts in the late 1980s. The original EMB-145 (now renamed ERJ 145) was launched in mid 1989 and would have been a stretched and jet engined EMB-120 Brasilia (with the two turbofans mounted forward of the wing as on most low wing turboprops). This design would have seated 45 to 50 passengers and featured 75% commonality with the Brasilia.

But by 1990 Embraer was studying a modified design with less commonality to the Brasilia as wind tunnel testing revealed that the original configuration would not meet its design performance objectives. Changes to this interim design included a mildly swept wing with winglets and conventional below wing mounted engines. However this design would have needed an unusually tall undercarriage.

Thus in late 1991 Embraer froze the definitive ERJ 145 design with rear fuselage mounted engines and T-tail, with a wing lacking winglets. Other features include Rolls-Royce (Allison) AE 3007A turbofans (similar to those that power the Citation X) and a Honeywell Primus 1000 EFIS avionics suite with five colour CRT screens in the flightdeck. The Brasilia's three abreast fuselage cross section was retained.

The ERJ 145's first flight took place on August 11 1995 with first deliveries from December 1996 to Continental Express. Continental's initial order for 25 was a major fillup for the program and opened the floodgates for a number of major sales.

Embraer has developed three ERJ 145 models, the initial ERJ 145ER, the higher max takeoff weight longer range ERJ 145LR introduced in 1998 and most recently the ERJ 145XR (Extra Long Range). The 145XR was launched at the 2000 Farnborough Airshow and is due to fly in the first quarter of 2001. It will feature uprated engines and increased fuel capacity for a 3705km (2000nm) range.

Other developments of the ERJ 145 are two radar equipped versions for the Brazilian air force (the AEW EMB-145 SA and remote sensing EMB-145RS) and the ERJ 135, 140 and Legacy, described separately.

Photo: A Luxair ERJ 145. (Viktor Lázló)

Embraer ERJ 170 & ERJ 190

Country of origin: Brazil

Type: 70, 98 and 108 seat regional airliners

Powerplants: ERJ 170 – Two 62.3kN (14,000lb) General Electric CF34-8E turbofans. ERJ 190 – Two 82.3kN (18,500lb) CF34-10Es.

Performance: ERJ 170 – Max cruising speed Mach 0.80 or 870km/h (470kt). Standard range with max passengers at long range cruising speed 3334km (1800nm), LR range at same conditions 3889km (2100nm). ERJ 190-100 – Speed same. Standard range with max passengers at long range cruising speed 3334km (1800nm), LR range at same conditions 4260km (2300nm). ERJ 190-200 – Speed same. Standard range with max passengers at long range cruising speed 2593km (1400nm), LR range at same conditions 3334km (1800nm).

Weights: ERJ 170 – Basic operating 20,150kg (44,422lb), standard max takeoff 35,450kg (78,153lb), LR max takeoff 36,850kg (81,239lb). ERJ 190-100 – Basic operating 26,200kg (57,760lb), standard max takeoff 45,990kg (101,389lb), LR max takeoff 48,500kg (106,922lb). ERJ 190-200 – Basic operating 27,100kg (59,744lb), standard max takeoff 46,990kg (103,593lb), LR max takeoff 48,990kg (108,003lb).

Dimensions: ERJ 170 – Wing span over winglets 26.00m (85ft 4in), length 29.90m (98ft 1in), height 9.67m (31ft 9in). ERJ 190-100 – Wing span over winglets 28.56m (93ft 8in), length 36.15m (118ft 7in), height 10.48m (34ft 5in). ERJ 190-200 – Same except length 38.56m (126ft 6in), height 10.49m (34ft 5in).

Capacity: Flightcrew of two. ERJ 170 – Standard seating for 70 at four abreast. ERJ-190-100 Standard seating for 98. ERJ 190-200 – Standard seating for 108.

Production: At late 2000 80 ERJ 170s & 30 ERJ 190-200s on order.

History: Embraer's ERJ 170 and ERJ 190 are all new entrants into the top end of the regional jet airliner market, with seating capacities spanning from 70 to 108.

Embraer announced development of the ERJ 170 and ERJ 190 in February 1999, and formally launched the program on June 14 that year at the Paris Airshow (with a $US4.9m launch order from Crossair).

The first member of the family to emerge will be the 70 seat ERJ 170, which is scheduled to fly in the fourth quarter of 2001 with certification and deliveries planned for the second half of 2002. The stretched ERJ 190, which is offered in 98 seat ERJ 190-100 and further stretched 108 seat ERJ 190-200 forms, should fly in the second quarter of 2003 with certification and first deliveries in the third quarter of 2004. All three variants are offered in standard and LR (long range) variants. A corporate jet version of the 170, the ECJ 170, is also planned.

Features of the ERJ 170/190 include new FADEC equipped GE CF34 engines (the most powerful CF34 variants), a new four abreast 'double bubble' fuselage cross section, a moderately swept wing with winglets (added to the design in mid 2000), fly-by-wire flight controls, and Honeywell Primus Epic EFIS avionics.

Some 16 companies are participating in the ERJ 170/190 program as risk sharing partners, led by GE and Honeywell. Other partners are Gamesa (rear fuselage and tail), Latecoere (centre fuselage), and Kawasaki (wing stub, leading and trailing edges, flaps, spoilers and control surfaces).

Photo: An impression of the ERJ 170 before winglets were adopted.

Enstrom F28, 280 & 480

Country of origin: United States of America

Type: Three and five seat light helicopters

Powerplant: F28A – One 155kW (205hp) Lycoming HIO-360-C1B flat four piston engine driving a three blade main rotor and two blade tail rotor. 280FX – One 170kW (225hp) Textron Lycoming HIO-360-F1AD with Rotomaster turbocharger. 480 – One 215kW (285shp) takeoff rated Rolls-Royce 250-C20W turboshaft.

Performance: F28A – Max cruising speed 161km/h (87kt). Initial rate of climb 950ft/min. Service ceiling 12,000ft. Hovering ceiling in ground effect 5600ft. Range with max fuel 380km (205nm). 280FX – Max speed 189km/h (102kt), economical cruising speed 172km/h (93kt). Initial rate of climb 1450ft/min. Certificated ceiling 12,000ft. Hovering ceiling out of ground effect 8700ft. Range with max fuel and no reserves 483km (260nm). 480 – Cruising speed 211km/h (114kt) at 1293kg (2850lb). Initial rate of climb 1500ft/min. Service ceiling 13,000ft. Hovering ceiling out of ground effect 12,200ft. Max range 806km (435nm).

Weights: F28A – Empty 657kg (1450lb), max takeoff 975kg (2150lb). 280FX – Empty equipped 719kg (1585lb), max takeoff 1179kg (2600lb). 480 – Empty 760kg (1675lb), max takeoff 1292kg (2850lb).

Dimensions: F28A – Main rotor diameter 9.75m (32ft 0in), length overall 8.94m (29ft 4in), fuselage length 8.56m (28ft 1in), height to top of rotor hub 2.79m (9ft 2in). Main rotor disc area 74.7m^2 (804sq ft). 280FX – Same except for length overall 8.92m (29ft 3in). 480 – Main rotor diameter 9.75m (32ft 0in), fuselage length 9.09m (29ft 10in), height to main rotor hub 2.92m (9ft 7in).

Capacity: Three seats in the F28 and 280, five seats in 480. Can also be fitted with agricultural spraying gear.

Production: Production of all versions exceeds 1000. Approximately 45 480s built.

History: This long running line of three, four and five place light helicopters dates back to the late 1950s and remains in production.

The Enstrom Helicopter Corporation was first formed in 1959, and the three place F28 was its first product. The first F28 prototype made its maiden flight on November 12 1960, with the production prototype flying in May 1962. Since that time numerous developments of the basic design have been built. These include the F28A which appeared in 1968; the Model 280 Shark from 1973, an improved version with a reprofiled airframe which supplemented the F28A in production; and the turbocharged F28C and 280C, which were certificated in 1975.

The prototype for the Allison (now Rolls-Royce) 250 turboshaft powered 480 five seater and TH-28 three seat trainer first flew in 1989 after a proof of concept 280FX powered by an Allison 250-C20W began test flying the previous year. The 480 was certificated in June 1993, the TH-28, which Enstrom unsuccessfully entered into a recent US Army competition for a new pilot training helicopter, was certificated in 1992 and is aimed at training and light patrol work.

Current Enstrom production models are the F28F Falcon which first appeared in 1981; the FLIR pod equipped F28F-P Sentinel which is optimised for police work; the three seat 280FX Shark which was certificated in early 1988; and the turbine powered 480 and TH-28.

Photo: An Enstrom 280FX Shark. (Dave Prossor)

Eurocopter AS 350 Ecureuil

Country of origin: France

Type: Light utility helicopter

Powerplant: AS 350B – One 546kW (732shp) Turbomeca Arriel 1D1 turboshaft (transmission takeoff rating 440kW/590shp) driving a three blade main rotor and two blade tail rotor. AS 350D – One 460kW (615shp) Textron (Avco) Lycoming LTS 101-600A2. AS 350B3 – One 632kW (848shp) Arriel 2B (transmission takeoff rating 500kW/671shp).

Performance: AS 350B2 – Max cruising speed 246km/h (133kt). Max rate of climb 1752ft/min. Hovering ceiling out of ground effect 8360ft. Range with max fuel 670km (362nm). AS 350D – Max cruising speed 230km/h (124kt). Max inclined rate of climb 1575ft/min. Range with max fuel and no reserves 760km (410nm). AS 350B3 – Max cruising speed 248km/h (134kt). Initial rate of climb 1791ft/min. Hovering ceiling out of ground effect 12,240ft. Range with max fuel 666km (360nm).

Weights: AS 350B2 – Empty 1171kg (2582lb), max takeoff 2250kg (4960lb). AS 350D – Empty 1070kg (2359lb), max takeoff 1950kg (4300lb), or 2100kg (4630lb) with a sling load. AS 350B3 – Empty 1175kg (2590lb), max takeoff 2250kg (4960lb).

Dimensions: Main rotor diameter 10.69m (35ft 1in), length with rotors turning 12.94m (42ft 6in), fuselage length 10.93m (35ft 11in), height overall 3.14m (10ft 4in). Main rotor disc area 89.8m² (966.1sq ft).

Capacity: Standard seating for six, including two forward seats and a four place rear bench seat.

Production: Approx 2400 AS 350s of all types (including military Fennecs) ordered by late 2000. In addition Helibras in Brazil has built under licence over 250 Esquilos.

History: Europe's most successful family civil helicopters, the Ecureuil (or Squirrel) is in extensive civil and military use worldwide undertaking a variety of wide ranging missions.

Aerospatiale development of the AS 350 Squirrel in the early 1970s culminated in the first flights of the Avco Lycoming LTS 101 powered prototype on June 27 1974 and the Turbomeca Arriel powered prototype on February 14 1975. These aircraft were followed by eight pre-production examples, the first of which flew in late 1977.

Customer deliveries began in April 1978. Initial models offered were the Arriel powered AS 350B, which was marketed outside North America, and the LTS 101 powered AS 350C AStar sold in the USA. The AS 350C was soon replaced by the D, with a more powerful engine.

Subsequent developments include the hot and high AS 350B1 with a 510kW (684shp) Arriel 1D; the AS 350BA which was certificated in 1991 and was in production through to 1998 and is fitted with the larger main rotors of the AS 350B2 (AS 350Bs can be retrofitted to BA standard); and the AS 350B2 (marketed in North America as the SuperStar) with a more powerful Arriel 1D1 turboshaft, and the main and tail rotors developed for the twin engine AS 355F Ecureuil 2 (described separately) and certificated in April 1989.

The AS 350B3 first flew on March 4 1997 and is a hot and high optimised model. Its most important change is a more powerful Arriel 2D engine. Deliveries began in January 1998.

Military Ecureuils are marketed as the AS 550 Fennec.

Photo: An AS 350 Ecureuil/Squirrel used for in support of Australia's Antarctic stations. (Tom Stokes)

Eurocopter AS 355 Ecureuil 2

Country of origin: France

Type: Twin engined light utility helicopter

Powerplants: AS 355F – Two 315kW (420shp) Allison 250-C20F turboshafts driving a three blade main rotor and two blade tail rotor. AS 355N – Two 302kW (406shp) max continuous rated Turbomeca TM 319 1A Arrius turboshafts.

Performance: AS 355F – Max cruising speed 224km/h (121kt). Initial rate of climb 1280ft/min. Hovering ceiling in ground effect 5900ft. Service ceiling 11,150ft. Range with max fuel and no reserves 703km (380nm). AS 355N – Max cruising speed 222km/h (120kt), economical cruising speed 217km/h (117kt). Initial rate of climb 1260ft/min. Hovering ceiling out of ground effect 2460ft. Range with max fuel 722km (390nm).

Weights: AS 355F – Empty 1305kg (2877lb), max takeoff 2540kg (5600lb) or 2600kg (5732lb) with external sling load. AS 355N – Empty 1436kg (3166lb), max takeoff 2600kg (5732lb).

Dimensions: Main rotor diameter 10.69m (35ft 1in), length overall rotors turning 12.94m (42ft 6in), fuselage length 10.91m (35ft 10in), height 3.14m (10ft 4in). Main rotor disc area 89.8m² (966.1sq ft).

Capacity: Standard seating for six, including two forward seats and a four place rear bench seat. Can be configured for police, ambulance, EMS and media missions.

Production: Orders for military AS 555s and civil AS 355s total over 860. Helibras of Brazil has built over 25 AS 355s under licence.

History: The twin engined member of the Ecureuil/Squirrel family, the AS 355 Ecureuil 2 offers greater performance, carrying capability and the increased redundancy of twin engines compared to the single engined AS 350.

Development of the first twin engine Ecureuil began early in the model's development life, with the first flying on September 28 1979. This prototype was powered by two Allison 250-C20F turboshafts, supplying power to the main and tail rotors through a combining gearbox. Put into production as the AS 355E, it was essentially a twin engined version of the AS 350 with detail changes made to the fuselage structure, fuel system, transmission and main rotor blades to support the twin engine configuration. In common with the AS 350, the AS 355 features the maintenance free Starflex main rotor hub, while the main rotor blades are of composite construction.

The AS 355F replaced the AS 355E from early 1982, and introduced new wider chord main rotor blades and a higher max takeoff weight. The AS 355F was followed by the F1 in January 1984 and F2 in December 1985, which introduced progressively higher maximum takeoff weights.

The current production model is the AS 355N Ecureuil 2 which introduced twin Turbomeca TM 319 Arrius turboshafts. It was certificated in 1989 and first deliveries took place from early 1992. It is marketed in North America as the TwinStar. As with the single engined AS 550, the twin engine military AS 555 is marketed as the Fennec (the AS 555SN is fitted with a chin mounted search radar for ASW).

Photo: An AS 355F1 over Auckland, New Zealand. The Ecureuil 2's enlarged engine fairings identify it from single engine models. (Peter Clark)

Eurocopter AS 332 Super Puma

Country of origin: France

Type: Medium lift utility helicopter

Powerplants: AS 332L – Two 1325kW (1755shp) Turbomeca Makila turboshafts driving a four blade main rotor and five blade tail rotor. AS 332L2 – Two 1375kW (1845shp) takeoff rated Turbomeca Makila 1A2 turboshafts.

Performance: AS 332L – Max cruising speed 277km/h (150kt). Max inclined rate of climb 1810ft/min. Hovering ceiling in ground effect 9840ft. Range 850km (635nm). AS 332L2 – High speed cruise 277km/h (150kt), economical cruising speed 252km/h (136kt). Rate of climb at 130km/h (70kt) 1447ft/min. Hovering ceiling out of ground effect 9380ft. Range with max fuel, economical cruising speed and no reserves 1490km (805nm), with standard fuel and same conditions 850km (460nm). Endurance 4hr 54min.

Weights: AS 332L – Empty 4370kg (9635lb), MTOW 9000kg (19,840lb). AS 332L2 – Empty 4686kg (10,331lb), MTOW 9300kg (20,502lb).

Dimensions: AS 332L – Main rotor diameter 15.08m (49ft 6in), length overall rotors turning 18.70m (61ft 4in), fuselage length 15.52m (50ft 11in), height overall 4.92m (16ft 1in). AS 332L2 – Main rotor diameter 16.20m (53ft 2in), length overall rotors turning 19.50m (63ft 11in), height overall 4.97m (16ft 4in). Main rotor disc area 206.1m^2 (2218.7sq ft).

Capacity: Flightcrew of one (VFR ops), or two (IFR ops) pilots. AS 332 seating for 17, AS 332L and AS 332L2 max seating for 24.

Production: Military and civil orders for all variants of the Super Puma total more than 550.

History: A larger development of the Puma (described under Aerospatiale), the Super Puma is a practical and proven medium lift twin helicopter, particularly popular for offshore oil rig support work.

The original SA 330 Puma, on which the Super Puma is based, flew for the first time in April 1965. The first Super Puma first flew in September 1978 and was essentially a more powerful version of the Puma, featuring 1270kW (1700shp) Turbomeca Makila turboshafts, new avionics, composite rotor blades and an enlarged fuselage. For a time Aerospatiale planned to fit the Super Puma with a Fenestron shrouded tail rotor, but testing revealed no significant performance benefits. Commercial versions were designated AS 332Cs.

The AS 332L (or SA 332L before 1980) Super Puma introduced a stretched fuselage (by 76.5cm/2.5ft), first flew on October 10 1980 and was certificated in 1983. The updated AS 332L1 with Makila 1A1 engines appeared in 1986. Bristow Helicopters ordered 31 customised AS 332Ls named Tiger for its North Sea offshore oil rig work.

The AS 332L remains in production but is progressively being replaced by the AS 332L2. The L2 Super Puma Mk 2 (known as the Cougar in military guise) features a further fuselage stretch permitting an additional row of seats, EFIS flight instrumentation, spheriflex rotor heads and longer main rotor blades with parabolic tips. It was certificated in 1992.

The Mk 2+ first flew on November 30 2000. It features Makila 1A4 engines (with FADEC), new main gearbox, a five blade main rotor, and a new glass cockpit with four LCDs. Certification is planned for late 2002.

Photo: Two AS 332L2s used for offshore oil rig support work.

Eurocopter AS 365N Dauphin 2 & EC 155

Country of origin: France

Type: Twin engine mid sized utility helicopter

Powerplants: AS 365N2 – Two 550kW (739shp) Turbomeca Arriel 1C2 turboshafts driving a four blade main rotor and Fenestron shrouded tail rotor. EC 155B – Two 635kW (851shp) takeoff rated Arriel 2C1s driving a five blade main rotor and Fenestron shrouded tail rotor.

Performance: AS 365N2 – Max cruising speed 285km/h (154kt), economical cruising speed 260km/h (140kt). Initial rate of climb 1380ft/min. Hovering ceiling in ground effect 8365ft, out of ground effect 5905ft. Range with standard fuel 900km (485nm). EC 155B – Max cruising speed 269km/h (145kt), economical cruising speed 265km/h (143kt). Hovering ceiling out of ground effect 2840ft. Max range with standard fuel 830km (448nm).

Weights: AS 365N2 – Empty 2240kg (4940lb), max takeoff 4250kg (9370lb). EC 155B – Empty 2528kg (5187lb), max takeoff 4800kg (10,582lb).

Dimensions: AS 365N2 – Main rotor diameter 11.94m (39ft 2in), length overall rotor turning 13.68m (44ft 11in), height 3.98m (13ft 1in). Main rotor disc area 111.9m^2 (1205sq ft). EC 155 – Main rotor diameter 12.60m (41ft 4in), length overall rotor turning 14.30m (46ft 11in), fuselage length 12.73m (41ft 9in), height 4.35m (14ft 3in). Main rotor disc area 124.7m^2 (1342.1sq ft).

Capacity: One pilot (VFR) or two pilots (IFR), and max seating for 13 passengers (with one pilot). Standard passenger seating for eight or nine. EC 155 – Standard seating for 14 including one or two pilots.

Production: Approximately 670 AS 365/366/565s ordered. 40 EC 155s ordered. Licence production in China as the Harbin 2-9.

History: The AS 365N Dauphin 2 is one of Eurocopter's most successful designs and has found widespread use in corporate, police, media, EMS and search and rescue roles worldwide.

The AS 365N is a much improved development of the original SA 365C Dauphin 2 (described under Aerospatiale). The AS 356N introduced more powerful Arriel 1C turboshafts, enlarged tail surfaces, revised transmission, main rotor, rotor mast fairing and engine cowling, and retractable tricycle undercarriage. The AS 365N first flew on March 31 1979. Deliveries began in early 1982.

The US Coast Guard took delivery of 99 AS 365N based HH-65 Dolphins. These aircraft are powered by Textron (Avco) Lycoming LTS 101s and are optimised for the USCG's search and rescue role.

Deliveries of the improved AS 365N2 commenced in 1990. It features upgraded Arriel 1C2 engines, improved gearbox, increased max takeoff weight, redesigned cabin doors, revised interior and optional EFIS instrumentation. The AS 365N3 is a hot and high development with FADEC equipped Arriel 2Cs. Deliveries began in December 1998.

Military AS 365Ns are offered as AS 565 Panthers.

The improved EC 155B (initially AS 365N4) development was announced at the 1997 Paris Airshow. It features twin Arriel 2Cs equipped with FADEC, a five blade Spheriflex main rotor and a 40% larger main cabin, achieved with bulged doors. First flight was on June 17 1997, with French and German certification awarded in December 1998. First delivery was in March 1999.

Photo: Germany's border guard service was the first EC 155 customer.

Eurocopter BO 105

Country of origin: Germany

Type: Five place light utility helicopter

Powerplants: BO 105 CBS & BO 105 CBS-5 – Two 313kW (420shp) Rolls-Royce 250-C20B turboshafts driving a four blade main rotor and two blade tail rotor.

Performance: BO 105 CBS-4 – Max cruising speed 240km/h (129kt), long range cruising speed 204km/h (110kt). Initial rate of climb 1457ft/min. Hovering ceiling out of ground effect 1500ft. Range with standard fuel and max payload 555km (300nm), ferry range with auxiliary fuel tanks 1020km (550nm). BO 105 CBS-5 – Max cruising speed 245km/h (132kt). Initial rate of climb 1870ft/min. Hovering ceiling out of ground effect 7960ft. Range 596km (321nm).

Weights: BO 105 CBS-4 – Empty 1300kg (2868lb), max takeoff 2500kg (5511lb).

Dimensions: Main rotor diameter 9.84m (32ft 4in), length incl rotors 11.86m (38ft 11in), fuselage length 8.81m (28ft 11in), height to top of main rotor mast 3.02m (9ft 11in). Main rotor disc area 76.1m² (818.6sq ft).

Capacity: Total seating for five, including two pilots or one pilot and passenger in front bucket seats, and three passengers on rear bench seat. Behind rear seats and below the engine is a freight/baggage compartment, accessible by two clamshell doors in the rear of the fuselage.

Production: Almost 1400 BO 105s of all models, including military versions, delivered thus far, including licence production in Canada, Indonesia, the Philippines and Spain.

History: In widespread military and civilian service, the BO 105 was MBB's (now part of Eurocopter) most successful helicopter design.

Construction of the first of three prototypes began in 1964, the first of which made the type's first flight on February 16 1967. This aircraft was powered by 236kW (317shp) Allison 250-C18 turboshafts and featured a conventional main rotor hub, but the subsequent prototypes incorporated a new rigid hub with feathering hinges, plus composite blades and MAN-Turbo 6022 engines. The BO 105 reverted back to Allison 250 power with the second of two pre-production aircraft, flying in this form in January 1971.

Initial production was of the BO 105C which was available from 1970. The Allison 250-C20 powerplant became standard from 1973. The BO 105 CB was introduced in 1975, and became the standard production model. It introduced uprated engines and a strengthened transmission. The BO 105 is now built in BO 105 CBS form with a slight 25cm (10in) fuselage stretch and extra window, allowing an additional passenger to be carried.

The BO 105 D has IFR instrumentation and was developed for the British offshore oil rig support market. The BO 105 L has more powerful engines and higher takeoff weight. The BO 105 LSA-3 is a hot and high version with Rolls-Royce (Allison) 250-C28C engines and built exclusively in Canada by Eurocopter Canada. The BO 105 LSA-3 Super Lifter has been developed for aerial crane work and has a 2850kg (6283lb) max takeoff weight.

The BO 105 CBS-5 (formerly EC Super Five) is an upgraded BO 105 CBS with new main rotor blades. It was certificated in late 1993 and has been the main production model since then.

Photo: An IPTN (Indonesia) built police NBO 105. (Robert Wiseman)

Eurocopter EC 135

Countries of origin: Germany and France

Type: Seven place light twin turbine utility helicopter

Powerplants: Either two 435kW (583shp) takeoff rated Turbomeca Arrius 2B1 or two 463kW (621shp) takeoff rated Pratt & Whitney Canada PW206B turboshafts driving a four blade main rotor and 10 blade shrouded Fenestron tail rotor.

Performance: Max cruising speed 256km/h (138kt). Max initial rate of climb 1500ft/min. Hovering ceiling out of ground effect 10,200ft. Range with standard fuel at sea level 620km (335nm) with Arrius 2Bs or 620km (340nm) with PW206Bs, ferry range with long range tanks 878km (474nm). Endurance with standard fuel 3hr 24min with Arrius 2B1s, 3hr 33min with PW206s.

Weights: Empty 1490kg (3284lb), max takeoff 2835kg (6250lb) or 2900kg (6393lb) with an external sling load.

Dimensions: Main rotor diameter 10.20m (33ft 6in), length overall rotor turning 12.16m (39ft 11in), fuselage length 10.20m (33ft 7in), height 3.62m (11ft 11in). Main rotor disc area 81.7m² (879.5sq ft).

Capacity: Designed for single pilot operation. Alternative cabin layouts are for five (two forward & three rear) or seven (two + three + two) in passenger roles. Alternative EMS layouts for one stretcher, three medical attendants and the pilot, or two stretchers, two attendants and pilot. Stretchers loaded through rear clamshell doors.

Production: By late 2000 orders stood at approx 200.

History: The EC 135 is intended as a replacement for Eurocopter's successful BO 105 light twin, and was developed from the BO 108 technology demonstrator.

The original MBB BO 108 was intended as an advanced technology helicopter demonstrator, and as such incorporated a range of high technology features including a hingeless main rotor (Sikorsky and Boeing adopted this design for their military RAH-66 Comanche), all composite bearingless tail rotor, shallow transmission (allowing greater cabin height) with special vibration absorbers, composite structures, improved aerodynamics, modern avionics and EFIS instrumentation. The first BO 108 was powered by Allison 250-C20R-3 turboshafts and flew on October 15 1988.

The success of the BO 108 test program led to MBB's announcement in January 1991 that it would develop a production version of the 108 with Arrius or PW206 engines as a replacement for the BO 105, with certification planned for 1994 and first deliveries in 1995. However the formation of Eurocopter (in January 1992) gave the program access to Aerospatiale's Fenestron shrouded tail rotor technology which was then incorporated into the design.

The combination of the BO 108 and the Fenestron led to the definitive EC 135 flying for the first time on February 15 1994. German certification was granted on June 14 1996, while US approval was given on July 31 that year, the same day as the first customer delivery.

The PW206 powered model is designated EC 135P1, the EC 135T1 has the Arrius 2B1. The improved PW207, but designated PW206B2, (with better single engine performance) will replace PW206Bs on the production line from May 2001.

The military EC 635 is also on offer.

Photo: The EC 135 is popular with EMS operators. (Eurocopter)

Eurocopter/CATIC/STAe EC 120 B Colibri

Countries of origin: France, Germany, China and Singapore

Type: Five place light utility helicopter

Powerplants: One 376kW (504shp) takeoff rated Turbomeca TM 319 Arrius 2F turboshaft driving a three blade main rotor and eight blade Fenestron shrouded tail rotor.

Performance: Max cruising speed 226km/h (122kt). Initial rate of climb 1300ft/min. Service ceiling 17,024ft. Range with no reserves 731km (3954nm). Endurance at 120km/h (65kt) 4hr 10min.

Weights: Empty 960kg (2116lb), max takeoff 1715kg (3781lb), max takeoff with a sling load 1800kg (3968lb).

Dimensions: Main rotor diameter 10.00m (32ft 9in), length overall rotor turning 11.52m (37ft 10in), fuselage length 9.60m (31ft 6in), height 3.40m (11ft 2in). Main rotor disc area 78.6m^2 (845.4sq ft).

Capacity: Typical seating for five, with pilot and passenger side by side with three passengers on rear bench seat. Could be configured for special missions roles. Max sling load 700kg (1543lb).

Production: First Colibri delivery (to Japan) in January 1998. At late 2000 more than 170 Colibris had been ordered. 100th delivered in May 2000.

History: Eurocopter's solution to develop a new light helicopter lay in forming a partnership with CATIC (Harbin) of China and Singapore Technologies Aerospace of Singapore.

Eurocopter (then Aerospatiale), CATIC and STA launched definition development of a new light helicopter, then designated P120L, in February 1990. The teaming arrangements for the helicopter saw Aerospatiale/Eurocopter take a 61% program share and leadership, CATIC with 24% and STAe with 15%. A development go-ahead contract for the new aircraft was signed in October 1992 (by which time Aerospatiale's helicopter activities had been merged into Eurocopter) and the EC 120 designation was announced in January 1993 (the Colibri [or Hummingbird] name came later). Design definition was completed in mid 1993.

Within the Eurocopter/CATIC/STAe partnership, Eurocopter is responsible for the design and manufacture of the rotor system and transmission, final assembly (at Marignane in France), flight testing and certification. CATIC builds the EC 120's fuselage, landing gear and fuel system, while STAe's areas of responsibility covers the tailboom, fin and doors.

Notable Colibri design features include a three blade main rotor with a Spheriflex hub integrated with the driveshaft and transmission, composite main and tail rotor blades and skid landing gear, a metal construction fuselage and a new eight blade Fenestron shrouded tail rotor. The Turbomeca TM 319 Arrius 1F turboshaft was selected to power at least the first 300 Colibris. The Colibri's cabin features standard seating for five including the pilot.

The first of two EC 120 prototypes first flew on June 9 1995 from Eurocopter France's Marignane facility. French DGAC certification was awarded in June 1997, while the first production Colibri first flew in December that year. First delivery was in January 1998, the 100th was delivered in May 2000.

Photo: The EC 120 B Colibri. The Colibri has proven to be a popular new entrant to the light helicopter market. (Peter Clark)

Eurocopter/Kawasaki BK 117 & EC 145

Countries of origin: Germany and Japan

Type: Twin engine utility helicopter

Powerplants: BK 117 A – Two 450kW (600shp) Avco (Textron) Lycoming LTS 101-650B-1 turboshafts driving a four blade main rotor and two blade tail rotor. BK 117 B-2 – Two 410kW (550shp) takeoff max continuous rated Honeywell LTS 101-750B-1s.

Performance: BK 117 A – Cruising speed 264km/h (143kt). Initial rate of climb 1970ft/min. Hovering ceiling in ground effect 13,450ft. Range with max payload 545km (295nm). BK 117 B-2 – Max cruising speed 248km/h (134kt). Initial rate of climb 1900ft/min. Hovering ceiling out of ground effect 7500ft. Range with standard fuel 540km (290nm), with internal long range fuel tank 706km (381nm).

Weights: BK 117 A – Empty 1520kg (3350lb), max takeoff 2800kg (6173lb). BK 117 B-2 – Empty 1745kg (3846lb), max takeoff 3350kg (7385lb), max takeoff with external payload.

Dimensions: Main rotor diameter 11.00m (36ft 1in), length overall 13.00m (42ft 8in), fuselage length 9.91m (32ft 6in), height rotors turning 3.85m (12ft 8in). Main rotor disc area 95.0m^2 (1023sq ft).

Capacity: One pilot and max seating for 10 passengers. Executive configuration seats six, standard MBB/Eurocopter configuration seats seven, standard Kawasaki version seats nine.

Production: Approx 370 BK 117s built, with 260 from Eurocopter/MBB and 110 from Kawasaki. Indonesia's IPTN licence built three BK 117s as NBK-117s.

History: The BK 117 was developed under a joint collaborative effort between MBB of Germany (now part of Eurocopter) and Kawasaki of Japan, resulting in production lines in both countries.

The BK 117 program replaced the independently developed BO 107 and Kawasaki KH-7 design studies. The BK 117 retains the former's overall configuration, with Eurocopter responsible for the helicopter's rotor system (which uses a scaled up version of the BO 105's four blade rigid main rotor), tail unit, hydraulic system and power controls, while Kawasaki has responsibility for the fuselage, transmission and undercarriage.

Development led to the BK 117's first flight on June 13 1979, the first production aircraft (built in Japan) flew December 1981, certification was awarded in December 1982, and first deliveries took place early in 1983. Initial production was of the BK 117 A-1, while the BK 117 A-3 with higher max takeoff weight and enlarged tail rotor with twisted blades was certificated in March 1985. The BK 117 A-4 introduced from 1987 features increased performance through an increased transmission limit at takeoff power, improved tail rotor head and, on German built aircraft, increased fuel.

The BK 117 B-1 (certificated in 1987) has more powerful engines and better performance, the BK 117 B-2 is currently in production and has an increased max takeoff weight. The BK 117 C-1 is a German development with Turbomeca Arriel engines.

The upgraded C-1 based EC 145 (formerly BK 117 C-2) first flew in mid 1999. At late 2000 Eurocopter had yet to formally unveil the EC 145 but improvements include a reprofiled EC 135 style nose, redesigned tail rotor and new avionics. It is optimised for EMS/SAR.

Photo: A BK 117 B-2. (Murray Hudson)

Extra 230, 300 & 200

Country of origin: Germany

Type: Unlimited competition aerobatic aircraft

Powerplant: 230 – One 150kW (200hp) Textron Lycoming AEIO-360 flat four piston engine driving a two blade c/s Mühlbauer propeller. 300 – One 225kW (300hp) Textron Lycoming AEIO-540-L1B5 flat six driving a three (or optionally four) blade Mühlbauer c/s prop.

Performance: 230 – Max speed 352km/h (190kt). Initial rate of climb 2950ft/min. Endurance with max fuel 2hr 30min. 300 – Max speed 343km/h (185kt), max manoeuvring speed 293km/h (158kt). Initial rate of climb 3300ft/min. Range with reserves 974km (526nm).

Weights: 230 – Empty 440kg (970lb), max takeoff 560kg (1235lb). 300 – Empty 630kg (1389lb), max aerobatic takeoff 870kg (1918lb), max takeoff 950kg (2094lb).

Dimensions: 230 – Wing span 7.40m (24ft 3in), length 5.82m (19ft 2in), height 1.73m (5ft 8in). 300 – Wing span 8.00m (26ft 3in), length 7.12m (23ft 4in), height 2.62m (8ft 7in). Wing area 10.7m² (115.17sq ft). 300S – Same except for wing span 7.50m (24ft 7in), length 6.65m (21ft 9in). Wing area 10.4m² (112sq ft).

Capacity: 300 and 200 seat two, 230 and 300S seat pilot only.

Production: Extra 230 production ceased in 1990. Approximately 190 Extra 300s delivered since 1988, approx 30 200s since 1996.

History: Extra's aerobatic light aircraft were designed from the outset for unlimited aerobatic competition flying.

The original wooden wing Extra 230 was designed by company founder Walter Extra to meet the requirements of competition pilots with the Swiss Aero Club. First flight occurred during 1983. Unusually for an aircraft of its type the Extra 230 features a wooden wing with dacron covering, while as on other aerobatic competition aircraft the 230's wing has 0° incidence for sustained inverted flight. Production ceased in 1990 as Extra couldn't source the correct type of wood.

Design work on the larger, two seat Extra 300 began in early 1987, culminating in the first flight of a prototype on May 6 1988 and certification in May 1990. Production began in October 1988.

Small numbers of Extra 260s were also built in the early 1990s. These aircraft were essentially downsized Extra 300s with seating for a pilot only and powered by a 195kW (260hp) IO-540 flat six. The Extra 260 was not certificated, the six that were built were able to fly under special permits.

The single seat Extra 300S first flew on March 4 1992 and was certificated that same month. The 300S differs from the 300 in having a single seat, shorter span wings and more powerful ailerons, while retaining the same powerplant and basic fuselage. The 300L has a low mounted wing. The strengthened 330L has a 245kW (330hp) AEIO-580 and larger control surfaces, and first flew in January 1998. The 330LX two seater first flew in early 1999.

Both the 300 and 300S are stressed for +10/-10g flight with a single pilot, have additional transparencies in the lower sides of the fuselage below the wings for pilot visibility, and a single piece canopy.

Extra's latest product is the 150kW (200hp) AEIO-360 powered Extra 200 two seater. It first flew in April 1996. Of similar construction to the 300, it replaces the earlier 230.

Photo: An Extra 300S. (Paul Merritt)

Fairchild (Swearingen) Merlin

Country of origin: United States of America

Type: Turboprop corporate transport

Powerplants: IIB – Two 495kW (665shp) AiResearch (Garrett) TPE-331-1-151G turboprops driving three blade constant speed propellers. IIIC – Two 670kW (900shp) Garrett TPE331-10U-503G turboprops driving four blade constant speed Dowty propellers.

Performance: IIB – Max cruising speed 475km/h (257kt). Initial rate of climb 2570ft/min. Service ceiling 29,000ft. Range with max fuel 2872km (1550nm). IIIC – Max cruising speed 556km/h (300kt). Initial rate of climb 2650ft/min. Range with max standard fuel at max cruising speed with six people on board 3590km (1938nm).

Weights: IIB – Empty 2926kg (6452lb), max takeoff 4540kg (10,000lb). IIIC – Empty equipped 3695kg (8150lb), max takeoff 5670kg (12,500lb).

Dimensions: IIB – Wing span 13.98m (45ft 11in), length 12.22m (40ft 1in), height 4.37m (14ft 4in). Wing area 26.0m² (279.74sq ft). IIIC – Wing span 14.10m (46ft 3in), length 12.85m (42ft 2in), height 5.13m (16ft 10in). Wing area 25.8m² (277.5sq ft).

Capacity: IIB – Flightcrew of one or two, with typical main cabin seating for six in executive layout or up to eight. III – Seating in main cabin for up to 11, or eight in a corporate configuration. Merlin IV seats up to 12 passengers in main cabin in a corporate configuration.

Production: Includes 33 Merlin IIAs, 87 Merlin IIBs, 92 Merlin III and IIIAs and 10 Merlin 300s. 160 Merlin IIIs and 84 IVs in service in 2000.

History: The Merlin series of turboprop executive transports was Swearingen's first manufacturing program.

Prior to the original Merlin II, Swearingen specialised in undertaking conversions of existing aircraft into corporate transports. The Merlin II (or SA26-T) for example is based on the Beech Queen Air and Twin Bonanza. The Merlin combined the wing of the Queen Air with the Twin Bonanza's undercarriage and an all new Swearingen designed pressurised fuselage and tail. The first Merlins were powered by two 300kW (400hp) Lycoming TIGO-540s, while the Merlin IIA was powered by Pratt & Whitney Canada PT6A-20 turboprops. The prototype IIA first flew on April 13 1965 and 33 were built before production switched to the AiResearch TPE331 powered Merlin IIB.

The improved and slightly larger Merlin III combined the Merlin II's fuselage but stretched slightly and with a new tail; and the wings and landing gear of the Metro II airliner (described separately) and more powerful engines. The Merlin III (or SA226-T) was certificated on July 27 1970. The improved IIIA introduced additional windows and avionics and systems changes, it was followed by the IIIB and then in 1981 (by which time Fairchild had acquired Swearingen) the IIIC, incorporating the wing from the Metro III.

The Merlin III was followed by the Merlin 300 which introduced aerodynamic improvements including winglets. Only 10 were built.

The Merlin IV designation applies to corporate configured versions of the Metro series of commuter airliners. The Merlin IVA designation covers the corporate versions of the original Metro II (which used a stretched Merlin II's fuselage coupled with a new wing, undercarriage and tail), the IVB is the executive equivalent of the Metro III, and the Merlin 23 is equivalent to the Metro 23.

Photo: A Swearingen Merlin IIIC. (Brian Wilkes)

Explorer Aircraft 500R, 500T & 750R

Countries of origin: Australia & USA

Type: Light utility aircraft

Powerplants: 500R – One 447kW (600hp) Orenda OE600A water cooled V8 piston engine driving a three blade prop. 500T – One 447kW (600shp) Pratt & Whitney Canada PT6A-135B driving a four blade prop. 750T – One 560kW (750shp) PT6A-60A driving a four blade prop.

Performance: 500R – Cruising speed 324km/h (175kt). Initial rate of climb 1000ft/min. Service ceiling 25,000ft. Max range 1760km (950nm). 500T – Max cruising speed 371km/h (200kt), cruising speed 333km/h (180kt). Other figures as per 500R. 750T – Cruising speed 352km/h (190kt). Initial rate of climb 1200ft/min. Service ceiling 25,000ft. Max range 1668km (900nm).

Weights: 500R & 500T – Empty 1732kg (3800lb), max takeoff 2812kg (6200lb). 750R – Empty 2267kg (5000lb), max takeoff 4082kg (9000lb).

Dimensions: 500R & 500T – Wing span 14.43m (47ft 4in), length 9.68m (31ft 9in), height 4.72m (15ft 6in). Wing area 18.4m² (197.6sq ft). 750T – Wing span 17.7m (58ft), length 12.3m (40ft 6in), height 4.72m (15ft 6in).

Capacity: Explorer 500R and 500T seat 10 (including pilot), Explorer 750T will seat 16 (including pilot). 500R & 500T payload 1090kg (2400lb), 750T payload 1816kg (4000lb).

Production: 500R and 500T deliveries planned from 2004, 750T deliveries from 2006.

History: The all new Explorer family of light utility aircraft was originally developed in Australia by Aeronautical Engineers Australia (AEA) but will be placed into production in the USA by Explorer Aircraft Inc.

AEA and Explorer Aircraft founder Peter Swannell first began looking at a new utility aircraft in the late 1980s, and initially considered developing a stretched and more powerful Cessna 206 conversion. But by 1993 Swannell had started design work on an all new aircraft, which evolved to become the Explorer 350R, an eight seater powered by a Teledyne Continental TSIO-550 flat six.

The proof of concept Explorer 350R first flew on January 23 1998. Apart from its 260kW (350hp) TSIO-550 engine, design features included a metal frame fuselage with a carbonfibre shell, conventional all metal wings and tail surfaces and retractable undercarriage.

The Explorer's basic configuration is optimised for its intended utility roles, with a high mounted, braced wing, rectangular and constant section, fuselage flat floor cabin, and large cabin windows.

Initially the Explorer 350R was intended to be the first production member of a family of utility aircraft. Instead Explorer Aircraft is focussing on the 10 seat PT6 turboprop powered 500T and the Orenda V8 piston powered 500R initially (which share the same airframe with the 350R), and the stretched, 16 seat PT6 powered 750T.

Explorer Aircraft formed in Denver, Colorado in the US in mid 1999 to develop and build the Explorer range. The proof of concept 350R was re-engined with a PT6A and flew as the 500T in June 2000. Production of the 500T is scheduled to begin in 2002 with full certification and production deliveries planned for 2004. 500R deliveries are planned for later in 2004, with deliveries of the 750T to follow in 2006. At late 2000 a decision on whether or not to build the 350R had not been made.

Photo: The Explorer 500T.

Fairchild Dornier 228

Country of origin: Germany

Type: 15-19 seat regional airliner and STOL utility transport

Powerplants: 100 – Two 535kW (715shp) Garrett TPE331-5 turboprops driving four blade constant speed Hartzell propellers. 212 – Two 560kW (776shp) Garrett/AlliedSignal TPE331-5-252Ds.

Performance: 100 – Max cruising speed 432km/h (233kt). Initial rate of climb 2050ft/min. Service ceiling 29,600ft. Range at max cruising speed 1730km (934nm), or 1970km (1064nm) at long range cruising speed. 212 – Max cruising speed 434km/h (234kt), cruising speed 408km/h (220kt). Initial rate of climb 1870ft. Service ceiling 28,000ft. Range with max pax and reserves at max cruising speed 1037km (560nm), range with a 775kg (1710lb) payload and reserves at long range cruising speed 2445km (1320nm).

Weights: 100 – Operating empty 3235kg (7132lb), max takeoff 5700kg (12,570lb). 212 – Empty 3258kg (7183lb), operating empty 3739kg (8243lb), max takeoff 6400kg (14,110lb).

Dimensions: 100 – Wing span 16.97m (55ft 7in), length 15.03m (49ft 3in), height 4.86m (15ft 9in). Wing area 32.0m² (345sq ft). 212 – Same except for length 16.56m (54ft 4in).

Capacity: Flightcrew of two. 100 – Typical passenger seating for 15. 212 – Typical passenger seating for 19 at two abreast and 76cm (30in) pitch. 228-212 based 228 Cargo has a max payload of 2340kg (5159lb). 212 based ambulance accommodates six stretchers and up to nine attendants or passengers.

Production: 238 Dornier 228s of all models built thus far, most of which have been delivered and are in service. Indian licence production of more than 80 228s (mostly for the Indian military).

History: In terms of civil sales the 228 series has been Dornier's most successful postwar design, with orders now in the region of 230.

The Dornier 228 incorporates the fuselage cross section of the earlier Do 28 and 128 combined with an all new supercritical wing and TPE331 turboprops. Two fuselage length versions, the 100 and 200, were developed concurrently, the 100 offering better range, the 200 more payload. The 100 was the first to fly, on March 28 1981, the first 200 followed on May 9 that year. The first 228 entered service in August 1982.

Composites were used in a number of secondary structure areas on the 228 including upper wing skins, nose and tail. At one stage Dornier also planned to offer the Pratt & Whitney Canada PT6A as an optional powerplant, but this never eventuated.

Dornier 228 developments include the 228-101 with reinforced structure and landing gear for higher weights, the corresponding 228-201 version of the -200, the 228-202 version built under licence production in India with HAL to meet that country's Light Transport Aircraft requirement, and the 228-212.

The -212 was the last Dornier (now Fairchild Dornier) production aircraft, its improvements include higher operating weights, structural strengthening and a lower empty weight, improvements to enhance STOL performance and modern avionics. The last of 238 Dornier built 228s was completed in 1999. HAL licence production continues.

Photo: A Dornier 228-200 of Malaysia's Pelangi Air in flight. (Fairchild Dornier)

Fairchild Dornier 328

Country of origin: Germany

Type: 30 seat regional turboprop airliner

Powerplants: Two 1625kW (2180shp) takeoff rated Pratt & Whitney Canada PW119B turboprops driving six blade Hartzell propellers.

Performance: 328-110 – Max cruising speed 620km/h (335kt). Design cruising altitude 25,000ft or optionally 31,000ft. Range with 30 passengers and reserves at max cruising speed and 25,000ft cruising altitude 1665km (900nm), at 31,000ft 1850km (1000nm).

Weights: 328-110 – Operating empty 8920kg (19,665lb), max takeoff 13,990kg (30,842lb).

Dimensions: Wing span 20.98m (68ft 10in), length 21.22m (69ft 8in), height 7.24m (23ft 9in). Wing area 40.0m² (430.6sq ft).

Capacity: Flightcrew of two. Typical passenger seating for 30 to 33 at three abreast, max seating for 39 at four abreast.

Production: Total 328 production of 112, incl 105 production aircraft.

History: The 30 seat Fairchild Dornier 328 is a modern regional turboprop airliner that offers high cruising speeds and advanced systems.

Development of the 328 traces back to Dornier's mid 1980s market research that indicated there existed a substantial market for regional airliners in the 30 seat class through to 2005. Firm 328 development work began in December 1988, culminating in the first development aircraft's first flight on December 6 1991.

The 328 was awarded certification in October 1993. First customer deliveries also occurred in October 1993.

The 328 design incorporated an all new fuselage section for three abreast seating (offering more width per passenger than the 727/737) combined with the same basic supercritical wing of the earlier Dornier 228. Clean aerodynamics give the 328 excellent high speed cruise and climb performance. Composite materials are used in a number of areas (particularly the tail) to reduce weight and the blades on the Hartzell props are composite. The flightdeck features a five screen Honeywell Primus 2000 EFIS avionics system, while with heads-up displays the 328 can be qualified for Cat IIIa landings.

Industrial partners on the 328 included Daewoo Heavy Industries (fuselage), Aermacchi (nose), Westland (nacelles) and Israel Aircraft Industries (wing), accounting for 40% of the aircraft's construction.

Variants of the 328 are the initial production standard 328-100, the standard 328-110 with heavier weights and greater range, the 328-120 with improved short field performance and the 328-130 with progressive rudder authority reduction with increasing airspeed.

Fairchild Aerospace acquired 80% of Dornier in mid 1996 to form Fairchild Dornier.

At various times Dornier and Fairchild Dornier have studied 50 seat stretches of the 328, but all have been abandoned. Dornier also studied building a 328 demonstrator powered by hydrogen. The liquid hydrogen fuel would have been stored in two external tanks under the wings and outboard of the engines.

The last 328 was delivered to Air Alps Aviation in Austria in October 1999, although at late 2000 some completed aircraft remained unsold.

The 328JET rejional jet development is described separately in the next entry.

Photo: An Air Proteus 328. (Rob Finlayson)

Fairchild Dornier 328JET & Envoy 3

Country of origin: Germany

Type: 32 seat regional jet airliner

Powerplant: Two 26.9kN (6050lb) Pratt & Whitney Canada PW306B turbofans.

Performance: 328JET – Max cruising speed 750km/h (405kt). Service ceiling 35,000ft. Range with payload and reserves 1370km (740nm), high gross weight version range with max payload and reserves 1666km (900nm). Envoy 3 – Range with optional long range fuel tank 3705km (2000nm).

Weights: 328JET – Standard operating empty 9344kg (20,600lb), standard max takeoff 15,200kg (33,510lb), high gross weight operating empty 4394kg (20,710lb), HGW max takeoff 15,660kg (34,524lb).

Dimensions: Wing span 20.98m (68ft 10in), length 21.28m (69ft 10in), height 7.24m (23ft 9in). Wing area 40.0m² (430.6sq ft).

Capacity: Flightcrew of two. Standard seating for 32 to 34 passengers three abreast at 79cm (31in). Envoy 3 seats 12 to 14 in a typical corporate configuration, or up to 19.

Production: At late 2000 orders and options stood at 122 with 40 in service.

History: The Fairchild Dornier 328JET has given a new lease of life to the basic 328 design and is pioneering a new class of airliner, that of the 30 seat regional jet.

Development of the 328JET was launched soon after Fairchild Aerospace took over Dasa's 80% stake in Dornier in mid 1996. Soon after Fairchild Dornier (for a time called Fairchild Aerospace) launched the 328JET, a jet engined development of the 328 turboprop, in February 1997.

The most obvious change to the 328 for the 328JET is the addition of FADEC equipped Pratt & Whitney Canada PW306 turbofans mounted in underwing pods. Aside from this though the 328JET was designed to be a minimum change development of the 328 turboprop. Just two fuselage frames (which the wing and landing gear attach to) required strengthening. A 10cm (4in) extension to the trailing edge flaps cuts aerodynamic drag. Other changes include strengthened landing gear and brakes, slight changes to the software of the Honeywell Primus 2000 EFIS avionics suite, and an APU is standard.

The first 328JET prototype was converted from the second 328 turboprop, and was rolled out on December 6 1997. It first flew from Munich in Germany on January 20 1998. Certification and first deliveries were in July 1999.

Fairchild Dornier has considered two stretched developments of the 328JET so far, the 50 seat 528JET and the 42 to 44 seat PW306B powered 428JET. The 428JET was formally launched in May 1998 and would have been assembled in Israel by IAI, but Fairchild Dornier suspended the program in August 2000 due to not being able to make a viable business case.

The 328JET is assembled at Fairchild Dornier's Oberpfaffenhofen, Germany plant. Fairchild Dornier in San Antonio, Texas, builds the wings, while Aermacchi in Italy builds the 328JET's fuselage.

The Envoy 3 is a corporate jet development of the 328JET, although at late 2000 none had been ordered.

Photo: An Atlantic Coast Airways 328JET. (Fairchild Dornier)

Fairchild Dornier 528JET, 728JET & 928JET

Country of origin: Germany

Type: Regional jet airliners

Powerplants: 728JET – Two 55.6kN (12,500lb) General Electric CF34-8D3 turbofans. 928JET – Two 68.8kN (15,400lb) or 76kN (17,100lb) CF34-10Ds.

Performance: 728JET – Cruising speed at 37,000ft Mach 0.81 or 852km/h (460kt). Max range 2965km (1600nm). 928JET – Max range 2965km (1600nm).

Weights: 728JET – Operating empty 20,880kg (46,032lb), max takeoff 35,200kg (77,602lb). 928JET – Operating empty 28,058kg (61,857lb), max takeoff 47,560kg (104,851lb).

Dimensions: 728JET – Wing span 26.62m (82.3ft), length 26.52m (87ft 0in), height 9.04m (29ft 8in). 928JET – Wing span 28.85m (94ft 6in). Wing area 84.4m² (908.5sq ft)

Capacity: Flightcrew of two. Typical seating for 70 to 85 passengers at five abreast in 728JET, 55 to 63 in 528JET and 100 in 928JET.

Production: At late 2000 Fairchild Dornier held orders and options for 276 728JETs, 28 Envoy 7s, and six 928JETs.

History: The 728JET family is Fairchild Dornier's ambitious bid to develop a range of regional jet airliners to supplement the smaller 328JET, and has attracted strong airline interest since launch.

Fairchild Dornier launched this new family of regional jets seating from 55 to 100 passengers on May 19 1998, with provisional launch orders from Crossair and Lufthansa for 120 new aircraft.

The lead aircraft in the program is the 70 to 85 seat 728JET, which is now due to fly in 2002 allowing service entry in 2003 (about two years after the original schedule to revisions to the design). In August 1998 Fairchild announced it had selected General Electric's FADEC equipped CF34-8D (which has 87% parts commonality with the CF34-8C1 selected to power the competing CRJ700) ahead of the SNECMA/Pratt & Whitney Canada SPW 14 to power the 728JET.

Other 728JET suppliers include Honeywell with its Primus Epic integrated EFIS avionics suite with flat panel LCDs, and APU and environmental control system, Lucas Aerospace (for the fly-by-wire flight control system), BFGoodrich (landing gear, wheels, tyres, brakes and fuel system), Hamilton Sundstrand (integrated electric system), and Parker Aerospace (hydraulics). CASA will build the wings and empennage.

Following the 728JET into service will be the stretched 100 seat 928JET and shortened 55 seat 528JET. The three types will feature a high degree of commonality, including engine type, and the same flightdeck, allowing a common pilot type rating.

The 928JET will fly in late 2003 and enter service in early 2005. Apart from the stretched fuselage – cabin length from behind the flightdeck will be 23.05m (75ft 7in) allowing typical seating for 100 passengers – it will also feature an increased span wing.

The 528JET will seat 55 to 63 passengers, with a fuselage length of 23.38m (76ft 9in) and a cabin length of 15.84m (52ft 0in).

Fairchild Dornier is also developing a corporate version of the 728JET, the Envoy 7, for delivery from mid 2004. Corporate 528JETs and 928JETs, the Envoy 5 and Envoy 7 respectively, will follow.

Photo: A computer generated image of a 728JET. (Fairchild)

Fairchild Metro II, III & 23

Country of origin: United States of America

Type: 19 seat regional airliner

Powerplants: Metro II – Two 700kW (940shp) Garrett AiResearch TPE331-3UW-303G turboprops driving three blade constant speed propellers. 23 – Two 745kW (1000shp) AlliedSignal TPE331-11U-612Gs, or 820kW (1100shp) TPE331-12UARs.

Performance: II – Max cruising speed 473km/h (255kt), long range cruising speed 450km/h (242kt). Service ceiling 27,000ft. Range with 19 passengers and reserves at max cruising speed 346km (187nm), with 15 pax and reserves at max cruising speed 1100km (595nm). 23 – Max cruising speed 542km/h (293kt). Service ceiling 25,000ft. Range with 19 passengers and reserves 2065km (1314nm), with 2268kg (5000lb) payload and reserves 988km (533nm).

Weights: II – Empty 3380kg (7450lb), max takeoff 5670kg (12,500lb). 23 – Operating empty 4309kg (9500lb), max takeoff 7484kg (16,500lb).

Dimensions: II – Wing span 14.10m (46ft 3in), length 18.09m (59ft 4in), height 5.08m (16ft 8in). Wing area 25.8m² (277.5sq ft). 23 – Same except for wing span 17.37m (57ft 0in). Wing area 28.7m² (309.0sq ft).

Capacity: Flightcrew of two. Passenger seating for 19 at two abreast and 76cm (30in) pitch. Merlin IV and 23 also seat 12 to 14 passengers in a corporate configuration. The Expediter I and 23 are freighters.

Production: 1028 Metros built, 412 in commercial service in 2000.

History: After a slow start to sales in the early 1970s, the Metro series of 19 seat commuters became one of the most popular of its class.

The Metro can trace its lineage back to the original Swearingen Merlin I executive transport. From the Merlin I Swearingen developed the turboprop powered II and III which were to form the basis of the new Metro commuter airliner. The Metro was Swearingen's first complete inhouse design and development work began in the late 1960s, resulting in the SA-226TC Metro's first flight on August 26 1969. The design was similar in appearance and layout to the earlier Merlins, and featured a pressurised fuselage, TPE331 turboprop engines and double slotted trailing edge flaps. Certification was awarded in June 1970 and the first example entered commercial service in 1973.

The Metro II superseded the I from 1975, with improvements to reduce cabin noise levels. The equivalent executive aircraft is the Merlin IV. In 1981 Fairchild introduced the Metro III (by which time Fairchild had taken over Swearingen), which was certificated to SFAR-41B allowing greater takeoff weights, while more efficient engines (including the option of Pratt & Whitney Canada PT6As on the IIIA) and greater wing span made the III more economical to operate. The Expediter freighter is based on the III.

The final production Metro model was the 23. Certificated to FAR Part 23 (Amendment 34) standards (hence the Metro 23 designation) it features a higher takeoff weight, more powerful engines and systems improvements first introduced on the military C-26. The Metro 23 EF has a bulged lower fuselage for greater baggage capacity, while the Merlin 23 and Expediter 23 models were also offered. In 1996 Fairchild studied a Metro with a significantly higher fuselage allowing stand-up headroom (in the style of the Raytheon Beech 1900D).

Metro production wound up in 1999.

Photo: A Metro 23. (Glenn Alderton)

Fokker F27 & Fairchild F-27 & FH-227

Country of origin: Netherlands

Type: 44-52 seat turboprop regional airliners

Powerplants: Mk 200/500/600 – Two 1730kW (2320ehp) Rolls-Royce Dart Mk 536-7R turboprops driving four blade Dowty Rotol propellers. FH-227E – Two 1715kW (2300shp) Dart 532-7Ls.

Performance: Mk 500 – Normal cruising speed 480km/h (260kt). Service ceiling 29,500ft. Range with 52 passengers and reserves 1741km (1935nm). FH-227 – Max cruising speed 473km/h (255kt), economical cruising speed 435km/h (236kt). Range with max payload 1055km (570nm), range with max fuel 2660km (1440nm).

Weights: Mk 500 – Empty 12,243kg (26,992lb), operating empty 12,684kg (27,964lb), max takeoff 20,410kg (44,996lb). FH-227 – Operating empty 10,398kg (22,923lb), max takeoff 20,639kg (45,500lb).

Dimensions: Mk 500 – Wing span 29.00m (95ft 2in), length 23.06m (82ft 3in), height 8.71m (28ft 7in). Wing area 70.0m² (753.5sq ft). FH-227 – Same except length 25.50m (83ft 8in), height 8.41m (27ft 7in).

Capacity: Flightcrew of two. Seating for 44 at four abreast and 76cm (30in) pitch in original fuselage length versions (Mks 100, 200, 300, 400, 600 & F-27). Standard seating for 52 and max seating for 60 at 72cm (28.5in) pitch in Mk 500. FH-227 seats 52 at 79cm (31in) pitch, or a maximum of 56.

Production: 581 F27s, 128 F-27s and 78 FH-227s built. Fokker production comprised 85 Mk 100s, 138 Mk 200s, 13 Mk 300s, 218 Mk 400 & 600s, 112 Mk 500s and six F27MPA Maritimes. 240 Fokker built and 27 Fairchild aircraft in service in late 2000. Additionally, six used as corporate transports.

History: Probably the closest to being the fabled DC-3 replacement, the Fokker F27 Friendship, including the Fairchild F-27 and FH-227, was built in greater numbers than any other western turboprop airliner.

The Fokker F27 started life as the P275 design study in 1950, a 32 seater powered by two Rolls-Royce Dart turboprops. With the aid of Dutch government funding the P275 evolved into the F27, which first flew on November 24 1955. This original prototype was powered by Dart 507s and would have seated 32, by the time the second prototype had flown (in January 1957) the fuselage length had grown to allow seating for 36.

By this stage Fokker had signed an agreement that would see Fairchild build Friendships in the USA. The first aircraft to enter service was in fact a Fairchild built F-27, in September 1958.

Fairchild F-27s differed from the initial Fokker F27 Mk 100s in having basic seating for 40, a lengthened nose capable of housing a weather radar, American avionics and additional fuel capacity.

Developments included the Mk 200/F-27A with more powerful engines, Mk 300/F-27B and primarily military Mk 400 Combi versions, the Mk 500 with a 1.50m (4ft 11in) fuselage stretch taking seating to 52 (first flight November 15 1967), and Mk 600 quick change freight/pax aircraft.

Fairchild independently developed the stretched FH-227, which first flew on January 27 1966, almost two years earlier than the Mk 500. The FH-227 featured a 1.83m (6ft 0in) stretch over standard length F27/F-27s, taking standard seating to 52.

Photo: An F27-600 quick change freighter/airliner. (David Daw)

Fokker 50

Country of origin: Netherlands

Type: Turboprop regional airliner

Powerplant: Series 100 – Two 1864kW (2500shp) Pratt & Whitney Canada PW125B turboprops driving six blade Dowty propellers. Series 300 – Two 2050kW (2750shp) PW127Bs.

Performance: Series 100 – Max cruising speed 532km/h (287kt), economical cruising speed 454km/h (245kt). Max operating altitude 25,000ft. Range with 50 passengers and reserves 2055km (1110nm), or 2822km (1524nm) for optional high gross weight version. Series 300 – Typical cruising speed 526km/h (284kt). Range with 50 passengers and reserves at high speed cruise 2033km (1097nm), or 3017km (1628nm) for high gross weight option at long range cruise.

Weights: Series 100 & 300 – Operating empty 12,520kg (27,602lb), max takeoff 19,950kg (43,980lb), or optionally 20,820kg (45,900lb).

Dimensions: Wing span 29.00m (95ft 2in), length 25.25m (82ft 10in), height 8.32m (27ft 4in). Wing area 70.0m² (753.5sq ft).

Capacity: Flightcrew of two. Standard seating for 50 at four abreast and 81cm (32in) pitch. Max high density seating for 58. Available with convertible passenger/freight configurations.

Production: 205 Fokker 50s built. Last delivered in May 1997. At late 2000 187 in commercial service and four used as corporate transports.

History: The Fokker 50 was the successor to Fokker's highly successful and long running F27 Friendship.

Fokker announced it was developing the 50 seat Fokker 50, together with the 100 seat jet powered Fokker 100, in November 1983. The Fokker 50 is based on the fuselage of the F27-500 Friendship, but incorporated a number of key design changes. Foremost of the improvements was the new generation Pratt & Whitney Canada PW125 turboprops driving advanced six blade props, giving a 12% higher cruising speed and greater fuel economy, and thus range. Other improvements include new avionics and an EFIS glass cockpit, limited use of composites, small 'Foklet' winglets, and more, albeit smaller, square main cabin windows.

Two prototypes were built based on F27 airframes (despite the fact that over 80% of Fokker 50 parts were new or modified), the first flying on December 28 1985. The first production aircraft flew on February 13 1987, certification was granted in May 1987, and first customer delivery, to Lufthansa Cityline, was in August that year.

The basic Fokker 50 production model was the Series 100. The Series 120 has three, instead of four doors. The hot and high optimised Series 300 has more powerful PW127B turboprops, and was announced in 1990. It has higher cruising speeds and better field performance, particularly at altitude.

The only significant development of the Fokker 50 to see the light of day was the Fokker 60 Utility, a stretched utility transport version ordered by the Royal Netherlands Air Force. Fokker built four for the Netherlands air force and looked at offering a passenger variant. The Fokker 60 was stretched by 1.62m (5ft 4in).

Fokker collapsed due to financial problems on March 15 1996 and the last Fokker 50 was delivered to Ethiopian Airlines in May 1997.

Photo: A Fokker 50 in the colours of Ansett owned Perth, Western Australia based regional airline Skywest. (Robert Wiseman)

Fokker F28 Fellowship

Country of origin: Netherlands

Type: Regional jet airliner

Powerplants: Mk 3000 & 4000 – Two 44.0kN (9900lb) Rolls-Royce RB183-2 Spey Mk 555-15P turbofans.

Performance: 3000 – Max cruising speed 843km/h (455kt), economical cruising speed 678km/h (366kt). Range at high speed cruise with 65 passengers 2743km (1480nm), at long range cruise with 65 passengers 3170km (1710nm). 4000 – Speeds same. Range at high speed cruise with 85 passengers 1900km (1025nm), at long range cruising speed with 85 passengers 2085km (1125nm).

Weights: 3000 – Operating empty 16,965kg (37,400lb), max takeoff 33,110kg (73,000lb). 4000 – Operating empty 17,645kg (38,900lb), max takeoff 33,110kg (73,000lb).

Dimensions: 3000 – Wing span 25.07m (82ft 3in), length 27.40m (89ft 11in), height 8.47m (27ft 10in). Wing area 79.0m² (850sq ft). 4000 – Same except for length 29.61m (97ft 2in).

Capacity: Flightcrew of two. Max seating for 85 at five abreast and 74cm (29in) pitch in Mk 4000, or 65 in Mk 3000. Mk 3000 offered with a 15 seat executive interior.

Production: Total F28 sales of 241, including some military customers. As at late 2000 approx 169 remained in commercial service.

History: The F28 Fellowship jet was developed to complement Fokker's highly successful F27 Friendship turboprop.

Fokker began development of the F28 in 1960 after perceiving a market for a higher performance (ie jet engined) and greater capacity airliner in comparison with the F27. First details of the F28 were made public in April 1962, at which stage it was to have been a 50 seater powered by two Bristol Siddeley BS.75 turbofans. By the time the F28 was launched in November 1965 it had grown to a 65 seater with simplified Rolls-Royce Spey turbofans (called the Spey Junior)

The first of three F28 prototypes first flew on May 9 1967, with certification award and first customer delivery (to LTU) both occurring on February 24 1969.

The F28 was developed into a range of models. Initial production was of the Mk 1000, which could typically seat between 55 and 65, and was powered by 43.8kN (9850lb) Spey Mk 555-15 turbofans. The Mk 2000 was essentially similar but featured a 2.21m (7ft 3in) fuselage stretch, increasing maximum seating to 79.

The Mks 5000 and 6000 were based on the 1000 and 2000 respectively, but introduced a longer span wing (by 1.49m/4ft 11in) and wing leading edge slats. Neither version attracted serious sales interest, and no 5000s and just two 6000s were built. Another version that did not come to fruition was the Mk 6600, which would have been stretched by a further 2.21m (7ft 3in), allowing for seating for 100 in a high density layout. It was aimed at Japanese airlines.

The final production models were the 3000 and 4000, again based on the 1000 and 2000 respectively. Both introduced a number of improvements, while the addition of two extra above wing emergency exits on the 4000 increased maximum seating to 85. Freight door equipped convertible versions of each model were offered, and are identified by a C suffix. The last F28 was delivered in July 1987.

Photo: An F28-4000. (Rob Finlayson)

Fokker 70

Country of origin: Netherlands

Type: 70 seat regional jet airliner

Powerplants: Two 61.6kN (13,850lb) Rolls-Royce Tay Mk 620 turbofans.

Performance: High speed cruise Mach 0.77. Range with 79 passengers and baggage at standard weights 2010km (1085nm), or 3410km (1840nm) for high gross weight option with extra fuel.

Weights: Operating empty 22,673kg (49,985lb), max takeoff standard aircraft 36,470kg (80,997lb), or optionally 38,100kg (83,996lb), or 39,915kg (87,997lb).

Dimensions: Wing span 28.08m (92ft 2in), length 30.91m (101ft 5in), height 8.50m (27ft 11in). Wing area 93.5m² (1006.4sq ft).

Capacity: Flightcrew of two. Standard single class passenger accommodation for 79 at five abreast at 81cm (32in) pitch. Fokker Executive Jet 70 interiors were fitted to customer requirements.

Production: 48 Fokker 70s built. Last delivered in April 1997. 43 in service in late 2000.

History: The Fokker 70 is a shortened development of the popular 100 seat class Fokker 100.

Fokker began development of the new derivative airliner in November 1992 despite the absence of firm orders, hopeful of snaring a large share of the forecast 2000 plus aircraft in the 70 to 125 seat class required through to 2010, and the replacement F28 market. The Fokker 70's 30.91m (101ft 4in) length is close to that of the F28-4000's 29.61m (97ft 2in), on which the Fokker 100 was originally based.

The first Fokker 70 was in fact the second Fokker 100 prototype which was modified by removing two fuselage plugs – one forward and one rear of the wing. Construction on this aircraft began in October 1992 (before the November 1992 program go-ahead), resulting in the type's first flight on April 4 1993. The first production Fokker 70 first flew in July 1994 and certification was awarded on October 14 1994. The first Fokker 70 (an Executive Jet 70) was delivered to Ford in the USA later that month.

A design aim of the Fokker 70 was to retain as much commonality with the larger Fokker 100 as possible. As a result they share essentially identical wings, airframes (except for length, and the removal of two emergency overwing exits on the Fokker 70) and systems, plus similar EFIS flightdecks. The Fokker 70 was offered with two flightdecks, one optimised for the 70's regional airline operations, the other essentially identical to the Fokker 100's to give operators of both types commonality. The Fokker 70 and 100 also share identical Tay Mk 620 powerplants, although the Tay Mk 650 that was offered for the 100 was not available on the 70. The 70 and 100 were built on a common production line.

As with the Fokker 100, a corporate shuttle, the Fokker Executive Jet 70, was offered (and attracted a small number of orders). The Fokker 70A was optimised for US carriers, while the Fokker 70ER (announced in late 1994) had extra fuel tankage and extended range.

With Fokker's collapse in 1996, the Fokker 70/100 production line closed in early 1997. Despite Fokker's financial failure the 70 remains popular with its operators and second hand examples are highly sought after.

Photo: A Malev Fokker 70. (Viktor László)

Fokker 100

Country of origin: Netherlands

Type: 100 seat regional jet

Powerplants: Two 61.6kN (13,850lb) Rolls-Royce Tay Mk 620-15 or 67.2kN (15,100lb) Mk 650-15 turbofans.

Performance: Max cruising speed 845km/h (456kt), long range cruising speed 737km/h (453kt). Range with 107 passengers and Tay 620s 2505km (1323nm), or high gross weight version with Tay 650s 3167km (1710nm).

Weights: Tay 620 – Operating empty 24,375kg (53,738lb), max takeoff 43,090kg (95,000lb). With Tay 650s – Operating empty 24,541kg (54,103lb), max takeoff 45,810kg (101,000lb).

Dimensions: Wing span 28.08m (92ft 2in), length 35.53m (116ft 7in), height 8.50m (27ft 11in). Wing area 93.5m² (1006.4sq ft).

Capacity: Flightcrew of two. Max single class high density seating for 122. Standard single class seating for 107 at five abreast and 81cm (32in) pitch. Two class seating for 12 first class passengers at four abreast and 91cm (36in) pitch, and 85 economy class passengers; or 55 business class at five abreast and 86cm (34in) pitch, and 50 economy class pax. Fokker 100QC Quick Change max payload of 11,500kg (25,353lb), comprising five LD9/LD7 containers and one half size container, or up to 11 LD3 containers.

Production: 283 Fokker 100s had been built when production ceased in early 1997. 273 in service in late 2000.

History: Fokker's largest aircraft, the Fokker 100 is a 100 seat jet airliner based on the F28 Fellowship, but stretched and thoroughly modernised.

Fokker announced it was developing the Fokker 100 simultaneously with the Fokker 50 turboprop in November 1983. The Fokker 100 is based on the basic F28 airframe, with the most important and obvious change being the stretched fuselage, increasing maximum seating to 122, compared with 85 in the F28-4000 (on which the 100 is based). Other changes include more economical Rolls-Royce Tay turbofans (which, unlike the F28's Speys, conform to Stage 3 noise limits), revised wing design with greater span and aerodynamic efficiency (Fokker claimed it to be 30% more efficient than the F28's), a modern EFIS glass flightdeck, redesigned cabin interior plus other systems and numerous equipment changes.

The Fokker 100's first flight occurred on November 30 1986, certification was awarded in November 1987 and the first customer delivery, to Swissair, occurred in February 1988.

The Fokker 100 was offered in a number of versions including higher gross weight options of the standard airliner, the Fokker 100QC Quick change airliner or freighter with a large forward freight door, and the Fokker Executive Jet 100 corporate shuttle or VIP transport, fitted with luxury interiors to customer requirements. It also forms the basis for the shorter Fokker 70, while the 130 seat class Fokker 130 had also been studied.

Fokker collapsed in 1996 due to on-going financial problems and wound up production early the following year. Subsequently Rekkof (Fokker spelt backwards) Restart unsuccessfully attempted to re-open the Fokker 70 and 100 lines.

Photo: The Fokker 100 comfortably outsold the F28. (Rob Finlayson)

Fuji FA-200 Aero Subaru

Country of origin: Japan

Type: Four seat light aircraft

Powerplant: FA-200-160 – One 120kW (160hp) Lycoming O-320-D2A flat four piston engine driving a two blade fixed pitch McCauley propeller. FA-200-180 – One 135kW (180hp) fuel injected IO-360-B1B driving a two blade constant speed McCauley prop.

Performance: FA-200-160 – Max speed 222km/h (120kt), max cruising speed 196km/h (106kt), long range cruising speed 164km/h (89kt). Initial rate of climb 680ft/min. Service ceiling 11,400ft. Max range with no reserves 1520km (820nm). FA-200-180 – Max speed 233km/h (126kt), max cruising speed 204km/h (110kt), long range cruising speed 167km/h (90kt). Initial rate of climb 760ft/min. Service ceiling 13,700ft. Range with no reserves 1400km (755nm).

Weights: FA-200-160 – Empty 620kg (1366lb), max takeoff 1059kg (2335lb). FA-200-180 – Empty 650kg (1433lb), max takeoff 1150kg (2535lb).

Dimensions: FA-200-160 – Wing span 9.42m (30ft 11in), length 7.96m (26ft 1in), height 2.02m (6ft 8in). Wing area 14.0m² (150.7sq ft). FA-200-180 – Same except for length 7.98m (26ft 2in).

Capacity: Typical seating for four.

Production: 299 Aero Subarus were built between 1965 and 1986. Series production lasted until 1977, when the Aero Subaru became available by firm order only through to 1986.

History: The Fuji FA-200 Aero Subaru was the first wholly Japanese designed light aircraft to enter series production, with the majority built for export orders.

A product of the Fuji Heavy Industries industrial conglomerate (which was formed through the merger of six different concerns, including WW2 fighter manufacturer Nakajima, and also builds Subaru cars), design work on the FA-200 began in 1964. A prototype, the FA-200-II, first flew on August 12 1965.

The basic FA-200 design was expected to form the basis of a family of light aircraft including the two seat side-by-side trainer FA-200-I powered by a 85kW (115hp) Lycoming O-235 and the single seat F-204 agricultural version. However only the four seat tourer, as represented by the prototype, entered production. This aircraft was of conventional low wing and fixed undercarriage design, and was aerobatic at reduced weights.

Three versions of the FA-200 entered production, the first being the 120kW (160hp) powered FA-200-160, which was also certificated with reduced weights in the Utility category with three seats, and the Aerobatic with two seats. The FA-200-180 was essentially similar but powered by a 135kW (180hp) fuel injected IO-360. Deliveries of both versions began in March 1968.

A third model joined the lineup from mid 1973, the FA-200-180AO. This was a reduced specification version of the FA-200-180 with a fixed pitch propeller and caburetted Lycoming O-360 engine.

The Aero Subaru remained in production until 1977 when 274 had been built. The type remained available to special order through to 1986, by which time a further 25 had been built.

Photo: An Australian registered Lycoming O-320 powered FA-200-160. (Gerard Frawley)

GAF N22 & N24 Nomad

Country of origin: Australia

Type: STOL utility transport

Powerplants: Two 313kW (420shp) Allison 250-B17C turboprops driving three blade Hartzell propellers.

Performance: Typical cruising speed 311km/h (168kt). Service ceiling N22B 21,000ft, N24A 20,000ft. Range with standard fuel, reserves and operating at 90% power 1352km (730nm). Search mission endurance at 259km/h (140kt) at 5000ft up to 8 hours.

Weights: N22B – Basic empty 2150kg (4741lb), max takeoff 3855kg (8500lb). N24A – Operating empty 2377kg (5241lb), max takeoff 4268kg (9400lb).

Dimensions: N22B – Wing span 16.52m (54ft 2in), length 12.56m (41ft 2in), height 5.52m (18ft 1.5in). Wing area 30.1m² (324.0sq ft). N24A – Same except length 14.36m (47ft 1in).

Capacity: Accommodation for two pilots although certificated for single pilot operation. Seating in main cabin at two abreast for 12 (N22) or 16 (N24). Searchmaster B patrol aircraft is fitted with a Bendix RDR 1400 search radar and has a normal crew of four. The more sophisticated Searchmaster L has a Litton LASR (AN/APS-504) search radar with 360 degree coverage in an undernose radar.

Production: Production ceased in late 1984 when 172 Nomads for civil and military customers had been built, including two prototypes. Approx 17 remain in service with commercial operators.

History: The Nomad STOL utility transport was developed by Australia's Government Aircraft Factory from the late 1960s to help provide the facility with work after construction of licence built Mirage jet fighters was completed.

First flight of the prototype Nomad N2 occurred on July 23 1971. A second prototype first flew on December 5 that year. First deliveries of the production N22 (to the Philippines military) began in 1975.

Features of the new utility design included retractable undercarriage, two Allison 250 turboprops, a braced, high mounted wing with full span double slotted flaps and a square sided fuselage.

The initial N22 was followed by the N22B with an increased maximum takeoff weight, which was certificated in 1975. The N22 also formed the basis for the Searchmaster coastal patrol aircraft which apart from military users also saw service with Australian and US customs services. The Floatmaster was a N22B fitted with Wipaire floats with retractable undercarriage.

The N22 was stretched by 1.14m (3ft 9in) resulting in the N24. Aimed more at regional airlines (and marketed as the Commuterliner) than utility operators, the main cabin could seat 16. Versions of the N24 offered included the Cargomaster freighter and the Medicmaster aerial ambulance.

Nomad production ceased in 1984, as much due to mismanagement by the Australian government departments entrusted with its development as any faults with the aircraft. However the aircraft is largely unloved in its home country.

It is interesting to note that GAF was renamed ASTA (Aerospace Technologies of Australia), which was acquired by Rockwell in 1996 and hence was subsequently inherited by Boeing late that year.

Photo: A New Zealand registered N24 Nomad. (Les Bushell)

Galaxy Aerospace (IAI) Astra

Country of origin: Israel

Type: Small to mid size corporate jet

Powerplants: 1125 – Two 16.2kN (3650lb) Garrett TFE731-3B-100G turbofans. SPX – Two 18.9kN (4250lb) Honeywell TFE731-40R-200Gs.

Performance: 1125 – Max cruising speed 862km/h (465kt). Initial rate of climb 3560ft/min. Service ceiling 41,500ft. Range with long range tanks and four passengers at Mach 0.72 cruising speed 5760km (3110nm). SPX – Max cruising speed at mid weight 895km/h (483kt), econ cruising speed 800km/h (432kt). Initial rate of climb 3805ft/min. Certificated altitude 45,000ft. Range with eight passengers and reserves 4235km (2286nm), with four passengers 5461km (2949nm).

Weights: 1125 – Basic operating empty 5747kg (12,670lb), max takeoff 10,660kg (23,500lb). SPX – Basic operating empty 6214kg (13,700lb), max takeoff 11,181kg (24,650lb).

Dimensions: Wing span 16.05m (52ft 8in), length 16.94m (55ft 7in), height 5.53m (18ft 2in). Wing area 29.4m² (316.6sq ft). SPX – Same except wing span over winglets 16.64m (54ft 7in).

Capacity: Flightcrew of two. Typical executive arrangements for six passengers, with max seating for nine passengers.

Production: Approx 120 Astras delivered by late 2000.

History: The IAI 1125 Astra is a comprehensively upgraded development of the successful 1124 Westwind, with a number of key changes to improve performance and increase cabin volume.

Israel Aircraft Industries began work on an improved development of its model 1124, initially known as the 1125 Westwind, in the early 1980s, with the first flight of the new type occurring on March 19 1984. A second prototype flew in October 1984, and a third was used for ground based static and fatigue testing. The first production Astra flew in March 1985, and the first customer delivery took place in mid 1986 after certification had been granted in August the previous year.

The Astra is based on the basic Westwind II fuselage and tail, mated with an all new high speed swept wing (initially lacking winglets). Aside from the aerodynamic and hence performance benefits of the new wing, it was also repositioned low on the fuselage (as opposed to mid mounted on the Westwind), where it does not intrude on internal cabin space. The repositioned wing plus reshaped fuselage frames means that headroom is increased by 20cm (8in). Other changes include a lengthened nose for greater avionics space and more extensive use of composites (mainly for control surfaces).

The original 1125 Astra was replaced in production by the Astra SP. The SP was first announced in 1989 and features a revised cabin interior, upgraded avionics, EFIS cockpit and some minor aerodynamic refinements. Thirty-seven were built before it was replaced by the SPX.

The SPX first flew in August 1994 and features more powerful FADEC equipped 18.9kN (4250lb) Honeywell TFE731-40R-200Gs, winglets and Collins Pro Line 4 avionics. Two were delivered to the US Air National Guard as C-38s for transport and medevac tasks.

IAI builds the Astra (and Galaxy) in Israel and the 'green' airframes are flown to Galaxy Aerospace Corporation in Texas in the US for interior outfitting. Galaxy holds the SPX and Astra type certificates and is responsible for marketing.

Photo: The Astra SPX. (IAI)

Galaxy Aerospace (IAI) Galaxy

Country of origin: Israel

Type: Super mid size corporate transport

Powerplants: Two 26.9kN (6040lb) Pratt & Whitney Canada PW306A turbofans.

Performance: Typical cruising speed 871km/h (470kt), long range cruising speed 797km/h (430kt). Max operating altitude 45,000ft. Max range with four passengers and reserves 6708km (3620nm).

Weights: Basic operating 8709kg (19,200lb), max takeoff 15,808kg (34,850lb).

Dimensions: Wing span 17.70m (58ft 1in), length 18.97m (62ft 3in), height 6.53m (21ft 5in). Wing area 34.3m^2 (369.0sq ft).

Capacity: Flightcrew of two. Seating for eight or more in executive style arrangements, or up to 18 in a three abreast corporate shuttle configuration.

Production: First deliveries January 2000. Galaxy estimates a market for over 200.

History: Marketed and supported by Galaxy Aerospace Inc, which is part owned by Israel Aircraft Industries, the IAI 1126 Galaxy is an all new 'super mid size' corporate jet.

Design work on the Galaxy (initially called the Astra Galaxy) began in the early 1990s and formal program launch was announced in September 1993. In 1995 a co-production arrangement was terminated that would have seen Yakovlev in Russia responsible for the design and manufacture of the Galaxy's fuselage, while IAI would be the main contractor responsible for final assembly, integration and marketing. Subsequently SOGERMA of France was selected to manufacture production Galaxy fuselages and tails.

The Galaxy was first expected to fly in 1996 but this was delayed until December 25 1997. A second prototype flew in May 1998 while the first production aircraft first flew in October that year. US FAA and Israeli certification was issued in December 1998. The first customer aircraft was delivered to TTI Industries in January 2000. (A Galaxy delivered to Lion Industries in Zurich in July 1999 was leased back by Galaxy Aerospace for use as a demonstrator.)

The Galaxy features a wing design based on the swept high speed unit of the Astra, but otherwise is a completely new design. It features a new 'widebody' fuselage, significantly wider and longer than the Astra's, with standup room. The rear fuselage is area ruled to reduce drag, while the wing features winglets. The Galaxy also features an EFIS Collins Pro Line 4 cockpit and nonstop trans Atlantic range.

IAI selected the Pratt & Whitney Canada PW306A turbofans for the Galaxy in January 1993 after studying competing designs from Allison (the AE 3007) and AlliedSignal/General Electric (the CFE738). The PW306A is a growth development (with increased fan diameter, improved hot end material and a forced mixer in the exhaust) of the PW305 series that powers the Hawker 1000 and Learjet 60.

IAI assembles and test flies Galaxies in Israel at its Tel Aviv facilities, while interior completion takes place at Galaxy Aerospace's new facilities at Alliance Airport, Fort Worth, Texas. Galaxy Aerospace Inc was established in August 1997 and also handles completions and customer support of the Astra SPX.

Photo: The first production Galaxy in flight.

Gippsland Aeronautics GA-200 Fatman

Country of origin: Australia

Type: Two seat agricultural aircraft

Powerplant: GA-200 – One 195kW (260hp) Textron Lycoming O-540-H2A5 flat six piston engine driving a two blade fixed pitch McCauley propeller, or alternatively a 185kW (250hp) O-540-A1D5.

Performance: GA-200 – Long range cruising speed 185km/h (100kt). Initial rate of climb 970ft/min.

Weights: GA-200 – Operating empty 770kg (1698lb), certificated max takeoff 1315kg (2899lb), max takeoff in agricultural operation 1700kg (3748lb).

Dimensions: Wing span 11.93m (39ft 2in), length in flying attitude 7.48m (24ft 7in), height on ground over cockpit 2.33m (7ft 8in). Wing area 19.6m^2 (211.0sq ft).

Capacity: Seating for two side-by-side. Hopper capacity 800 litres (211US gal/176Imp gal).

Production: Approx 60 built by late 2000. Planned annual production rate by 2002 50.

History: The Gippsland Aeronautics GA-200 Fatman is an all new ag aircraft developed in Australia.

The GA-200 is Gippsland Aeronautics' first inhouse design, and results from more than two decades of experience in modifying other aircraft. In particular Gippsland Aeronautics has extensive experience in modifying the Piper Pawnee, but despite the visual similarity the GA-200 is an all new design.

Features of the GA-200 include a braced low mounted wing, a Textron Lycoming O-540 flat six engine and 800 litre (211US gal/176Imp gal) integral chemical hopper forward of the cockpit. It is of conventional construction with a low mounted braced wing. The single slotted flaps can be extended for tighter turns during spraying operations.

Australian CAA certification in normal and agricultural categories to US airworthiness standards was awarded on March 1 1991. US FAA certification to FAR Pt 23 was awarded in October 1997.

The GA-200 is offered in standard agricultural aircraft and Ag-trainer form. The Ag-trainer is an ag pilot trainer fitted with a smaller chemical hopper and dual controls.

The GA-8 has won a number of export orders, including several to China. Other aircraft have been built for customers in New Zealand and the USA. Aircraft sold in the US have their airframe sections shipped from Australia with components such as the engine and avionics fitted locally.

Gippsland Aeronautics studied a development of the GA-200 powered by an Australian developed magnesium block V8 engine that would have run on unleaded mogas (the GA-200 already has Australian approval to operate using premium grade unleaded mogas for its O-540).

However the company instead focussed its efforts on the more powerful GA-200C powered by an uprated 225kW (300hp) O-540 and an increased max takeoff weight. A hopper upgrade to 1060 litres (280USgal/233Imp gal). The prototype GA-200C first flew in early 1998 and it is now the standard production model.

Photo: A GA-200 on Lord Howe Island, off Australia's east coast. (Peter Phillipps)

Gippsland Aeronautics GA-8 Airvan

Country of origin: Australia

Type: Eight seat utility light aircraft

Powerplants: One 225kW (300hp) IO-540-KA5 Textron Lycomng fuel injected flat six driving a three blade constant speed propeller.

Performance: Never exceed speed 342km/h (185kt) IAS, long range cruising speed 222km/h (120kt). Takeoff distance 457m (1500ft). Endurance at long range cruising speed with no reserves 6hrs.

Weights: Empty 997kg (2200lb), max takeoff 1815kg (4000lb).

Dimensions: Wing span 12.37m (40ft 7in), length 8.79m (28ft 10in), height 2.82m (9ft 3in). Wing area 19.3m^2 (208.0sq ft).

Capacity: Single pilot and passenger side-by-side with up to six passengers in the main cabin behind them. Main cabin can also configured to carry freight or two stretchers and a medical attendant.

Production: Sixth Airvan due to fly in December 2000. By late 2001 Gippsland Aeronautics plans to be building 20 Airvans a year. Price in 2000 $A550,000.

History: The GA-8 Airvan is the second all new aircraft design from Australian manufacturer Gippsland Aeronautics, and has been designed as a utility transport to replace the popular Cessna 206/207 series and others such as the de Havilland Canada Beaver. Envisaged roles include passenger and freight carriage, police work, aerial survey amd skydiving.

Design work on the Airvan began in early 1994 and prototype construction commenced soon after. This prototype flew for the first time on March 3 1995 and publicly appeared at the Australian International Airshow and Aerospace Expo at Avalon later that month after having completed just eight flying hours.

At that time Gippsland Aeronautics anticipated that the Airvan could be certificated within 12 months. Unfortunately the prototype subsequently crashed during spinning trials in February 1996, pushing back the planned certification and entry into service dates.

The prototype Airvan was powered by a 185kW (250hp) Textron Lycoming O-540 driving a two blade propeller. A second prototype flew in August 1996, powered by a 225kW (300hp) IO-540. This was to be replaced with a 225kW (300hp) IO-580 but production aircraft will have an IO-540-K as detailed above. Useable fuel capacity is 332 litres.

Other Airvan design feature include its strut braced, high mounted two spar wing which is based on the unit on the GA-200 ag aircraft, the square sided large volume fuselage with a large sliding freight door on the port side and flat floor, and fixed landing gear designed for rough field operations.

The first productionAirvan (the fifth Airvan built) was in November 2000 following Australian certification, which was awarded on October 27 2000 (US certification is planned). A second production aircraft was due to fly before the end of the year.

In 2000 Gippsland Aeronautics was focussing on introducing the GA-8 into production, but further developments of the aircraft are planned, with more powerful IO-580 and turbine Rolls-Royce 250-C20 powered variants on the drawing board. Canadian operators in particular have shown interest in a floatplane equipped version.

Photo: The first production GA-8 Airvan. This aircraft was delivered in November 2000. (Mark Bathie)

Grob G 115

Country of origin: Germany

Type: Two seat basic and aerobatic trainer

Powerplant: G 115A – One 85kW (115hp) Textron Lycoming O-235-H2C flat four piston engine driving a two blade fixed pitch or optional constant speed Hoffmann propeller. G 115D – One 135kW (180hp) Textron Lycoming fuel injected AEIO-360 driving a two blade constant speed prop.

Performance: G 115A – Max speed 220km/h (119kt), cruising speed 205km/h (110kt). Initial rate of climb 690ft/min. Range with max fuel 1000km (540nm). G 115D – Max speed 270km/h (146kt), cruising speed 250km/h (135kt). Initial rate of climb 1500ft/min. Range with no reserves 963km (520nm).

Weights: G 115A – Basic empty 590kg (1300lb), max takeoff 850kg (1874lb). G 115D – Basic empty 660kg (1455lb), max takeoff 920kg (2028lb).

Dimensions: G 115A – Wing span 10.00m (32ft 10in), length 7.36m (24ft 2in), height 2.75m (9ft 0in). Wing area 12.2m^2 (131.4sq ft). G 115D – Wing span 10.00m (32ft 10in), length 7.44m (24ft 5in), height 2.75m (9ft 0in). Wing area 12.2m^2 (131.4sq ft).

Capacity: Standard seating for two.

Production: 110 G 115s and G 115As built by late 1992. Production switched to the G 115C and G 115D in late 1993. Approximately 200 have been built of all models.

History: Grob is a company well known for its sailplanes and powered gliders, having produced over 3500 aircraft since the early 1970s, so it is perhaps not surprising that its G 115 is the first aircraft made from Glass Fibre Reinforced Plastics to be certificated by the US FAA.

Development of the G 115, sometimes referred to as the T-Bird, dates back to the early 1980s and Grob's two earlier two seat trainers. The initial G 110 first flew in 1982 and was built in small numbers, while the G 112 flew in 1984 in prototype form only. Nevertheless the two types formed the basis of the G 115, the prototype (powered by an O-235 engine) of which made its first flight in November 1985. The first prototype was representative of the production G 115 model, a second prototype differed in having a constant speed propeller, a taller fin and rudder and relocated tailplane, and represented the G 115A. The G 115 and G 115A remained in production until 1990. The line re-opened with improved models in late 1992.

The current Grob G 115 models include: the 115B, essentially a 115A with a more powerful 120kW (160hp) O-320 engine (which can be retrofitted to earlier A models); the G 115C with the same O-320, plus fuel in the wings and other minor improvements; the similar G 115C1 Acro; 135kW (180hp) O-360 powered G 115C2; the fully aerobatic 135kW (180hp) AEIO-360G powered 115D which can also be used as a glider tug; and 120kW (160hp) AEIO-320 powered G 115D2. The G 115 Bavarian was built for a US flying club. It features fuel in the wing, a revised instrument panel and more glass.

Another aircraft to bear the G 115 designation is the G 115TA Acro, but this is similar to other G 115s in name and basic configuration only. Powered by a 195kW (260hp) AEIO-540, it is aimed primarily at military customers.

Photo: A Grob G 115D.

Grumman American AA-1

Country of origin: United States of America

Type: Two seat light aircraft

Powerplant: AA-1A – One 81kW (108hp) Lycoming O-235-C2C flat four piston engine driving a two blade fixed pitch propeller. AA-1C – One 85kW (115hp) O-235-L2C.

Performance: AA-1A – Max speed 222km/h (120kt), max cruising speed 203km/h (110kt), long range cruising speed 180km/h (97kt). Initial rate of climb 765ft/min. Service ceiling 13,750ft. Range with no reserves 805km (435nm). AA-1C – Max speed 233km/h (126kt), max cruising speed 217km/h (117kt), long range cruising speed 178km/h (96kt). Initial rate of climb 700ft/min. Max range with reserves 648km (350nm).

Weights: AA-1A – Empty 442kg (975lb), max takeoff 680kg (1500lb). AA-1C – Empty 485kg (1066lb), max takeoff 726kg (1600lb).

Dimensions: Wing span 7.47m (24ft 6in), length 5.87m (19ft 3in), height 2.32m (7ft 7in). Wing area 9.4m² (101sq ft).

Capacity: Typical seating for two.

Production: Over 1100 built by American Aviation of all models. Grumman production of over 600.

History: What became Grumman's first light aircraft came from the drawing board of noted kit aircraft designer Jim Bede.

The AA-1 began life as the Bede BD-1, a compact design using just 385 parts and bonded honeycomb construction. The original BD-1 was powered by a 65kW (90hp) Continental C90-14, and first flew on July 11 1963. Unlike other Bede designs however the BD-1 was not intended for kit building, instead Bede renamed his company the American Aviation Corporation, and placed the BD-1 in series production at the company's Cleveland plant.

Production aircraft differed from the prototype in having a revised wing layout and vertical tail, a wider track undercarriage and a more powerful Lycoming O-235. First production aircraft were designated the AA-1 Yankee and the first were delivered in 1968, the last in 1971.

The Yankee was replaced in production by the AA-1A Trainer, with a modified wing and equipped for pilot training. It flew for the first time on March 25 1970 and was certificated in January 1971. A superior spec deluxe version of the AA-1A, the Tr-2, had an upmarket interior trim, wheel fairings and more comprehensive standard avionics fit. It was introduced in October 1971.

Following Grumman Corporation's acquisition of American Aviation, all AA-1s and Tr-2s were produced under the Grumman American Aviation Corporation banner. The first new development from the new company was the AA-1B, a revised version of the Trainer with greater takeoff weights.

Grumman introduced the further improved AA-1C, T-Cat and Lynx in 1978 with greater takeoff weights, a more powerful O-235 engine and revised tail surfaces. The AA-1C was the standard production model, the T-Cat and Lynx offering progressively higher levels of standard equipment.

Gulfstream acquired Grumman American in 1978, and discontinued AA-1 production shortly afterwards.

Photo: A simple and well balanced design has made the two seat Grumman (in this case a Tr-2) a popular trainer. (Gary Gentle)

Grumman American AA-5

Country of origin: United States of America

Type: Four seat light aircraft

Powerplants: AA-5 – One 110kW (150hp) Lycoming O-320-E2G flat four piston engine driving a two blade fixed pitch propeller. AG-5B – One 135kW (180hp) Textron Lycoming O-360-A4K.

Performance: AA-5 – Max speed 240km/h (130kt), max cruising speed 225km/h (122kt), typical cruising speed 207km/h (112kt). Initial rate of climb 660ft/min. Service ceiling 12,650ft. Range with reserves 805km (435nm). AG-5B – Max cruising speed 265km/h (143kt). Service ceiling 13,800ft. Range with max fuel at 75% power 1020km (550nm).

Weights: AA-5 – Empty 545kg (1200lb), max takeoff 998kg (2200lb). AG-5B – Empty 595kg (1310lb), max takeoff 1088kg (2400lb).

Dimensions: Wing span 9.60m (31ft 6in), length 6.71m (22ft 0in), height 2.40m (8ft 0in). Wing area 13.0m² (140sq ft).

Capacity: Standard seating for four.

Production: Production totals include over 1000 Tigers, plus over 100 American General Aircraft AG-5Bs.

History: The AA-5 four seaters are the bigger developments of the two seat AA-1, sharing 60% structural commonality.

The first AA-5 prototype (built by American Aviation) flew on August 21 1970. Primary differences from the AA-1 included the stretched fuselage allowing seating for four, greater span wing, higher max takeoff weight and more powerful 110kW (150hp) Lycoming O-320 engine. Production deliveries began in December 1971, at which time two basic models were offered, the standard AA-5 and the upmarket Traveler. The Traveler featured a comprehensive instrument fit with dual controls. The Traveler was instantly popular, especially with its higher cruising speeds than those for other 110kW (150hp) powered light singles including the 172.

Significant improvements were introduced when Grumman American (following Grumman's 1972 acquisition of American Aviation) released the AA-5B. Performance was boosted considerably with a more powerful 135kW (180hp) Lycoming O-360 (giving performance more like that of 150kW/200hp powered retractable gear singles), while the maximum takeoff weight was increased. Other revisions included increased span horizontal tail surfaces, larger rear cabin windows, greater fuel capacity, revised wheel fairings and deletion of the ventral fin fitted to earlier Traveler models. An up spec model with a greater standard equipment list was also sold as the Tiger. The AA-5B was offered alongside the AA-5.

The basic AA-5 was modernised in 1976 with the aerodynamic improvements introduced on the AA-5B, optional extra fuel and other improvements to boost speed slightly. Base aircraft of this model were the AA-5A, the corresponding higher level standard equipment model was the Cheetah.

Production of the AA-5A and AA-5B continued through the late 1970s until 1978 when Gulfstream purchased Grumman American. The production rights to the series were then put up for sale. Over a decade later the American General Aircraft Corporation restarted production of a revised AA-5B in 1990 as the AG-5B. However American General ceased trading in mid 1994 due to poor sales and financial problems.

Photo: An AA-5 Traveler. (Lance Higgerson)

Grumman G-21 Goose

Country of origin: United States of America

Type: Eight seat utility amphibian

Powerplants: G-21A – Two 335kW (450hp) Pratt & Whitney R-985-AN-6 Wasp nine cylinder piston radial engines driving two blade constant speed propellers. Turbo-Goose – Two 505kW (680shp) Pratt & Whitney Canada PT6A-27 turboprops driving three blade propellers.

Performance: G-21A – Max speed 323km/h (175kt), cruising speed 307km/h (166kt). Initial rate of climb 1300ft/min. Service ceiling 22,000ft. Range with max fuel 1285km (695nm). Turbo-Goose – Max speed 390km/h (210kt). Service ceiling 20,000ft. Range with standard fuel 2575km (1390nm).

Weights: G-21A – Empty 2460kg (5425lb), max takeoff 3630kg (8000lb). Turbo-Goose – Empty equipped 3040kg (6700lb), max takeoff weight 5670kg (12,500lb).

Dimensions: G-21A – Wing span 14.95m (49ft 0in), length 11.70m (38ft 4in), height 3.66m (12ft 0in). Wing area 34.8m² (375sq ft). Turbo-Goose – Wing span 15.49m (50ft 10in), length 12.06m (39ft 7in). Wing area 35.1m² (377.6sq ft).

Capacity: Flightcrew of two. Main cabin passenger seating for six or seven in piston engined Goose, Turbo-Goose seats up to 12.

Production: Total Goose production exceeded 300 aircraft, most of which were originally delivered to military customers. Production ceased in 1945. Small numbers of radial and turbine powered Gooses remain in service worldwide.

History: The Goose began life in the pre WW2 days as Grumman's first design intended for civilian use, but most of the type's production ultimately was against military orders placed during WW2.

The Goose's first flight occurred in June 1937. Grumman's already extensive experience in building carrier based fighters for the US Navy was reflected in the Goose's rugged construction, features of which included a braced tailplane and deep two step hull. Retractable undercarriage was another feature. Initial civil production machines were designated the G-21A.

The arrival of WW2 saw the Goose (a name originally bestowed on the aircraft by Britain's Royal Air Force) enter military service with a number of allied air arms, the largest operator being the US Navy. Military orders from the US, Britain and Canada accounted for much of the Goose's 300 unit production run.

Postwar, surplus Gooses found their way into service with commercial operators worldwide, their unique amphibious capability and rugged construction ensuring their popularity in the coming decades.

Some Goose aircraft have been converted to turboprop power, McKinnon Enterprises (initially based in the US, and then Canada) first fitted Gooses with four 255kW (340hp) Lycoming GSO-480 six cylinder geared and turbocharged piston engines as the G-21C and G-21D, and then with two Pratt & Whitney Canada PT6As.

Models were the G-21C and G-21D Turbo Gooses with PT6A-20s, and then the 507kW (680shp) PT6A-27 powered G-21G Turbo-Goose with a range of improvements (options included enlarged windows and increased fuel capacity) and the more straightforward Turboprop Goose conversion.

Photo: A US registered G-21C Goose. (Keith Gaskell)

Grumman G-44 Widgeon

Country of origin: United States of America

Type: Light utility amphibian

Powerplants: G-44A – Two 150kW (200hp) Ranger 6-440C-5 six cylinder, inverted, inline piston engines driving two blade propellers. Super Widgeon – Two 200kW (270hp) Lycoming GO-480-B1D flat sixes driving three blade constant speed Hartzell propellers.

Performance: G-44A – Max speed 257km/h (139kt), typical cruising speed 209km/h (113kt). Initial rate of climb 1000ft/min. Super Widgeon – Max speed 306km/h (165kt), typical cruising speed 282km/h (152kt). Initial rate of climb 1750ft/min. Service ceiling 18,000ft. Range with max fuel and reserves 1600km (865nm).

Weights: G-44A – Empty 1470kg (3240lb), max takeoff 2052kg (4525lb). Super Widgeon – Empty 1724kg (3800lb), max takeoff 2500kg (5500lb).

Dimensions: Wing span 12.19m (40ft 0in), length 9.47m (31ft 1in), height 3.48m (11ft 5in). Wing area 22.8m² (245sq ft).

Capacity: Maximum accommodation for six, including pilot.

Production: More than 266 Widgeons built, including 176 for military use during World War 2, and postwar 50 Grumman built G-44As and 40 SCAN-30 French built G-44As. McKinnon converted more than 50 G-44s to Lycoming powered Super Widgeon configuration.

History: The smallest of Grumman's amphibians developed, the Widgeon was conceived as a light personal and executive transport, following the success of the larger Goose.

The prototype Widgeon first flew in July 1940, but America's impending entry into WW2 stalled plans for civilian production. The first production Widgeon was the military J4F-1, a three seat anti submarine patrol and utility version for the US Navy. The US Navy and US Army Air Force ordered large numbers of Widgeons throughout the war years, others saw service with the US Coast Guard and 15 were supplied to Britain's Royal Navy, that service originally calling the aircraft Gosling. In all, 176 Widgeons were built for military service during the conflict.

After the war, Grumman refined the Widgeon for commercial use by altering the hull profile for improved handling on water and increasing seating capacity for up to six. Grumman built 50 of these as the G-44A, while a further 40 were built in France as the SCAN-30. Most SCAN-30s were delivered to customers in the USA.

US firm McKinnon Enterprises offered conversions during the 1960s to both the Grumman Goose and Widgeon. McKinnon's Super Widgeon conversion involved fitting G-44As with Lycoming GO-480 flat six cylinder engines driving three blade Hartzell propellers, which significantly boosted top speed, climb performance and range through improved fuel economy and extra fuel capacity. Other changes incorporated on the Super Widgeon were then modern IFR avionics, enlarged cabin windows, more soundproofing, an emergency escape hatch, and as an option retractable wingtip floats. Modifications to the hull and structure meanwhile allowed an increase in the Super Widgeon's maximum takeoff weight.

Small numbers of Widgeons and Super Widgeons still fly, mostly in private hands.

Photo: A McKinnon Super Widgeon. (Jim Thorn)

Grumman G-73 Mallard

Country of origin: United States of America

Type: 10 seat utility amphibious transport

Powerplants: G-73 — Two 450kW (600hp) Pratt & Whitney R-1340-S3H1 Wasp nine cylinder piston radial engines driving three blade constant speed propellers. G-73T — Two 530kW (715shp) Pratt & Whitney Canada PT6A-27 or PT6A-34 turboprops.

Performance: G-73 — Max speed 346km/h (187kt), cruising speed 290km/h (157kt). Initial rate of climb 1290ft/min. Service ceiling 23,000ft. Range with max fuel 2220km (1655nm). G-73T — Max cruising speed 354km/h (191kt), economical cruising speed 346km/h (187kt). Initial rate of climb 1350ft/min. Service ceiling 24,500ft. Range with max fuel and no reserves 2595km (1400nm), with max payload and no reserves 1388km (750nm).

Weights: G-73 — Empty 4240kg (9350lb), max takeoff 5783kg (12,750lb). G-73T — Empty equipped 3970kg (8750lb), max takeoff 6350kg (14,000lb).

Dimensions: G-73/G-73T — Wing span 20.32m (66ft 8in), length 14.73m (48ft 4in), height on undercarriage 5.72m (18ft 9in). Wing area 41.3m² (444sq ft).

Capacity: Crew of two. Main cabin seating for up to 10 passengers. Many aircraft used as executive transports with customised interiors.

Production: 59 Mallards built between 1946 and 1951. Small numbers later converted to turboprop power.

History: Following in the footsteps of the smaller Goose and Widgeon before it, Grumman developed the G-73 Mallard amphibian for commercial use.

Developed in the immediate postwar years, the Mallard is of similar overall configuration to Grumman's earlier amphibious designs in that it features twin radial engines on a high mounted wing with underwing floats, retractable undercarriage and an unswept tail unit. Unlike the earlier aircraft the Mallard features tricycle undercarriage, a stressed skin two step hull and fuel can be carried in the wingtip tanks.

The Mallard prototype first flew on April 30 1946, and the type entered service shortly afterwards in September that year with a Canadian operator. The Mallard was designed for regional airline operations with two pilots and 10 passengers, but most of the 59 delivered were for corporate use. Today only a small number remain in use, but their unique amphibious capability means they remain popular, particularly with tourist operators.

Like the earlier and smaller Goose, the Mallard has been fitted with Pratt & Whitney Canada PT6A turboprops. Frakes Aviation in the USA re-engined a small number of Mallards as G-73Ts in the early 1970s, their PT6A-27s substantially boosting performance and operating economy. The first Frakes conversion first flew in 1969 and an FAA supplemental type certificate was awarded in October 1970.

In early 1994 an ambitious plan emerged which would see the Mallard re-enter production in the Czech Republic. Aero and Levov of the Czech Republic, and Duncan Aviation of the USA hoped to raise the necessary capital to restart the line in the late 1990s. These plans have since lapsed.

Photo: Few, if any, aircraft can match the Mallard's amphibian qualities and load carrying capability. (Lenn Bayliss)

Grumman G-111 Albatross

Country of origin: United States of America

Type: Amphibious airliner and light utility transport

Powerplants: Two 1100kW (1475hp) Wright R-1820-982C9HE3 nine cylinder radial piston engines driving three blade constant speed propellers.

Performance: Max speed 380km/h (205kt), max cruising speed 362km/h (195kt), long range cruising speed 200km/h (108kt). Initial rate of climb (with METO power) 1250ft/min. Range with 28 passengers and reserves 750km (405nm) from water or 505km (273nm) from land, max ferry range with no reserves 2740km (1480nm).

Weights: Operating empty 10,660kg (23,500lb), max takeoff from land 13,970kg (30,800lb), max takeoff from water 14,130kg (31,150lb).

Dimensions: Wing span 29.46m (96ft 8in), length 18.67m (61ft 3in), height 7.87m (25ft 10in). Wing area 96.2m² (1035sq ft).

Capacity: Flightcrew of two. G-111 conversion seats 28 passengers in main cabin at 81cm (32in) pitch.

Production: Production for military customers of 418, built between 1947 and 1961. Grumman purchased 57 ex military Albatrosses for conversion to civil G-111 configuration in the early 1980s, but only 12 were converted. Other ex USN Albatrosses fly in private hands.

History: The Albatross is easily the largest of Grumman's series of utility amphibians, and was the only one originally developed specifically for military service.

The Albatross resulted from a late 1940s US Navy requirement for a general purpose amphibious transport. The first Albatross prototype flew on October 24 1947, with more than 400 production HU-16s subsequently delivered to the US Navy, US Coast Guard and 12 other nations. Military Albatross missions included general reconnaissance, maritime patrol, anti submarine warfare (in which role it could be armed with torpedoes and depth charges) and search and rescue.

In the late 1970s, Grumman and major US flying boat operator Resorts International began work on a program to convert the Albatross for civil airline service. The conversion incorporated numerous changes to the basic Albatross, including a 28 seat passenger interior, a galley and provision for a flight attendant, upgraded avionics and other improved systems. The airframes were also stripped down, inspected, components were replaced or repaired, and the whole airframe was zero timed. Military equipment was removed and the engines were stripped down and rebuilt.

The first such G-111 Albatross conversion flew for the first time on February 13 1979 and US FAA certification was awarded in April 1980.

Grumman purchased 57 Albatrosses for conversion and foresaw a potential market for up to 200 modified amphibians, however this prediction proved somewhat optimistic. In all only 12 aircraft were converted, all for Resorts International.

A more developed version powered by Garrett TPE331 turboprops and a firebomber were also studied but not developed. Later in 1986 Frakes International proposed re-engining Albatrosses with Pratt & Whitney Canada PT6A or PW120 turboprops, but these plans also did not eventuate.

Photo: A PT6A powered G-111 Albatross pictured at Nassau, the Bahamas. (Jim Thorn)

Grumman G-159 Gulfstream I

Country of origin: United States of America

Type: Corporate transport and regional airliner

Powerplants: Two 1485kW (1990hp) Rolls-Royce Dart Mk 529-8X or -8E turboprops driving four blade Rotol propellers.

Performance: I – High speed cruise 560km/h (302kt), economical cruising speed 463km/h (250kt). Range with a 1245kg (2740lb) payload, max fuel and reserves 4087km (2206nm). I-C – Max cruising speed 555km/h (300kt). Range with max payload 805km (435nm).

Weights: I – Empty equipped 9942kg (21,900lb), max takeoff 15,935kg (35,100lb). I-C – Empty 10,747kg (23,639lb), max takeoff 16,300kg (36,000lb).

Dimensions: I – Wing span 23.92m (78ft 6in), length 19.43m (63ft 9in), height 6.94m (22ft 9in). Wing area 56.7m² (610.3sq ft). I-C – Same except for length 22.97m (75ft 4in), height 7.01m (23ft 0in).

Capacity: I – Flightcrew of two. Typical corporate layouts seat between 10 and 14 passengers. Commuter airliner seating for 19 or high density seating for up to 24. I-C – Flightcrew of two. Seating for between 32 and 38 at three abreast.

Production: 200 Gulfstream Is built when production ceased in February 1969 in favour of the jet powered Gulfstream II. Approximately 111 remained in corporate use in 2000 while a further 36 were in airline service. Five Gulfstream G-1C conversions performed. In 2000 two were in use as corporate transports.

History: Grumman developed the Gulfstream I turbine powered executive transport to replace the many hundreds of war surplus piston twins performing such missions in the mid 1950s.

Design work began in 1956, with first flight of the Gulfstream I prototype occurring on August 14 1958. FAA Type certification was awarded on May 21 1959 and deliveries of production aircraft followed from that June. Notably, the Gulfstream I was the first US twin engined corporate transport to be certificated to cruise at 30,000ft.

As the first in the Gulfstream line, the GI established the basic fuselage cross section that carries through today to the Gulfstream IV and V. Other features were the Rolls-Royce Dart turboprops (beginning a long standing association with RR that remains to this day) giving the I good high speed cruise performance, and an auxiliary power unit allowing independent operations from remote strips, providing power for the air conditioning and electrical systems prior to engine start.

While primarily designed as a corporate transport, a large number of the standard fuselage Gulfstream Is were also used as commuter airliners, seating up to 24 passengers. Military Gulfstream Is were built for the US Navy (navigator training TC-4s) and US Coast Guard (VIP VC-4s). Production of the standard fuselage I ceased in 1969.

In 1979, by which time Grumman's design rights had been purchased by the newly established Gulfstream American Corporation, Gulfstream began offering stretched airliner conversions of the base GI. These aircraft were stretched by 3.25m (10ft 8in), allowing seating for up to 38 passengers at three abreast. Called the G-159C Gulfstream I-C, the first conversion flew on October 25 1979, and production conversions (five were undertaken) were delivered from November 1980.

Photo: A US registered Gulfstream I. (Wally McLeod)

Grumman Gulfstream II & Gulfstream III

Country of origin: United States of America

Type: Long range large corporate jet

Powerplants: Gulfstream II & III – Two 50.7kN (11,400lb) Rolls-Royce Spey turbofans.

Performance: GII – Max cruising speed 935km/h (505kt), economical cruising speed 795km/h (430kt). Initial rate of climb 4350ft/min. Range with max fuel and reserves 6880km (3715nm). GIII – Max cruising speed 928km/h (500kt), economical cruising speed 818km/h (442kt). Initial rate of climb 3800ft/min. Max operating ceiling 45,000ft. Range with eight passengers and reserves 7600km (4100nm).

Weights: GII – Operating empty 16,740kg (36,900lb), max takeoff 29,710kg (65,500lb). GIII – Empty 14,515kg (32,000lb), operating empty 17,235kg (38,000lb), max takeoff 31,615kg (69,700lb).

Dimensions: GII – Wing span 20.98m (68ft 10in), length 24.36m (79ft 11in), height 7.47m (24ft 6in). Wing area 75.2m² (809.6sq ft). GIII – Wing span 23.72m (77ft 10in), length 25.32m (83ft 1in), height 7.43m (24ft 5in). Wing area 86.8m² (933sq ft).

Capacity: Flightcrew of two. Main cabin seating for up to 19 in GII or 21 in GIII in a high density configuration, eight to 12 in a typical corporate configuration.

Production: Total Gulfstream II and III production amounted to 464 aircraft, comprising 258 GIIs and 206 GIIIs. 244 GIIs and 198 GIIIs were in service in 2000.

History: Collectively the most successful members of the Gulfstream corporate aircraft family, the Gulfstream II and Gulfstream III are Spey powered developments of the original turboprop powered Gulfstream I.

The Rolls-Royce Dart turboprop powered Grumman Gulfstream I proved to be quite successful as a large long range corporate transport, while the availability of an appropriately sized turbofan in the form of the Rolls-Royce Spey meant that a jet powered successor was a logical development. Grumman launched this aircraft, named the Gulfstream II (or GII), in May 1965.

While based on the original Gulfstream I – the GII shares the same forward fuselage and cross section – there are more differences than similarities. The most obvious difference is the two rear mounted Spey turbofans, others include a new swept wing and T-tail. A similar size fuselage to the GI seats 10 in a typical executive configuration.

No prototype GII was built, instead the first to fly was a production standard aircraft, which recorded its maiden flight on October 2 1966. Certification and first production deliveries occurred on October 19 and December 6 1967 (to National Distillers & Chemical Corporation) respectively.

The improved Gulfstream III followed Gulfstream American's purchase of Grumman's GA lines in 1978. The Gulfstream III first flew on December 2 1979. Changes compared with the GII include a revised wing of greater span and area with drag reducing winglets, more fuel tankage and thus range, a reprofiled nose and a 97cm (3ft 2in) fuselage stretch. Gulfstream IIBs are GIIs retrofitted with the GIII's wing.

Production deliveries of GIIIs began in late 1980 and continued until 1986 when production ceased in favour of the Gulfstream IV.

Photo: A US registered GIII. North America is home to 166 GIIIs. (Robert Wiseman)

Gulfstream Aerospace Gulfstream IV

Country of origin: United States of America

Type: Long range large corporate jet

Powerplants: Two 61.6kN (13,850lb) Rolls-Royce Tay Mk 611-8 turbofans.

Performance: IV – Normal cruising speed 850km/h (460kt). Initial rate of climb 4000ft/min. Range with max payload and reserves 6732km (3633nm), range with eight passengers and reserves 7815km (4220nm). IV-SP – Max cruising speed 936km/h (505kt), normal cruising speed 850km/h (460kt). Initial rate of climb 4122ft/min. Max certificated altitude 45,000ft. Range with max payload and reserves 6182km (3338nm), range with eight passengers and reserves 7815km (4220nm).

Weights: IV – Empty 16,102kg (35,500lb), max takeoff 33,203kg (73,200lb). IV-SP – Empty same, max takeoff 33,838kg (74,600lb).

Dimensions: Wing span 23.72m (77ft 10in), length 26.92m (88ft 4in), height 7.45m (24ft 5in). Wing area 88.3m² (950.39sq ft).

Capacity: Flightcrew of two. Main cabin seating for between 14 and 19, plus flight attendant. SRA-4 special missions version can be configured for freight work.

Production: Approximately 420 Gulfstream IVs and IV-SPs delivered by late 2000. Military C-20s built for the US Air Force, Navy, Marines and Army, other military customers include Sweden and Japan.

History: The Gulfstream IV is a significantly improved, larger, longer ranging and advanced development of the earlier II and III.

The most significant improvement with the GIV over the earlier Gulfstream models are the Rolls-Royce Tay turbofans, which bring significant fuel burn and noise emission improvements despite their higher thrust output than the II and III's Speys. Other changes over the GIII include a stretched fuselage and aerodynamically and structurally improved wing with 30% fewer parts, greater fuel capacity and range, increased span tailplane and an EFIS avionics suite with six colour CRT displays.

Design work on the IV began in early 1983, with the first of four production prototypes making the type's first flight on September 19 1985. FAA certification was awarded on April 22 1987. The improved Gulfstream IV-SP (SP = Special Performance), with higher payload and landing weights and improved payload range performance, replaced the IV from September 1992.

A third development is the special mission SRA-4. Designed primarily for military roles (such as maritime patrol and electronic surveillance, depending on equipment fit) it is also offered as a freighter for priority cargo transport (the US Navy operates four and the Marines one as C-20G operations support aircraft capable of accommodating 26 passengers or three freight pallets). The US Army also operates one C-20F, the US Air Force two VIP C-20Hs.

Both the Gulfstream IV and IV-SP have set a number of records. A Gulfstream IV flew west around the world over 36,800km (19,890nm) in June 1987 in a time of 45hr 25min, setting 22 class world records, another flew east around the world in February 1988, setting 11 class world records. In March 1993 a IV-SP set new world speed and distance records on a routine business flight from Tokyo to Alberquerque in the USA. In all the IV-SP holds 74 records.

Photo: A Gulfstream IV-SP. (Gulfstream)

Gulfstream Aerospace Gulfstream V

Country of origin: United States of America

Type: Ultra long range large corporate jet

Powerplants: Two 65.6kN (14,750lb) Rolls-Royce BR710-48 turbofans.

Performance: GV – Max cruising speed 924km/h (499kt), long range cruising speed 850km/h (459kt). Initial rate of climb 4188ft/min. Initial cruise altitude 41,000ft, max certificated altitude 51,000ft. Max range with four crew and eight passengers and reserves at design cruising speed 12,045km (6500nm), flight time for which would be approximately 14hr 28min.

Weights: GV – Basic operating with four crew 21,228kg (46,800lb), max takeoff 40,370kg (89,000lb).

Dimensions: GV – Wing span over winglets 28.50m (93ft 4in), length 29.39m (96ft 5in), height 7.87m (25ft 10in). Wing area 105.6m² (1137.0sq ft).

Capacity: Flightcrew of two. Typical passenger load of eight but seats 15 to 19. Typically equipped with a crew rest room, a business work station with satcom, computer and fax, a dining/conference area with seating for four, a three seat couch that converts into a bed, five other reclining seats, two galleys and a restroom fitted with a toilet and shower.

Production: 100th GV delivered late 2000. A Gulfstream V delivered in September 1997 was the 1000th Gulfstream built.

History: The Gulfstream V is the largest and latest development of the Gulfstream line of corporate transports, designed to fly intercontinental distances.

Gulfstream Aerospace first announced it was studying a stretched ultra long range corporate transport based on the Gulfstream IV at the annual NBAA convention in October 1989, while the program was officially launched at the 1992 Farnborough Airshow. First flight was on November 28 1995, with certification and first deliveries planned for late 1996. Provisional FAA certification was awarded in December 1996, full certification was granted in April 1997, with the first customer delivery on July 1 1997. By September 1997 the GV had set no fewer than 36 world city pair, class time to climb and altitude records.

The Gulfstream V is based on the Gulfstream IV, but features a number of substantial changes to suit its different design objectives. The fuselage is stretched, but perhaps the two most important changes are the new wing and new Rolls-Royce BR710 turbofans (the GV was the first application for this engine). The all new wing is built by Northrop Grumman, and is optimised for high speed flight (it was developed using Computer Aided Design and NASA developed computational fluid dynamics). The flightdeck is built around a six screen Honeywell EFIS avionics suite and features head-up displays.

Gulfstream is now working on the enhanced Gulfstream V-SP which is due to fly in the fourth quarter of 2001 with deliveries from late 2003. Improvements include a 227kg (500lb) increase in max takeoff weight, aerodynamic improvements for better range at higher cruising speeds – 9265km (5000nm) at Mach 0.87 or 12,507km (6750nm) at Mach 0.80 – slightly reduced takeoff length, reconfigured main cabin, a seventh fuselage window on the forward right-hand side, and Gulfstream's new PlaneView flightdeck including improved head-up displays, CNS/ATM compatibility, and forward looking infrared camera.

Photo: A Gulfstream V in flight. (Gulfstream)

Grumman/Schweizer Ag-Cat

Country of origin: United States of America

Type: Agricultural aircraft

Powerplants: G-164A Super Ag-Cat – One 335kW (450hp) Pratt & Whitney R-985 series nine cylinder radial piston engine driving a two blade constant speed propeller. G-164B Ag-Cat Super-B Turbine – Choice of 373kW (500shp) Pratt & Whitney Canada PT6A-11AG, or 510kW (680shp) PT6A-15AG, or 560kW (750shp) PT6A-34AG turboprops, driving a three blade constant speed prop.

Performance: G-164A – Max speed 237km/h (128kt), typical working speed range 130 to 160km/h (70 to 86kt). Initial rate of climb 1080ft/min. Super-B Turbine with PT6A-15AG – Working speed 210km/h (113kt). Range with max fuel 318km (172nm).

Weights: G-164A – Empty equipped for spraying 1220kg (2690lb), max certificated takeoff 2040kg (4500lb). Super-B Turbine – Empty equipped for spraying 1429kg (3150lb), max takeoff 3184kg (7020lb).

Dimensions: G-164A – Wing span 10.95m (35ft 11in), length 7.11m (23ft 4in), height 3.27m (10ft 9in). Wing area 20.5m² (328sq ft). Super Turbine B – Wing span upper 12.92m (42ft 5in), lower 12.36m (40ft 7in); length 8.41m (27ft 8in), height 3.68m (12ft 1in). Wing area 36.5m² (392.7sq ft).

Capacity: Usually pilot only. Hopper capacity 1514 litres (400US gal/333Imp gal). Some converted with a second cockpit (seating two) for joyflights.

Production: Schweizer built 2628 under contract for Grumman between 1959 and 1979, including more than 400 G-164s, 1330 G-164As and 833 G-164Bs. Some built under licence in Ethiopia.

History: The Ag-Cat biplane is a purpose designed agricultural aircraft, built between 1959 and the late 1990s.

The Grumman designed G-164 Ag-Cat biplane first flew on May 27 1957. Some 400 initial G-164 Ag-Cats were delivered from 1959, fitted with a variety of radial engines including various Continentals, the 180kW (240hp) Gulf Coast W-670-240, the 185kW (245hp) Jacobs L-4 or 205 to 225kW (275 to 300hp) Jacobs R-755 engines.

The G-164A followed. In its basic A/450 form it was powered by a 335kW (450hp) Pratt & Whitney R-985, and featured a greater maximum takeoff weight and additional fuel. The A/600 has a 450kW (600hp) R-1340 engine. The B/450 is based on the A/450 but with increased span wings, while the B/525 is powered by a 390kW (525hp) Continental/Page R-975.

The longer fuselage 450kW (600hp) R-1340 powered C/600 meanwhile forms the basis for the Pratt & Whitney Canada PT6A powered Turbo Ag-Cat D.

Recent models include the 450kW (600hp) R-1340 powered Super-B/600 and the PT6A powered Ag-Cat Super-B Turbine (various PT6A models were offered ranging from 375 to 560kW/680 to 750shp).

Schweizer built all production Ag-Cats until 1992, firstly under contract for Grumman between 1959 and 1979, and again from 1981 when it bought the design and production rights. In 1995 Schweizer sold the Ag-Cat's manufacturing rights to the Ag-Cat Corp of Malden, Missouri, who built small numbers of Ag-Cat Super-B turbines until entering bankruptcy.

Photo: A G-164A Ag-Cat. (Lance Higgerson)

Gulfstream GA-7

Countries of origin: United States of America

Type: Four place light twin

Powerplants: GA-7 – Two 119kW (160hp) Lycoming O-320-D1D flat four piston engines driving two blade constant speed propellers. TB 360 – Two 134kW (180hp) Textron Lycoming O-360-A1G6.

Performance: GA-7 – Max speed 311km/h (168kt), max cruising speed 296km/h (160kt), typical cruising speed 260km/h (140kt). Initial rate of climb 1150ft/min. Service ceiling 17,400ft. Max range with no reserves 2170km (1170nm). TB 360 – Max speed 322km/h (174kt), cruising speed at 75% power 306km/h (165kt), at 45% power 222km/h (120kt). Initial rate of climb 1400ft/min. Service ceiling 20,000ft. Range with max fuel at 75% power 1480km (800nm), at 45% power 2110km (1140nm).

Weights: GA-7 – Empty 1174kg (2588lb), MOTW 1725kg (3800lb).

Dimensions: GA-7 – Wing span 11.23m (36ft 10in), length 9.09m (29ft 10in), height 3.16m (10ft 4in). Wing area 17.1m² (184.0sq ft).

Capacity: Standard seating for four.

Production: GA-7s were built in 1978 and 1979.

History: The GA-7 Cougar light twin saw limited production with Gulfstream in the late 1970s. France's Socata has been developing an improved version, the TB 360 Tangara.

The GA-7 prototype first flew on December 20 1974, but three years passed before production began. By this time Grumman's light aircraft lines had been acquired by Gulfstream, which delivered production GA-7s from February 1978.

The GA-7 design featured two 120kW (160hp) Lycoming O-320s and the bonded honeycomb construction used on the Grumman AA-1 and AA-5. The initial GA-7 design featured a sliding cockpit canopy and two cabin windows per side. Changes for production aircraft included the adoption of a conventional cabin roof enclosing an enlarged cabin with an entry door on the right hand side. The prototype's single spar wing design was changed to a twin spar design allowing an integral wet wing fuel tank, and on production GA-7s the main undercarriage units retracted outwards, rather than inwards.

Gulfstream built two basic variants, the standard GA-7 and the GA-7 Cougar with a more comprehensive avionics fit and improved interior fittings. However sales of both aircraft were slow, in part because of the GA-7's relatively low combined power output of 240kW (320hp). Production ceased in 1979 with Gulfstream's departure from light aircraft manufacture.

In 1995 Socata purchased the rights to the GA-7 with the intention of placing it back into production as the TB 320 Tangara. In June 1996 Socata announced its plans to redevelop the aircraft as the TB 360 Tangara with 135kW (180hp) O-360s.

So far three modified GA-7s have flown as Tangara prototypes, the first had a 120kW (160hp) and a 135kW (180hp) engine and flew in mid 1996, the third, which first flew in February 1997, was in full TB 360 configuration. French certification was awarded in December 1997 but in 1999 Socata announced it was suspending development due to strong demand for its other products, and that instead it was looking for a partner to place the TB 360 into production.

Photo: A Grumman Cougar. (Bill Lines)

Handley Page Herald

Country of origin: United Kingdom

Type: Turboprop airliner and freighter

Powerplants: 200 – Two 1605kW (2150shp) Rolls-Royce Dart 527 turboprops driving four blade propellers.

Performance: 200 – Max cruising speed 440km/h (238kt), economical cruising speed 426km/h (230kt). Range with max payload 450km (280nm), range with max fuel 1400km (870nm).

Weights: 200 – Operating empty 11,700kg (25,800lb), max takeoff 19,505kg (43,000lb).

Dimensions: 200 – Wing span 28.88m (94ft 4in), length 23.01m (75ft 6in), height 7.34m (24ft 1in). Wing area 82.3m² (886sq ft).

Capacity: Flightcrew of two. Series 100 max passenger seating for 47, series 200 max seating for 56. Last survivor configured for freight work, series 200 max payload 5100kg (11,240lb).

Production: Total production of 50, comprising four Series 100s, 38 Series 200s and eight Series 400s for the Royal Malaysian Air Force. Two survive in Guatemala.

History: A contemporary of the BAe 748 and Fokker F27 Friendship, the Handley Page Herald was a less than successful attempt at providing a replacement for the ubiquitous Douglas DC-3.

The Herald was designed by Handley Page's Reading facility, which was formerly the Miles Aircraft Company. Bearing a superficial resemblance to the smaller and older Miles Marathon, the Herald originally was powered by four 650kW (870hp) Alvis Leonides Major radial piston engines.

Handley Page optimised the Herald design for operations from underdeveloped airfields with operators which it thought would prefer piston rather than turbine power. The first Herald prototype flew on August 25 1955, a second flew on August 3 1956.

However, by this time the Vickers Viscount had proven the reliability and economical operation of turboprops and consequently Handley Page made the decision to switch to turboprops for the Herald in May 1957. Both of the piston powered prototypes were converted with two Rolls-Royce Darts in place of the four Alvis Leonides Majors. The first flight of a Herald in the new configuration occurred on March 11 1958. The first Series 100 production Herald first flew on October 30 1959.

Only four Series 100s were built before production switched to the larger capacity and stretched (by 1.09m/3ft 7in) Series 200 in late 1961. The prototype 200 first flew on April 8 1961 and it became the major production model. The only other Herald derivative built was the Series 400, a military version of the 200 for Malaysia, which took delivery of eight. Brazil's VASP ordered 10 Herald Series 700s with more powerful engines but cancelled the order and the partially completed airframes were scrapped.

The Herald failed to attract many orders success, its poor sales further contributing to the decline of Handley Page. Herald production ceased in August 1968, while Handley Page collapsed in late 1969.

Channel Express retired the world's last airworthy Herald in 1999. In 2000 two Heralds survived in Guatemala, although it seems very unlikely that these machines will fly again.

Photo: Channel Express retired Herald 401 G-BEYF in 1999. (Keith Gaskell)

Harbin Y-11 & Y-12 & CAG Twin Panda

Country of origin: China

Type: Commuter airliners and utility transports

Powerplants: Y-11B – Two 260kW (350hp) Teledyne Continental TSIO-550-B flat six piston engines driving three blade variable pitch props. Y-12 (II) – Two 460kW (620shp) Pratt & Whitney Canada PT6A-27 turboprops driving three blade constant speed Hartzell props.

Performance: Y-11B – Max speed 265km/h (143kt), max cruising speed 235km/h (127kt), economical cruising speed 200km/h (108kt). Initial rate of climb 1100ft/min. Service ceiling 19,685ft. Range with max payload 300km (163nm), with max fuel 1080km (590nm). Y-12 (II) – Max cruising speed 292km/h (157kt), economical cruising speed 250km/h (135kt). Initial rate of climb 1595ft/min. Service ceiling 22,960ft. Range at economical cruising speed with max fuel and reserves 1340km (725nm).

Weights: Y-11B – Empty equipped 2505kg (5250lb), max takeoff 3500kg (7715lb). Y-12 (II) – Max takeoff 5300kg (11,685lb).

Dimensions: Y-11B – Wing span 17.08m (56ft 1in), length 12.12m (39ft 9in), height 5.19m (17ft 0in). Wing area 34.2m² (367.7sq ft). Y-12 (II) – Wing span 17.25m (56ft 7in), length 14.86m (48ft 9in), height 5.68m (18ft 8in). Wing area 34.3m² (368.88sq ft).

Capacity: Flightcrew of two. Main cabin seats six to eight passengers in Y-11. Y-12 can seat up to 17 at three abreast and 75cm (30in) pitch.

Production: Approx 40 Y-11s, two prototype and one production Y-11Bs and over 105 Y-12s built by late 2000. 35 Twin Pandas on order.

History: The piston powered Y-11 and turboprop Y-12 are Chinese developed regional airliners and utility transports.

Design of the type 11 transport aircraft, or Yun-shu 11 (Y-11) began during the mid 1970s as a replacement for the Antonov An-2 utility biplane in Chinese service (licence built in China as the Y-2). A prototype was built and flown at Shenyang in 1975, while production began at what is now the Harbin Aircraft Manufacturing Company in 1980. Features include two radial engines, capability for rough field operations and STOL performance. Y-11s have seen service as commuter airliners and have also been configured and used for ag spraying.

The Y-11B is an improved development powered by Teledyne Continental engines to overcome single engine altitude performance shortfalls. The first Y-11B's maiden flight was on December 25 1990.

The Y-12 is a turboprop powered development and has been built in greater numbers than the Y-11. Work on a turboprop powered Y-11 began in the early 1980s, and a Pratt & Whitney Canada PT6A powered and enlarged cabin Y-12 prototype (previously the Y-11T) first flew on August 16 1984. Current production is of the Y-12 (II), while the further improved Y-12 (IV) was granted US certification in March 1995.

Canadian Aerospace Group (CAG) offers a developed Y-12 as the Twin Panda, which it aims at the Twin Otter replacement market. The Twin Panda is based on the Y-12 (IV) but features more powerful PT6A-34 engines, strengthened landing gear, and upgraded avionics and interior. Upgraded avionics are optional. Production Twin Pandas will be built in China and outfitted in Canada prior to delivery. In 2000 Canadian Aerospace Group said it had orders for 35 Twin Pandas.

Photo: A Harbin Y-12 (IV) with sweptback wingtips. (Sebastian Zacharias)

Hawker Siddeley HS.125

Country of origin: United Kingdom

Type: Mid size corporate jet

Powerplants: Srs 400 – Two 14.9kN (3360lb) Rolls-Royce Viper 522 turbojets. Srs 600 – Two 16.7kN (3750lb) Rolls-Royce Viper 601 turbojets.

Performance: Srs 400 – Long range cruising speed 724km/h (390kt). Initial rate of climb 4800ft/min. Range with 454kg (1000lb) payload and reserves 2835km (990nm). Srs 600 – Long range cruising speed 810km/h (427kt). Initial rate of climb 4900ft/min. Range with max fuel and reserves 3020km (1630nm).

Weights: Srs 400 – Typical operating empty 5557kg (12,260lb), max takeoff 10,569kg (23,300lb). Srs 600 – Max takeoff 11,340kg (25,000lb).

Dimensions: Srs 400 – Wing span 14.32m (47ft 0in), length 14.42m (47ft 5in), height 5.26m (17ft 3in). Wing area 32.8m² (353sq ft). Srs 600 – Same except length 15.37m (50ft 6in).

Capacity: Flightcrew of two. Various optional interior configurations offered depending on customer preference. Max main cabin seating for 12 in Srs 400 or 14 in Srs 600.

Production: Total sales of HS.125s up to and including the Series 600 reached 358, including the Srs 2 Dominie for Britain's RAF. More than 230 remained in use in 2000.

History: One of the British aviation industry's most successful postwar designs, the Hawker Siddeley HS.125 was one of the most popular first generation business jets and in developed form remains in production with Raytheon (refer separate entry).

The HS.125 started life as a de Havilland project before that company became part of the Hawker Siddeley group. As the DH.125 this mid size corporate jet first flew on August 13 1962. For a time the DH.125 was named the Jet Dragon, while just eight initial Series 1 production aircraft were built before deliveries switched to the more powerful Series 1A (the A suffix denoting North America) and Series 1B (the B denoting sales for world markets). A total of 77 was built. The Series 2 meanwhile was a military derivative built for Britain's Royal Air Force as the Dominie navigation trainer.

The improved Series 3A and 3B (29 built) had a higher gross weight, while the 3A-R and 3B-R (36 built) were heavier still with extra fuel for greater range.

When de Havilland merged into Hawker Siddeley, the Series 4, which featured numerous minor refinements, was marketed as the Series 400A and 400B and 116 were built.

The final Viper turbojet powered 125 built was the Series 600A and 600B. The Series 600 features a stretched fuselage taking standard main cabin seating from six to eight, or up to 14 in a high density configuration. Other changes included more powerful Rolls-Royce Viper 601-22 turbojets, lengthened vertical tail and ventral fin, and a fuel tank in the extended dorsal fin.

The 600 first flew on January 21 1971 and it became the standard production model until the Garrett TFE731 turbofan powered 700 series was introduced (described separately) in 1976. Some Series 600s were re-engined with TFE731s as HS.125-600Fs.

Photo: A HS.125 Series 600B.

Helio Courier

Country of origin: United States of America

Type: Four/six seat STOL utility light aircraft

Powerplants: H-250 – One 185kW (250hp) Lycoming O-540-A1A5 flat six piston engine driving a three blade constant speed propeller. H-295 – One 229kW (295hp) geared GO-480-G1D6.

Performance: H-250 – Max speed 257km/h (140kt), max cruising speed 245km/h (132kt), long range cruising speed 214km/h (116kt). Initial rate of climb 830ft/min. Service ceiling 15,200ft. Range with standard fuel and no reserves 1035km (560nm), with optional fuel 2073km (1120nm). H-295 – Max speed 270km/h (145kt), max cruising speed 265km/h (143kt), long range cruising speed 240km/h (130kt). Initial rate of climb 1150ft/min. Service ceiling 20,500ft. Range with standard fuel and no reserves 1060km (575nm), with optional fuel 2220km (1200nm).

Weights: H-250 – Empty 890kg (1960lb), max takeoff 1542kg (3400lb). H-295 – Empty 943kg (2080lb), max takeoff 1542kg (3400lb).

Dimensions: H-250 & H-295 – Wing span 11.89m (39ft 0in), length 9.45m (31ft 0in), height 2.69m (8ft 10in). Wing area 21.5m² (231sq ft).

Capacity: Early models up to the H-250 could seat four, the H-395 five or six, the H-250 and subsequent models six.

Production: More than 500 Couriers of all models built, including 130 U-10s for the US Air Force.

History: The Helio Courier has proven to be a versatile utility aircraft, highly regarded for its superb STOL abilities.

The Courier traces back to a much modified experimental development of the two seat Piper Vagabond known as the Koppen-Bolinger Helioplane. This Helioplane featured numerous aerodynamic modifications to enhance low speed handling and STOL performance, and many of its features were subsequently incorporated into the all new and much larger Courier.

The Courier was initially known as the Helioplane Four and first appeared in 1952. In its original form it was powered by a 197kW (264hp) Lycoming GO-435 and seated four. First flight occurred during 1953 and deliveries of the initial production model, the H-391B, got underway in 1954. Subsequent development led to a number of derivatives, beginning with the H-392 Strato Courier of 1957. Intended for high altitude photographic work, the H-392 was powered by a 255kW (340hp) supercharged GSO-435.

The H-395, featuring a 220kW (295hp) GO-485 and seating for five or six, was the first major production version and it appeared in 1957. The H-395A was similar but its engine could operate on 80 octane fuel, making it suitable for operations in remote areas. Next came the H-250 (with a 185kW/250hp O-540) and H-295 Super Courier (220kW/295hp GO-480) from 1965, and the tricycle undercarriage HT-295 from 1974. The H-250 remained in production until 1972, the H-295 until 1976.

A development of the H-295 with an eight cylinder 300kW (400hp) Lycoming IO-720, the Courier 800, plus the 260kW (350hp) TIO-540 powered Courier 700 were put into production by the newly established Helio Aircraft Company from 1983, but production was limited and ceased in the late 1980s.

Photo: A H-250 Courier at Cairns on the north Queensland coast, Australia. (Martin Grimm)

Hiller UH-12

Country of origin: United States of America

Type: Light utility helicopter

Powerplant: UH-12E4T – One 315kW (420shp) Allison 250-C20B turboshaft driving two blade main and tail rotors. UH-12E3 – One 255kW (340hp) Textron Lycoming VO-540-C2A flat six piston engine.

Performance: UH-12E4T – Max speed 154km/h (83kt). Range with auxiliary tanks 565km (305nm). UH-12E3 – Max speed 154km/h (83kt), cruising speed 145km/h (78kt). Initial rate of climb 1290ft/min. Service ceiling 15,000ft. Hovering ceiling out of ground effect 6800ft. Range with reserves 278km (150nm), or 585km (316nm) with optional fuel.

Weights: UH-12E4T – Empty 750kg (1650lb), max takeoff 1406kg (3100lb). UH-12E3 – Empty 798kg (1759lb), max takeoff 1406kg (3100lb).

Dimensions: UH-12E4T – Main rotor diameter 10.80m (35ft 5in), length overall 12.41m (40ft 9in), fuselage length 9.08m (29ft 10in), height 3.08m (10ft 2in). Main rotor disc area 92.0m² (990.0sq ft). UH-12E3 – Same except fuselage length 8.69m (28ft 6in).

Capacity: Seating for three on a bench seat, or for four (two forward and two behind) in UH-12E4 and -12E4T.

Production: Over 2300 of all versions built, including military H-23s.

History: The UH-12 series of light helicopters has had one of the longest and most sporadic production runs in history.

The UH-12 first flew in 1948. The initial variant was the Model 12 which was powered by a 133kW (178hp) Franklin 6V4-178-B33 engine. The Model 12A followed from 1952, it introduced a semi enclosed cockpit, while the distinctive goldfish bowl cockpit first appeared on the 12C, which also introduced all metal rotor blades (the 12C, plus the 12A and 12B were powered by a 150kW/200hp or 155kW/210hp engine). The definitive UH-12E was first delivered from May 1959.

Developments on the UH-12E theme include the four seat UH-12E4 with a stretched fuselage and the Allison 250 turboshaft powered UH-12ET and UH-12E4T. Kits were offered allowing the conversion of -12Es into -12E4s, while piston powered aircraft could be retrofitted with the Allison turboshaft. Large numbers of military Hillers were also built for the US military as H-23 Ravens.

The production history of the UH-12 is chequered, with design and initial production undertaken by the original Hiller company. Hiller, and then Fairchild Hiller, built over 2000 up until the late 1960s. The newly formed Hiller Aviation acquired design and production rights in 1973 and restarted UH-12E production. Hiller Aviation was then acquired by Rogerson Aircraft in 1984, the first UH-12Es manufactured under the new company banner coming off the line in mid 1984. Rogerson subsequently changed its name to Rogerson Hiller, and relaunched UH-12E production in 1991.

The final chapter of the UH-12 story so far opened in mid 1994 when the original designer and owner Stanley Hiller, in conjunction with Thai investors, acquired the program from Rogerson. The new Hiller Aircraft Corporation planned to build small numbers of UH-12E3s (the first, a conversion of an existing UH-12E, flew on June 2 1995) for its Thai partners, and also flew the Allison 250 turboprop powered UH-12E3T, but did not resume production.

Photo: The UH-12E has proven successful worldwide.

Hindustan Advanced Light Helicopter

Country of origin: India

Type: Medium utility helicopter

Powerplants: Prototypes – Two 746kW (1000shp) takeoff rated Turbomeca TM 333-2B turboshafts driving a four blade main rotor and a four blade tail rotor. Production civil aircraft – Two 970kW (1300shp) LHTEC CTS 800s.

Performance: Max speed 290km/h (156kt), max cruising speed 245km/h (132kt). Initial rate of climb 2360ft/min. Service ceiling 19,680ft. Hovering ceiling in ground effect over 9840ft. Range with max fuel 800km (430nm), range with a 700kg (1543lb) payload 400km (215nm). Endurance 4hr.

Weights: Army version – Empty equipped 2500kg (5511lb), max takeoff 4000kg (8818lb). Naval version – Empty 2500kg (5511lb), max takeoff 5000kg (11,023lb).

Dimensions: Main rotor diameter 13.20m (43ft 4in), length overall rotors turning 15.87m (52ft 1in), fuselage length tail rotor turning 13.43m (44ft 1in), height overall tail rotor turning with skids 4.98m (16ft 4in), with wheels 4.91m (16ft 2in). Main rotor disc area 136.9m² (1473.0sq ft).

Capacity: Flightcrew of two. Main cabin seating for 10 to 14, depending on configuration. Max external sling load army variant 1000kg (2205lb), naval variant 1500kg (3307lb).

Production: The Indian government plans to buy 300 for that country's military. HAL foresees civil and military domestic orders for approx 650.

History: The Advanced Light Helicopter is the first indigenous helicopter design of the growing Indian aircraft industry, and will be built in different versions for the Indian Army, Navy, Coast Guard and Air Force, as well as for civil customers.

In the early 1980s India approached Germany's MBB (now Eurocopter Deutschland) to help it design and build a mid size multirole helicopter for both military and civil use. Subsequently a cooperation agreement was signed in July 1984, covering design support, development and production. Design work began in November that year, while the first flight of the first of four prototypes was on August 20 1992.

ALH design features include a hingeless four blade main rotor with swept back tips and composite construction main and tail rotor blades. The first three prototypes are powered by TM 333s but a final engine choice for production aircraft has yet to be made. Civil aircraft will feature LHTEC CTS 800s.

The Advanced Light Helicopter will be built in two distinct military versions, one for the Indian air force and army, and one for the navy. Army and air force versions will feature skids, and will be used for a number of missions including ground attack, troop transport and SAR. Naval versions will be fitted with retractable tricycle undercarriage and a folding tail boom. The civil version will feature tricycle landing gear and will be certificated to western standards. The first civil ALH is due to fly in early 2001.

The Indian government plans to buy around 300 ALHs for its military, to replace a variety of helicopters including Chetaks and Cheetahs. The first firm order, for 100, was placed in late 1996. First deliveries were due in the first quarter of 2001.

Photo: The first prototype ALH, Z 3182. (Hindustan)

IAI Arava

Country of origin: Israel

Type: STOL utility transport

Powerplants: 201 – Two 560kW (750shp) Pratt & Whitney Canada PT6A-34 turboprops driving three blade constant speed Hartzell propellers.

Performance: 201 – Max speed 326km/h (176kt), max cruising speed 320km/h (172kt), economical cruising speed 310km/h (168kt). Initial rate of climb 1290ft/min. Service ceiling 25,000ft. Range with max payload and reserves 260km (140nm), max range with a 1585kg (3500lb) payload and reserves 1000km (540nm).

Weights: 201 – Operating empty 4000kg (8816lb), max takeoff 6804kg (15,000lb).

Dimensions: 201 – Wing span 20.96m (68ft 9in), length 13.03m (42ft 9in), height 5.21m (17ft 1in). Wing area 43.7m² (470.2sq ft).

Capacity: Flightcrew of two. Seating for 19 passengers four abreast in an airline configuration in 101B, 20 in 102 and 24 in 201. 201 can carry 2350kg (5184lb) of freight. 102 can carry up to 12 passengers in an executive configuration, other configurations offered include aerial ambulance, mapping and mineral exploration.

Production: Total Arava production of more than 90 mainly for military customers. In 2000 nine in service as corporate transports, six in commercial service.

History: The Arava STOL utility transport was IAI's first design to enter production that was intended for both military and civil customers, but was built in only small numbers.

IAI began design work on the Arava in 1966. Design objectives included STOL performance, the ability to operate from rough strips, and the carriage of 25 troops or bulky payloads. To achieve this the Arava design was of a fairly unusual configuration, featuring a barrel-like short but wide fuselage, the rear of which is hinged and swings open for easy loading and unloading, plus long span wings, twin tails mounted on booms that run from the engine nacelles, and two Pratt & Whitney Canada PT6A turboprops.

The Arava first flew on November 27 1969, while a second prototype flew for the first time on May 8 1971. US FAA certification for the initial Arava 101 was granted in April 1972.

The Arava 101 was not put into production, but formed the basis for the 101B, 102 and 201 production models. The 101B was marketed in the USA as the Cargo Commuterliner and differed from the 101 in having an improved 19 seat interior in passenger configuration and more powerful PT6A-36s. The 102 had a 20 seat passenger interior, or alternatively a 12 passenger executive interior or all freight configuration.

The 201 is primarily a military version. More than 70 were built, mainly for air arms of developing nations. The final Arava development was the 202, which is easily recognised by its large Whitcomb winglets, boundary layer fences inboard of each wingtip and slightly stretched fuselage. The winglets and boundary layer fences were offered as a kit for retrofitting to existing Aravas.

Arava production ceased in the late 1980s.

Photo: The Arava's twin tail booms and high wing configuration allow an unobstructed fuselage for rear loading. (IAI)

IAI Westwind

Country of origin: Israel

Type: Small to mid size corporate jet

Powerplants: 1123 – Two 13.8kN (3100lb) General Electric CJ610-9 turbojets. 1124A – Two 16.5kN (3700lb) Garrett TFE731-1-100G turbofans.

Performance: 1123 – Max cruising speed 870km/h (470kt), economical cruising speed 755km/h (408kt). Initial rate of climb 4040ft/min. Service ceiling 45,000ft. Max range 3410km (1840nm), range with max payload 2575km (1390nm). 1124A – Max speed 868km/h (469kt), economical cruising speed 723km/h (390kt). Range with max payload and reserves 4430km (2390nm), range with four passengers and max fuel 5385km (2905nm).

Weights: 1123 – Operating empty 5330kg (11,750lb), max takeoff 9390kg (20,700lb). 1124A – Operating empty 6010kg (13,250lb), max takeoff 10,660kg (23,500lb).

Dimensions: 1123 – Wing span 13.65m (44ft 5in), length 15.93m (52ft 3in), height 4.81m (15ft 10in). Wing area 28.6m² (308.3sq ft). 1124A – Same.

Capacity: Flightcrew of two. Standard seating for seven in typical corporate layout, max seating for 10. Many configured as freighters.

Production: 150 1121s built. More than 250 Westwinds built, incl 36 with turbojets. 51 1121s, 25 1123s and 242 1124s in service in 2000.

History: The IAI Westwind has become one of the success stories of the small but effective Israeli aviation industry.

The Westwind started life as the Aero Commander 1121 Jet Commander, a General Electric CJ610 turbojet powered small executive jet based on Aero Commander's successful piston and turboprop twin line (described separately under Rockwell). The first 1121 flew on January 27 1963, with deliveries of slightly stretched production aircraft from January 1965. However North American shortly afterwards acquired Aero Commander, and as it was already building the Sabreliner (described under Rockwell), the Jet Commander line had to be sold off because of anti-trust laws. Thus the design and production rights for the Jet Commander were sold to Israel Aircraft Industries (IAI) in 1967.

IAI continued production of the Jet Commander as the improved 1121A and 1121B Commodore Jet (total US/Israeli 1121 production was 150, production was transferred to Israel between 1967 and mid 1969). IAI then developed the 1123 Westwind (originally Commodore Jet Eleven 23) with a stretched fuselage allowing seating for 10 passengers. The Westwind first flew on September 28 1970. Thirty-six turbojet powered 1123s were built before production transferred to the Garrett TFE731 turbofan powered 1124 (known as the Westwind I from 1981), the first of which were delivered in mid 1976. The 1124N Sea Scan was announced in 1976 and is a radar equipped maritime patrol and surveillance derivative.

Development of the basic 1124 led to the 1124A Westwind 2 with improved hot and high performance, better fuel economy and longer range. Delivered from May 1980, changes over the 1124 included a modified wing section, winglets, flat cabin floor and other interior improvements. Production ceased in 1987 in favour of the 1125 Astra (described separately under Galaxy Aerospace).

Photo: A 1124 Westwind chartered to the UN. (Gary Flanagan)

Ibis Aerospace Ae270

Countries of origin: Czech Republic & Taiwan

Type: Turboprop utility & corporate transport

Powerplants: Ae270 P – One 634kW (850shp) flat rated Pratt & Whitney Canada PT6A-42 turboprop driving a four blade propeller. Ae270 HP – One PT6A-66A.

Performance: Ae270P – Max cruising speed at 20,000ft 407km/h (220kt). Initial rate of climb 1920ft/min. Certificated ceiling 25,000ft. Range at 25,000ft with reserves 2915km (1575nm). Ae270 HP – Max cruising speed at 20,000ft 481km/h (260kt). Initial rate of climb 1900ft/min. Certificated ceiling 25,000ft. Range at 25,000ft with reserves 2915km (1575nm).

Weights: Ae270 P – Empty 1788kg (3942lb), max takeoff 3300kg (7275lb). Ae270 HP – Empty 1966kg (4400lb), max takeoff 3515kg (7750lb).

Dimensions: Wing span 13.82m (45ft 4in), length 12.23m (40ft 1in), height 4.78m (15ft 8in). Wing area 21.0m^2 (226.0sq ft).

Capacity: Flightcrew of one or two pilots. Main cabin seating for up to eight in a passenger configuration, or six or seven forward facing seats or four seats in a club arrangement in corporate configurations. Can be configured for freight.

Production: Deliveries following certification planned for late 2001. $US1.995 for the Ae270 P.

History: The single engine Ibis Ae270 turboprop is aimed at corporate, commuter airliner and utility operators, and is being developed by Czech and Taiwanese interests.

The Ae270 was originally designed by Czech Republic based Aero, a company better known for its L-29 and L-39 military jet trainers (in fact Aero has built more jet trainers than any other company in the world). Aero announced it was working on the L-270 (as the Ae270 was then designated) in 1990, with design configuration finalised the following year. Aero had planned to build two L-270 models, the basic Motorlet M 601 E powered, unpressurised, fixed landing gear Ae270 U, and the pressurised, retractable undercarriage, P&WC PT6A-42 powered Ae270 MP equipped with Bendix-King avionics. In 1993 Aero adopted the Ibis name for the aircraft and refined the two models with the Ae270 MP evolving to become the Ae270P with AlliedSignal avionics (EFIS will be optional), with the Ae270 U becoming the Ae270 W.

After some delays, in 1997 Aero and Taiwan's AIDC formed Ibis Aerospace as a 50:50 joint venture company to develop and produce the Ae270. Under the new joint venture company arrangement final assembly will take place in the Czech republic, while the wings and landing gear will be built in Taiwan.

The Ae270 P prototype was rolled out on December 10 1999 with first flight on July 25 2000. Certification is planned for late 2001 with deliveries soon after.

At the NBAA's annual convention in New Orleans in October 2000 Ibis announced development of the improved performance Ae270 HP, which it is aiming at the corporate market. Compared with the Ae270 P the HP will have a more powerful PT6A-66A engine and will cruise at higher speeds. Meanwhile at late 2000 the future of the Ae270 W was under review.

Photo: The first Ae270 P prototype. (Ibis Aerospace)

Ilyushin Il-18

Country of origin: Russia

Type: Medium range turboprop airliner

Powerplants: Il-18D – Four 3170kW (4250shp) Ivchenko AI-20M turboprops driving four blade propellers.

Performance: Max cruising speed 675km/h (365kt), economical cruising speed 625km/h (337kt). Range with max payload and reserves 3700km (1995nm), with max fuel and reserves 6500km (3510nm).

Weights: Empty equipped (with 90 seats) 35,000kg (77,160lb), max takeoff 64,000kg (141,095lb).

Dimensions: Wing span 37.40m (122ft 9in), length 35.90m (117ft 9in), height 10.17m (33ft 4in). Wing area 140m² (1507sq ft).

Capacity: Flightcrew of five comprising two pilots, flight engineer, navigator and radio operator. Initial Il-18s seated 75, the Il-18B 84, Il-18C 90 to 100, Il-18D and Il-18E 110 or max 122 at six abreast.

Production: Estimated production of over 600 aircraft for civilian operators, all initially delivered to airlines in the former Soviet Union, Eastern Europe, China, Cuba and various client states in Africa and Asia. Approximately 50 remain in service.

History: The Ilyushin Il-18 enjoyed one of the longest production runs of any turboprop airliner in the world and played a significant role in developing air services in Russia's remote regions in the 1960s and 1970s.

The Il-18 was developed in response to a mid 1950s Aeroflot requirement for an economical 75 to 100 seat medium range airliner. The prototype Il-18 (named *Moskva*) was powered by four 2985kW (4000shp) Kuznetsov SN-4 turboprops and flew for the first time on July 4 1957. The first Il-18 entered Aeroflot service on April 20 1959.

Initial production Il-18s could seat 75 passengers and the first 20 were powered by the Kuznetsov engines before the 2985kW (4000shp) Ivchenko AI-20 became the standard powerplant on the Il-18B. From there on only minor changes characterised the Il-18's development life.

The Il-18B was the first major production model and featured a reconfigured interior to seat 84 passengers. The Il-18V entered service in 1961. It became the standard Aeroflot version and could seat up to 111 passengers, depending on configuration.

The Il-18D and domestic Il-18E were developed from the Il-18I prototype and introduced more powerful 3170kW (4250ehp) AI-20Ms, and could seat up to 122 passengers due to the rear cabin pressue bulkhead being moved further aft. The Il-18D is similar to the E but has extra fuel capacity with an additional centre section tank. During winter Aeroflot's Il-18Es would be reconfigured with fewer seats with the addition of a rear coat closet. On the Il-18D and E the APU is in the belly of the fuselage, rather than in the tail.

Il-18 production ceased in 1968.

The Il-18 has the NATO reporting name of 'Coot'. Like the Lockheed Electra, the Il-18 also formed the basis of a maritime patrol and anti submarine warfare aircraft, the Il-38 'May'.

Most Il-18s are now flown by secondary operators on regional routes and on charters as they have been replaced by more modern and efficient jet equipment on primary routes.

Photo: An Equatorial Guinea registered Il-18 on approach to Dubai in the UAE. (Paul Merritt)

Ilyushin Il-62

Country of origin: Russia

Type: Medium to long range medium capacity airliner

Powerplants: Il-62 – Four 103.0kN (23,150lb) Kuznetsov NK-8-4 turbofans. Il-62M – Four 107.9kN (24,250lb) Soloviev D-30KU turbofans.

Performance: Il-62 – Cruising speed 820 to 900km/h (440kt to 485kt). Range with max payload and reserves 6700km (3610nm), range with 10 tonne (22,045lb) payload 9200km (4965nm). Il-62M – Speeds same. Range with max payload 7800km (4210nm), range with 10 tonne (22,045lb) payload 10,000km (5400nm).

Weights: Il-62 – Empty 66,400kg (146,390lb), operating empty 69,400kg (153,000lb), max takeoff 162,200kg (375,150lb). Il-62M – Operating empty 71,500kg (157,360lb), max takeoff 165,500kg (363,760lb).

Dimensions: Wing span 43.20m (141ft 9in), length 53.12m (174ft 4in), height 12.35m (40ft 6in). Wing area 279.6m² (3009sq ft).

Capacity: Flightcrew of five comprising two pilots, flight engineer, navigator and radio operator. Max seating for 174 in Il-62M, 186 in Il-62 and 195 in Il-62MK at six abreast in two cabins. Alternative configurations include 114 at five abreast, or 85 first class passengers.

Production: Over 250 of all models built, of which over 75 were exported. Production ceased in 1994. Over 105 in service in 2000.

History: The four engined Il-62 was the Soviet Union's first long range jetliner designed for intercontinental flights such as Moscow to New York nonstop.

The prototype Il-62 was first unveiled in September 1962, and like the contemporary British Vickers VC10 (which first flew four months earlier) its design featured a T-tail and four rear mounted engines. Due to the unavailability of the chosen Kuznetsov NK-8 turbofans this aircraft made the type's first flight, in January 1963, powered by four 75.0kN (16,750lb) Lyulka AL-7 turbojets. Other design features included a wing sweep of 35°, three section ailerons, double slotted trailing edge flaps, two upper surface spoilers and fixed drooping leading edge extension on the outer two-thirds of the wings to combat limited control at low speed, a characteristic of T-tail aircraft. The four engines are rear mounted either side of the fuselage in pairs with only the outer two engines fitted with thrust reversers.

Prolonged development due to deep stall problems (a problem encountered by other T-tail aircraft) and problems with the NK-8 turbofan meant the Il-62 did not enter passenger revenue service until March 1967, while its first intercontinental service was in September 1967 between Moscow and Montreal.

The improved Il-62M appeared at the 1971 Paris Airshow and introduced more economical Soloviev D-30KU turbofans, increased fuel capacity, greatly improving payload-range performance, as well as an improved flightdeck and modified mechanised cargo holds capable of housing containers. The Il-62M entered service in 1974.

The Il-62MK was announced in 1978. It features an increased max takeoff weight of 167,000kg (368,170lb) which allows a maximum of 195 passengers to be carried.

Low rate production of the Il-62 ceased in 1994 when the final two aircraft were completed.

Photo: An East Line Il-62M. (Sam Chui)

Ilyushin Il-76

Country of origin: Russia

Type: Freighter

Powerplants: Four 117.7kN (26,455lb) Aviadvigatel (Soloviev) D-30KP turbofans. Il-76MF – Four 156.9kN (35,275lb) Aviadvigatel PS-90ANs.

Performance: Il-76T – Max speed 850km/h (460kt), cruising speed 750 to 800km/h (405 to 430kt). Max range with reserves 6700km (3615nm), range with 40 tonne (88,185lb) payload 5000km (2700nm). Il-76TD – Speeds same. Range with max payload 3650km (1970nm), with 20 tonne (44,090lb) payload 7300km (3940nm). Il-76MF – Cruising speed range 750 to 780km/h (405 to 420kt). Range with 40 tonne (88,185lb) payload 5200km (2805nm).

Weights: Il-76T – Max takeoff 170,000kg (374,785lb). Il-76TD – Max takeoff 190,000kg (418,875lb). Il-76MF – Operating empty 101,000kg (222,665lb), max payload 52,000kg (114,640lb), max takeoff 200,000kg (440,925lb).

Dimensions: Wing span 50.50m (165ft 8in), length 46.59m (152ft 10in), height 14.76m (48ft 5in). Wing area 300.0m^2 (3229.2sq ft). Il-76MF – Same except length 53.20m (174ft 6in).

Capacity: Flightcrew of five including two pilots, flight engineer, navigator and radio operator, plus two freight handlers. Il-76MP firefighting conversion can carry 44 tonnes (97,000lb) of fire retardant in two tanks.

Production: Over 800 Il-76s of all models built, most for the Russian military. Approx 295 were in commercial service in 2000.

History: The Ilyushin Il-76 (NATO reporting name 'Candid') was developed as a replacement for the turboprop Antonov An-12, mainly for military use.

Development under the design leadership of G V Novozhilov in the late 1960s resulted in the type's first flight on March 25 1971. Series production commenced in 1975 and the first examples entered Aeroflot service that year.

The Il-76 design features a high mounted wing, four engines, T-tail, rear loading ramp and freight doors. It was also designed with short field performance in mind, operating from austere strips. To this end the Il-76 features wide span triple slotted trailing edge flaps, upper surface spoilers and near full span leading edge slats, and it rides on 20 low pressure tyres, the front nose unit featuring four wheels, the main wheel bogies having two rows of four tyres each. Freight handling is largely mechanised, requiring only two freight handlers which can be carried as part of the standard crew complement of seven.

Civil versions developed from the basic Il-76 include the Il-76T with additional fuel; the Il-76TD with increased takeoff and payload weights and D-30KP-2s which retain their power output to higher altitudes; and the Il-76MP firefighter. Military Il-76MDs (equivalent to the TD) are also in commercial service.

The stretched Aviadvigatel PS-90AN powered Il-76MF, which first flew on August 1 1995, will be built in Tashkent. Stage 3 compliant, it was originally intended for the Russian air force (service entry is now planned for 2001). In 2000 10 Il-76MFs were in production. Civil aircraft would be designated Il-96TF. Ilyushin also plans to build a CFM56-5 powered version of the Il-76MF, which would be designated Il-76MF-100.

Photo: An Il-76TD. (Tony Senden)

Ilyushin Il-114

Countries of origin: Russia & Uzbekistan

Type: Turboprop regional airliner

Powerplants: Il-114 – Two 1840kW (2466shp) Klimov TV7-117S turboprops driving six blade SV-34 propellers

Performance: Il-114 – Max speed 500km/h (270kt), cruising speed 470km/h (254kt). Range with 64 passengers and reserves 1000km (540nm), with a 1500kg (3300lb) payload 4800km (2590nm).

Weights: Il-114 – Operating empty 15,000kg (33,070lb), max takeoff 23,500kg (50,045lb).

Dimensions: Il-114 – Wing span 30.00m (98ft 5in), length 26.88m (88ft 2in), height 9.32m (30ft 7in). Wing area 81.9m^2 (881.6sq ft).

Capacity: Flightcrew of two. Seating for 64 at four abreast and 75cm (30in) pitch. Il-114T freighter can carry a 6500kg (14,315lb) payload 1000km (540nm).

Production: Total 15 built thus far including development aircraft. Two Il-114Ts in service with Uzbekistan Airways with 13 Il-114-100s on order (first delivery due late 2000).

History: The Ilyushin Il-114 was designed to replace ageing fleets of turboprop airliners, including the Antonov An-24, in service on regional routes within the USSR.

Ilyushin finalised the Il-114's basic design and configuration in 1986, although the first prototype did not fly until March 29 1990. In total, three prototypes were built plus two static test airframes, with the original intention being to achieve certification and service entry in 1993. However the test program was delayed, caused at least in part by the crash of one of the prototypes on takeoff during a test flight in mid 1993. Russian certification was finally awarded on April 26 1997.

The Il-114 is of conventional configuration, but 10% of its structure by weight is of composites and advanced metal alloys, including titanium. It features low noise six blade composite construction propellers, and it can operate from unpaved airfields.

The Il-114 is the basic airliner and forms the basis for a number of developments. The Il-114T is a freighter developed for Uzbekistan Airlines. It is fitted with a 3.31 x 1.78m (10ft 10in x 5ft 10in) freight door in the rear port fuselage and a removable roller floor. The Il-114T entered service with Uzbekistan Airlines in 1998 and so far that airline is the only Il-114 operator. The Il-114-N200S would feature a rear loading freight ramp.

The Il-114-100 (formerly Il-114PC) is powered by Pratt & Whitney Canada PW127 turboprops, increasing fuel economy and range. Ilyushin and P&WC signed a joint venture covering Il-114-100 development in June 1997 and the first example first flew on January 26 1999. Russian certification was awarded on December 27 that year.

The Il-114M would feature more powerful TV7M-117 engines and increased max takeoff weight allowing a payload of 7000kg (15,430lb) to be carried. The Il-114MA would feature the increased MTOW and P&WC engines, giving a cruising speed up to 650km/h (351kt).

The Il-114P is a military maritime patrol variant while the Il-114FK is designed for elint, reconnaissance and cartographic work and would feature a glazed nose and raised flightdeck.

The Il-114 is assembled in Tashkent in Uzbekistan.

Photo: The PW127 powered Il-114-100. (Paul Merritt)

Ilyushin Il-86

Country of origin: Russia

Type: Medium range widebody airliner

Powerplants: Four 127.5kN (28,660lb) KKBM (Kuznetsov) NK-86 turbofans.

Performance: Max cruising speed 950km/h (513kt), typical cruising speed between 900km/h (485kt) and 950km/h (513kt). Design range with 40 tonne (88,185lb) payload 3600km (1945nm), with max fuel 4600km (2485nm).

Weights: Max takeoff 208,000kg (458,560lb).

Dimensions: Wing span 48.06m (157ft 8in), length 59.94m (195ft 4in), height 15.81m (51ft 10in). Wing area 320m² (3444sq ft).

Capacity: Flightcrew of three comprising two pilots and flight engineer, with provision for a navigator. Max seating for 350 at nine abreast. Mixed two class seating for 234 comprising 28 six abreast in forward cabin and 206 eight abreast in other two cabins. Lower deck freight holds can accommodate up to 16 standard LD3 containers if some lower deck carry on baggage racks are omitted.

Production: 103 built (including four military command posts). Approximately 90 were in service in late 2000, all with Russian and CIS operators and one Chinese airline.

History: Russia's first widebody airliner, the Ilyushin Il-86 has endured a chequered career. It has suffered from poor fuel economy, and failed to meet its modest design range, and was built in relatively small numbers.

Il-86 development was announced at the 1971 Paris Airshow. But a protracted development program followed and the first examples did not enter service until almost a decade later in late 1980. Antonov, Tupolev and Ilyushin were all asked to respond to Aeroflot's requirement for a widebody airliner, with Ilyushin's design proving successful.

The Il-86 initially was similar in configuration to the narrowbody Il-62, with four rear mounted turbofans and a T-tail. However the same problems that affects most T-tail designs such as poor low speed handling, plus the heavy structural weight needed to support the four engines caused a rethink, resulting in the adoption of a conventional tail and under wing mounted engine configuration.

Although a conventional design, one unusual feature of the Il-86 is that – where airport aerobridges are not provided – passengers can board the aircraft via airstairs leading to a lower deck baggage stowage area, before climbing a fixed internal staircase to the main passenger cabin.

The Il-86 prototype was unveiled in prototype form in 1976. The first of two prototypes first flew on December 22 1976, while the first production aircraft flew on October 24 1977. Airline service began in December 1980 (Aeroflot had previously hoped to have it in service in time for the 1980 Moscow Olympic Games). Just over 100 had been built when production ended in 1994, the only change to the design to that time being a slight increase in max takeoff weight.

Plans to equip the Il-86 with CFM International CFM56 turbofans to dramatically improve fuel economy, range and reducing noise levels to within ICAO Stage 3 limits have been discussed at various times, but the cost of such an upgrade has so far proved prohibitive.

Photo: China Xinjiang Airlines operates three Il-86s. (Rob Finlayson).

Ilyushin Il-96-300

Country of origin: Russia

Type: Medium to long range widebody airliner

Powerplants: Four 156.9kN (35,275lb) Aviadvigatel (Soloviev) PS-90A turbofans.

Performance: Cruising speed 850 to 900km/h (460 to 485kt). Range with max payload and reserves 7500km (4050nm), with 30 tonne (66,140lb) payload 9000km (4860nm), with 15 tonne (33,070lb) payload 11,000km (5940nm).

Weights: Operating empty 117,000kg (257,940lb), max takeoff 216,000kg (476,200lb).

Dimensions: Wing span over winglets 60.11m (197ft 3in), length 55.35m (181ft 7in), height 17.55m (57ft 7in). Wing area 391.6m² (4215.0sq ft).

Capacity: Flightcrew of three, comprising two pilots and flight engineer. Basic single class seating for 300 at nine abreast in two cabins. Three class arrangement seats 235 comprising 22 first class at six abreast and 102cm (40in) pitch, 40 business class at eight abreast and 90cm (35in) pitch, and 173 economy class at nine abreast and 87cm (34in) pitch. Aeroflot aircraft being refurbished with new interiors seating 12 first, 21 business class and 180 economy class passengers. Forward lower freight hold accommodates six LD3 containers or pallets, rear hold accommodates 10 LD3s or pallets.

Production: Fourteen Il-96-300s built so far, comprising three prototypes and 11 production aircraft.

History: Despite resembling the larger Il-86, the Il-96-300 is essentially a new design, incorporating a number of advanced technologies and new engines aimed at improving on the poor performing Il-86.

Development of Russia's second widebody airliner began in the mid 1980s, resulting in the Il-96's first flight on September 28 1988. In all, three flying prototypes were built, plus two airframes to use for static and ground testing. Commonality in some areas with the Il-86 allowed a 1200 flight hour certification program, resulting in Russian certification being awarded on December 29 1992. The Il-96-300 entered service with Aeroflot Russian International Airlines the following year. Initial reliability proved poor.

The Il-96-300 features a number of new technologies previously the exclusive domain of modern western built airliners. These include a triplex fly-by-wire flight control system, a six screen EFIS flightdeck (however a flight engineer is retained, unlike modern western designs), some composite construction (including the flaps and main deck floors), and winglets. The modern PS-90A turbofans comply with ICAO Stage 3 noise limits (the Il-86 does not) and the Il-86's unique lower deck airstair design was deleted.

The basic Il-96-300 is in service with Aeroflot (which has a further six on order for delivery in 2001-2003), Atlant-Soyuz and Domodedovo. The VIP Il-96PU is used by the Russian government as a presidential transport, while in 1999 Vnukovo Airlines ordered the longer range Il-96V (with 2220km/1200nm increased range), although the status of this order is unclear.

The Il-96-300 also forms the basis for the stretched and westernised Il-96M and Il-96T, described separately.

Photo: A Domodedovo Il-96-300. (Richard Hall).

Ilyushin Il-96M & Il-96T

Country of origin: Russia

Type: Long range widebody airliner (Il-96M) and freighter (Il-96T)

Powerplants: Four 164.6kN (37,000lb) Pratt & Whitney PW2337 turbofans.

Performance: Il-96M – Typical cruising speed 830km/h (448kt). Range with 30 tonne (66,138lb) payload and reserves 11,482km (6195nm). Il-96T – Typical cruising speed range 850 to 870km/h (459 to 469kt). Range with a 58 tonne (127,870lb) payload 9700km (5237nm).

Weights: Operating empty 132,400kg (291,887lb), max takeoff 270,000kg (595,238lb).

Dimensions: Il-96M – Wing span over winglets 60.11m (197ft 3in), length 64.70m (212ft 3in), height 15.72m (51ft 7in). Wing area 391.6m² (4215.0sq ft). Il-96T – Same except length 63.94m (209ft 9in).

Capacity: Flightcrew of two. Three class seating for 18 first class passengers at 152cm (60in) pitch, 44 business class at 92cm (36in) pitch and 250 economy class at 86cm (34in) pitch. Two class seating for 85 business class and 250 economy class passengers. Single class seating for 375 passengers in three separated cabins seating 124, 162 and 89. Underfloor freight holds can accommodate up to 32 standard LD3 containers. Il-96T freighter can carry max payload of 92 tonnes (202,820lb) with international standard containers or pallets.

Production: At late 2000 30 Il-96M/-96T firm orders held, including from Aeroflot (17 Il-96Ms and 3 Il-96Ts), Transaero (six Il-96Ms) and Volga Dnepr (four Il-96Ts).

History: The Ilyushin Il-96M long range airliner and Il-96T freighter are modernised and stretched developments of the Il-96-300 equipped with western engines and avionics. The Il-96T is also the first Russian transport to be awarded US FAA certification.

Compared with the Il-96-300 the Il-96M and -96T features a fuselage stretch taking max single class passenger accommodation back to over 350 (like the Il-86). The longer fuselage also means that the Il-96M's vertical tail can be smaller. Perhaps the most important changes are the Pratt & Whitney PW2337 turbofans giving greater fuel economy and reliability, and Rockwell Collins avionics including a modern two crew six screen EFIS flightdeck. (Pratt & Whitney and Rockwell have invested more than $US80m and $US50m in the program, respectively.)

The first Il-96M/T to fly was the Il-96MO prototype, a conversion of an Il-96-300, on April 6 1993. The first production aircraft was a Il-96T freighter which was rolled out on April 26 1997. The first new build Il-96M was due to fly during 1998 however the M has been delayed by several years. Russian certification for the Il-96T was awarded on March 31 1998, followed by US FAA certification on June 2 1999.

Production Il-96Ms/-96Ts are built in Voronezh.

Possible developments of the Il-96M under study include the Il-96MK, which would be powered with ducted engines in the 175 to 195kN (38,000 to 43,000lb) thrust class, and the twin engine Il-98, which would be powered by western turbofans such as the GE90, Trent 800 or P&W PW4000 series.

Photo: The first production Il-96T in Aeroflot colours. (Paul Merritt)

Ilyushin Il-103

Country of origin: Russia

Type: Four/five seat light aircraft

Powerplants: One 157kW (210hp) Teledyne Continental IO-360-ES2B fuel injected flat six piston engine driving a two blade variable pitch Hartzell propeller.

Performance: Max speed 220km/h (119kt), cruising speed 180km/h (97kt). Initial rate of climb 623ft/min. Max range with pilot, 270kg (595lb) payload and reserves 800km (432nm).

Weights: Empty 900kg (1984lb), max takeoff (utility) 1285kg (2832lb).

Dimensions: Wing span 10.56m (34ft 8in), length 8.00m (26ft 3in), height 3.13m (10ft 4in). Wing area 14.7m² (158.4sq ft).

Capacity: Seating for four or five, with rear bench seat for either two or three.

Production: Approximately 30 were flying by late 2000, with aircraft in service with Russian flying clubs and five exported to the Peruvian air force. Unit price approx $US156,000.

History: The Il-103 is one of the Russian aerospace industry's first attempts at designing and building a light aircraft for both eastern and western certification.

The Il-103 was originally conceived in response to a Russian requirement for 500 military and civil basic trainers. Program go-ahead for this new tourer and trainer was given in 1990. First flight was originally planned for the second half of 1993, although this was delayed until May 17 1994.

The Il-103 is fairly conventional in design and construction. It is powered by a 157kW (210hp) Teledyne Continental IO-360 driving a two blade variable pitch propeller, but has a surprisingly slow cruising speed compared with similarly powered western light aircraft. It features fixed tricycle undercarriage with a castoring nosewheel and anti lock brakes on main wheels, control sticks with columns optional, and a 200 litre fuel capacity. Floats and skis are optional.

Il-103 construction is largely of aluminium, but the firewall frame and wingroot attachments are made from titanium, and the wingtips are from bonded glass fibre reinforced plastic.

Ilyushin has now received both Russian and US FAA FAR Part 23 certification. Russian AP-23 certification (equivalent to FAR Part 23) was awarded in February 1996, with first deliveries to local customers taking place later that year, while US certification was awarded in December 1998.

The Il-103 is being developed in three basic models. The basic Il-103 is intended for the Russian market. The Il-103-10 is the export version with upgraded avionics, while the Il-103-11 is for export but with partially upgraded avionics compared to the Russian baseline fit.

Ilyushin has looked at certificating the Il-103 with a 1460kg (3218lb) max takeoff weight and a development with a 194kW (260hp) class Teledyne Continental or Textron Lycoming engine.

The Il-103's export sale was an order for five for the Peruvian air force, which were delivered in 1999. Others are in service with Russian aero clubs and flying schools, although no sales to the west had been recorded by late 2000.

Photo: An Il-103 with big brother Il-96M in the background. This is the first prototype. (Rob Finlayson)

Indonesian Aerospace N-250

Country of origin: Indonesia

Type: 64/68 seat turboprop regional airliner

Powerplants: Two 2439kW (3271shp) Rolls Royce AE 2100C turbo-props driving six blade constant speed Dowty Rotol propellers.

Performance: N-250-50 – Max cruising speed 610km/h (330kt), economical cruising speed 555km/h (300kt). Initial rate of climb 1970ft/min. Service ceiling 25,000ft. Range with 50 passengers and standard fuel 1480km (800nm), range with 50 passengers and optional fuel 2040km (1100nm).

Weights: N-250-50 – Operating empty 13,665kg (30,125lb), max takeoff 22,000kg (48,500lb). N-250-100 – Operating empty 15,700kg (34,612lb), max takeoff 24,800kg (54,675lb).

Dimensions: N-250-50 – Wing span 28.00m (91ft 11in), length 26.30m (86ft 4in), height 8.37m (27ft 6in). Wing area 65.0m² (700sq ft). N-250-100 – Same except length 28.12m (92ft 3in), height 8.78m (28ft 10in).

Capacity: Flightcrew of two. Typical accommodation in N-250-50 for 50 to 54. N-250-100 will seat up to 62 to 64 passengers at four abreast at 81cm (32in) pitch, 68 at 76cm (30in) pitch, or 60 at 81cm (32in) with optional extra cargo.

Production: At late 2000 reconfirmable orders stood at over 27.

History: The advanced N-250 is the Indonesian aerospace industry's most ambitious project yet but in late 2000 its future remained unclear due to a lack of funding.

IPTN (now Indonesian Aerospace/IAe, or Dirgantara Indonesia) announced development of the N-250 at the 1989 Paris Airshow. Prototype construction began in 1992 but by this stage calculations showed that the 50 seater would be overweight, and so IPTN decided to stretch the basic aircraft to seat 64 to 68 passengers. At the time only the first prototype was to be built to the 50 seat N-250 standard, subsequent aircraft would have been to the larger N-250-100 specification. However in late 1995 this plan was amended and the 50 seat N-250-50 was again added to the model line-up alongside the larger N-250-100.

Features of the N-250 include fly-by-wire, a glass EFIS Rockwell Collins Pro Line 4 avionics system and Rolls-Royce (Allison) AE 2100 turboprops.

The N-270 was a planned 70 seat, 3m (10ft) stretched development which would have been built in the USA by AMRAI (American Regional Aircraft Industries) at Mobile, Alabama but the project has collapsed. In 1997 IPTN also negotiated with Euro Regional Aircraft Industry (ERAI) to build the N-250-100 in Germany.

PA1, the 50 seat first prototype, first flew on August 10 1995, while PA2, the first N-250-100 development aircraft, began test flying in 1997. Work on a third prototype had virtually come to a complete stop due to the Asian financial crisis and a lack of funding precludes its completion.

Indonesian certification was originally scheduled for mid 1997 and US certification for late 1997, but certification compliance issues and the Asian financial crisis conspired to delay the program and possibly stall it all together. Indonesian Aerospace needs about $US90m in funding to complete certification testing.

Photo: The N-250-50 prototype. (Paul Merritt)

Kaman K-Max

Country of origin: United States of America

Type: Aerial crane and utility helicopter

Powerplant: One 1119kW (1500shp) Honeywell T53-17A-1 turboshaft flat rated to 1007kW (1350shp) for takeoff driving two intermeshing two blade main rotors.

Performance: Max normal operating speed 185km/h (100kt) or 130km/h (75kt) with an external load. Initial rate of climb 2500ft/min. Hovering ceiling out of ground effect 29,120ft. Range with max fuel 555km (300nm).

Weights: Operating empty 2334kg (5145lb), max takeoff without jettisonable load 2948kg (6500lb), with jettisonable external load 5443kg (12,000lb).

Dimensions: Rotor diameter (each) 14.73m (48ft 4in), length overall rotors turning 15.85m (52ft 0in), height to centre of hubs 4.14m (13ft 7in). Total rotor disc area 340.9m² (3669.0sq ft).

Capacity: Accommodates pilot only but certificated with fuselage side mounted external seats (one either side). Designed to lift external loads such as Bambi firefighting buckets. The K-Max's maximum hook lifting capability is 2720kg (6000lb).

Production: The first K-Max was delivered in January 1994. Over 35 built by late 2000.

History: Kaman's first civil helicopter since the Ka-225 was certificated in 1949, the K-Max is a specialised helicopter designed specifically for aerial crane work.

The unusual looking K-2100 K-Max is easily identified by its characteristic intermeshing main rotors. The two main rotors have the dual advantages of allowing a low rotor disc area loading and that all the engine's power produces lift, and none is 'wasted' driving an anti torque tail rotor. The two main rotors are also fitted with trailing edge servo flaps that control the blades' angle of attack, negating the need for hydraulic power.

Power is supplied by a Honeywell (formerly AlliedSignal and Lycoming) T53-17A-1 turboshaft (equivalent to the military T53-L-703), the T53 also powers the Bell UH-1 Iroquois series (and the equivalent commercial Bell 204 and 205, described separately). The extremely high power to weight ratio of the K-Max means it can lift loads of up to 2720kg (6000lb).

The prototype K-Max first flew on December 23 1991. Certification was delayed somewhat by an early decision to improve the rotor system to increase performance margins, changes including lengthening the main rotors' diameters and increasing the rating of the transmission. US FAA certification was awarded in September 1994.

Recognising that the K-Max's high power to weight ratio may place inexperienced operators in difficult situations, Kaman took a very cautious approach to marketing the aircraft and leased out the first six production aircraft while flight experience was gained.

As an aerial crane the K-Max is suited to firefighting operations carrying various size Bambi buckets, logging, construction, surveying and aerial spraying. It has also been demonstrated to the US Navy in the vertrep (vertical replenishment) role (due to USN requirements Kaman certificated the K-Max for IFR operations, awarded in 1999).

Photo: The K-Max features intermeshing twin rotors.

Kamov Ka-26 & Ka-226

Country of origin: Russia

Type: Light twin utility helicopters

Powerplants: Ka-26 – Two 240kW (325hp) Vedeneyev M-14V-26 radial piston engines driving two counter rotating main rotors.

Performance: Ka-26 – Max level speed 170km/h (90kt), max cruising speed 150km/h (80kt), economical cruising speed 90 to 110km/h (60 to 70kt), typical agwork operating speeds 30 to 115km/h (15 to 62kt). Service ceiling 9840ft. Range with seven passengers and reserves 400km (215nm), max range with auxiliary fuel tanks 1200km (647nm). Endurance at economical cruising speed 3hr 40min.

Weights: Ka-26 – Basic aircraft operating empty 1950kg (4300lb), max takeoff 3250kg (7165lb).

Dimensions: Ka-26 – Main rotor diameter (each) 13.00m (42ft 8in), fuselage length 7.75m (25ft 5in), height 4.05m (13ft 4in). Disc area of each main rotor 132.7m^2 (1430sq ft).

Capacity: Ka-26 – Seating for eight including one pilot and passenger separated from modular main cabin which seats six. For agwork can be fitted with a 900kg (1985lb) capacity hopper and spraybars in place of cabin. In air ambulance configuration can accommodate two stretchers and three seated casualties or medical attendants. For freight work it can carry a sling load or be operated with an open platform in place of the cabin module.

Production: Ka-26 – Estimated 850 built for civil and military roles, with operators in over 15 countries.

History: The unusually configured Kamov Ka-26 remains in widespread civil service in many former Soviet states.

The Ka-26 (which has the NATO reporting name 'Hoodlum') first flew in prototype form in 1965, but it did not enter service until 1970. More than 850 were built, mostly for civil applications.

The Ka-26 features two counter rotating main propellers, a Kamov design characteristic that negates the need for an anti torque tail rotor. Other features include the two podded radial piston engines mounted either side of the fuselage, and the removable and exchangeable rear fuselage.

The interchangeable cabin means that the Ka-26 can perform a wide variety of missions, including passenger and freight transport, air ambulance, aerial survey, and search and rescue, among others, with a special mission specific rear fuselage pod fitted as needed. The fuselage pod can also be removed and the aircraft instead equipped with a chemical hopper and booms for crop spraying, or it can work as an aerial crane and can also carry sling loads of freight.

Ka-26 production evidently ceased in the late 1970s, although the design was developed into the turbine powered and modernised Ka-126 which first flew in 1986. Development of the Ka-126 continued into the mid 1990s but production was never undertaken.

Kamov is currently working on the improved Ka-226A. Enhancements include a new rotor system with hingeless hubs and glass fibre blades, and changes to the airframe including a reprofiled nose. Power is from two 335kW (450shp) Rolls-Royce (Allison) 250-C20R/2 turboshafts. First flight was on September 4 1997. Kamov plans to achieve US certification for the Ka-226.

Photo: The Ka-226. (Sabastian Zacharias)

Kamov Ka-32

Country of origin: Russia

Type: Medium utility helicopter

Powerplants: Ka-32T – Two 1635kW (2190shp) Klimov TV3-117V turboshafts driving two counter rotating three blade main rotors.

Performance: Ka-32T – Max speed 250km/h (135kt), max cruising speed 230km/h (125kt). Service ceiling 16,400ft. Hovering ceiling out of ground effect 11,480ft. Range with max fuel 800km (430nm). Endurance with max fuel 4hr 30min.

Weights: Ka-32T – Empty 6500kg (14,330lb), normal loaded 11,000kg (24,250lb), max flight weight with sling load 12,600kg (27,775lb).

Dimensions: Ka-32T – Main rotor diameter (each) 15.90m (52ft 2in), fuselage length 11.30m (37ft 1in), height 5.40m (17ft 9in). Rotor disc area (each) 198.5m^2 (2138sq ft).

Capacity: Pilot and navigator on flightdeck. Main cabin seats 16 passengers, or can be configured for freight carriage or as an air ambulance. Max internal payload is 4000kg (8820lb), max sling load weight is 5000kg (11,025lb).

Production: Approx 170 Ka-32s delivered, with approx 130 in service. A number have been leased by western companies and others operate throughout the globe on charter from their Russian owners.

History: The Kamov Ka-32 (NATO reporting name 'Helix-C') is a utility helicopter based on the military Ka-27.

Kamov began design work on the Ka-27 in 1969, its principle design objective being to provide a shipborne anti submarine warfare helicopter to replace the Ka-25 ('Hormone'). The Ka-27 prototype first flew in December 1974 and served as a prototype for the planned military and civil (Ka-32) variants. The Ka-27 was first noted in Soviet navy service in 1981, the same year that the first civil Ka-32 was publicly exhibited at Minsk. The Ka-27 and -32 feature the same overall configuration of the Ka-25, including the Kamov trademark of counter rotating propellers (negating the need for a tail rotor), plus twin vertical tails.

A number of versions of the basic Ka-32 have appeared thus far. The Ka-32T is the standard utility version, and is in use for a range of missions including passenger transport, air ambulance or flying crane. Although it features only basic avionics, it has been produced in greater numbers than the other Ka-32 derivatives. The Ka-32S meanwhile is fitted with a comprehensive IFR avionics suite for operations in poor weather conditions. Equipped for maritime operations, it is used from icebreakers, for maritime search and rescue, and offshore oil rig support, among other tasks.

The Ka-32K is optimised for use as a flying crane and features a retractable gondola beneath the fuselage for a second pilot who can manoeuvre the aircraft when positioning it. The Ka-32A is similar to the Ka-32T but is certificated (awarded in June 1993) to the Russian equivalent of US FAR Pt 29/Pt 33 airworthiness standards, and is offered with advanced avionics. In May 1998 the Ka-32A11BC was certificated by Transport Canada to FAR Pt 29, the first time a Russian helicopter had been awarded western certification.

Kamov is now working on the improved Ka-32M with 1839kW (2466hp) TV3-117VMA-SB3 turboshafts.

Photo: The Canadian certificated Ka-32A11BC.

Lake LA-4, Buccaneer & Renegade

Country of origin: United States of America

Type: Four/six seat amphibious light aircraft

Powerplant: LA-4 – One 135kW (180hp) Lycoming O-360-A1A flat four piston engine driving a two blade fixed pitch propeller. LA-4-200 – One 150kW (200hp) fuel injected IO-360-A1B. Turbo 270 – One 185kW (250hp) turbocharged Textron Lycoming TIO-540-AA1AD flat six.

Performance: LA-4 – Max speed 217km/h (117kt), max cruising speed 210km/h (114kt), typical cruising speed 200km/h (109kt). Initial rate of climb 800ft/min. Service ceiling 14,000ft. Max range 1010km (545nm). LA-4-200 – Max speed 248km/h (134kt), max cruising speed 240km/h (130kt), long range cruising speed 213km/h (115kt). Initial rate of climb 1200ft/min. Service ceiling 14,700ft. Max range 1327km (717nm). Turbo 270 – Max cruising speed 287km/h (155kt). Service ceiling 23,800ft. Max range with no reserves at 55% power 2075km (1120nm).

Weights: LA-4 – Empty 715kg (1575lb), max takeoff 1090kg (2400lb). LA-4-200 – Empty 705kg (1555lb), max takeoff 1220kg (2690lb). Turbo 270 – Empty equipped 875kg (1930lb), max takeoff 1383kg (3050lb).

Dimensions: LA-4 & LA-4-200 – Wing span 11.58m (38ft 0in), length 7.59m (24ft 11in), height 2.84m (9ft 4in). Wing area 15.8m² (170.0sq ft). Turbo 270 – Wing span 11.68m (38ft 4in), length 8.64m (28ft 4in), height 3.05m (10ft 0in). Wing area 15.2m² (164.0sq ft).

Capacity: Normal seating for four in LA-4 and Buccaneer; Renegade and Turbo Renegade seat six.

Production: Over 1000 built, including over 300 Renegades.

History: This successful family of light amphibians has been by far the largest selling series of its type (exceeding Republic's Seabee), and one of a very small number of such aircraft to enter production.

The LA-4 series dates back to the Colonial C-1 Skimmer, a three place light amphibian which first flew in July 1948. The C-1 eventually entered production powered by a 110kW (150hp) Lycoming O-320 in 1955, and small numbers of it and the four seat 135kW (180hp) O-360 powered C-2 Skimmer IV were built before Lake Aircraft purchased the manufacturing and design rights in October 1959.

Lake's prototype LA-4P was a development of the Skimmer IV, and first flew in November 1959. Put into production in August 1960, the production LA-4 differed from the Skimmer IV in having greater wing span, strengthened structure and higher weights. The LA-4 remained in production until 1972 (small numbers of seaplane only LA-4Ts were built), by which stage the improved LA-4-200 Buccaneer had been in production for two years. The main difference in the two models was the LA-4-200's more powerful engine, extra fuel and higher weights.

Further development led to the LA-250 Renegade being certificated in 1983. It introduced a number of changes over the Buccaneer including the more powerful six cylinder IO-540 engine and a stretched fuselage with seating for six. It was joined by the turbocharged (TIO-540-AA1AD powered) Turbo 270 Renegade. The Special Edition Seafury and Special Edition Turbo Seafury were based on the Renegade and Turbo Renegade respectively, and featured enhancements for salt water operations. Production ceased in the mid 1990s.

Photo: An LA-4-200 Buccaneer. (Gary Gentle)

Lancair Columbia 300 & 400

Country of origin: United States of America

Type: High performance four seat light aircraft

Powerplant: 300 – One 225kW (300hp) Teledyne Continental IO-550-N2B flat six piston engine driving a three blade constant speed Hartzell prop. 400 – One turbocharged 236kW (310hp) TSIO-550-G.

Performance: 300 – Normal cruising speed at 75% power 353km/h (191kt). Initial rate of climb 1340ft/min. Service ceiling 18,000ft. Range 2038km (1100nm). 400 – Cruising speed approx 426km/h (230kt) at 18,000ft.

Weights: 300 – Empty 998kg (2200lb), max takeoff 1542kg (3400lb).

Dimensions: 300 – Wing span 11.00m (36ft 1in), length 7.67m (25ft 2in), height 2.74m (9ft 0in). Wing area 13.1m² (141.2sq ft).

Capacity: Standard seating for four.

Production: 300 – More than 300 on order by late 2000. First delivery in February 2000. 400 – First deliveries planned for late 2001. Lancair aims to build one aircraft a day from late 2001.

History: Lancair's Columbia 300 and 400 are high performance, composite construction factory built aircraft from a company famous for its high performance kit aircraft.

While the Columbia 300 is Lancair's first production aircraft, the Redmond, Oregon based Lancair was established in 1984 by Lance Neibauer, and has built more than 1500 high performance aircraft kits.

Lancair announced it was developing the Columbia, then designated the LC-40, in 1996. An aerodynamic prototype of the design began test flying in July 1996 while the first certification prototype first flew in early 1997. The type's first public appearance was at the 1997 Oshkosh Airshow as the Columbia 300. Certification was awarded on October 1 1998. Deliveries of production aircraft (built at a new factory at Redmond's Bend Municipal Airport) began in February 2000.

In common with Lancair's kitplanes, the Columbia 300 features composite construction allowing a smooth, low drag external finish. Power is from a six cylinder 225kW (300hp) Continental IO-550. The 300 features a 402 litre (106US gal/82Imp gal) fuel capacity in two tanks, advanced IFR avionics and fixed undercarriage.

Lancair announced the even quicker turbocharged Columbia 400 in early 2000. The 400 is based on the 300 but features a twin turbocharged, twin intercooled 231kW (310hp) Teledyne Continental TSIO-550-G, giving a cruising speed of 426km/h (230kt) at 18,000ft. First flight was in June 2000. When deliveries begin in late 2001 the Columbia 400 will take the mantle of the world's fastest production fixed undercarriage light aircraft from the Columbia 300.

The 400 will also introduce Lancair's HITS (Highway In The Sky) advanced IFR avionics platform, designed with AvroTec (displays), Avidyne (software) and Seagull, under sponsorship of NASA's AGATE program, for improved IFR situational awareness. HITS features a primary flight display that presents flight data in an integrated format, and a multifunction display for moving map displays, StormScope, radar, up-linked weather and traffic avoidance programs. Another advanced feature to be introduced with the 400 will be a FADEC engine management system, allowing single lever control for power, mixture and the propeller. HITS and FADEC will be offered as options on the 300 in 2001.

Photo: The Columbia 300 in flight. (Lancair)

Learjet 23, 24, 25, 28 & 29

Country of origin: United States of America

Type: Light corporate jets

Powerplants: 23 – Two 12.7kN (2850lb) General Electric CJ610-4 turbojets. 25D & 29 – Two 13.1kN (2950lb) CJ610-8As.

Performance: 23 – Max speed 860km/h (465kt), max cruising speed 850km/h (460kt), economical cruising speed 817km/h (440kt). Range with max fuel and reserves 2660km (1436nm). 25D – Cruising speed 860km/h (465kt). Range with four passengers and reserves 2663km (1438nm). 29 – Max speed 883km/h (477kt), max cruising speed 836km/h (452kt), economical cruising speed 756km/h (408kt). Service ceiling 51,000ft. Range with four passengers, max fuel and reserves 2550km (1376nm).

Weights: 23 – Empty 2974kg (6550lb), max takeoff 5675kg (12,500lb). 25D – Empty equipped 3465kg (7640lb), MTOW 6805kg (15,000lb). 29 – Empty 3730kg (8224lb), MTOW 6805kg (15,000lb).

Dimensions: 23 – Wing span 10.84m (35ft 8in), length 13.18m (43ft 3in), height 3.73m (12ft 3in). Wing area 21.5m² (231.8sq ft). 25D – Same except for length 14.50m (47ft 7in). 29 – Same as 25 except for wing span 13.35m (43ft 10in). Wing area 24.6m² (264.5sq ft).

Capacity: 23 & 24 – Flightcrew of two. Max seating in main cabin for six, typical seating for four. 25 & 28 – Flightcrew of two. Main cabin seating for up to eight passengers. 29 – Flightcrew of two and seating for six passengers.

Production: 745 turbojet power Learjets built, comprising 363 23/24s; 373 25s; five 28s and four 29s. In late 2000 34 23s, 211 24s, 314 25s, five 28s and four 29s were in service worldwide.

History: One of the world's largest, fastest, best selling and well known series of business jets, the Learjet family began with the original six to eight seat Learjet 23 which first flew on October 7 1963.

The 23 was designed and conceived by William (Bill) Lear in Switzerland as the SAAC-23, later named the Learjet 23. The diminutive 23 pioneered a new market segment for the light business jets, and proved very successful. The first production 23 was delivered in October 1964, but was replaced by the improved Model 24 in 1966 after 104 had been built. The 24, which introduced uprated engines and a number of detail changes, first flew in February 1966 and was delivered from the middle of that year. Developments of the 24 included the 24D, E and F, introducing improvements such as increased weights, thrusts, and range.

The Learjet 25 introduced a 1.27m (4ft 2in) fuselage stretch allowing seating for up to eight passengers and was first flown on August 12 1966. A number of subsequent developments of the 25 were built, including the B, D, F and G.

The unsuccessful Learjet 28 and 29 Longhorns are based on the 25 but introduced a new, increased span wing fitted with winglets. These improved fuel efficiency and overall performance, particularly payload range and fuel economy. The Longhorn 28 seats up to eight passengers, the Longhorn 29 sacrifices two seats for extra range. They are otherwise similar. Production of the family ceased in 1982.

Learjets are known for their tight accommodation. Max internal cabin width is just 1.50m (4ft 11in), max height 1.32m (4ft 4in).

Photo: The diminutive Learjet 23. (Gary Gentle)

Let L-40 Meta-Sokol

Country of origin: Czech Republic

Type: Three/four seat light aircraft

Powerplant: Late production aircraft – One 85kW (115hp) with 5 min supercharged 105kW (140hp) rating Walter M332 inline inverted four cylinder piston engine driving a two blade constant speed propeller.

Performance: Late production aircraft – Max speed 237km/h (128kt), max cruising speed 208km/h (112kt). Initial rate of climb 630ft/min. Service ceiling 14,765ft. Max range 850km (460nm).

Weights: Late production aircraft – Empty 520kg (1147lb), max take-off 920kg (2030lb).

Dimensions: Late production aircraft – Wing span (without wingtip tanks) 10.00m (32ft 10in), length 7.54m (28ft 9in), height 2.47m (8ft 1in). Wing area 14.6m² (156.0sq ft).

Capacity: Initial production aircraft had seating for three with a single passenger seated behind pilot and passenger. Late production aircraft had seating for four.

Production: Approximately 200 Meta-Sokols built between 1954 and 1961. Almost all production was of the four seat model, with only small numbers of the initial three seat model built. Small numbers survive in use.

History: One of the more lesser known light aircraft to emerge from behind the Iron Curtain, the unusually configured Meta-Sokol three/four seat light aircraft was a development of the Let Mraz M.1 Sokol.

The M.1 Sokol was a three seat light aircraft developed in the late 1940s. It was used in a variety of roles, mainly for training, and a number were built for Czechoslovak flying schools. The wooden construction M.1 Sokol featured tail dragger undercarriage and a 80kW (105hp) Walter Minor 4-III inline inverted four cylinder engine.

Like the M.1 Sokol, early production Meta-Sokols seated three people and were powered by the same 80kW (105hp) Walter Minor engine. However the Meta-Sokol introduced a number of new features and design changes including metal construction, a rearwards sliding cockpit canopy, a very tall vertical tail, and a unique undercarriage system.

The Meta-Sokol's undercarriage features a reverse tricycle arrangement, with the main undercarriage legs extending from the front of the wing, with the third leg mounted from under the fuselage. Unlike the original fixed undercarriage M.1 Sokol, the Meta-Sokol's undercarriage retracts, although the rearward retracting main landing gear remains exposed in flight.

The prototype L-20 Meta-Sokol flew for the first time during 1954. This original three seat model was built in only small numbers before it was superseded by the definitive four seater, which also introduced a more powerful M332 engine. The M332 was notable in that its normal maximum power output could be boosted for up to five minutes with supercharging.

Like the majority of Eastern European aircraft of its time, most Meta-Sokols were exported to countries within the Soviet sphere of influence, although a number were sold in western Europe, North America and Australia. Production continued through to 1961.

Photo: An L-40 Meta-Sokol. Note the reverse tricycle undercarriage, rear sliding canopy and tall vertical tail. (Bill Lines)

Let L-200 Morava

Country of origin: Czech Republic

Type: Four/five seat light twin

Powerplants: L-200A – Two 155kW (210hp) Walter Minor M337 fuel injected inverted inline piston engines driving two blade variable pitch propellers. L-200D – Same except three blade constant speed props.

Performance: L-200A – Max speed 305km/h (165kt), max cruising speed 293km/h (158kt), long range cruising speed 256km/h (138kt). Initial rate of climb 1150ft/min. Service ceiling 20,340ft. Range with max fuel 1770km (955nm). L-200D – Max speed 290km/h (157kt), max cruising speed 282km/h (152kt), long range cruising speed 256km/h (138kt). Initial rate of climb 1260ft/min. Service ceiling 18,700ft. Range with max fuel 1710km (923kt).

Weights: L-200A – Empty 1275kg (2810lb), max takeoff 1950kg (4300lb). L-200D – Empty 1330kg (2932lb), max takeoff 1950kg (4300lb).

Dimensions: Wing span 12.31m (40ft 5in), length 8.61m (28ft 3in), height 2.25m (7ft 4in). Wing area 17.3m² (186sq ft).

Capacity: Typical accommodation for four or five, with pilot and passenger in individual seats and two or three passengers on rear bench seat.

Production: Total L-200 production over 1000, including approximately 160 L-200As.

History: The Let L-200 Morava retractable four seat light twin was one of the few light aircraft to be exported from behind the Iron Curtain during the Cold War era, although in small numbers.

Ladislav Smrek of the Czechoslovakian State Aircraft Factory designed the L-200 in the mid 1950s to replace the early postwar vintage Aero 45 and 145 light twins. His resulting design is similar in many ways to its contemporary western twins, with a four or five place cabin, a low wing, wingtip tanks, metal construction and retractable undercarriage. However the Morava is distinguishable by its twin tails, standard thermal wing de-icing equipment and inverted inline engines.

The prototype XL-200 Morava flew for the first time on April 8 1957. The XL-200 prototype and a series of preproduction L-200s were powered by 120kW (160hp) Walter Minor 6-III inline sixes. Initial production was of the L-200A, which differed from the L-200 in being powered by two 155kW (210hp) fuel injected M337s, and had greater weights, a reprofiled cabin and hydraulically (rather than electrically) operated undercarriage and flaps.

Let built 160 L-200s before production switched to the improved L-200D. Features include a strengthened undercarriage, improved hydraulic and electrical systems and constant speed three blade propellers. The L-200D remained in production until 1969, and a number were licence built in Slovenia (then part of Yugoslavia). A turboprop powered development was studied but not built.

Most L-200 production was for customers within the Soviet Bloc – Aeroflot for example operated several hundred in a range of roles including air taxi, air ambulance and communications duties. However small numbers were exported to western Europe, the USA and other western countries.

Photo: An Australian registered L-200A. The type is quite rare in the west. (Bill Lines)

Let L 410 & L 420

Country of origin: Czech Republic

Type: 19 seat turboprop regional airliners

Powerplants: L 410 UVP-E – Two 560kW (750shp) Motorlet M 601 E turboprops driving five blade Avia propellers. L 420 – Two 580kW (775shp) M 601 Fs.

Performance: L 410 UVP-E – Max cruising speed 388km/h (210kt), economical cruising speed 365km/h (197kt). Initial rate of climb 1378ft/min. Service ceiling 24,300ft. Range with max fuel (including wingtip tanks), 920kg (2030lb) payload and reserves 1318km (707nm). 420 – Max cruising speed 390km/h (210kt). Initial rate of climb 1400ft/min. Range with max payload 560km (302nm), range with a 1015kg (2237lb) payload and max fuel including tip tanks 940km (507nm), range with max fuel excluding tip tanks 940km (507nm).

Weights: L 410 UVP-E – Empty 3920kg (8720lb) to 4020kg (8863lb), operating empty 4120kg (9083lb) to 4180kg (9215lb), max takeoff 6600kg (14,550lb). L 420 – Basic empty 4065kg (8962lb), operating empty 4225kg (9314lb), max takeoff 6600kg (14,550lb).

Dimensions: Wing span over tip tanks 19.98m (65ft 7in), span excluding tip tanks 19.48m (63ft 11in), length 14.43m (47ft 4in), height 5.83m (19ft 2in). Wing area 34.9m² (375.2sq ft).

Capacity: Flightcrew of two. Typical commuter passenger seating for 17 or 19 at three abreast. Executive version seats 15 plus flight attendant. Cargo version equipped to handle special containers. Air ambulance version configured for six stretcher patients and six sitting passengers, either injured or medical attendants.

Production: Almost 1100 L 410s of all variants built, including 31 L 410As, 110 L 410Ms and 560 L 410 UVP-Es, with over 340 in service. One L 420 built.

History: The L 410 is very successful commuter which was first built in response to Soviet requirements, but has sold widely around the globe.

Design studies of the original 15 seat L 410 began in 1966. The resulting design was named the Turbolet, and was developed to be capable of operations from unprepared strips. The powerplant chosen was the all new Walter or Motorlet M 601, but this engine was not sufficiently developed enough to power the prototypes, and Pratt & Whitney Canada PT6A-27s were fitted in their place. First flight occurred on April 16 1969, and series production began in 1970. Initial production L 410s were also powered by the PT6A, and it was not until 1973 that production aircraft L 410Ms featured the M 601.

The basic L 410 was superseded from 1979 by the L 410 UVP with a 47cm (1ft 7in) fuselage stretch, M 601B engines and detail refinements. The UVP was in turn replaced by the M 601E powered UVP-E in which the toilet and baggage compartments were repositioned allowing more efficient seating arrangements for up to 19 passengers. The UVP-E is the definitive production version.

The L 420 is an improved variant with more powerful M 601F engines, higher weights and improved performance designed to meet western certification requirements. It first flew on November 10 1993 and was awarded US FAA certification in March 1998.

Ayres took control of Let in September 1998 but Let suspended aircraft production in mid 2000 due to financial problems.

Photo: A Slovakian registered L 410. (Viktor László)

Let L 610

Country of origin: Czech Republic

Type: 40 seat regional airliner

Powerplants: L 610G – Two 1305kW (1750shp) General Electric CT7D-9D turboprops driving four blade constant speed Hamilton Standard HS14RF-23 propellers.

Performance: L 610G – Max cruising speed 450km/h (243kt), long range cruising speed 282km/h (152kt). Initial rate of climb 1673ft/min. Service ceiling 23,620ft. Range with 40 passengers and reserves 1230km (615nm), range with max fuel 2420km (1306nm).

Weights: L 610G – Empty 8950kg (19,713lb), operating empty 9220kg (20,327lb), max takeoff 14,500kg (31,967lb).

Dimensions: Wing span 25.60m (84ft 0in), length 21.72m (71ft 3in), height 8.19m (26ft 11in). Wing area 56.0m² (602.8sq ft).

Capacity: Flightcrew of two. Standard seating for 40 passengers at four abreast and 76cm (30in) pitch. Combi mixed passenger/freight and all freight layouts available, the latter can carry six pallets.

Production: Czech airline CSA is a provisional L 610 G customer. Small numbers of L 610 Ms were delivered to Aeroflot. Status of program in doubt at late 2000.

History: The Let L 610 40 seat turboprop regional airliner was originally designed for a Soviet requirement, but in its westernised L 610 G form has been marketed worldwide.

The L 610 was conceived in the mid 1980s to meet a Soviet Union requirement for a new 40 seat turboprop airliner. A production run of 500 was envisaged for primary customer Aeroflot, and the L 610's design was optimised to suit that carrier's requirements (including operations from austere airfields). Although it bears a resemblance to the small L 410 Turbolet, the L 610 was an all new design, and in basic L 610M form for Aeroflot was powered by two 1358kW (1822shp) Motorlet M 602 turboprops. The L 610 M first flew on December 28 1988, and a small number were delivered to Aeroflot during 1991 before Let suspended deliveries, stating that they would not resume unless western currency was used for payment.

With the collapse of communism in Czechoslovakia Let was able to development a westernised version of the L 610 which it could market internationally. This resulted in the L 610 G which features General Electric CT7 turboprops, Collins Pro Line II digital EFIS avionics, Collins weather radar and autopilot.

The L 610 G prototype first flew on December 18 1992 (four years after the L 610M), however delays have meant that US FAA certification still had not been achieved by late 2000.

Let has had high hopes that the L 610 would prove popular in world markets. Certainly the Czech Republic's lower labour costs would see the aircraft priced competitively but at late 2000 its future was unclear. In 1998 US manufacturer Ayres purchased a 93.8% stake in Ayres but despite this the Czech manufacturer has continued to suffer financial problems. In mid 2000 Let's workforce was placed on enforced leave and aircraft production had been suspended, leaving the future of the L 610 in question.

Photo: The General Electric CT7 powered L 610 G has been marketed as the Ayres 7000. The family resemblance to the L 410 is obvious but the L 610 is an all new design. (Paul Merritt)

Lockheed L-188 Electra

Country of origin: United States of America

Type: Turboprop airliner and freighter

Powerplants: L-188C – Four 2800kW (3750shp) Allison 501-D13 turboprops driving four blade constant speed propellers.

Performance: L-188C – Max cruising speed 652km/h (352kt), economical cruising speed 602km/h (325kt). Service ceiling 27,000ft. Range with max payload 3450km (1910nm), with max fuel 4023km (2180nm).

Weights: L-188C – Operating empty 27,895kg (61,500lb), max takeoff 52,664kg (116,000lb).

Dimensions: Wing span 30.18m (99ft 0in), length 31.81m (104ft 6in), height 10.01m (32ft 10in). Wing area 120.8m² (1300sq ft).

Capacity: Flightcrew of three. Single class seating for up to 104 passengers. Most aircraft now configured as freighters, max payload weight is approximately 12 tonnes (26,000lb).

Production: Total Electra production of 170, including 55 L-188Cs. Approximately 50 remained in commercial service in late 2000.

History: Lockheed's Electra provided a number of airlines with their introduction to turbine powered aircraft. Today it remains popular with freight operators.

The Lockheed L-188 Electra was developed to meet a 1954 American Airlines requirement for a domestic short to medium range 75 to 100 sear airliner. In June 1955 American ordered 35 of Lockheed's design, the L-188. Many other airlines shared American's interest in the L-188, and by the time the first prototype flew on December 6 1957, the order book stood at 144. Service entry was with Eastern Airlines (due to a pilots' strike at American) on January 12 1959.

However, any optimism Lockheed would have felt about a strong sales future would have been short lived, as a number of crashes in 1959 and 1960 (two of which where the aircraft broke up in flight) contributed to a number of order cancellations.

As an interim measure following the crashes, speed restrictions were imposed while the problem was resolved. Investigations uncovered a design defect with the engine mountings where the wing would shake and eventually brake up. Lockheed undertook a significant modification program where the nacelles, nacelle mountings and wing structure were strengthened, and the speed restrictions were eventually lifted in 1961. After that the Electra proved reliable and popular in service, but the damage had been done and production wound up in 1961 after 170 had been built.

Lockheed built two basic versions of the Electra. The L-188A was the basic production aircraft, and accounted for most Electra sales. The L-188C entered service with KLM in 1959 and had greater fuel capacity and higher weights, and thus improved payload range performance.

Most Electras currently in service are configured as freighters. From 1967 Lockheed converted 41 Electras to freighters or convertible freighter/passenger aircraft, fitting a strengthened floor and a large cargo door forward of the wing on the left side. Other companies have also converted Electras to freighters. However, a small number remain in passenger service, mainly in South America.

The Electra also formed the basis for the P-3 Orion maritime patrol aircraft – more than 600 were built.

Photo: A Renown Aviation Electra freighter. (Keith Gaskell)

Lockheed JetStar

Country of origin: United States of America

Type: Large size corporate jet

Powerplants: JetStar – Four 14.7kN (3300lb) Pratt & Whitney JT12A-8 turbojets. JetStar II – Four 16.5kN (3700lb) Garrett TFE731-3 turbofans.

Performance: JetStar – Max speed 911km/h (492kt), economical cruising speed 816km/h (440kt). Range with max fuel and reserves 3595km (1940nm). JetStar II – Max cruising speed 880km/h (475kt), economical cruising speed 817km/h (440kt). Max initial rate of climb 4200ft. Service ceiling 36,000ft. Range with max fuel and reserves 5132km (2770nm), range with max payload and reserves 4818km (2600nm).

Weights: JetStar – Operating empty 10,012kg (22,074lb), max takeoff 19,051kg (42,000lb). JetStar II – Operating empty 10,967kg (24,178lb), max takeoff 19,844kg (43,750lb).

Dimensions: Wing span 16.60m (54ft 5in), length 18.42m (60ft 5in), height 6.23m (20ft 5in). Wing area 50.4m² (542.5sq ft).

Capacity: Flightcrew of two. Typical seating for eight to 10 passengers.

Production: 164 turbojet powered JetStars built by mid 1973. Lockheed built 40 new build turbofan powered JetStar IIs from 1976, while Garrett converted an additional 53 to JetStar 731 configuration. Approx 20 JT12 powered JetStars, 38 JetStar IIs and 44 JetStar 731s in service at late 2000.

History: The four engined JetStar was initially designed as a private venture but was also selected to fulfil a US Air Force requirement for a multi engined crew trainer and light transport.

The first JetStar prototype first flew on September 4 1957. Two prototypes were built powered by two Bristol Siddeley Orpheus turbojets, one of these was re-engined with four Pratt & Whitney JT12s in 1959 when an agreement to licence assemble the Orpheus in the United States could not be negotiated. The JT12 was selected for production aircraft, and the first of these flew in mid 1960.

Civil certification for the JetStar was awarded in August 1961, making the JetStar the first civil certificated business jet. Meanwhile the JetStar entered service with the USAF in late 1961 as the VC-140 VIP transport and in 1962 as the C-140 navaid calibration aircraft – the service had dropped its plans to use the aircraft as an aircrew trainer.

The JT12 turbojet powered JetStar was built through until mid 1973. The initial Dash 6 JetStar (or JetStar 6) with 10.7kN (2400lb) JT12A-6s and then 11.4kN (2570lb) JT12A-6As was replaced by the more powerful 14.7kN (3300lb) JT12A-8 powered Dash 8 JetStar (or JetStar 8) from 1967.

The improved JetStar II features four Garrett (previously AiResearch) TFE731 turbofans with their significantly improved fuel consumption, giving the aircraft better operating economics and range, plus lower noise levels. The first JetStar II flew on August 18 1976, with certification following in December that year. The II remained in production until 1979.

AiResearch meanwhile had already flown its own TFE731 powered conversion of the JetStar in July 1974. The first production AiResearch 731 JetStar conversion flew in March 1976.

Photo: A Lockheed JetStar II. (Paul Howard)

Lockheed Martin L-100 Hercules

Country of origin: United States of America

Type: Medium range freighter

Powerplants: L-100-30 – Four 3362kW (4508shp) Allison 501-D22A turboprops driving four blade constant speed propellers.

Performance: L-100-30 – Max cruising speed 571km/h (308kt). Range with max payload 2472km (1334nm), range with no payload 8950km (4830nm).

Weights: L-100-30 – Operating empty 35,260kg (77,736lb), max takeoff 70,310kg (155,000lb).

Dimensions: L-100-30 – Wing span 40.41m (132ft 7in), length 34.37m (112ft 9in), height 11.66m (38ft 3in). Wing area 162.1m² (1745.0sq ft).

Capacity: L-100-30 – Flightcrew of three or four. Max payload of 23,158kg (51,054lb) comprising pallets or containers.

Production: Approximately 40 civil standard L-100s are in commercial service, while others had been built for military use. No L-100Js had been ordered at late 2000.

History: Lockheed's L-100 freighters are the civil equivalents of the venerable military C-130 Hercules, and have proven to be of great utility, particularly in undeveloped countries.

Lockheed initiated design of the Hercules in response to a 1951 US Air Force requirement for a turboprop powered freighter. This resulted in the C-130 Hercules, which first flew in prototype form on August 23 1954. Design features included the high mounted wing, four Allison 501/T56 turboprops and the rear loading freight ramp. The USAF ordered the C-130 into series production in September 1952, and since that time more than 2200 have been built.

The C-130's appeal to freight operators led Lockheed to develop a civil version. The first commercial versions were based on the C-130E model, and a demilitarised demonstrator first flew in April 1964. This initial civil development, the Model 382, was awarded civil certification in February 1965. This model was soon followed up by the 382B, or the L-100, which introduced an improved freight handling system.

Sales of these initial versions were slow, leading Lockheed to develop the 2.54m (8ft 4in) stretched L-100-20 (Model 382E), which offered better freight capacity and operating economics. The L-100-20 was certificated in October 1968, but was soon followed by the even longer L-100-30. The -30 was 2.03m (6ft 8in) longer than the -20, first flew in August 1970, and was delivered from December that year. Most civil Hercules sales have been of the L-100-30 variant. The last L-100 was built in 1992, while the last military Allison 501/T56 powered C-130 was delivered in 1996.

The L-100J would be a commercial derivative of the new generation C-130J Hercules II. Improvements would include new Rolls-Royce (Allison) AE 2100 advanced turboprop engines driving six blade props, two crew glass flightdeck and significantly lower maintenance and operating costs. The C-130J first flew on April 5 1996, while US FAA civil certification was awarded in September 1998. The L-100J would be based on the stretched fuselage C-130J-30 but in 2000 the program was frozen as Lockheed Martin focussed on the military variants.

Photo: An L-100-30 operated by Safair of South Africa in UN colours. Safair is the world's largest civil Hercules operator. (Gary Flanagan)

Lockheed L-1011 TriStar

Country of origin: United States of America

Type: Medium to long range widebody airliner

Powerplants: L-1011-1 – Three 187kN (42,000lb) Rolls-Royce RB211-22B turbofans. L-1011-200 – Three 213.5kN (48,000lb) RB211-524s or 222.4kN (50,000lb) -524B or B4s.

Performance: L-1011-1 – Max cruising speed 973km/h (526kt), economical cruising speed 890km/h (463kt). Max range 5760km (3110nm). L-1011-200 – Speeds same. Range with max pax payload 6820km (3680nm), range with max fuel 9111km (4918nm).

Weights: L-1011-1 – Operating empty 109,045kg (240,400lb), max takeoff 195,045kg (430,000lb). L-1011-200 – Operating empty 112,670kg (248,000lb), max takeoff 211,375kg (466,000lb).

Dimensions: Wing span 47.34m (155ft 4in), length 54.17m (177ft 8in), height 16.87m (55ft 4in). Wing area 320.0m^2 (3456.0sq ft).

Capacity: Flightcrew of three. Max seating for 400 at 10 abreast and 76cm (30in) pitch. Typical two class seating for 256 at six abreast and nine abreast. Underfloor holds can accommodate 16 LD3 containers.

Production: Total TriStar production of 250, of which 200 were standard fuselage length -1, -100, -200 and -250 models. Approx 137 TriStars in commercial service in 2000, of which 109 were standard fuselage models, including 11 freighters. Production ceased 1983, the prototype was sold to be broken up for spares in 1986.

History: The Lockheed TriStar was the second widebody airliner to be launched, and although it was dogged with early financial and development problems, particularly with the engine, it went on to gain an excellent reputation in service for its reliability, economy of operation and low noise emissions.

The L-1011 TriStar was the last Lockheed airliner to be developed and was launched in March 1968 in response to an American Airlines requirement (that also resulted in the DC-10) for a large capacity medium range airliner. Lockheed initially studied a twin engined layout, but it was decided that three engines would be necessary to ensure it could takeoff at max weights from existing runways.

Work on the L-1011 prototype began early in 1969, resulting in a November 16 1970 first flight. The engine choice of Rolls-Royce's advanced three shaft design RB211 however dogged the TriStar's early career. Rolls-Royce went bankrupt in February 1970 largely due to higher than estimated RB211 development costs, severely harming both Lockheed and the TriStar sales program. The problems were able to be resolved after the British government nationalised Rolls-Royce, guaranteeing the supply of production engines. Despite the initial problems the RB211 proved to be extremely reliable and efficient in service and grew into a family of variants.

The first L-1011 model that entered service with Eastern and TWA in April 1972 was the initial domestic L-1011-1 (which was built in greater numbers than any other TriStar variant). Subsequent models to be developed were the -100 with more fuel and higher weights, the -200 with higher thrust engines, and the long range -500, described separately. The -250 was a conversion of the -1 with RB211-524B4 engines (as on the -500) for US carrier Delta.

A small number have been converted to freighters.

Photo: An L-1011-1 gets airborne.

Lockheed L-1011-500 TriStar

Country of origin: United States of America

Type: Long range widebody airliner

Powerplants: Three 222.4kN (50,000lb) Rolls-Royce RB211-524B or -525B4 turbofans.

Performance: Max cruising speed 960km/h (518kt), economical cruising speed 894km/h (483kt). Range with max pax payload 9905km (5345nm), range with max fuel 11,260km (6100nm).

Weights: Operating empty 111,310kg (245,500lb), max takeoff 231,330kg (510,000lb).

Dimensions: Wing span 50.09m (164ft 4in), length 50.05m (164ft 3in), height 16.87m (55ft 4in). Wing area 329.0m^2 (3540.0sq ft).

Capacity: Flightcrew of three. Max seating for 330 in a single class 10 abreast layout at 76cm (30in) pitch. Typical two class seating for 24 premium class at six abreast and 222 economy at nine abreast. Underfloor cargo holds can accommodate 19 standard LD3 containers.

Production: 50 L-1011-500s built when production ceased in 1983, of which 28 were in commercial service in late 2000. 3 used as corporate transports.

History: Lockheed developed the shortened fuselage L-1011-500 as a long range, smaller capacity TriStar based on the L-1011-200 series.

Launched in August 1976, the key changes incorporated in the -500 over the standard L-1011s are the 4.11m (13ft 6in) shorter fuselage, greater takeoff weights and more powerful RB211-524 engines. The shortened fuselage reduces seating capacity to a maximum of 330, 70 less than the standard length TriStars, while the below deck galleys that had been a feature of the L-1011 family were replaced with conventional main deck units.

Other improvements include enhanced wing-to-fuselage and fuselage-to-rear engine intake fairings, automatic braking and automatic thrust control. Most have three, rather than four, doors/emergency exits on each side of the fuselage. The design changes combine to give the -500 a maximum range of 11,260km (6100nm), approximately 2000km (1300nm) further than the long range -200.

The L-1011-500 first flew on October 16 1978 and entered service with British Airways in May 1979.

Soon after the -500 also introduced the active aileron improvements first pioneered on the Advanced TriStar, which was the original prototype TriStar fitted with a number of advanced features intended for introduction to the TriStar production line. The Advanced TriStar incorporated increased span wings to reduce drag, with active, automatic operation of the ailerons used to cope with the increased weight and aerodynamic loads instead of strengthening the wing structure.

The first -500 with active ailerons and extended wingtips flew in November 1979 and deliveries of -500s with the new wing tip extension began the following year, while in 1981 it became a standard feature. Lockheed began retrofitting the active aileron wingtip extension to all previously built L-1011-500s from 1981. Production ceased in 1983 after 50 had been built, although the last 500 was not delivered until 1985.

Nine ex PanAm and British Airways -500s are operated by Britain's Royal Air Force as long range tanker-transports.

Photo: An AirTransat L-1011-500. (Gary Gentle)

Luscombe Model 8 Silvaire

Country of origin: United States of America

Type: Two seat light aircraft

Powerplant: 8A – One 50kW (65hp) Continental A-65 flat four piston engine driving a two blade fixed pitch propeller. 8F Special – One 65kW (90hp) Continental C-90 flat four.

Performance: 8A – Max speed 185km/h (100kt), cruising speed at 75% power 165km/h (90kt). Initial rate of climb 900ft/min. Range 595km (320nm). 8F – Max speed 206km/h (111kt), max cruising speed 193km/h (104kt). Initial rate of climb 900ft/min. Range 804km (435nm).

Weights: 8A – Empty 302kg (665lb), max takeoff 545kg (1200lb). 8F Special – Empty 395kg (870lb), max takeoff 635kg (1400lb).

Dimensions: 8A & 8F Special – Wing span 10.68m (35ft 0in), length 6.10m (20ft 0in), height 1.78m (5ft 10in). Wing area 13.0m² (140.0sq ft).

Capacity: Seating for two side by side.

Production: Over 7500 Model 8s built between 1938 and 1960.

History: The Luscombe 8 Silvaire was a highly successful two seat high wing light aircraft which remains popular as a classic aircraft.

Prior to introducing the Silvaire into production in 1937, Luscombe had built a small number of two seat high wing light aircraft, the most popular of which was the Phantom, which was powered by a 108kW (145hp) Warner Super Scarab radial engine. The initial Model 8A Silvaire was similar to the Phantom in configuration but differed in that it was powered by a 50kW (65hp) Continental A-65 engine. A more up-market model was also built from 1939, featuring a higher level of standard equipment and improved cabin trim. The 8B was similar to the 8A other than it was powered by a 50kW (60hp) Lycoming.

In 1941 Luscombe released the 8C which featured a 55kW (75hp) Continental engine, and the 8D, which differed in having wingtip fuel tanks. Over 1200 Model 8s were built through to early 1942 when production ceased due to the United States' entry into WW2.

After the war in late 1945 Luscombe resumed Silvaire production to meet the booming demand experienced by all US light aircraft manufacturers as returned military pilots wanted to continue flying in civilian life. From 1946 all Luscombes featured a new metal wing with a single strut. The first Silvaire to feature the new wing was the 8E, which was powered by a 65kW (85hp) Continental C-85-12 engine.

The final Silvaire production model was the 8F, which featured a 65kW (90hp) Continental C-90. The 8A Sky Pal meanwhile was a lower powered variant of the 8F with a Continental C-65.

Financial difficulties forced Luscombe to cease trading in 1949. US company Temco took over production and built a small number before it too ceased production in 1950. Finally, some Silvaires were built in Colorado between 1955 and 1960.

In 1998 Renaissance Aircraft revealed plans to reintroduce the 8F to production. Georgia based Renaissance's 8F features a 110kW (150hp) Textron Lycoming O-320 driving a metal propeller, dramatically improving performance, giving an estimated top speed of 243km/h (131kt) and a max rate of climb of 1500ft/min. A Luscombe built 8F was refurbished to serve as the prototype in 1999, production was due to get underway in 2000. Base price is projected to be $US71,200. Options include wheel spats, leather interior and IFR avionics.

Photo: A Silvaire at Hillsboro Airport, Oregon. (Keith Myers)

Luscombe Spartan

Country of origin: United States of America

Type: Four seat light aircraft

Powerplants: 185 – One 138kW (185hp) Teledyne Continental IO-360-ES4 flat six piston engine driving a two blade fixed pitch propeller. 210 – One 156kW (210hp) IO-360-ES driving a two blade constant speed propeller.

Performance: 185 – Normal cruising speed 209km/h (113kt). Initial rate of climb 950ft/min. Service ceiling 18,000ft. Range 852km (460nm). 210 – Normal cruising speed 225km/h (122kt). Initial rate of climb 1050ft/min. Range 1448km (782nm).

Weights: 185 – Empty 612kg (1350lb), max takeoff 1035kg (2280lb). 210 – Empty 658kg (1450lb), max takeoff 1035kg (2280lb).

Dimensions: Wing span 11.73m (38ft 6in), length 7.24m (23ft 9in), height 2.69m (8ft 10in). Wing area 15.5m² (167.0sq ft).

Capacity: Standard seating for four.

Production: Approximately 300 ordered by late 1998. Altus factory could build up to 500 Spartans a year. 185 VFR base price at late 1998 $US138,500.

History: The Spartan is a modern tricycle reincarnation of the late 1940s Luscombe 11A Sedan.

The four seat taildragger Sedan was based on the popular Silvaire (over 6000 built) and first flew on September 11 1946. Production ceased in 1949 by when 198 had been built. In the mid 1950s aeronautical engineer Alfred Ney purchased a damaged 11A and through until 1988 developed a number of changes for the aircraft which aided eventual development of the 11E. Ney's improvements included tricycle undercarriage, improvements to the handling characteristics and a more spacious cabin.

In 1992 Land Air Sales and Leasing Corporation purchased the 11's type certificate and then transferred it to the newly established Luscombe Aircraft Corporation which has set about re-engineering the 11 for its return to production as the 185-11E Spartan. Further changes included a redesigned wing which will be easier to manufacture, and a lower empty weight.

Las Vegas based Luscombe Aircraft Corporation converted a Sedan (N1674B) to act as a proof of concept aircraft while the first new build 185-11E prototype first flew on June 19 1998. Certification for the basic aircraft, still pending at late 2000, would allow first deliveries (from the new 11,150m²/120,000sq ft factory at Altus, Oklahoma) to follow soon after.

The Spartan's most important changes compared with the Sedan are tricycle undercarriage and a six cylinder Teledyne Continental IO-360 (derated from 157kW/210hp to 138kW/185hp). Other changes include a revised cowl shape for the new engine, a reprofiled windscreen, two overhead windows, modern avionics, soundproofing, inertia reel shoulder harnesses and dual vacuum pumps. Two optional avionics packages are offered.

A family of Spartan models is envisaged, including a 185 with a constant speed propeller, the higher performance 157kW (210hp) IO-360 powered Spartan 210 and a turbocharged 210 variant.

Photo: The first prototype Spartan 185-11E which first flew on June 19 1998. (Luscombe)

Maule M-4 to M-7

Country of origin: United States of America

Type: 4-5 seat STOL light aircraft

Powerplant: M-4C – One 108kW (145hp) Continental O-300-A flat six piston engine driving a two blade fixed pitch propeller. MX-7-235 – One 175kW (235hp) Textron Lycoming O-540-J1A5D flat six or fuel injected IO-540-W1A5D driving a two or three blade prop.

Performance: M-4C – Max speed 245km/h (132kt), max cruising speed 233km/h (125kt). Initial rate of climb 700ft/min. Service ceiling 12,000ft. Max range with no reserves 1130km (610nm). MX-7-235 (with IO-540) – Max speed 273km/h (147kt), max cruising speed 257km/h (140kt). Initial rate of climb 2000ft/min. Service ceiling 20,000ft. Range with standard fuel 790km (425nm), range with auxiliary fuel 1496km (807nm).

Weights: M-4C – Empty 500kg (1100lb), max takeoff 953kg (2100lb). MX-7-235 – Empty 669kg (1475lb), max takeoff 1247kg (2750lb).

Dimensions: M-4C – Wing span 9.04m (29ft 8in), length 6.71m (22ft 0in), height 1.89m (6ft 3in). Wing area 14.2m² (152.5sq ft). MX-7-235 – Wing span 9.40m (30ft 10in), length 7.16m (23ft 6in), height 1.93m (6ft 4in). Wing area 15.4m² (165.6sq ft).

Capacity: Standard seating for four, M-7-235 has seats for five.

Production: More than 2000 of all variants produced.

History: The origins of this rugged series of STOL light aircraft lie in the Bee Dee M-4 (named after its designer Belford D Maule).

Although the M-4, which first flew on September 8 1960, was planned to be a kitbuilt aircraft, it was placed into series production and a prolific series of variants and sub variants followed.

The first of the line was the M-4 series, which was in production between 1962 and 1973. The initial M-4, or later M-4C Jetasen, was quite basic, featuring a 108kW (145hp) O-300 and fixed pitch prop. Other M-4 variants were the 155kW (210hp) Continental IO-360 powered M-4-210C Rocket and the 118kW (220hp) Franklin 6A-350 powered M-4-220C Strata-Rocket.

The M-5 series went into production in 1973 and featured a large swept back vertical tail surface, four cabin doors, optional extra fuel and the cambered wingtips first introduced on later series M-4s. Variants included the Franklin powered M-5-220C and Lycoming O-540 powered M-5-225C Lunar Rockets; the Continental powered M-5-210C and M-5-180C (with a four cylinder O-360); and the turbocharged Lycoming TIO-360 powered M-5-210TC.

The M-6 was only built in small numbers but introduced changes such as greater wing span and fuel tankage.

Maule Aircraft Production ceased in 1975, while Maule Air Inc was formed in 1984 to build the M-5 and improved M-7.

The M-7, which introduced a stretched cabin and increased fuel capacity, forms the basis of a prolific family of subvariants. Current production M-7s are built with four powerplant options: the 120kW (160hp) O-320 powered MX-7-160 and tricycle undercarriage MXT-7-160 family; the 175kW (235hp) M-7-235 and MT-7-235 series; the 194kW (260hp) O-540/IO-540 powered M-7-260 and MT-7-260 range; and 313W (420shp) Rolls-Royce 250-B17C turboprop powered MMT--7-420. Numerous subvariants with equipment changes are offered.

Photo: An M-5-180C. (Bob Grimstead)

McDonnell Douglas DC-9-10, -20 & -30

Country of origin: United States of America

Type: Short range airliners

Powerplants: -10 – Two 54.5kN (12,250lb) Pratt & Whitney JT8D-5 turbofans. -30 – Two 64.5kN (14,500lb) JT8D-9s, or two 66.7kN (15,000lb) JT8D-11s, or two 71.2kN (16,000lb) JT8D-17s.

Performance: -10 – Max cruising speed 903km/h (488kt), economical cruising speed 885km/h (478kt). Range with max payload 1055km (570nm). -30 – Max cruising speed 907km/h (490kt), long range cruise 798km/h (430kt). Range at high speed cruise with 64 passengers and reserves 2150km (1160nm), range at long range cruise with 80 passengers and reserves 3095km (1670nm).

Weights: -10 – Operating empty 22,635kg (49,900lb), max takeoff 41,140kg (90,700lb). -30 – Empty 25,940kg (57,190lb), max takeoff 54,885kg (121,000lb).

Dimensions: -10 – Wing span 27.25m (89ft 5in), length 31.82m (104ft 5in), height 8.38m (27ft 6in). Wing area 86.8m² (934sq ft). -30 – Same except for length 36.37m (119ft 4in), wing span 28.47m (93ft 5in). Wing area 93.0m² (1000.7sq ft).

Capacity: Flightcrew of two. -10 – Seating for 80 in a single class at five abreast and 86cm (34in) pitch. Max seating for 90. -30 – Max seating for 115 in a single class, five abreast and 81cm (32in) pitch, standard single class seating for 105. DC-9-30CF can carry over eight cargo pallets.

Production: 976 DC-9s of all models built including 137 -10s, 10 -20s and 662 -30s (including military C-9s). 75 DC-9-10s, 5 DC-9-20s and 451DC-9-30s in airline service at late 2000. 1 DC-9-10, 8 DC-9-15s and 3 DC-9-30s used as corporate jets at late 2000.

History: No other airliner in history has undergone more development than the prolific DC-9/MD-80/MD-90/717 series, which started life with the 70 seat DC-9-10 of the early sixties.

Douglas developed the DC-9 as a short range airliner complementing the much larger DC-8. Development was launched on April 8 1963, with a launch order from Delta following soon after. The DC-9 was an all new design, featuring rear fuselage mounted engines, a T-tail, moderately swept wings and seats for up to 90 passengers.

Construction of the prototype began in July 1963 with first flight on February 25 1965. Certification and service entry was on November 23 and December 8 1965, respectively.

From the outset the DC-9 had been designed with stretched larger capacity developments in mind. The first stretch resulted in the biggest selling DC-9, the 4.54m (14ft 11in) longer, 105 seat DC-9-30, which entered service with Eastern on February 1 1967. Subsequent stretched versions are described separately.

Small numbers of developed versions of the DC-9-10 were also built. The DC-9-20 featured the DC-9-10's fuselage with the -30's more powerful engines and longer span wings, giving better hot and high performance. The DC-9-15 was basically a -10 but with more fuel and higher weights. Factory built convertibles and pure freighters were also offered, while a number of DC-9-30s have been converted to freighters, and/or are having Stage 3 hushkits fitted, further extending their useful service lives.

Photo: An Austral Air DC-9-30. (Rob Finlayson)

McDonnell Douglas DC-9-40 & -50

McDonnell Douglas MD-80

Country of origin: United States of America

Type: Short to medium range airliners

Powerplants: -40 – Two 64.5kN (14,500lb) Pratt & Whitney JT8D-9 turbofans, or two 69.0kN (15,500lb) JT9D-15s, or two 71.2kN (16,000lb) JT8D-17s. -50 – Two 69.0kN (15,500lb) JT8D-15s, or two 71.2kN (16,000lb) JT8D-17s.

Performance: -40 – Max cruising speed 898km/h (485kt), long range cruising speed 820km/h (443kt). Range at high speed cruise with 70 passengers and reserves 1725km (930nm), range with 87 passengers and reserves at long range cruising speed 2880km (1555nm). -50 – Speeds same except for max speed 926km/h (500kt). Range at long range cruising speed with 97 passengers and reserves 3325km (1795nm).

Weights: -40 – Empty 26,612kg (58,670lb), max takeoff 54,885kg (121,000lb). -50 – Empty 28,068kg (61,880lb), max takeoff 54,885kg (121,000lb).

Dimensions: -40 – Wing span 28.47m (93ft 5in), length 38.28m (125ft 7in), height 8.53m (28ft 0in). Wing area 93.0 m² (1000.7sq ft). -50 – Same except for length 40.72m (133ft 7in).

Capacity: Flightcrew of two. -40 – Seating for up to 125 passengers at five abreast. -50 – Seating up to 139 passengers at five abreast and 79cm (31in) pitch.

Production: Total DC-9 production of 976, including 71 Series 40s and 96 Series 50s. Approximately 66 -40s and 85 -50s remained in service in late 2000.

History: The DC-9-40 and DC-9-50 are stretched developments of the DC-9-30 and predecessors to the later further lengthened MD-80 and MD-90 series.

The DC-9-40 was developed in response to a Scandinavian Airline System (SAS) requirement for a larger capacity development of the DC-9. Compared with the DC-9-30, the DC-9-40 is 1.91m (6ft 4in) longer, raising seating capacity in a single class configuration to 125. Apart from the fuselage stretch and more powerful engine options, the -40 was much the same as the -30. First flight occurred on November 28 1967, and the -40 entered service with SAS on March 12 the following year.

The DC-9-50 is the largest member of the DC-9/MD-80/MD-90/717 family to bear the DC-9 designation. Launched in mid 1973 and delivered from August 1975, the DC-9-50 is a further 2.44m (8ft 0in) longer than the DC-9-40, or 4.34m (14ft 3in) longer than the DC-9-30, and has maximum seating for 139 passengers. The DC-9-50 introduced a new look cabin interior designed to make more efficient use of the space available and give the impression of a more spacious widebody interior, plus other improved features such as an improved anti skid braking system and quieter engines compared with the DC-9-40.

The DC-9-40 and -50 sold only in fairly modest numbers before the arrival of the further stretched MD-80 series. The largest DC-9-40 customer was SAS, while Northwest continues to operate a large fleet of DC-9-40s and -50s (it is currently the largest DC-9 operator in the world).

Photo: A Northwest DC-9-40 on pushback from a bleak Toronto. (Gary Gentle)

Country of origin: United States of America

Type: Short to medium range airliner

Powerplants: MD-81 – Two 82.3kN (18,500lb) Pratt & Whitney JT8D-209 turbofans. MD-88 – Two 93.4kN (21,000lb) JT8D-219s.

Performance: MD-81 – Max speed 925km/h (500kt), long range cruising speed 813km/h (440kt). Range with 155 passengers and reserves 2897km (1564nm). MD-88 – Speeds same. Range with 155 passengers and reserves 4850km (2620nm).

Weights: MD-81 – Operating empty 35,329kg (77,888lb), max takeoff 63,505kg (140,000lb), or 67,810kg (149,500lb) with JT8D-217As. MD-88 – Operating empty 35,369kg (77,976lb), max takeoff 67,810kg (149,500lb).

Dimensions: Wing span 32.87m (107ft 10in), length 45.06m (147ft 10in), height 9.02m (29ft 7in). Wing area 112.3m² (1209sq ft).

Capacity: Two Flightcrew. Max seating for 172. Typical two class seating for 142 (14 premium and 128 economy class).

Production: MD-80 series (inc MD-87) orders totalled 1191 aircraft, of which over 1165 were in service in 2000.

History: The popular MD-80 series was a stretched and improved development of the McDonnell Douglas DC-9.

The origins of the MD-80 lie in 1975 testing where a standard DC-9 was fitted with improved, more efficient, higher bypass ratio JT8D-200 series turbofans. MDC originally proposed fitting the new engines (which meet Stage 3 noise limits) to a development designated the DC-9-55, which would have featured two JT8D-209s and a 3.86m (12ft 8in) stretched fuselage over the -50.

Instead MDC developed the DC-9 Super 80 (or DC-9-80), combining the new engines with a further stretched fuselage, increased span wing and other improvements. Launched in October 1977, the Super 80 first flew on October 18 1979. Certification for the initial Super 80 model, the 81, was granted on August 16 1980. The first customer delivery was to Swissair in September 1980.

McDonnell Douglas renamed the DC-9-80 the MD-80 in 1983. The generic MD-80 designation applies to the series with separate designations for different model types. The specific MD-80 models are the initial MD-81, the MD-82 with more powerful JT8D-217s, the extended range MD-83 with extra fuel and more efficient JT8D-219s, and the MD-88 (first flight August 1987) with the JT8D-219s, weights and fuel capacity of the MD-82 with an EFIS flightdeck and redesigned cabin interior, plus other improvements. The shorter fuselage but longer range MD-87 is described separately.

Early sales of the Super 80 were slow until American Airlines placed an initial order for 67 MD-82s (with options on 100) in early 1984 (American operates over 260 MD-80s), kickstarting what went on to become a highly successful program – the 1000th MD-80 was delivered in March 1992.

Following the 1997 merger of Boeing and McDonnell Douglas the future of the MD airliners was reviewed. In December 1997 Boeing announced its decision to drop the MD-80 and MD-90 once current orders were fulfilled. The 1191st and last MD-80, an MD-83 named *Spirit of Long Beach,* was delivered to TWA on December 21 1999.

Photo: An MD-81 of Argentine airline Dinar. (Rob Finlayson)

McDonnell Douglas MD-87

Country of origin: United States of America

Type: Short to medium range airliner

Powerplants: Two 89.0kN (20,000lb) Pratt & Whitney JT8D-217C turbofans. Other JT8D-200 series engines were available optionally.

Performance: Max speed 925km/h (500kt), long range cruising speed 811km/h (438kt). Range with 130 passengers and reserves 4393km (2372nm), or optionally 5248km (2833nm). Range with max fuel 5522km (2980nm), or optionally 6764km (3650nm).

Weights: Operating empty with standard fuel 33,237kg (73,274lb), operating empty with optional fuel 33,965kg (74,880lb), max takeoff 63,505kg (140,000lb), optionally 67,810kg (149,500lb).

Dimensions: Wing span 32.86m (107ft 10in), length 39.75m (130ft 5in), height 9.30m (30ft 6in). Wing area 112.3m² (1209.0sq ft).

Capacity; Flightcrew of two. Max seating for 139 passengers at five abreast at 81cm (32in) pitch. Two class seating for 117.

Production: Of total MD-80 sales of over 1100, 75 were for MD-87s. 70 were in commercial service in 2000, 4 were in use as corporate transports.

History: The MD-87 is a shortened version of the successful MD-80 series, with typical seating for 117.

A reversal of the trend from the DC-9 to the MD-80 series, the MD-87 combines the advanced features introduced on the MD-80 (most notably the more fuel efficient, quieter Pratt & Whitney JT8D-200 engines) with a 5.3m (17ft 5in) shorter length fuselage which is similar in length to the DC-9-30.

The MD-87 features a 39.75m (130ft 5in) fuselage length; plus an EFIS flightdeck (the MD-87 was the first aircraft of the MD-80 series to introduce EFIS, with two dual flight management systems and glass displays) and an optional Sundstrand Head-Up Display; Pratt & Whitney JT8D-217C turbofans (which are approximately 2% more efficient than the -217A); the cruise performance package improvements introduced on late production MD-80s, including the extended low drag tail cone, fillet fairing between the engine pylons and the fuselage and low drag flap hinge fairings; and increased height fin to compensate for the shorter fuselage.

The MD-87 was optionally available with extra front and rear cargo compartment auxiliary fuel tanks to extend range, and other engines in the JT8D-200 series. In other respects the MD-87 is similar to the rest of the MD-80 series.

McDonnell Douglas launched development of the MD-87 on January 3 1985, following the placement of launch orders from Finnair and Austrian in December 1984. First flight took place on December 4 1986 and US FAA certification was granted on October 21 1987.

MD-87 sales were relatively small and mainly to traditional Douglas customers. Notable operators include Iberia (with 24), SAS (18) and Japan Air System (eight). Smaller operators include Finnair, Aero Lloyd, Aeromexico, Great American, Austrian and American (which inherited its from Reno Air).

By the time Boeing and McDonnell Douglas merged in August 1997 all MD-87 orders had been fulfilled and Boeing ceased marketing the type.

Photo: Iberia is the largest MD-87 operator. (Keith Gaskell)

McDonnell Douglas MD-90

Country of origin: United States of America

Type: Short to medium range narrowbody airliner

Powerplants: MD-90-30 – Two 111.2kN (25,000lb) International Aero Engines V2525-D5 turbofans.

Performance: MD-90-30 – Typical cruising speed 809km/h (437kt). Range with 153 passengers 3862km (2085nm), or 4023km (2172nm) for standard -30ER, or 4425km (2389nm) for long range -30ER.

Weights: MD-90-30 – Operating empty 39,915kg (88,000lb) max takeoff 70,760kg (156,000lb).

Dimensions: Wing span 32.87m (107ft 10in), length 46.51m (152ft 7in), height 9.33m (30ft 7in). Wing area 112.3m² (1209.0sq ft).

Capacity: Flightcrew of two. Two class seating for 12 premium class and 141 economy class passengers in MD-90-30, or max single class seating for 172.

Production: Total MDC/Boeing MD-90 production of 114, completed in 2000. Two MD-90-30Ts are being completed in China under the Trunkliner program.

History: The MD-90, a stretched, IAE V2500 powered development of the MD-80, is the largest member of the Douglas/McDonnell Douglas/Boeing DC-9/MD-80/MD-90/717 family.

McDonnell Douglas launched the MD-90 program in November 1988, first flight occurred on February 22 1993, and certification was awarded on November 16 1994. Launch customer Delta took delivery of the first of 31 MD-90s it ordered on February 25 1995 (Delta is now replacing them with 737-800s).

The MD-90's most significant change over the MD-80 is its two V2500 turbofans. Interestingly, at 111kN (25,000lb) thrust, the MD-90's V2500s are the largest, heaviest and most powerful engines to be rear mounted on any airliner.

Other changes over the MD-80 include the 1.37m (4ft 6in) fuselage stretch forward of the wing, allowing seating for an extra 10 passengers (in a two class arrangement). The stretch is forward of the wing to compensate for the extra weight of the engines. The MD-90 also features an EFIS glass flightdeck based on that in the MD-88, and other detail improvements such as a revised passenger interior.

The basic MD-90 model is the MD-90-30 while the extended range MD-90-30ER has an increased max takeoff weight and optional auxiliary fuel tank (just two were built, for Egypt's AMC Aviation). The MD-90-50 was offered but not ordered. It was a further extended range version with a higher maximum takeoff weight and extra fuel. The MD-90-50 based MD-90-55 high capacity variant would have been capable of seating 187 passengers in a single class with two extra doors in the forward fuselage to meet emergency evacuation requirements.

Under a 1992 agreement SAIC in China was to build 20 MD-90-30T Trunkliners (with double bogey main landing gear) under licence. However China abandoned the Trunkliner program in mid 1998 and just two MD-90-30Ts were expected to be completed.

Following the 1997 merger of Boeing and McDonnell Douglas, Boeing decided to cancel MD-90 production once outstanding orders were fulfilled. The last of 114 US built MD-90s was completed in 2000.

Photo: A Delta MD-90 (in the carrier's old colours) at Washington National Airport. (Mike McHugh)

McDonnell Douglas DC-10 & Boeing MD-10

Country of origin: United States of America

Type: Medium to long range widebody airliner

Powerplants: DC-10-10 – Three 178kN (40,000lb) General Electric CF6-6D turbofans, or 182.4kN (41,000lb) CF6-6D1s. DC-10-30 – Three 218kN (49,000lb) CF6-50As, 226.9kN (51,000lb) CF6-50Cs, or 233.5kN (52,500lb) CF6-50C1s or C2s, or 240.2kN (54,000lb) CF6-50C2Bs. DC-10-40 – Three 219.6kN (49,400lb) Pratt & Whitney JT9D-20s, or 235.8kN (53,000lb) JT9D-59As.

Performance: DC-10-30 – Max speed 982km/h (530kt), max cruising speed 908km/h (490kt). Range with max fuel and no payload 12,055km (6505nm), range with max payload 7415km (4000nm). DC-10-40 – Range with max fuel and no payload 11,685km (6305nm), range with max payload (& JT9D-59As) 7505km (4050nm).

Weights: DC-10-30 – Empty 121,198kg (267,197lb), max takeoff 263,085kg (580,000lb). DC-10-40 – Empty 122,951kg (271,062lb), max takeoff 259,450kg (572,000lb).

Dimensions: Wing span 50.40m (165ft 5in), length 55.50m (182ft 1in), height 17.70m (58ft 1in). Wing area 367.7m² (3958.0sq ft).

Capacity: Flightcrew of three. Max seating for 380 passengers at nine abreast and 81cm (32in) pitch. Mixed class seating arrangements vary between 250 and 270. DC-10-30F – 23 pallets on main deck.

Production: 386 civil DC-10s built with 318 in airline service in late 2000. FedEx has ordered 89 MD-10 conversions.

History: Designed in response to the same American Airlines requirement as the Lockheed TriStar, the DC-10, despite a sometimes troubled past, was the more successful of the two widebody trijets.

Originally conceived as a twinjet, the DC-10 gained a third engine at the base of its vertical tail to meet an American Airlines requirement that the aircraft be capable of operating from existing runways. The DC-10 subsequently was launched in February 1968 with orders from American and United. First flight took place on August 29 1970.

The first transcontinental range DC-10-10s entered service with American in August 1971. By then work was already underway on the intercontinental range DC-10-30 which introduced more powerful engines, additional fuel tanks and a third main undercarriage unit.

Most DC-10s built were -30s (including convertible -30CFs and pure freight -30Fs), while the -40 is a Pratt & Whitney JT9D powered variant ordered by Northwest and JAL. The United States Air Force ordered 60 CF6 powered DC-10s as KC-10 Extender tanker transports.

A number of major and catastrophic accidents marred the DC-10's service record in the mid to late 1970s, but the various causes of these accidents were overcome and the DC-10 went on to operate successfully and reliably. Production ceased in 1989.

The Boeing MD-10 conversion initiated for FedEx involves fitting DC-10s (both existing freighters and new freighter conversions) with a two crew Honeywell VIA 2000 EFIS flightdeck with six LCD screens. The instrument panel layout is identical to that in the MD-11, and pilots can be qualified to fly the two interchangeably. First flight was on April 4 1999, while the first of 89 MD-10 conversions for FedEx was delivered on May 9 2000 (the same day the conversion was certificated). Boeing is offering the MD-10 conversion to other DC-10 operators.

Photo: A JALways DC-10-40. (John Adlard)

MD Helicopters/Hughes 500

Country of origin: United States of America

Type: Light utility helicopters

Powerplant: 500C – One 207kW (278shp) Allison 250-C20 turboshaft driving a four blade main rotor and two blade tail rotor. MD 530F – One 280kW (375shp) max continuous rated Rolls-Royce 250-C30 driving a five blade main rotor and two or optionally four blade tail rotor.

Performance: 500C – Max cruising speed 232km/h (125kt), long range cruising speed 217km/h (117kt). Initial rate of climb 1700ft/min. Hovering ceiling in ground effect 13,000ft. Range 605km (325nm). MD 530F – Max cruising speed 249km/h (135kt), economical cruising speed 228km/h (123kt). Initial rate of climb 2070ft/min. Service ceiling 18,700ft. Range with standard fuel and no reserves 429km (232nm).

Weights: 500C – Empty 493kg (1088lb), max takeoff 1157kg (2550lb). MD 530F – Empty 722kg (1591lb), max takeoff 1406kg (3100lb), max overload takeoff 1610kg (3550lb), max takeoff with sling load 1700kg (3750lb).

Dimensions: 500C – Main rotor diameter 8.03m (26ft 4in), fuselage length 7.01m (23ft 0in), height 2.48m (8ft 2in). MD 530F – Main rotor diameter 8.33m (27ft 4in), length overall rotors turning 9.94m (32ft 7in), fuselage length 7.49m (24ft 7in), height to top of rotor head (std skids) 2.67m (8ft 9in). Main rotor disc area 54.6m² (587.5sq ft).

Capacity: Typical seating for five. Alternatively can accommodate two stretchers and medical attendant, plus pilot.

Production: Approximately 4850 Hughes 500s and MD 500s have been built, including large numbers for military customers.

History: One of the world's most successful and useful light turbine helicopters, the Hughes 500/MD 500 series was originally developed in response to a US Army requirement for a light observation helicopter.

Hughes won the US Army observation helicopter contest against competition from Bell and Hiller with its Allison 250 powered OH-6 Cayuse, which first flew in February 1963. By then Hughes was already working on a civil variant, to be marketed as the Hughes 500 (Hughes Model 369). It was offered in basic five and seven seat configurations, and the 500U, later 500C, utility version with a more powerful engine.

From 1976 deliveries were of the 500D, an improved version with a more powerful engine, a T-tail, and new five blade main and optional four blade tail rotors. The 500D was followed by the 500E from 1982 with recontoured nose and various interior improvements including greater head and leg room. The 530F (first delivery January 1984) is a more powerful version optimised for hot and high work.

McDonnell Douglas acquired Hughes Helicopters in January 1984, and from August 1985 the 500E and 530F were built as the MD 500E and MD 530F Lifter. Following the August 1997 Boeing/McDonnell Douglas merger Boeing put the line up for sale. Bell was an early suitor, but its plans were thwarted by the US Federal Trade Commission (FTC) in 1998. Then in January 1999 Boeing announced the sale of the light helicopter lines to MD Helicopters, a newly formed division of Netherlands based RDM Holdings. The sale was finalised in February 1999. In April 2000 MD Helicopters contracted Kaman to build the fuselages for the single engine MDs.

Military variants are marketed under the MD 500 Defender name.

Photo: A Kawasaki built Hughes 500C. (Theo van Loon)

MD Helicopters MD 520N

Country of origin: United States of America

Type: Light utility helicopter

Powerplant: One 280kW (375shp) Rolls-Royce 250-C20R turboshaft driving a five blade main rotor.

Performance: Max cruising speed at S/L 250km/h (135kt). Initial rate of climb 1850ft/min. Service ceiling 14,175ft. Hovering ceiling in ground effect 11,200, out of ground effect 6000ft. Range at S/L 424km (229nm). Endurance at S/L 2hr 24min.

Weights: Empty 742kg (1636lb), max takeoff 1520kg (3350lb), or 1745kg (3850lb) with an external sling load.

Dimensions: Rotor diameter 8.33m (27ft 4in), length overall rotor turning 9.78m (33ft 2in), fuselage length 7.77m (25ft 6in), height with standard skids 2.74m (9ft 0in), height with extended skids 3.01m (9ft 11in). Rotor disc area 54.5m² (586.8sq ft).

Capacity: Standard seating for five.

Production: Over 100 MD 520Ns ordered.

History: The MD 520N introduced a revolutionary advance in helicopter design as it dispensed with a conventional tail rotor in favour of the Hughes/McDonnell Douglas developed NOTAR (NO TAil Rotor) system.

Development of the revolutionary NOTAR system dates back to late 1975 when Hughes engineers began initial concept development work. In December 1981 Hughes flew an OH-6A fitted with NOTAR for the first time. A more heavily modified prototype demonstrator first flew in March 1986 (by which time McDonnell Douglas had acquired Hughes).

Although the concept, known as the Coanda effect, took some time to refine, the NOTAR system is simple in theory and works to provide directional control the same way a wing develops lift. Low pressure air is forced through two slots on the right side of the tailboom, causing the downwash from the main rotor to hug the tailboom, producing lift, and thus a measure of directional control. This is augmented by a direct jet thruster and vertical stabilisers.

The NOTAR system benefits include far lower external noise (the MD 520N is the quietest certificated helicopter in the world), increased safety due to the lack of a tail rotor, improved handling and performance, reduced vibration and easier maintainability.

In applying the NOTAR technology to production helicopters, McDonnell Douglas originally intended to develop the standard MD 520N alongside the more powerful hot and high optimised MD 530N (both were launched in January 1989 and were based on the conventional MD 500E). The MD 530N was the first to fly, on December 29 1989, the MD 520N first flew on May 1 1990. Development of the MD 530N was suspended when McDonnell Douglas decided that the MD 520N met most customer requirements for the 530N. Certification for the MD 520N was awarded on September 13 1991, and the first was delivered on December 31 that year.

Following the 1997 Boeing/McDonnell Douglas merger, Boeing sold the former MD civil helicopter lines to MD Helicopters in early 1999.

At the 2000 Farnborough Airshow MD Helicopters announced enhancements to the MD 520N including an improved RR 250-C20R+ engine with 3-5% more power for better performance on warm days, and, with changes to the diffuser and fan rigging, increased range.

Photo: An MD 520N.

MD Helicopters MD 600N

Country of origin: United States of America

Type: Eight place light utility helicopter

Powerplant: One 603kW (808shp) Rolls-Royce 250-C47 turboshaft, derated to 447kW (600shp) for takeoff and 395kW (530shp) for max continuous operation driving a six blade main rotor.

Performance: Max cruising speed to 5000ft 248km/h (134kt). Initial rate of climb 1350ft/min. Max operating altitude 20,000ft. Hovering ceiling in ground effect 11,100ft, out of ground effect 6000ft. Max range at 5000ft 707km (382nm) or 633km (342nm) at sea level.

Weights: Empty 952kg (2100lb), max takeoff with internal load 1860kg (4100lb), max takeoff with sling load 2131kg (4700lb).

Dimensions: Rotor diameter 8.38m (27ft 6in), length overall rotor turning 11.79m (35ft 5in), fuselage length 8.99m (29ft 6in), height to top of rotor head 2.65m (8ft 9in), or 2.74m (9ft 0in) with extended skids. Rotor disc area 55.2m² (594.0sq ft)

Capacity: Typical seating for eight.

Production: Deliveries began mid 1997. 45 ordered by US Border Patrol. Approx 50 in service at late 2000.

History: The MD 600N is a stretched eight seat development of the five seat MD 520N helicopter.

McDonnell Douglas Helicopter Systems (MD Helicopters since 1999) first announced it was developing a stretched MD 520N in late 1994, and surprised the world helicopter community the following year when it unveiled the first flying prototype of the new helicopter, at that time designated the MD 630N, at the Heli Expo in Las Vegas in January 1995. This prototype, a modified MD 530F, had made its first flight on November 22 1994. The MD 630N created high levels of interest at the Heli Expo and McDonnell Douglas gave the go-ahead for the production aircraft, redesignated the MD 600N, in March 1995.

The prototype was modified to MD 600N standard with a production standard engine and tail boom and flew in November 1995, followed the next month by the first MD 600N production prototype. Unfortunately this second prototype was destroyed by fire following a forced landing in May 1996, caused by the main rotor contacting the tail boom during extreme control reversal tests.

Thus the third prototype, which first flew on August 9 1996, featured modifications to increase the main rotor-tail boom clearance. Certification was awarded on May 15 1997 with deliveries beginning in June that year. Further performance improvements were certificated in mid 1998.

McDonnell Douglas stretched the MD 520N fuselage by inserting a plug aft of the cockpit/cabin bulkhead and stretching the NOTAR tail boom. The larger fuselage allows for an extra (middle) row of seats. Other differences compared with the MD 520N include a new six blade main rotor (the MD 520N has a five blade unit) and a more powerful Allison (now Rolls-Royce) 250 turboshaft.

Following the 1997 Boeing/McDonnell Douglas' merger, Boeing sold the former MD civil helicopter lines to Dutch owned MD Helicopters in early 1999.

MD Helicopters is developing a yaw stability augmentation system for the MD 600, to reduce pilot workload, to be available in 2001.

Photo: Australia's first MD 600N. (Lance Higgeron)

MD Helicopters MD Explorer

Country of origin: United States of America

Type: Light twin helicopter

Powerplants: Two 469kW (629shp) takeoff rated Pratt & Whitney Canada PW206E turboshafts driving a five blade main rotor.

Performance: Max cruising speed at S/L 248km/h (134kt). Initial rate of climb 2250ft/min. Service ceiling 18,000ft. Hovering ceiling in ground effect 10,400ft (ISA), out of ground effect 12,2000ft (ISA). Max range with standard fuel 543km (293nm). Max endurance 3.2hr.

Weights: Standard empty 1531kg (3375lb), max takeoff 2835kg (6250lb), or 3130kg (6900lb) with external sling load.

Dimensions: Rotor diameter 10.31m (33ft 10in), length overall 11.83m (38ft 10in), fuselage length 9.85m (32ft 4in), height 3.66m (12ft 0in). Main rotor disc area 83.5m² (899.0sq ft).

Capacity: One pilot and passenger on front bucket seats with six passengers in main cabin in club seating arrangement. Max seating for 10 (including pilot). Alternatively can be configured with stretchers and seating for medical attendants.

Production: Approximately 60 delivered by late 2000.

History: The MD Explorer light twin helicopter is the first all new design to incorporate the unique NOTAR (NO TAil Rotor) system.

McDonnell Douglas Helicopters launched the Explorer as the MDX in January 1989. First flight took place on December 18 1992. Full certification for the initial PW206B powered Explorer (unofficially designated MD 900) version was granted in December 1994.

One of the most advanced helicopters in its market segment, the MD Explorer features Boeing's unique NOTAR anti torque system (described in detail under the MD 520N entry), with benefits including increased safety, far lower noise levels and performance and controllability enhancements. (Boeing retains the design rights to the NOTAR technology despite selling the former McDonnell Douglas civil helicopter line to MD Helicopters in early 1999.)

The Explorer also features an advanced bearingless five blade main rotor with composite blades, plus carbonfibre construction tail and fuselage (designed and built in Australia, although production is being transferred to Turkey).

Initial Explorers were powered by two Pratt & Whitney Canada PW206Bs (the Explorer was the first application for the PW200 series), while plans to offer the Turbomeca Arrius as an option were dropped. In September 1997 a range of improvements were introduced, including PW206E turboshafts with higher single engine inoperative ratings, revised engine air inlets, improved NOTAR inlet design and a more powerful stabiliser control system. Benefits include improved range and endurance and an increased max takeoff weight. This enhanced explorer was unofficially designated the MD 902.

On August 31 1998 the Explorer became the first helicopter to be validated by Europe's JAA JAR Part 27 Category A guidelines, which requires helicopters be capable of safely continuing flight during takeoff or landing on a single engine.

From September 2000 the Explorer has been delivered with the further improved PW207E turboshaft, with improved hot and high and one engine inoperative performance.

Photo: Boeing's stewardship of the Explorer was shortlived.

Mil Mi-8, Mi-17 & Mi-171

Country of origin: Russia

Type: Medium lift utility helicopters

Powerplants: Mi-8T – Two 1250kW (1677shp) Klimov (Isotov) TV2-117AG turboshafts driving a five blade main rotor and three blade tail rotor. Mi-171 – Two 1545kW (2070shp) TV3-117VM.

Performance: Mi-8T – Max speed 250km/h (135kt), max cruising speed 225km/h (121kt). Service ceiling 14,765ft. Hovering ceiling in ground effect 5905ft, out of ground effect 2785ft. Range with standard fuel 570km (307nm), with auxiliary fuel 985km (531nm). Mi-171 – Max speed 250km/h (135kt), max cruising speed 230km/h (124kt). Service ceiling 18,700ft. Hovering ceiling out of ground effect 13,055ft. Range with standard fuel 570km (307nm), range with two auxiliary tanks 1065km (575nm).

Weights: Mi-8T – Empty 7149kg (15,760lb), max takeoff (for vertical takeoff) 12,000kg (26,455lb). Mi-171 – Empty equipped 7055kg (15,555lb), max takeoff 13,000kg (28,660lb).

Dimensions: Mi-8T – Main rotor diameter 21.29m (69ft 10in), length overall 25.24m (82ft 10in), fuselage length 18.17m (59ft 8in), height 5.54m (18ft 2in). Main rotor disc area 356.0m² (3932sq ft). Mi-171 – Same except for length overall 25.35m (83ft 2in), fuselage length 18.42m (60ft 6in).

Capacity: Flightcrew of two, with provision for flight engineer. Primarily used for freight transport, internal and/or with external sling loads. Can carry up to 32 passengers in Mi-8, or 24 in Mi-8T. Mi-8 Salon executive version seats 11 passengers. As air ambulance can accommodate 12 stretchers.

Production: Over 12,000 Mi-8s, Mi-17s and Mi-171s built, but majority for military service.

History: Built in greater numbers than any other Russian helicopter, the Mi-8/Mi-17/Mi-171 series (NATO codename 'Hip') was designed primarily as a military transport, but is also in widespread civil use.

The Mi-8 was designed as a replacement for the piston engined Mi-4, with design work beginning in May 1960. First flight of the prototype (powered by a single Soloviev turboshaft driving a four blade main rotor) occurred in June 1961, while a production standard Mi-8 flew in August 1962 and production began shortly afterwards. Versions of the Mi-8 built for civil use have square windows and include the Mi-8 passenger version, Mi-8T utility transport, Mi-8TM passenger transport with weather radar and Mi-8 Salon executive transport.

Production of the Mi-8 ceased in favour of the re-engined Mi-17, which was first publicly revealed to the west at the 1981 Paris Airshow. The Mi-17 introduced TV3 turboshafts and the tail rotor was relocated to the port side of the tailboom. Civil versions include the base Mi-17P (with square windows), and the Mi-171 and Mi-17M, which both feature more powerful TV3-117VM turboshafts, and are built by Ulan-Ude Aviation and Kazan Helicopters respectively.

The Kazan/Mil developed Mi-17KF is designed to meet western certification standards and features an EFIS instrument panel with colour displays, rounded 'dolphin' nose with space for radar, and a rear loading ramp in place of the clamshell doors. The latter two features are also incorporated on the Kazan/Mil Mi-17MD and Mi-17N.

Photo: A Kazan Mi-171. (Gary Flanagan)

Mil Mi-26

Country of origin: Russia

Type: Ultra heavy lift utility helicopter

Powerplants: Two 7457kW (10,000shp) ZMKB Progress (Lotarev) D-136 turboshafts driving an eight blade main rotor and five blade tail rotor.

Performance: Max speed 295km/h (160kt), typical cruising speed 255km/h (137kt). Service ceiling 15,100ft. Hovering ceiling in ground effect 14,765ft. Range with max internal fuel at max takeoff weight with reserves 800km (432nm), range with four auxiliary fuel tanks 1920km (1036nm).

Weights: Empty 28,200kg (62,170lb), normal takeoff 49,600kg (109,350lb), max takeoff 56,000kg (123,450lb).

Dimensions: Main rotor diameter 32.00m (105ft 0in), tail rotor diameter 7.61m (25ft 0in), length overall rotors turning 40.03m (131ft 4in), fuselage length 35.91m (117ft 10in), height to top of rotor head 8.15m (26ft 9in), height tail rotor turning 11.60m (38ft 1in). Main rotor disc area 804.3m² (8657sq ft), tail rotor disc area 45.5m² (489.5sq ft).

Capacity: Flightcrew of four comprising two pilots, flight engineer and navigator, plus loadmaster. Four seat passenger compartment behind flightdeck. Main cabin typically accommodates freight (max payload 20 tonnes/44,090lb), but can seat 63 passengers at four abreast. Firefighting version can carry 7500 litres (1650Imp gal/1980US gal) of fire retardant. Medical version comprehensively equipped with operating theatre and accommodation for stretcher patients and medical attendants.

Production: Approximately 70 built, mostly for military use.

History: Mil's Mi-26 is the largest helicopter in the world by a significant margin. It has a maximum takeoff weight greater than that of the Fokker 100, and more than twice that of the Boeing Chinook, and an internal freight hold similar in size to that in the L-100 Hercules.

Development of the Mi-26 began in the early 1970s and resulted in a first flight on December 14 1977. Although mainly in military use, the original design requirement stated that the helicopter would be for civil use, and that it should have a maximum takeoff weight one and a half times that of any previous helicopter. Preproduction machines were built from 1980, production machines sometime after that. The first Mi-26s became operational with the Soviet military during 1983.

The Mi-26 is notable for its eight blade main rotor, powerful 7457kW (10,000shp) D-136 turboshaft engines and massive size. Several civil versions have been developed or proposed. These include the basic freighter Mi-26T, Mi-26MS medevac version, Mi-26P airliner version with seating for 63 passengers at four abreast, Mi-26TM flying crane with fuselage side mounted gondola for a pilot/sling load supervisor to oversee sling load operations, Mi-26TM firefighter which can carry 15,000 litres internally or 17,260 litres in an underslung bucket (one was delivered to the Moscow fire brigade in 1999) and Mi-26TZ fuel tanker.

The improved Mi-26M remains under development and will feature new 10,700kW (14,350shp) class ZMKB Progress D-127 turboshafts, better hot and high performance, increased maximum payload, composite main rotor blades, improved aerodynamics and EFIS flightdeck.

Photo: An Mi-26T of Cyprus based Nutshell. (Paul Merritt)

Mooney M-20A to M-20F

Country of origin: United States of America

Type: Four seat high performance light aircraft

Powerplant: M-20C – One 135kW (180hp) Lycoming O-360-A1D flat four piston engine driving a two blade constant speed prop. M-20E – One 150kW (200hp) Lycoming IO-360-A1A fuel injected flat four.

Performance: M-20C – Max speed 288km/h (156kt), max cruising speed 272km/h (147kt), economical cruising speed 236km/h (127kt). Initial rate of climb 800ft/min. Service ceiling 17,200ft. Range with reserves 1464km (790nm). M-20E – Max speed 317km/h (171kt), max cruising speed 301km/h (163kt), economical cruising speed 270km/h (146kt). Initial rate of climb 1120ft/min. Service ceiling 19,500ft. Max range with no reserves 1648km (890nm).

Weights: M-20C – Empty 692kg (1525lb), max takeoff 1168kg (2575lb). M-20E – Empty 714kg (1575lb), max takeoff 1168kg (2575lb).

Dimensions: M-20C/E – Wing span 10.67m (35ft 0in), length 7.06m (23ft 2in), height 2.54m (8ft 4in). Wing area 15.5m² (167.0sq ft).

Capacity: Typical seating for four.

Production: Over 5000 early model M-20 series aircraft built from the mid 1950s to the mid 1970s.

History: Mooney's first design was the 1948 wooden single seat M-18 Mite, but work was soon underway on the much larger M-20 four seater with metal and wood construction and fabric covering.

This M-20 first flew on August 10 1953. Powered by a 105kW (145hp) six cylinder Continental O-300 flat six engine, the M-20 also had retractable undercarriage and introduced the distinctive forward swept tail. Mooney placed it into production soon after with a 110kW (150hp) Lycoming O-320, and a prolific series of developments followed.

These included the 700 plus M-20As with a 135kW (180hp) O-360, and the similarly powered M-20C Mark 21. Very successful with 400 built in its first year, the Mark 21 featured an all metal structure and higher takeoff weight. A lower spec fixed undercarriage version, the M-20D Master, was also offered. The subsequent M-20E Super 21 first flew in July 1963 and featured a more powerful fuel injected 150kW (200hp) IO-360 engine, combining the M-20E's clean aerodynamics and the more powerful engine to give a claimed top speed of 317km/h (171kt). From the mid 1960s all models gained a small fin fillet and a larger squared off rear cabin window.

The M-20F Executive 21 of 1965 was based on the M-20E Super 21 and had a 25cm (10in) fuselage stretch and an extra cabin window on each side, new cabin fittings and extra fuel. In 1967 the range was renamed, the M-20C becoming the Ranger, the M-20F continued as the Executive, the M-20E was discontinued for a time until reappearing as the Chaparral, and a new model, the M-20G Statesman (with the Executive's fuselage and a 135kW/180hp engine) appeared (although only 183 were built).

For a time from 1970 Mooney was known as the Aerostar Aircraft Corporation, and the Ranger became the Aerostar 200, the Chaparral the 201 and Executive the 220. However this company ceased production in early 1972, and it was not until 1973 that revised models were built under the Mooney banner (described separately).

Photo: A Mooney M-20E Super 21. (Les Bushell)

Mooney M-20J to M20S

Country of origin: United States of America

Type: High performance four seat light aircraft

Powerplant: Eagle – One 182kW (244hp) Teledyne Continental IO-550-G fuel injected flat six driving a two blade c/s prop. Bravo – One 200kW (270hp) Textron Lycoming TIO-540-AF1B turbocharged and fuel injected flat six piston engine driving a three blade c/s prop.

Performance: Eagle – Cruising speed 324km/h (175kt). Service ceiling 18,500ft. Range at economical cruising speed 2242km (1210nm). Bravo – Cruising speed at 25,000ft 407km/h (220kt). Initial rate of climb 1230ft/min. Service ceiling 25,000ft. Range with max fuel 1945km (1050nm).

Weights: Eagle – Basic empty 995kg (2194lb), max takeoff 1451kg (3200lb). Bravo – Empty 1029kg (2268lb), max takeoff 1527kg (3368lb).

Dimensions: Eagle/Bravo – Wing span 11.00m (36ft 1in), length 8.15m (26ft 9in), height 2.54m (8ft 4in). Wing area 16.3m² (175.0sq ft).

Capacity: Standard seating for four.

Production: Over 2300 of all models delivered since the mid 1970s.

History: Mooney's new owners, the Republic Steel Company, placed the M-20 line back into production in late 1973.

All three then current models, the Ranger, Chaparral and Executive, were returned to production, but new design efforts centred around the M-20F Executive design. The first model developed was the M-20J 201, with improvements aimed at reducing drag, giving a theoretical top speed of 323km/h (175kt), or 201mph. The 201 entered production in 1976, replacing the Executive, while the Ranger remained in production until 1979.

Models included the M-20K 231 from late 1978, powered by a turbocharged six cylinder Continental TSIO-360, and the 201LM (Lean Machine) from 1986 with only basic options. The 201 evolved into the M-20J 205 with rounded cabin windows and redesigned wingtips, slightly increasing top speed. A Special Edition 'SE' luxury options package was also offered. The M-20K 252TSE (Turbo Special Edition) was a development of the 231 with a top speed of 405km/h (220kt), or 252mph, and combined the 205's airframe mods with a 155kW (210hp) turbocharged, intercooled Continental TSIO-360. The Porsche PFM 3200 powered M-20L was built between 1987 and 1991.

The top of the line Bravo – formerly the M20M TLS (Turbo Lycoming Sabre) – was introduced in 1989. It features a slightly stretched fuselage, a turbocharged and intercooled Lycoming TIO-540 and three blade prop. The Bravo name was adopted in 1996.

The Allegro – formerly the M20J MSE 205 – development is powered by a 150kW (200hp) Textron Lycoming IO-360-A3B6D.

Introduced in 1994, the M20R Ovation was based on the Bravo fuselage but is powered by a 210kW (280hp) Continental IO-550G flat six. The Ovation2 was introduced in late 1999 and features a two blade prop which is more efficient than the three blade unit it replaced.

In 1997 Mooney introduced the short lived 370km/h (200kt) cruise M20K Encore which was powered by a turbocharged TSIO-360.

Deliveries of the new entry level M20S Eagle, which combines the extended length fuselage with a 182kW (244hp) Continental IO-550, began in 1999. It effectively replaced the Allegro in the Mooney line-up.

Photo: A Mooney Ovation. (Paul Sadler)

Mitsubishi MU-2

Country of origin: Japan

Type: Twin turboprop utility transport

Powerplants: MU-2B – Two 430kW (575shp) Garrett AiResearch TPE331-25A turboprops driving three blade constant speed propellers. Marquise – Two 535kW (715shp) Garrett TPE331-10-501Ms driving four blade constant speed propellers.

Performance: MU-2B – Max cruising speed 500km/h (270kt), economical cruising speed 440km/h (237kt). Initial rate of climb 2220ft/min. Max range with reserves 1930km (1040nm). Marquise – Max cruising speed 571km/h (308kt), economical cruising speed 547km/h (295kt). Service ceiling 29,750ft. Range with max fuel and reserves 2585km (1395nm).

Weights: MU-2B – Empty 2422kg (5340lb), max takeoff 4050kg (8930lb). Marquise – Empty equipped 3470kg (7650lb), max takeoff 5250kg (11,575lb).

Dimensions: MU-2B – Wing span 11.94m (39ft 2in), length 10.13m (33ft 3in), height 3.94m (12ft 11in). Wing area 16.5m² (178sq ft). Marquise – Same except for length 12.01m (39ft 5in), height 4.17m (13ft 8in).

Capacity: Flightcrew of one or two. Short fuselage models had typical seating for seven in main cabin, longer fuselage models up to 11. Many aircraft in various corporate configurations, or used as freighters.

Production: Over 800 built. Production comprised three MU-2As, 34 MU-2Bs, four military MU-2Ds, 18 MU-2Ds, 16 military SAR MU-2Es, 95 MU-2Fs, 46 MU-2Gs, 108 MU-2Js, 83 MU-2Ks, 36 MU-2Ls, 27 MU-2Ms, 36 MU-2Ns, 31 MU-2Ps, 130 plus Marquise and 60 plus Solitaires. Over 500 were in use as corporate aircraft in 2000.

History: The MU-2 was one of postwar Japan's most successful commercial aircraft types.

Development of the MU-2, Mitsubishi's first indigenous postwar aircraft design, began in the late 1950s. Designed as a light twin turboprop transport suitable for a variety of civil and military roles, the MU-2 first flew on September 14 1963. This first MU-2 and the handful of MU-2As built were powered by Turbomeca Astazou turboprops, all other models from the MU-2B onwards had Garrett TPE331s.

The MU-2 lineup can be divided up into two basic types, the standard fuselage and stretched fuselage models. The MU-2B, E, F, K, M, P and Solitaire feature the short fuselage, the others, including the Marquise, the stretched fuselage. The first stretched fuselage MU-2G flew on January 10 1969.

The MU-2 was progressively improved and upgraded throughout its production life. Notable changes include improved and more powerful TPE331 engines, and four blade propellers from the N and P models.

Mitsubishi established a production facility for MU-2s in San Angelo, Texas in the USA in 1967 to build MU-2s for the North American and world markets. The San Angelo Mitsubishi International facility became the sole source of MU-2 production until 1986 when the line finally closed.

Today over 500 MU-2s are in use as corporate transports (mainly in the USA), while many have been converted as freighters.

Photo: A long fuselage MU-2. The type is popular with overnight freight and charter operators. (Gary Gentle)

NAMC YS-11

Country of origin: Japan

Type: Twin turboprop regional airliner

Powerplants: YS-11A-200 – Two 2280kW (3060shp) Rolls-Royce Dart 542-10K turboprops driving four blade propellers.

Performance: -200 – Max cruising speed 470km/h (253kt), economical cruising speed 452km/h (244kt). Range with max payload and no reserves 1090km (590nm), range with max fuel and no reserves 3215km (1736nm).

Weights: -200 – Operating empty 15,419kg (33,993lb), max takeoff 24,500kg (54,010lb).

Dimensions: Wing span 32.00m (105ft 0in), length 26.30m (86ft 4in), height 8.98m (29ft 6in). Wing area 94.8m² (1020.4sq ft).

Capacity: Flightcrew of two. Typical single class seating in main cabin for 60 at four abreast and 86cm (34in) pitch. The combi YS-11A-300 accommodates freight in the forward portion of the main cabin with seating for 46 behind that.

Production: 182 YS-11s built comprising two prototypes, 48 series 100s, 83 Series 200s, 31 series 300s, eight series 400s, two series 500s and eight series 600s. Production total includes 23 for Japanese military. 51 remained in service at late 2000.

History: Still the only Japanese airliner to enter production since WW2, the YS-11 achieved a degree of success in its domestic market and in North America.

The YS-11 was a product of the Nihon Aircraft Manufacturing Company (or NAMC), a consortium of Fuji, Kawasaki, Mitsubishi, Nippi, Shin Meiwa (now Shin Maywa) and Showa. NAMC was formed on June 1 1959 to design and develop a short to medium range airliner, with particular attention being paid to meeting the specific operating requirements of the Japanese domestic airlines.

NAMC selected the Rolls-Royce Dart over the Allison 501 to power the new airliner. Fuji was given responsibility for the tail unit, Kawasaki the wings and engine nacelles, Mitsubishi the forward fuselage and final assembly, Nippi the ailerons and flaps, Shin Meiwa the rear fuselage and Showa the light alloy honeycomb structural components.

The YS-11 first flew on August 30 1962 (a second prototype flew that December), and was awarded Japanese certification in August 1964. By that time the first production aircraft were under construction, and the type entered service with Toa Airways (now JAS) in April 1965. Initial production was of the YS-11-100, the follow up YS-11A-200 (first flight November 1967) was designed for export markets and featured an increased max takeoff weight. The YS-11A-300 was a combi passenger/freight model, while the YS-11A-400 was a pure freighter with a forward freight door.

The YS-11A-500, -600 and -700 were equivalent to the -200, -300 and -400, but with a 500kg (1100lb) greater max takeoff weight. Production ceased in February 1974.

By late 2000 51 YS-11s remained in commercial service. The largest operators were the Philippines' Aboitiz Air (8), Air Nippon (7) and Japan Air Commuter (12).

Photo: A Japan Air Commuter YS-11A-500. The YS-11 was noteworthy for employing the most powerful version of the RR Dart to go into operation. (Rob Finlayson)

North American/Ryan Navion

Country of origin: United States of America

Type: High performance four/five seat light aircraft

Powerplant: Super 260 – One 195kW (260hp) Lycoming GO-435-C2 flat six piston engine driving a two blade propeller. Model H – One 215kW (285hp) Continental IO-520-B fuel injected flat six piston engine driving a two blade constant speed McCauley prop.

Performance: Super 260 – Max speed 280km/h (151kt). Model H – Max speed 307km/h (166kt), max cruising speed at 75% power 298km/h (161kt). Initial rate of climb 1300ft/min. Service ceiling 21,500ft. Range with max fuel 2560km (1397nm).

Weights: Super 260 – Max takeoff 1293kg (2850lb). Model H – Empty 882kg (1945lb), max takeoff 1504kg (3315lb).

Dimensions: Super 260 – Wing span 10.19m (33ft 5in), length 8.38m (27ft 6in). Model H – Wing span 10.59m (34ft 9in), length 8.38m (27ft 6in), height 2.54m (8ft 4in). Wing area 17.1m² (184.3sq ft).

Capacity: Usually four, five in Rangemaster.

Production: Approx 2500 of all models built, incl 1109 by North American (inc L-19s), 1240 by Ryan (inc L-19s), and 140 NAC Rangemasters. Approx 1500 still flying.

History: The Navion was designed in the late 1940s and built by four different companies through until the mid 1970s.

The company responsible for the original Navion was North American Aviation (famous for its WW2 P-51 Mustang fighter). The end of WW2 saw massive military contracts cancelled en masse and so North American designed the original four seat NA-145 to diversify out of military production. The NA-145 Navion was powered by a 140kW (185hp) Continental and North American built more than 1100 in 1946 and 1947. North American also built a number of L-17 observation aircraft based on the Navion for the US military.

Production and development of the Navion then transferred to Ryan. The standard Ryan production model was the Navion 205 or Navion A, which differed from the NA-145 in that it was powered by a 155kW (205hp) Continental E-185. More than 100 were built between 1948 and 1950. Ryan also built a few hundred Navion Super 260s or Navion Bs between 1950 and 1951 (when Ryan ceased Navion production). These were powered by a 195kW (260hp) Lycoming GO-435. In addition Ryan also built almost 200 L-17s (some saw service in Korea).

The basic Navion design resurfaced in 1960 when the Navion Aircraft Company developed a five seater variant called the Rangemaster. The Rangemaster was powered by the same 195kW (260hp) Lycoming engine as the Navion Super 260, but instead of the rear sliding canopy of earlier Navions, the Rangemaster had a reprofiled, more streamlined five seat cabin. Later production Rangemasters had a smaller tail.

The Rangemaster was last built by the Navion Rangemaster Aircraft Corporation between 1974 and 1976 in improved G and H form.

Camair in the USA also converted a small number of Navions of various models to twin engine configuration, the first flew in 1953.

Navion Aircraft purchased the manufacturing rights to the Navion in 1995 with the intention of returning an improved version of the Rangemaster to production. Changes would include a reprofiled nose and new avionics.

Photo: NA and Ryan Navions feature a rear sliding canopy.

Noorduyn Norseman

Country of origin: Canada

Type: 10 seat utility transport

Powerplant: Norseman V – One 450kW (600hp) Pratt & Whitney R1340-AN-1 Wasp nine cylinder radial piston engine driving a three blade propeller.

Performance: V – Normal cruising speed 238km/h (128kt). Time to climb to 5000ft 6.5min, time to climb to 15,000ft 28.5min. Service ceiling 17,000ft. Range at 75% power cruising speed with max fuel 1850km (998nm).

Weights: V – Empty 2007kg (4420lb), loaded 3360kg (7400lb).

Dimensions: V – Wing span 15.75m (51ft 8in), length 9.85m (32ft 4in), height 3.12m (10ft 3in).

Capacity: V – Pilot and up to nine passengers on bench seats. Often configured for freight.

Production: Norseman production ran from the late 1930s through until 1946 with Noorduyn, and then with Canadian Car and Foundry until 1959, by which time 904 had been built by both manufacturers. Approximately 20 remain in use in Canada, while one or two may be flying in other countries.

History: The rugged Norseman bush aircraft first flew in the mid 1930s, and so its long in service record equals that of the legendary Douglas DC-3.

The Norseman was designed by Robert Noorduyn, who was born in Holland and later worked for several prominent aircraft companies in England and the USA, including Armstrong Whitworth, British Aerial Transport Sopwith, Fokker (in the USA where he worked on the F.VII/3m), Bellanca and Pitcairn. In 1934 Noorduyn formed Noorduyn Aircraft Ltd (Noorduyn Aviation from 1938). Later in 1934 Noorduyn began work on the Norseman, resulting in the first flight of the float equipped prototype Norseman I from the St Laurence River on November 14 1935.

The Norseman I was powered by a 315kW (420hp) Wright Whirlwind, featured spruce wing spars and a metal tubing fuselage frame with fabric covering. It was the first Canadian aircraft with flaps.

Further development resulted in the heavier Norseman II and the 335kW (450hp) P&W Wasp Junior powered Norseman III. The 415kW (550hp) Norseman IV was the subject of significant Royal Canadian Air Force and civil orders in 1938.

The USA's entry into WW2 in late 1941 saw the US Army Air Force take delivery of 746 Norsemans in C-64A, UC-64A and C-64B variants. These aircraft operated in many theatres and were often equipped with floats or skis. The Norseman V is the civil equivalent of the C-64A.

With the aircraft no longer needed for war, Noorduyn production ceased in 1945 and its Cartierville plant was taken over by Canadair. However through to 1959 Canadian Car and Foundry built small numbers of Norseman Vs for civil customers.

After the war many ex military Norsemans found gainful use with civil operators, and currently as many as 20 are still airworthy in Canada.

Photo: A surprising number of Norsemans remain in commercial use, primarily in Canada. This float equipped Norseman V is in service with Huron Air of Armstrong, Ontario. (Rodney Kozar)

Pacific Aerospace CT-4 Airtrainer

Country of origin: New Zealand

Type: Two/three seat basic trainer

Powerplant: CT-4A – One 155kW (210hp) Teledyne Continental IO-360-D fuel injected flat six piston engine driving a two blade constant speed propeller. CT-4B – One 155kW (210hp) IO-360-HB9.

Performance: CT-4A – Max speed 285km/h (155kt), cruising speed 240km/h (130kt), long range cruising speed 235km/h (127kt). Initial rate of climb 1345ft/min. Range at long range cruising speed 1300km (700nm). CT-4B – Max speed 267km/h (144kt), 75% power cruising speed 260km/h (140kt). Initial rate of climb 1250ft/min. Range with max fuel at normal cruising speed 1110km (600nm).

Weights: CT-4A – Empty 690kg (1520lb), max takeoff 1090kg (2400lb) or 1203kg (2650lb). CT-4B – Max takeoff 1203kg (2650lb).

Dimensions: Wing span 7.92m (26ft 0in), length 7.06m (23ft 2in), height 2.59m (8ft 6in). Wing area 12.0m² (129.0sq ft).

Capacity: Normally two seats side by side, with space for optional third seat or baggage behind.

Production: 112 CT-4s of all models built, mainly for military orders. The largest civil user is BAE Systems Flight Training Australia (formerly the BAe/Ansett Flying College) which operates 12 CT-4Bs and 10 ex RNZAF CT-4As. Many (30+) ex RAAF CT-4As are now flying in civil hands mainly in Australia, some in New Zealand and the USA. 24 CT-4Es built.

History: Affectionately dubbed the Plastic Parrot in Royal Australian Air Force service, the CT-4 Airtrainer was primarily designed as a military trainer, but is also in limited civilian use.

The CT-4 was developed from the Australian Victa Airtourer series (described separately). Victa had developed the four place Aircruiser (first flight in mid 1966) based on the Airtourer, but development work ceased and instead the production rights for the Aircruiser were purchased by Aero Engine Services Ltd (or AESL) of New Zealand in 1969, which already had the rights to the Airtourer series.

AESL made a number of changes to the basic Aircruiser design, including adding a new clamshell canopy, structural strengthening for aerobatic work, and stick controls, making it suitable for military basic training. The first such CT-4A Airtrainer flew on February 23 1972. Primary customers were the Australian, New Zealand and Thai air forces. Production by NZAI (New Zealand Aircraft Industries), as AESL had become, continued until 1977.

In 1990 Pacific Aerospace Corporation (the successor to NZAI) resumed production of the improved CT-4B against an order from the BAe/Ansett Flying College (now BAE Systems Flight Training) in Tamworth, Australia, providing the impetus for further developments of the line.

A turboprop Allison 250 powered CT-4C flew on January 21 1991, and a retractable undercarriage version, the CT-4CR was proposed. Development of the 225kW (300hp) IO-540 powered CT-4E was aimed for the US Air Force's Enhanced Flight Screening competition. Twenty-four CT-4Es have been built, including 13 for the Royal New Zealand Air Force to replace CT-4As (10 of which were refurbished and sold to BAE Systems Flight Training in Australia).

Photo: PAC's CT-4E demonstrator. (Peter Clark)

Pacific Aerospace Fletcher FU-24 & Cresco

Country of origin: New Zealand

Type: Agricultural aircraft

Powerplant: FU-24-954 – One 300kW (400hp) Textron Lycoming IO-720-A1A or -A1B fuel injected flat eight piston engine driving a three blade constant speed Hartzell propeller. Cresco 08-750 – One 560kW (750shp) Pratt & Whitney Canada PT6A-34AG turboprop.

Performance: FU-24-954 – Max speed 233km/h (126kt), max cruising speed 209km/h (113kt), typical operating speed range 165 to 210km/h (90 to 115kt). Initial rate of climb 805ft/min. Service ceiling 16,000ft. Range with max payload and reserves 709km (383nm). 08-750 – Max speed 291km/h (157kt), max cruising speed at 75% power 261km/h (141kt). Initial rate of climb 1657ft/min. Service ceiling 26,000ft. Range with standard fuel and no reserves 726km (392nm).

Weights: FU-24-954 – Empty equipped 1188kg (2620lb), max takeoff 2465kg (5430lb). 08-850 – Empty equipped 1315kg (2900lb), normal max takeoff 2925kg (6450lb), ag (restricted) category max takeoff 3742kg (8250lb).

Dimensions: FU-24-954 – Wing span 12.81m (42ft 0in), length 9.70m (31ft 10in), height 2.84m (9ft 4in). Wing area 27.3m² (294.0sq ft). 08-750 – Same except for length 11.07m (36ft 4in), height 3.63m (11ft 11in).

Capacity: Typical arrangement seats pilot and passenger, and chemical hopper (capacity 1210 litres in FU-24-954, 1770 litres in Cresco). Can also be configured for freight work, or can seat six in rear compartment (earlier models can seat five or six passengers).

Production: Almost 300 FU-24s built in the USA and New Zealand (70 in US, balance in NZ) since 1955. Approx 30 Crescos built.

History: Fletcher in the USA originally developed the FU-24 largely for agwork in New Zealand.

The FU-24 flew for the first time in June 1954, and production and deliveries began during 1955, following certification on July 22. Seventy 195kW (260hp) Continental IO-470-D powered FU-24s and slightly larger FU-24As were built in the USA before Fletcher ceased production in 1964, and Air Parts (now Pacific Aerospace) of New Zealand acquired the production rights.

Initial New Zealand production was of two models, one powered by a 215kW (285hp) Continental, the other a 225kW (300hp) unit. The subsequent FU-24-950 was powered by a 300kW (400hp) eight cylinder Lycoming IO-720, and was followed up by the similarly powered FU-24-954 from 1979.

Like many ag aircraft, the Fletcher was a natural candidate for conversion to turboprop power. The resulting Cresco first flew on February 28 1979 powered by a 450kW (600shp) Avco Lycoming (now Textron Lycoming) LTP 101. Nine such aircraft were built, while a tenth was fitted with a 560kW (750shp) PT6A-34AG.

Although PAC announced it would cease aircraft manufacture in 1994, PAC's new owners placed the Cresco back into production. Initial production was of the LTP 101 powered Cresco 08-600, now the focus is on the PT6A powered Cresco 08-750.

In 2000 PAC was working on a Cresco optimised for carrying skydivers with an enlarged fuselage.

PAC also offers turbine FU-24 conversions with PT6s or Walter 601s.

Photo: A Cresco 08-600 used for skydiving. (Michael Johnson)

Piaggio P.166

Country of origin: Italy

Type: Commuter airliner and utility transport

Powerplants: P.166 – Two 255kW (340hp) Lycoming GSO-480-B1C6 geared and supercharged flat six piston engines driving three blade constant speed propellers. P.166DL3SEM – Two 450kW (600shp) AlliedSignal LTP 101-700 turboprops.

Performance: P.166 – Max speed 357km/h (193kt), max cruising speed 333km/h (180kt), economical cruising speed 280km/h (151kt). Initial rate of climb 1240ft/min. Service ceiling 25,000ft. Max range 1930km (1040nm). P.166-DL3SEM – Max speed 400km/h (215kt). Range with max payload 1390km (750nm), range with max fuel 2130km (1150nm).

Weights: P.166 – Empty 2350kg (5180lb), max takeoff 3680kg (8115lb). P.166-DL3SEM – Empty equipped 2688kg (5926lb), max takeoff 4300kg (9480lb).

Dimensions: P.166 – Wing span (without tip tanks) 14.25m (46ft 9in), length 11.61m (38ft 1in), height 5.00m (16ft 5in). Wing area 26.6m² (286sq ft). P.166-DL3SEM – Same except for wing span over tip tanks 14.69m (48ft 3in), length (including chin mounted radar) 11.88m (39ft 0in).

Capacity: Flightcrew of one or two and standard seating for eight or nine in main cabin in airliner configuration. Max seating for 12 in P.166C. Executive configuration seats five or six with toilet and bar. Air ambulance can carry two stretchers and two medical attendants.

Production: Approximately 145 P.166s of all models built. New production aircraft built on demand.

History: The Piaggio P.166 has been built in only small numbers but has been used in a wide variety of utility missions.

Intended for civil use when designed in the late 1950s, the P.166 features a large cabin which has been put to use in a variety of civil, military and quasi military roles, while its gull wing with tip tanks and pusher engines configuration like that on from the P.136 amphibian, ensures it is easily identified.

The prototype P.166 first flew on November 16 1957, and deliveries of the initial P.166 production model took place from April 1959. Just 23 were built before production switched to the P.166B Portofino, which featured more powerful 285kW (380hp) engines and an increased max takeoff weight of 3800kg (8377lb). Five Portofinos were built, while several earlier P.166s were converted to that standard with the more powerful engines.

The P.166C was introduced in 1964 and featured a larger cabin and 3950kg (8708lb) max takeoff weight. It could seat 12 passengers but only two were built.

The turboprop LTP 101 powered P.166.DL3 first flew in 1976 and was certificated in 1978. Alitalia has taken delivery of several for use as crew trainers, but most have been for the Italian government and military. Production of the radar and FLIR equipped P.166-DL3SEM continued into the 1990s for the Italian coast guard and today it remains available on demand. The 459kW (615shp) PT6A-121 powered P.166-DP1 first flew in May 1999 – eight have been ordered by Italian customs and coastguard authorities.

Photo: An Australian registered P.166. (Bill Lines)

Piaggio P.180 Avanti

Country of origin: Italy

Type: Twin turboprop executive transport

Powerplants: Two 634kW (850shp) Pratt & Whitney Canada PT6A-66 turboprops driving five blade constant speed Hartzell props.

Performance: Max speed 732km/h (395kt), max cruising speed 644km/h (348kt). Initial rate of climb 2950ft/min. Service ceiling 41,000ft. Range with one pilot, six passengers and IFR reserves 2595km (1400nm).

Weights: Empty equipped 3400kg (7500lb), max takeoff 5240kg (11,550lb).

Dimensions: Wing span 14.03m (46ft 1in), length 14.41m (47ft 4in), height 3.94m (12ft 11in). Wing area 16.0m² (172.2sq ft).

Capacity: Flightcrew of one or two (certificated for single pilot operation). Max seating in main cabin for nine in high density airliner configuration. Standard seating for seven in individual seats. Executive/VIP seating for five.

Production: 30 Avantis built by early 1995, production resumed late 1998.

History: The innovative Avanti has been a slow seller despite its modern features, jet like performance and turboprop operating costs.

Development of the Avanti dates back to program launch in 1981. Gates Learjet participated in Avanti development from 1983 and would have built the Avanti's forward fuselage, but instead withdrew from the program in January 1986. Not deterred by Gates' withdrawal, Piaggio assumed total control of the program, and all tooling and three forward fuselages for what would have been the Learjet P.180 were transferred to Italy.

Piaggio flew the first of two P.180 prototypes on September 23 1986, the second flew in May 1987. Italian certification was granted in March 1990, the first production Avanti flew that May and the first customer delivery took place in September 1990.

The unorthodox Avanti remains unique for a corporate aircraft in that it features three flying surfaces – the canard foreplane, wing and tail. This arrangement not only offers the benefits of the canard, but meant the wing could be positioned in the rear of the fuselage, so that it didn't intrude on available interior cabin space. The small natural laminar flow wing was designed by the Ohio State University. The pusher engine configuration was chosen to reduce cabin noise.

Composites are used in a number of areas, including the tail, engine nacelles, canards, outboard wing flaps, landing gear doors and the tail cone, but generally, unlike the Beech Starship, most construction is conventional. A two multifunction display (plus weather radar display) Rockwell Collins EFIS glass flightdeck is standard, a five screen suite has been offered as an option.

Twice Piaggio has increased the P.180's maximum weight, thus improving its payload range.

Avanti production ceased in 1995 when Piaggio was placed under administration. Under new ownership the company was resurrected in November 1998 and Avanti production resumed.

The Italian air force is the Avanti's biggest operator, while another noted owner is Formula 1 car racer Ralf Schumacher.

Photo: A Canadian registered Avanti. (Gary Gentle)

Pilatus PC-6 Porter & Turbo Porter

Country of origin: Switzerland

Type: STOL utility transport

Powerplant: PC-6-H2 – One 255kW (340hp) Lycoming GSO-480-B1A6 geared and supercharged six cylinder piston engine driving a three blade constant speed propeller. PC-6/B2-H4 – One 410kW (550shp) flat rated Pratt & Whitney Canada PT6A-27 turboprop.

Performance: PC-6-H2 – Max speed 233km/h (126kt), max cruising speed 216km/h (117kt), economical cruising speed 190km/h (103kt). Initial rate of climb 550ft/min. Service ceiling 17,400ft. Max range with no reserves 1500km (810nm). PC-6/B2-H4 (Utility version) – Economical cruising speed 213km/h (115kt). Initial rate of climb 940ft/min. Max operating ceiling 25,000ft. Range with max payload at economical cruising speed and no reserves 730km (395nm), range with max internal fuel 925km (500nm), with external fuel 1610km (870nm).

Weights: PC-6-H2 – Empty 1250kg (2755lb), max takeoff 2200kg (4850lb). PC-6/B2-H4 – Empty 1130kg (2491lb), max takeoff 2800kg (6173lb), max takeoff with skis 2600kg (5732lb).

Dimensions: PC-6-H2 – Wing span 15.14m (49ft 8in), length 10.20m (33ft 6in), height tail down 3.20m (10ft 6in). Wing area 28.8m² (310sq ft). PC-6/B2-H4 – Wing span 15.87m (52ft 1in), length 10.90m (35ft 9in), height 3.20m (10ft 6in). Wing area 30.2m² (324.5sq ft).

Capacity: Pilot and passenger on flightdeck, with standard seating for six in main cabin. Max seating for 11 including pilot. Alternative layouts include two stretchers and three medical attendants, or 10 skydivers. Some equipped for agricultural spraying.

Production: Over 540 Porters of all versions have been built, including 100 under licence in the USA and against various military orders.

History: The Pilatus Porter and Turbo Porter STOL utilities are renowned for their exceptional STOL performance and low speed handling and have sold strongly on the strength of their performance.

The high wing taildragger Porter was designed to perform a range of utility roles, and first flew on May 4 1959. The first production aircraft built were delivered from 1960 and were powered by a six cylinder GSO-480 piston engine, but it was not long after that a turboprop powered development flew.

The first PC-6/A Turbo Porter flew in May 1961, powered by a 390kW (523shp) Turbomeca Astazou II turboprop. The majority of PC-6s are PC-6/Bs, powered by the Pratt & Whitney Canada PT6A. PC-6/Cs were powered by a 310kW (575shp) AiResearch TPE331, and were first delivered in 1965.

Smaller numbers of piston powered Porters have been built in parallel with Turbo Porters with Lycoming GSO-480s and IGO-540s.

The PC-6/B was first delivered from 1964 and remains in production today. Initial models were powered by the 410kW (550shp) PT6A-6 or -20. The PC-6/B2-H2 first flew in 1970 and introduced the PT6A-27 and an increased maximum takeoff weight.

The current Porter production model is of the PC-6/B2-H4 which was introduced in 1985. It features a further increase in max takeoff weight, larger dorsal fin fillet, revised wingtips, strengthened airframe structure and improved undercarriage. The H-4's improvements can be retrofitted to the H-2.

Photo: A South African police Turbo Porter. (Keith Gaskell)

Pilatus PC-12

Country of origin: Switzerland

Type: Corporate, utility and regional airliner turboprop

Powerplant: One 895kW (1200shp) takeoff rated Pratt & Whitney Canada PT6A-67B turboprop driving a four blade constant speed Hartzell propeller.

Performance: Max cruising speed at 25,000ft 500km/h (270kt), economical cruising speed 430km/h (232kt). Initial rate of climb 1680ft/min. Max operating altitude 30,000ft. Max range at economical cruising speed with VFR reserves 4187km (2260nm). Range at max cruising speed with IFR reserves 2965km (1600nm).

Weights: PC-12 – Standard empty 2600kg (5732lb), max takeoff 4500kg (9920lb).

Dimensions: Wing span 16.23m (52ft 3in), length 14.40m (47ft 3in), height 4.26m (14ft 0in). Wing area 25.8m² (277.8sq ft).

Capacity: Flightcrew of one or two pilots (certificated for single pilot). Seating for nine in main cabin in regional airliner configuration. Corporate/executive transport configurations typically seat six in main cabin. Combi passenger/freight version seats four passengers in main cabin plus freight pallet.

Production: The 200th PC-12 was delivered in March 2000. Current production rate 60 per year.

History: The PC-12 is a King Air class and size turboprop aimed at the corporate transport and regional airliner markets. It is the latest in a line of single engined PT6 powered Pilatus products.

Pilatus announced it was developing the PC-12 at the National Business Aviation Association's annual convention in October 1989. First flight of the first of two prototypes occurred on May 31 1991. Certification was originally planned for mid 1993, but after a redesign of the wings with the addition of winglets to ensure performance guarantees were met, Swiss certification was awarded on March 30 1994 and US FAA FAR Part 23 approval followed on July 15 1994.

Compared to the King Air 200 twin, its major competitor, the PC-12's most significant design feature (apart from it being a more modern design) is its use of a single PT6A-67B turboshaft. Internally the PC-12's cabin is also longer (by 6cm/2.4in) and wider (by 15cm/6in) than the King Air 200's, and the same height. The cockpit features EFIS displays and the PC-12 is certificated for single pilot operation while each PC-12 built features a standard cargo door in the rear fuselage. Weather radar is an option but has been fitted to all production aircraft thus far. From 1997 the increased 4.5 tonne MTOW has been standard. New, smaller winglets were introduced in 1998.

The PC-12 is offered in standard nine seat airliner form, in a four passenger seat/freight combi version and as a six place corporate transport. A pure freighter model has also been considered. The PC-12 Eagle is a military special missions platform.

Most PC-12s built thus far have been corporate transports, but important regulatory changes in Australia, Brazil, Canada and the USA in the late 1990s cleared single engine turboprops for IFR RPT operations in those nations. This opened up new markets for the PC-12 as a regional airliner, replacing older King Airs and elderly piston twins such as the Navajo Chieftain and Cessna 400 series.

Photo: An RFDS PC-12 over central Australia. (Brian Maginnity)

Piper Cub

Country of origin: United States of America

Type: Two seat light aircraft

Powerplant: J-3C-65 – One 50kW (65hp) Continental A-65-1 flat four piston engine driving a two blade fixed pitch propeller. PA-12 – One 75kW (100hp) Lycoming O-235 flat four.

Performance: J-3C-65 – Max speed 148km/h (80kt), typical cruising speed 132km/h (71kt). Initial rate of climb 450ft/min. Service ceiling 12,000ft. Range 402km (217nm). PA-12 – Max speed 183km/h (99kt), normal cruising speed 170km/h (90kt). Service ceiling 12,600ft. Range 580km (313nm).

Weights: J-3C-65 – Empty 290kg (640lb), max takeoff 500kg (1100lb). PA-12 – Empty 430kg (950lb), max takeoff 795kg (1750lb).

Dimensions: Wing span 10.75m (35ft 3in), length 6.79m (22ft 3in), height 2.03m (6ft 8in). Wing area 16.6m² (178.5sq ft). PA-12 – Wing span 10.83m (35ft 6in), length 6.74m (22ft 1in), height 2.08m (6ft 10in). Wing area 16.7m² (179.3sq ft).

Capacity: Typical seating for two in tandem in the Cub, Cub Coupe and Cub Special, three in the Cub Cruiser and Super Cruiser, and four in the Family Cruiser.

Production: Production includes 5795 prewar J-3s, 8252 postwar J-3C-65s, 1248 J-4 Cub Coupes, over 1410 J-5 Cub Cruisers, more than 430 PA-11 Cub Specials, 3761 PA-12 Super Cruisers and 521 PA-14 Family Cruisers. Wartime construction of 5687 L-4s.

History: The simple and economical Cub is one of the most well loved light aircraft of all time, and helped make flying an affordable pastime for thousands of pilots in the years surrounding World War 2.

The Piper Cub began life as the Taylor E-2 Tiger Kitten, which was powered by a tiny 15kW (20hp) Brownbach engine. The Tiger Kitten was grossly underpowered and the Taylor Brothers' Airplane Company went bankrupt before a more powerful engine could be found. Businessman William Piper, who had made large profits from the oil industry, purchased a majority holding in the Taylor company in 1931 for $US1000. The company continued building derivatives of the E-2 under the Taylor banner through the 1930s. The first aircraft to be called Cub was the E-2 powered by a Continental A-40. Small numbers were built from 1931.

In 1937 Piper adopted his own name for the company, and the first J-3 Cubs were built. The J-3 was an improved J-2, resulting from a redesign of the three cylinder radial powered H-2 by Walter Janouneay. The affordable J-3 Cub became a runaway sales success and several thousand were sold before the USA's entry into WW2 saw all J-3 production built for the US Army as the L-4. Prewar Piper also built the J-4 Cub Coupe with side by side seating and the three seat J-5 Cub Cruiser.

Postwar Piper reverted to civilian production with the J-3 later becoming the PA-11 Cub Special. Late build PA-11s were powered by a 65kW (90hp) Continental C-90 and had increased range. The PA-12 Super Cruiser has seating for three and a more powerful Lycoming O-235 engine, while the four seat PA-14 Family Cruiser formed the basis for the Super Cub.

Photo: J-3 Cubs were built in their thousands and painted in this distinctive yellow scheme with black lightning strike. (Gerard Frawley)

Piper PA-18 Super Cub

Country of origin: United States of America

Type: Two seat utility light aircraft

Powerplant: PA-18-95 – One 65kW (90hp) Continental C-90-12F or -8F flat four piston engine driving a two blade fixed pitch propeller. PA-18-150 – One 110kW (150hp) Lycoming O-320.

Performance: PA-18-95 – Max speed 180km/h (97kt), max cruising speed 161km/h (87kt). Initial rate of climb 710ft/min. Service ceiling 15,750ft. Max range with no reserves 580km (313nm). PA-18-150 – Max speed 210km/h (113kt), max cruising speed 185km/h (100kt), economical cruising speed 170km/h (90kt). Initial rate of climb 960ft/min. Service ceiling 19,000ft. Range at max cruising speed and no reserves 740km (400nm).

Weights: PA-18-95 – Empty 367kg (910lb), max takeoff 680kg (1500lb). PA-18-150 – Empty 429kg (946lb), max takeoff 794kg (1750lb).

Dimensions: PA-18-95 – Wing span 10.73m (35ft 3in), length 6.83m (22ft 5in), height 2.02m (6ft 9in). Wing area 16.6m² (178.5sq ft). PA-18-150 – Same except for length 6.88m (22ft 7in).

Capacity: Typical seating for two in tandem.

Production: Almost 7500 Super Cubs (including 1700 military) built until 1981 when production originally ceased. Piper production for WTA between 1982 and 1988 totalled 250. Piper production between 1988 and 1994 approximately 100.

History: The Super Cub is one of Piper's most successful and long lived aircraft programs, with production spanning over four decades.

The PA-18 Super Cub was the ultimate development of Piper's original aircraft, the J-3 Cub (described separately). The four seat development of the Cub, the PA-14 Cub Cruiser, was the basis for the Super Cub, but the later differed in having seating for two in tandem (as on the Cub), all metal wings and, in its initial form, a 65kW (90hp) Continental C-90 in the PA-18-90 or a 80kW (108hp) Lycoming O-235 engine in the PA-18-105. The Super Cub flew for the first time in 1949, and certification was awarded on November 18 that year. The first production Super Cubs were delivered from late 1949, the type replacing the PA-11 Cub Special on Piper's production lines.

The 100kW (135hp) Lycoming O-290 powered PA-18-135 appeared in 1952, while the definitive 110kW (150hp) Lycoming O-320 powered PA-18-150 was certificated on October 1 1954 and delivered from the following year.

The Super Cub remained in production with Piper through until 1981, when almost 7500 had been built over an uninterrupted 32 year production run. Piper continued building Super Cubs on behalf of Texas based WTA who held the manufacturing and marketing rights from 1981 until 1988. In 1988 Piper resumed marketing responsibility for the Super Cub and continued low rate production. Financial troubles meant that Super Cub production ceased in 1992, before resuming once more the following year. Finally in late 1994 Piper announced that the Super Cub would not form part of its model line for 1995 and that it would cease production after the last of 24 on order for distributor Muncie Aviation were completed.

Photo: A PA-18-150 Super Cub. The Super Cub is larger and more powerful than the basic J-3/PA-11 Cub. (Michael Johnson)

Piper PA-20 Pacer & PA-22 Tri-Pacer & Colt

Country of origin: United States of America

Type: Two and four seat light aircraft

Powerplant: PA-22-108 Colt – One 80kW (108hp) Lycoming O-235-C1B flat four piston engine driving a two blade fixed pitch propeller. PA-22-160 Tri-Pacer – One 119kW (160hp) Lycoming O-320-B2A.

Performance: PA-22-108 – Max speed 193km/h (104kt), max cruising speed 173km/h (93kt). Initial rate of climb 610ft/min. Service ceiling 12,000ft. Max range with no reserves 1110km (600nm). PA-22-160 – Max speed 227km/h (123kt), max cruising speed 216km/h (117kt). Initial rate of climb 800ft/min. Service ceiling 16,500ft. Range with standard fuel and no reserves 862km (465nm), with optional fuel 1054km (569nm).

Weights: PA-22-108 – Empty 447kg (985lb), max takeoff 748kg (1650lb). PA-22-160 – Empty 503kg (1110lb), max takeoff 907kg (2000lb).

Dimensions: PA-22-108 – Wing span 9.14m (30ft 0in), length 6.10m (20ft 0in), height 1.91m (6ft 3in). Wing area 13.66m² (147sq ft). PA-22-160 – Wing span 8.92m (29ft 3in), length 6.28m (20ft 7in), height 2.53m (8ft 4in). Wing area 13.7m² (147.5sq ft).

Capacity: Pacer and Tri-Pacers (including Caribbean) typically seat four, while the Colt seats two side by side. Seaplane versions of the Tri-Pacer could seat three.

Production: Total PA-22 production of 9495 comprising 7688 Tri-Pacers and 1827 Colts, while 1699 PA-20 Pacers were built.

History: The Pacer and Tri-Pacer designs were Piper's volume selling four seaters from 1949 through to the introduction of the Comanche and Cherokee in the early 1960s, while the Colt was a two seat training derivative of the Tri-Pacer.

The original tail dragger PA-20 Pacer was introduced in 1949 alongside the two seat Super Cub, and was powered by a 85kW (115hp) Continental engine. Improvements were made in 1950, including a larger tail, while a 93kW (125hp) variant was added. From 1952 to 1954 when production ceased the Pacer was offered in 93kW (125hp) and 100kW (135hp) variants.

The tricycle undercarriage Tri-Pacer (with the same engine options) initially augmented the Pacer in production from 1950 until Pacer production ceased in 1954. The Tri-Pacer gained a 110kW (150hp) engine and a higher takeoff weight from 1955, and a 120kW (160hp) O-320 from 1957. From 1958 Piper offered a lower spec, less expensive version of the Tri-Pacer as the PA-22-150 Caribbean.

The two seat Colt was derived from the Tri-Pacer but had a less powerful 85kW (108hp) engine, lower maximum takeoff weight, no rear cabin windows, the removal of a rear door and less fuel capacity, but otherwise the two airframes were identical. Piper introduced the Colt to its lineup in late 1960, and the type remained in production for just over two years until the two seat Cherokee could be introduced. Colt production ceased in 1963 after almost 2000 had been built.

The Tri-Pacer and Colt were Piper's only high wing tricycle undercarriage aircraft, and the last in production to feature metal tubing and fabric covering construction.

Photo: This PA-22-108 Colt has been modified with tail dragger undercarriage. (Robert Wiseman)

Piper PA-23 Apache & Aztec

Country of origin: United States of America

Type: Four seat light twins

Powerplant: PA-23-235 Apache – Two 175kW (235hp) Lycoming O-540-B1A5 flat six piston engines driving two blade constant speed Hartzell propellers. PA-23-250T Aztec F – Two 185kW (250hp) turbocharged and fuel injected Lycoming TIO-540-C1As.

Performance: PA-23-235 – Max speed 325km/h (176kt), max cruising speed 307km/h (166kt). Initial rate of climb 1450ft/min. Service ceiling 17,200ft. Max range with no reserves 1907km (1030nm). PA-23-250T – Max speed 408km/h (220kt), max cruising speed 390km/h (211kt), economical cruising speed 335km/h (181kt). Initial rate of climb 1470ft/min. Service ceiling 24,000ft. Range at max cruising speed 1797km (970nm), at economical cruising speed 2309km (1246nm).

Weights: PA-23-235 – Empty 1241kg (2735lb), MTOW 2177kg (4800lb). PA-23-250T – Empty 1508kg (3323lb), MTOW 2360kg (5200lb).

Dimensions: PA-23-235 – Wing span 11.32m (37ft 2in), length 8.41m (27ft 7in). Wing area 19.2m² (207sq ft). PA-23-250T – Wing span 11.39m (37ft 4in), length 9.53m (31ft 3in), height 3.08m (10ft 1in). Wing area 19.2m² (207sq ft).

Capacity: Apache seats four. Aztec As seat five, later Aztecs seat six.

Production: Almost 7000 PA-23s built, comprising 2047 Apaches and 4929 Aztecs, including a small number of military variants.

History: The origins of the Apache (one of the first widely available GA twins and Piper's first 'Indian') and the larger and more powerful Aztec lie in the early postwar Twin Stinson design.

Piper acquired the assets of Consolidated Vultee's Stinson Aircraft division in 1948, inheriting a design study for a new four place light twin. Piper left the design dormant for a few years until 1952 when it built a prototype aircraft, designated 23-01, based on the Stinson design. The low wing four seat twin was powered by 93kW (125hp) Lycoming engines, had fabric covering, fixed undercarriage and a twin fin tail design.

Unsatisfactory flight trials led Piper to substantially redesign the 23-01, introducing more powerful 110kW (150hp) engines, metal construction, retractable undercarriage and a conventional tail unit. Designated the PA-23 Apache, the redesigned twin flew for the first time on March 2 1952. Production deliveries began in March 1954.

Apache A, B, C, D and E subvariants of the initial PA-23-150 were built before production switched to the more powerful PA-23-160 Apache F in late 1958. Subsequent Apache developments were the Apache F with a third cabin window, and the Apache 235, a lower powered development of the Aztec A.

The Aztec is an enlarged and more powerful development of the Apache powered by two six cylinder 185kW (250hp) O-540s, and Aztec As were first delivered from early 1960. The Aztec B introduced a longer nose and seating for six, the Aztec C fuel injected engines, the optional Aztec C Turbo was turbocharged, while the Aztec D, E and F and corresponding turbo models introduced detail changes. Production ceased in 1982.

Photo: A PA-23-150 Apache D. Total PA-23-250 production was 1231 units through to 1958.

Piper PA-24 Comanche

Country of origin: United States of America

Type: Four seat high performance light aircraft

Powerplant: PA-24-250 – One 185kW (250hp) Lycoming O-540-A1A5 flat six driving a constant speed propeller. PA-24-400 – One 300kW (400hp) Lycoming IO-720-A1A flat eight driving a three blade c/s prop. PA-24-260 Turbo C – One 200kW (260hp) turbocharged and fuel injected IO-540-R1A5 flat six driving a two blade c/s prop.

Performance: PA-24-250 – Max speed 306km/h (165kt), max cruising speed 291km/h (157kt). Initial rate of climb 1350ft/min. Service ceiling 20,000ft. Max range with optional fuel 2665km (1440nm). PA-24-400 – Max speed 360km/h (194kt), max cruising speed 343km/h (185kt). Initial rate of climb 1600ft/min. Service ceiling 19,500ft. Range with standard fuel 2012km (1086nm), with optional fuel 2478km (1338nm). PA-24-260 Turbo C – Max speed 390km/h (210kt), max cruising speed 318km/h (172kt). Initial rate of climb 1320ft/min. Operating ceiling 25,000ft. Max range 2052km (1108nm), with optional fuel 2398km (1295nm).

Weights: PA-24-250 – Empty 767kg (1690lb), max TO 1315kg (2900lb). PA-24-400 – Empty 957kg (2110lb), max TO 1633kg (3600lb). PA-24-260 Turbo C – Empty 860kg (1894lb), max takeoff 1450kg (3200lb).

Dimensions: PA-24-250 – Wing span 10.97m (36ft 0in), length 7.59m (24ft 11in), height 2.29m (7ft 6in). Wing area 16.5m² (178sq ft). PA-28-400 – Wing span 10.97m (36ft 0in), length 7.84m (25ft 8in), height 2.39m (7ft 10in). Wing area 16.5m² (178sq ft). PA-24-260 Turbo C – Wing span 10.97m (36ft 0in), length 7.62m (25ft 0in), height 2.29m (7ft 6in). Wing area 16.5m² (178sq ft).

Capacity: Standard seating for four, Comanche B and C could have optional fifth and sixth seats.

Production: Total PA-24 production 4856, including 1143 180s, 2537 250s, 1028 260s and 260 Ts, and 148 400s.

History: Piper's PA-24 Comanche was a high performance retractable undercarriage single designed to challenge the established Beech Bonanza.

Piper's first low wing single engine design, the Comanche featured a retractable tricycle undercarriage, swept back tail, flying tail or 'stabilator' horizontal tail surfaces, laminar flow wing and all metal construction, a stark contrast to Piper's earlier high wing fabric covered designs. The Comanche first flew on May 24 1956 and was delivered to customers from late 1957 in PA-24-180 form.

Since then through to the cessation of production in June 1972 (due to flooding of Piper's Lock Haven plant), a number of progressively higher performance variants were released. These included 1958's 185kW (250hp) PA-24-250 and the 300kW (400hp) PA-24-400.

Just 148 400s were built, despite Piper claiming it to be the fastest production four seat single available at the time. Its massive eight cylinder IO-720 engine consumed fuel at a prodigious rate, so it was expensive to operate, and there were problems with cooling the rear cylinders. Today however it has something of a mini cult status.

Following the PA-24-400 was the PA-24-260 from 1964, with a 195kW (260hp) O-540 or IO-540, and finally the Rajay turbocharger fitted PA-24-260 Turbo C, available from 1970.

Photo: Initial Comanches were PA-24-180s and -250s. (Gary Gentle)

Piper PA-28 Cherokee Series

Country of origin: United States of America

Type: Two and four seat light aircraft

Powerplant: PA-28-161 Warrior II – One 110kW (160hp) Lycoming O-320-A2B flat four piston engine driving a two blade fixed pitch propeller. PA-28-181 Archer III – One 135kW (180hp) Textron Lycoming O-360-A4M flat four.

Performance: PA-28-161 – Max speed 235km/h (127kt), max cruising speed 233km/h (126kt), long range cruising speed 195km/h (105kt). Initial rate of climb 644ft/min. Service ceiling 11,000ft. Max range with reserves 1185km (637nm). PA-28-181 – Max speed 246km/h (133kt), normal cruising speed 237km/h (128kt). Initial rate of climb 667ft/min. Service ceiling 13,240ft. Range with reserves at 75% power 820km (443nm), at 55% power 924km (499nm).

Weights: PA-28-161 – Empty 613kg (1352lb), max takeoff 1105kg (2440lb). PA-28-181 – Empty equipped 752kg (1658lb), max takeoff 1155kg (2550lb).

Dimensions: PA-28-161 – Wing span 10.67m (35ft 0in), length overall 7.25m (23ft 10in), height 2.22m (7ft 4in). Wing area 15.8m² (170sq ft). PA-28-181 – Same as PA-28-161.

Capacity: Seating for four, two in some dedicated trainer versions.

Production: Over 30,000 fixed undercarriage PA-28 Cherokee series built, including approximately 10,100 PA-28-140s, 10,200 PA-28-180s & -181s, 5000 PA-28-151 & -161s, and 2800 PA-28-235 & 236s.

History: The initial PA-28-150 and PA-28-160 Cherokees were introduced in 1961 as replacements for Piper's PA-22 Tri-Pacer and Colt.

Unlike the PA-22 series the new PA-28 was a low wing design with metal construction. The prototype Cherokee was powered by a 120kW (160hp) engine, and flew for the first time on January 14 1960. Production aircraft were powered by either 110kW (150hp) or 120kW (160hp) engines and were delivered from early 1961.

From 1962 a 135kW (180hp) version was added to the lineup. The 175kW (235hp) flat six Lycoming O-540 powered Cherokee 235 was introduced in 1963, while the two seat trainer optimised Colt replacement PA-28-140 entered the marketplace in 1964. With these models the basic PA-28 lineup was in place (the retractable PA-28R and larger PA-32 are described separately).

Subsequent variants include the Cherokee B and Cherokee C, the 180D, 235C, 140 Flite Liner two seat trainer PA-28-140, 180F, 235E, PA-28-180 Cherokee Challenger and PA-28-235 Cherokee Charger, the PA-28-180 Cherokee Archer and PA-28-235 Cherokee Pathfinder, PA-28-151 Cherokee Warrior which introduced the new tapered wing that would become a feature of subsequent PA-28s, PA-28-181 Cherokee Archer II and PA-28-236 Dakota (the Cherokee prefix was later dropped for the Archer II and Warrior), the PA-28-161 Warrior II, PA-28-236T Turbo Dakota and PA-28-161 Cadet.

Small numbers of Warriors, Dakotas and Archers were built in the early 1990s. The Archer III was introduced in 1994, and features a new, streamlined cowling. 1999 models gained new paint, improved interior and a new avionics package. The PA-28-161 Warrior III features a new instrument panel and was introduced in late 1994. Since 1995 Piper has had new owners, and the brand has enjoyed a strong resurgence.

Photo: Piper has built almost 400 Archer IIIs since 1995. (Paul Sadler)

Piper PA-28R Cherokee Arrow

Country of origin: United States of America

Type: Four seat light aircraft

Powerplant: PA-28R-180 – One 135kW (180hp) Lycoming IO-360-B1E fuel injected flat four piston engine driving a two blade constant speed Hartzell propeller. PA-28R-201T – One 150kW (200hp) Continental TSIO-360-FB turbocharged and fuel injected flat six.

Performance: PA-28R-180 – Max speed 274km/h (148kt), typical cruising speed 260km/h (140kt), long range cruising speed 230km/h (124kt). Initial rate of climb 875ft/min. Service ceiling 15,000ft. Range at economical cruising speed 1600km (865nm). PA-28R-201T – Max speed 330km/h (178kt), max cruising speed 320km/h (172kt), long range cruising speed 284km/h (153kt). Initial rate of climb 940ft/min. Range with reserves 1667km (900nm).

Weights: PA-28R-180 – Empty 626kg (1380lb), max takeoff 1134kg (2500lb). PA-28R-201T – Empty 786kg (1732lb), max takeoff 1315kg (2900lb).

Dimensions: PA-28R-180 – Wing span 9.14m (30ft 0in), length 7.38m (24ft 3in), height 2.44m (8ft 0in). Wing area 14.2m² (160sq ft). PA-28R-201T – Wing span 10.80m (35ft 5in), length 8.33m (27ft 3in), height 2.52m (8ft 3in). Wing area 15.9m² (170sq ft).

Capacity: Typical seating for four.

Production: Approx 6000 PA-28Rs built, incl 81 PA-28R-180Bs, 1664 PA-28R-200s and -201s, and 1291 PA-28R-201Ts and PA-28RT-201Ts.

History: The PA-28R began life as a retractable undercarriage variant of the PA-28 Cherokee.

The original PA-28-180R Cherokee Arrow was a relatively simple adaptation of the existing PA-28-180 Cherokee D, but incorporated electro-hydraulically operated retractable undercarriage (complete with a self lowering system that safeguarded against the pilot failing to do so, automatically lowering when airspeed reached 170km/h/91kt and a certain engine manifold pressure), a fuel injected version of the PA-28-180's O-360, a constant speed propeller and an increased max takeoff weight.

Production switched to the PA-28R-180 and more powerful 150kW (200hp) IO-360-C1C powered PA-28R-200 Cherokee Arrow II. Changes included the same 12.7cm (5in) stretched fuselage introduced on the Cherokee Challenger and Cherokee Charger, with greater rear legroom and baggage capacity, plus larger horizontal tail and dorsal fin fillet.

The PA-28R-201 Arrow III first flew in September 1975, and was introduced from 1976. The major change (also introduced on the fixed undercarriage PA-28s at that time) was a new wing with longer tapered span, while the maximum takeoff weight was increased. The turbocharged PA-28R-201T was also offered.

The PA-28RT-201 and -201T Arrow IV introduced a new all moving T-tail. Production of the Arrow IV ceased in 1982, and resumed again in 1989, but ceased once more in 1992. Instead Piper returned the conventional tailed Arrow III back into production. Very small numbers were built in the early 1990s while Piper was under bankruptcy protection. Since the emergence of New Piper Inc in 1995 the Arrow III has been part of the expanded Piper line-up, although only small numbers have been built.

Photo: A PA-28R-201 Arrow III. (Gary Gentle)

Piper PA-32 Cherokee Six, Lance & Saratoga

Country of origin: United States of America

Type: Six seat high performance light aircraft

Powerplant: PA-32RT-300 Lance II – One 225kW (300hp) Lycoming IO-540-K1G5 fuel injected flat six piston engine driving a two blade c/s prop. PA-32R-301T Saratoga II TC – One 225kW (300hp) turbocharged Textron Lycoming TIO-540-AH1A driving a three blade c/s prop.

Performance: PA-32RT-300 – Max speed 306km/h (165kt), max cruising speed 293km/h (158kt), long range cruising speed 258km/h (139kt). Initial rate of climb 1000ft/min. Service ceiling 14,600ft. Max range with reserves 1600km (865nm). PA-32R-301T – Max speed 346km/h (187kt), cruising speed at 10,000ft 324km/h (175kt), at 15,000ft 343km/h (185kt). Max certificated ceiling 20,000ft. Range at long range cruise power and 10,000ft 1756km (948nm).

Weights: PA-32RT-300 – Empty 912kg (2011lb), max takeoff 1633kg (3600lb). PA-32R-301T – Empty equipped 1118kg (2465lb), max takeoff 1633kg (3600lb).

Dimensions: PA-32RT-300 – Wing span 9.99m (32ft 10in), length 8.44m (27ft 9in), height 2.90m (9ft 6in). Wing area 16.2m² (174.5sq ft). PA-32T-301T – Wing span 11.02m (36ft 2in), length 8.23m (27ft 0in), height 2.59m (8ft 6in). Wing area 16.6m² (178.3sq ft).

Capacity: Standard seating for six, some with an optional seventh seat.

Production: Approximately 700 PA-32s of all versions have been built, including over 100 Saratoga II HPs/TCs since 1993.

History: The PA-32 series began life as the Cherokee Six, a significantly modified six seat development of the PA-28 Cherokee series.

While similar in configuration to the Cherokee, the Cherokee Six differed in a number of major areas. Two of the big differences were implied in its name, a six cylinder O-540 or IO-540 powerplant, and the six seat configuration. While the wing was based on the Cherokee's, the fuselage was substantially larger, with strengthened undercarriage and a larger tail.

The Cherokee Six first flew on December 6 1963, while deliveries of production PA-32-260s began from mid 1965. Development led to a range of improved models, starting with the 225kW (300hp) fuel injected IO-540 powered Cherokee Six-300 (PA-32-300). Production of the -260 and -300 ended in the late 1970s, but in the meantime they had been joined by the Cherokee Lance. The Cherokee Lance, or just Lance from mid 1977 with the introduction of the improved Lance II, was a retractable undercarriage development. The Lance II and turbocharged PA-32R-300T Turbo Lance also introduced a T-tail and remained in production to late 1979.

The Lance II and Cherokee Six were replaced by the Saratoga. Available in fixed or retractable undercarriage form, with standard or turbocharged powerplants, the major change was the new increased span tapered wing.

Production of the Saratoga ceased in 1985, but Piper reintroduced the Saratoga II HP in 1993 with aerodynamic improvements and a revised instrument panel and interior. The turbocharged Saratoga II TC was introduced in 1997. 1999 models introduced new Garmin and S-TEC avionics. A five seat interior with a entertainment/workstation console (similar to that in the Seneca V) is optional.

Photo: A Saratoga II HP. (Gary Gentle)

Piper PA-25 Pawnee & PA-36 Pawnee Brave

Country of origin: United States of America

Type: Agricultural aircraft

Powerplant: PA-25-235 – One 175kW (235hp) Lycoming O-540-B2B5 flat six piston engine driving a two blade fixed pitch McCauley propeller. PA-36-375 – One 280kW (375hp) Lycoming IO-720-DICD fuel injected flat eight driving a three blade constant speed Hartzell prop.

Performance: PA-25-235 – Max speed 188km/h (102kt), cruising speed 170km/h (91kt), typical spraying speed 145km/h (78kt). Initial rate of climb 630ft/min. Service ceiling 13,000ft. PA-36-325 – Max speed 216km/h (116kt), cruising speed 210km/h (113kt), spraying speed range 161 to 193km/h (87 to 104kt). Initial rate of climb 550ft/min. Service ceiling 15,000ft. Range 772km (417nm).

Weights: PA-25-235 – Empty 585kg (1288lb), max takeoff 1317kg (2900lb). PA-36-375 – Empty 1162kg (2560lb), max takeoff 2180kg (4800lb).

Dimensions: PA-25-235 – Wing span 11.02m (36tft 2in), length 7.55m (24ft 9in), height 2.19m (7ft 2in). Wing area 17.0m² (183sq ft). PA-36-375 – Wing span 11.82m (38ft 10in), length 8.39m (27ft 6in), height 2.29m (7ft 6in). Wing area 21.0m² (225.65sq ft).

Capacity: Seating for pilot only, but can be fitted with an optional jump seat. PA-25-235 – Hopper capacity 568 litres (150US gal/125Imp gal), or 545kg (1200lb). PA-36-375 – Hopper capacity 1041 litres (275US gal/229Imp gal), or 1000kg (2200lb).

Production: Total PA-25 Pawnee production 5015. PA-36 Pawnee Brave production ceased in 1982.

History: The Piper Pawnee was one of the first single seat light aircraft to be specifically designed and built for agricultural spraying and dusting. It was also one of the most successful, with several thousand built, and with licence production in a number of countries.

The PA-25 Pawnee was originally designed by Fred Weick as the Ag-3, and flew in prototype form during 1957. The design was originally powered by a 110kW (150hp) Lycoming O-320, the fuselage structure was designed to absorb impact forces in a crash, the high cockpit had excellent all round vision, the braced wing was fitted with spray bars, while a jump seat could be fitted in the hopper.

Initial production was of the 110kW (150hp) powered Pawnee, which was delivered from August 1959. The Pawnee was replaced by the 175kW (235hp) powered Pawnee B with an enlarged hopper, the Pawnee C followed with oleo type shock absorbers, while the ultimate Pawnee model, the Pawnee D, had a 195kW (260hp) O-540. Production ceased in 1982.

The PA-36 Pawnee Brave meanwhile was a much larger new design, although of the same overall configuration to the Pawnee. The result of Piper research on Pawnee operations, the Pawnee Brave (originally the Pawnee II) was available from 1971. Initial production was of the 210kW (285hp) Continental O-285 Tiara powered PA-36-285. The 225kW (300hp) Lycoming IO-540 powered Brave 300, 280kW (375hp) IO-720 powered Brave 375, and 300kW (400hp) IO-720 powered Brave 400 followed.

Pawnee Brave production ceased in 1982.

Photo: A PA-36 Pawnee Brave 300. (Robert Wiseman)

Piper PA-30 & PA-39 Twin Comanche

Country of origin: United States of America

Type: Six seat light twin

Powerplants: PA-30-160 – Two 120kW (160hp) Lycoming IO-320-B1A fuel injected flat four piston engines driving two blade constant speed Hartzell propellers. PA-39T – Two 120kW (160hp) counter rotating Lycoming IO-320-C1As.

Performance: PA-30-160 – Max speed 330km/h (178kt), max cruising speed 312km/h (168kt), long range cruising speed 267km/h (144kt). Initial rate of climb 1460ft/min. Service ceiling 18,600ft. Max range with no reserves and standard fuel 1795km (970nm), or with tip tanks 2190km (1182nm). PA-39T – Max speed 376km/h (203kt), max cruising speed 357km/h (193kt), economical cruising speed 327km/h (177kt). Initial rate of climb 1460ft/min. Service ceiling 25,000ft. Range at max cruising speed 2373km (1282nm), range at economical cruising speed 2582km (1395nm).

Weights: PA-30-160 – Empty 1002kg (2210lb), max takeoff 1633kg (3600lb), or 1690kg (3725lb) with tip tanks. PA-30-160 – Empty 1097kg (2416lb), max ramp 1690kg (3725lb).

Dimensions: Wing span 10.97m (36ft 0in) or 11.22m (36ft 10in) with tip tanks, length 7.67m (25ft 2in), height 2.49m (8ft 2in). Wing area 16.5m² (178sq ft).

Capacity: Typical seating for four, including pilot in Twin Comanche. Up to six including pilot in Twin Comanche B.

Production: Total Twin Comanche production was 2156, comprising 2001 PA-30s and 155 PA-39s.

History: As its name implies, the Twin Comanche is a twin engine development of the PA-24 Comanche. When in production, it was Piper's premier four/six place light twin, replacing the Apache 235 and positioned beneath the larger and more powerful Aztec.

The Twin Comanche was originally proposed as early as 1956, when the single engine Comanche was undergoing initial development, however the project was delayed while Piper worked on the Comanche and the Aztec twin. So it was not until 1962 that a Comanche was converted to a twin configuration with two 120kW (160hp) IO-320s (originally two 110kW/150hp engines were planned), with first flight on November 7 1962. First flight of a production Twin Comanche was in May 1963, with first deliveries later that year.

The Twin Comanche differed little from its single engine brethren other than changes associated with its twin engine layout, and it quickly proved to be very popular. Improvements to the PA-30 resulted in the introduction of the Twin Comanche B in 1965, which featured a stretched fuselage allowing seating for up to six, as on the equivalent Comanche B single, while turbocharged engines and wingtip tanks were offered as options.

From 1970 the Twin Comanche C featured a slightly higher cruising speed and interior improvements, while the PA-39 Twin Comanche C/R was fitted with counter rotating engines.

Production of the Twin Comanche ceased in 1972 – by which time only the PA-39 was available – due to the flooding of Piper's Lock Haven factory.

Photo: The Twin Comanche B, C and C/R had optional seating for six. (Gary Gentle)

Piper PA-34 Seneca

Country of origin: United States of America

Type: Six place light twin

Powerplants: PA-34-200 – Two 150kW (200hp) Lycoming IO-360-A1A fuel injected flat fours driving two blade c/s props. Seneca V – Two 165kW (220hp) Teledyne Continental L/TSIO-360-RB turbocharged, intercooled fuel injected counter rotating flat sixes driving two blade Hartzell or optional three blade McCauley c/s props.

Performance: PA-34-200 – Max speed 314km/h (170kt), max cruising speed 300km/h (160kt), long range cruising speed 267km/h (144kt). Initial rate of climb 1360ft/min. Service ceiling 19,400ft. Max range with no reserves 1818km (982nm). Seneca V – Max speed 379km/h (205kt), max cruising speed at 10,000ft 341km/h (184kt), at 18,500ft 367km/h (198kt), normal cruising speed at 10,000ft 322km/h (174kt), at 16,500ft 352km/h (190kt). Initial rate of climb 1550ft/min. Max certificated altitude 25,000ft. Range at max range power with reserves at 10,000ft 1295km (700nm), at 18,500ft 1222km (660nm).

Weights: PA-34-200 – Empty 1190kg (2623lb), max takeoff 1905kg (4200lb). Seneca V – Empty equipped 1532kg (3377lb), max takeoff 2155kg (4750lb).

Dimensions: PA-34-200 – Wing span 11.85m (38ft 11in), length 8.69m (28ft 6in), height 3.02m (9ft 11in). Wing area 19.2m² (206.5sq ft). Seneca V – Same except length 8.72m (28ft 8in). Wing area 19.4m² (208.7sq ft).

Capacity: Seating for six in all but Seneca V which seats five.

Production: Approx 4750 Senecas built by Piper (incl approx 200 Vs), plus approx 20 Seneca IIs licence built in Poland by PZL Mielec as the M-20 Mewa, and over 870 in Brazil by Neiva as the EMB-810.

History: The most successful six place light twin since its introduction, the Seneca is a twin engine development of the Cherokee Six.

Seneca development began when Piper flew a converted trimotor Cherokee Six, designated PA-32-3M, fitted with two additional 85kW (115hp) Lycomings O-235 on either wing. The subsequent twin engine prototype PA-34 Seneca first flew with two 135kW (180hp) Lycomings, while the definitive standard third Seneca prototype first flew in October 1969 with fuel injected 150kW (200hp) IO-360s. Production deliveries of the initial PA-34-200 model began in late 1971.

Handling and performance criticisms were addressed from the 1974 model year with the PA-34-200T Seneca II which introduced changes to the flight controls and, more importantly, two turbocharged Continental TSIO-360-Es. Piper originally planned that the follow-on Seneca III would feature a T-tail, but these plans were dropped and the main changes introduced were counter rotating 165kW (220hp) TSIO-360s and a revised interior and instrument panel. Introduced in 1981, the Seneca III was replaced by New Piper's improved Seneca IV in 1994 with aerodynamic refinements, axisymetric engine inlets and a revised interior.

The current Seneca V was introduced in January 1997. It features intercooled turbocharged L/TSIO-360-RB engines which maintain rated power to 19,500ft, and seating for five, with a standard entertainment/executive workstation with extendable worktable and optional phone/fax. A sixth seat in place of the workstation is optional.

Photo: The Seneca V. (Piper)

Piper PA-38 Tomahawk

Country of origin: United States of America

Type: Two seat light aircraft and basic trainer

Powerplant: One 85kW (112hp) Avco Lycoming O-235-L2A or -L2C flat four piston engine driving a two blade fixed pitch Sensenich propeller.

Performance: Max speed 202km/h (109kt), max cruising speed 200km/h (108kt), normal cruising speed 185km/h (100kt). Initial rate of climb 718ft/min. Service ceiling 13,000ft. Max range with reserves 867km (468nm).

Weights: Empty 512kg (1128lb), max takeoff 757kg (1670lb).

Dimensions: Wing span 10.36m (34ft 0in), length 7.04m (23ft 1in), height 2.77m (9ft 1in). Wing area 11.6m² (124.7sq ft).

Capacity: Seating for two side by side.

Production: 2497 Tomahawks were built between 1978 and 1983.

History: The Piper PA-38 Tomahawk (nicknamed Tommy for short) was the first all new two seat trainer built by one of the USA's big three GA manufacturers in almost three decades when it was introduced.

The PA-38-112 Tomahawk was designed as a relatively inexpensive to acquire and operate two seat trainer to tackle the firmly established definitive basic trainer in the 1970s, the Cessna 150 and 152, and to take over the spot in Piper's model range then occupied by two seat variants of the PA-28 Cherokee series.

Design input for the Tomahawk came from a questionnaire Piper distributed randomly to 10,000 flight instructors during the mid 1970s. With their responses in mind (ideal characteristics included night lighting, dual toe brakes, a fuel selector accessible to both student and instructor, low noise levels, position lights and the ability to spin), Piper developed the PA-38. The resulting aircraft featured a T-tail and NASA Whitcomb GA(W)-1 design low set wing of constant chord and thickness (also featured on the competing but less successful Beech Skipper), a cabin wider than the Cherokee's (and thus much wider than the Cessna 150/152's) with 360° vision and a Lycoming O-235 powerplant. Many parts, such as the main undercarriage wheels and elevators, were interchangeable.

Piper announced it was developing the Tomahawk during late 1977 and first deliveries were made in early 1978. Despite an initial mixed reaction to the new trainer from the flying public, the Tomahawk was an instant sales success with over 1000 built in the first year of production alone. In service the Tomahawk proved to be economical to operate, but the aircraft was dogged by quality control problems (some 19 Airworthiness Directives were issued by the FAA in the PA-38's first four years) and unpredictable stalling characteristics, resulting in a number of stall/spin accidents.

Flow strips were added to the wing on late production Tomahawk Is to improve the much criticised stall characteristics, while a number of other problems, including the poor quality control, were addressed in the improved Tomahawk II, which was introduced for the 1981 model year. Enhancements included improved sound proofing, windscreen defrosting, door latching and nose wheel design.

Piper ceased production of the Tomahawk during 1983.

Photo: The Tomahawk features a NASA Whitcomb GA(W)-1 constant chord and thickness wing, T-tail and car style door. (Paul Sadler)

Piper PA-31 Navajo

Country of origin: United States of America

Type: Six/eight seat corporate transport and commuter airliner

Powerplants: PA-31-310 – Two 230kW (310hp) Lycoming TIO-540-A turbocharged and fuel injected flat six piston engines driving three blade constant speed propellers. PA-31P – Two 317kW (425hp) Lycoming TIGO-541-E1A geared, turbocharged and fuel injected engines.

Performance: PA-31-310 – Max speed 420km/h (227kt), max cruising speed 404km/h (218kt), long range cruising speed 273km/h (147kt). Initial rate of climb 1445ft/min. Service ceiling 27,300ft. Range with reserves 2398km (1295nm). PA-31P – Max speed 451km/h (244kt), max cruising speed 428km/h (231kt), long range cruising speed 306km/h (165kt). Initial rate of climb 1740ft/min. Operational ceiling 29,000ft. Range with reserves 2150km (1160nm).

Weights: PA-31-310 – Empty equipped 1843kg (4062lb), max takeoff 2950kg (6500lb). PA-31P – Empty equipped 2380kg (5250lb), max takeoff 3540kg (7800lb).

Dimensions: PA-31-310 – Wing span 12.40m (40ft 8in), length 9.94m (32ft 8in), height 3.97m (13ft 0in). Wing area 21.3m^2 (229sq ft). PA-31P – Same except for length 10.52m (34ft 6in), height 4.04m (13ft 3in).

Capacity: Configured to seat six (including pilot) in standard and executive layouts, and eight in commuter layout.

Production: Total PA-31 Navajo production of 2044, including 259 Pressurised Navajo PA-31Ps.

History: The highly successful Navajo six/eight seat cabin class twin has been adapted and operated in a number of commuter, charter, air taxi, light freight and executive transport roles, and has spawned a series of developments.

The PA-31 was developed at the request of company founder William T Piper, and the program for a new larger twin was given the project name Inca. The first prototype PA-31 made the type's first flight on September 30 1964 and was Piper's largest aircraft to be built to that time.

Deliveries began in the first half of 1967, with two basic models offered, the 225kW (300hp) IO-540-M powered PA-31-300 Navajo, and the PA-31-310 Turbo Navajo, with turbocharged 230kW (310hp) TIO-540 engines and a higher max takeoff weight. Both featured Piper's distinctive Tiger Shark engine nacelles with optional nacelle lockers. The improved Turbo Navajo B was released in late 1971 (the normally aspirated PA-31-300 was dropped at the same time). The Navajo C and the Navajo C/R, which had more powerful 242kW (325hp) TIO-540-F counter rotating engines, appeared in 1974.

Aimed at the corporate aircraft market, the pressurised Navajo PA-31P had three windows per side of the cabin, geared, turbocharged and fuel injected TIGO-541-E1A engines, a higher takeoff weight and strengthened structure and undercarriage, optional extra fuel, a lengthened nose, and most importantly a cabin pressurisation system. The PA-31P first flew in March 1968, first deliveries took place from 1970, and it remained in production until 1984.

Meanwhile production of the PA-31-310 had ceased in 1983. Further developments of the Navajo, including the Chieftain, Mojave and Cheyenne, are described separately.

Photo: A PA-31-300 Navajo. (Rob Finlayson)

Piper PA-31 Mojave, Chieftain & T-1040

Country of origin: United States of America

Type: Eight/10 seat corporate transport and commuter airliner

Powerplants: PA-31P-350 Mojave – Two 260kW (350hp) Lycoming TIO-540-V2AD turbocharged and fuel injected flat six piston engines driving three blade constant speed Hartzell propellers. PA-31-350 Chieftain – Two 260kW (350hp) Lycoming TIO-540-J2BD turbocharged and fuel injected flat sixes.

Performance: PA-31P-350 – Max speed 447km/h (241kt), max cruising speed 435km/h (235kt), long range cruising speed 361km/h (195kt). Initial rate of climb 1220ft/min. Service ceiling 30,400ft. Max range with reserves 2260km (1220nm). PA-31-350 – Max speed 428km/h (231kt), max cruising speed 320km/h (173kt), long range cruising speed 254km/h (137kt). Initial rate of climb 1120ft/min. Operational ceiling 24,000ft. Max range with reserves and standard fuel 1760km (950nm), with optional fuel 2390km (1290nm).

Weights: PA-31P-350 – Empty equipped 2495kg (5500lb), max takeoff 3265kg (7200lb). PA-31-350 – Empty equipped 1988kg (4383lb), max takeoff 3175kg (7000lb).

Dimensions: PA-31P-350 – Wing span 13.56m (44ft 6in), length 10.52m (34ft 6in), height 3.96m (13ft 0in). Wing area 22.0m^2 (237sq ft). PA-31-350 – Wing span 12.40m (40ft 8in), length 10.55m (34ft 8in), height 3.96m (13ft 0in). Wing area 21.3m^2 (229sq ft).

Capacity: Standard seating in Mojave for seven, including one pilot and passenger, or two pilots on flightdeck, with seating for five behind them. Chieftain has max seating for 10.

Production: Mojave production approx 50. 1825 Chieftains built.

History: The PA-31P-350 Mojave was the last pressurised version of the PA-31 series to be built, while the PA-31-350 Chieftain was a stretched Navajo.

The stretched Navajo Chieftain first appeared in 1973, after Piper began design work in 1971 (delays were caused by the destruction of the second prototype and early production aircraft due to flooding at Piper's Lock Haven plant in June 1972). Originally dubbed the Navajo II, the Navajo Chieftain was intended to compete against the Cessna 402 and to a lesser extent the turboprop powered Beech 99. Changes over the basic Navajo were many, including a 61cm (2ft) fuselage stretch, six side cabin windows, larger doors (an extra crew door was optional), and more powerful and counter rotating 260kW (350hp) TIO-540 engines. From the 1980 model year the PA-31-350 became simply as the Chieftain. Production continued until October 1984.

Small numbers were also built of the airline optimised T-1020 (based on the Chieftain but 'hardened' for airline operations) and Pratt & Whitney Canada PT6A powered T-1040 (PA-31T-3). The latter combined the Chieftain's fuselage with the Cheyenne I's PT6A-11 engines, nose and tail, the Cheyenne IIXL's wings and landing gear, and the Cheyenne III's nacelles and baggage lockers.

The Mojave was a development of the PA-31P, and its airframe was essentially similar to the turboprop powered PA-31T Cheyenne I's. Changes included less powerful 260kW (350hp) counter rotating IO-540-V2As, a lower cabin pressure differential, and longer span wings. Mojaves were built between 1983 and 1986.

Photo: A New Zealand registered Piper T-1040. (Les Bushell)

Piper PA-31T Cheyenne

Country of origin: United States of America

Type: Twin turboprop corporate transports

Powerplants: PA-31T Cheyenne – Two 460kW (620shp) Pratt & Whitney Canada PT6A-28 turboprops driving three blade constant speed Hartzell propellers. PA-31T2-620 Cheyenne IIXL – Two 560kW (750shp) PT6A-135s.

Performance: PA-31T – Max speed and max cruising speed 516km/h (280kt), economical cruising speed 452km/h (244kt). Initial rate of climb 2800ft/min. Service ceiling 29,000ft. Range at max cruising speed 1555km (840nm). PA-31T2-620 – Max speed 510km/h (275kt), max cruising speed 500km/h (270kt), economical cruising speed 385km/h (208kt). Service ceiling 32,400ft. Range at max cruising speed 2608km (1408nm), at economical cruising speed with max fuel 2740km (1478nm).

Weights: PA-31T – Empty equipped 2260kg (4983lb), max takeoff 4082kg (9000lb). PA-31T2-620 – Empty equipped 2580kg (5680lb), max takeoff 4335kg (9540lb).

Dimensions: PA-31T – Wing span 13.01m (42ft 8in), length 10.57m (34ft 8in), height 3.89m (12ft 9in). Wing area 21.3m² (229sq ft). PA-31T2-620 – Same except for length 11.18m (36ft 8in).

Capacity: Cheyenne II, I, IA, and IIXL typically seat six, including pilot, or optionally eight.

Production: Total PA-31T Cheyenne production of approximately 825, comprising 526 Cheyenne IIs, 215 Cheyenne I & IIAs and 82 Cheyenne IIXLs. At late 2000 over 700 PA-31Ts were in corporate use.

History: The Piper Cheyenne is a family of turboprop corporate aircraft based on the popular Navajo and Chieftain piston twins

Although the first Cheyenne was not delivered until mid 1974, work on a turboprop version of the Pressurised Navajo dates back almost a decade earlier to the mid 1960s. The prototype of the Cheyenne first flew on August 29 1969, but Piper had to redesign the flight control systems to handle the increased loads on the airframe due to the higher speeds. Production deliveries were further delayed due to flooding at Piper's Lock Haven plant in June 1972.

Certification had been granted on May 3 1972, while the first production aircraft (powered by 462kW/620shp PT6A-28s) first flew on October 22 1973.

Piper introduced the lower powered (373kW/500shp PT6A-11s) and less expensive Cheyenne I in 1978, and renamed the original Cheyenne the Cheyenne II. Refinements to the Cheyenne I made in 1983, including more powerful engines, revised cowlings and interior, resulted in the Cheyenne IA.

Meanwhile the stretched Cheyenne IIXL had been introduced in 1979. Compared with the standard length Cheyennes, the IIXL was 61cm (2ft) longer, featured an extra cabin window on the left side, 180kg (400lb) increased max takeoff weight and 560kW (750shp) PT6A-135s.

An improved IIXLA was planned, but did not enter production.

The further stretched and T-tail PA-42 Cheyenne III was also introduced in 1978, and is described separately.

Photo: The IIXL variant featured the largest cabin in the Cheyenne I & II family. (Gary Gentle)

Piper PA-42 Cheyenne III, IIIA & 400LS

Country of origin: United States of America

Type: Twin turboprop corporate transports

Powerplants: PA-42-720 Cheyenne III – Two 535kW (720shp) Pratt & Whitney Canada PT6A-41 turboprops driving three blade constant speed Hartzell propellers. PA-42-1000 Cheyenne 400LS – Two 1225kW (1645shp) derated to 745kW (1000shp) Garrett TPE331-14A/Bs driving four blade Hartzell props.

Performance: PA-42-720 – Max speed 537km/h (290kt), max cruising speed 461km/h (250kt), economical cruising speed 413km/h (223kt). Initial rate of climb 2235ft/min. Service ceiling 33,000ft. Range at max cruising speed 3100km (1675nm). PA-42-1000 – Max speed 650km/h (351kt), max cruising speed 594km/h (320kt), economical cruising speed 506km/h (273kt). Initial rate of climb 3242ft/min. Range at max cruising speed 3015km (1630nm), range at economical cruising speed 3500km (1890nm).

Weights: PA-42-720 – Empty 2900kg (6389lb), max ramp weight 5125kg (11,285lb). PA-42-1000 – Empty 3412kg (7522lb), max takeoff 5466kg (12,050lb).

Dimensions: PA-42-720 – Wing span (over tip tanks) 14.53m (47ft 8in), length 13.23m (43ft 5in), height 4.50m (14ft 9in). Wing area 27.2m² (293.0sq ft). PA-42-1000 – Same except for height 5.18m (17ft 0in).

Capacity: One or two pilots on flightdeck, with main cabin seating for between six and nine passengers. Typical seating for six in main cabin in corporate configuration.

Production: PA-42 Cheyenne production totals approximately 185 aircraft, of which approximately 145 are Cheyenne IIIs and IIIAs. At late 2000 183 PA-42s were in use.

History: Aimed directly at Beech's successful King Air twin turboprop series, the PA-42 Cheyennes are larger developments of the earlier PA-31T Cheyennes (in turn themselves turboprop developments of the PA-31 Navajo).

The PA-42 Cheyenne III was announced in September 1977. The first production Cheyenne III first flew on May 18 1979 and FAA certification was granted in early 1980. Compared with the Cheyenne II the PA-42 was about 1m (3ft) longer, was powered by 537kW (720shp) PT6A-41 turboshafts and introduced a T-tail, the most obvious external difference between the PA-31T and PA-42. Deliveries of production Cheyenne IIIs began on June 30 1980.

Development and improvement of the III led to the PA-42-720 Cheyenne IIIA, with PT6A-61 engines, a higher service ceiling and revised systems and interior.

The higher powered and significantly faster PA-42-1000 is basically similar to the PA-42-720 except for its far more powerful 745kW (1000hp) Garrett TPE331 turboprops driving four blade propellers. Piper's largest and fastest production aircraft to date, the PA-42-1000 was initially called the Cheyenne IV, before becoming known as the Cheyenne 400LS, and then simply the Cheyenne 400. First flown in 1983, the Cheyenne 400 was delivered from late 1984. Both the Cheyenne IIIA and 400 were available on special order through to the early 1990s.

Photo: A PA-42-720 Cheyenne III. (Brian Wilkes)

Piper PA-44 Seminole

Country of origin: United States of America

Type: Four seat light twin

Powerplants: PA-44-180 – Two 135kW (180hp) Lycoming O-360-E1AD flat four piston engines driving two or optionally three blade constant speed Hartzell propellers. PA-44-180T – Two 135kW (180hp) Lycoming TO-360-E1A6D turbocharged flat fours driving two blade constant speed props.

Performance: PA-44-180 – Max speed 311km/h (168kt), max cruising speed 309km/h (167kt), long range cruising speed 280km/h (151kt). Initial rate of climb 1200ft/min. Service ceiling 17,100ft. Range with reserves 1630km (880nm). PA-44-180T – Max speed 363km/h (196kt), max cruising speed 343km/h (185kt), long range cruising speed 293km/h (158kt). Initial rate of climb 1290ft/min. Range with reserves 1520km (820nm).

Weights: PA-44-180 – Empty 1070kg (2360lb), max takeoff 1723kg (3800lb). PA-44-180T – Empty 1116kg (2461lb), max takeoff 1780kg (3925lb).

Dimensions: Wing span 11.77m (38ft 8in), length 8.41m (27ft 7in), height 2.59m (8ft 6in). Wing area 17.1m^2 (183.8sq ft).

Capacity: Typical seating for four.

Production: Total Seminole production through to 1990 of 469, including 87 Turbo Seminoles. Approx 30 PA-44-180s built by New Piper since 1995.

History: The PA-44 Seminole was developed during the heyday of the GA industry in the mid to late 1970s but fell victim to the depressed market from the early 1980s plus the growing reliability and popularity of high performance big singles. As a result it has been built in only fairly modest numbers.

A contemporary of the Gulfstream GA-7 Cougar and Beechcraft Duchess, the Seminole was conceived in part as a Twin Comanche replacement, aimed at the self flying businessperson and the twin engine training market. Developed from the mid 1970s, the Seminole is based on the PA-28R Arrow series, with the Arrow's single engine replaced by two counter rotating 135kW (180hp) Lycoming O-360s, plus a new T-tail and semi tapered wings. The prototype first flew in May 1976. Production machines, designated PA-44-180, were delivered from May 1978.

The turbocharged PA-44-180T was introduced from 1980. Aside from turbocharged TO-360s, the Turbo Seminole introduced prop de-icing and an oxygen system. Just 87 PA-44-180Ts were built when Piper ceased production for the first time in late 1981. Piper reopened the Seminole line in 1988, with 30 non turbocharged PA-44s built before once more suspending production in 1990, due to its parlous financial position at the time.

Once again the PA-28-180 Seminole is back in production, with manufacture restarting in 1995 although sales have been relatively modest. Piper currently offers two avionics packages for the Seminole, a standard fit and an Advanced Training Group package.

Interestingly the PA-44 is the only T-tail Piper currently in production, even though in the late 1970s most Piper aircraft had been modified to feature a T-tail.

Photo: A new production PA-44-180. (Piper)

Piper (Ted Smith) Aerostar

Country of origin: United States of America

Type: Six seat high performance light twin

Powerplants: 600A – Two 215kW (290hp) Lycoming IO-540-K1J5 fuel injected flat six piston engines driving three blade constant speed Hartzell propellers. PA-60-700P – Two 260kW (350hp) turbocharged and counter rotating TIO-540-U2As.

Performance: 600A – Max speed 418km/h (226kt), long range cruising speed 357km/h (193kt). Initial rate of climb 1800ft/min. Service ceiling 21,200ft. Max range with reserves 2225km (1200nm). PA-60-700P – Max speed 490km/h (264kt), max cruising speed 484km/h (261kt), economical cruising speed 390km/h (211kt). Initial rate of climb 1755ft/min. Service ceiling 25,000ft. Range at max cruising speed 1250km (675nm), at economical cruising speed with max fuel 2150km (1160nm).

Weights: 600A – Empty 1695kg (3757lb), max takeoff 2495kg (5500lb). PA-60-700P – Empty 1940kg (4275lb), MTOW 2864kg (6315lb).

Dimensions: 600A – Wing span 10.41m (34ft 2in), length 10.61m (34ft 10in), height 3.89m (12ft 1in). Wing area 15.8m^2 (170sq ft). PA-60-700P – Same except for wing span 11.18m (36ft 8in). Wing area 16.6m^2 (178.2sq ft).

Capacity: Typical seating for six.

Production: 1010 Aerostars built, including 519 by Piper.

History: The Aerostar – which in its higher powered forms can lay claim to being the fastest piston twin GA aircraft built – was designed by Ted Smith, who was also responsible for the Aero Commander twins.

Smith's original intention in designing the Aerostar was to develop a family of single and piston twins, twin turboprop and even twin jet powered versions of the same basic aircraft. However the Aerostar appeared in piston twin form only. Smith began design work on the Aerostar in late 1964, with a prototype making its first flight two years later in November 1966.

The prototype was powered by 120kW (160hp) Lycoming IO-320s, but the Aerostar was placed into production from 1968 as the Aerostar 600 with 215kW (290hp) IO-540s. The turbocharged Aerostar 601 followed the 600 into production shortly afterwards, while the turbocharged and pressurised 601P went into production in 1972. By this time Butler Aviation had acquired the production rights of the Aerostar in 1970, producing a small number as Butler Aerostars. Smith bought the line back again in 1972, and his new company, Ted R Smith and Associates, resumed Aerostar manufacture, including of the improved 601B with the same span wings as on the 601P, until Piper acquired the Aerostar line in March 1978.

Piper continued production of the 600A, 601B and 601P at Ted Smith's Santa Maria plant, and introduced the 602P with low compression TIO-540-AA1A5 engines.

When Piper transferred production to its new Vero Beach, Florida factory in early 1982, only the 602P was in production, and this was redesignated the PA-60-602P. The PA-60-700P was the last Aerostar version, and just 25 were built. In production between 1983 and 1985, the 700P has more powerful engines, a higher max takeoff weight and optional extra fuel capacity.

Photo: A Piper built PA-60-602P Aerostar . (Rob Finlayson)

Piper PA-46 Malibu & Malibu Mirage

Country of origin: United States of America

Type: Six seat high performance light aircraft

Powerplant: PA-46-310P – One 230kW (310hp) Continental TSIO-520-BE turbocharged and fuel injected flat six piston engine driving a two blade constant speed Hartzell propeller. PA-46-350P – One 260kW (350hp) Textron Lycoming TIO-540-AE2A.

Performance: PA-46-310P – Max speed 434km/h (234kt), max cruising speed 398km/h (215kt), long range cruising speed 363km/h (196kt). Initial rate of climb 1170ft/min. Service ceiling 25,000ft. Max range at long range cruising speed and altitude with reserves 2880km (1555nm). PA-46-350P – Max speed at mid cruise weight 407kt (220kt), cruising speed 394kt (213kt). Service ceiling 25,000ft. Range with max fuel and reserves at normal cruising speed and optimum altitude 1953km (1055nm).

Weights: PA-46-310P – Empty 1066kg (2350lb), max takeoff 1860kg (4100lb). PA-46-350P – Empty equipped 1397kg (3080lb), max takeoff 1968kg (4340lb).

Dimensions: PA-46-310P – Wing span 13.11m (43ft 0in), length 8.66m (28ft 5in), height 3.44m (11ft 4in). Wing area 16.3m² (175sq ft). PA-46-350P – Same except for length 8.81m (28ft 11in).

Capacity: Typical seating for pilot and five passengers.

Production: More than 900 PA-46s delivered, comprising 404 PA-46-310Ps and over 500 PA-46-350Ps.

History: According to Piper the all new Piper Malibu was the first pressurised cabin class piston single. Certainly it promised to be one of the first of a new generation of light aircraft introduced from the early 1980s before recession and oppressive liability laws in the USA strangled the GA industry. Nevertheless, the PA-46 remains in production today and is selling relatively strongly.

Announced in November 1982, the Malibu was intended to compete against Cessna's pressurised P210 Centurion, plus older light business twins. Designed with the aid of CAD/CAM (Computer Aided Design/Computer Aided Manufacture), the prototype first flew in 1980. Certification was awarded in September 1983, with production deliveries from that November.

Features of the first production model PA-46-310P included the specially developed turbocharged 230kW (310hp) Continental TSIO-520, a high aspect ratio wing, a relatively roomy cabin with club seating for four behind the pilot, a rear airstair style door, IFR avionics as standard, and cabin pressurisation.

The improved PA-46-350P Malibu Mirage replaced the -310P Malibu in production from October 1988. The major change introduced on the Malibu Mirage was the more powerful 260kW (350hp) Textron Lycoming TIO-540-AE2A, while other changes included a new electrical system and revised interior.

New Piper has made a number of minor improvements to the Malibu Mirage, including to the brakes, autopilot and air-conditioning. In 1999 the Mirages gained the strengthened wing of the turboprop Malibu Meridian development, allowing an 18kg (40lb) increase in max takeoff weight. The Mirage is also offered with conventional and EFIS avionics packages.

Photo: A PA-46-350P Malibu Mirage. (Bob Grimstead)

Piper PA-46-500TP Malibu Meridian

Country of origin: United States of America

Type: Six seat corporate turboprop

Powerplant: One 373kW (500shp) takeoff rated Pratt & Whitney Canada PT6A-42A turboprop driving a four blade constant speed Hartzell propeller.

Performance: Max cruising speed at 30,000ft and mid cruise weight 485km/h (262kt). Initial rate of climb 1741ft/min. Certificated altitude 30,000ft. Range at max cruising speed at 30,000ft with reserves 1982km (1070nm). Endurance 4.37hr.

Weights: Standard equipped 1471kg (3243lb), max takeoff 2200kg (4850lb).

Dimensions: Wing span 13.11m (43ft 0in), length 8.98m (29ft 6in), height 3.44m (11ft 4in). Wing area 17.0m² (183.0sq ft).

Capacity: Typical seating for pilot and five passengers.

Production: First production aircraft handed over November 2000 at which stage Piper held orders for 135. Price approx $US1.375m. Production target 60 per year.

History: The Malibu Meridian is the first major aircraft program from New Piper Aircraft Inc and is a high performance turboprop development of the popular Malibu Mirage.

New Piper announced development of the Meridian at the 1997 NBAA convention. An aerodynamic conforming prototype was rolled out at Piper's Vero Beach, Florida facilities on August 13 1998 and flew for the first time on August 21 that year. Three further Meridian prototypes entered the flight test program during 1999. Certification was awarded on September 27 2000, with the first customer delivery on November 7 2000.

The Meridian's most obvious feature compared with the Malibu is its Pratt & Whitney Canada PT6A-42A turboprop. The -42A has a thermodynamic rating of 901kW (1029shp) but on the Meridian is derated to 373kW (500shp) for takeoff. This allows the engine to maintain max power through to the aircraft's 30,000ft ceiling, giving a 485km/h (262kt) cruising speed.

Major sections of the Meridian's fuselage are common with the Malibu's, but the turboprop features a number of significant changes, including a stainless steel firewall, chord lengthening wing root gloves which increase wing area to ensure a relatively low stall speed, increased area horizontal tail and rudder, and increased fuel capacity.

The Meridian also gains a completely new instrument panel. Standard equipment includes a three axis S-TEC 550 autopilot which is coupled to the dual 13cm (5in) colour LCD Garmin GNS 530 integrated GPS displays (incorporating IFR GPS and VOR/ILS receiver with glidescope), and a Meggitt Engine Instrument Display System comprising dual LCDs presenting engine information (such as torque, temperatures and pressures, propeller RPM, outside air temperature and fuel level at destination and time to destination calculations).

An optional Electronic Flight Display System (EFDS) presents flight information on four Meggitt colour LCDs (two per side), comprising dual primary flight displays and dual navigation displays. Conventional flight instrumentation is standard.

Photo: One of three Meridian certification flight test aircraft. The family resemblance with the Mirage is obvious. (Piper)

PZL M-18 Dromader

Country of origin: Poland

Type: Ag spraying and firefighter aircraft

Powerplant: One 745kW (1000hp) PZL Kalisz (Shvetsov) ASz-62IR supercharged nine cylinder radial piston engine driving a four blade constant speed propeller.

Performance: M-18 & M-18A (with ag equipment) – Max cruising speed 237km/h (128kt), typical operating speed range 170 to 190km/h (90 to 103kt). Initial rate of climb 1115ft/min. Service ceiling 21,235ft. Max range with no reserves with max fuel and no ag equipment 970km (520nm). M-18A (without ag equipment) – Max speed 256km/h (138kt), cruising speed 205km/h (110kt), typical operating speed 230km/h (124kt). Initial rate of climb 1360ft/min. Service ceiling 21,235ft. Max range with no reserves with max fuel and no ag equipment 970km (520nm).

Weights: M-18A – Empty 2690kg (5930lb), max takeoff 4700kg (10,360lb) but restricted to 4200kg (9230lb) under FAR Pt 23.

Dimensions: M-18A – Wing span 17.70m (58ft 1in), length 9.47m (31ft 3in), height over tail 3.70m (12ft 2in). Wing area 40.0m² (430.5sq ft).

Capacity: M-18 seats pilot only, M-18A has second seat for a ground loader or mechanic behind the pilot, M-18AS and BS have a second cockpit with instrumentation for an instructor. M-18B hopper capacity of 2500 litres (550Imp gal/660US gal) of liquid or 2200kg (4850lb) of dry chemicals.

Production: By 2000 over 700 Dromaders built, most for export. M-18 single seater production ceased in 1984 after 230 had been built.

History: The M-18 Dromader agricultural aircraft has been one of Poland's most successful aircraft exports.

PZL Swidnik designed the Dromader in collaboration with Rockwell International in the US during the mid 1970s. From the outset the aim was to certificate the aircraft to western standards. The first prototype of the basic single seat M-18 flew on August 27 1976, a second prototype flew that October. Poland awarded certification for the Dromader during September 1978, series production began in 1979.

The basic Dromader design was conventional, with power supplied by a nine cylinder radial engine, while the outer wing panels were based on those on the Rockwell Thrush Commander.

The basic single seat M-18 was in production for five years until 1984 when it was replaced by the two seat M-18A. The two seat M-18A was developed to allow the carriage of either a mechanic or chemical loader to austere fields. In the meantime PZL Mielec had developed a firebombing derivative which first flew in 1978. The M-18AS trainer has a second cockpit for flight instruction. Since 1996 the M-18B, with a 5300kg (11,684lb) max takeoff weight, has been the standard production model. The M-18BS is a two seat trainer based on the M-18B. The M-18C with 895kW (1200hp) Kalisz K-9 engine flew in 1995 but has not entered production.

In the USA, Melex (part owned by PZL Mielec) developed a PT6A turboprop development dubbed the T45 Turbine Dromader. The Turbine Dromader first flew during 1985 and the US FAA issued it a Supplementary Type Certificate in April 1986. Others have been converted with TPE331s.

Photo: An M-18A Dromader. (Howard Geary)

PZL Swidnik (Mil) Mi-2 & Kania

Countries of origin: Poland & Russia

Type: Light twin utility helicopter

Powerplants: Mi-2 – Two 300kW (400shp) Isotov designed Polish built GTD-350 turboshafts driving a three blade main rotor and two blade tail rotor. Kania – Two 315kW (720shp) Allison 250-C20B turboshafts driving a three blade main and two blade tail rotor.

Performance: Mi-2 – Max cruising speed 200km/h (108kt), long range cruising speed 190km/h (102kt). Max rate of climb 885ft/min. Service ceiling 13,125ft. Hovering ceiling in ground effect 6560ft. Range with max payload and reserves 170km (91nm), range with max fuel 440km (237nm), range with optional fuel 580km (313nm). Kania – Max cruising speed 215km/h (116kt), economical cruising speed 190km/h (102kt). Initial rate of climb 1722ft/min. Service ceiling 13,120ft. Hovering ceiling out of ground effect 4510ft. Range with max fuel and reserves 435km (234nm), with auxiliary fuel and reserves 800km (432nm). Endurance with auxiliary fuel 4hr.

Weights: Mi-2 – Empty equipped 2402kg (5295lb) in passenger version, or 2372kg (5229lb) in transport version; max takeoff 3550kg (7826lb). Kania – Basic empty 2000kg (4410lb), max takeoff 3550kg (7826lb).

Dimensions: Mi-2 – Main rotor diameter 14.50m (47ft 7in), length overall 17.48m (57ft 4in), fuselage length 11.94m (39ft 2in), height (no tail rotor) 2.70m (8ft 10in). Main rotor disc area 166.4m² (1791.1sq ft). Kania – Same except for fuselage length 12.03m (39ft 6in).

Capacity: Mi-2 – Two pilots or one pilot and passenger on flightdeck, main cabin seating for seven. Ambulance configurations can accommodate four stretchers and one medical attendant or two stretchers and two attendants. Kania – Pilot and eight passengers in passenger configuration, pilot and five passengers in corporate configuration. Two stretchers, one seated patient and two medical attendants in ambulance configuration. Ag version capacity 1000kg (2205lb) of chemicals.

Production: More than 5500 mainly military Mi-2s built. 15 Kanias built, last delivered in 1997, but it remains available to order.

History: Poland's most successful helicopter was originally developed in Russia by Mil, and in its Allison powered Kania (Kitty Hawk) version has been granted US certification.

Mil originally designed the light utility Mi-2 in Russia during the early 1960s, resulting in a first flight in September 1961. In January 1964 an agreement between the USSR and Poland transferred development and production to the latter country, which commenced in 1965. The Mi-2 evolved since that time and remained in low rate production into the 1990s. The main civil variant is simply designated Mi-2, while Swidnik also developed a diverse number of military variants.

The Kania (Kitty Hawk) is an upgrade of the basic Mi-2, with Allison 250-C20B turboshafts, western avionics, and composite main and tail rotor blades. It also holds US FAR Pt 29 certification. Developed in cooperation with Allison, the Kania first flew on June 3 1979, and US certification was granted in February 1986. The Kania has never entered full scale production but remains on offer, both as a new build aircraft and as an upgrade of existing Mi-2s.

Photo: A Hungarian registered Mi-2. (Viktor László)

PZL Swidnik W-3 Sokol

Countries of origin: Poland

Type: Mid size twin utility helicopter

Powerplants: Two 670kW (900shp) takeoff rated WSK-PZL Rzeszów PZL-10W turboshafts driving a four blade main rotor and three blade tail rotor.

Performance: W-3A – Max cruising speed 243km/h (131kt). Initial rate of climb 2008ft/min. Hovering ceiling (at max takeoff weight) out of ground effect 6220ft. Service ceiling 19,680ft. Max range with reserves 745km (402nm), with auxiliary fuel and reserves 1290km (696nm), with max payload and no reserves 200km (108nm).

Weights: W-3A – Basic operating empty 3850kg (8488lb), max takeoff 6400kg (14,110lb).

Dimensions: Main rotor diameter 15.70m (51ft 6in), length overall rotors turning 18.79m (61ft 8in), fuselage length 14.21m (46ft 8in), height overall 5.14m (16ft 10in), height to top of rotor mast 4.20m (13ft 10in). Main rotor disc area 193.6m² (2034sq ft).

Capacity: Two pilots or pilot and flight engineer or passenger on flightdeck. Main cabin seating for 12 in passenger configuration, or three medical attendants and eight rescued survivors in SAR Anaconda version, or four stretchers and medical attendant in ambulance configuration, one stretcher and medical attendants in critical care EMS version, or five/six passengers in executive configuration. Can carry a 2100kg (4630lb) sling load.

Production: Approximately 130 Sokols of all models have been built, including against Polish military orders.

History: The W-3 Sokol (Falcon) is the first helicopter to be fully designed and built in Poland, and is PZL Swidnik's most promising sales prospect in the near to medium future.

Developed during the mid 1970s, the Sokol made its first flight on November 16 1979, and has since been certificated in Poland, Russia, the US, South Korea and Germany. Following a fairly protracted development program, low rate production of the Sokol commenced during 1985. Initial sales of the general purpose Sokol were within Poland and in the Eastern Bloc, before the collapse of communism allowed PZL Swidnik to broaden its sales base. To do this PZL Swidnik developed the improved W-3A Sokol aimed at achieving western certification. Certification to US FAR Pt 29 standards was granted in May 1993, while German certification was granted in December that year.

The Sokol is of conventional design and construction, with two PZL-10W turboshafts. (These are based on the Russian designed TVD-10B turboprops that power the Polish built An-28). Composites are used in the tail and main rotor blades.

The Sokol is offered in a number of variants and is capable of performing a range of helicopter missions, including passenger transport, VIP, cargo, EMS, medevac, firefighting and search and rescue (the W-3 RM Anaconda).

An upgraded version of the Sokol is currently under development. The SW-5 (a provisional designation) would have twin FADEC equipped 745kW (1000shp) Pratt & Whitney Canada PT6B-67B turboshafts, Sextant supplied avionics, a simplified rotor head and greater use of composites.

Photo: A German police W-3A Sokol. (Grzegorz Holdanowicz)

PZL Swidnik SW-4

Country of origin: Poland

Type: Light utility helicopter

Powerplants: One 335kW (450shp) (283kW/380shp max continuous rated) Rolls-Royce 250-C20R/2 turboshaft driving a three blade main rotor and two blade tail rotor. Option of one 460kW (615shp) Pratt & Whitney Canada PW200/9 turboshaft.

Performance: RR 250 engine – Max speed 232km/h (125kt), normal cruising speed 200km/h (108kt). Initial rate of climb 1973ft/min. Service ceiling 17,820ft. Max range with standard fuel and no reserves 860km (464nm). Endurance 5hr 8min.

Weights: RR 250 engine – Empty 850kg (1874lb), max takeoff (internal load) 1600kg (3527lb), max takeoff with sling load 1800kg (3968lb).

Dimensions: Main rotor disc diameter 9.00m (29ft 6in), length overall rotors turning 10.55m (34ft 8in), fuselage length including tailskid 9.08m (29ft 9in), height overall 3.05m (10ft 10in). Main rotor disc area 63.6m² (684.8sq ft).

Capacity: Standard seating for four or five (including pilot). In medevac configuration accommodation for one stretcher patient and two medical attendants. Max sling load 750kg (1655lb).

Production: Two flying prototypes and one static prototype built.

History: The origins of PZL Swidnik's SW-4 five seat light utility helicopter date back to the early 1980s.

Swidnik began development of a new four/five place light utility helicopter in 1981. This original SW-4 was to have been powered by a 300kW (400shp) PZL Rzeszow GTD-350 turboshaft and was built in mock-up form. It would have had a top speed of 240km/h (130kt) and a max range with auxiliary fuel of 900km (485nm).

The collapse of the Iron Curtain allowed Swidnik to substantially redesign the SW-4, based around the Rolls-Royce (Allison) 250 turboshaft. Aside from the powerplant, design changes included a more streamlined fuselage and revised tail and tailboom.

The first prototype, a non flying ground test aircraft, was rolled out in December 1994. Two flying prototypes have been built, the first of which was completed in 1996 and first flew on October 26 that year. At late 2000 the status of the program was unclear.

PZL Swidnik aims to attain US FAA FAR Part 27 certification for the SW-4. The program was delayed somewhat when PZL Swidnik decided to redesign the rotor head, enlarge the horizontal stabiliser and improve the hydraulic system.

Once the basic Rolls-Royce powered SW-4 is certificated and in production PZL Swidnik wants to develop a Pratt & Whitney Canada PW200 powered variant. A twin engine model has also been considered to allow the helicopter to meet new European regulations which restrict single engine helicopter operations under some conditions.

The SW-4 is expected to be able to fulfil a range of utility missions ranging from executive transport to medevac and police roles. Border patrol and military pilot training are other planned missions.

The helicopter features Bendix King avionics, including an optional IFR instrument package.

Photo: The non flying SW-4 prototype. The future of the SW-4 program is unclear. (PZL Swidnik)

PZL Warszawa-Okecie PZL-104 Wilga

Country of origin: Poland

Type: Four seat light utility aircraft

Powerplant: 35A – One 195kW (260hp) PZL AI-14RA nine cylinder radial piston engine driving a two blade c/s prop. 2000 – One 225kW (300hp) Textron Lycoming IO-540 flat six driving a three blade constant speed prop.

Performance: 35A – Max speed 194km/h (105kt), cruising speed at 75% power 157km/h (85kt). Initial rate of climb 905ft/min. Service ceiling 13,250ft. Range with max fuel and reserves 510km (275nm). 2000 – Cruising speed at 75% power 190km/h (103kt). Max range 1500km (810nm).

Weights: 35A – Empty equipped 870kg (1918lb), max takeoff 1300kg (2866lb). 2000 – Empty 900kg (1984lb), max takeoff 1400kg (3086lb).

Dimensions: 35A/2000 – Wing span 11.12m (36ft 6in), length 8.10m (26ft 7in), height 2.96m (9ft 9in). Wing area 15.5m² (166.8sq ft).

Capacity: Typical seating for four including pilot. Rear two seats can be replaced with fuel tank. Ambulance configuration accommodates two stretchers and medical attendants.

Production: More than 965 Wilgas built since the mid 1960s. Small numbers of Wilga 2000s built, first delivery in 1998.

History: The rugged STOL PZL-104 Wilga has been one of Poland's most successful light aircraft exports.

Poland's Light Aircraft Science and Production Centre in Warsaw began development of the Wilga in the early 1960s as a replacement for the general purpose Czechoslovak L-60 Brigadyr utility. The prototype Wilga 1 was powered by a 135kW (180hp) Narkiewicz WN-6B radial and first flew on April 24 1962. A redesign of the basic aircraft followed, and a modified Wilga 2 with a new fuselage and tail and a 145kW (195hp) WN-6RB engine flew in August 1963. That December the 170kW (225hp) Continental O-470 powered Wilga C or (Wilga 32) flew and Lipnur Gelatnik later built 39 in Indonesia.

Poland's first production Wilgas were the 3A four seat utility and 3S ambulance which introduced the 195kW (260hp) Ivchenko designed AI-14 radial. Soon after PZL reconfigured the Wilga's cabin and landing gear, resulting in the definitive production version, the Wilga 35. The prototype Wilga 35 first flew on July 28 1967.

The Wilga 35 remains in production essentially unchanged, and several variants have been offered, while the Wilga 80 is identical to the 35 other than its further rear positioned carburettor air intake. The Wilga 35A and 80A are designed for flying club operations and are fitted with a hook for glider towing, the 35H and 80H are float equipped, the 35P is usually fitted with four seats, the 35R and 80R are agricultural aircraft fitted with a 270kg (595lb) under fuselage chemical hopper and spray bars, and the 35P is an ambulance variant capable of carrying two stretchers.

The PZL-104M Wilga 2000 is an improved development aimed at western customers. It is powered by a 225kW (300hp) Textron Lycoming Continental IO-540 flat six in a reprofiled nose, and features Allied-Signal avionics and extra fuel. First flight was on August 21 1996, while FAA certification was awarded in 1997, with first delivery (to the Polish border guards) the following year.

Photo: A Wilga 80. (Dave Fraser)

PZL Warszawa-Okecie Koliber

Country of origin: Poland

Type: Four seat light aircraft

Powerplant: 160A – One 120kW (160hp) Textron Lycoming O-320-D2A flat four piston engine driving a two blade fixed pitch Sensenich propeller. 235A – One 175kW (235hp) Textron Lycoming O-540-B4B5 flat six driving a two blade McCauley or three blade Hartzell constant speed prop.

Performance: 160A – Max speed 220km/h (119kt), cruising speed at 75% power 194km/h (105kt). Service ceiling 11,475ft. Max range at 75% power 919km (496nm), at 65% power 960km (518nm). 235A – Max speed 260km/h (140kt), cruising speed at 75% power 248km/h (134kt). Service ceiling 14,755ft. Max range at 75% power 734km (396nm), at 65% power 958km (517nm).

Weights: 160A – Empty 607kg (1337lb), max takeoff 850kg (1874lb). 235A – Empty 705kg (1553lb), max takeoff 1150kg (2533lb).

Dimensions: 160A & 235A – Wing span 9.75m (32ft 0in), length 7.37m (24ft 2in), height 2.80m (9ft 2in). Wing area 12.7m² (136.5sq ft).

Capacity: Typical seating for four.

Production: Total Franklin powered Series I, II and III production approximately 40 units. Approx 75 Lycoming powered Kolibers built.

History: The Koliber (Hummingbird) is a licence built development of the Socata Rallye.

The Rallye was still in production when PZL Warszawa-Okecie acquired a licence to build and develop the Rallye 100ST in Poland. The prototype Koliber was powered by a 87kW (116hp) PZL-F (Franklin) four cylinder engine (Poland had earlier purchased the design and production rights to Franklin engines) and flew on April 18 1978.

Initial production Kolibers featured the 86kW (116hp) engine, later aircraft a more powerful 95kW (125hp) Franklin engine. Franklin powered versions of the Koliber were the Series I, the initial production model, with 10 built and first flight occurring in May 1979; the Series II developed for Polish aero clubs which was capable of limited aerobatics (25 built); and the improved Series III (45 built). Franklin powered Koliber production ceased in 1988.

The Textron Lycoming O-320 powered Koliber 150 first flew in September 1988. The 150A (Koliber II in the USA) was developed for export and was granted US FAR Part 23 certification in early 1994. According to the type's US and Asia Pacific distributor, this was the first time that a four place fixed undercarriage light aircraft had been fully certificated in the USA in over a decade. The first Koliber 150A delivery was made to a US customer in mid 1994, while Koliber 150s have been delivered to a number of European countries.

The PZL-111 Koliber 235A Senor is a more powerful, higher performance development of the Koliber 150A, powered by a 175kW (235hp) Textron Lycoming O-540. It first flew on September 14 1995 and was awarded Polish certification in December 1996.

The latest model is the 120kW (160hp) O-320-D2A powered Koliber 160A which was introduced in 1998, replacing the Koliber 150/150A in production. The first two Koliber 160As were delivered to the UK PZL distributor in late 1999.

Photo: The Koliber is a development of the 'light series' Rallye. This is a Koliber 150A. (Paul Sadler)

Raytheon Beechcraft Bonanza

Country of origin: United States of America

Type: Four to six seat high performance light aircraft

Powerplant: C33 – One 170kW (225hp) Continental fuel injected IO-470-K flat six driving a two blade constant speed propeller. A36 – One 225kW (300hp) Teledyne Continental IO-550-B engine driving a three blade constant speed McCauley propeller. B36TC – One 225kW (300hp) turbocharged Teledyne Continental TIO-520-UB engine.

Performance: C33 – Max speed 312km/h (168kt), max cruising speed 298km/h (161kt), long range cruising speed 248km/h (134kt). Initial rate of climb 930ft/min. Range with standard fuel and no reserves 957km (515nm), with optional tanks 1818km (980nm). A36 – Max speed 340km/h (184kt), max cruising speed 326km/h (176kt). Initial rate of climb 1208ft/min. Range with 45 minute reserves 1694km (914nm). B36TC – Max speed 394km/h (213kt), high speed cruise 370km/h (200kt). Initial rate of climb 1053ft/min. Range with 45 minute reserves 2022km (1092nm).

Weights: C33 – Empty 807kg (1780lb), max takeoff 1383kg (3050lb). A36 – Empty 1040kg (2295lb), max takeoff 1665kg (3650lb). B36TC – Empty 1104kg (2433lb), max takeoff 1746kg (3850lb).

Dimensions: C33 – Wing span 10.00m (32ft 6in), height 2.51m (8ft 3in). Wing area 16.5m² (177.6sq ft). A36 – Wing span 8.38m (27ft 6in), length 8.13m (26ft 8in), height 2.62m (8ft 7in). Wing area 16.8m² (181sq ft). B36TC – Same as for A36.

Capacity: All Model 33s seat four with some models having an optional fifth seat, all Model 36s seat six.

Production: 3352 Model 33s built through to 1996. Approx 3380 normally aspirated Model 36s/A36s built with production continuing. Over 650 turbocharged models built. Annual production rate of around 90 to 100 units.

History: First conceived in the late 1950s as a lower cost derivative of the V-tail Bonanza, the conventional tail Bonanza remains in production today.

Compared with the equivalent Model 35, the first model 33 Debonair introduced a conventional three surface tail, a less powerful engine and a more austere interior fit. It first flew on September 14 1959 and was included in Beech's model range the following year.

The subsequent A33 and B33 Debonairs offered a small number of changes, while the C33 introduced a third cabin window and restyled interior. The Debonair was dropped from the range in 1967, by which time the C33A had been released, an aircraft very similar in performance and trim level to the V-tail Bonanzas, and the name Bonanza was adopted for this model range as well. Development of the 33 continued with the E33 and 155kW (285hp) E33A, the aerobatic E33C, the economy G33 and the F33, available in 155kW (285hp) A and aerobatic C models. The F33A remained in production until 1996.

The larger six seat Model 36 was first released in 1968, featuring a stretched cabin, 155kW (285hp) engine and greater takeoff weights. This aircraft remains in production today as the A36. The four seat A36AT (Airline Trainer)'s IO-500 is limited to 216kW (290hp).

The turbocharged 225kW (300hp) A36TC first appeared in 1979, production switched to the current B36TC in 1981.

Photo: A B36TC Bonanza. (Raytheon)

Raytheon Beechcraft Baron

Country of origin: United States of America

Type: Four or six place business & utility twin

Powerplants: B55 – Two 140kW (260hp) Continental IO-470-L fuel injected horizontally opposed flat six piston engines driving two blade constant speed propellers. 58 (current production) – Two 225kW (300hp) Teledyne Continental IO-550-C Raytheon Special Edition engines driving three blade constant speed Hartzell propellers.

Performance: B55 – Max speed 373km/h (201kt), max cruising speed 348km/h (188kt), long range cruising speed 320km/h (173kt). Initial rate of climb 1693ft/min. Range with reserves 1836km (990nm). 58 – Max speed 386km/h (208kt), max cruising speed 376km/h (203kt), cruising speed 356km/h (192kt), economical cruising speed 300km/h (162kt). Initial rate of climb 1735ft/min. Range with reserves 2432km (1313nm).

Weights: B55 – Empty 1468kg (3236lb), max takeoff 2313kg (5100lb). 58 – Empty 1633kg (3600lb), max takeoff 2495kg (5500lb).

Dimensions: B55 – Wing span 11.53m (37ft 10in), length 8.53m (28ft 0in), height 2.92m (9ft 7in). Wing area 18.5m² (199.2sq ft). 58 – Wing span 11.53m (37ft 10in), length 9.09m (29ft 10in), height 2.97m (9ft 9in). Wing area 18.5m² (199.2sq ft).

Capacity: Models 55 and 56 had standard seating for four, with some models offering an optional fifth seat. Model 58 has optional fifth and sixth seats, with optional club seating arrangement.

Production: More than 2600 of all variants built by late 2000.

History: The successful and long running Baron line is widely regarded as the most successful of its class, and has comfortably outlasted its main rivals from Piper and Cessna.

Development of the Baron began in the late 1950s. The first to fly, the Model 95-55 on February 29 1960, was essentially a re-engined development of the Model 95 Travel Air (Beech's first light twin, which first flew in August 1956). As a result the Baron can lay claim to Bonanza and T-34 Mentor lineage, as the Travel Air combined the fuselage of the former with the tail of the latter, plus twin engines, a new wing and other new features. Some 720 Travel Airs were built from the late 1950s to the late 1960s.

The first Barons were delivered during early 1961, although these early production examples were soon followed off the line in 1962 by the improved A55. The subsequent B55 of 1965 remained in production until 1982, during which time it was continually refined. During the B55's model life other variants entered production, these included the more powerful C55, D55 and E55. In the meantime the turbocharged Baron 56TC appeared in 1967 and the A56TC in 1970, although these were produced only in limited numbers.

The IO-550 powered Model 58 is a stretched version of the 55, and first entered production in 1970. It remains in production today, having evolved somewhat in production during that time. Versions include the pressurised 58P and the turbocharged 58TC, both powered by 240kW (325hp) Teledyne Continental TSIO-520s.

Current production (under the Raytheon Aircraft Company banner) runs at around 45 per year.

Photo: A small number of Jaguar Special Edition Baron 58s were built in 1999. (Raytheon)

Raytheon Beechcraft King Air 90 & 100

Country of origin: United States of America

Type: Twin turboprop corporate and utility transport

Powerplants: 90 – Two 373kW (500shp) Pratt & Whitney Canada PT6A-6 turboprops driving three blade c/s Hartzell propellers. B100 – Two 533kW (715shp) Garrett TPE331-6-252Bs driving three blade props. C90B – Two 410kW (550shp) PT6A-21s driving four blade props.

Performance: 90 – Max speed 450km/h (243kt), max cruising speed 435km/h (235kt). Initial rate of climb 1900ft/min. Range with reserves 2520km (1360nm). B100 – Max speed 491km/h (265kt). Initial rate of climb 2140ft/min. Range at max cruising speed 2343km (1264nm), at economical cruising speed 2455km (1325nm). C90B – Max cruising speed 457km/h (247kt). Range at economical cruising speed at 24,000ft 2375km (1282nm).

Weights: 90 – Empty equipped 2412kg (5318lb), max takeoff 4218kg (9300lb). B100 – Empty equipped 3212kg (7092lb), max takeoff 5352kg (11,800lb). C90B – Empty 3040kg (6702lb), max takeoff 4580kg (10,100lb).

Dimensions: 90 – Wing span 13.98m (45ft 11in), length 10.82m (35ft 6in), height 4.47m (14ft 8in). Wing area 25.9m^2 (279.7sq ft). B100 – Wing span 14.00m (45ft 11in), length 12.17m (39ft 11in), height 4.70m (15ft 5in). Wing area 26.0m^2 (279.7sq ft). C90B – Wing span 15.32m (50ft 3in), length 10.82m (35ft 6in), height 4.34m (14ft 3in). Wing area 27.3m^2 (293.9sq ft).

Capacity: 90 – Typical seating for six, max seating for eight. 100 – Six to eight in corporate configuration, or max seating for 13.

Production: Approx 1840 of all variants of the King Air 90 family built (including 226 military orders). Approx 350 King Air 100s built.

History: The Model 90 King Air was the first model in the largest and most successful family of corporate turboprop twins yet built.

The King Air began life as a turboprop development of the Queen Air designed to meet a US Army requirement for a staff/utility transport. A prototype PT6 powered Queen Air Model 65-80 (later 65-90T) began test flying in 1963 and the type was subsequently ordered by the US Army as the U-21A. The civil equivalent, the model 90 King Air, introduced pressurisation and first flew on January 20 1964. Deliveries of production civil aircraft began in late 1964.

Development resulted in several civil variants, including the A90 and B90 with PT6A-20 engines; the C90 with PT6A-21s; the E90 with more powerful PT6A-34Bs; and the F90 which introduced the T-tail of the 200 (described separately), four blade props and other mods. The less expensive 90SE Special Edition was released during 1994, but is no longer offered. The latest variant to appear was the C90B Jaguar Special Edition. Announced in January 1998 it features the Jaguar car company's green and gold colours including the leaping cat logo on the tail and a Connolly leather interior with walnut and boxwood cabinets.

The King Air 100 series was announced in May 1969. Compared with the 90 series it was 1.27m (4ft 2in) longer, allowing greater seating capacity, and featured a reduced wing span and larger rudder. The A100 is a military version, while the B100 is powered by 535kW (715shp) Garrett TFE331s. Production of the 100 ceased in 1984.

Photo: A Canadian registered King Air 100. (Gary Gentle)

Raytheon Beechcraft King Air 200

Country of origin: United States of America

Type: Twin turboprop corporate, passenger & utility transport

Powerplants: 200 – Two 635kW (850shp) Pratt & Whitney Canada PT6A-41 turboprops driving three blade constant speed propellers. B200 – Two 635kW (850shp) P&WC PT6A-42s.

Performance: 200 – Max speed 536km/h (289kt), max cruising speed 515km/h (278kt). Initial rate of climb 2450ft/min. Range with reserves at max cruising speed 3254km (1757nm), at econ cruising speed 3495km (1887nm). B200 – Max speed 541km/h (292kt), max cruising speed at 27,000ft 531km/h (287kt), econ cruising speed at 27,000ft 411km/h (222kt). Initial rate of climb 2450ft/min. Range at max cruising speed at 18,000ft 2142km (1157nm), with max fuel at econ cruising speed at 31,000ft 3442km (1859nm).

Weights: 200 – Empty 3318kg (7315lb), max takeoff 5670kg (12,500lb). B200 – Empty 3716kg (8192lb), max takeoff 5670kg (12,500lb).

Dimensions: Wing span 16.61m (54ft 6in), length 13.36m (43ft 10in), height 4.52m (14ft 10in). Wing area 28.2m^2 (303.0sq ft).

Capacity: Flightcrew of one or two. Accommodation for a maximum of 13 passengers in main cabin, plus a further passenger beside the pilot on flightdeck. Typical corporate seating layout for six in main cabin.

Production: Over 1840 King Air 200s have been delivered to civil and commercial buyers, while 397 have been delivered to military forces. Current production rate approx 50 per annum.

History: The King Air 200 is the most popular member of the King Air family, and was introduced with new features including the distinctive T-tail, more powerful engines, greater wing span and area, increased cabin pressurisation, greater fuel capacity and higher operating weights.

Beech began design work on the Super King Air 200 in October 1970, resulting in the type's first flight on October 27 1972. Certificated in mid December 1973, the King Air 200 went on to be the most successful aircraft in its class, eclipsing such rivals as the Cessna Conquest and Piper Cheyenne. Today the King Air 200 is the only one of the three in production.

The improved B200 entered production in May 1980, this version features more efficient PT6A-42 engines, increased zero fuel max weight and increased cabin pressurisation. Subvariants include the B200C with a 1.32m x 1.32m (4ft 4in x 4ft 4in) cargo door, the B200T with removable tip tanks, and the B200CT with tip tanks and cargo door (four built). The Special Edition B200SE was certificated in October 1995 and introduced an EFIS avionics suite. It is no longer available but current production B200s feature a Collins Pro-Line II EFIS suite as standard, while a three screen suite is optional.

Various special mission King Air 200s and B200s have been built, including for navaid calibration, maritime patrol and resource exploration. In addition several hundred Super King Airs have been built for the US military under the designation C-12. C-12s perform a range of missions from electronic surveillance to VIP transport.

The 1500th commercial King Air 200 was built in 1995. In 1996 Raytheon dropped the 'Super' prefix.

Photo: A Beech 200 King Air. (Rob Finlayson)

Raytheon Beechcraft King Air 300 & 350

Country of origin: United States of America

Type: Twin turboprop corporate and utility aircraft

Powerplants: Two 783kW (1050shp) Pratt & Whitney Canada PT6A-60A turboprops driving four blade Hartzell propellers.

Performance: 300 – Max cruising speed 583km/h (315kt), economical cruising speed 568km/h (307kt). Initial rate of climb 2844ft/min. Range with max fuel and reserves 3630km (1960nm). 350 – Max speed 584km/h (315kt), max cruising speed 576km/h (311kt), typical cruising speed at 24,000ft 558km/h (301kt). Initial rate of climb 2731ft/min. Range at max cruising power and 18,000ft 1911km (1032nm), at max range power and 35,000ft 3357km (1813nm).

Weights: 300 – Empty 3850kg (8490lb), max takeoff 6350kg (14,000lb). 350 – Empty 4132kg (9110lb), max takeoff 6804kg (15,000lb).

Dimensions: 300 & 300LW – Wing span 16.61m (54ft 6in), length 13.36m (43ft 10in), height 4.37m (14ft 4in). Wing area 28.2m² (303sq ft). 350 – Wing span 17.65m (57ft 11in), length 14.22m (46ft 8in), height 4.37m (14ft 4in). Wing area 28.8m² (310.0sq ft).

Capacity: 300 – One or two pilots on flightdeck, with standard layout for six passengers in main cabin. Alternative high density seating for 15 (including pilot). 350 – Typical passenger seating for eight in main cabin, optional seating for an extra two, plus one in toilet compartment and one on flightdeck next to the pilot, making a total of 13.

Production: 219 King Air 300s were built when production ended in 1991. Production of the 300LW ceased in 1994 after 35 had been built. Over 320 King Air 350s delivered.

History: The King Air 300 is an updated version of the successful B200 series, and was itself replaced by the further improved King Air 350, the latest model in this long running and very successful line of corporate and utility transports.

Work on an improved development of the successful King Air B200 began in August 1981, the 14 month design effort resulting in the first flight of the new 300 model in October the following year. Improvements over the B200 were numerous, with the main change being the installation of more powerful PT6A-60A turboprops in place of the -42s of the earlier model. Other changes included reprofiled and more aerodynamically clean engine cowls and exhausts and extended wing leading edges, plus minor internal changes. Both empty and max takeoff weights were also increased.

The max weight was reduced for the 300LW or 'Light Weight', intended to minimise weight based airways user fees, particularly in Europe. The 300AT was an airline pilot trainer.

The King Air 300 has been replaced by the 350, its major improvements being a stretched fuselage lengthened by 86cm (2ft 10in) and winglets. The latest member of the King Air family, it had its first flight in 1988, and has been in production since late 1989. The King Air 350C features a built-in airstair and a 132 x 132cm (52 x 52in) freight door. The 350 is also available in a range of special missions and military variants. The 350 is available with three or five screen Collins EFIS avionics suites.

The 'Super' prefix was dropped from the King Air name in 1996.

Photo: A King Air 350. (Raytheon)

Raytheon Beechcraft 1900

Country of origin: United States of America

Type: Regional airliner and corporate transport

Powerplants: 1900C – Two 820kW (1100shp) Pratt & Whitney Canada PT6A-65B turboprops driving four blade constant speed Hartzell propellers. 1900D – Two 954kW (1279shp) P&WC PT6A-67D turboprops.

Performance: 1900C – Max cruising speed 495km/h (267kt). Range with 10 pax at long range cruising speed with reserves 2907km (1570nm). 1900D – Max cruising speed 533km/h (288kt). Range with 10 pax and reserves at long range cruising speed 2776km (1498nm).

Weights: 1900C – Empty 4327kg (9540lb), max takeoff 7530kg (16,600lb). 1900D – Typical empty 4831kg (10,650lb), max takeoff 7688kg (16,950lb).

Dimensions: 1900C – Wing span 16.60m (54ft 6in), length 17.63m (57ft 10in), height 4.54m (14ft 11in). Wing area 28.2m² (303sq ft). 1900D – Wing span (over winglets) 17.67m (58ft 0in), length 17.63m (57ft 10in), height 4.72m (15ft 6in). Wing area 28.8m² (310.0sq ft).

Capacity: Flightcrew of two. Standard passenger accommodation for 19 at two abreast. Executive and corporate shuttle configurations range for between 10 to 18, depending on customer requirements.

Production: 207 civil Beech 1900Cs were built when production ended. Approx 400 1900Ds delivered by late 2000.

History: The Beech 1900 19 seat commuter was chosen along with the smaller 1300, both developments of the King Air 200, and the C99 for Beech's re-entry into the regional airliner market in 1979.

The most obvious change from the King Air 200 to the 1900C is the substantially lengthened fuselage (17.63m/57ft 10in compared to 13.34m/43ft 9in). Other changes include more powerful engines, a modified tail with tailets, and stabilons on the lower rear fuselage.

Development of the 1900 commenced in 1979, with first flight on September 3 1982. US FAA certification was awarded in November 1983, prior to the 1900C's service entry in February the following year. The first Exec-Liner corporate transport version was delivered in mid 1985.

During the course of 1900C production a wet wing was introduced, increasing fuel capacity by 927 litres (204Imp gal/245US gal), while military transport, maritime patrol and electronic surveillance versions were offered.

Beech announced the improved 1900D at the US Regional Airlines Association meeting in 1989, with the prototype, a converted 1900C, first flying on March 1 1990. Production switched to the improved model in 1991, with first deliveries (to Mesa Air) that November. The main change introduced on the 1900D was the substantially deeper fuselage with stand-up headroom. In addition it also introduced larger passenger and freight doors and windows, twin ventral strakes and auxiliary horizontal fixed tails, while more powerful engines and winglets improve hot and high performance. The cockpit features a four screen Rockwell Collins EFIS suite.

The 1900D has sold particularly well. For example the 1900D's biggest customer is Mesa Airlines, a United Airlines feeder, which operates 63. A 1900D delivered to Impulse Airlines in Australia in March 1997 was the 500th 1900 built.

Photo: A Beech 1900D. (Gary Gentle)

Raytheon Beechjet 400

Country of origin: United States of America

Type: Light corporate jet

Powerplants: Two 13.9kN (2965lb) takeoff rated Pratt & Whitney Canada JT15D-5 turbofans.

Performance: 400 – Max speed 837km/h (452kt), cruising speed 748km/h (404kt). Range with four pax, max fuel and reserves 3572km (1929nm). 400A – Max speed 867km/h (468kt), typical cruising speed 834km/h (450kt), long range cruising speed 726km/h (392kt). Initial rate of climb 3770ft/min. Service ceiling 43,450ft. Range with max fuel and reserves cruising at 796km/h (430kt) 2915km (1574nm), at 746km/h (403kt) 3098km (1673nm).

Weights: 400 – Basic empty 4225kg (9315lb), max takeoff 7158kg (15,780lb). 400A – Operating empty (including crew) 4921kg (10850lb), max takeoff 7303kg (16,100lb).

Dimensions: Wing span 13.25m (43ft 6in), length 14.75m (48ft 5in), height 4.24m (13ft 11in). Wing area 22.4m² (241.4sq ft).

Capacity: Flightcrew of one or two pilots, with standard passenger arrangement in main cabin for six with an entertainment/executive console, or seven without (plus provision for an eighth passenger in toilet compartment with seat belt installed).

Production: Total Beechjet 400 production 64 (62 still in service in 2000). Approx 540 400As delivered by late 2000, including 180 modified 400As built for the US Air Force as T-1A Jayhawk tanker/transport trainers.

History: The Raytheon Beechjet traces its origins back to the Mitsubishi Diamond 2 bizjet, which Beechcraft acquired the design and production rights to in the mid 1980s.

The original Mitsubishi MU-300 Diamond 1 first flew in August 1978, powered by two 11.1kN (2500lb) P&WC JT15D-4 turbofans. The subsequent Diamond 2 flew on June 20 1984, with the first production aircraft flying in January 1985. Only 11 Diamond 2s were built before Beech purchased the design and production rights, resulting in the Model 400 Beechjet.

Beech re-engined the Diamond 2 with P&WC JT15D-5 turbofans, developed a new interior, and incorporated a number of other minor refinements. Deliveries of the Beechjet began in June 1986, with low rate production continuing until that model was replaced by the Model 400A, which was delivered from November 1990.

The new 400A incorporated a number of improvements over its predecessor. A higher max takeoff weight and greater operating ceiling improved performance, while repositioning the rear fuselage fuel tank increased cabin volume. The flightdeck features Collins Pro Line 4 EFIS with three colour displays – two primary flight displays (PFDs) and a multifunction display (MFD) with a second MFD optional.

Following customer feedback Raytheon developed a new luxury standard interior for the Beechjet which was introduced in 1996.

The Beechjet 400A also serves as the basis for the military T-1 Jayhawk tanker and transport aircrew trainer – 180 were delivered between 1992 and 1997. The Japan Air Self Defence Force has also taken delivery of 10 T-400 aircrew trainers (Beechjet 400Ts).

Photo: This Beechjet 400A was delivered to China's Hainan Airlines in February 1999. (Raytheon)

Raytheon Premier I

Country of origin: United States of America

Type: Light corporate jet

Powerplants: Two 10.2kN (2300lb) Williams-Rolls FJ44-2A turbofans.

Performance: Max cruising speed 854km/h (461kt). Max certificated operating altitude 41,000ft. Takeoff length at MTOW at S/L less than 915m (3000ft). Max range at long range cruising speed with IFR reserves 2780km (1500nm).

Weights: Basic operating including single pilot 3627kg (7996lb), max takeoff 5670kg (12,400lb).

Dimensions: Wing span 13.56m (44ft 6in), length 14.02m (46ft 0in), height 4.66m (15ft 4in). Wing area 23.0m² (247.0sq ft).

Capacity: One or two pilots on flightdeck (will be certificated for single pilot). Main cabin seats six in standard configuration with four seats in a club arrangement and two seats behind them. Toilet in rear fuselage. Baggage compartments in nose and tail.

Production: More than 140 orders held at late 2000. First deliveries planned for early 2001.

History: The promising Premier I is the first new product of Raytheon Aircraft (following Raytheon's September 1994 merger of its Beech and Hawker subsidiaries). It is an all new entry level corporate jet to compete head on with Cessna's highly successful CitationJet/CJ1 series.

Beech began design work on the Premier I in early 1994 under the designation PD374 (later PD390). Raytheon authorised development gc-ahead in early 1995, and initial details of the new jet were released in mid 1995. Raytheon publicly launched the Premier I at the National Business Aviation Association convention in Las Vegas in September 1995, where a full size cabin mock-up was on display.

Construction of the first Premier I began in late 1996 and rollout was on August 19 1998, followed by first flight on December 22 that year. Four Premier Is have been used in the flight test program leading to certification planned for late 2000 (over two years later than originally scheduled).

The Premier I was designed using CATIA computer aided design. Features include its composite carbonfibre/epoxy honeycomb fuselage, swept metal construction wings, T-tail and two Williams-Rolls FJ44 turbofans.

The composite fuselage has a number of benefits. Advanced production techniques (using computer controlled automated fibre placement machines) means a Premier I fuselage can be constructed in one week, whereas a conventional airframe would require one to two weeks to complete. The composite construction also allows greater (approx 13%) internal cabin space compared with a conventional construction fuselage of the same external dimensions (it lacks internal frames), while weight is 20% lower than otherwise would be the case.

The Premier I will be certificated for single pilot operations. The flightdeck will feature the new Collins Pro Line 21 EFIS avionics suite with two 20 x 25cm (8 x 10in) flat panel LCDs (one a primary flight display, the other a multifunction display).

Raytheon intends that the Premier I will form the basis of a new family of business jets with the stretched Premier II and Premier III planned.

Photo: The second prototype Premier I first flew on June 4 1999.

Raytheon Hawker 800 & BAe 125-700

Countries of origin: United Kingdom and USA

Type: Mid size corporate jet

Powerplants: 700 – Two 16.6kN (3700lb) Garrett TFE731-3-RH turbofans. 800XP – Two 20.7kN (4660lb) Honeywell TFE731-5BR-1Hs.

Performance: 700 – Max cruising speed 808km/h (436kt), economical cruising speed 723km/h (390kt). Service ceiling 41,000ft. Range with max fuel, payload and IFR reserves 4725km (2550nm). 800XP – Max speed and max cruising speed 845km/h (456kt), economical cruising speed 740km/h (400kt). Max initial rate of climb 3100ft/min. Max certificated altitude 43,000ft. Range with max payload 4222km (2280nm), range with max fuel and VFR reserves 5472km (2955nm).

Weights: 700 – Empty 5825kg (12,845lb), max takeoff 11,567kg (25,500lb). 800XP – Basic empty 7380kg (16,270lb), max takeoff 12,700kg (28,000lb).

Dimensions: 700 – Wing span 14.33m (47ft 0in), length 15.46m (50ft 9in), height 5.36m (17ft 7in). Wing area 32.8m² (353.0sq ft). 800XP – Wing span 15.66m (51ft 5in), length 15.60m (51ft 2in), height 5.36m (17ft 7in). Wing area 34.8m² (374.0sq ft).

Capacity: Flightcrew of two. Typical seating for eight passengers in corporate layout, or max seating for 14.

Production: 215 125-700s and 275 Hawker 800s built. Approx 200 Hawker 800XPs built. Over 1000 125 series aircraft ordered including military versions.

History: The 125-700 and Hawker 800 are two more recent versions of the world's longest running corporate jet production program.

The 125-700 and Hawker 800 are direct developments of the DH.125 (later the HS.125), which first flew in August 1962. This aircraft was developed into a number of variants through to the HS.125-600, all of which are powered by the Rolls-Royce Viper turbojet and are described separately under Hawker Siddeley.

The introduction of the BAe 125-700 in 1976 brought with it significant performance and fuel economy benefits as the -700 incorporated Garrett TFE731 turbofans. The 125-700 first flew on June 19 1976, and remained in production until it was replaced by the 125-800 in 1984.

The 125-800 first flew on May 26 1983 and it introduced a number of improvements. Aerodynamic changes included a reprofiled nose and windscreen, extended fin leading edge, and greater span wing which decreased drag and increased lift and fuel capacity. Range was boosted further by a larger ventral fuel tank. More powerful TFE731s improved field performance, while a redesigned interior made more efficient use of the space available. The 800 was also the first corporate jet to feature an EFIS cockpit. The 800A was specifically aimed at the US market, the 800B for non US markets.

The 125-800 became the Hawker 800 from mid 1993 when Raytheon purchased BAe's Corporate Jets division. Production was transferred to Wichita in the USA (the first US built 800 flew on November 5 1996, the last UK built 800 on April 29 1997).

Current production is of the 800XP (Extended Performance) which was certificated in 1995 and has improved engines for better climb and cruise performance. A new interior was introduced in 1999. At late 2000 Raytheon was evaluating new avionics for the aircraft.

Photo: A BAe 125-700. (Gary Gentle)

Raytheon (BAe) Hawker 1000

Countries of origin: United Kingdom and USA

Type: Mid size corporate jet

Powerplants: Two 23.1kN (5200lb) Pratt & Whitney Canada PW305 turbofans.

Performance: Max cruising speed 867km/h (468kt), economical cruising speed 745km/h (402kt). Service ceiling 43,000ft. Range with max payload 5750km (3105nm), range with max fuel and NBAA VFR reserves 6205km (3350nm).

Weights: Empty 7810kg (17,220lb), max takeoff 14,060kg (31,000lb).

Dimensions: Wing span 15.66m (51ft 4in), length 16.42m (53ft 10in), height 5.21m (17ft 1in). Wing area 34.8m² (374.0sq ft).

Capacity: Flightcrew of two. Standard main cabin seating for eight comprising club seating for four at the front of the cabin, a three seat couch and a single seat. Max seating for 15.

Production: Production ceased after 52 built, almost all are in service in North America.

History: The Hawker 1000 was the largest member of the DH/HS/BAe 125/Hawker 800 series of corporate jets.

The Hawker 1000 was based on the smaller Hawker 800, and until 1997 the two types were in production side by side in the famous de Havilland plant in Hatfield in England. The 1000 differs from the 800 in a number of respects however and features a stretched fuselage. The 1000 is identifiable via its seven main cabin windows per side, whereas the 800 has six, and the 0.84m (2ft 9in) stretch (achieved by small fuselage plugs in front of and behind the wing) allowing an increase in max seating to 15. However as it is optimised for long range intercontinental work, the typical Hawker 1000 configuration seats one less than the smaller Hawker 800.

Other important changes include Pratt & Whitney Canada PW305 turbofans (in place of the AlliedSignal TFE731s on the Hawker 800), extra fuel in the extended forward wing fairing, new lightweight systems, revised and more efficient cabin interior with increased headroom, EFIS glass cockpit and certification to the latest US FAR and European JAR requirements.

British Aerospace launched the BAe 1000 program in October 1989. The first BAe 1000 development aircraft first flew on June 16 1990, with a second following on November 26 that year. These two were followed by the first production aircraft which participated in an 800 hour flight test development program, culminating in UK certification being granted on October 21 1991 (FAA certification followed on October 31 1991). The first production aircraft was delivered in December 1991.

As is the case with the BAe 125-800, the BAe 1000 became the Hawker 1000 from mid 1993 when Raytheon purchased British Aerospace's Corporate Jets division. However, the 1000 never enjoyed the popularity of the 800 and production ceased in 1997 with the delivery of the 52nd aircraft.

The 1000's largest customer was the Net Jets fractional ownership scheme which has 17 in service (including 13 of the last 14 built).

Photo: Although it looks similar to its predecessor, the Hawker 1000 is recognisable by its stretched fuselage and larger engine nacelles. (Raytheon)

Raytheon Hawker Horizon

Country of origin: United States of America

Type: Super mid size corporate jet

Powerplants: Two 28.9kN (6500lb) Pratt & Whitney Canada PW308A turbofans.

Performance: Max cruising Mach 0.84 or 896km/h (484kt). Certificated ceiling 45,000ft. Max range 6300km (3400nm), range at Mach 0.82 with six passengers and NBAA IFR reserves 5745km (3100nm).

Weights: Basic operating 9494kg (20,930lb), max takeoff 16,330kg (36,000lb).

Dimensions: Wing span 18.82m (61ft 9in), length 21.08m (69ft 2in), height 5.97m (19ft 7in). Wing area 49.3m² (531.0sq ft).

Capacity: Flightcrew of two. Typical main cabin layout will seat eight, with a toilet in the aft fuselage.

Production: Certification and first deliveries planned for the northern spring of 2001. Over 150 orders held at late 2000.

History: Raytheon's Hawker Horizon is an all new 'super mid size' corporate jet.

Design work on what became the Horizon was already underway when Raytheon Corporate Jets and Beech merged in early 1995 to form Raytheon Aircraft. The new design, initially labelled PD376 and later Horizon 1000, was one of three projects the new Raytheon Aircraft was working on, along with what became the Premier I. Raytheon worked closely with potential customers during design definition.

Raytheon formally announced the Hawker Horizon immediately prior to the National Business Aviation Association's annual convention in November 1996. The originally planned first flight date of late 1999 has slipped (in part due to delays with the Premier I) to the first quarter of 2001, with US FAA certification scheduled for late 2002.

One of Raytheon's design philosophies in developing the Horizon is to combine the earlier Hawkers' popular characteristics with advanced technologies. Experienced Hawker designers formed the core of the Horizon's design team and the aircraft has been designed to look and feel like a Hawker.

Compared to the Hawker 1000 the Horizon will have a wider, slightly longer fuselage with a flat floor and stand up headroom and a two tonne heavier max takeoff weight. The Horizon features an all composite fuselage manufactured using the automated fibre placement technology developed for the Premier I. Raytheon says the composite fuselage saves weight and increases cabin volume. The empennage features an aluminium sub structure and carbonfibre skin.

Power will be from two digitally controlled Pratt & Whitney Canada PW308A turbofans. P&WC is a risk sharing partner in the program, as is avionics integrator Honeywell (the Horizon will feature Honeywell's Primus Epic avionics suite with five flat panel colour LCDs and cursor control devices – comprising touchpad, joystick, light pen, trackball and soft keys).

The Horizon's new metal construction supercritical 30° sweep, aft loaded wing will be built by Fuji Heavy Industries of Japan, another risk sharing partner, and will pass beneath the fuselage. Other suppliers/partners include Messier-Dowty (landing gear), Sundstrand, Vickers and Honeywell (APU and environmental control system).

Photo: The Horizon will feature a composite fuselage. (Raytheon)

Republic RC-3 Seabee

Country of origin: United States of America

Type: Four seat amphibious light aircraft

Powerplant: One 160kW (215hp) Franklin 6A8-215-B8F six cylinder inline piston engine driving a two blade propeller.

Performance: Max speed 193km/h (104kt), max cruising speed 166km/h (90kt). Initial rate of climb 700ft/min. Service ceiling 12,000ft. Range 900km (485nm).

Weights: Empty 885kg (1950lb), max takeoff 1360kg (3000lb).

Dimensions: Wing span 11.48m (37ft 8in), length 8.51m (27ft 11in), height 2.92m (9ft 7in). Wing area 18.2m² (196sq ft).

Capacity: Typical seating for four.

Production: Total Seabee production of 1060 built between 1946 and 1947.

History: One of the few amphibious light aircraft to be built in large numbers, the Republic Seabee was a product of the same company that built the legendary World War 2 P-47 Thunderbolt fighter.

The Seabee was conceived during the latter stages of World War 2 when Republic began to look beyond its massive wartime contracts to a basis for sustained peacetime production. The original concept was one that was quite popular during the 1940s – to provide a four seat light aircraft that would cost little more to purchase and operate than a family car. To an extent Republic succeeded in its aims, more than 1000 Seabees were built in just one year of production.

The original prototype Seabee was designated the RC-1 (Republic Commercial design number one) and first appeared during 1944. The RC-1 was a three seat design powered by a 130kW (175hp) six cylinder Franklin 6ALG-365 piston engine. First flown during November 1944, the conventional all metal construction RC-1 for a time was dubbed the Thunderbolt Amphibian.

A comprehensive testing and development program ensued, during which the RC-1 was punishingly tested. One test that illustrated that the RC-1 encompassed Republic aircraft's legendary abilities to absorb punishment involved intentionally making a wheels-up landing on a concrete runway. The RC-1 passed this test without incident, the only damage being a small metal shaving from the keel.

While the RC-1's structural integrity was beyond dispute, Republic nevertheless decided to redesign the RC-1, mainly to significantly reduce production and acquisition costs. What resulted was the RC-3 Seabee, a four seater powered by a 160kW (215hp) Franklin 6A8-215-B8F piston engine. Aside from the increased seating capacity, the Seabee differed from the RC-1 in being lighter, built with far fewer components (450 compared with 1800 in the RC-1), required 25% less tooling to manufacture and, most importantly, cost half of what the RC-1 would have.

Seabee production began in mid 1946, but lasted only until October 1947, when ironically Republic decided to concentrate on its once more lucrative military business (with the development of the F-84 fighter), despite healthy Seabee sales.

The decision to cease Seabee production also terminated development plans for twin engined and landplane developments.

Photo: This photograph shows to good effect the Seabee's stepped hull, outrigger floats and undercarriage. (Randall Krebbs)

Robin DR 400 & DR 500

Country of origin: France

Type: Four/five seat light aircraft

Powerplant: DR 400/120 Dauphin – One 84kW (112hp) (Textron) Lycoming O-235-L2A flat four piston engine driving a two blade fixed pitch propeller. DR 400/180 – One 135kW (180hp) Textron Lycoming O-360-A.

Performance: DR 400/120 – Max speed 241km/h (130kt), max cruising speed 215km/h (116kt). Initial rate of climb 600ft/min. Service ceiling 12,000ft. Range with standard fuel and no reserves at max cruising speed 860km (465nm). DR 400/180 – Max speed 278km/h (150kt), max cruising speed 260km/h (140kt), economical cruising speed 245km/h (132kt). Initial rate of climb 825ft/min. Service ceiling 15,475ft. Range at economical cruising speed 1450km (783nm).

Weights: DR 400/120 – Empty equipped 535kg (1180lb), max takeoff 900kg (1985lb). DR 400/180 – Empty equipped 600kg (1320lb), max takeoff 1100kg (2425lb).

Dimensions: Wing span 8.72m (28ft 7in), length 6.96m (22ft 10in), height 2.23m (7ft 3in). Wing area 13.6m^2 (146.4sq ft).

Capacity: Most DR 400 models typically seat four.

Production: Over 1700 DR 400s of all variants built.

History: The Robin DR 400 series of light aircraft owes its origins to the Jodel series of wooden construction light aircraft.

Avions Pierre Robin was formed by Pierre Robin and the principal designer of Jodel Aircraft, Jean Delemontez, in October 1957 as Centre Est Aeronautique. The company's initial production was of developments of the basic Jodel series of tail draggers, and it was these aircraft that evolved into the DR 400 series. Initial production was of the DR 100 and the DR 1050/1051, while the DR 220, DR 221 and DR 250 featured the Jodel's basic wing with a four seat fuselage. The final links between the Jodels and the DR 400 were the DR 253 and DR 300 series, tricycle developments of the DR 220 series.

First flight of the DR 400 occurred during June 1972, both a DR 400/ 125 and a DR 400/180 taking flight that month.

Since that time a number of developments have been offered. The least powerful version is the DR 400/120, and it remains in production today as the DR 400/120 Dauphin 2+2. Powered by an 84kW (112hp) O-235, the DR 400/120 is really a two seater, although it can seat two children on a rear bench seat. The DR 400/125i has a 93kW (125hp) fuel injected IO-240 and was revealed in 1995. The DR 400/140 Dauphin is powered by a 120kW (160hp) O-320 and is a full four seater. The four seat DR 400/160 Chevalier meanwhile also features a 120kW (160hp) Lycoming O-320 and seats four. It first flew in June 1972. With a different prop, more fuel capacity and slightly different wing it became the DR 400/160 Major from 1980.

The four/five seat DR 400/180 Regent and DR 400 Remo 180R are powered by the 135kW (180hp) (Textron) Lycoming O-360, the Remo being optimised for glider towing. Also optimised for glider tug work is the DR 400/200R Remo 200, the most powerful DR 400 model (powered by a 150kW/200hp IO-360, driving a constant speed prop).

The DR 500i President was unveiled at the 1997 Paris Airshow as the DR 400/200i. It features a 150kW (200hp) IO-360 driving a constant speed prop and widened and taller cabin. Deliveries began in 1998.

Photo: The DR 500i President. (Bob Grimstead)

Robin HR 200 & R 2000 Alpha

Country of origin: France

Type: Two seat aerobatic light aircraft

Powerplant: HR 200 Club – One 80kW (108hp) Lycoming O-235-C2A flat four piston engine driving a two blade fixed pitch propeller. R 2160 Alpha Sport – One 120kW (160hp) Lycoming O-320-D.

Performance: HR 200 – Max speed 230km/h (124kt), max cruising speed 215km/h (116kt). Initial rate of climb 670ft/min. Service ceiling 13,000ft. Range with max fuel 1078km (582nm). 2160 – Max speed 257km/h (138kt), max cruising speed 242km/h (130kt), cruising speed 234km/h (126kt). Initial rate of climb 1025ft/min. Service ceiling 15,000ft. Range with max fuel 795km (430nm).

Weights: HR 200 – Empty 500kg (1100lb), max takeoff 760kg (1670lb). 2160 – Empty 550kg (1213lb), max takeoff 800kg (1765lb).

Dimensions: HR 200 – Wing span 8.40m (27ft 7in), length 6.68m (21ft 11in), height 2.18m (7ft 2in). Wing area 12.6m^2 (135.6sq ft). 2160 – Wing span 8.33m (27ft 4in), length 7.10m (23ft 4in), height 2.13m (7ft 0in). Wing area 13.0m^2 (140.0sq ft).

Capacity: Typical seating for two side by side.

Production: Approx 160 200s and 130 R 2000s built.

History: This series of two seat aerobatic aircraft was designed during the 1970s specifically for flying school use, and has been developed in two major variants, both of which are back in production.

The original HR 200 was the second all metal aircraft designed for Robin by Christophe Heintz (previous Robins had been designed by Jean Delemontez, who was also responsible for the earlier Jodel series). It first flew on July 19 1971 powered by an 80kW (108hp) O-235, while the first production aircraft flew in April 1973.

Three initial versions were built, the 80kW (108hp) powered Club or HR 200/100, the more powerful Acrobin 125 or HR 200/125 (with a 95kW/125hp O-235) and the Acrobin 160 or HR 200/160 (with a 120kW/160hp IO-320). The HR 200 remained in production until the late 1970s, and is once again on offer. Robin has now recommenced production of the HR 200/120B, powered by an 88kW (118hp) Textron Lycoming O-235-L2A and a new instrument panel. The HR 200/160 is powered by the 120kW (160hp) O-320 and was introduced in 1999.

The R 2000 Alpha series meanwhile was a redevelopment of the HR 200. The HR 200's basic fuselage was retained, but changes included an all new wing and enlarged rudder and vertical tail to improve spinning characteristics. The prototype R 2000 was powered by a 135kW (160hp) IO-320 and flew for the first time on January 15 1976. Deliveries of production aircraft began in 1977.

Three developments of the R 2000 series were built, the R 2100, the R 2112 and R 2160 Alpha Sport, with the main differences between the three being the powerplant fitted. The R 2100 is powered by an 80kW (108hp) O-235, the R 2112 has an 84kW (112hp) O-235, and the R 2160 has a 120kW (160hp) O-320.

Of the three, the R 2160 Alpha Sport has been the most popular. Production of the R 2000 series (by Robin factories in France and Canada) originally ceased in 1983, however Robin restarted production of the R 2160 in 1994. Current production is of the R 2160 D and the R 2160i with a fuel injected AEIO-320.

Photo: An R 2160 Alpha Sport.

Robin R 3000

Country of origin: France

Type: Two/four seat light aircraft

Powerplant: R 3000/100 – One 87kW (116hp) Lycoming O-235 flat four piston engine driving a two blade fixed pitch propeller. R 3000/160 – One 135kW (180hp) Textron Lycoming O-320-D2A flat four.

Performance: R 3000/100 – Max speed 230km/h (124kt), max cruising speed 210km/h (113kt), normal cruising speed 200km/h (108kt). Initial rate of climb 590ft/min. Service ceiling 13,000ft. Range with standard fuel and no reserves 1120km (605nm), with optional fuel 1420km (767nm). R 3000/160 – Max speed 270km/h (146kt), max cruising speed 255km/h (138kt), economical cruising speed at 65% power 238km/h (128kt). Initial rate of climb 875ft/min. Service ceiling 15,000ft. Range with standard fuel at 75% power cruising speed 1490km (804nm), at 65% power cruising speed 1610km (868nm).

Weights: R 3000/100 – Empty 580kg (1280lb), max takeoff 900kg (1985lb). R 3000/160 – Empty 650kg (1433lb), max takeoff 1150kg (2535lb).

Dimensions: Wing span 9.81m (32ft 2in), length 7.51m (24ft 8in), height 2.66m (8ft 9in). Wing area 14.5m² (155.8sq ft).

Capacity: Seating for two in R 3000/100, three in R 3000/120 and four in R 2000/140 and R 3000/160.

Production: 76 examples of all versions of the R 3000 delivered, the last in 1996.

History: Robin began development of the R 3000 in the late 1970s as part of a model range modernisation drive.

Robin originally proposed offering a wide range of R 3000 models, although only a few have seen production. Models that were proposed but never saw the light of day include the R 3180S with a turbocharged engine and retractable undercarriage; the fixed gear, but turbocharged R 3180T; the R 3180GT1 and R 3180GT2 with a larger cabin (the GT1 would have been turbocharged, the GT2 turbocharged with retractable gear); and the R 3140T with a solid cabin roof.

A 1981 agreement saw Aerospatiale, GA manufacturer Socata's parent, become responsible for R 3000 marketing between 1983 and 1987, which meant that Robin concentrated on lower power models so as to not compete with Socata's TB range (described separately), and plans for the higher performance models were dropped.

The metal construction R 3000 features a Jodel based wing and forward sliding cockpit canopy and an aerodynamically efficient airframe, and is distinguishable by its T-tail. The first R 3000 model to fly was the R 3140, its first flight occurred on December 8 1980, a second prototype flew in June 1981 and introduced the definitive tapered wings. Production aircraft have been delivered since 1985.

The R 3140, later the R 3000/140, was joined in production by the two seat 87kW (116hp) O-235 powered R 3000/100; the three seat R 3120; R 3000/120 (R3120); four seat 105kW (140hp) powered R 3000/140; and the 135kW (180hp) R 3000/180R glider tug.

The last two models built were R 3000/140 and R 3000/160, a development of the R 3000/120 (which went of production in 1988) with a 119kW (160hp) O-360-D2A.

No R 3000s have been built since 1996.

Photo: A Robin R 3000/120.

Robinson R22

Country of origin: United States of America

Type: Two seat light helicopter

Powerplant: R22 – One 93kW (124hp) Lycoming O-320-A2B flat four piston engine driving two blade main and tail rotors. R22 Beta II – One 98kW (131hp) derated Textron Lycoming O-360-B2C.

Performance: R22 – Max speed 180km/h (97kt), 75% power cruising speed 174km/h (94kt), economical cruising speed 153km/h (82kt). Initial rate of climb 1200ft/min. Service ceiling 14,000ft. Hovering ceiling in ground effect 6500ft. Range with max payload and no reserves 385km (207nm). R22 Beta II – Max speed 180km/h (97kt), 70% power cruising speed 177km/h (96kt), economical cruising speed 153km/h (82kt). Hovering ceiling in ground effect 9400ft. Range with max payload, normal fuel and no reserves over 320km (173nm), with max payload, maximum fuel and no reserves over 482km (260nm). Endurance 3hr 20min.

Weights: R22 – Empty 361kg (796lb), max takeoff 590kg (1300lb). R22 Beta II – Empty 388kg (855lb), max takeoff 620kg (1370lb).

Dimensions: Main rotor diameter 7.67m (25ft 2in), length overall rotors turning 8.76m (28ft 9in), fuselage length 6.30m (20ft 8in), height overall 2.72m (8ft 11in). Main rotor disc area 46.2m² (497.4sq ft).

Capacity: Typical seating for two, side by side. R22 Agricultural is fitted with a 150 litre (33Imp gal/40US gal) capacity chemical tank.

Production: Approx 3180 R22s of all versions have been built (including some against military orders) by late 2000.

History: The Robinson R22 undisputedly has been the world's most popular light helicopter since its introduction in the late 1970s.

The R22 was designed by the founder of the Robinson Helicopter Company, Frank Robinson. He conceived the R22 to be an efficient, cheap to acquire, reliable and economical to operate multi purpose two seat light helicopter.

Design work on the R22 began in the 1970s, and an 85kW (115hp) Lycoming O-235 powered prototype first flew on August 28 1975. Certification of the R22 was delayed somewhat to March 1979 due to the loss of the prototype. Despite this setback the R22 was an overnight success, and several hundred had been ordered by the time the first were delivered from October 1979.

A number of variants and developments of the R22 have been offered. These include the improved R22 Alpha introduced in 1983, and the more powerful R22 Beta from 1985. The R22 Mariner is equipped with floats; the R22 Police version is fitted with special communications gear, a searchlight, siren and loudspeaker; the R22 Agricultural is fitted with tanks and booms for agricultural spraying; while the R22 IFR is fitted with IFR instrumentation for helicopter IFR flight training.

The latest R22 model is the R22 Beta II, powered by a 120kW (160hp) O-360 derated to 98kW (131hp) for takeoff for improved hot and high performance (as takeoff power can be maintained up to 7500ft). The Beta II was introduced into production in 1995 and was certificated in early 1996. It is also offered in IFR, Police, Agricultural and Mariner versions.

R22 uses are varied and include helicopter pilot training, cattle mustering, traffic reporting and police work.

Photo: An R22 Mariner. (Robinson)

Robinson R44

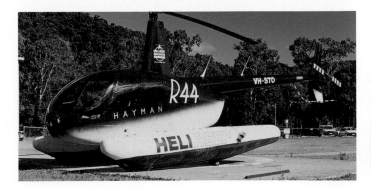

Country of origin: United States of America

Type: Four place piston engined light helicopter

Powerplant: One 195kW (260hp) Textron Lycoming O-540 flat six piston engine derated to 165kW (225hp) for takeoff and 153kW (205hp) for continuous operation driving a two blade main rotor and two blade tail rotor.

Performance: Cruising speed at 75% power 209km/h (113kt). Initial rate of climb 1000ft/min. Service ceiling 14,000ft. Hovering ceiling in ground effect 6400ft, out of ground effect 5100ft. Max range with no reserves approx 645km (350nm).

Weights: Standard empty 635kg (1400lb), max takeoff 1090kg (2400lb).

Dimensions: Main rotor diameter 10.06m (33ft 0in), length overall rotors turning 11.76m (38ft 7in), height 3.28m (10ft 9in). Main rotor disc area 79.5m² (855.3sq ft).

Capacity: Typical seating for four, with two passengers on bench seat behind pilot and passenger.

Production: Over 500 R44s have been delivered since production began in late 1992. 2000 production rate six per week.

History: Robinson's R44 light four place piston helicopter has proven a great success, it is currently the world's best selling helicopter.

While bearing a resemblance to the two place R22, the R44 is much larger and is almost as long as the turbine powered Bell JetRanger. Robinson's aim in developing the R44 was to provide a relatively fast (205 to 215km/h [110 to 115kt] cruising speed) and useful four seat light helicopter that had performance close to that of turbine powered aircraft, yet with an acquisition cost of just a third of turbines and significantly lower maintenance costs.

Robinson Helicopter Company president and founder Frank Robinson first began design work on a light four seat piston engined helicopter during 1986. First flight occurred on March 31 1990 following extensive structural and dynamic component fatigue testing. US FAA certification was awarded on December 10 1992, with deliveries from Robinson's Torrance, California plant commencing soon after.

The R44 uses the same simple design, construction and operating philosophies behind the smaller two place R22. A 194kW (260hp) Textron Lycoming O-540 flat six (derated to 165kW/225hp for takeoff) drives two blade main and tail rotors, while other features include an electronic throttle governor, rotor brake and automatic clutch.

Until mid 2000 the standard R44 model was the R44 Astro. Variants included the float equipped R44 Clipper (certificated in July 1996); the R44 Police law enforcement machine with IR sensor or television camera mounted in a gyrostabilised nose turret, video monitor, a searchlight and bulged door windows (certificated in July 1997); IFR certificated R44 IFR; and the R44 Newscopter which can carry a TV camera in a nose turret.

The R44 Raven is the new standard R44 production model, and features a hydraulic flight control system. The Raven has proven so popular that Robinson decided to drop the Astro from production. The first Raven was delivered in mid 2000, and it is offered in the same special mission forms as the Astro was.

Photo: An R44 Clipper. (Robert Wiseman)

Rockwell (Ayres) Thrush Commander

Country of origin: United States of America

Type: Agricultural aircraft

Powerplant: Thrush Commander-600 – One 450kW (600hp) Pratt & Whitney R-1340 Wasp nine cylinder piston radial engine driving a two blade propeller. S2R-R1820/510 – One 895kW (1200shp) R-1820 Cyclone radial driving a three blade prop.

Performance: 600 – Max speed 225km/h (122kt), max cruising speed at 70% power 200km/h (108kt), typical working speed range 170 to 185km/h (91 to 100kt). Initial rate of climb 900ft/min. Service ceiling 15,000ft. Ferry range with max fuel at 70% power 648km (350nm). S2R-R1820/510 – Max speed 256km/h (138kt), cruising speed 249km/h (135kt), working speed 161-241km/h (87-130kt). Initial rate of climb 2033ft/min. Ferry range 1078km (582nm).

Weights: 600 – Empty equipped 1678kg (3700lb), max takeoff (agricultural category) 2720kg (6000lb). S2R-R1820/510 – Empty equipped 2263kg (4990lb), typical operating 4536kg (10,000lb).

Dimensions: 600 – Wing span 13.51m (44ft 4in), length 8.95m (29ft 5in), height 2.79m (9ft 2in). Wing area 30.3m² (326.6sq ft). S2R-R1820/510 – Same except wing span 13.54m (44ft 5in), height 9.60m (31ft 6in). Wing area 30.3m² (326.6sq ft).

Capacity: Pilot only, second seat optional.

Production: Over 1650 piston powered Thrushes built.

History: The original Snow S-2 was designed by Leland Snow, who incorporated his knowledge as an experienced ag pilot into the S-2's design.

The Snow S-2 prototype flew for the first time in 1956 and production deliveries began in 1958. S-2 variants differed in engine options, which included the 165kW (220hp) Continental W-670 powered S-2A, the S-2B and S-2C with a Pratt & Whitney R-985, and the R-1340-AN-1 powered S-2C-600.

Aero Commander acquired the design and production rights to the S-2 series in 1965 and built the improved S-2D Ag Commander. The S-2 changed hands once more in 1967 when North American Rockwell (later Rockwell) acquired Aero Commander, continuing the series as the Thrush Commander. Rockwell built the Thrush in two basic models, the basic Thrush Commander-600 with a 450kW (600hp) R-1340 and 1514 litre (400US gal) chemical hopper and the Thrush Commander-800 with a 595kW (800hp) Wright R-1820 Cyclone and larger 1930 litre (510US gal) hopper.

Design and production rights changed hands a final time in 1977 when Ayres (who had previously carried out turboprop conversions to Thrush Commanders) acquired the rights to the Thrush Commander -600 and -800 and their production facilities from Rockwell.

Ayres continued to build the Thrush Commander-600, variously named the Thrush-600, S2R-R1340 Thrush and S2R-600. For a time Ayres also offered a Polish PZL-3 Pezetel radial powered version, the Pezetel Thrush. In the early 1980s Ayres re-introduced the Thrush Commander-800 to production as the Bull Thrush S2R-R1820, which at the time it claimed to be the most powerful agricultural aircraft in production.

Ayres ceased production of the piston Thrushes in the mid 1990s.

Photo: A Rockwell Thrush Commander. (Keith Myers)

Rockwell Darter & Lark Commanders

Country of origin: United States of America

Type: Four seat light aircraft

Powerplant: Darter – One 110kW (150hp) Lycoming O-320-A flat four piston engine driving a two blade fixed pitch propeller. Lark – One 135kW (180hp) O-360-A2F.

Performance: Darter – Max speed 214km/h (115kt), max cruising speed 206km/h (111kt). Initial rate of climb 785ft/min. Service ceiling 11,000ft. Range at max cruising speed 820km (443nm). Lark – Max speed 222km/h (120kt), max cruising speed 212km/h (114kt). Initial rate of climb 750ft/min. Service ceiling 13,000ft. Range at max cruising speed 845km (456nm).

Weights: Darter – Empty 580kg (1280lb), max takeoff 1020kg (2250lb). Lark – Empty 658kg (1450lb), max takeoff 1110kg (2450lb).

Dimensions: Darter – Wing span 10.67m (35ft 0in), length 6.86m (22ft 6in), height 2.84m (9ft 4in). Wing area 16.8m² (181sq ft). Lark – Same except for length 7.59m (24ft 11in), height 3.07m (10ft 1in).

Capacity: Typical seating for four.

Production: Approximately 200 Model 100s/Darter Commanders and 250 Lark Commanders built.

History: Aero Commander developed the high wing four seat 100 series in an effort to expand its product range.

The Aero Commander 100 began life as a three seat design from Volaircraft of Aliquippa, Pennsylvania. The basic design was known as the Volaire 10 and first flew during 1960. Features included a high wing, 360° all round visibility and metal construction. A handful of production aircraft, the 1035 powered by a 100kW (135hp) O-290-D and the four seat 110kW (150hp) O-320 powered 1050, were built before Aero Commander purchased the design and manufacturing rights for both in 1965.

Aero Commander only made a small number of changes before the 1035 and 1050 were placed into production as the Aero Commander 100A and 100 respectively in the second half of 1965. In 1966 Aero Commander incorporated a small number of changes including revised windscreen and rear cabin window designs.

By the time the first major changes to the basic design were introduced, Aero Commander had been taken over by North American Rockwell in 1967, and the aircraft was renamed the Model 100/150 Darter Commander. Darter production continued into 1969.

North American Rockwell also introduced the improved 100/180 Lark Commander in 1967 (FAA Type Approval was awarded on September 26 that year). Changes included a more powerful 135kW (180hp) O-360-A2F engine, a swept back fin, reprofiled cowling and 91kg (200lb) increase in max takeoff weight. The aerodynamic changes gave the Lark Commander a sleeker appearance, and the more powerful engine boosted performance. However Rockwell dumped Lark production in 1971, as it had been outsold and out performed by the less powerful Piper Cherokee and Cessna 172.

Rockwell sold design and production rights for both the Darter (which had been out of production since 1969) and the Lark to Phoenix Aircraft in 1971, but the latter company did not undertake production.

Photo: The Aero Commander 100 bears a superficial resemblance to the Cessna 172. (Mike McHugh)

Rockwell Commander 112 & 114

Country of origin: United States of America

Type: Four seat high performance light aircraft

Powerplant: 112B – One 140kW (200hp) Lycoming IO-360-C1D6 fuel injected flat four piston engine driving a two blade constant speed propeller. 114 – One 195kW (260hp) Lycoming IO-540-T4A5D fuel injected flat six driving a three blade constant speed prop.

Performance: 112B – Max speed 277km/h (150kt), max cruising speed 251km/h (135kt), long range cruising speed 222km/h (120kt). Initial rate of climb 880ft/min. Service ceiling 15,200ft. Max range with reserves 1085km (585nm), or 1647km (890nm) with optional fuel. 114 – Max speed 307km/h (166kt), max cruising speed 290km/h (157kt), long range cruising 254km/h (137kt). Initial rate of climb 1088ft/min. Service ceiling 17,400ft. Max range with reserves 1355km (730nm).

Weights: 112B – Empty 804kg (1773lb), max takeoff 1270kg (2800lb). 114 – Empty 885kg (1885lb), max takeoff 1425kg (3140lb).

Dimensions: Wing span 10.85m (35ft 8in), length 7.63m (25ft 1in), height 2.57m (8ft 5in). Wing area 15.2m² (164sq ft). 114 – Same except wing span 9.98m (32ft 9in). Wing area 14.1m² (152.0sq ft).

Capacity: Typical seating for four.

Production: Production of the 112 and 114 series ceased in 1979.

History: The Rockwell Commander 112 and 114 are high performance, retractable undercarriage light aircraft.

Rockwell's General Aviation Division began development of the original Commander 111 and 112 during the late 1960s, and announced its new range in late 1970. Both models featured conventional construction and a low wing configuration, while the 111 had fixed undercarriage and the 112 had retractable gear. The prototype 112 first flew on December 4 1970, and was powered by a 135kW (180hp) Lycoming O-360, while a prototype 111 first flew late in 1971. The loss of the 112 prototype during flight testing due to the structural failure of the tail unit delayed certification and production of both models until a fix was found. Deliveries of production aircraft took place from late 1972.

Production 111s were powered by 135kW (180hp) O-360s, production 112s were powered by more powerful 150kW (200hp) IO-360s. Only a few 111s were built before Rockwell decided to concentrate on the higher performance retractable gear 112. The updated 112A appeared in 1974 with a higher max takeoff weight, improved cabin ventilation and detail refinements, while the turbocharged 156kW (210hp) TO-360 powered 112TC was introduced in 1976. It also featured a longer span wing and increased max takeoff weight.

Also introduced in 1976 was the 114, which is basically a 112 with a more powerful 194kW (260hp) six cylinder IO-540. The 114 remained in production basically unchanged until 1979, by which stage it had been named the Gran Turismo Commander. Meanwhile the improved 112B had appeared in 1977, featuring the increased max takeoff weight and the extended wingtips introduced on the 112TC. By that stage the 112TC was designated the 112TC-A, later it became known as the Alpine Commander.

The Commander Aircraft Company began building the 114 based improved 114B and 114TC in 1992, these are described separately.

Photo: A Commander 112TC-A. This aeroplane was later named the Alpine Commander. (Gary Gentle)

Rockwell (Aero) Commander 500/560/680

Country of origin: United States of America

Type: Utility and corporate transports

Powerplants: 685 – Two 325kW (435hp) Lycoming GTSIO-520-F geared, turbocharged and fuel injected flat six piston engines driving three blade constant speed propellers. Rockwell 500S – Two 215kW (290hp) Lycoming IO-540-E1B5.

Performance: 685 – Max speed 449km/h (242kt) at 20,000ft, max cruising speed 412km/h (222kt), long range cruising speed 281km/h (152kt). Initial rate of climb 1490ft/min. Operational ceiling 25,000ft. Max range at 20,000ft with reserves 2125km (1147nm), with optional fuel 2858km (1543nm). 500S – Max speed 346km/h (187kt), max cruising speed 326km/h (176kt), long range cruise 298km/h (161kt). Initial rate of climb 1340ft/min. Service ceiling 19,400ft. Max range with reserves 1915km (1035nm).

Weights: 685 – Empty 2742kg (6046lb), max takeoff 4082kg (9000lb). 500S – Empty 2102kg (4635lb), max TO 3060kg (6750lb).

Dimensions: 685 – Wing span 13.43m (44ft 1in), length 13.10m (43ft 0in), height 4.56m (15ft 0in). Wing area 22.5m² (242.5sq ft). 500S – Wing span 14.95m (49ft 1in), length 11.22m (36ft 10in), height 4.56m (15ft 0in). Wing area 23.7m² (255.0sq ft).

Capacity: Seating in standard length Commanders for five to seven, including pilot. Stretched Grand Commander seats up to 11.

Production: Total includes 150 520s; 182 560As; 70 560Es; 254 680 Supers; 41 680Es and 13 720s.

History: The origins of this prolific series of twins lies with two former Douglas employees (one of whom was Ted Smith) who formed the Aero Design and Engineering Corporation in December 1944 after failing to interest their employer in a design they were working on.

Their original design was the six to seven seat L-3805, which first flew on April 23 1948. This aircraft formed the basis for the first Aero Commander production model, the 520, which seated five to seven people and was powered by two 195kW (260hp) Lycoming GO-435s. Production began in late 1951.

Approximately 150 Aero Commander 520s were built through to 1954. Subsequent development led to the more powerful 560 series (1954) with geared engines, the 680 series (1955) with supercharged engines, and the direct drive normally aspirated 500 series (1958). Variants include the 560A which introduced the 25cm (10in) stretched fuselage that became the standard short fuselage length, the 560E which introduced the definitive wing span, the 720 Alti-Cruiser pressurised development of the 680, and the later pressurised 680PF.

The 560 and 680 were joined by the stretched 680FL Grand Commander from 1962. The 500 was introduced to production in 1958 and was originally intended as a low cost model.

In 1967 North American Rockwell took over Aero Commander and the Grand Commander became the Courser Commander and the 500 became the Shrike Commander (gaining its distinctive pointed nose at the same time). The Shrike Commander was the last Commander to remain in production, manufacture ending in 1980.

The final piston powered model was the Rockwell 685 Commander, which was a piston powered Turbo Commander.

Photo: A Commander 560. (Lance Higgerson)

Rockwell Turbo Commander

Country of origin: United States of America

Type: Twin turboprop utility and corporate transports

Powerplants: 690A – Two 520kW (700shp) Garrett AiResearch TPE331-5-251K turboprops driving three blade constant speed propellers. Jetprop 1000 – Two 730kW (980shp) Garrett TPE331-10-501Ks flat rated to 610kW (820shp).

Performance: 690A – Max speed 528km/h (285kt), econ cruising speed 465km/h (251kt). Initial rate of climb 2850ft/min. Range with max payload and reserves 1370km (740nm). 1000 – Max speed 571km/h (308kt), econ cruising speed 474km/h (256kt). Initial rate of climb 2802ft/min. Max certificated altitude 35,000ft. Range with max payload and reserves 2430km (1311nm), with max fuel and reserves 3855km (2080nm).

Weights: 690A – Empty 2778kg (6126lb), loaded 4650kg (10,250lb). 1000 – Empty equipped 3307kg (7289lb), max TO 5080kg (11,200lb).

Dimensions: 690A – Wing span 14.22m (46ft 8in), length 13.52m (44ft 5in), height 4.56m (15ft 0in). Wing area 24.7m² (266sq ft). 1000 – Wing span 15.89m (52ft 2in), length 13.10m (43ft 0in), height 4.55m (15ft 0in). Wing area 26.0m² (279.4sq ft).

Capacity: Pilot and passenger or copilot on flightdeck. Main cabin seating for six to eight. Jetprop 1000 can seat 10 in main cabin.

Production: Approximate production of 1075 includes Gulfstream production of 122 Jetprop 840s, 42 Jetprop 900s, 84 Jetprop 980s and 108 Jetprop 1000s. Production ceased in 1985.

History: The turboprop powered developments of the Aero Commander family of light twins enjoyed a two decade long production run, and were built by three companies before production ceased.

The original Turboprop Commander was based on the 680FLP, and first flew on December 31 1964, but instead of piston engines power was supplied by 450kW (605shp) Garrett AiResearch TPE331 turboprops. This initial Turbo Commander model was designated the 680T and entered production in 1965.

Progressively improved developments of the basic Turbo Commander appeared, including the 680V, which introduced an increased maximum takeoff weight, and the 680W with improved engines. Following North American Rockwell's takeover of Aero Commander and the introduction of the further improved Model 681, the name Hawk Commander was adopted for a time, but it was dropped from 1971 with the release of the 681B.

By the time of the introduction of the 681B, Rockwell was already flight testing the upgraded Turbo Commander 690, which first flew on March 3 1968 and was certificated in July 1971. Rockwell introduced the improved 690A soon after.

In 1979 Rockwell flew the Jetprop Commander 840 and 980, developments of the 690 powered by 625kW (840shp) Garrett TPE331-5 and 730kW (980shp) TPE331-10 turboprops respectively. These went into production with Gulfstream, who had purchased Rockwell's GA lines in 1979. The Jetprop 1000 was similar in overall dimensions but introduced a revised interior that made better use of the available space and the 980's engines. The Jetprop 900 meanwhile combined the revised interior with the 840's engines. Production ceased in 1985.

Photo: A Rockwell Turbo Commander 690A. (Richard Hall)

Rockwell Sabreliner

Country of origin: United States of America

Type: Mid size corporate jet

Powerplants: 40 – Two 14.7kN (3300lb) Pratt & Whitney JT12A-8 turbojets. 75A – Two 20.2kN (4500lb) General Electric CF700-2D-2 turbofans.

Performance: 40 – Max cruising speed 810km/h (440kt), economical cruising speed 743km/h (400kt). Max rate of climb 4700ft/min. Service ceiling 45,000ft. Range with max fuel, four passengers and reserves 3240km (1750nm). 75A – Max cruising speed 906km/h (490kt), economical cruising speed 772km/h (417kt). Service ceiling 45,000ft. Max range with max fuel, four passengers and reserves 3174km (1713nm).

Weights: 40 – Empty equipped 5102kg (11,250lb), max takeoff 9150kg (20,172lb). 75A – Empty equipped 5990kg (13,200lb), max takeoff 10,435kg (23,000lb).

Dimensions: 40 – Wing span 13.61m (44ft 8in), length 14.30m (46ft 11in), height 4.88m (16ft 0in). Wing area 31.8m² (342.1sq ft). 75A – Wing span 13.61m (44ft 8in), length 14.38m (47ft 2in), height 5.26m (17ft 3in). Wing area 31.8m² (342.1sq ft).

Capacity: Flightcrew of two. Main cabin seats up to 10 in high density layout. Various other seating arrangements possible.

Production: Over 600 civil Sabreliners built, plus 200 T-39s. Over 380 remained in use in late 2000 including 33 T-39s in civil use and 124 Sabreliner 60s.

History: The Sabreliner was successfully developed for both military and civil use.

North American Aviation began work on the Sabreliner as a private venture but it was formally launched in August 1956 in response to the US Air Force's UTX (Utility Trainer Experimental) requirement for a utility jet aircraft capable of performing transport and combat readiness training missions. A civil configured prototype (designated NA264) first flew on September 16 1958 powered by General Electric YJ85 turbojets. Soon after the US Air Force ordered the Sabreliner into production, and it and the US Navy went on to order several Pratt & Whitney JT12 turbojet powered versions, including the T-39A pilot proficiency and support transport and the T-39B/D radar trainer.

The first civil aircraft, the NA265-40, was equivalent to the T-39A and was certificated in April 1963. The Series 40 followed from June 1966 and featured a higher cruising speed and greater internal cabin space. The Series 60 was stretched by 97cm (3ft 2in) and is identifiable by its five, rather than three, cabin windows per side. The Series 60A introduced aerodynamic changes over the 60. The Sabreliner 75 meanwhile is based on the 60 and 60A, but has a deeper fuselage with greater headroom.

Turbofan power was introduced to the Sabreliner family in 1973 (by which time North American had become part of Rockwell International) with the introduction of the General Electric CF700 turbofan powered 75A. The 75A also introduced aerodynamic, cabin, equipment and systems improvements. The Series 65A meanwhile is similar to the 60A and 75 but is powered by Garrett AiResearch TFE731-3-1D turbofans. It was delivered from December 1979. Sabreliner production ceased in 1981.

Photo: A turbojet powered Sabreliner 60A. (Gary Gentle)

Saab 340

Country of origin: Sweden

Type: Twin turboprop regional airliner

Powerplants: 340A – Two 1295kW (1735shp) General Electric CT7-5A2 turboprops driving four blade constant speed Dowty or Hamilton Standard props. 340B – Two 1305kW (1750shp) CT7-9Bs.

Performance: 340A – Max cruising speed 515km/h (278kt), economical cruising speed 484km/h (260kt). Range with max payload 1455km (785nm), range with max fuel 3975km (2145nm). 340B – Max cruising speed 523km/h (282kt), long range cruising speed 467km/h (252kt). Range with 35 passengers and reserves at max cruising speed 1490km (805nm), at long range cruising speed 1735km (935nm).

Weights: 340A – Operating empty 7810kg (17,215lb), max takeoff 12,370kg (27,275lb). 340B – Operating empty 8140kg (17,945lb), max takeoff 13,155kg (29,000lb).

Dimensions: Wing span 21.44m (70ft 4in), length 19.73m (64ft 9in), height 6.97m (22ft 11in). Wing area 41.8m² (450.0sq ft).

Capacity: Flightcrew of two. Main cabin seats up to 37, or typically 33 to 35 with a galley at three abreast and 76cm (30in) pitch. Combi seats 19 passengers and 1500kg (3310lb) of cargo. A small number of 340s are outfitted in corporate configurations.

Production: 458 Saab 340s built to 1998. 340A production ended in September 1989 with 159 built. At late 2000 418 were in airline service, with a further three used as corporate transports.

History: The Saab 340 proved to be a highly popular regional airliner that helped to pioneer the 30 seat turboprop class, but slow sales in the late 1990s forced Saab to cease production.

In 1979 Saab-Scania of Sweden and Fairchild in the USA reached an agreement to conduct joint feasibility and development studies on a 30 to 40 seat commuter airliner. The resulting SF340 design was launched in September 1980 with the aim of capturing 25 to 30% of its market. Within the 65/35 Saab-Fairchild partnership split Saab was responsible for the fuselage, fin and final assembly, while Fairchild was responsible for the wings, engine nacelles and empennage. The two companies selected the General Electric CT7 (a commercial development of the T700 which powers Sikorsky's S-70 series of military helicopters) to power the new airliner.

The first of three SF340 prototypes first flew on January 25 1983, while the first production aircraft flew in early March 1984. US and European certification was awarded that June. From November 1 1985 Saab assumed overall responsibility for the SF340 following Fairchild's decision to drop out of the program. Saab initially retained the SF340 designation but later changed it to 340A.

The first improved development of the Saab 340 was the 340B. More powerful engines improved hot and high performance, while other changes included a greater span tailplane, a higher max takeoff weight and better range. Deliveries began in September 1989.

The last development of the 340 was the 340B Plus, which introduced changes developed for the larger Saab 2000, including an improved cabin interior. The first 340B Plus was delivered in March 1994. However lack of sales and profitability forced Saab to cease 340 and 2000 production, which wound up in 1998.

Photo: An Air Rarotonga Saab 340. (Wayne Grant)

Saab 2000

Country of origin: Sweden

Type: 50 seat twin turboprop regional airliner

Powerplants: Two 3096kW (4152shp) Allison AE 2100A turboprops driving six blade constant speed Dowty propellers.

Performance: Max cruising speed 682km/h (368kt) at 25,000ft, long range cruising speed 594km/h (321kt). Initial rate of climb 2250ft/min. Service ceiling 31,000ft. High speed range with 50 passengers and reserves 2185km (1180nm), range at long range cruising speed 2868km (1549nm).

Weights: Operating empty 13,800kg (30,423lb), max takeoff 22,800kg (50,2650lb).

Dimensions: Wing span 24.76m (81ft 3in), length 27.28m (89ft 6in), height 7.73m (25ft 4in). Wing area 55.7m^2 (600.0sq ft).

Capacity: Flightcrew of two. Normal passenger accommodation for 50 at three abreast and 81cm (32in) pitch. Max seating for 58 at three abreast and 76cm (30in) pitch, with repositioned galley and wardrobe.

Production: 63 Saab 2000s built to 1998. In 2000 54 were in airline service with three used as corporate transports.

History: The Saab 2000 was a stretched 50 seat, faster development of the successful 340.

The Saab 2000, with a cruise speed of over 665km/h (360kt), is one of the fastest turboprop airliners developed. Saab marketing said it combines near jet speeds, including near jet climb and descent rates, with turboprop economy. Saab launched development of the 2000 in mid December 1988 with a launch order from Crossair for 25 (plus a further 25 on option) following definition and design studies that revealed a market for a high speed regional turboprop.

The initial Saab 2000 development plan would have seen the 2000 in service in the second half of 1993, but delays pushed this back until the second half of 1994. The Saab 2000's first flight took place on March 26 1992, and European and US certification was granted in March and April 1994 respectively. Service entry with Crossair occurred a few months later.

While retaining the same cross section as the Saab 340, the 2000 is 7.55m (24ft 9in) longer (seating 15 more passengers), while the same wing section was retained but the 2000's wing span is 15% greater than the 340's, and the engines are positioned further outboard.

The 2000 was the first civil application of the advanced Allison (now Rolls-Royce) AE 2100 turboshaft (derived from the military T406 developed for the V-22 Osprey tiltrotor). They are equipped with FADEC and drive slow turning six blade props. The flightdeck features a Collins Pro Line 4 EFIS avionics suite with six colour CRT displays. Cabin noise is reduced by an active noise control system comprising 72 microphones and 36 speakers which generate anti phase noise.

Several European aerospace firms participated in the Saab 2000 manufacturing program including CASA, which designed and built the wing, Westland, which manufactured the rear fuselage, and Valmet of Finland, which built the tail.

Lack of sales and profitibility forced Saab to cease 340 and 2000 production, with the lines winding up in 1998. The last 2000 was delivered to Crossair in April 1999.

Photo: A Saab 2000 used for navaid calibration in Japan. (John Adlard)

Schweizer/Hughes 300 (& 269)

Country of origin: United States of America

Type: Light utility helicopter

Powerplant: 300C – One 142kW (190hp) Textron Lycoming HIO-360-D1A fuel injected flat four derated from 168kW (225hp) driving a three blade main rotor and two blade tail rotor.

Performance: 300C – Max cruising speed 159km/h (86kt), max range cruising speed 124km/h (67kt). Initial rate of climb 750ft/min. Hovering ceiling in ground effect 10,800ft, out of ground effect 8600ft. Service ceiling 10,200ft. Range with max normal fuel and no reserves 386km (208nm). Max endurance 3hr 48min.

Weights: 300C – Empty 499kg (1100lb), max takeoff 930kg (2050lb), or 975kg (2150lb) with an external sling load.

Dimensions: Main rotor diameter 8.18m (26ft 10in), length overall 9.40m (30ft 10in), fuselage length 6.80m (22ft 0in), height to top of rotor head 2.66m (8ft 9in). Main rotor disc area 52.5m^2 (565.5sq ft).

Capacity: Typical seating for three on a bench seat in 300 or two in 269. Many aircraft equipped for agricultural spraying and fitted with chemical hoppers and spray booms. Can lift a 475kg (1050lb) payload in an external sling load.

Production: Total 269/TH-58/300 production over 3500 aircraft, of which 2800 were built by Hughes before production transferred to Schweizer. Total includes military production.

History: The Hughes/Schweizer 300 is one of the most successful piston powered helicopters built, with over three and a half thousand produced by the two manufacturers over four decades.

Development of this versatile utility helicopter dates back to the mid 1950s when Hughes flew the two seat Model 269 for the first time in October 1956. The 269 sparked US Army interest and it ordered five as the YHO-2HU for evaluation in the scout and observation roles. Deliveries of the commercial equivalent Model 269A began in 1961.

The 269A program received a huge boost when Hughes won a US Army contract for a light helicopter primary trainer. In all, 792 were built as the TH-55A Osage and more than 60,000 US Army helicopter pilots learnt to fly in the type.

Hughes followed the two seat 269A with the slightly larger three seat 269B, which it marketed as the Hughes 300, which first flew in 1964. The 300 was followed from 1969 by the improved 300C, which introduced a more powerful 140kW (190hp) Lycoming HIO-360 engine and increased diameter main rotor, giving an increase in payload of 45%, plus performance improvements. The 300C (or 269C) flew in August 1969 and today remains in production basically unchanged.

Since 1983 the 300C has been built by Schweizer in the USA. Schweizer built the 300C initially under licence for Hughes, and then acquired all rights to the helicopter in 1986. Under Schweizer's stewardship more than 250 minor improvements have been made to the 300C, but the basic design has been left unchanged. Schweizer also offers a version optimised for police work. Named the Sky Knight, it is available with options such as a search light and infrared sensors. For military pilot training the 300C is marketed as the TH-300C.

The latest 300 model is the 300CB trainer powered by a HO-360-C1A and delivered from late 1995.

Photo: A Schweizer 300C.

Schweizer 330 & 333

Country of origin: United States of America

Type: Light utility helicopters

Powerplant: 330SP – One 315kW (420shp) Rolls-Royce 250-C20W turboprop rated at 175kW (235shp) for takeoff and 165kW (220hp) for max continuous operation driving a three blade main rotor and two blade tail rotor.

Performance: 330SP – Normal cruising speed 193km/h (104kt), economical cruising speed 185km/h (100kt). Max initial rate of climb 1380ft/min. Hovering ceiling in ground effect 13,600ft, out of ground effect 10,500ft. Max range with no reserves 590km (319nm), endurance 4hr 12min.

Weights: 330SP – Empty 517kg (1140lb), max takeoff 1025kg (2260lb).

Dimensions: 330SP – Main rotor diameter 8.31m (27ft 3in), length overall rotors turning 9.46m (31ft 1in), height overall 3.35m (11ft 0in). Main rotor disc area 52.5m² (565.5sq ft).

Capacity: Typical seating for three, optional seating for four.

Production: 330 Deliveries began in mid 1993. Approx 35 built. 333 deliveries began mid 2000.

History: The turbine Schweizer 330 and 333 are turbine developments of the Hughes/Schweizer 300 series of two/three seat light piston engine helicopters.

Schweizer, a firm well known for its production of gliders, acquired the production and manufacturing rights to the Hughes 300, which it had been building under licence since 1983, from McDonnell Douglas in November 1986. In 1987 Schweizer announced it was developing an improved turbine powered version. The new model was dubbed the 330 and it was designed to fulfil a number of utility roles.

The Schweizer 330 uses the dynamic components, rotors, controls and systems of the 300C, combined with a Rolls-Royce (previously Allison) 250-C20 turboshaft. The engine has been derated to just 165kW (220hp), giving the 330 excellent hot and high performance. For example the powerplant will reach its max rated power output right up to 18,000ft. Other changes compared with the piston 300C include an essentially all new fuselage, new vertical tail surfaces and a new tail fairing.

The 330 first flew on June 14 1988 (a converted 300C). FAA certification was awarded in September 1992 and first deliveries took place from mid 1993.

The improved 330SP was announced in May 1997. Compared to the basic 330 it features a larger main rotor hub, increased chord main blades and raised skids. These modifications can also be retrofitted to existing 330s.

To enhance its appeal as a trainer the 330 is offered with a third set of flight controls, allowing the carriage of two students and an instructor on training flights.

Schweizer announced the further improved 333 at Heli-Expo in February 2000. Improvements include upgraded dynamic system components, new rotor blades and standard high ground clearance skids. It has a 30% greater useful load than the 330SP. Deliveries began in mid 2000 (to the San Antonio Police Department).

Photo: The 333, announced in early 2000. (Schweizer)

Scottish Aviation Twin Pioneer

Country of origin: United Kingdom

Type: Utility transport

Powerplants: Series 3 – Two 475kW (640hp) Alvis Leonides 531 seven cylinder radial piston engines driving three blade constant speed propellers.

Performance: Series 3 – Max cruising speed 257km/h (140kt), economical cruising speed 210km/h (114kt). Initial rate of climb 1370ft/min. Service ceiling 18,000ft. Max range at economical cruising speed 1287km (695nm), range with 1590kg (3500lb) payload 322km (175nm).

Weights: Series 3 – Empty 4630kg (10,200lb), max takeoff 6628kg (14,600lb).

Dimensions: Series 3 – Wing span 23.33m (76ft 6in), length 13.80m (45ft 3in), height 3.74m (12ft 3in). Wing area 62.3m² (670.0sq ft).

Capacity: Flightcrew of two. Main cabin seats 16 in passenger configuration, or can hold 1540kg (3400lb) of freight. Has also been used as a platform for aerial photography.

Production: Total Twin Pioneer production of 91, including 32 CC.1s and seven CC.2s for Britain's Royal Air Force and others for the Royal Malayan Air Force. Production ceased in 1964.

History: The Scottish Aviation Twin Pioneer utility transport saw limited commercial and military service, mainly in the UK and some Commonwealth countries.

Despite its name, the Twin Pioneer is an all new aircraft compared with the Scottish Aviation Pioneer. The original Pioneer was a high wing single engined five seat light aircraft powered by an Alvis radial piston engine which was built in small numbers for the Royal Air Force for liaison duties.

The Twin Pioneer is also powered by Alvis radials and features a high wing, but is much larger overall, capable of seating up to 16 passengers in the main cabin. Designed for both civil and military applications, the Twin Pioneer was also one of the few postwar aircraft to feature a high wing and tailwheel undercarriage, while its triple vertical tail arrangement makes it easily recognisable.

The prototype Twin Pioneer first flew on June 25 1955, and the first production examples were delivered from April 28 1956. By mid 1964, when production ceased, 94 of three different models had been built. The Royal Air Force in Britain was the largest customer, taking delivery of 39 Twin Pioneers.

The RAF used its Twin Pioneers for a variety of transport and liaison roles, and they could carry 13 troops, or 11 paratroops, or six stretchers and five sitting casualties or medical attendants. Another military operator was Malaya/Malaysia.

The initial Twin Pioneer production model was the Series 1, powered by two 410kW (550hp) Alvis Leonides 514/8 radials. The Series 2 was powered by Pratt & Whitney R-1340 radials. Final production was of the Series 3 (described above), powered by 475kW (640hp) Leonides 531/8 radials.

In 2000 only a handful of Twin Pioneers remained in service, including two Series 3s registered in Australia.

Photo: A Twin Pioneer used for tourist operations in Australia. (Peter Easton)

Shorts Skyvan & Skyliner

Country of origin: United Kingdom

Type: STOL utility transport and regional airliner

Powerplants: Srs 3 – Two 535kW (715shp) Garrett TPE331-2-201A turboprops driving three blade Hartzell propellers.

Performance: Srs 3 – Max cruising speed 324km/h (175kt), normal cruising speed 311km/h (168kt), economical cruising speed 278km/h (150kt). Initial rate of climb 1640ft/min. Service ceiling 22,500ft. Range at long range cruising speed with reserves 1115km (600nm), range in typical freighter configuration with a 1815kg (4000lb) payload and reserves at economical cruising speed 300km (162nm).

Weights: Srs 3 – Basic operating 3331kg (7344lb) for Skyvan or 4055kg (8940lb) for Skyliner, max takeoff 5670kg (12,500lb).

Dimensions: Srs 3 – Wing span 19.79m (64ft 11in), length 12.21m (40ft 1in), or 12.60m (41ft 4in) with weather radar, height 4.60m (15ft 1in). Wing area 35.1m² (378sq ft).

Capacity: Flightcrew of one or two. Seating for up to 19 passengers at three abreast in Skyliner, or nine passengers in executive configuration.

Production: 150 Skyvans and Skyliners built between the mid 1960s and 1986, almost all of which were Series 3s (including almost 60 military Series 3Ms).

History: The boxy and rugged Shorts Skyvan and Skyliner date back to the postwar Miles Aerovan project.

In 1958 Short Brothers (or Shorts) acquired the design rights to the HDM.106 Caravan, a development of Miles' HDM.105, an Aerovan fitted with the very high aspect ratio Hurel Dubois designed wing. Shorts thoroughly revised the Caravan design, resulting in the SC.7 Skyvan, featuring a box-like 1.98m x 1.98m (6ft 6in x 6ft 6in) square fuselage (allowing seating for 19 or freight), a rear loading freight ramp, and a reduced span version of the Hurel Dubois wing. Prototype construction began in 1960 but the Series 1 prototype, powered by two Continental 291kW (390hp) GTSIO-520 piston engines, did not fly until January 17 1963 due to problems with the Belfast transport.

Unlike the prototype, initial production SC.7s were powered by 545kW (730shp) Turbomeca Astazou XII turboprops. The original piston powered Series 1 prototype was the first Astazou powered Skyvan to fly (with 390kW/520shp Astazou IIs), in October 1963. The re-engined prototype was designated the Series 1A, while early Astazou powered production aircraft were designated Series 2. The first Series 2 flew in October 1965.

Early on in the SC.7's production run Shorts decided to switch the powerplant choice to 535kW (715shp) Garrett TPE331-201s, resulting in the definitive Series 3 (first flight December 15 1967). Many Series 2 Skyvans were also converted to Garrett power.

The basic Series 3 and the higher takeoff weight Series 3A can perform a number of utility missions including passenger transport, ambulance, aerial survey and freight work, and are called Skyvans. The Skyliner airliner features an improved level of interior equipment and furnishing, while military Skyvans are designated Series 3M and 3M-200 with a higher max takeoff weight.

Low rate production continued to January 1986.

Photo: With its rear freight ramp the Skyvan is a popular skydiving aircraft. (Michael Johnson)

Shorts Belfast

Country of origin: United Kingdom

Type: Heavy lift turboprop freighter

Powerplants: Four 4275kW (5730shp) Rolls-Royce Tyne RTy 12 turboprops driving four blade constant speed propellers.

Performance: Max cruising speed 566km/h (306kt), typical cruising speed 510km/h (275kt). Service ceiling 30,000ft. Range with max payload and reserves approximately 1575km (850nm), range with 10 tonne (22,000lb) payload 6200km (3350nm), range with max fuel and reserves 8530km (4605nm).

Weights: Operating empty 59,020kg (130,000lb), max takeoff 104,325kg (230,000lb). Max payload over 32,000kg (70,485lb).

Dimensions: Wing span 48.41m (158ft 10in), length 41.58m (136ft 5in), height 14.33m (47ft 0in). Wing area 229.1m² (2466sq ft).

Capacity: Flightcrew of three or four comprising two pilots, a flight engineer and possibly a navigator. Can accommodate a wide variety of oversize and heavy cargoes such as heavy machinery, industrial equipment such as generators and small aircraft and helicopters. Can be fitted with a roller floor to handle palletised freight.

Production: Only 10 Belfasts built specifically for the UK's Royal Air Force. Two in commercial service with Heavylift in 2000.

History: With a maximum takeoff weight of over 100 tonnes (220,500lb), Shorts' Belfast is one of the largest turboprop powered aircraft built, behind the massive 250 tonne (551,250lb) max takeoff Antonov An-22 (described separately) and Douglas' C-133 Cargomaster of the 1950s.

The Belfast was developed in response to a Royal Air Force requirement for a heavy lift freighter capable of carrying a wide range of military hardware, including artillery pieces, 200 plus troops, helicopters and/or guided missiles over relatively long ranges. Shorts had studied a number of large freighter designs during the late 1950s, and what became the Belfast began life as the SC.5/10, design work on which began in February 1959.

Development of the SC.5/10 design resulted in the first flight of the Belfast on January 5 1964. Design features of this big aircraft included four Rolls-Royce Tyne turboprops mounted on a high wing, an 18 wheel undercarriage (comprising two eight wheel main bogeys and two wheel nose undercarriage system) and beaver tail rear loading doors and ramp.

When the Belfast entered service with the RAF in January 1966 it was the largest aircraft to be operated by that service.

The Belfast's military career was relatively short lived, and all 10 were retired in 1976. Heavylift (then TAC Heavylift) acquired five Belfasts for commercial service in 1977, and three were placed into service in 1980. Marshall of Cambridge performed a number of modifications on the Belfast which allowed it to be certificated to civil standards on March 6 1980.

Since then Heavylift's Belfasts have given the company a very useful capability to carry heavy and awkward sized loads, bettered only by its An-124s. In late 2000 two were in operation (G-HLFT and G-BEPS) and Heavylift anticipated flying them for at least another year, depending on maintenance costs and spares availability.

Photo: Heavylift's G-HLFT, one of its two Belfasts. (Mike McHugh)

Shorts 330

Country of origin: United Kingdom

Type: Regional airliner and utility freighter

Powerplants: 330-100 – Two 875kW (1173shp) Pratt & Whitney Canada PT6A-45 turboprops driving five blade constant speed Hartzell propellers. 330-200 – Two 893kW (1198shp) PT6A-45Rs.

Performance: 330-100 – Max cruising speed 356km/h (192kt), long range cruising speed 296km/h (160kt). Initial rate of climb 1200ft/min. Range with 30 passengers and reserves 590km (320nm). 330-200 – Max cruising speed 352km/h (190kt), long range cruising speed 294km/h (159kt). Range with max payload 660km (473nm), range with max fuel and no reserves 1695km (915nm).

Weights: 330-100 – Empty equipped in airliner configuration 6577kg (14,500lb), max takeoff 10,160kg (22,400lb). 330-200 – Operating empty 6697kg (14,764lb), max takeoff 10,387kg (22,900lb).

Dimensions: Wing span 22.76m (74ft 8in), length 17.69m (58ft 1in), height 4.95m (16ft 3in). Wing area 42.1m² (453.0sq ft).

Capacity: Flightcrew of two. Typical passenger accommodation for 30 at three abreast and 76cm (30in) pitch in 10 rows of seats. In combi freight/passenger configuration the 330 houses freight in the front of the cabin and 18 passengers in the rear.

Production: 330 production wound up in September 1992 after 136 had been built, including military C-23 Sherpas and 330UTs. Approximately 35 were in airline service at late 2000.

History: The Shorts 330 (sometimes called the 'Shed') was developed to be a simple, inexpensive and reliable 30 seat regional airliner.

The Shorts 330 is a stretched development of the SC.7 Skyvan. Beginning life designated the SD3-30, the 330 retained the Skyvan's overall configuration, including the slab sided fuselage cross section, supercritical, braced, above fuselage mounted wing design (lengthened by 2.97m/9ft 9in) and twin tails. Compared with the Skyvan the fuselage is stretched by 3.78m (12ft 5in), allowing seating for over 10 more passengers. Power is from two Pratt & Whitney PT6A turboprops driving five blade props, while a more aerodynamic pointed nose and retractable undercarriage were added. More than 60% greater fuel capacity boosts range significantly over the Skyvan.

Following project go-ahead for the SD3-30 in May 1973 an engineering prototype of the 330 first flew on August 22 1974. A production prototype flew on July 8 1975. The first true production aircraft followed that December. The 330 entered airline service with Time Air of Canada in August 1976.

Initial Shorts 330s were powered by PT6A-45As and -45Bs and are known as 330s or 330-100s. The definitive 330-200 (announced at the 1981 Paris Airshow) features more powerful PT6A-45Rs and a number of detail improvements, while items previously available as options were made standard equipment.

Various freighter versions of the 330 have been developed, including the Sherpa with a rear loading ramp (in service with the US Air Force and Army as the C-23), and the military 330UTT.

The last civil 330, a UTT for the Quebec provincial government, was delivered in June 1991, the last 330 of any model, a C-23B for the USAF, was delivered in September 1992.

Photo: A Fijian registered 330-200. (Francis Nickelson)

Shorts 360

Country of origin: United Kingdom

Type: 36 seat regional airliner

Powerplants: 360 – Two 990kW (1327shp) Pratt & Whitney Canada PT6A-65R turboprops driving five blade constant speed Hartzell propellers. 360-300 – Two 1062kW (1424shp) PT6A-67Rs driving six blade props.

Performance: 360 – Max cruising speed 390km/h (210kt). Range at max cruising speed with 36 passengers 426km (230nm), range with max fuel 1055km (570nm). 360-300 – Typical cruising speed 400km/h (216kt). Initial rate of climb 952ft/min. Range with 36 passengers and reserves at typical cruising speed 745km (402nm), with 31 passengers and reserves at 337km/h (182kt) cruising speed 1178km (636nm).

Weights: 360 – Operating empty 7530kg (16,600lb), max takeoff 11,657kg (25,700lb). 360-300 – Typical operating empty 7870kg (17,350lb), max takeoff 12,292kg (27,100lb).

Dimensions: Wing span 22.80m (74ft 10in), length 21.58m (70ft 10in), height 7.27m (23ft 10in). Wing area 42.2m² (454.0sq ft).

Capacity: Flightcrew of two. Typical passenger seating for 36 at three abreast and 76cm (30in) pitch in 12 seat rows. Optional seating for 39 in a high density configuration. Freighter 360-300F can house up to five standard LD3 containers or pallets.

Production: Last 360 completed in 1991 after 164 had been built. Approx 115 were in airline service in late 2000.

History: The Shorts 360 is a stretched, larger capacity and improved 36 seat derivative of the 30 seat Shorts 330.

The relative success of the rugged Shorts 330 (and deregulation in the US which allowed commuter airlines to fly aircraft with more than 30 seats) prompted the Northern Ireland based manufacturer to develop a stretched derivative. Shorts announced it was developing the 360 in mid 1980, and a prototype 360 first flew on June 1 1981.

The first production 360 flew in August 1982 and certification was awarded on September 3 that year. The 360 entered service with Suburban Airlines in the US in November 1982.

The two Shorts airliners are very close in overall dimensions and size, but the later 360 is easily identified by its new conventional tail unit mounted on a revised rear fuselage. The 360 is also 91cm (3ft) longer than the 330, allowing two more seat rows and six extra passengers to be carried, while the extra length reduces drag. Power is supplied by two Pratt & Whitney PT6A-65Rs, and the 360's wing span is slightly greater. Otherwise the 330 and 360 are very similar, and share a high degree of commonality (both are unpressurised).

Shorts marketed a number of 360 developments, the first of which was the 360 Advanced with 1062kW (1424shp) PT6A-65ARs. The 360 Advanced was introduced in late 1985, but was soon followed by the further improved 360-300, which entered service in March 1987. The 360-300 introduced advanced six blade propellers, more powerful PT6A-67R engines giving a higher cruise speed and improved hot and high performance, plus other aerodynamic improvements. The 360-300 was also built in 360-300F freighter form.

Shorts 360 production wound up in 1989 but the last 360 was not assembled and flown until 1991.

Photo: A Gill Airways 360. (Dave Fraser)

SIAI-Marchetti S.205 & S.208

Country of origin: Italy

Type: Four seat light aircraft

Powerplant: S.205-20 – One 150kW (200hp) Lycoming IO-360-A1B6D fuel injected flat four piston engine driving a two blade constant speed propeller. S.208 – One 185kW (260hp) Lycoming O-540-E4A5 flat six.

Performance: S.205-20 – Max speed 270km/h (146kt), max cruising speed 250km/h (136kt), normal cruising speed 243km/h (131kt). Initial rate of climb 826ft/min. Service ceiling 15,575ft. Range 1260km (680nm). S.208 – Max speed 320km/h (173kt), max cruising speed 300km/h (162kt). Initial rate of climb 985ft/min. Service ceiling 17,725ft. Range with tip tanks 1800km (970nm).

Weights: S.205-20 – Empty 760kg (1677lb), max takeoff 1300kg (2865lb). S.208 – Empty 827kg (1823lb), max takeoff 1500kg (3307lb).

Dimensions: S.205-20 – Wing span 10.86m (35ft 8in), length 8.00m (26ft 3in), height 2.89m (9ft 6in). Wing area 16.1m² (173sq ft). Same except span over tip tanks 11.23m (36ft 10in), length 8.09m (26ft 7in).

Capacity: Typical seating for four in S.205, up to five in S.208.

Production: Approx 620 S.205s, including 62 S.220 Velas assembled by Waco in the USA. Approx 120 S.208s built, including 40 for the Italian air force.

History: SIAI-Marchetti designed this series of four seat light aircraft to re-enter the GA market.

When SIAI-Marchetti began work on the four seat S.205, the company intended to develop a series of aircraft with various powerplant and other options, such as retractable undercarriage and constant speed propellers. To this end the company was modestly successful, with several hundred S.205s and larger S.208s built, with most sold to European customers.

The first of three S.205 prototypes flew during 1965. This initial aircraft was powered by a 135kW (180hp) Lycoming O-360 and featured fixed undercarriage. In production it became the S.205-18/F (18 for 180hp, F for fixed undercarriage). The first production S.205-18/F flew in February 1966 and deliveries commenced later that year.

The model lineup was expanded to include the 150kW (200hp) fuel injected IO-360 powered and higher max takeoff weight S.205-20/F, and the retractable undercarriage S.205-18/R and S.205-20/R. The most powerful member of the S.205 family was the S.205-22/R. This aircraft was powered by a 165kW (220hp) Franklin 6A-350-C1 flat six and was also assembled in the USA by Waco as the S.220 Vela.

Production of the S.205 initially ceased in 1975, although SIAI-Marchetti returned it to production as the improved S.205AC from 1977 until 1980 to meet an order for 140 for the Italian aero club.

The S.208 is based on the S.205 but has a larger cabin with seating for five. First flown on May 22 1967, it is powered by a 195kW (260hp) Lycoming O-540 and has retractable undercarriage, a third cabin window per side, optional tip tanks and strengthened structure. Deliveries commenced in 1968, and 44 S.208Ms were built for the Italian air force for liaison and training work.

Production ceased in 1975 and then resumed in 1977 alongside the S.205AC until finally winding up again in 1980.

Photo: An Australian registered 205-18/F. (Lance Higgerson)

Sikorsky S-55

Country of origin: United States of America

Type: Mid size utility helicopter

Powerplant: S-55C – One 520kW (700hp) Pratt & Whitney R-1340-3 nine cylinder radial piston engine driving a three blade main rotor and two blade tail rotor. S-55T – One 625kW (840shp) Garrett AiResearch TSE331-3U-303 turboshaft derated to 485kW (650shp).

Performance: S-55C – Max speed 163km/h (88kt), cruising speed 137km/h (74kt). Initial rate of climb 700ft/min. Hovering ceiling in ground effect 2000ft. Service ceiling 10,500ft. Range 645km (350nm). S-55T – Max speed 183km/h (99kt), cruising speed 157km/h (85kt). Initial rate of climb 1200ft/min. Hovering ceiling out of ground effect 6700ft. Range with reserves 595km (320nm).

Weights: S-55C – Empty 2245kg (4950lb), max takeoff 3265kg (7200lb). S-55T – Empty equipped 2132kg (4700lb), MTOW 3265kg (7200lb).

Dimensions: Main rotor diameter 16.16m (53ft 0in), fuselage length 12.87m (42ft 3in), height 4.06m (13ft 4in).

Capacity: Flightcrew of two. Typical seating in main cabin for eight to 12 passengers. Many aircraft configured in executive configurations or to carry freight. Can also carry an external sling load.

Production: Total Sikorsky S-55 production of 1281 aircraft, most for military service with US forces, 44 built under licence in Japan and 400 as Westland Whirlwinds. Approximately 40 S-55T conversions.

History: Like many Sikorsky helicopters, the S-55 started out as a military helicopter for the US armed forces that was later adapted for commercial service.

Sikorsky developed the S-55 in response to a US military requirement for a large general purpose helicopter. The US Defense Department awarded Sikorsky a contract to develop such a helicopter in 1948, and the first prototype flew on November 10 1949. As the H-19 Chickasaw the S-55 saw widespread US military service. Civil certification for the commercial S-55 series was first awarded on March 25 1952.

The initial civil variant was the S-55, powered by a 450kW (600hp) Pratt & Whitney Wasp radial piston engine. Later civil variants include the S-55A which introduced a 520kW (700hp) Wright R-1300 radial piston engine, while the S-55C had a P&W R-1340 engine and the repositioned tail boom of the S-55A.

Westland in the UK licence built 400 S-55s as the Whirlwind for mainly military but also commercial use. Early Whirlwinds were similar to the S-55 save for their Alvis Leonides radial engine, later developments were powered by a 785kW (1050shp) Rolls-Royce Bristol Gnome H.1000 turboshaft. S-55 licence manufacture was also undertaken in Japan and France.

In January 1971 Aviation Specialties was awarded a type certificate for its turboprop powered conversion of the S-55, dubbed the S-55T. Aviation Specialties formed the Helitec Corp to market and convert S-55s, and approximately 40 were fitted with a Garrett AiResearch TSE331 turboshaft. The conversion reduced the S-55's empty weight by approximately 410kg (900lb).

Photo: An S-55B. A feature of the S-55 is its nose mounted engine, with the driveshaft to the main rotor passing over the main cabin and behind the flightdeck. (Dave Prossor)

Sikorsky S-58

Country of origin: United States of America

Type: Mid size utility helicopter

Powerplant: S-58 – One 1140kW (1525hp) Wright R-1820-84 radial piston engine driving four blade main and tail rotors. S-58T – One 1340kW (1800shp) Pratt & Whitney Canada PT6T-3 Twin Pac turboshaft (two PT6s linked through a combining transmission) or one 1400kW (1875shp) PT6T-6.

Performance: S-58 – Max speed 198km/h (107kt), max cruising speed 158km/h (85kt). Initial rate of climb 1100ft/min. Hovering ceiling out of ground effect 2400ft. Range with max fuel and reserves 450km (243nm). S-58T (with PT6T-6s) – Max speed 222km/h (120kt), cruising speed 158km/h (85kt). Hovering ceiling out of ground effect 6500ft. Range with reserves 480km (260nm).

Weights: S-58 – Empty equipped 3461kg (7630lb), max takeoff 5895kg (13,000lb). S-58T – Empty 3355kg (7400lb), max TO 5895kg (13,000lb).

Dimensions: S-58 – Main rotor diameter 17.07m (56ft 0in), length overall rotors turning 17.27m (56ft 8in), fuselage length 14.25m (46ft 9in), height 4.36m (14ft 4in). Main rotor disc area 228.5m² (2460sq ft). S-58T – Same except for fuselage length 14.41m (47ft 3in).

Capacity: Flightcrew of two. Main cabin seating capacity for between 10 and 16 passengers or freight. Can also carry external sling loads.

Production: 1821 S-58s built mainly for military but also civil use between 1954 and 1970.

History: The Sikorsky S-58 was one of the most successful piston powered mid size helicopters built.

Sikorsky developed the S-58 in response to a US Navy requirement for an anti submarine warfare helicopter. Design features included a single Wright R-1820 radial piston engine mounted in the nose, one of the largest fuselages to be designed for a single piston powered helicopter, and a raised flightdeck. As the XHSS-1 the S-58 first flew on March 8 1954.

Hundreds of S-58s were built to serve with the US Navy in anti submarine warfare roles as the SH-34G and SH-34J Seabat, and in utility roles with the US Marines as the UH-34D Seahorse. The US Army operated large numbers as the CH-34 Choctaw while many other allied countries operated the S-58 in various military service.

In the UK Westland licence built a Rolls-Royce Gnome turboshaft development called the Wessex, some of which saw civil service.

Smaller numbers of piston powered S-58s saw civil service with most delivered to customers within the USA. The S-58 offered a very large fuselage and good lifting capability, but its piston engine made it expensive to operate.

In 1970 Sikorsky announced it was developing a turboprop conversion package for the S-58. Turboprop powered S-58s are designated the S-58T and were initially powered by a 1340kW (1800shp) Pratt & Whitney PT6T-3 Twin-Pac, later aircraft a 1400kW (1875shp) PT6T-6. The first S-58T conversion flew on August 19 1970. Sikorsky set up a production line to convert customer S-58s, offered kits for S-58 operators to perform the conversion themselves, and purchased used S-58s, converted them to turbine power and offered them for resale. Small numbers remain in commercial service.

Photo: An S-58T. (Paul Merritt)

Sikorsky S-61L & S-61N

Country of origin: United States of America

Type: Medium lift utility helicopter

Powerplants: S-61N Mk II – Two 1120kW (1500shp) General Electric CT58-140-1 or 140-2 turboshafts driving five blade main and tail rotors.

Performance: S-61N Mk II – Economical cruising speed 222km/h (120kt). Service ceiling 12,500ft. Hovering ceiling out of ground effect 8700ft. Range with max fuel and reserves 833km (450nm).

Weights: S-61N Mk II – Empty 5595kg (12,336lb), max takeoff 8620kg (19,000lb). S-61L Mk II – Empty 5,308kg (11,701lb).

Dimensions: Main rotor diameter 18.90m (62ft 0in), length overall rotors turning 22.20m (72ft 10in), fuselage length 17.96m (58ft 11in), height 5.32m (17ft 6in). Main rotor disc area 280.5m² (3019.0sq ft).

Capacity: Flightcrew of two. Main cabin seating for up to 26 in early production aircraft and 30 in later production aircraft. Payloader can lift a 4990kg (11,000lb) external sling load.

Production: Production ceased in 1979 when 116 S-61Ns and S-61Ls had been delivered.

History: The Sikorsky S-61N and S-61L are based on SH-3/S-61A/B Sea King series originally developed in the late 1950s. They are widely used as oil rig support helicopters.

In September 1957 the US Navy awarded Sikorsky a development contract to produce what became the Sea King, an amphibious anti submarine warfare helicopter capable of detecting and attacking submarines. The prototype first flew on March 11 1959, while deliveries of production Sea Kings took place from September 1961. Power for initial production aircraft was supplied by two 930kW (1250shp) General Electric T58-GE-8B turboshafts.

Development of a civil version was undertaken almost concurrently, with the commercial S-61L flying for the first time on November 2 1961 (certification was awarded on November 2 1961). While based on the Sea King, the S-61L is 1.27m (4ft 3in) longer, allowing it to carry a substantial payload of freight or passengers. Power for initial production S-61Ls was supplied by two 1005kW (1350shp) GE CT58-140 turboshafts, the civil equivalent of the T58. Other changes include a modified rotor head and stabiliser. Unlike the Sea King, the S-61L features a modified landing gear without float stabilisers.

The S-61N, which first flew on August 7 1962, retains the floats, making it suitable for overwater operations, particularly for oil rig support. Both the S-61L and S-61N were subsequently updated to Mk II standard with improvements including more powerful CT58-110 engines giving better hot and high performance, vibration damping and other detail refinements.

A third civil development of the S-61 series to be offered was the Payloader, a stripped down machine optimised for aerial crane work. The Payloader features the fixed undercarriage of the S-61L, but with an empty weight almost 900kg (2000lb) less than the standard S-61N.

S-61 production ceased in 1979.

The S-61 Shortsky is a shortened (1.6m/50in) conversion of the S-61N and L, designed to increase single engine performance and external payload. The conversion first flew in February 1996 and was developed by Helipro in Washington State in the USA.

Photo: A Bristow S-61N. (Keith Gaskell)

Sikorsky S-76

Country of origin: United States of America

Type: Mid size corporate & utility helicopter

Powerplants: S-76 Mk II – Two 485kW (650shp) takeoff rated Allison 250-C30S turboshafts driving four blade main and tail rotors. S-76C+ – Two 638kW (856shp) takeoff rated Turbomeca Arriel 2S1s.

Performance: S-76 Mk II – Max cruising speed 287km/h (155kt), long range cruising speed 232km/h (125kt). Initial rate of climb 1350ft/min. Service ceiling 15,000ft. Range with 12 passengers, standard fuel and reserves 748km (404nm), with eight passengers, auxiliary fuel and reserves 1112km (600nm). S-76C+ – Max speed 287km/h (155kt), cruising speed 269km/h (145kt). Initial rate of climb 1625ft/min. Hovering ceiling out of ground effect 1800ft. Range at 259km/h (140kt) with reserves 713km (385nm).

Weights: S-76 Mk II – Empty (standard equipment) 2540kg (5600lb), max takeoff 4672kg (10,300lb). S-76C+ – Empty (executive configuration) 3691kg (8138lb), max takeoff 5307kg (11,700lb).

Dimensions: Main rotor diameter 13.41m (44ft 0in), length overall 16.00m (52ft 6in), fuselage length 13.22m (43ft 4in), height overall 4.41m (14ft 6in). Main rotor disc area 141.3m² (1520.5sq ft).

Capacity: Flightcrew of two. Max seating for 12 or 13 passengers at 79cm (31in) pitch in oil rig support aircraft. VIP configurations offered in six or eight passenger seat form. EMS configured aircraft accommodate one or two stretchers and four medical attendants.

Production: Total S-76 production in late 1998 of approximately 480, comprising 284 S-76As, 101 S-76Bs, 17 S-76A+, 43 S-76Cs and approx 70 S-76C+s. Over 70 S-76As converted to S-76A+ standard. 500th S-76 registered in May 1999.

History: Sikorsky's S-76 is a popular mid size corporate and oil rig support helicopter.

Sikorsky began development work on the S-76 (for a time named Spirit) in the mid 1970s and used technologies and experience gained from the military S-70 Black Hawk program. The resulting S-76A was powered by two Allison 250-C30S turboshafts and could seat 12. First flight was on March 13 1977 and FAA certification was awarded in November 1978.

The first improved model was the S-76 Mark II (introduced in March 1982) with more powerful Allison engines and 40 detail refinements. The S-76B is powered by two Pratt & Whitney Canada PT6B-36s (the 101st and last B was due to be delivered in December 1998), while the S-76C is powered by two Turbomeca Arriel 1S1 engines. The S-76A+ designation covers undelivered S-76As subsequently fitted and delivered with Arriel engines, and S-76As converted to Arriel power.

Current production is of the S-76C+ with 18% more powerful FADEC equipped Arriel 2S1 engines. Certification of the C+ was awarded in mid 1996. Forthcoming improvements include composite blades, a quiet tail rotor with curved blades, an active noise and vibration control system, and an advanced health and usage monitoring system. A three LCD screen integrated instrument display system (IIDS) for engine and rotor information is now standard, supplementing the four screen Honeywell EFIS suite.

Photo: Canada's Heli-Jet Airways operates five S-76s on passenger services linking Victoria with Vancouver and Seattle. (Paul Merritt)

Sikorsky S-92 Helibus

Country of origin: United States of America

Type: Medium to heavy lift airliner and utility helicopter

Powerplants: S-92A – Two 1790kW (2400shp) takeoff rated General Electric CT7-8 turboshafts driving four blade main and tail rotors.

Performance: S-92A – Max cruising speed 287km/h (155kt), economical cruising speed 260km/h (140kt). Hovering ceiling out of ground effect 7300ft. Range with reserves 741km (400nm).

Weights: S-92A – Empty 7030kg (15,500lb), max takeoff 11,430kg (25,200lb), max takeoff with sling load 12,020kg (26,500lb).

Dimensions: Main rotor diameter 17.71m (56ft 4in), length overall rotors turning 20.85m (68ft 5in), fuselage length 17.32m (56ft 10in), height 6.45m (21ft 2in). Main rotor disc area 231.6m² (2492.4sq ft).

Capacity: Flightcrew of two. Accommodation in main cabin for 19 passengers or up to three standard LD3 containers.

Production: Certification and first deliveries planned for 2001 and 2002 respectively.

History: The S-92A Helibus is a new medium/heavy lift helicopter Sikorsky is developing with a number of international partners.

Development of the S-92 was first announced in 1992 when Sikorsky unveiled a mockup of the new helicopter. However in 1993 Sikorsky postponed launching the S-92 due to the international helicopter market downturn and instead began searching for international risk sharing partners. By 1995 Sikorsky had formed its Team S-92 grouping and formally launched the S-92 at that year's Paris Airshow.

Sikorsky has built five prototype S-92s, four of which are flying aircraft. The first is a civil S-92A, which first flew on December 23 1998. The international utility/military S-92IU development has been dropped with the S-92A filling civil and military roles. S-92A certification to FAR/JAR Pt 29 and first deliveries are scheduled for 2002.

As originally envisaged the S-92 was to combine upgraded dynamic system components of the H-60/S-70 series with a larger cabin. However the S-92 is essentially an all new helicopter, with larger, composite construction, swept, tapered and anhedral tipped main rotor blades, new tail rotor, and a new four stage transmission based on the three stage S-70 unit.

Some 40% of the aircraft is of composite construction. The S-92's main cabin is wider and longer than the S-70's and features a rear loading freight ramp, while the cockpit will feature a Sanders EFIS system (based on that in the Lockheed Martin C-130J Hercules) with four colour liquid crystal displays, with provision for a fifth. Power is from two FADEC equipped GE CT7-8D turboshafts. RR Turbomeca RTM322s could be a future alternative engine.

Team S-92 members include risk sharing partners Mitsubishi Heavy Industries (7.5%, responsible for the main cabin), Gamesa of Spain (7% – cabin interior and transmission housing) and China's Jingdezhen Helicopter Group/CATIC (2% – tail pylon and tailplane), while Taiwan's AIDC (6.5% – flightdeck) and Embraer (4% – sponsons and fuel system) are fixed price suppliers/partners.

The S-92 is similar in size to the S-61 and is aimed at being a modern replacement for the later helicopter. The S-92 is also in the same class as the popular Super Puma.

Photo: The S-92A first prototype. (Sikorsky)

Sino Swearingen SJ30-2

Country of origin: United States of America

Type: Light corporate jet

Powerplants: Two 10.2kN (2300lb) Williams Rolls FJ44-2A turbofans.

Performance: High speed cruise Mach 0.80, long range cruising speed Mach 0.78 or 828km/h (447kt). Max certificated altitude 49,000ft. Takeoff balanced field length 1167m (3830ft). Range with one pilot and three passengers and NBAA IFR reserves 4635km (2500nm).

Weights: Empty equipped 3493kg (7700lb), operating empty 3583kg (7900lb), max takeoff 5987kg (13,200lb).

Dimensions: Wing span 12.90m (42ft 4in), length 14.31m (47ft 0in), height 4.34m (14ft 3in). Wing area 17.7m² (190.7sq ft).

Capacity: Typically pilot and passenger (or copilot) on flightdeck (will be certificated for single pilot operation). Typical main cabin seating for five with four in a club arrangement and fifth seat opposite main cabin door.

Production: At late 2000 158 orders held. First deliveries scheduled for late 2001.

History: The promising but oft delayed Sino Swearingen SJ30-2 is a seven place entry level corporate jet.

The SJ30 concept was for an advanced technology and relatively high performance, yet low cost entry level corporate jet. It will compete against the Cessna CJ1 and Raytheon Premier I.

Development work dates back to the SA-30 Fanjet which was announced in October 1986. Swearingen Engineering and Technology, under the leadership of Ed Swearingen (designer of the Metro and Merlin turboprops), began to design and develop the SA-30 for Gulfstream. Gulfstream planned to market the aircraft as the SA-30 Gulfjet, however it withdrew from the program in September 1989. Instead the Jaffe Group took Gulfstream's place. Construction of a prototype began in San Antonio, Texas, but in 1990 the Jaffe Group also withdrew from the then SJ30 program.

The first SJ30 prototype first flew on February 13 1991 and development progressed slowly until the 1994 announcement that Swearingen would form a joint venture with Taiwanese investors to create Sino Swearingen to build the SJ30 at a new factory in Martinsburg, West Virginia.

Sino Swearingen decided to enlarge the basic SJ30, resulting in the 1.32m (4ft 4in) stretched, increased wing span SJ30-2. The SJ30 prototype was modified to represent the SJ30-2 and flew in this configuration in November 1996. The definitive, more powerful FJ44-2A turbofans were installed on this aircraft in September 1997. Three new build production representative prototypes are due to undertake a 1400hr flight test program (the first of these flew on November 30 2000), clearing the way for certification and first deliveries about 12 months later.

Features of the SJ30-2 include a Honeywell Primus Epic avionics suite with three 20 x 25cm (8 x 10in) colour, flat panel LCDs and IC-615 integrated avionics computer, a 32° swept wing, increased fuel capacity compared with the basic SJ30 design, a Mach 0.80 cruise speed and a 4635km (2500nm) range.

Photo: The first production representative SJ30-2 prototype.

Socata (Morane-Saulnier) Rallye

Country of origin: France

Type: Series of two/four seat light aircraft

Powerplant: MS 880B – One 75kW (100hp) Continental O-200-A flat four piston engine driving a two blade constant speed propeller. 235 GT – One 175kW (235hp) Lycoming O-540-B4B5 flat six driving a three blade constant speed propeller.

Performance: MS 880B – Max speed 195km/h (105kt), max cruising speed 174km/h (94kt). Initial rate of climb 540ft/min. Service ceiling 10,500ft. Max range 853km (460nm). 235 GT – Max speed 275km/h (150kt), max cruising speed 245km/h (132kt), normal cruising speed 231km/h (125kt). Initial rate of climb 980ft/min. Service ceiling 14,750ft. Max range with reserves 1090km (590nm).

Weights: MS 880B – Empty 450kg (990lb), max takeoff 770kg (1695lb). 235 GT – Empty 695kg (1530lb), max TO 1200kg (2645lb).

Dimensions: MS 880B – Wing span 9.61m (31ft 6in), length 6.97m (22ft 11in), height 2.69m (8ft 10in). Wing area 12.3m² (132sq ft). 235 GT – Wing span 9.74m (31ft 11in), length 7.25m (23ft 10in), height 3.67m (9ft 2in). Wing area 12.8m² (137.3sq ft).

Capacity: Seating for three adults or two adults and two children in MS 880B Rallye-Club/Rallye 100, Rallye 125 and the MS 886 Super Rallye/Rallye 150T. All other variants seat four adults.

Production: More than 3500 Rallyes built by Sud Aviation and Socata.

History: The prolific Rallye family is Europe's most successful light aircraft series, today it remains in production in Poland as the Koliber.

Morane Saulnier designed the Rallye in response to a late 1950s French government competition for a light aircraft. Morane Saulnier's proposal resulted in the Rallye, which first flew on June 10 1959. This first MS 880A prototype was powered by a 67kW (90hp) Continental C90 flat four engine.

Sud Aviation and then Socata developed a wide range of Rallye models. The main two/three seat production version was the 75kW (100hp) Continental O-200 powered MS 880B Rallye-Club. Other Rallye-Clubs were the 78kW (105hp) Potez powered MS 881 and 85kW (115hp) Lycoming O-235 powered MS 883. A more powerful Rallye-Club development was the 110kW (145hp) Continental O-300 flat six powered Super Rallye (later to become the Rallye 150 S, then 150 ST and later still the Garnament).

The first true four seater was the MS 890 Rallye Commodore (deliveries began in 1964), which differed from the Super Rallye in having a higher max takeoff weight and strengthened structure. Developments of the Commodore included the 110kW (150hp) Lycoming O-320 powered MS 892 Commodore 150 (later the Rallye 150 GT), the 135kW (180hp) O-360 powered MS 893 Commodore 180 (later the Rallye 180 GT and then the Gaillard) and the 165kW (220hp) Franklin 6A-350 powered MS 894 Rallye Minerva (later the Rallye 220 GT and sold in the US as the Waco Minerva).

Product improvements led to the Rallye-Club based Rallye 100S with two seats and 100ST with three and then with a 82kW (110hp) engine the Rallye 100 ST Galopin; the Rallye 125; the glider towing 180 T Galerien; the 235 GT (later the Gabier); and the tail dragger Gaucho ag sprayer. French production ceased in 1983.

Photo: An O-200 powered MS 880B Rallye-Club. (Bill Lines)

Socata GY-80 Horizon & ST10 Diplomate

Country of origin: France

Type: Four seat light aircraft

Powerplant: GY-80-160 – One 120kW (160hp) Lycoming O-320-D flat four piston engine driving a two blade fixed pitch or optional constant speed propeller. ST10 – One 150kW (200hp) Lycoming IO-360-C fuel injected flat four driving a two blade fixed pitch or optional constant speed propeller.

Performance: GY-80-160 – Max speed 240km/h (130kt), cruising speed 234km/h (126kt). Initial rate of climb 690ft/min. Service ceiling 13,940ft. Range with max fuel 950km (515nm). ST10 – Max speed 280km/h (151kt), cruising speed 265km/h (143kt). Initial rate of climb 1005ft/min. Service ceiling 16,400ft. Range with four people on board 1385km (745nm).

Weights: GY-80-160 – Empty 620kg (1365lb), max takeoff 1100kg (2425lb). ST10 – Empty 723kg (1594lb), max takeoff 1220kg (2690lb).

Dimensions: GY-80-160 – Wing span 9.70m (31ft 10in), length 6.64m (21ft 10in), height 2.60m (8ft 6in). Wing area 13.0m² (139.9sq ft). ST10 – Same except length 7.26m (22ft 10in), height 2.88m (9ft 6in).

Capacity: Typical seating for four.

Production: Approximately 260 GY-80 Horizons of all models and 55 ST10 Diplomates were built. Production ceased in 1974.

History: The Horizon and Diplomate are relatively high performance retractable undercarriage four seaters which were built in relatively modest numbers.

The initial GY-80 Horizon began life as a privately developed design penned by Yves Gardan, who had also been responsible for a number of other postwar light aircraft designs. Gardan built a prototype which flew on July 21 1960. Two years later, Sud Aviation (now Aerospatiale) acquired the design and production rights for the GY-80 and placed the type into production. Sud Aviation built three preproduction development aircraft before placing the GY-80 into series production in late 1963.

A key aspect to the GY-80 was its simple design and method of construction. The GY-80 was of conventional construction, featuring retractable tricycle undercarriage, Frise slotted ailerons and Fowler flaps (the flaps, ailerons and horizontal tail pieces were interchangeable to reduce maintenance costs). The Horizon was built using car assembly techniques, with just 11 production jigs.

Three versions of the Horizon were built, differing in powerplant and fuel tankage. These were the 110kW (150hp) Lycoming O-320-A powered GY-80-150, the 120kW (160hp) O-320-D powered GY-80-160, and the 135kW (180hp) Lycoming O-360-A powered GY-80-180. These were built firstly by Sud Aviation, and then by its newly established light aircraft division Socata from 1966.

Socata flew an improved development of the GY-80, initially called the Super Horizon 200, on November 7 1967. This new development featured a stretched cabin and a more powerful 150kW (200hp) fuel injected Lycoming IO-360-C. In production between 1969 and 1974, the Super Horizon was renamed Provence, and then the ST10 Diplomate, the latter becoming the type's definitive name.

Photo: A GY-80-160D Horizon. (Jim Thorn)

Sud (Aerospatiale) Caravelle

Country of origin: France

Type: Short range airliner

Powerplants: Caravelle 10B – Two 64.4kN (14,500lb) Pratt & Whitney JT8D-9 turbofans. Earlier Caravelle versions (Mk I, IA, III and VI) were powered by two 48.9 to 56.0kN (11,000 to 12,600lb) thrust class Rolls-Royce RA.29 Avon turbojets.

Performance: Caravelle 10B – Max cruising speed 825km/h (445kt). Range with max payload 2650km (1450nm), range with max fuel 3640km (1965nm).

Weights: 10B – Operating empty 30,055kg (66,260lb), max takeoff 56,000kg (123,460lb). Earlier series Avon powered versions max takeoff weights range from 46,000kg (101,413lb) for the Mk III to 50,000kg (110,230lb) for the Mk VI-R.

Dimensions: Caravelle 10B – Wing span 34.30m (112ft 6in), length 33.01m (108ft 3.5in), height 8.72m (28ft 7in). Wing area 146.7m² (1579sq ft). Caravelle Mks I, IA, III and VI same except for length 32.01m (105ft 0in). Caravelle 12 featured 3.21m (10ft 7in) fuselage stretch over the Caravelle 10.

Capacity: Caravelle 10 – Flightcrew of two pilots and one flight engineer. Max passengers 100 at five abreast in a high density layout. Typical accommodation for 91 passengers in a mixed class arrangement. Maximum payload 9100kg (20,600lb).

Production: 282 production Caravelles built between 1958 and 1972. 10 remained in commercial service in late 2000.

History: The twinjet Caravelle was the first jet airliner to enter production in continental Europe and the first with rear mounted engines.

The Caravelle was designed in response to a French Secretariat General of Commercial and Civil Aviation requirement for a 1600 to 2000km (865 to 1080nm) range airliner (allowing operations between France and its North African dependants) with a 6000 to 7000kg (2725 to 3180lb) payload requirement at a speed of 620km/h (335kt). SNCASE (Societe Nationale de Constructions Aeronautiques de Sud-Est, later Sud Aviation, and subsequently merged into Aerospatiale), responded with a trijet design designated the X120, with three rear mounted SNECMA Atar turbojets. This design then matured to feature two rear mounted Rolls-Royce Avons.

The French government ordered two flying and two static prototypes of the twinjet in 1953, resulting in the type's first flight on May 27 1955. Entry into service of the SE 210 Caravelle I with Air France was on May 12 1959 on the Paris/Rome/Istanbul route.

Subsequent to the Caravelle I and similar IA models were the Caravelle III with 50.7kN (11,400lb) Avon RA.29 Mk 527s (one Caravelle III was powered by General Electric CJ805-23C turbofans, but production never eventuated); the 54.3kN (12,200lb) Avon RA.2 Mk 531 powered VI-N; and the VI-R with a modified windscreen and thrust reversers.

The Caravelle 10R (first delivery July 1965) introduced more fuel efficient Pratt & Whitney JT8D turbofans, while the 11R was a convertible passenger/freighter based on the 10R. The ultimate Caravelle model was the 3.20m (10ft 6in) stretched Caravelle 12. It could seat up to 128 single class passengers. Caravelle 10s and 12s are often called Super Caravelles.

Photo: A Caravelle 10. (Gianfranco Beting)

Sukhoi Su-26, Su-29 & Su-31

Taylorcraft

Country of origin: Russia

Type: Single and two seat aerobatic light aircraft

Powerplant: Su-29 – One 265kW (255hp) VOKBM M-14PT nine cylinder radial piston engine driving a constant speed three blade propeller. Su-31T – One 294kW (394hp) M-14PF driving a three blade constant speed prop.

Performance: Su-29 – Max speed 325km/h (175kt). Initial rate of climb 3150ft/min. Service ceiling 13,120ft. Range with max fuel 1200km (648nm). Su-31T – Max speed 330km/h (178kt). Initial rate of climb 4725ft/min. Service ceiling 13,125ft. Range with internal fuel 290km (155nm), max ferry range up to 1200km (648nm).

Weights: Su-29 – Empty 735kg (1620lb), MTOW 1204kg (2654lb). Su-31T – Empty equipped 670kg (1480lb), MTOW 968kg (2134lb).

Dimensions: Su-26M – Wing span 8.20m (26ft 11in), length 7.29m (23ft 11in), height 2.89m (9ft 6in). Wing area 12.2m² (127.0sq ft). Su-31T – Wing span 7.80m (25ft 7in), length 6.90m (22ft 8in), height 2.76m (9ft 1in). Wing area 11.8m² (127.0sq ft).

Capacity: Accommodation for pilot only in Su-26, Su-26M, Su-31T and Su-31U. Seating for two in tandem in Su-29.

Production: Over 170 Su-29s, Su-26s and Su-31s built.

History: Sukhoi's highly regarded aerobatic aircraft have won numerous international aerobatic events.

Sukhoi is perhaps better known as one of the two pre-eminent Russian high performance combat aircraft designers (the other being Mikoyan), but it turned its attention to design and flying a single seat aircraft for unlimited aerobatics competitions in the early 1980s. The prototype of the single seat Su-26, the first of the series, first flew in June 1984, and remarkably competed in the World Aerobatic Championships held in Hungary only two months later.

Features introduced on the initial Su-26 include the Vedneyev, now VOKBM, M-14 nine cylinder piston radial engine, which is highly regarded for its simplicity, power to weight ratio, fuel economy and low oil consumption. The airframe itself is extremely strong, capable of withstanding +11 and -9g, while the wing's aerofoil section is symmetrical and attached to the airframe at zero incidence and dihedral for similar positive and negative angle of attack flight characteristics.

Modifications to the Su-26 including a squared off vertical tail and less glass led to the Su-26M, which participated in the 1986 World Aerobatic Championships in the UK. The Su-26MX is an export version.

The success of the Su-26 led Sukhoi to design a two seat, dual control development, the Su-29, which first flew during 1991. Differences include the second seat, greater span wing and increased length. The Su-29M has an improved M-14 based M-9F engine (with 309kW/414hp).

The ultimate development is the Su-31, which first flew in June 1992 as the Su-29T. The Su-31 is a single seater based on the Su-29 but with a more powerful engine. The basic version is the Su-31T, the Su-31X is for export and the Su-31U has retractable undercarriage. Production began in 1994. The Su-29M has a pilot extraction system, the Su-29M2 (introduced in 1999) has an M-9F engine and lightened structure.

Photo: An Su-31. (Daryl Williams)

Country of origin: United States of America

Type: Two seat light aircraft

Powerplant: BC-12D – One 50kW (65hp) Continental A-65 flat four piston engine driving a two blade fixed pitch propeller. F-21 – One 88kW (118hp) Avco Lycoming O-235-L2C flat four.

Performance: BC-12D – Max speed 177km/h (96kt), cruising speed 153km/h (83kt). Initial rate of climb 600ft/min. Service ceiling 17,000ft. Max range 805km (435nm). F-21 – Max cruising speed at 75% power 196km/h (106kt). Initial rate of climb 875ft/min. Service ceiling 18,000ft. Range with max fuel 645km (347nm).

Weights: BC-12D – Empty 304kg (670lb), max takeoff 522kg (1150lb). F-21 – Empty 450kg (990lb), max takeoff 680kg (1500lb).

Dimensions: BC-12D – Wing span 10.98m (36ft 0in), length 6.71m (22ft 0in), height 2.03m (6ft 8in). Wing area 17.1m² (183.5sq ft). F-21 – Wing span 10.98m (36ft 0in), length 6.78m (22ft 3in), height 1.98m (6ft 6in). Wing area 17.1m² (183.5sq ft).

Capacity: Seating for two, except in the Model 15 Tourist, which seats four.

Production: Taylorcraft production includes 100 prewar Model As, 1800 military L-2s, more than 2800 postwar BC-12Ds, and more than 120 F-19 Sportsmans.

History: The Taylorcraft series has one of the most chequered production histories of any light aircraft.

The original Taylor Brother's Airplane Company was responsible for the Piper Cub design, and William T Piper purchased the company and its designs in 1931 when it ran into financial difficulties. Gilbert Taylor stayed on as president with the company under Piper's ownership (the Taylor name was initially retained) until 1935 when he resigned to establish his own company, this time named Taylorcraft.

Taylorcraft's first aircraft was similar to the Piper Cub except that it seated two side by side and was powered by a 30kW (40hp) Continental engine. Prewar it was built in A, B, D and D Tandem Trainer form, the latter seating two in tandem.

The Tandem Trainer formed the basis for the wartime L-2, nicknamed Grasshopper, and more than 1600 were built during World War 2 for the US Army Air Force.

Postwar Taylorcraft resumed production of the prewar B-12 as the BC-12D. Almost 3000 BC-12Ds were built before the company encountered financial troubles and the firm was bought out by Gilbert Taylor again, in March 1947. The new Taylorcraft Inc then built the two seat Ace, Traveller, De Luxe and Sportsman; the four seat Tourist, Ranch Wagon, Topper agricultural aircraft and the float equipped Seabird and Zephyr.

Once more Taylorcraft ceased trading, and did not reform until 1968 when it was set up to support existing aircraft. In 1973 this company began building the Continental O-200 powered F-19 Sportsman 100, and from 1983 the Lycoming O-235 powered F-21, which were based on the prewar Model B, but production ceased in 1986. Then in January 1990 Taylorcraft flew the improved Textron Lycoming O-235-L2C powered F-22, small numbers of which were built before production ceased for the final time in October 1992.

Photo: The F-21B was built between 1985 and '86. (Bill Lines)

Tupolev Tu-134

Country of origin: Russia

Type: Short range airliner

Powerplants: Tu-134 – Two 64.5kN (14,490lb) Soloviev D-30 turbofans. Tu-134A – Two 66.7kN (14,990lb) Soloviev D-30 Series IIs.

Performance: Tu-134 – Max cruising speed 900km/h (485kt), economical cruising speed 750km/h (405kt). Normal operating ceiling 39,730ft. Range with 7000kg (15,420lb) payload and reserves 2400km (1295nm), with 3000kg (6600lb) payload 3500km (1890nm). Tu-134A – Max cruising speed 900km/h (485kt), economical cruising speed 750km/h (405kt). Range with 5000kg (11,025lb) payload and reserves 3020km (1630nm).

Weights: Tu-134 – Operating empty 27,500kg (60,627lb), max takeoff 44,500kg (98,105lb). Tu-134A – Operating empty 29,050kg (64,045lb), max takeoff 47,000kg (103,600lb).

Dimensions: Tu-134 – Wing span 29.00m (95ft 2in), length 34.35m (112ft 8in), height 9.02m (29ft 7in). Wing area 127.3m² (1370.3sq ft). Tu-134A – Same except length 37.05m (121ft 7in), height 9.14m (30ft 0in).

Capacity: Flightcrew of three, comprising two pilots and a navigator. Tu-134 seats 72 in a single class. Tu-134A seats up to 84 passengers in a single class at four abreast, or 12 first class and 54 economy class at four abreast in a two class arrangement. Tu-134B-3 can seat up to 96 in a single class.

Production: Production estimated at over 700, most for Aeroflot, but approximately 170 exported to various east European airlines and other Soviet client states. Approx 325 were in service in late 2000.

History: For many years the Tupolev Tu-134 was the standard short haul jet airliner in the Soviet Union and eastern Europe.

The Tupolev design bureau was responsible for the Soviet Union's first jet powered airliner, the Tu-104 (which was based on the Tu-16 'Badger' bomber), and the Tu-104's smaller brother, the Tu-124. Both of these short range jetliners suffered from a number of performance shortfalls however, thus prompting development of the Tu-134.

The initial Tu-134 design was based fairly closely on the Tu-124, and for a time was designated the Tu-124A. However Tupolev decided to reconfigure the aircraft to feature rear fuselage mounted engines and a T-tail, resulting in the new designation.

Six development Tu-134s were built, with the first flying on July 29 1963. Production began in 1964 although it was not until September 1967 that Aeroflot launched full commercial services.

Initial production was of the standard fuselage length Tu-134, while the stretched Tu-134A entered Aeroflot service in the second half of 1970. Seating up to 76 in a single class, the Tu-134A differed from the Tu-134 in having a 2.10m (6ft 11in) fuselage stretch, a reprofiled nose (many without glazing and with weather radar), more powerful D-30 engines and an APU.

Other versions created by conversion are the Tu-134B with a forward facing position for the third crew member between and behind the pilots, the Tu-134B-1 which has a revised interior to seat up to 90 passengers without a galley, and the Tu-134B-3 which can seat 96 with full galley and toilet facilities retained.

Photo: A Tu-134A. (Viktor László)

Tupolev Tu-154

Country of origin: Russia

Type: Medium range airliner

Powerplants: Tu-154 – Three 93.2kN (20,950lb) Kuznetsov NK-8-2 turbofans. Tu-154M – Three 103.6kN (23,380lb) Aviadvigatel (Soloviev) D-30KU-154-II turbofans.

Performance: Tu-154 – Max cruising speed 975km/h (527kt), economical cruising speed 900km/h (486kt), long range cruising speed 850km/h (460kt). Range with max payload and reserves 3460km (1870nm), range with max fuel and 13,650kg (31,100lb) payload 5280km (2850nm). Tu-154M – Max cruising speed 950km/h (513kt). Range with max payload 3700km (1997nm), range with max fuel and 5450kg (12,015lb) payload 6600km (3563nm).

Weights: Tu-154 – Operating empty 43,500kg (95,900lb), max takeoff 90,000kg (198,415lb). Tu-154M – Basic operating empty 55,300kg (121,915lb), max takeoff 100,000kg (220,460lb).

Dimensions: Wing span 37.55m (123ft 3in), length 47.90m (157ft 2in), height 11.40m (37ft 5in). Wing area 201.5m² (2168.4sq ft).

Capacity: Flightcrew of three or four. Typical single class seating for 158 to 164 at six abreast, or 167 in a high density layout for Tu-154; Tu-154M seats a maximum of 180 at six abreast and 75cm (29.5in) seat pitch.

Production: Approximately 900 Tu-154s of all models have been built, including approximately 325 Tu-154Ms. About 570 were in service in late 2000.

History: Tupolev's Tu-154 trijet remains the standard medium range airliner within many states of the former Soviet Union and is still in fairly widespread use.

The Tu-154 was developed to replace the turbojet powered Tupolev Tu-104, plus the An-10 and Il-18 turboprops. Design criteria in replacing these three relatively diverse aircraft included the ability to operate from gravel or packed earth airfields, to be able to fly at high altitudes above most Soviet Union air traffic, and good field performance. To meet these aims the initial Tu-154 design featured three Kuznetsov (now KKBM) NK-8 turbofans (which also powered the larger, longer range Il-62) giving a relatively good thrust to weight ratio, double bogey main undercarriage units which retract into wing pods, and a rear engine T-tail configuration.

The Tu-154 first flew on October 4 1968. The first production example was delivered to Aeroflot in early 1971, although regular commercial service did not begin until February 1972.

Three Kuznetsov powered variants of the Tu-154 were built, the initial Tu-154, the improved Tu-154A with more powerful engines and a higher max takeoff weight, and the Tu-154B with a further increased max takeoff weight. Tu-154C is a freighter version of the Tu-154B.

Current production is of the Tu-154M, which first flew in 1982. The major change introduced on the M was the far more economical, quieter and reliable Soloviev (now Aviadvigatel) turbofans. Low rate production look set to wind up in 2000. A handful of converted Tu-154M-100s have modernised interiors and new Russian avionics.

The proposed Tu-154M2 with two PS-90A turbofans remains unbuilt while a re-engining program with CFM56s has also been studied.

Photo: A Hungarian registered Tu-154M. (Viktor László)

Tupolev Tu-204, Tu-214, Tu-224 & Tu-234

Country of origin: Russia

Type: Medium range airliner

Powerplants: Tu-204 – Two 158.3kN (35,580lb) Aviadvigatel PS-90A turbofans. Tu-204-220 – Two 191.7kN (43,100lb) Rolls-Royce RB211-535E4 or -535F5 turbofans.

Performance: Tu-204 – Cruising speed 810km/h to 850km/h (437 to 460kt). Range with max payload 2430km (1312nm), with design payload 3400km (1835nm). Tu-204-220 – Speeds same. Range with max payload 4600km (2483m).

Weights: Tu-204 – Operating empty 58,300kg (128,530lb), max takeoff 94,600kg (208,550lb). Tu-204-220 – Operating empty 59,000kg (130,070lb), max takeoff 110,750kg (244,155lb).

Dimensions: Tu-204 – Wing span 41.80m (137ft 2in), length 46.10m (151ft 3in), height 13.90m (45ft 7in). Wing area 182.4m² (1963.4sq ft).

Capacity: Flightcrew of two, although original Aeroflot requirement specified a flight engineer. Tu-204-200 seats up to 212 six abreast at 82cm (32in) pitch, or two class seating for 30 business class at 96cm (38in) pitch at six abreast and 154 economy at 81cm (32in) pitch and six abreast. Tu-224/-234 seats 166 in a single class.

Production: 15 Tu-204s in airline service in 2000.

History: The Tupolev Tu-204 is a medium range narrowbody twinjet and was the first Russian airliner to fly with western engines.

Tupolev began development of the Tu-204 to meet an Aeroflot requirement for a replacement for the medium range Tu-154 trijet. This all new twin featured a supercritical wing, while engine designer Soloviev (now Aviadvigatel) specifically developed the PS-90 turbofan. Other Tu-204 design features include fly-by-wire and a six screen EFIS flightdeck. First flight was on January 2 1989.

The Tu-204 is offered in a number of models. The base model is the Tu-204, while the Tu-204-100 and -200 have higher max takeoff weights, more fuel and greater range. The Tu-204C and Tu-204-100C are freighters with a forward main deck freight door, the Tu-214C³ is a combi convertible development.

Tupolev was keen to develop a westernised development of the Tu-204 to broaden the type's market appeal, resulting in the Rolls-Royce RB211-535 powered Tu-204-120, which first flew on August 14 1992. All but the first five feature Honeywell's VIA 2000 EFIS avionics suite.

Rolls-Royce powered variants include the Tu-204-120C freighter, -122 with Rockwell Collins avionics, increased weight -220 and equivalent cargo -220C, and the -222 with Collins avionics. Air Cairo of Egypt became the launch operator when it took delivery of a Tu-204-120 and -120C in November 1998.

Tupolev is also developing a shortened development of the Tu-204, in the form of the 166 seat RB211-535E4 powered Tu-224 and the 158kN (35,580lb) PS-90P powered Tu-234. The Tu-234 prototype (converted from the Tu-204 prototype) was publicly displayed at the 1995 Moscow Airshow. Lack of funding has delayed first flight.

Other proposed developments include a Pratt & Whitney PW2240 powered model, the 250 seat stretched Tu-204-400, a business jet and a maritime patrol platform.

Photo: A Tu-204-120C. (Paul Merritt)

Tupolev Tu-334

Country of origin: Russia

Type: Short to medium range airliner

Powerplants: Tu-334-100 – Two 73.6kN (16,535lb) ZMKB Progress D-436T1 turbofans. Tu-334-200 – Two 80.5kN (18,100lb) D-436T2s or Rolls-Royce BR715-55s.

Performance: Tu-334-100 – Typical cruising speeds at 35,000ft 800 to 820km/h (430 to 442kt). Range with max payload passengers 2000km (1080nm). Tu-334-200 – Range with max payload 2200km (1187nm).

Weights: Tu-334-100 – Empty 30,050kg (66,250lb), max takeoff 46,100kg (101,630lb). Tu-334-200 – Empty 34,375kg (75,785lb), max takeoff 54,800kg (120,815lb).

Dimensions: Tu-334-100 – Wing span 29.77m (97ft 8in), length 31.26m (102ft 7in), height 9.38m (30ft 9in). Wing area 83.2m² (895.8sq ft). Tu-334-200 – Wing span 32.61m (107ft 0in), length 35.16m (115ft 5in). Wing area 100.0m² (1076.4sq ft).

Capacity: Tu-334-100 – Flightcrew of two or three. Seats 102 in a single class arrangement at six abreast, or 72 in two classes (12 first and 60 economy class). Tu-334-200 – 126 single class passengers.

Production: Aeroflot has 20 Tu-334-220s on order. Production aircraft would be built at MAPO, Aviacor and Aviant (the latter in the Ukraine).

History: The Tupolev Tu-334 100 seat jet is being developed as a replacement for the ageing Tu-134.

Development of a replacement for the Tu-134 has been underway since the late 1980s, but it was not until August 1995 at the Moscow Airshow that the first prototype was displayed publicly. This aircraft made its first flight on December 8 1999.

The Tu-334 is based on the much larger Tu-204 twinjet with Tupolev using as many Tu-204 features in the new design as practical to reduce development time and costs. Examples of this include an identical flightdeck and a shortened Tu-204 fuselage. In addition the Tu-334's wing is based on the Tu-204's, although the latter's is a significantly larger unit.

Apart from commonality with the Tu-204, other notable Tu-334 design features are the rear fuselage mounted Progress D-436 turbofans, T-tail and fly-by-wire flight controls.

The Tu-334 is being developed in a number of versions. The first is the basic Tu-334-100, while the Tu-334-120D is planned to be powered by Rolls-Royce BR710-48 turbofans (the third prototype is being built to this configuration). The Tu-354-200 (alternatively Tu-354) is a stretched, 35m (115ft) long, 110 to 126 seater (in a single class). Apart from the fuselage stretch, changes will include more powerful D436T2 or BR715-55 turbofans, an increased span wing and four wheel main undercarriage units. The similar Tu-334-220 has BR715-55s and a further increased MTOW. The Tu-334-200C would be a Combi variant of the -200.

The Tu-334-100D will be a longer range Tu-334-100 featuring the -100's standard length fuselage but with more powerful engines, increased fuel capacity, a higher max takeoff weight and the increased span wings of the Tu-334-200. Tupolev has also studied the Tu-334C, which would be a freighter and even the cyrogenic fuelled Tu-336.

Photo: The prototype Tu-334-100. (Paul Merritt)

Transavia Airtruk & Skyfarmer

Country of origin: Australia

Type: Agricultural aircraft

Powerplant: PL12-U – One 225kW (300hp) Continental IO-520-D fuel injected flat six piston engine driving a two blade constant speed McCauley propeller. T-300A – One 225kW (300hp) Textron Lycoming IO-540 fuel injected flat six driving a three blade c/s Hartzell prop.

Performance: PL12-U – Max cruising speed 188km/h (102kt). Initial rate of climb 800ft/min. Service ceiling 10,500ft. Range with max payload 1205km (650nm), with max fuel 1295km (700nm). T-300A – Max speed 196km/h (106kt), max cruising speed (75% power) 188km/h (102kt). Initial rate of climb 515ft/min. Service ceiling 12,500ft.

Weights: PL12-U – Empty 830kg (1830lb), max takeoff 1723kg (3800lb). T-300A – Typical empty 955kg (2100lb), max takeoff (ag category) 1925kg (4244lb).

Dimensions: PL12-U – Wing span 12.15m (39ft 11in), length 6.35m (20ft 10in), height 2.79m (9ft 2in). Wing area 23.5m² (252.7sq ft). T-300A – Wing span 11.98m (39ft 4in), length 6.35m (20ft 10in), height 2.79m (9ft 2in). Wing area (including lower stub wing) 24.5m² (264.0sq ft).

Capacity: Single pilot in all versions. PL12, T-300 and T-400 – Seats for two passengers and fitted with a chemical hopper. PL12-U seats five with no hopper.

Production: Total production of 120 plus, including 18 assembled in New Zealand. Production ceased in 1993.

History: The Airtruk and Skyfarmer owe their origins to New Zealand's first commercial aircraft, the Waitomo Airtruck.

The original Waitomo Airtruck was designed by Luigi Pellarini in the mid 1950s, and used a number of components from the WW2 North American T-6 Texan/Harvard piston engine military advanced trainer. These components included main undercarriage wheels, the front undercarriage assembly, fuel tanks and the 410kW (550hp) Pratt & Whitney R-1340 radial piston engine. The Airtruck also featured a fairly tall and squat fuselage that accommodated a pilot, two passengers and a chemical hopper, tricycle undercarriage, a high mounted wing and boom mounted twin tails. The unusual twin tail configuration was adopted as it solved the problem of chemicals contaminating the rear fuselage, while it also allowed easier loading of the chemical hopper. The Airtruck first flew on August 2 1960.

The Airtruck was not built in New Zealand, and instead was further developed in Australia by Transavia as the PL12 Airtruk. The Airtruk differed from the Airtruck in having a flat six Continental engine and additional lower stub wings. It was delivered from December 1966.

The PL12-U utility seats five and has the chemical tank deleted. It was delivered from 1971. The T-300 and T-300A Skyfarmers are improved developments of the PL12 with a Textron Lycoming IO-540 engine; the T-300 first flew in July 1971, the T-300A, which introduced aerodynamic improvements, first flew in 1981. The final development was the 300kW (400hp) flat eight IO-720 powered T-400, four were delivered to China. Production ceased in 1993.

Photo: An Airtruk. Note the rear fuselage cabin which seats two. (Lance Higgerson)

Vickers Viscount

Country of origin: United Kingdom

Type: Turboprop airliner and freighter

Powerplants: V.700D – Four 1297kW (1740ehp) Rolls-Royce Dart 510 turboprops driving four blade constant speed propellers. V.810 – Four 1485kW (1990ehp) Dart 525s.

Performance: V.700D – Max cruising speed 537km/h (290kt), economical cruising speed 521km/h (282kt). Service ceiling 25,500ft. Range with max payload and no reserves 2140km (1157nm), range with max fuel and 43 passengers 2768km (1496nm). V.810 – Max cruising speed 587km/h (318kt), economical cruising speed 565km/h (305kt). Range with 64 passengers 2780km (1500nm), range with max fuel 2832km (1530nm).

Weights: V.700D – Basic empty 17,200kg (37,918lb), max takeoff 29,257kg (64,500lb). V.810 – Operating empty 19,959kg (43,200lb), max takeoff 32,866kg (72,500lb).

Dimensions: V.700 – Wing span 28.56m (93ft 9in), length with radar 24.94m (81ft 10in), height 8.16m (26ft 9in). Wing area 89.5m² (963sq ft). V.800 – Same except for length 26.11m (85ft 8in).

Capacity: Flightcrew of two or three. V.700 – Typical layouts included 40 passengers at four abreast, or between 47 to 63 at five abreast. V.800 – Typical seating for 65 at five abreast and 97cm (38in) pitch.

Production: Total Viscount orders reached 438, plus development aircraft. Approx 10 Viscounts in service in late 2000, all in Africa.

History: Vicker's Viscount was the first turboprop airliner from any nation to enter service.

The Viscount was one of the results of the UK's wartime Brabazon Committee, which was set up to encourage postwar commercial aviation in the UK. Discussions between the committee and Vickers designers in late 1944, who had already been working on the VC1 Viking airliner development of the Wellington bomber, resulted in what was eventually to become the Viscount. The committee's requirement was for a 24 seat, 1000 mile (1600km/868nm) range airliner, and by the end of 1945 Vickers had selected the Rolls-Royce Dart turboprop engine that was then under development to power the new aircraft.

In March 1946 the British government placed a contract with Vickers to build two prototypes of its design (called Viceroy), one powered by Darts, the other by Armstrong Siddeley Mamba turboprops. By the time of the Dart powered prototype's first flight on July 16 1948 the design had grown to seat 34. Airline indifference to the 34 seat Viscount and the availability of more powerful Dart variants however led Vickers to stretch the design to seat 40. This development was designated the Type 700, and first flew on April 19 1950.

Airline interest in the Viscount 700 was much stronger, and after receiving certification on April 17 1953 it entered service with BEA the following day. The Viscount was the subject of numerous large orders including from North America, its smoothness, good operating economics and pressurisation contributing to its success.

Capitalising on the 700's success Vickers developed the stretched 800 with seating for up to 69, while the final Viscount development was the 810 with more powerful engines and higher weights.

Photo: A former British World Viscount 800 operated by Heli-Jet Aviation in South Africa. (Keith Gaskell)

Victa Airtourer

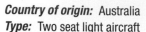

Country of origin: Australia

Type: Two seat light aircraft

Powerplant: 115 – One 85kW (115hp) Lycoming O-235 flat four piston engine driving a two blade fixed pitch propeller. T4 – One 110kW (150hp) Lycoming O-320.

Performance: 115 – Max speed 228km/h (123kt), max cruising speed 210km/h (113kt), long range cruising speed 177km/h (96kt). Initial rate of climb 900ft/min. Service ceiling 14,000ft. Max range with no reserves 1140km (617nm). T4 – Max speed 241km/h (130kt), max cruising speed 225km/h (122kt), long range cruising speed 198km/h (107kt). Initial rate of climb 1100ft/min. Service ceiling 15,500ft. Max range with no reserves 1005km (543nm).

Weights: 115 – Empty 490kg (1080lb), max takeoff 750kg (1650lb). T4 – Empty 528kg (1165lb), max takeoff 793kg (1750lb).

Dimensions: Wing span 7.92m (26ft 0in), length 6.55m (21ft 6in), height 2.13m (7ft 0in). Wing area 11.2m² (120sq ft).

Capacity: Seating for two, side by side.

Production: 170 Victa built 100s and 115s, AESL production of 94.

History: The popular Airtourer was designed by Australian Dr Henry Millicer (chief aerodynamicist of Australia's Government Aircraft Factory) in response to a Royal Aero Club (in the UK) sponsored Light Aircraft Design competition.

Millicer's design won the competition, and the Ultra Light Aircraft Association of Australia formed the Air Tourer Group to build a 50kW (65hp) Continental powered wooden prototype, which first flew on March 31 1959.

The wooden prototype aroused the interest of Victa (an Australian company more known for its lawnmowers), who in 1960 decided to commercially design and produce the Airtourer series. Victa's first all metal prototype of the Airtourer was powered by a 75kW (100hp) Continental, and first flew on December 12 1961. The first production Airtourer 100 flew in June 1962, and type approval was awarded the following month. The more powerful Airtourer 115 flew for the first time in September 1962.

Victa built 170 production Airtourers before its inability to compete against cheap American imports (which were aided by a favourable exchange rate) which were swamping the Australian market forced production to end. Plans to build the four seat Aircruiser development (described under Millicer) were dropped.

However New Zealand's AESL (Aero Engine Services Ltd) purchased the Airtourer design and production rights in early 1967. AESL (later NZAI and now PAC) built the Airtourer 115, the more powerful 110kW (150hp) model Airtourer 150, and constant speed prop fitted Super 150. Later the 115 became the T2, the 150 the T4 and the Super 150 the T5. The T3 was powered by a 95kW (130hp) RR Continental O-240, while the T6 was a militarised version based on the T5 built for New Zealand. NZAI production ceased in 1974.

In December 1997 Australia's Millicer Aircraft Industries purchased the Airtourer's production rights and it planned to deliver new build M10-140 and M10-160 AirTourers from 1999. However the promising venture was wound up in 2000.

Photo: A Victa Airtourer 115. (Gerard Frawley)

VisionAire Vantage

Country of origin: United States of America

Type: Single engine corporate jet

Powerplants: One 12.9kN (2900lb) Pratt & Whitney Canada JT15D-5 turbofan.

Performance: Max cruising speed 648km/h (350kt), economical cruising speed 463km/h (250kt). Initial rate of climb 4000ft/min. Max certificated altitude 41,000ft. Range at max cruising speed 1857km (1002nm), at economical cruising speed 2870km (1550nm).

Weights: Standard empty 1950kg (4300lb), max takeoff 3402kg (7500lb).

Dimensions: Wing span 14.49m (47ft 6in), production aircraft length 12.65m (41ft 6in). Wing area 20.6m² (222.0sq ft).

Capacity: One pilot and passenger on flightdeck. Main cabin seats four in standard configuration in a club arrangement. Toilet and baggage compartment in rear of cabin.

Production: At late 2000 VisionAire held orders for 110 Vantages. First two production aircraft due to be completed in 2002, certification and first deliveries planned for 2003.

History: The innovative Vantage is an all new single engine entry level corporate jet, designed to compete against the CitationJet and TBM 700 turboprop.

Self flying businessman James O Rice Jr established VisionAire in St Louis in 1988 after deciding that there existed a significant market for a low cost entry level business jet. Design aims with the new jet include jet comfort and altitude, good short field performance, a large cabin and low acquisition and operating costs.

The Vantage was designed by VisionAire with the assistance of Scaled Composites (whose president is Burt Rutan), with the aircraft's definitive arrangement settled upon in 1993. In February 1996 VisionAire contracted Scaled Composites to design and build a proof of concept prototype, and this aircraft was rolled out from the latter's Mojave, California facility on November 8 1996.

This aircraft successfully flew for the first time on November 16 1996 and it was used to demonstrate performance and handling characteristics before a production configuration was settled upon. VisionAire now aims to achieve certification for the Vantage in 2003. Scaled Composites will build Vantage's wing and vertical and horizontal stabilisers at VisionAire's new Ames, Iowa production facility where final assembly will be undertaken. AAR of Florida has been contracted to build production forward and rear fuselages.

The Vantage's most notable feature is its single JT15D turbofan engine, which is buried in the rear fuselage and fed by two air inlets on either side of the fuselage. The JT15D has been in operation since 1982 on the Beechjet 400 and Citation V, and VisionAire says the proven engine would have a shutdown rate per aircraft of once every 250 to 500 years if flown 500 hours per annum. Other notable features include the mid fuselage mounted forward swept wing of relatively large area, and graphite composite airframe. It will be certificated to FAR Part 23 Amendment 51.

Photo: The proof of concept Vantage prototype. The first two production aircraft will be completed in 2002 and used in the certification program. (VisionAire)

VulcanAir (Partenavia) P.68

Country of origin: Italy

Type: Six/seven seat light twin

Powerplants: P.68B – Two 150kW (200hp) Lycoming IO-360-A1B fuel injected flat four piston engines driving two blade constant speed propellers. P.68TC – Two 155kW (210hp) turbocharged Textron Lycoming TIO-360-C1A6Ds.

Performance: P.68B – Max speed 322km/h (174kt), max cruising speed 306km/h (165kt), economical cruising speed 295km/h (160kt). Initial rate of climb 1600ft/min. Service ceiling 20,000ft. Range at economical cruising speed 1700km (920nm). P.68TC – Max speed 352km/h (190kt), max cruising speed 324km/h (175kt), economical cruising speed 278km/h (150kt). Initial rate of climb 1550ft/min. Service ceiling 27,000ft. Range with max payload 555km (300nm), range with max fuel 1924km (1040nm).

Weights: P.68B – Empty 1200kg (2645lb), max takeoff 1960kg (4321lb). P.68TC – Empty equipped 1300kg (2866lb), max takeoff 1990kg (4387lb).

Dimensions: P.68B – Wing span 12.00m (39ft 5in), length 9.35m (30ft 8in), height 3.40m (11ft 2in). Wing area 18.6m² (200.0sq ft). P.68TC – Same except for length 9.55m (31ft 4in).

Capacity: Standard seating arrangement for seven, comprising one pilot and six passengers, or two pilots and five passengers.

Production: Partenavia built 403 P.68s through to 1994, incl 13 preproduction P.68As and 150 P.68B Victors. VulcanAir production began in 1998. Production rate of one a month to double in 2001.

History: Partenavia designed the P.68 as an efficient multirole twin capable of performing a number of utility roles.

The P.68 Victor first flew on May 25 1970 and it soon demonstrated performance similar to that of aircraft in its class (such as the Seneca) which had retractable undercarriage. The high wing design also incorporated a large degree of glass fibre reinforced plastic construction in non load bearing areas. Thirteen preproduction P.68As were built between 1971 and 1973 before the improved production standard P.68B, with a longer cabin, increased takeoff weight and redesigned instrument panel, was delivered from 1974. A retractable undercarriage variant, the P.68R, was trialled over 1976/77 but did not enter production.

The P.68C replaced the B in 1979 and introduced a longer nose to house weather radar and more avionics, extra fuel, revised cabin interior and redesigned wheel fairings. The turbocharged TC was introduced in 1980 and features two turbocharged 157kW (210hp) TIO-360s. Observer versions of both the P.68B and P.68C have been built, these featuring a clear nose section for helicopter-like visibility.

A turboprop development, the AT.68TP-300 Spartacus, first flew in 1978, and led to the larger AP.68TP Viator, which is in Italian government service.

Partenavia ceased production in 1994 following its bankruptcy. The company's assets were purchased by Santo de Fe in 1997 and he renamed the company VulcanAir in 1998. VulcanAir resumed P.68 production in 1998 and deliveries began in November 1999. Models offered are the P.68C and P.68C-TC (both also offered in Observer form).

Photo: A New Zealand registered P.68B. (Les Bushell)

Weatherly 201, 620 & 620TP

Country of origin: United States of America

Type: Agricultural aircraft

Powerplants: 201C – One 335kW (450hp) Pratt & Whitney R-985 nine cylinder radial piston engine driving a two blade constant speed Hartzell propeller. 620 – Same except for a three blade constant speed prop. 620TP – One 375kW (500shp) Pratt & Whitney Canada PT6A-11AG turboprop.

Performance: 201C – Typical cruising speed 170km/h (91kt). Initial rate of climb 960ft/min. 620 – Endurance 2hr 30min. 620TP – Endurance 2hr 0min.

Weights: 201C – Empty 1157kg (2550lb), max takeoff restricted category 2177kg (4800lb). 620 – Empty 1270kg (2800lb), max takeoff restricted category 2495kg (5500lb), design takeoff 1815kg (4000lb). 620TP – Empty 1135kg (2500lb), max takeoff restricted category 2450kg (5400lb), design takeoff 1815kg (4000lb).

Dimensions: 201C – Wing span 11.89m (39ft 0in), length 8.29m (27ft 3in), height 2.48m (8ft 2in). Wing area 23.3m² (251.5sq ft). 620 & 620TP – Wing span 12.50m (41ft 0in), or 14.33m (47ft 0in) with optional wingtip guide vanes.

Capacity: Pilot only in all models. Hopper capacity in 201C is 1022 litres (270US gal/225Imp gal); hopper capacity in 620 is 1268 litres (335US gal/280Imp gal); hopper capacity in 620TP is 1287 litres (340US gal/283Imp gal).

Production: Weatherlys in production between 1967 and 1982. The three model types were built in relatively small numbers (including more than 100 Model 201s).

History: The Weatherly 201 and 620 agricultural aircraft were built in relatively small numbers between the late 1960s and early 1980s.

The Weatherly 201 and its successors date back to the Weatherly WM-62C agricultural aircraft built between January 1961 and late 1965 (19 were made). The WM-62s were conversions of the basic Fairchild M-62 airframe, fitted with a chemical hopper, spray booms and either a Wright W670 or Pratt & Whitney R-985 radial engine.

Weatherly used its experience in designing and converting the WM-62s in developing its own agricultural aircraft design. The resulting Model 201 was a larger aircraft overall of conventional ag aircraft configuration, with a low wing, a Pratt & Whitney R-985 radial, integral chemical hopper and spray booms and an enclosed cockpit for the pilot. The initial production 201 was certificated in 1967, the improved 201C was granted its type certificate in 1975. A unique feature was the use of wingtip vanes which were developed to increase the effective swath width, while reducing the amount of chemicals lost from the spraying swath (they could be folded back beneath the wings for hangar storage).

The Model 620 replaced the 201C in production from 1980. The 620 featured a longer span wing with optional wingtip vanes and a larger chemical hopper, but the same R-985 engine.

The Pratt & Whitney Canada PT6A-11AG turboprop powered 620TP joined the 620 in production in 1980, and featured a longer nose and a slightly larger chemical hopper. Production of the 620 and 620TP ceased in 1982.

Photo: A Weatherly 620B fitted with the wingtip vanes. (Bill Lines)

Yakovlev Yak-18T

Country of origin: Russia

Type: Four seat light aircraft

Powerplant: One 265kW (355hp) Vedneyev/VOKBM M-14P nine cylinder radial piston engine driving a two blade variable pitch metal propeller.

Performance: Max speed 295km/h (159kt), max cruising speed 250km/h (135kt), economical cruising speed 210km/h (113kt). Initial rate of climb 985ft/min. Service ceiling 18,120ft. Range with four people, max fuel and reserves 580km (313nm).

Weights: Empty 1217kg (2683lb), max takeoff (with four people) 1650kg (3637lb).

Dimensions: Wing span 11.16m (36ft 7in), length 8.39m (27ft 7in), height 3.40m (11ft 2in). Wing area 18.8m² (202.4sq ft).

Capacity: Typical seating for four with rear bench seat removable. New production aircraft seat six.

Production: Estimated Yak-18T production of 200, with more than 150 still in service in Russia. Production initially ceased in 1989, but resumed by the Smolensk Aircraft Factory in 1993. New batch of 15 started in 1999.

History: One of the very few four seat light aircraft to be built in the Soviet Union during the Cold War years, the rugged Yak-18T has its basis in the Yak-18 series of two seat military trainers.

The Yak-18 first flew in 1946 and went on to be built in massive numbers (including more than 8000 for the Soviet air force which used it as its standard military basic trainer for many decades). Most production was of the Yak-18A. Several single seat models were built for competition aerobatics, including the Yak-18P, Yak-18PM and Yak-18PS. Many have since appeared in the west.

The four seat Yak-18T was the last production model, and the most extensively modified. Compared with the single and two seat Yak-18 models, the Yak-18T introduced a much enlarged cabin with seating for four, tricycle undercarriage (single seat Yak-18PMs had tricycle undercarriage also), plus the 265kW (355hp) Vedneyev (now VOKBM) M-14 nine cylinder radial engine.

First flight occurred in mid 1967 and the Yak-18T was then subsequently placed into series production in Smolensk. The Yak-18T went on to become the standard basic trainer with Aeroflot flight schools, while small numbers also entered service with the Soviet air force as liaison and communications aircraft. After approximately 200 were built, mainly for Aeroflot, production ceased in the late 1980s.

In 1993 the Smolensk Aircraft Factory placed the -18T back into production against a number of new contracts, including 20 for the Philippines air force. Several Yak-18Ts have also found their way into the west. Recent improvements include a two piece windscreen, increased fuel capacity and seating for six (with leather seats), improvements originally developed for the Technoavia SM-94 development which would have had further improvements. The small number of SM-94s that have been built are basically standard Yak-18Ts.

Compared with western four seat light aircraft, the Yak-18T is much larger, heavier and less economic to operate with a far more powerful engine, although it was never intended for private pilot operation. It has an aerobatic capability, while its handling is described as docile.

Photo: A Yak-18T. (Sebastian Zacharias)

Yakovlev Yak-40

Country of origin: Russia

Type: Regional jet airliner

Powerplants: Yak-40 – Three 14.7kN (3300lb) Ivchenko AI-25 turbofans. Yak-40V – Three 17.2kN (3858lb) AI-25Ts.

Performance: Yak-40 – Max cruising speed 550km/h (297kt), economical cruising speed 470km/h (254kt). Range with max payload of 32 passengers 1450km (780nm), range with max fuel 1800km (970nm).

Weights: Yak-40 – Operating empty 9400kg (20,725lb), max takeoff 16,000kg (35,275lb). Yak-40V – Max takeoff 16,500kg (36,375lb).

Dimensions: Wing span 25.00m (82ft 0in), length 20.36m (66ft 10in), height 6.50m (21ft 4in). Wing area 70.0m² (735.5sq ft).

Capacity: Flightcrew of two. Typical passenger seating arrangement for 27 at three abreast and 78cm (30in) pitch. Maximum seating for 32 in a high density four abreast configuration. Some fitted with corporate interiors.

Production: Estimated total Yak-40 production is 1000, of which approximately 750 were built for Aeroflot. Approximately 490 in airline service in late 2000. Others used as corporate transports.

History: The Yak-40 was the first jet powered airliner in its class in service in large numbers anywhere in the world, preceding the ERJ 135 and 328JET by three decades.

Design of the Yak-40 resulted from a mid 1960s Aeroflot requirement for a replacement for the thousands of Lisunov Li-2s (Soviet built DC-3s), Ilyushin Il-12s and Il-14s then in service. Aeroflot attached great significance to the Yak-40 program, as the aircraft was intended to operate regional services that accounted for 50% of Aeroflot's passenger traffic.

A S Yakovlev (after whom the design bureau is named) led the Yak-40 design team, and the program's existence was revealed on October 21 1966, when the prototype first flew. The type went into production in 1967 and entered service with Aeroflot in September 1968. Production continued until 1978, with around 1000 built.

The Yak-40's most noticeable design feature is its trijet configuration, with three specially developed Ivchenko AI-25 two shaft turbofans. The three jet engine layout was chosen for increased redundancy (and hence better one engine out performance, allowing good short field performance) – operating economics was a lesser priority. The unswept, high aspect ratio wing is also designed for good field performance. An APU and a ventral airstair in the rear fuselage allow autonomous operation at remote airfields.

The Yak-40 remained basically unchanged during its production life, with the only variant to enter production being the Yak-40V, an export model with a higher max takeoff weight and more powerful engines. In addition a number of developments were proposed, including the 40 seat stretched Yak-40M.

In the early 1980s US company, ICX Aviation, planned to build the type in the USA with western avionics and three more efficient Garrett TFE731 turbofans. In 1991 the Yak-40TL twin engine conversion was also proposed. The main difference would have been the replacement of the Yak-40's three engines with two Lycoming LF 507s.

Photo: A Yak-40 of Bulgarian based Hemus Air. (Viktor László)

Yakovlev Yak-42

Country of origin: Russia

Type: Short range airliner

Powerplants: Three 63.7kN (14,330lb) ZMKB Progress (Lotarev) D-36 turbofans.

Performance: Yak-42 – Max cruising speed 810km/h (437kt), economical cruising speed 750km/h (405kt). Range with max payload and reserves 1380nm (745nm), with 120 passengers 1900km (1025nm), with 104 passengers 2300km (1240nm), with max fuel and 42 passengers 4100km (2215nm). Yak-42D – Range with 120 passengers 2200km (1185nm).

Weights: Yak-42 – Empty equipped with 104 seats 34,500kg (76,058lb), with 120 seats 34,515kg (76,092lb); max takeoff 57,000kg (125,660lb). Yak-42D – Max takeoff 57,500kg (126,765lb).

Dimensions: Wing span 34.88m (114ft 5in), length 36.38m (119ft 4in), height 9.83m (32ft 3in). Wing area 150.0m^2 (1614.6sq ft).

Capacity: Flightcrew of two pilots, with provision for a flight engineer. High density single class seating for 120 at six abreast. Two class seating for eight at four abreast and 96 economy class at six abreast.

Production: More than 180 built, with low rate production continuing at Saratov. Approx 145 were in commercial service in 2000.

History: The Yak-42 trijet was developed as a replacement for Tupolev's Tu-134 twinjet and Antonov's An-24 turboprop.

The Yak-42 is an all new design, although, like the smaller Yak-40, it features a three engine configuration for increased redundancy and good short field performance. A moderately swept wing was a compromise between the need for good field performance and high speed cruise capabilities. An integral airstair, APU and double main undercarriage are all incorporated into the Yak-42 design for austere airfield operations. The Lotarev turbofan meanwhile was one of the first true turbofans to be developed in the Soviet Union.

The first of three prototypes flew on March 7 1975. Development flying revealed the need for increased wing sweep back, and the change of wing sweep angle and suspected development problems with the new three shaft turbofans delayed service entry to late 1980.

Most production was of the basic Yak-42. The Yak-42D with increased range was introduced in 1989.

The Yak-42D-100 meanwhile is a development with a four screen Honeywell EFIS cockpit and Stage 3 noise level compliance, among other improvements. One was displayed at the 1993 Paris Salon (as the Yak-142). One version that could enter production is the Yak-42A, based on the D but with more fuel, new Russian avionics and some of the improvements developed for the Yak-42D-100.

The Yak-242 was an all new design study with the Yak-42's cross section, two PS-90A turbofans and seating for up to 180.

The Yak-42-200 was announced in 1997, it would feature a 6.03m (19ft 10in) stretch, increasing all economy class seating to 150. Max takeoff weight would be 65,000kg (143,300lb). The Yak-42T is a freighter design study. It would be fitted with a main deck freight door.

At the 2000 Singapore Airshow, Swiss company Airline Partners launched the CityStar 100 which would feature western avionics and a new interior, both fitted in Switzerland.

Photo: A Chinese Yak-42 at Guangzhou. (John Adlard)

Yakovlev Yak-55 & Yak-54

Country of origin: Russia

Type: Aerobatic aircraft

Powerplants: Yak-55M – One 265kW (355hp) VOKBM M-14P nine cylinder radial piston driving a two blade variable pitch propeller. Yak-54 – Same except three blade prop.

Performance: Yak-55M – Max speed 360km/h (194kt). Initial rate of climb 3050ft/min. Rate of roll 345°/sec. G limits +9/-6. Yak-54 – Never exceed speed 450km/h (243kt). Initial rate of climb 2950ft/min. Rate of roll 345°/sec. Ferry range 700km (377nm). G limits +9/-7.

Weights: Yak-55M – Max takeoff 840kg (1852lb). Yak-54 – Max takeoff 990kg (2182lb).

Dimensions: Yak-55M – Wing span 8.10m (26ft 7in), length 7.00m (23ft 0in), height 2.80m (9ft 2in). Wing area 12.8m^2 (137.8sq ft). Yak-54 – Wing span 8.16m (26ft 9in), length 6.91m (22ft 8in). Wing area 12.9m^2 (138.8sq ft).

Capacity: Yak-55M – Pilot only. Yak-54 – Seating for two in tandem.

Production: 120 Yak-55s built for the DOSAAF paramilitary training organisation through to 1991. Over 100 Yak-55Ms built, many exported included to the US. Approx 15 Yak-54s have been built.

History: Yakovlev's Yak-55, Yak-55M and Yak-54 are competition standard aerobatic aircraft, all powered by Russia's ubiquitous M-14 radial piston engine.

The Yak-55 made an unexpected public debut at the 11th World Aerobatics Championships being held in Spitzerberg, Austria in August 1982. At the time it was thought the new Yakovlev was an evolution of the Yak-18/Yak-50 series. However, despite featuring a common powerplant, the Vedneyev (now VOKBM) M-14P radial, the Yak-55 was an all new, smaller aircraft, featuring all metal construction, with a mid mounted wing, seating for the pilot only and tailwheel undercarriage.

However inflight structural failures necessitated a complete redesign of the basic aircraft including a new wing, the Yak-55 appearing in its new form at the 1984 World Aerobatic Championships. Through to 1991 some 120 Yak-55s were built, primarily for the Soviet paramilitary training organisation DOSAAF, four of these were later exported to the United States.

In 1991 production began of the improved Yak-55M, which introduced further improvements. About 60 were believed to be built for DOSAAF, but many of these were subsequently sold, with a number making their way to the US. In all about 100 were built to early 1996, many of which were for export.

The Yak-54 two seater is essentially an all new aircraft compared with the Yak-55M, but again is powered by the M-14P. Like the Yak-55M, the 54's mid mounted wing is symmetrical with no angle of incidence, dihedral or anhedral.

The Yak-54 first flew on December 24 1993, with production beginning at Saratov in 1995, since which time approximately 15 built, with many of these exported to the USA. Two variants of the Yak-54 have been proposed, the retractable undercarriage Yak-56 trainer and the single seat Yak-57.

Photo: A Yak-54 in flight. Compared with the similar Sukhoi Su-26 series, the Yak features a mid, rather than low, mounted wing. (Sebastian Zacharias)

Zlin Trener & Akrobat

Country of origin: Czech Republic

Type: One and two seat aerobatic and training light aircraft

Powerplant: Z 226 – One 120kW (160hp) Walter Minor 6-III inverted inline six cylinder piston engine driving a two blade fixed pitch propeller. Z 526F – One 135kW (180hp) Avia M 137 A inverted inline six driving a two blade constant speed propeller.

Performance: Z 226 – Max speed 220km/h (120kt), normal cruising speed 195km/h (105kt). Initial rate of climb 950ft/min. Service ceiling 17,390ft. Range 485km (260nm). Z 526F – Max speed 244km/h (132kt), normal cruising speed 210km/h (113kt). Initial rate of climb 1180ft/min. Service ceiling 17,060ft. Range with standard fuel 475km (256nm), range with wingtip tanks 837km (452nm).

Weights: Z 226 – Empty 570kg (1257lb), max takeoff 820kg (1808lb). Z 526F – Empty 665kg (1465lb), max takeoff 975kg (2150lb).

Dimensions: Z 226 – Wing span 10.29m (33ft 9in), length 7.80m (25ft 7in), height 2.06m (6ft 9in). Wing area 14.9m² (160.4sq ft). Z 526F – Wing span 10.60m (34ft 9in), length 8.00m (26ft 3in), height 2.06m (6ft 9in). Wing area 15.5m² (166.3sq ft).

Capacity: Seating for two in Z 26, Z 126, Z 226, Z 326, Z 526 and Z 726. Pilot only in Z 226A, 326A, 526A, Z 526AF and Z 526AFS.

Production: More than 1400 of all variants built, many against military and government flying school orders.

History: The renowned Zlin series of two seat Trener trainers and single seat Akrobat aerobatic aircraft was a great success, winning numerous world aerobatic championship titles during the 1960s.

The original Z 26 Trener was designed in response to a Czechoslovak government requirement for a two seat basic trainer for flying school and military use. The Z 26 was powered by a 78kW (105hp) Walter Minor 4-III inline four cylinder engine, featured wooden construction and fixed, taildragger undercarriage. The prototype first flew in 1947 and 16 production Z 26s were built before it was replaced from 1953 by the metal construction Z 126.

Development over a three decade production run resulted in numerous further improved variants. In 1952 Zlin introduced the Z 226 Trener-6 which featured a more powerful 120kW (160hp) six cylinder Walter Minor 6-III engine. The Z 226 was also built in single seat Z 226A Akrobat, glider tug Z 226B and Z 226T trainer forms.

The similar Z 326 Trener-Master and single seat Z 326A Akrobat introduced retractable undercarriage, a feature that became standard on all subsequent models. Deliveries began in 1959. The Z 526 differed in that the pilot flew the aircraft from the rear, rather than the front seat, with optional tip tanks and a constant speed prop. The Z 526F introduced in 1968 had a 135kW (180hp) Avia M 137A engine. The otherwise similar Z 526L differed in being powered by a 150kW (200hp) Lycoming AIO-360 flat four and was intended for export.

Single seat Z 526s were the Z 526A, Z 526AS, and Z 526AFS.

The Z 526 AFM was built between 1981 and 1984 and was powered by a 155kW (210hp) Avia M337 engine, had tip tanks and the Z 526AFS's lengthened fuselage.

Final development was the Z 726 series, the Z 726 Universal had reduced span wing, the Z 726K a 155kW (210hp) Avia M 337 engine.

Photo: A Hungarian registered Zlin Trener. (Viktor László)

Zlin Z 42, Z 43, Z 142, Z 242 & Z 143

Country of origin: Czech Republic

Type: Two/four seat light aircraft

Powerplant: Z 43 – One 155kW (210hp) Avia M 337 six cylinder inline inverted piston engine driving a two blade propeller. Z 242 L – One 150kW (200hp) Textron Lycoming AEIO-360-A1B6 flat four driving a three blade c/s prop. Z 143 – One 175kW (235hp) Textron Lycoming O-540-J3A5 flat six driving a three blade variable pitch Mühlbauer prop.

Performance: Z 43 – Max speed 235km/h (127kt), cruising speed 210km/h (113kt). Initial rate of climb 690ft/min. Range with max fuel 1100km (595nm). Z 242 L – Max speed 236km/h (127kt), max cruising speed 214km/h (114kt). Initial rate of climb 1102ft/min. Range with max fuel 1056km (570nm). Z 143 – Max speed 265km/h (143kt), max cruising speed at 75% power 235km/h (127kt), econ cruising speed at 60% power 216km/h (226kt). Initial rate of climb 1457ft/min. Range at 65% power 1335km (720nm).

Weights: Z 43 – Empty 730kg (1609lb), max TO 1350kg (2976lb). Z 242 L – Basic empty 730kg (1609lb), max TO 1090kg (2403lb). Z 143 – Empty equipped 830kg (1830lb), max TO 1350kg (2976lb).

Dimensions: Z 43 – Wing span 9.76m (32ft 0in), length 7.75m (25ft 5in), height 2.91m (9ft 7in). Wing area 14.5m² (156.1sq ft). Z 242 L – Wing span 9.34m (30ft 8in), length 6.94m (24ft 9in), height 2.95m (9ft 8in). Z 143 – Wing span 10.14m (33ft 3in), length 7.58m (24ft 11in), height 2.91m (9ft 7in). Wing area 14.8m² (159.1sq ft).

Capacity: Seating for two in tandem in Z 42, Z 142 and Z 242, seating for four in Z 43 and Z 143.

Production: Total production includes more than 350 142s, approx 80 Z 242 Ls and 35 Z 143s, including military orders.

History: This series of two seat trainers and four seat light aircraft was initially developed to replacement for the successful Zlin Trener.

The initial Z 42 was developed during the mid 1960s and seats two side by side. It flew for the first time on October 17 1967. The improved Z 42M meanwhile introduced a constant speed propeller and the larger tail developed for the Z 43 four seater, and replaced the Z 42 in production in 1974.

Development of the two seat line continued with the further improved Z 142, which first flew on December 29 1979. Changes included a larger cockpit canopy and faired undercarriage. The Z 142 remained in production in Z 142C form to the mid 1990s. The latest two seater of this family to be developed is the 150kW (200hp) Textron Lycoming AEIO-360 flat four powered Z 242 L. Changes aside from the engine include a three blade constant speed prop and revised engine cowling profile. First flight was on February 14 1990.

Development of the four seat models, the Z 43 and Z 143, has followed that of the two seaters. The Z 43 appeared a year after the Z 42, first flying on December 10 1968. The Z 42 and Z 43 share the same basic airframe, but differ in that the Z 43 features a larger and wider cabin with seating for four, and a more powerful engine.

The current Z 143 L first flew on April 24 1992, and is similar in structure to the Z 242, but again differs in having a larger cabin with seating for four and a more powerful Textron Lycoming O-540 flat six engine.

Photo: A Zlin Z 242 L. (Lance Higgerson)

International Aircraft Registration Prefixes

Prefix	Country	Prefix	Country	Prefix	Country
AP	PAKISTAN	OE	AUSTRIA	VR-B	BERMUDA
A2	BOTSWANA	OH	FINLAND	VR-C	CAYMAN ISLANDS
A3	TONGA	OK	CZECHIA	VR-G	GIBRALTAR
A40	OMAN	OM	SLOVAKIA	VT	INDIA
A5	BHUTAN	OO	BELGIUM	V2	ANTIGUA & BARBUDA
A6	UNITED ARAB EMIRATES	OY	DENMARK	V3	BELIZE
A7	QATAR	P	KOREA (DPRK)	V4	ST KITTS-NEVIS
A9C	BAHRAIN	PH	NETHERLANDS	V5	NAMIBIA
B	CHINA (Peoples Republic of)	PJ	NETHERLANDS ANTILLES	V7	MARSHALL ISLANDS
B	CHINA (Taiwan)	PK	INDONESIA	V8	BRUNEI
C/CF	CANADA	PP/PT	BRAZIL	XA/XB/XC	MEXICO
CC	CHILE	PZ	SURINAM	XT	BURKINA FASO
CN	MOROCCO	P2	PAPUA NEW GUINEA	XU	KAMPUCHEA
CP	BOLIVIA	P4	ARUBA	XY	MYANMAR
CS	PORTUGAL	RA	RUSSIA	YA	AFGHANISTAN
CU	CUBA	RDPL	LAOS	YI	IRAQ
CX	URUGUAY	RP	PHILIPPINES	YJ	VANUATU
C2	NAURU	SE	SWEDEN	YK	SYRIA
C3	ANDORRA	SP	POLAND	YL	LATVIA
C5	GAMBIA	ST	SUDAN	YN	NICARAGUA
C6	BAHAMAS	SU	EGYPT	YR	ROMANIA
C9	MOZAMBIQUE	SX	GREECE	YS	EL SALVADOR
D	GERMANY	S2	BANGLADESH	YU	YUGOSLAVIA
DQ	FIJI	S5	SLOVENIA	YV	VENEZUELA
D2	ANGOLA	S7	SEYCHELLES	Z	ZIMBABWE
D4	CAPE VERDE ISLANDS	S9	SAO TOME	ZA	ALBANIA
D6	COMORO ISLANDS	TC	TURKEY	ZK	NEW ZEALAND
EC	SPAIN	TF	ICELAND	ZP	PARAGUAY
EI	EIRE	TG	GUATEMALA	Z3	MACEDONIA
EK	ARMENIA	TI	COSTA RICA	3A	MONACO
EL	LIBERIA	TJ	CAMEROON	3B	MAURITIUS
EP	IRAN	TL	CENTRAL AFRICAN REPUBLIC	3C	EQUATORIAL GUINEA
ER	MOLDOVA	TN	CONGO BRAZZAVILLE	3D	SWAZILAND
ES	ESTONIA	TR	GABON	3X	GUINEA
ET	ETHIOPIA	TS	TUNISIA	4K	AZERBAIJAN
EW	BELARUS	TT	CHAD	4L	GEORGIA
EX	KYRGYZSTAN	TU	IVORY COAST	4R	SRI LANKA
EY	TAJIKISTAN	TY	BENIN	4U	UNITED NATIONS
EZ	TURKMENISTAN	TZ	MALI	4X	ISRAEL
E3	ERITREA	T2	TUVALU	5A	LIBYA
F	FRANCE	T3	KIRIBATI	5B	CYPRUS
G	GREAT BRITAIN	T7	SAN MARINO	5H	TANZANIA
H4	SOLOMON ISLANDS	UK	UZBEKISTAN	5N	NIGERIA
HA	HUNGARY	UN	KAZAKHSTAN	5R	MADAGASCAR
HB	SWITZERLAND & LIECHTENSTEIN	UR	UKRAINE	5T	MAURITANIA
HC	ECUADOR	VH	AUSTRALIA	5U	NIGER
HH	HAITI	VN	VIETNAM	5V	TOGO
HI	DOMINICAN REPUBLIC	VP-F	FALKLAND ISLANDS	5W	WESTERN SAMOA
HK	COLOMBIA	VP-LA	ANGUILLA	5X	UGANGA
HL	REPUBLIC OF KOREA	VP-LM	MONTSERRAT	5Y	KENYA
HP	PANAMA	VP-LV	BRITISH VIRGIN ISLANDS	6O	SOMALIA
HR	HONDURAS	VQ-T	TURKS & CAICOS ISLANDS	6V	SENEGAL
HS	THAILAND			6Y	JAMAICA
HV	THE VATICAN			7O	YEMEN
HZ	SAUDI ARABIA			7P	LESOTHO
I	ITALY			7Q	MALAWI
JA	JAPAN			7T	ALGERIA
JY	JORDAN			8P	BARBADOS
J2	DJIBOUTI			8Q	MALDIVES
J3	GRENADA			8R	GUYANA
J5	GUINEA BISSAU			9A	CROATIA
J6	ST LUCIA			9G	GHANA
J7	DOMINICA			9H	MALTA
J8	ST VINCENT & GRENADINES			9J	ZAMBIA
LN	NORWAY			9K	KUWAIT
LV	ARGENTINA			9L	SIERRA LEONE
LX	LUXEMBOURG			9M	MALAYSIA
LY	LITHUANIA			9N	NEPAL
LZ	BULGARIA			9Q	ZAIRE
MT	MONGOLIA			9U	BURUNDI
N	USA			9V	SINGAPORE
OB	PERU			9XR	RWANDA
OD	LEBANON			9Y	TRINIDAD & TOBAGO

THE PHONETIC ALPHABET

A	Alpha	N	November
B	Bravo	O	Oscar
C	Charlie	P	Papa
D	Delta	Q	Quebec
E	Echo	R	Romeo
F	Foxtrot	S	Sierra
G	Golf	T	Tango
H	Hotel	U	Uniform
I	India	V	Victor
J	Juliet	W	Whiskey
K	Kilo	X	X-ray
L	Lima	Y	Yankee
M	Mike	Z	Zulu

Civil Aircraft Index